The History of the Village of the Small Huts

To Ken
Cameron
who likes
Art more than
People / or is
it the other way
round

Praise for Michael Hollingsworth

"Three cheers for Michael Hollingsworth! ... The land of the beaver will never be the same."—*Globe and Mail*

"One thing can certainly be said for Michael Hollingsworth—he plays no favourites. In his monumental vision of Canada's past ... everyone and everything is potential fodder for his comical and ironic retelling of history."—*NOW Magazine*

"Something completely different, history with a unique Hollingsworth spin: It's riotous, outrageous ... it's rollicking good fun."
—*The Toronto Star*

"Hollingsworth's dialogue [is] an axe, endlessly sharpened and then used to hack down all the hopelessly colonial views of history that Canadians have been force fed since childhood."
—*The St. Albert Gazette*

"When Hollingsworth puts the audience into the middle of the language rights, separatist, federal/provincial powers, and free trade issues of Laurier's day, his ironic commentary forces us to associate it with the same issues as they face us now."—*Canadian Theatre Review*

"Michael Hollingsworth's history plays shine a bright light into dusty corners of Canada's past."—*NOW Magazine*

"Hollingsworth has perfected the quick-hit, over-the-top style."
—*Globe and Mail*

THE HISTORY OF THE VILLAGE OF THE SMALL HUTS

PARTS I ~ VIII

by Michael Hollingsworth

Blizzard Publishing • Winnipeg

The History of the Village of Small Huts: Parts I to VIII
first published 1994 by
Blizzard Publishing Inc.
73 Furby Street, Winnipeg, Canada R3C 2A2

Cover design by Rick Simon.

Photo Credits
New France: Gary Farmer as Donnacona. [© Rick Simon]
The British: The Cast. [© Michael Cooper]
The Mackenzie-Papineau Rebellion: Arturo Fresolone as Papineau and Eric Keenleyside as Mackenzie.
Confederation and Riel: Arturo Fresolone as Louis Riel, Graham Greene as Gabriel Dumont, and Bruce Vavrina as a Métis. [© Michael Cooper]
Laurier: Stephen Ouimette as Wilfrid Laurier and Deanne Taylor as Emilie Lavergne. [© Michael Cooper]
The Great War: Janet Burke, Cliff Saunders, Mackenzie Gray, Alan Bridle, and Hugo Dan. [© Joanne Hovey]
The Life and Times of Mackenzie King: The Cast. [© Michael Cooper]
World War II: Edward Roy as Lord Mountbatten and Alan Bridle as Lord Montgomery. [© Michael Cooper]

Printed in Canada by Best Gagne Book Manufacturers.
Published with the assistance of
the Canada Council and the Manitoba Arts Council.

Canadian Cataloguing in Publication Data

Hollingsworth, Michael
The history of the village of the small huts
A play.
ISBN 0-921368-42-9
1. Canada – History – Drama. I. Title.
PS8565.0634H5 1994   C812'.54   C94-920259-2
PR9199.3.H643H5 1994

Contents

Playwright's Preface, page viii

Introduction by Michèle White, page ix

New France

Part One: The Beginnings, page 2

Part Two: Champlain, page 7

Part Three: Brébeuf, page 20

Part Four: Radisson, page 30

Part Five: Frontenac, page 39

The British

Part One: The Plains of Abraham, page 52

Part Two: The Conspiracy of Pontiac, page 73

Part Three: The Loyalists, page 84

Part Four: The War of 1812, page 104

The Mackenzie-Papineau Rebellion

Act One, page 128

Act Two, page 150

Confederation and Riel

Act One, page 168

Act Two, page 190

Laurier

Act One, page 216

Act Two, page 234

The Great War

Act One, page 252

Act Two, page 267

The Life and Times of Mackenzie King

Act One, page 284

Act Two, page 303

World War II

Act One, page 322

Act Two, page 343

Cast of Characters, page 361

Production Credits, page 368

VideoCabaret is grateful for the faithful support of the Canada Council for the Arts, the Ontario Arts Council, the Municipality of Metropolitan Toronto, Cultural Affairs Division, the City of Toronto through the Toronto Arts Council, the Laidlaw Foundation, and the Chalmers Foundation for financing the development and presentations of the play cycle known as *The History of the Village of the Small Huts.*

Michael Hollingsworth wishes to thank Shain Jaffe, Deanne Taylor, Jim Plaxton, Brent Snyder, Shadowland, Astrid Janson, Leslie Lester, Rick Simon, and the dozens of artists who helped translate the work from the page to the stage, also Theatre Passe Muraille, Toronto Free Theatre, and the Theatre Centre for co-producing and presenting the cycle.

For Deanne

Playwright's Preface

Canada is an Iroquois word, translated as "village of the small huts." *The History of the Village of the Small Huts* is a comedy of manners satirizing the various colonial periods of Canada. It follows the story lines of the three founding nations—the Native, the French, and the British. It is an historical epic for an audience raised on rock music and TV. In the age of electric information, sixty scenes an hour sets a proper pace. It is the goons of history in their very own "Goon Show." It is the Canadian "Book of the Dead," a merry tale told by ghosts and demons.

Voltaire once said: "L'Histoire n'est que le tableau des crimes et des malheurs." Translation: History is but a picture of crime and misfortune.

In this country we are all victims of the maxim "God can not change the past, but historians can." Tell the big lie long enough and the people believe it.

The lie: The history of Canada is dull.

It is anything but dull.

It is ferocious, crazy, cruel, wild, irreverent, and entertaining.

The first eight parts of *The History of the Village of the Small Huts* contained in this book are the chronicles of the French and British imperial periods of Canadian history.

Canada is state-of-the-art colonialism.

It is perfect, immaculate, pure.

Canadian double-think is a seminal characteristic of citizenship. Blink your eyes and you're a nation, blink your eyes and you're a colony. Blink your eyes ...

The next instalments in *The History of the Village of the Small Huts* will chronicle Canada's place in the American Nation Planet. The only thing one knows for sure is that the new boss will be the same as the old boss.

What is going to happen has already happened.

M.H.
September, 1994

Introduction

by Michèle White

History is a visual experience for Michael Hollingsworth. A single still image—the photo of the Queen handing Canada's patriated constitution to Prime Minister Trudeau in 1982—represents the moment he believes Canada acquired nation status. Simultaneously, it is the image which initiated his multipart play cycle *The History of the Village of the Small Huts.*

Hollingsworth's writing process begins with a combing through of *The Dictionary of Canadian Biography* and related documents for characters and plot. From these he sifts out adjectives which describe his subjects. Then he adds an inventory of visual references—everything from period genre paintings to the portraits of prime ministers on our paper currency. For the satirical voice at the heart of the entire epic project, he invokes Monty Python, the Goon Show, and the British television puppet show Spitting Image.

Hollingworth's vision, as the *Histories'* playwright and director, continues to develop through what he describes as a political alignment with the VideoCabaret production team. An implicit compatibility with the sensibilities of his scenographers allows Hollingsworth to give these visualizers scope in illustrating the text. Designers, like Shadowland Productions, Astrid Janson, or Teresa Przybylski, add dimensions which he rarely alters.

Shadowland's visual imprimatur is evident throughout the *Histories.* It combines the philosophy of the *arte povère* movement with the English theatre collective Welfare State International's community based improvisational techniques and adds the visual strategies of Trinidad's Carnival. For instance, in *Part Two: The British,* party favour materials, such as the plastic leis used to decorate school gyms, are turned into an elaborate arrangement of overskirts and underskirts for the political machinator/queen-of-the-prom figure, Madame Pean. In *Part Eight: World War Two*, life-size German and Canadian tanks, artillery cannons, and landing craft are cut and shaped out of painted cardboard and manipulated across the stage by the actors. This bin-picking and foraging eclecticism, due to both philosophical and financial requirements of economy, pragmatism and expediency, consummately partners Hollingsworth's crash-and-burn approach to raiding history and pillaging contemporary media sources for reference material.

In a theatre where economic necessity becomes an aesthetic principle, Hollingsworth's association with another key visual collaborator, Jim Plaxton, has allowed him to eliminate scenery, stage furniture and every other physical reference to time and place on stage. Plaxton invented the original set space from which the staging of the *Histories* has evolved. Starting with his own dictum that "where there's a light, there's a stage," the lighting and stage designer has psychologically constructed the village of small huts. Plaxton's lights puncture a black box stage, creating domes in which the director sculpts his *tableaux vivant* enactments of history. Because it dispenses with the conventions of stage machinery, this design has allowed Hollingsworth to realize his requirement of hundreds of blackouts which bracket innumerable scenes peopled with dozens of characters, played out at rapid-fire pace in a highly compressed period of time.

Hollingsworth, the director, moves the whole visual experience along with the pacing of television. Incorporating technology into theatre is a premise of the VideoCabaret company. Here it is evident through the performance ritual. Against a black void, the actors, in an exercise of sheer precision, move in tandem with hundreds of computerized lighting cues. They act out the hyperbolic facial and body gestures which the lighting technique and absence of physical location demands of them. Through body language created almost entirely from their heads and trunks, in their overblown physical attire, the performers, alone, must signal to the audience all the sense of place the text requires—from the muddy street of Hochelaga to the beaches of Dieppe.

Blackouts surround scenes of a few moments' or mere seconds' duration in which the stage box is illuminated by parallel and intersecting pimpoints of light from outside and behind. The resulting chiaroscruro focuses attention solely on the stage figures. Eliminated is the spill of theatre lights uncontrolled by the designer. The action plays out of the impenetrable darkness of an indefinable space where the performers speak their pieces and fade back in a wash of blackness. Significant moments are frozen in a dissolving spotlight. The claustrophobia of the chamber is released, periodically, when the room is flooded briefly with light or when a pattern of squares and rectangles splays over the box.

Appropriate to the VideoCabaret idiom, the effect is, variably, that of the first cinema machines, or of film noir clips looping through a projector, illuminated for seconds, then gone. The film score style of Brent Snyder's music for the first seven *Histories* and the evocation of period music in Andrew J. Paterson's sound collage for *Part Eight: World War Two* amplify this effect.

VideoCabaret and Shadowland productions frequently place the audience inside the performance space or carve out the playing area from within a crowd. Production plans for a post-*Histories* play, or series of plays, to be called *The Global Village*, a homage to Marshall McLuhan, allow for the use of a more interactive, technological enviroment to reflect the fact that the post-World War Two period is not yet history with a capital "H". Hollingsworth feels it is still in the process of being interpreted by historians, and so, for the moment, it is an organic mass of information which can be processed through VideoCabaret formats.

By contrast, the completed *Histories'* black box picture framing device deliberately distances the audience from the performance as if it were a moving comic strip. Still, the impulse to infiltrate the audience space is compelling for VideoCabaret. In *Part Five: Laurier*, the stage expanded into Theatre Passe Muraille through interjected, kinetic, cardboard silhouettes of bowing musicians. For *Part Two: The British*, Jim Plaxton transformed the same theatre into a tiered 18th century opera house with boxes, four foot chandeliers, frescoes and Italian drawn plush red curtains, all built out of painted cardboard.

Into these physical containers, Hollingsworth, the playwright, pours his dramatis personae. A raggle-taggle band of anti-heroes, they are vile and greedy, stupid and self-interested, but never, ever boring in the way that we may have come to imagine them through the normal channels of absorbing Canadian history. In appearance, they are parodies of the sanctified linear engravings and drawings of C. W. Jefferys and Charles Manley MacDonald which school children inherited as the visualization of Canadian history. Larger-than-life sized wigs, inflated costumes in vibrant primary colours vivid against the enveloping blackness, overblown two-dimensional props and the white-faced make-up of the mime, whose features must be expanded to express any dimension, are some of the devices through which these source materials are lampooned.

Familiar historical figures, such as Sir Wilfrid Laurier, are immediately identifiable through gross exaggeration of their hair style or jacket cut. The rouge Prime Minister, symbolically dressed in brilliant red against a pasty complexion, looks more like the Mad Hatter from Sir Alfred Tenniel's drawings for *Alice's Adventures in Wonderland* than any historical or official image. He reads a giant copy of Machiavelli's *The Prince* which, like many of Shadowland's props for the *Histories*, acts as a metaphor. Canadian history as a madcap trip down the rabbit-hole seems entirely plausible when characters like Laurier's mistress, Emilie Lavergne, flounces into the light in lime-green Jello chiffon with polka dots, feathers and pleats, rouche sleeves, honey-dew melon breast plates all topped by a head of carrot red curls.

While characters like these play on the viewer's retina liberally throughout an entire play, others must transmit their identity and role in a matter of seconds. This puts an enormous premium on dress, make-up, hair, props, and acting style to communicate instantly with the audience. Many of the *Histories'* costumes have crisp, hard, two-dimensional shapes and the static, strong delineation of engravings, daguerreotypes, and toy theatre. They also spring out of traditions of satirical social commentary in the visual arts of the periods in which the *Histories* are set. Sources such as James Gillray's political cartoons and caricatures, engraved and hand-tinted in glowing colours, or George Grosz' watercolours and prints of mutilated misfits ravaged by two wars are evoked. This deliberately visual strategy draws on the audience's capacity to make these associations thereby adding whole dimensions to the characters without depending on text. The strong images permit Hollingsworth to retain a sparkling economy of text in the *Histories* and to race through the complexities of history at lightening speed.

Hollingsworth ransacks the history of art and image throughout these plays. The dramatic tableaux the director sets up on stage frequently draw on devices of two-dimensional visual representation. Frozen-framed scenes signal references to images and icons and turn the live action back into a page from history before the viewers' eyes. In *Part Five: Laurier*, Bourget, the monstrous book-burning Bishop of Montreal, draped in blood red satin streaming with ribbons and cast in dramatic chiaroscuro, lies in his death scene like a perverse caricature of Caravaggio's painting of Christ's deposition or—a modern-day equivalent—an Evergon photograph which itself satirically appropriates art historical visualizations.

These plays are laced with parodic form and ironic voice. This is illustrated in the costume construction throughout the *Histories*. In *Part One: New France*, a courtesan, attired in more wig than dress, wears pink bloomers, ribbons and stockings and a flounced skirt, circa 1700, which is, in fact, a hooped mechanism made from a transparent plastic shower curtain—simultaneously an hilariously funny sight gag, a feminist critique of the patriarchy and a Dadaist kinetic sculpture.

Popular stereotypes of indigenous peoples is lampooned through prop pieces such as full-length headdresses worn by native characters. Obviously made from papier mache with fake-fur, these worl and bear masks come replete with bulbous, blood-shot eyes and animal trap teeth.

Organized religion receives its share of the scenographers' unstinting irony through characters like a nun in white face, with hideously pronounced eyes, wearing twigs wound round her head in a crown of thorns with red ribbons as drops of blood. On her chest a three-dimensional red satin heart, bound in wire with more red ribbons dripping off it, is pierced by a twig with a mirror shard on the end for an arrow-head.

Hollingsworth also parodies theatrical formats or pays homage to parodic formats in his writing. These formats locate the plays in sequential time while the lit and costumed actors locate them geographically. *Part One: New France* begins the cycle by recalling both the mystery plays of the Jesuit priests performed for native peoples and commedia dell'arte as adapted by Molière. *Part Two: The British* is written as a satirical comedy of manners set in a period opera house.

Part Three: The Mackenzie-Papineau Rebellion traces the historical thread through a Punch and Judy show, the most popular theatrical form of the time. The analogy of the players to puppets is unavoidable. The actors perform within the box set like marionettes, a visual device which emphasizes the political machinations behind the scenes. This, like many other devices Hollingsworth employs, signals the artifice and illusion of theatre and history simultaneously. The self-consciously contrived theatricality, overblown and played for the extremes, creates associations with historical entertainments devised to communicate basic notions of good and evil to an illiterate audience. It thereby alludes to a contemporary widespread and prevalent ignorance of Canadian history, which the cycle is designed, in part, to address.

Part Four: Confederation and Riel mixes Victorian melodrama with Gilbert and Sullivan operetta. *Part Five: Laurier* moves from melodrama in the first act to farce in the second, the popular theatrical formats of the era it spans. The stereotyped characters and extravagant exaggeration of the farce format, played out through clowning, physical comedy, and caricature, all surface exuberantly in the fifth play. The figures of Canadian history are made over into the figures popularized by Feydeau—cuckolds, silly wives, foreigners, the aged and the deformed—delivering their performances at a rapid-fire pace. The visual style of the acting matches the theatrical formats and is inextricable from the overall visual styling of these productions.

The twentieth-century *Histories* pay homage to the formats of expressionistic music hall,

Brecht, Artaud, and theatre of the absurd. Specifically, *Part Six: The Great War* is built from Hollingsworth's affinity for the Dada movement, the Cabaret Voltaire and Heinrich Boll. The format for *Part Seven: The Life and Times of MacKenzie King* is described by the playwright as both a depression era docudrama and an Anglo-American tip-of-the-hat to the theatrical styles of Clifford Odets and Noel Coward as a deliberate comment on the politics of Canadian national identity. *Part Eight: World War Two* pastiches agitprop and group theatre realism. Because he grew up in Wales and has the objectivity of the outsider, Hollingsworth is able to debunk the pop mythologies of both John Wayne Hollywood war movies glamorizing the U.S. and British "how we won the war" formula films. He has written, as a result, a play which is Canada-centric.

The encyclopedic use of different formats to express a consistent and evolving content is characteristic of contemporary art production. The artist ranges back and forth between historical precedents and the forms of the immediate present, often sharply juxtaposing them, in an attempt to find a container which both serves the idea and addresses the viewing patterns and attention span of an audience saturated with television and film-watching experience.

Hollingsworth is structuring a theatre borne out of historical precedents and contemporary influences—a vast web of sources which includes, as he describes it, Milton and Led Zepplin. Less a process of appropriation than a synthesis of sources, it rises out of a generation's collective experience. In The art/music production of the Queen Street West area of Toronto, where VideoCabaret and Michael Hollingsworth are quartered, the use of parody as form and irony as voice has predominated over the past two decades.

Hollingsworth's particular use of parody is multi-levelled. The *Histories* package centuries of stories and personages for present day consumption. On one level, he is concerned that a lack of national self-esteem prevents an audience from sustaining its interest in a history play cycle unless the writer resorts to a humorous form. As a result he has pulled out all the stops to entice viewers either inured to, or unfamiliar with, the basic facts. On another level, he calls upon the Roman definition of satire "as truth in the guise of humour" and uses it as a critical tool. The playwright sets out the past in order to create in the viewer an objective distance from the present. When Hollingsworth puts the audience into the middle of issues of land or language rights, separatism, federal/provincial powers, free trade, or participation in foreign wars, his ironic commentary forces us to associate the historical precedent with contemporary manifestations.

Linda Hutcheon writes in her book, *A Theory of Parody*, that "modern artists seem to have recognized that change entails continuity, and have offered us a model for the process of transfer or reorganization of that past. Their double-voiced parodic forms play on the tensions created by this historical awareness." She could well have been referring to Michael Hollingsworth and VideoCabaret and their apparent "desire to 'refunction' those forms to their own needs."

Hollingsworth, the immigrant, has understood that there is little or no indigenous context for Canadian theatre. The parodying of European theatrical formats follows his awareness that there has been no distinct history of theatre in Canada as in Europe, in either content or form. In part, this strategy rebounds upon the Canadian capacity to adopt the creativity of other cultures without developing its own or embracing what it does develop. In this context, parody becomes both a symptom and a mode of critique. It is "not a matter of nostalgic imitation of past models; it is a stylistic confrontation, a modern recoding which establishes difference at the heart of similarity," to draw further on Hutcheon's thesis. Recoding is used by many artists, in contemporary practice, to address issues of identity. Michael Hollingsworth, in *The History of the Village of the Small Huts*, establishes difference at the heart of similiarity, holding up the past as a mirror to the present, to forge a Canadian identity.

New France

Part One of The History of the Village of the Small Huts

Part One

The Beginnings

Scene One

(The sound of drums, rattles, chanting. The lights fade in. ODODHARHO enters.)

ODODHARHO: Our ancestors came from the ground. We are the original men. We are Men of Men. We make the whole earth tremble. As a tree grows it is our right to rule. We are kings of this forest. Wherever our shadow is cast that land is ours. Iroquois will never fight Iroquois. We will make all nations sit beneath this tree and as these roots are deep we must rise up and speak the language of our nature. I am Ododharho. The maker of the Great Peace.

(The lights fade.)

Scene Two

(In another playing area the lights fade in. AGOUHANNA enters holding an effigy of the sun.)

AGOUHANNA: Sun, are you listening? We know you love war. We only fight when you are watching. Well today is your day to smile. Oh mighty shining Sun, you have done us great wrong, you have put men on this earth who love their own shadow more than you.

(The sound of thunder.)

Sun, do not cry. Today those men are going to die. In this war I will take many slaves. And I will make a necklace from the ears of the warriors who will not obey me. In this forest everything that breathes, bites. I am Agouhanna, Huron Chief, the wolf that never sleeps. If you look in my eyes you will see a graveyard of snakes. I will never surrender.

(ODODHARHO enters.)

ODODHARHO: I am the snake eater, Ododharho, Iroquois Chief. When I dream I see serpents eating eagles. Three times I have offered you the Great Peace.

AGOUHANNA: You mean the Great Slavery.

ODODHARHO: And three times you have refused. I now offer you the Great War. I have come for your bones. Prepare to die.

AGOUHANNA: I will take my knife and cut out your brain and crush it between two rocks.

ODODHARHO: And I will eat your heart and drink your blood.

AGOUHANNA: You are going on a great journey to nowhere. Prepare to die.

(They strike a warlike pose. The lights fade.)

Scene Three

(In another playing area the lights fade in. Two Huron warriors enter, ATIRONTA and TESSOUAT.)

ATIRONTA: They make me feel like a fool because I am young.

TESSOUAT: Don't be sad Atironta. You will get scalp yet.

ATIRONTA: I had his head in my hands and my knife at his temple, and he escaped. Why?!

(TESSOUAT holds up a scalp.)

TESSOUAT: Here this is mine. This will cheer you up.

ATIRONTA: Why?!

TESSOUAT: You should talk with the Old One.

ATIRONTA: The Head Piercer?

TESSOUAT: Yes, the Head Piercer. I want to watch. He will tell you why you did not take scalp.

(AGOUHANNA enters.)

AGOUHANNA: Because you are a fool. I am surprised he did not take your scalp. But I am tired of talking about war. I live for peace.

ATIRONTA: But how will I prove myself if I do not have a war.

AGOUHANNA: You will hunt. I expect many bearskins from you.

ATIRONTA: I kill with knife I am so angry.

TESSOUAT: I will watch you kill bear with knife I am so angry.

ATIRONTA: I kill right now.

(The lights fade.)

Scene Four

(In another playing area the lights fade in. TESSOUAT enters. There are faces in the darkness. He smiles.)

TESSOUAT: This august body sits on its bum all day and what does it do? It talks all day. Talk, talk, talk and because they have their knees up around their ears they can't hear what anyone says. So they talk, talk, talk. And when they are not talking they are smoking their pipes. Well smoke this: Aenons was killed and eaten by two Iroquois warriors.

FACE ONE: How do you know this?

TESSOUAT: My mother's brother told me.

FACE TWO: Did anyone see Iroquois kill and eat?

TESSOUAT: Son of my mother's brother.

FACE ONE: And where is he?

(ATIRONTA enters wearing a bearskin.)

ATIRONTA: He is here. I demand revenge. The blood of my blood has been consumed by a demon. I demand revenge.

(The lights fade. Sounds of war chants, screams, drums, and rattles—a cacophony.)

Scene Five

(In another playing area the lights fade in. ATIRONTA enters holding a head.)

ATIRONTA: Behold. The head of the demon that ate my brother. And look, friend of demon.

(In another playing area the lights fade in. An IROQUOIS WARRIOR is tied to the stake.)

This is my slave. Know that if it had been my desire I could have eaten him. But I brought him to my village. Am I not a great warrior?

VOICES: *(Off.)* Ho.

(The sound of a drum and rattle is heard.)

ATIRONTA: What does my slave have to say?

IROQUOIS WARRIOR: I want you all to amuse yourselves by killing me. When you stick the knife in, I will laugh. Ha! I am Iroquois, I hate you.

ATIRONTA: Oh this man is going to die. You not believe what I am going to do to you.

IROQUOIS WARRIOR: I will laugh and sing. I want you all to have a feast in my honour. I want to watch as you munch your corn. You corn munchers.

ATIRONTA: Oh this man is going to die.

IROQUOIS WARRIOR: Now bring out your dancing girls. I want to see them dance the dance of death.

ATIRONTA: Oh, this man is going to die. You will beg for mercy. But you will be given none. And when the sun rises you will die. We will start by burning his legs.

(The IROQUOIS WARRIOR shows his legs.)

IROQUOIS WARRIOR: Get to it.

(The lights fade.)

Scene Six

(In another playing area the lights fade in. ATIRONTA and TESSOUAT enter. Offstage is the sound of pandemonium.)

ATIRONTA: He did not cry out.

TESSOUAT: It is a bad sign.

ATIRONTA: His spirit will not leave this village.

TESSOUAT: We will drive him out. He was demon.

(The lights fade.)

Scene Seven

(In another playing area the lights fade in. ATIRONTA and TESSOUAT are hunting beavers.)

ATIRONTA: I am walking, talking bad luck story. I once saw a maiden who made my blood run hot. She was daughter of Giant Snowflake. So one day I see Giant Snowflake smoking his pipe. And I run into his hut and say "I want to marry your daughter." Giant Snowflake looks up from his pipe as if I am mouse and say "I will think about it." Look at me as if I am mouse.

TESSOUAT: Sssssssh.

ATIRONTA: Two days later, I am still standing there, and he is still smoking his pipe, thinking about—

TESSOUAT: Sssssssh, listen. The beavers are happy and proud we are here.

ATIRONTA: Come out beavers. Have the courage to be caught. I will respect your bones.

TESSOUAT: Sssssssh ... Look.

(TAIGNOAGNY enters.)

TAIGNOAGNY: This is my river. How dare you hunt beavers on my river.

(ATIRONTA and TESSOUAT speak in unison.)

ATIRONTA and TESSOUAT: No, this river is my river. That beaver is my beaver.

TAIGNOAGNY: That beaver is in my shadow. You are in my shadow. Sing me your death song because I am going to tell you all about Ododharho.

(ATIRONTA and TESSOUAT spit.)

Ah, my friend, you will regret that. I will eat mush from the skull of your grandmother.

ATIRONTA: Sing me your death song because I am going to tell you all about Nanabozho.

TAIGNOAGNY: No, Nanabozho.

ATIRONTA: Nanabozho.

TAIGNOAGNY: Ododharho.

ATIRONTA: Nanabozho

TAIGNOAGNY: Ododharho.

ATIRONTA: Nanabozho!

TAIGNOAGNY: Ododharho!

ATIRONTA: Nanabozho!

TAIGNOAGNY: Ododharho!

ATIRONTA: Nanabozho!

TAIGNOAGNY: Ododharho!

(In another playing area the lights fade in. JACQUES CARTIER enters.)

CARTIER: I, Jacques Cartier, on this fine day, claim all this land and all the rivers and lakes that flow into this land for the King of France.

(CARTIER brandishes a sword.)

You are now beloved subjects of Le Roi Majeste de France.

(The lights fade.)

TAIGNOAGNY: Ododharho!!

ATIRONTA: Nanabozho!!

(The lights fade.)

Scene Eight

(In another playing area the lights fade in. CARTIER, DONNACONA, and TAIGNOAGNY enter.)

TAIGNOAGNY: This is Donnacona, the Great Leveler, the Head Piercer. If you look at this man the wrong way he will eat your brain. This Donnacona, Iroquois Chief.

CARTIER: What is this place called?

DONNACONA: This place is called Canada.

CARTIER: What does that word mean?

DONNACONA: It means, what does it mean? ... it means "village of the small huts." Welcome. You are a trader. I have many furs and fish.

CARTIER: I am not a fisherman.

DONNACONA: Then you have gew-gaws.

CARTIER: Oh Donnacona, Great Chief. Your son has told me about gold and silver.

DONNACONA: Ah, yes the Saguenay. The stories I could tell. Oh the Saguenay. Oh the Saguenay.

(The lights fade.)

Scene Nine

(In another playing area the lights fade in. CARTIER enters holding a cross and a sword.)

CARTIER: I am only an instrument of God, a tool, a mere spearhead. Hear that trees. That's good for a laugh, isn't it? Where are your demons? Come out my demons and dance for me. You're a bunch of lucky bastards. If I had any sense I would burn my ships and stay here forever and kill you all. I have seen the sign. I saw an eagle eating a serpent. This land is mine.

(The lights fade.)

Scene Ten

(In another playing area the lights fade in. CARTIER and DONNACONA, who chants and mutters to himself, enter.)

DONNACONA: Oh the Saguenay. Oh the Saguenay. Oh the Saguenay.

CARTIER: There is no gold, no God, no diamonds, no nutmeg, no silk, no path to China in this place.

DONNACONA: Oh the Saguenay.

CARTIER: Nothing. Just you.

DONNACONA: And the Saguenay. Ah the stories I could tell about the Saguenay. In the Saguenay the shit of God is everywhere.

CARTIER: What's that?

DONNACONA: Gold. I have seen golden idols in the Saguenay.

CARTIER: Really?

DONNACONA: And diamonds as big as pumpkins in the Saguenay.

CARTIER: Really?

DONNACONA: And the people that live in the Saguenay have no head, they have face on belly. Oh the Saguenay. And they have no legs so they walk around on arms all day. Oh the Saguenay. And they sing the most beautiful songs you have ever heard. Singing all the time. Oh the Saguenay.

CARTIER: You must take me there.

DONNACONA: Oh the Saguenay.

CARTIER: I will wait out the winter.

DONNACONA: Oh the Saguenay.

CARTIER: Are the winters cold?

DONNACONA: Oh the Saguenay. *(He rubs his hands.)* Oh the Saguenay.

(The lights fade.)

Scene Eleven

(In another playing area the lights fade in. CARTIER enters holding a pistol in one hand and small sticks in the other. The voices of scurvy victims are heard from the shadows.)

VOICES: I've got scurvy. My teeth are falling out. My head is falling off. My mouth is a rotting hole. I'm ready to dig up the dead and start eating. Don't look at me like that. I'm not dead yet.

CARTIER: The winters are cold, food is scarce, the natives are hostile. If you must amuse yourselves, do so with games of odd and even. Anyone who prefers to find amusement in murder and cannibalism will be executed. And there will be no debate about it. If you try to eat me, if you even think about it, I will kill you. Many of you have spent years in irons. If I put you in irons you will rot in them. I will tie you to a post and sit you in the snow and you can tell your troubles to the Indians. They will have sympathetic ears. They will listen to your story as they cut the top of your head off.

Now we all have scurvy. Let us be thankful it is not the plague. In the spring we return home. There is no God, no gold, and no path to China in this place. Only furs and fish, but at least that is something. This is without a doubt the land that God gave to Cain as his inheritance.

Now, I have burned our Bibles. There is only one cure for scurvy, fresh food. Do you men believe in Fate, in Destiny? You all came from prison. Your were meant to die in Hell. You are like slime that lives. I can't stand looking at you anymore. You are wretches. And one of you is going to be the wretched. We are going to draw sticks. The man who pulls the short stick pulls on hard luck. Now draw.

(CARTIER cocks the pistol and extends the hand holding the sticks. The lights fade.)

Scene Twelve

(In another playing area the lights fade in. CARTIER on his knees.)

CARTIER: The stench of rotting flesh is in my nostrils forever. I will never forget the smell, ever. We are in the death grip of winter.

(The sound of a howling wind is heard.)

Listen to the demons singing for our blood. The ice in the river is crushing our ships and plague rages. It is hopeless. But the Indians, bless their hearts, have given us this.

(CARTIER holds up a jug.)

This is spruce juice. I have seen savages with the plague drink this and become cured. It is foul tasting stuff. Worse than piss, but you're all going to die anyway. So you may as well drink it. Now, who wants to drink the devil's brew?

(Offstage: faint feeble voices say "Me, me, me." The lights fade.)

Scene Thirteen

(In another playing area the lights fade in. DONNACONA is chanting and muttering to himself.)

DONNACONA: Oh the Saguenay. Oh the Saguenay. Oh the Saguenay.

(In another playing area the lights fade in. CARTIER enters.)

CARTIER: Half our men are dead, but the other half are cured. We are like the healthy vine. Let us give praise to the Virgin Mary, and to our patron saint, St. Lawrence.

Oh blessed saint, we were about to say "Roll me over, this side is done." But the magic juice restored us. We are going to leave this place. But not before stealing Donnacona. May the Saguenay be wondrous and good. Oh the Saguenay.

(The lights fade.)

DONNACONA: Oh the Saguenay.

(The lights fade.)

Part Two

Champlain

Scene One

(In another playing area the lights fade in. A MAN pretending to be Neptune the Sea God, holds a trident.)

MAN: I am Neptune, Ruler of the Sea. Everybody listen to me. I am Neptune, Ruler of the Sea. Everybody look at me. I am Neptune, I will not tell you again because I am here to welcome Samuel de Champlain.

(CHAMPLAIN enters clapping his hands, and a PRIEST enters.)

CHAMPLAIN: Bravo, enough, enough, bravo.

MAN: We tried to do it in the latest Paris fashion but—

CHAMPLAIN: And it was. Well done. Gentlemen it is time to eat. I hereby inaugurate the Order of the Good Time. Let us toast our good fortune. The winter is cold but our belly is full.

(Noises offstage.)

MAN: Old bumshaker is here.

(MEMBERTOU enters.)

MEMBERTOU: I am Membertou. Today I am one hundred.

MAN: You are always one hundred.

(MEMBERTOU looks at the PRIEST. The PRIEST makes the sign of the cross. MEMBERTOU laughs.)

MEMBERTOU: I have been worshipping Satan for one hundred years. You have French ears and I a savage tongue. Cut off your ears and you will understand me. Or perhaps you think I am a little animal in the forest and you are a great creature?

(The PRIEST looks to the heavens.)

Speak great creature.

PRIEST: Oh Lord, oh Saviour, oh Jesus, have mercy on this man.

MEMBERTOU: This one never stops talking to his Oki. Never stops.

MAN: Except when there is food on the table.

MEMBERTOU: Look I have brought my spoon. Is this not proof that I have been invited to a feast. A feast of friends. I am ready to feast, and I make vow to eat everything that is put on my plate. Everything.

CHAMPLAIN: You are our honoured guest. Sit, Membertou, sit.

(The lights fade. During the darkness the sound of meal taking and laughter.)

Scene Two

(The lights fade in. MEMBERTOU, CHAMPLAIN, MAN and PRIEST enter. MEMBERTOU and CHAMPLAIN hold cups.)

MEMBERTOU: Ah Mr Champlain. What can I say that I have not said? I am like the beaver, happy and proud you are here. You Frenchmen, you make me laugh. You laugh at our wigwams, and tell us about your French houses. You say men who are six feet tall live in houses sixty feet tall, as if that is a great thing. You Frenchmen. You say your homeland is a great paradise and yet you come to this little Hell. Each year you risk your life to come to this place. Each year you abandon your wives, your children, your old ones. Why? When you speak it makes me wonder. You Frenchmen. You say you are superior to us in every way, and yet you covet our rags. All of you would fight, perhaps kill each other for the piece of beaver skin that is between my legs. Well you can have it. If you cannot see its value, hold it up to your nose and smell it. You Frenchmen.

(CHAMPLAIN holds up his cup.)

Ah, I see the man who smiles all the time is smiling again.

CHAMPLAIN: Gentlemen, a toast. To spruce bark and good health to you all.

(They drink.)

And to this man.

(MEMBERTOU nods his head and laughs.)

This is my best friend. My oldest ally.

(MEMBERTOU laughs.)

MEMBERTOU: I knew you would say something like that. You always say such nice things to me. And to prove I am friend of Frenchmen. I accept the Jesus God as my saviour.

CHAMPLAIN: Can we baptize you?

MEMBERTOU: Because I am friend of Frenchmen, black robe over there can put the death water on me anytime.

(CHAMPLAIN and others applaud. MEMBERTOU holds up his cup.)

To Frenchmen. May they live ... like the seal that lives on the bottom of the ocean and eats the crab and smiles and then rises up and barks for breath.

(MEMBERTOU drinks. They all drink.)

CHAMPLAIN: Thank you, Membertou, thank you.

MEMBERTOU: Last night Membertou have dream. Dream that you all go away. If you ever make that dream come true, you will make this hundred-year-old man cry. I am addicted to French peas and biscuits.

CHAMPLAIN: There will be others. I go where the stars shine. Where the fur is thick and the skin is thin. To Quebec.

MEMBERTOU: I knew you were going to say that. This is good firewater. Makes you very sad.

(The lights fade.)

Scene Three

(In another playing area the lights fade in. MEMBERTOU and CHAMPLAIN enter. CHAMPLAIN looks as if he has just awakened from a nightmare.)

MEMBERTOU: You had a dream, a nightmare.

CHAMPLAIN: I was at an Eat-All feast. I was eating and eating, I ate everything. Then I went for a walk in the forest. And all of a sudden I was being chased by a wolf.

MEMBERTOU: A monstrous wolf.

CHAMPLAIN: Yes, the wolf chased me for days until I was exhausted.

MEMBERTOU: And you fell to the ground.

CHAMPLAIN: I was incapable of getting up and running. And I laid my head on the ground.

MEMBERTOU: And you started to fall asleep.

CHAMPLAIN: And I could hear the snarling growling wolf, breaking the bush coming toward me.

MEMBERTOU: Closer and closer.

CHAMPLAIN: And I was just about to fall asleep.

MEMBERTOU: And what happened then?

CHAMPLAIN: And then ... you were shaking me and I woke up.

MEMBERTOU: That's right. When a man sleeps, he dreams. The dream is always true. And if a man sleeps in his dream, he dies—and never wakes, and never dreams again. To sleep within sleep is to die. Remember that.

(The lights fade.)

Scene Four

(In another playing area the lights fade in. ANADABIJOU, Montagnais Chief, and ATIRONTA, Huron Chief, enter.)

ATIRONTA: These knives are good knives.

ANADABIJOU: And this tomahawk is better than our tomahawk. Hold this.

(ANADABIJOU gives ATIRONTA a tomahawk.)

ATIRONTA: Ooooooooh! I must meet these Frenchmen.

ANADABIJOU: No, no, no, no. Frenchmen trade with me, I trade with you. Besides you don't want to meet these Frenchmen.

ATIRONTA: Why not?

ANADABIJOU: They have face like evil Manitou. Look like demon, act like demon.

Frenchmen have only one foot and only one leg. Hop around like grasshopper. And Frenchmen have no asshole, so when he speak shit come out mouth. Oh, you don't want to meet Frenchmen. You tell me what you want I get it for you.

(The lights fade.)

Scene Five

(In another playing area the lights fade in. CHAMPLAIN enters sketching a map. ANADABIJOU enters.)

CHAMPLAIN: So this is Quebec. What does that word mean?

ANADABIJOU: Quebec. It means "the narrowing."

CHAMPLAIN: The narrowing, eh. I see why. One could build a great fort here.

ANADABIJOU: Put your wigwam here and you will be king of this land.

CHAMPLAIN: Yes, I will build my habitation here.

(The lights fade.)

Scene Six

(In another playing area the lights fade in. Two MUTINEERS are drinking from a bottle.)

MUTINEER ONE: Chop wood, draw water, drop dead. That's all we do. This is worse than prison. I hate him so much.

MUTINEER TWO: He is killing us with work. We will die like slaves building his crappy habitation.

MUTINEER ONE: I came to this country to get out of jail, and to be rich, not to work.

MUTINEER TWO: There is a Spanish ship trading for furs. If we cut Champlain's throat and give this crap hole to the Spanish we will be rich.

MUTINEER ONE: Or we could shoot him in the back and blame it on the Indians.

(CHAMPLAIN enters.)

CHAMPLAIN: You men are the scum of the earth. I got you out of a brothel. And you out of a prison. I gave you gainful employment building my habitation. And you show gratitude by making plans to murder me.

MUTINEER TWO: I liked it in the brothel.

CHAMPLAIN: Good because you are going to the most Hellish whorehouse imaginable.

MUTINEER TWO: Good, I prefer the bondage of Satan to this craphole.

(CHAMPLAIN shouts offstage.)

CHAMPLAIN: I want each of their heads on a stick.

(CHAMPLAIN faces the MUTINEERS.)

When the sun rises, you will be bird food.

(The lights fade.)

Scene Seven

(In another playing area the lights fade in. CHAMPLAIN and ANADABIJOU enter.)

ANADABIJOU: The spirit shot arrows into the ground and they turned into men.

CHAMPLAIN: No. Man was made from clay and one night while he was sleeping God took a rib and made a woman.

ANADABIJOU: Arrows.

CHAMPLAIN: I am going to convert you. You will believe in Jesus before I am through with you.

(ANADABIJOU shakes his head.)

ANADABIJOU: If you kill the Iroquois I will believe in Jesus.

CHAMPLAIN: Why do you want to kill the Iroquois?

ANADABIJOU: Many tribes think the Iroquois are possessed by a demon. When you meet them, you will think so too. If you would join with me against the Iroquois, many allies—the Algonquin, the Huron—would come to give them a knock on the head they would never forget. And you would meet my friends.

CHAMPLAIN: If I joined you on this … adventure, you would trade your furs with me.

ANADABIJOU: If you are at Tadoussac instead of the traders I will trade with you. But if the traders are at Tadoussac—

CHAMPLAIN: They won't be. My company owns all the furs in this forest. When you bring them to Tadoussac I will trade you at a better price, because you are my oldest ally.

(ANADABIJOU smiles. The lights fade.)

Scene Eight

(In another playing area the lights fade in. Noises offstage. CHAMPLAIN jumps up with a start.)

CHAMPLAIN: What's all that shouting?

(ÉTIENNE BRÛLÉ enters.)

Well, manservant.

BRÛLÉ: One of our men mistook Marcel for the wild pig and shot him. The natives think this is a bad omen.

(ATIRONTA enters.)

ATIRONTA: Did you dream?

CHAMPLAIN: No. Stop asking me that question.

(ATIRONTA shouts offstage.)

ATIRONTA: He did not dream.

(The lights fade.)

Scene Nine

(In another playing area the lights fade in. CHAMPLAIN is sleeping. ATIRONTA and ANADABIJOU enter.)

ATIRONTA: He doesn't dream.

ANADABIJOU: He must dream.

(ANADABIJOU wakes up CHAMPLAIN.)

Did you dream?

CHAMPLAIN: Yes. I dreamed that I killed three Iroquois chiefs.

(ATIRONTA shouts offstage.)

ATIRONTA: The dream is good!

VOICE: *(From off.)* Good because the Iroquois are here.

(The lights fade.)

Scene Ten

(In another playing area the lights fade in. ANADABIJOU stands with arms folded, smiling and laughing. From the darkness come Iroquois taunts and laughter.)

VOICE ONE: You are the stuff that comes out the dog's bum.

VOICE TWO: You are worse than that. You are nothing.

VOICE THREE: You are worse than nothing. You are useless.

(ANADABIJOU holds up his hands and gestures "Talk , talk , talk.")

VOICE ONE: You are worse than useless. You are hopeless.

VOICE TWO: Wait until you see what we are going to do to you.

VOICE THREE: I am so happy the sun will be a witness when I scalp you.

ANADABIJOU: When thunderstick speak, you will be quiet.

(Laughter is heard.)

I have heard it speak. You not believe what is going to do to you.

(Drumbeats and chanting. CHAMPLAIN enters holding an arquebus. ANADABIJOU and ATIRONTA enter.)

CHAMPLAIN: Ah, I see them.

(CHAMPLAIN aims his arquebus.)

They are in my sights. They are dead men.

ATIRONTA: Shake!

(CHAMPLAIN pulls the trigger. There is a loud explosion. The musket recoils against his shoulder.)

CHAMPLAIN: Three Iroquois chiefs, one shot.

(ANADABIJOU and ATIRONTA raise their tomahawks and scream. The lights fade.)

Scene Eleven

(In another playing area the lights fade in. ATIRONTA and ANADABIJOU enter with an IROQUOIS PRISONER.)

ATIRONTA: Now we will hear your death song.

IROQUOIS WARRIOR: I will not sing for you. No matter how great the pain.

ANADABIJOU: We will see. Look at this. This is steel knife, not stone knife.

ATIRONTA: Your fathers and brothers have done terrible things to us.

ANADABIJOU: You wait until you see what we are going to do to you.

ATIRONTA: You are going to die by fire.

ANADABIJOU: But before that we are going to cut off your fingers and feet.

IROQUOIS WARRIOR: I will not sing.

ATIRONTA: And then skin you alive.

ANADABIJOU: And then scalp you.

(CHAMPLAIN enters holding a pen and drawing board.)

CHAMPLAIN: And after you have finished with him I want to baptize him.

ATIRONTA: Whatever is left you can baptize. No problem.

(ATIRONTA, ANADABIJOU and the IROQUOIS WARRIOR exit.)

CHAMPLAIN: I am going to write the word Jesus on every tree in this forest. Goblins live here.

(Lights fade.)

Scene Twelve

(In another playing area, the lights fade in. Sounds of the Iroquois being tortured. CHAMPLAIN and ANADABIJOU enter.)

ANADABIJOU: This is a great day. We killed fifty Mohawk and took twelve prisoners. What a night this is going to be.

(Offstage a scream and laughter is heard)

CHAMPLAIN: Oh my God, this must stop.

(A scream.)

Good Lord. What are you doing?

ANADABIJOU: We are killing him … slowly.

CHAMPLAIN: Let me put him out of his misery.

ANADABIJOU: No, no, no, no. Painful death for this one. Not easy death.

CHAMPLAIN: You are skinning him alive.

ANADABIJOU: Yes. We will give you head as honour.

(A scream.)

CHAMPLAIN: Oh this is intolerable. I can bare this no longer. That man must die. Now.

(A loud scream.)

ANADABIJOU: Very well, you can kill him. He is brave like the hedgehog is brave. He has heart of baby. We will feed it to other prisoners.

(CHAMPLAIN exits.)

CHAMPLAIN: *(Off.)* Stand back.

(A gunshot is heard. ATIRONTA enters holding a head.)

ATIRONTA: I will put flowers in this one's hair.

(ATIRONTA and ANADABIJOU laugh. CHAMPLAIN enters.)

You are great warrior, great warrior. Evil demon live inside this thing. I am Atironta, Huron Chief. No one in my nation has ever seen what I have seen today. I see you cannot take your eyes off my friend. When you come to Huron village you can talk with him. But we must attack the Iroquois again, or they will attack us. Thundersticks will be victorious.

CHAMPLAIN: If I join you on this … expedition, will you then believe in Jesus?

ATIRONTA: Aataensic is our God.

CHAMPLAIN: Your God is a fool. My God is more powerful.

ATIRONTA: I cannot promise you that we will believe in your God, but I promise you we will trade our furs for your gew-gaws.

CHAMPLAIN: Done. Little by little I will change you.

(The lights fade.)

Scene Thirteen

(In another playing area the lights fade in. CHAMPLAIN and ANADABIJOU enter.)

CHAMPLAIN: I understand you captured some Onodaga men and women.

ANADABIJOU: That's right, Great Musket.

CHAMPLAIN: And you cut off the fingers of a woman.

ANADABIJOU: That's right Great Knife Holder.

CHAMPLAIN: Leave the women alone. You must not do that. I forbid you to touch the women.

ANADABIJOU: But they are worse than the men. You haven't seen what they do to prisoners. They deserve it.

CHAMPLAIN: But they are women.

(Noises offstage.)

What's all that shouting.

(BRÛLÉ enters.)

BRÛLÉ: The Iroquois have come out of their fort.

CHAMPLAIN: We must attack but we have lost the element of surprise.

ANADABIJOU: So what? They know we are here. Let us show them why we are here. Attack with us and my warriors will not torture the women … only men.

CHAMPLAIN: Allez.

(The lights fade. In the darkness the sound of the battle: curses, taunts, screams, war cries, gun shots, chants, lamentations.)

Scene Fourteen

(The lights fade in. CHAMPLAIN enters with an arrow in his neck, and in his knee.)

Fools, fools, you fools.

(BRÛLÉ enters.)

They run, they take scalps and run. I fear I have made a grievous error. The Iroquois are formidable and fearless.

BRÛLÉ: Come your wounds are terrible. We will winter with the Huron.

(ATIRONTA enters.)

ATIRONTA: This is a great victory, a great victory.

CHAMPLAIN: How can this be a great victory? We are retreating.

(ATIRONTA holds up scalps and laughs.)

ATIRONTA: With scalps.

BRÛLÉ: Come, Iroquois are coming.

CHAMPLAIN: Ah, Étienne, you are so good to me.

(The lights fade.)

Scene Fifteen

(In another playing area the lights fade in. GARAKONTIE enters.)

GARAKONTIE: I am the sun that always advances. I am Garakontie, Iroquois Chief. Each day our wayward brothers, the Huron, give us more reason to hate them. The Huron do not fight fair anymore. Why should we fight fair anymore? Twice we have been attacked by Men of Iron with thundersticks. We should fight like the no-see-'ems that comes to feast, like the mosquito that drinks your blood all day and all night but is never seen drinking. The Huron have white devil on their side. Well we can have white devil on our side too. Man who look sick all the time with the big yellow eyes, ugly Dutchman hate ugly Frenchman. My brethren, let us not forget the wisdom of our fathers. When among wolves, howl.

(The lights fade.)

Scene Sixteen

(In another playing area the lights fade in. CHAMPLAIN, ATIRONTA, and BRÛLÉ enter.)

CHAMPLAIN: So spring is here and my wounds have healed.

ATIRONTA: Flowers will grow in those wounds.

CHAMPLAIN: Not where I am going. I am expecting missionaries from France, Franciscan Friars. I will send them to you. In the past we have talked about Jesus, they will pursue the matter.

ATIRONTA: And if they are like you, they are welcome.

CHAMPLAIN: Hmmm-hmmm. My manservant, Étienne Brûlé, will stay with you.

(CHAMPLAIN turns to BRÛLÉ.)

You will be my eyes and ears. Learn their ways and one day you will be a founding father of New France.

(BRÛLÉ grunts.)

Hide your squaws in their wigwams. He is addicted to women.

ATIRONTA: We know that all ready. We are expecting many of his pumpkins to blossom this summer.

(CHAMPLAIN smiles. The lights fade.)

Scene Seventeen

(In another playing area the lights fade in. CHAMPLAIN and JOSEPH LE CARON, the Recollet priest, enter.)

LE CARON: Show me the hordes of Hell. I thirst for them.

CHAMPLAIN: They await you in the forest.

LE CARON: And I am prepared.

(LE CARON holds up a Bible and a crucifix.)

CHAMPLAIN: Is my wife with you?

LE CARON: Not likely pilgrim, but there was a woman.

(The lights fade.)

Scene Eighteen

(In another playing area the lights fade in. CHAMPLAIN and his WIFE enter.)

CHAMPLAIN: You are like an angel.

CHAMPLAIN'S WIFE: And you are ... old.

CHAMPLAIN: Yes, with grey hair. When we married you were this big.

(CHAMPLAIN holds his hand knee high.)

CHAMPLAIN'S WIFE: I remember the day well.

CHAMPLAIN: And now you are a woman. Let me hold you.

CHAMPLAIN'S WIFE: I want to be a nun.

CHAMPLAIN: What? But you are my wife!

CHAMPLAIN'S WIFE: I want to be the wife of God.

CHAMPLAIN: But he has many wives. Wait till I die, then be his wife. When I die I will smile at that union. Come, you will like it here. In the wintertime it is beautiful.

CHAMPLAIN'S WIFE: Is it cold in the winter?

CHAMPLAIN: Some people think it is. Others ... you will see.

(The lights fade.)

Scene Nineteen

(In another playing area the lights fade in. LE CARON and ATIRONTA enter.)

LE CARON: And God made Adam and Eve, and they were imperfect. And what did he do?

ATIRONTA: He made new ones.

LE CARON: No. He damned them to Hell, and all the children of Adam and Eve were damned to Hell, and all the children of the children. They didn't go to heaven.

ATIRONTA: Is there moose meat in heaven?

LE CARON: No.

ATIRONTA: Remember that day when you make shadow creatures with hands? Well we catch many fish that day. Do that again.

LE CARON: No.

ATIRONTA: Remember that woman who was going to die and you baptized her and she lived? Well she is sick again, and is going to die for sure this time. Baptize her again.

LE CARON: No. I saved her soul once, that is enough.

ATIRONTA: But she will die.

LE CARON: Then she will be a trophy for Jesus.

ATIRONTA: Why are you doing this? You are here as our guests.

LE CARON: Will you live like a Frenchman.

ATIRONTA: How does a Frenchman live? I see these Frenchmen, these traders, they live like us.

LE CARON: Don't do what they do.

ATIRONTA: They do what I do. I don't do what they do.

(LE CARON holds up the crucifix.)

LE CARON: And God made Adam and Eve, and they were imperfect. And what did he do?

ATIRONTA: He made new ones.

LE CARON: No. He damned them to Hell. And all the children of Adam and Eve were damned, and all the children of the—

(ATIRONTA shakes his head. The lights fade.)

Scene Twenty

(In another playing area the lights fade in. CHAMPLAIN and his WIFE enter. CHAMPLAIN holds a proclamation.)

CHAMPLAIN: This is tremendous. C'est magnifique. Cardinal Richelieu has formed the Company of the One Hundred Associates. God be praised my dreams come true. I thought our king only wanted furry animals to live here, not people. One day this city of sixty will be an empire, God willing. Richelieu, he is a great man.

(CHAMPLAIN reads further.)

"... and in accordance with this the Society of Jesus will replace the Franciscans and—"

CHAMPLAIN'S WIFE: Jesuits. My dreams come true.

CHAMPLAIN: Jesuits. You don't know what they are like.

CHAMPLAIN'S WIFE: Oh yes, I do. Richelieu, he is a great man.

CHAMPLAIN: Yes.

(CHAMPLAIN reads further. The lights fade.)

Scene Twenty-one

(In another playing area the lights fade in. CHAMPLAIN and LE CARON enter.)

LE CARON: They are too primitive to be converted. We have an easier time converting Hindu Nabobs and Buddhists to the love of Jesus than these people. We have only one hope. We must make them like Frenchmen, like human beings. Then we can convert them. The Native way of life is the way of Satan. The thought of leaving this place makes me sigh and groan, and staying makes me groan and sigh. Confrontations make me tremble like a leaf.

CHAMPLAIN: It is a difficult task.

LE CARON: Yes, but my eyes are blue and my faith is strong.

(JEAN DE BRÉBEUF enters.)

BRÉBEUF: Your habitation is lovely.

CHAMPLAIN: The Franciscans like it.

(BRÉBEUF raises an eyebrow.)

LE CARON: So you are the Jesuit I have heard so much about. Jean de Brébeuf. I am Joseph Le Caron.

(LE CARON tries to shake hands—BRÉBEUF refuses.)

BRÉBEUF: I am here to give the word to the Red Man. And if need be, suffer just a little for my saviour.

CHAMPLAIN: I hope you will get along with the Franciscans.

BRÉBEUF: Ah, yes, the jolly Friars. When Satan farts the Franciscans purify the air. But when Satan goes one step further, put your faith in Jesuit care.

CHAMPLAIN: Well I am sure you and the Franciscans will be able to work it out.

BRÉBEUF: Without a doubt

(The lights fade.)

Scene Twenty-two

(In another playing area the lights fade in. CHAMPLAIN, his WIFE, and BRÉBEUF enter. CHAMPLAIN's WIFE wears a pendant containing a small mirror around her neck.)

CHAMPLAIN'S WIFE: This place is awful. It's damp, draughty, and the Indians he brings home.

CHAMPLAIN: They are my friends, I like them.

CHAMPLAIN'S WIFE: They leer at me.

CHAMPLAIN: They think you hold them near to your heart. They look at themselves in that little mirror around your neck.

CHAMPLAIN'S WIFE: They look at more than themselves. And I want to be a nun. And they leer at me. And these winters are terrible.

BRÉBEUF: She wants to go back to France, Mr. Champlain. You must be patient. She is not a saint. She has humble ambitions.

CHAMPLAIN: Then why do you wear those dresses?

CHAMPLAIN'S WIFE: I am tired of dressing like a drudge.

BRÉBEUF: She's a woman.

CHAMPLAIN'S WIFE: Yes, I am a woman, not a tree. A woman. I want to go back to France.

CHAMPLAIN: Give it time. Wait till the springtime and you hear all the little birds tweeting their little hearts out. It is beautiful.

(The lights fade.)

Scene Twenty-three

(In another playing area the lights fade in. BRÉBEUF is wearing a dunce cap. The words "I am a sinner" are written on the cap.)

BRÉBEUF: Oh Lord I am a sinner. Beat me with clubs and put me on the rack and tear my flesh. Roll me naked over hot coals and stomp me gently. Oh to be a eunuch and a slave and then slain by Satan's gladiators. Oh Lord this country is filled with atheists, pagans, heretics, imps, gargoyles, and monsters. But do not fear oh Lord. Your strength is my strength. I will have them gibbering and howling at my feet. And I will pray to St. Joseph for a happy death. Oh Lord I am a sinner.

(The lights fade.)

Scene Twenty-four

(In another playing area the lights fade in. CHAMPLAIN enters.)

CHAMPLAIN: Did I not prove that I was your friend when I slew the Iroquois? Have I not helped you in your wars? Have I not been a fair trader? You are my brothers in blood and your friendship flows within my heart. You have asked me to visit your villages more times than I have been able to honour. Well Champlain, the Great Musket, now honours those offers. Behold the Man.

(In another playing area the lights fade in. BRÉBEUF enters.)

In the longhouse you call me the Man of Iron. This is the Man of God. With hands of steel and benevolent patience he will embrace you and you will come to love him. He will instruct the young and the old, the big and the little, and you will come to know something about something. If you want to be my friend, if you want to be friends with the French, you must take this man. And we will trade as we have traded. Are we agreed? Good.

(Lights fade.)

Scene Twenty-five

(In another playing area the lights fade in. CHAMPLAIN and ATIRONTA enter.)

ATIRONTA: Oh Gou-Gou. Oh Gou-Gou.

CHAMPLAIN: If the food tastes as bad as it smells I will die.

ATIRONTA: Oh Gou-Gou.

CHAMPLAIN: Hear that knees, die of gout.

ATIRONTA: Oh Gou-Gou.

CHAMPLAIN: We are not eating fish bellies again, are we?

ATIRONTA: Oh Gou-Gou.

CHAMPLAIN: What is Gou-Gou?

ATIRONTA: Oh Gou-Gou. Gou-Gou is a terrible monster, terrible monster. Oh Gou-Gou. Gou-Gou is a cannibal giant, big as tree, hold club as big as canoe. Oh Gou-Gou. Gou-Gou eat bears for breakfast. Gou-Gou eat all the time, drink everyone's blood. Oh Gou-Gou. Gou-Gou look like woman but not woman. Gou-Gou has teeth like wolf and snake between legs. Gou-Gou hiss all the time. Hissssss. Oh Gou-Gou.

CHAMPLAIN: Where does Gou-Gou live?

ATIRONTA: In forest. I have seen him.

(Sound of thunder.)

Oh Gou-Gou is a terrible monster, terrible monster. Gou-Gou will suck out your blood. Gou-Gou is thirsty. Gou-Gou suck out the reason we live, suck out a man's macho juice. Even worse suck out the yellow water. Oh you don't want to meet Gou-Gou.

CHAMPLAIN: Is Gou-Gou real?

ATIRONTA: If you meet Gou-Gou you will not have time to ask "Are you real?" because Gou-Gou will be up your nose drinking your snot. Gou-Gou is so thirsty.

CHAMPLAIN: Gou-Gou.

(ATIRONTA nods his head.)

ATIRONTA: Oh Gou-Gou.

(The lights fade.)

Scene Twenty-six

(In another playing area the lights fade in. CHAMPLAIN, BRÛLÉ and BRÉBEUF enter.)

BRÉBEUF: This man is vile and vicious. He gambles, he swears, he blasphemes, he drinks liquor. And I have seen him with his women. He fornicates in the Longhouse, in the cornfields. This man fornicates in the forest.

BRÛLÉ: I am Étienne Brûlé. I fuck all night, I fuck all day.

CHAMPLAIN: Don't say that word in this man's presence.

BRÉBEUF: He speaks the language of Hell all the time.

BRÛLÉ: What do you speak?

BRÉBEUF: And that's another point. When I give him the Lord's word, he doesn't translate it properly.

BRÛLÉ: The Huron think you're the biggest joke in the world.

BRÉBEUF: When I say Jesus will save them from sin, that's not what he tells them.

BRÛLÉ: First of all, there is no word for sin. I've told you that at least a hundred times.

BRÉBEUF: Whenever he translates what I say, they laugh at me. You are an animal.

BRÛLÉ: And what are you, a man? You trying to make me laugh.

BRÉBEUF: He is an enemy of the faith.

(BRÛLÉ sneers.)

CHAMPLAIN: Manservant, is that true?

BRÛLÉ: I have always done your bidding, always.

BRÉBEUF: He gets liquor from the Dutch.

CHAMPLAIN: Manservant.

BRÉBEUF: And he has betrayed your friendship with the Huron by trading with the Iroquois.

CHAMPLAIN: Manservant, is this true? Speak manservant, what has possessed you?

BRÛLÉ: I am not your manservant. I am Étienne Brûlé, freeman.

CHAMPLAIN: Get out of my sight, I never want to see you again.

BRÛLÉ: You don't know what it's like out there.

CHAMPLAIN: Get out of my sight. You are no longer a Frenchman.

(BRÛLÉ spits while BRÉBEUF brandishes the cross. The lights fade.)

Scene Twenty-seven

(In another playing area the lights fade in. The sound of the tweeting of birds. CHAMPLAIN and his WIFE sit in chairs ten feet apart. CHAMPLAIN's WIFE wears a shawl as she knits.)

CHAMPLAIN: Husband and wife should live like … husband and wife. Not like monk and nun. What kind of life is that?

CHAMPLAIN'S WIFE: It is a pure life.

CHAMPLAIN: Yes it is. Eat and sleep, and then die. A basic life.

(The WIFE sneers.)

CHAMPLAIN'S WIFE: You have ruined my life by bringing me here. If you had let me stay in France I would still love you.

CHAMPLAIN: But if you had stayed in France that would have ruined my life. Which is the greater injustice?

CHAMPLAIN'S WIFE: I am too cold to think.

(CHAMPLAIN gets up from his chair.)

CHAMPLAIN: But you are the only educated person here that I can talk with.

CHAMPLAIN'S WIFE: What about your friend the witch doctor. You think he is quite learned. Talk with him.

CHAMPLAIN: I do. He tells me funny stories.

CHAMPLAIN'S WIFE: I don't want to hear his funny stories.

CHAMPLAIN: He gives me very good recipes.

CHAMPLAIN'S WIFE: Oh yes. How to make Iroquois soup. With vegetable or without. Why don't you and him go out on a scalping party.

CHAMPLAIN: Please.

CHAMPLAIN'S WIFE: I hate him so much. He just walks in here, never knocks. Just walks in. I can never get him to leave. And every time he comes here, he stays for supper, and will not leave until he has gorged himself on God knows what. And watching him eat is an ordeal.

CHAMPLAIN: He's my friend.

CHAMPLAIN'S WIFE: Last week I saw him eating and going to the bathroom at the same time. I was completely revolted. I don't want him here.

CHAMPLAIN: But—

(ANADABIJOU enters.)

ANADABIJOU: Greetings, Great Musket.

CHAMPLAIN'S WIFE: Him!

ANADABIJOU: Kiss my moccasins, I am Montagnais Chief.

CHAMPLAIN'S WIFE: That does it. I want to go back to France on the next ship. It's back to France for me. Good night.

(CHAMPLAIN's WIFE exits. ANADABIJOU sits in the chair vacated by her.)

ANADABIJOU: I have made you sad. I should have not made that remark to your wife.

CHAMPLAIN: No, I suppose … Anadabijou?

ANADABIJOU: Yes, Great Musket.

CHAMPLAIN: Would you like to drink some firewater with me?

ANADABIJOU: In all the time I have known you I have never seen you drink the firewater. Bring it out. This is a great honour.

(The lights fade.)

Scene Twenty-eight

(In another playing area the lights fade in. CHAMPLAIN and ANADABIJOU, intoxicated, are singing "Alouette." CHAMPLAIN holds up the bottle.)

CHAMPLAIN: This is the last one.

ANADABIJOU: Good, more firewater.

(ANADABIJOU holds up a cup.)

My cup is thirsty. Fill. I am ready to lose my body. Beware, Great Musket. When I drink this one, I will turn into God.

CHAMPLAIN: Do you have any trouble with women?

ANADABIJOU: Who me? Never, not once. You should tell your woman that there is too much water in the river. Any woman who will not skin my meat, cut my fish, can go for a long walk in snowstorm. There is a reason I bring home the caribou.

CHAMPLAIN: Do you like women?

ANADABIJOU: Does the caribou wait patiently for the spear?

CHAMPLAIN: Answer my question.

ANADABIJOU: I just did. Go hunting and one day you will know something about something.

(Pause.)

Let's sing the bird song again.

CHAMPLAIN: Yes … lets.

(The lights fade.)

Scene Twenty-nine

(In another playing area the lights fade in. CHAMPLAIN and SETTLERS enter. CHAMPLAIN paces in an agitated state while listening to the voices of the English invaders.)

VOICE: *(Off.)* Your supply of ships has been intercepted. Surrender swine. We know your stocks are low, that your cannons do not have any balls, that food is scarce, and that many of your settlers are scavenging in the forest.

CHAMPLAIN: How do they know this?

(Various SETTLERS shrug.)

VOICE: *(Off.)* If you do not surrender, we will not take prisoners. Surrender and we will feed you.

(CHAMPLAIN looks at the SETTLERS. They hang their heads. The lights fade.)

Scene Thirty

(In another playing area the lights fade in. ENGLISH SOLDIERS enter with DAVID KIRKE, BRÛLÉ, and CHAMPLAIN. The Union Jack is raised.)

KIRKE: Hip hip hooray. Long live the King.

(KIRKE and the ENGLISH SOLDIERS laugh. CHAMPLAIN looks at BRÛLÉ.)

CHAMPLAIN: You have forsaken France. How could you do this?

BRÛLÉ: I am no longer a Frenchman. I am Canadien.

CHAMPLAIN: May you die by torture and be damned for eternity.

KIRKE: That's enough. If I had known Jesuits were here I would have pounded this place to Kingdom come. You and the sons of Satan are going to an English prison … move dog.

(KIRKE turns to BRÛLÉ.)

And you, of course, you have your freedom.

CHAMPLAIN: This then is the end.

KIRKE: Yes.

(The lights fade.)

Scene Thirty-one

(In another playing area the lights fade in. BRÛLÉ and ANADABIJOU enter.)

BRÛLÉ: Hey, Great Moccasin, what is this place?

ANADABIJOU: This place is called Ongawa.

BRÛLÉ: What does that word mean?

ANADABIJOU: It means "meeting place."

BRÛLÉ: Meeting place … Hmmm.

(ANADABIJOU puts a knife to BRÛLÉ's throat.)

ANADABIJOU: Yes traitor, meeting place. Come, you are going to meet our dogs. They are hungry.

(The lights fade.)

Scene Thirty-two

(In another playing area the lights fade in. ANADABIJOU, with a bottle of rum, is singing "Alouette." CHAMPLAIN enters.)

ANADABIJOU: You are like a dream. Are you real?

CHAMPLAIN: Will you think I am real if I crawl up your nose and start drinking your snot?

ANADABIJOU: Hey, Great Musket. I saw you leave in chains and now—

CHAMPLAIN: What is taken by the powers of Europe is also given. God works in strange ways.

ANADABIJOU: Yes.

CHAMPLAIN: What is this?

ANADABIJOU: English rum.

CHAMPLAIN: This is what Satan drinks.

ANADABIJOU: Yes. I have bitten off many noses since you left. But dogs in red would not trade me kettles for my furs ... only this. Gou-Gou live inside this bottle.

CHAMPLAIN: Give me this.

ANADABIJOU: If you drink that, Gou-Gou will be inside you.

CHAMPLAIN: This is pure poison.

ANADABIJOU: But it keeps me warm in my wig-wam.

CHAMPLAIN: Tell me, Anadabijou, that man who betrayed me, Étienne Brûlé, do you know what has happened to him.

(ANADABIJOU burps.)

Good.

(The lights fade.)

Scene Thirty-three

(In another playing area the lights fade in. CHAMPLAIN and BRÉBEUF enter.)

CHAMPLAIN: I remember the wars when our beloved King Henry ...

BRÉBEUF: The Protestant?

CHAMPLAIN: Yes, yes, the Protestant. He gave me my commission to come here personally.

BRÉBEUF: Hmmm-hmm.

CHAMPLAIN: I remember on one of my journeys across the ocean to see him ... I saw the peril and the icebergs, wind and storms and icebergs.

BRÉBEUF: Yes.

CHAMPLAIN: And I remember in Paris when that traitor Ravaillac murdered our ... King Henry.

BRÉBEUF: Oh yes.

CHAMPLAIN: The crowd tore him limb from limb, drawn and quartered, ripped out his heart and ate it, put his head on a stick, then crushed it and put hot molten lead in every gaping wound before he died.

BRÉBEUF: Yes.

CHAMPLAIN: You knew him, didn't you?

BRÉBEUF: Ravaillac?

CHAMPLAIN: Yes.

BRÉBEUF: Uh ... I can't place the face but I have heard of him.

CHAMPLAIN: Yes, I remember the civil war when I would lead troops into villages, and of course others would lead other troops.

BRÉBEUF: Yes.

CHAMPLAIN: And it didn't matter if the village was Protestant or Catholic, and it didn't matter if the invading army was Protestant or Catholic, the inhabitants would always run for the forest, and the forest was infested with wolves. I have seen so many faces with no eyes ... and they would run into the forest.

BRÉBEUF: You look weary Samuel.

CHAMPLAIN: Wolves, always wolves.

BRÉBEUF: Drink, Samuel, drink.

(BRÉBEUF holds up a liquor bottle. The lights fade.)

Scene Thirty-four

(In another playing area the lights fade in. CHAMPLAIN and ANADABIJOU enter.)

CHAMPLAIN: This place exists more in my brain than in reality. I have such terrible nightmares. While I am sleeping I feel like a demon is sitting on my chest smiling at me. Do you ever feel like that?

ANADABIJOU: No, Great Musket. But I am not surprised you feel like that. You have demons living with you. I am sure they visit your dreams.

(BRÉBEUF enters.)

The Head Demon.

BRÉBEUF: Samuel, Samuel.

CHAMPLAIN: Ah, Père Brébeuf.

BRÉBEUF: Samuel, my precious. I have brought you your mustard seed.

(BRÉBEUF holds up a small bag.)

CHAMPLAIN: Oh good.

(CHAMPLAIN grabs a handful of "Spangle Dust.")

This protects me from demons.

ANADABIJOU: How?

CHAMPLAIN: Before demons attack us they have to stop and count each mustard seed.

ANADABIJOU: Why?

CHAMPLAIN: Because they are demons.

(CHAMPLAIN casts his mustard seed.)

Save me from demons. Protect me from fiends.

(CHAMPLAIN casts his mustard seed.)

BRÉBEUF: And Gou-Gou. Don't forget Gou-Gou.

(BRÉBEUF and ANADABIJOU stare at each other.)

CHAMPLAIN: And Gou-Gou.

(CHAMPLAIN casts his mustard seed. The lights fade.)

Scene Thirty-five

(In another playing area, the lights fade in. CHAMPLAIN and BRÉBEUF enter.)

BRÉBEUF: And he hung up the sword at the altar of the Lord. And so ends the life of St. Ignatius.

CHAMPLAIN: What a beautiful story. I never tire from hearing it. Of all the saints I like him the best.

BRÉBEUF: Oh well said. As above, so below.

CHAMPLAIN: As above, so below.

BRÉBEUF: One day if you play your cards right. You will be a saint. St. Samuel, how does that sound?

CHAMPLAIN: I think that pleasure will deny me. I have yet to meet Jesus in the forest.

BRÉBEUF: What a shame. I see him all the time. Now before we eat, would you like to confess your sins?

CHAMPLAIN: Yes. Last night I had a dream … a nightmare.

BRÉBEUF: Oh yes.

CHAMPLAIN: I dreamed I was being chased by a wolf. I kept running but, it was terrifying.

BRÉBEUF: Was this wolf male or female?

CHAMPLAIN: It was … man wolf. Ferocious.

BRÉBEUF: The wolf that never sleeps. To be devoured by a wild beast is a good sign. I will pray that the wolf will leave only the large bones. Remember Samuel, the moment of death is the birthday of eternal life. Drink Samuel, drink.

(BRÉBEUF gives a wine bottle to CHAMPLAIN.)

CHAMPLAIN: This wine must have been a very bad year. It gives me terrible headaches.

BRÉBEUF: They will soon pass. Drink Samuel, drink.

(CHAMPLAIN looks at the wine bottle, then at BRÉBEUF. BRÉBEUF smiles. The lights fade.)

Scene Thirty-six

(In another playing area the lights fade in; BRÉBEUF and two JESUITS are in earnest, silent conversation. In another playing area the lights fade in; ANADABIJOU and a HABITANT enter.)

HABITANT: On this day, December 25th, 1635, the anniversary of the virgin birth, Samuel de Champlain, explorer, missionary, soldier, founder of New France, passes away. This is a sad day. And yet we should take heart knowing that some men die so that others may live, and of course, some men live so that others may die, but—

ANADABIJOU: What are you saying?

HABITANT: I don't know. I am so upset, so upset.

ANADABIJOU: Come, we should bury our friend.

(The lights fade on ANADABIJOU and the HABITANT. BRÉBEUF and the two JESUITS continue their silent conversation. The lights fade.)

Part Three

Brébeuf

Scene One

(In another playing area the lights fade in. LALEMANT leafs through an almanac. BRÉBEUF stands aside, as if in a trance.)

LALEMANT: Ah ha, an eclipse on August 4th. Excellent. Jean there is—What is it, Jean?

BRÉBEUF: I see a cross in the sky.

LALEMANT: How large, Jean, how large?

BRÉBEUF: Large enough to crucify us all.

(BRÉBEUF smiles ecstatically. The lights fade.)

Scene Two

(In another playing area the lights fade in. LALEMANT, ISAAC JOGUES, and BRÉBEUF enter.)

LALEMANT: I feel like I am living in a dream. In the forest empire of Satan. I keep expecting the earth to part and his Infernalness to appear at any moment. Can you imagine how they would respond?

BRÉBEUF: With every oblation imaginable.

JOGUES: And that savage over there thinks he is the greatest creature that has ever walked the earth.

LALEMANT: I walked into the longhouse yesterday, and they were copulating like dogs. And the "great creature," if nothing else, is certainly a great lover.

BRÉBEUF: The women are mad for him.

JOGUES: And the "great creature" over there ... every time he sees me he does this.

(JOGUES shakes his groin area.)

Every time. I don't look at him anymore except when I sneak a glance out of the corner of my eye, to see if he's looking at me, and of course, he always is and he does this.

(JOGUES makes an obscene gesture.)

LALEMANT: Really.

JOGUES: Thank God they have built us a cabin.

BRÉBEUF: Praise Jesus.

LALEMANT: Praise Jesus.

(The lights fade.)

Scene Three

(In another playing area the lights fade in. BRÉBEUF, ATIRONTA, AGONA, and a SHAMAN enter.)

BRÉBEUF: Paradise is heaven. Only those who die baptized, go there.

ATIRONTA: Do they hunt and feast in heaven?

BRÉBEUF: Of course not.

ATIRONTA: When I die, can I take my pipe and smoke it?

BRÉBEUF: No.

ATIRONTA: Then I don't want to go.

BRÉBEUF: But you must go. Do you want to burn in Hell?

ATIRONTA: If I can take my pipe, yes.

BRÉBEUF: Your children died without being baptized.

AGONA: Is it true that my children are burning in Hell?

(BRÉBEUF nods his head.)

BRÉBEUF: I can see them now. The flames of Hell are burning the flesh off their bones. The devil has the head of your son in his jaws, and is eating his soul. They scream for their mother but they burn in hell. Now I can baptize you.

AGONA: No. When I die I want to be with my children.

(BRÉBEUF holds up a picture of Jesus.)

BRÉBEUF: This is a picture of Jesus. He is the Supreme Manitou. The Oki of Okies.

(BRÉBEUF holds up a picture of Mary.)

This is a picture of Mary. This is the mother of Jesus Christ.

(A SHAMAN enters shaking a rattle.)

SHAMAN: Who was father?

BRÉBEUF: Father was God. God was father.

SHAMAN: Show us picture of him.

BRÉBEUF: No.

SHAMAN: Why not? You show us picture of Virgin Mother, show us picture of Jesus, well show us picture of God.

BRÉBEUF: That is not possible because the father of Jesus—

SHAMAN: —Was Nanabozho.

BRÉBEUF: No. Nanabozho was father of nothing, was father of worse than nothing. Nanabozho was father of shit.

(SHAMAN shakes his rattle.)

SHAMAN: Nanabozho!

BRÉBEUF: Jesus, oh Jesus.

SHAMAN: What kind of God is this Jesus God that say don't kill, then kill everybody.

BRÉBEUF: Shut up, imp.

SHAMAN: We think Jesus God is a crazy God.

BRÉBEUF: Shut up, ape.

SHAMAN: When our God say don't kill, we don't kill.

BRÉBEUF: Quiet, fiend.

SHAMAN: When our God say kill, we kill.

BRÉBEUF: Be quiet. Do you think French knives are superior to Huron knives?

ATIRONTA: Yes.

BRÉBEUF: Do you think French tomahawks are superior to Huron tomahawks?

ATIRONTA: Yes.

BRÉBEUF: Do you think French God is superior to Huron God?

ATIRONTA: No.

BRÉBEUF: Do you want to go to heaven?

ATIRONTA: No.

BRÉBEUF: Why not?

ATIRONTA: We think heaven is full of Frenchmen. I want to be with my relatives in hell. I am not afraid of Jesuit torture.

(The SHAMAN shakes his rattle.)

SHAMAN: We think Jesus is a heartless monster God. We will receive more mercy from the Iroquois than we will from Jesus.

BRÉBEUF: Oh Lord, how weak are the judgments of men.

SHAMAN: And where some see lies others see truth.

(The SHAMAN shakes his rattle. The lights fade.)

Scene Four

(In another playing area the lights fade in. ATIRONTA mimes holding a fish net.)

ATIRONTA: Fish. I am ready for you.

(ATIRONTA throws the net.)

Come on fish. Have the courage to be caught. I will respect your bones.

(The lights fade.)

Scene Five

(In another playing area the lights fade in. BRÉBEUF sits at a wooden table.)

BRÉBEUF: Oh these fish just keep appearing. Oh we will make merry with this fish. Miracle. A miracle. I see a cross on this fish.

(BRÉBEUF claps his hands.)

Oh what a holy supper this is going to be. Eating fish so that we may be fishers of men. Oh I will rejoice and be glad. Of this kingdom there is no end.

(The lights fade.)

Scene Six

(In another playing area the lights fade in. ATIRONTA and AGONA enter.)

ATIRONTA: He talks to himself all the time in the forest, all the time. He is a great sorcerer. He talks to demons all day.

AGONA: What does he say?

ATIRONTA: He puts on a hat like this.

(ATIRONTA puts on the dunce cap.)

And then says … Oh Lord, you have taught me the rules I have no doubt about the rewards. Then he does this.

(ATIRONTA presses the dunce cap against his groin.)

Oh Lord, I'm going to take that woman. Oh Lord, I'm going to take that woman.

(The lights fade.)

Scene Seven

(In another playing area the lights fade in. BRÉBEUF with the dunce cap.)

BRÉBEUF: Oh to be crucified with arrows. Oh Lord put me in a cauldron and let me stew in my own juice. I am ready for you. Whoever Abraham was, I am. I see a mountain covered with virgins. Oh what flagellating ecstasy. Fill my dungeon with light.

(BRÉBEUF searches the darkness.)

I saw you. I know you're spying on me. I see you. Come out my pet, I see you.

(ATIRONTA enters.)

What do you think you're doing?

(The sound of a rattle is heard.)

Ah, stupid question.

(The SHAMAN enters.)

Satan himself has come to visit me. Well, Satan, a fine day, isn't it. Do you worship Baphomet in the form of a cat?

SHAMAN: Do I worship who in the form of a what?

BRÉBEUF: I know you do. You are a heretic, an apostate, an idolater.

SHAMAN: What are you?

BRÉBEUF: I command you to say the Lord's Prayer without stuttering.

SHAMAN: I know you are mad and cruel. Just don't bite anyone. You are a crazy Frenchman, sent to plague us.

BRÉBEUF: Oh to be flogged while my parents burn at the stake.

SHAMAN: If this man puts on the skin of a bear, he will go berserk, I can tell.

BRÉBEUF: Oh demons are everywhere. Sitting on a lettuce leaf, as numerous as bees.

SHAMAN: I have met one Frenchman in my life and it is one too many.

(The lights fade.)

Scene Eight

(In another playing area the lights fade in. LALEMANT and BRÉBEUF enter. LALEMANT holds a pen and paper.)

LALEMANT: How many fleas bit you last night?

BRÉBEUF: Six hundred and sixty-six.

(LALEMENT writes on the paper.)

LALEMANT: What did you eat today?

BRÉBEUF: Some corn, twelve kernals mixed with some tree bark and some rock moss.

(LALEMANT writes on the paper.)

LALEMANT: And what did it taste like?

BRÉBEUF: I closed my eyes and it tasted good.

(LALEMANT writes on the paper.)

LALEMANT: What did you dream last night?

(Pause.)

Were you visited by temptation?

BRÉBEUF: I dreamed … it was a nightmare.

LALEMANT: Oh yes.

BRÉBEUF: I dreamed I was caught in the cleft of the buttocks of Mary.

(LALEMENT writes on the paper.)

LALEMANT: Did you escape this embrace?

BRÉBEUF: Yes, in a way.

LALEMANT: How many times have you examined your conscience today.

BRÉBEUF: Seven times.

LALEMANT: Why so few?

(The lights fade.)

Scene Nine

(In another playing area the lights fade in. JOGUES and ATIRONTA enter.)

JOGUES: Oh my bed is infested with fleas.

ATIRONTA: Change your blankets.

JOGUES: No, the fleas are on my body.

(JOGUES holds up a magnifying glass for ATIRONTA to look through.)

Big, aren't they. Oh this is the first plague of Moses. More to come.

(The lights fade.)

Scene Ten

(In another playing area the lights fade in. LALEMANT and BRÉBEUF enter.)

BRÉBEUF: And with corpse-like submission, statue-like indifference, and stick-like humility, you will obey all my commands.

LALEMANT: And with corpse-like submission, statue-like indifference, and stick-like humility I will obey all your commands.

BRÉBEUF: Good. Now sing our song.

LALEMANT: The Pope to rule the world. The Jesuits to rule the Pope.

BRÉBEUF: More feeling.

LALEMANT: The Pope to rule to world. The Jesuits to rule the Pope.

BRÉBEUF: Again.

(The lights fade.)

Scene Eleven

(In another playing area the lights fade in. JOGUES kneels in prayer.)

JOGUES: The Savages call me Ondessonk. It means "bird of prey." It has been very good hunting. Oh Lord, protect this man on his journey. He takes our beavers to market. May he trade wisely. As I enter the gate of the enemy there will be nothing between me and thee. As you put your hand under the thigh of Isaac and sent him forth … send me forth.

(The lights fade.)

Scene Twelve

(In another playing area the lights fade in. BRÉBEUF enters.)

BRÉBEUF: She will be Sarah. She is a fair woman to look upon. I will plant my seed inside her.

(ATIRONTA enters with a rattle.)

ATIRONTA: Echon, hark. Isaac has been captured by the Iroquois.

BRÉBEUF: And the wicked shall perish and the righteous with them. And with fire in one hand and a knife in the other Isaac was taken as a token … Oh Lord accept him as a burnt offering.

(ATIRONTA shakes his rattle. The lights fade.)

Scene Thirteen

(In another playing area the lights fade in. ATIRONTA and AGONA enter.)

AGONA: He is a great sorcerer. Everyone he puts the death water on dies. He is unstoppable. If he sees someone sick and he does not have his water shaker, he goes crazy and starts crying and screaming, and then evil spirit enters him and he starts shaking his tears on the sick, and then they die.

ATIRONTA: Stay away from that man. He is possessed by a demon.

(The lights fade.)

Scene Fourteen

(In another playing area the lights fade in. BRÉBEUF and LALEMANT enter.)

BRÉBEUF: The cross was the symbol of Satan's victory over Christ.

LALEMANT: Jean, what has come into your head.

BRÉBEUF: We are like the wandering monks. Free to think.

LALEMANT: Jean, we are the hands and feet of God. Nothing else. Now let us pray to the Infanta.

(BRÉBEUF kneels in prayer and hallucinates.)

BRÉBEUF: Speak Lord and I will listen.

(BRÉBEUF makes facial contortions and then bawls like an ox.)

LALEMANT: What is it Jean?

BRÉBEUF: I have been given the word. I will judge this house with cruel measure. Oh my Lord, False Gods, make this land unclean.

(ATIRONTA enters shaking a rattle.)

In this forest I renounce everything.

LALEMANT: Except Jesus.

BRÉBEUF: My Saviour. The most beautiful man in the world.

ATIRONTA: Shake! *(He shakes his rattle.)*

BRÉBEUF: Life is the love of vanity. It is the love of unhealthy joy, lusts, adulteries, incests, sacrileges, heresies, swindles.

ATIRONTA: Shake! *(He shakes his rattle.)*

BRÉBEUF: Idealism without power is fantasy.

ATIRONTA: Shake! *(He shakes his rattle.)*

BRÉBEUF: He who wills the end must will the means.

ATIRONTA: Shake! *(He shakes his rattle.)*

BRÉBEUF: Ad majorem Dei gloriam.

ATIRONTA: Shake! *(He shakes his rattle.)*

BRÉBEUF: To the greater glory of God.

ATIRONTA: Shake! *(He shakes his rattle.)*

BRÉBEUF: There is no yoke too heavy for me to lift.

ATIRONTA: Shake! *(He shakes his rattle.)*

BRÉBEUF: I am an ox fit only for burden.

ATIRONTA: Shake!

(ATIRONTA shakes his rattle. BRÉBEUF bawls like an ox. The lights fade.)

Scene Fifteen

(In another playing area the lights fade in. The Iroquois Chief, TEGANNISSORENS and an ENGLISH OFFICER enter.)

ENGLISH OFFICER: Don't worry about the Dutch. The Dutch are nothing compared to the English. Nothing. My leader is a Great Mucka Muck. When he is angry snakes come out of his head.

TEGANNISSORENS: Snakes come out of his head when he is happy. There is a story my friend, I will tell it to you. It is about an owl with big eyes who was visited by crows. These crows told awful lies to the owl with the big eyes. The owl would say to the crows "Does the moon shine at night?" And the crows would say "No." And the owl had big eyes. And the owl would ask them "Are you crows?" And the crows would cry "No."

ENGLISH OFFICER: I don't understand this story.

TEGANNISSORENS: Speak truth.

ENGLISH OFFICER: On my word as an officer and a gentleman, and an Englishman, every word in that treaty is true. And the words of an Englishman are never broken.

(TEGANNISSORENS bends an arrow.)

TEGANNISSORENS: My father signed a treaty with an Englishman.

ENGLISH OFFICER: That was then, this is now. Attack the French and the English king with the snakes in his head will be good to you. Is it a deal? And your land is your land. Is it a deal?

TEGANNISSORENS: Deal.

(The lights fade.)

Scene Sixteen

(In another playing area the lights fade in. LALEMANT and BRÉBEUF enter.)

LALEMANT: I finished translating the Lord's Prayer into Huron. Do you know what it sounds like? It sounds like the Lord's Prayer backwards.

BRÉBEUF: Sign of the Devil.

(BRÉBEUF coughs.)

LALEMANT: You have a cough, Jean.

BRÉBEUF: It's nothing.

LALEMANT: Hope to God you haven't got what the Indians have got.

(BRÉBEUF shakes his head.)

They all suffer from consumption.

BRÉBEUF: We must heal, and failing that, baptize them before they die.

LALEMANT: They think we are the cause of their illness. The witch doctors here, do not suffer us gladly.

BRÉBEUF: The Black Hole is coming.

LALEMANT: The Black Hole.

BRÉBEUF: August the fourth.

(BRÉBEUF coughs. The lights fade.)

Scene Seventeen

(In another playing area the lights fade in. BRÉBEUF, AGONA and ATIRONTA enter.)

BRÉBEUF: The more one suffers on earth the happier one is in heaven. Listen to me you knaves, ruffians, louts, and wretches. Listen.

The more one suffers on earth the happier one is in heaven. Believe in Jesus, you sinners.

(ATIRONTA and AGONA laugh. ATIRONTA shakes his rattle.)

BRÉBEUF: Convert before it is too late. Convert I say. Oh Jesus, make them believe, give them a taste of your medicine. Eat the sun Jesus, eat the sun. The Black Hole is coming.

(Lighting change to evoke an eclipse. Pandemonium.)

Believe in Jesus before he eats your soul.

AGONA: Jesus, Jesus, oh Jesus.

BRÉBEUF: Jesus, Jesus, oh Jesus.

ATIRONTA: Jesus, Jesus, oh Jesus.

(The lights fade.)

Scene Eighteen

(In another playing area the lights fade in. BRÉBEUF, AGONA, and ATIRONTA enter.)

BRÉBEUF: Now that you have eaten the flesh of Jesus and drank his blood, how do you feel?

ATIRONTA: More.

BRÉBEUF: Exactly. Has it made you strong? It has made me strong.

ATIRONTA: More.

BRÉBEUF: Oh, you will get more.

(BRÉBEUF looks at AGONA.)

As honey is sweet, this woman is beautiful. My sweet.

ATIRONTA: I know you are a powerful sorcerer, but I do not fear you. I will burn in Hell with Jesuits, but you will burn in Hell here if you do not leave—

(BRÉBEUF turns to AGONA)

BRÉBEUF: Would you like to see me turn him into a toad?

AGONA: No.

BRÉBEUF: Perhaps a turtle.

AGONA: No.

(BRÉBEUF turns to ATIRONTA.)

BRÉBEUF: Who do you love?

ATIRONTA: This woman.

BRÉBEUF: Who do you love?

AGONA: Jesus.

BRÉBEUF: Oh blessed bliss-laden word. A bolt of lightning is going to strike this man down. Get him out of my sight before the snakes come out of my head.

(BRÉBEUF turns to ATIRONTA.)

Leave me. She is in my flock, as you will be. I will crush your soul and then fill the void with Jesus.

ATIRONTA: If I was master of this land, your story would be over.

BRÉBEUF: But you are not the master of this land. I am.

(The lights fade.)

Scene Nineteen

(In another playing area the lights fade in. LALEMANT is on his knees reciting "Hail Mary." BRÉBEUF enters. He shakes a rattle. Then, like a shaman, he makes a magic circle around LALEMANT. BRÉBEUF starts to massage his hair.)

BRÉBEUF:I will comb the snakes out of my hair and then wear the deer horns, and my enemies will be a heap of bones before me.

(BRÉBEUF shakes his rattle. LALEMANT stops reciting.)

LALEMANT: But I have only said two thousand this morning.

(BRÉBEUF shakes his rattle.)

BRÉBEUF: I will comb the snakes—

LALEMANT: I see no snakes in your hair—

BRÉBEUF: In order to be nearer to Christ we must tempt Providence.

LALEMANT: Oh Father in Heaven, have mercy on this man.

(BRÉBEUF holds up a whip.)

A devil has entered the servant of the servant.

(BRÉBEUF starts whipping LALEMANT. The lights fade.)

Scene Twenty

(In another playing area the lights fade in. AGONA enters holding a bible.)

AGONA: And the book says ... thou shalt not worship another God ... because you are a jealous God and quick to anger. And the book says … thou shalt not take your name in vain … because that makes you crazy and then you kill everybody. And the book says … thou shalt not—

(BRÉBEUF enters.)

BRÉBEUF: —suffer a witch to live.

(AGONA closes the book.)

What are Iroquois?

AGONA: Enemies of faith.

BRÉBEUF: Good. And what are Huron?

(AGONA's eyes light up.)

AGONA: Believers in faith.

BRÉBEUF: Good. Now jump up.

(AGONA jumps up.)

BRÉBEUF: Now I want you to tell me about your religion.

AGONA: I thought you found our religion silly.

BRÉBEUF: No, I find it very interesting. Here, sit on my knee and speak.

(AGONA sits on BRÉBEUF's knee.)

AGONA: There were six men. No land. The men wandered like the wind in search of land. Instead they found woman in heaven. One man, Hogaho the wolf, climbed a tree and saw the woman drinking water. The great Spirit became angry and threw the woman out of heaven. She landed on a turtle. The turtle dug up clay and made island. The woman made love to turtle and had two children who fight. Strong one kill weak one and woman give birth. Strong kill weak and woman give birth. Strong kill weak and woman give birth.

(The lights fade.)

Scene Twenty-one

(In another playing area the lights fade in. TEGANNISSORENS enters.)

TEGANNISSORENS: Imagine the beaver without his fur. He would die. We are like the beaver. If we do not have his fur we will die. The English firearms, the knives, the kettles, the tomahawks, we need them. Is there any man who will debate that? Then we are agreed. Now we all dream. We dream the good life. A kettle full of fish, moose meat on every stump, cornfields as far as the eye can see. But our dreams will be fantasies if we do not have the things the English can give us. It is life, or it is death. We are kings of this forest. We rule all the beavers. But all our beavers have left us. They chew our trees in the land of the Algonquin, in the land of the Huron. The French think the Huron are the "Good Iroquois." They think the Iroquois are the "Bad Iroquois." The Frenchman who thinks like that—I would eat his brain so he could never think like that ever again. Only Iroquois are Iroquois.

(The lights fade.)

Scene Twenty-two

(In another playing area the lights fade in. JOGUES, BRÉBEUF, and LALEMANT enter.)

BRÉBEUF: It is a miracle that you are here. A miracle.

LALEMANT: And your hands. Let me kiss your scabs. Your fingers I must kiss them, I must.

(JOGUES holds up two stumps. BRÉBEUF holds up a silver goblet.)

BRÉBEUF: In this chalice is the blood of Jesus. Drink martyr.

(BRÉBEUF holds the goblet to the mouth of JOGUES. JOGUES drinks.)

LALEMANT: Oh Lazarus you are risen.

BRÉBEUF: And now you are going back to represent God to the Iroquois.

JOGUES: I have unshakable faith in Jesus.

BRÉBEUF: Jesus, oh blessed bliss-laden word.

JOGUES: When I was first captured by the Mohawk they hung me upside down and did unspeakable things with my crucifix. Then they chewed off my fingers, cut off my thumbs, and hoisted me over a fire and started roasting me alive. As my back was burning I thought of St. Lawrence and shouted to them "This side is done, roll me over." I was taken to their village where the work began in earnest, but in that dungeon of demons I did not wither. When I was in extremes I feared that in my pain I would curse my tormentors. But I prayed for strength. As he forgave I forgave and not a word or a whimper passed my lips.

BRÉBEUF: Jesus is the most beautiful man in the world.

LALEMANT: Oh bliss-laden word.

JOGUES: And now I go back to face my tormentors and love them to death. I escaped before I had the time to say "I am finished."

BRÉBEUF: Ecce Homo.

LALEMANT: Ecce Homo.

(The lights fade.)

Scene Twenty-three

(In another playing area the lights fade in. Chanting, banging of drums, shouting, shaking of rattles. BRÉBEUF and LALEMANT enter.)

LALEMANT: What is that racket?

BRÉBEUF: The plague rages. They are frightening away their devils.

LALEMANT: They certainly are. If they don't stop this noise … I shall leave.

BRÉBEUF: They blame us for the plague. They say we are sorcerers. When we walk together to other villages the natives shout "Famine and pest are coming, prepare to die, famine and pest are coming." The devil is desperate. He is causing great strife because we have saved so many souls from His Infernalness. This is an unspeakable happiness. Subduing a den of devils to our will. We will beard Satan yet.

LALEMANT: Providing the tools of Lucifer do not kill us.

BRÉBEUF: We will pray to St. Joseph nine times. He will deliver us.

(The lights fade.)

Scene Twenty-four

(In another playing area the lights fade in. The SHAMAN enters shaking his rattle.)

SHAMAN: Black robes, black magic. They ask everybody their name, and then kneel before the fire, and mutter to themselves, and then the named die. There are now too many dead for the living to bury. Everyone is a dog's supper. I make it known right now, that if someone will kill these men, I will have no objection.

(The SHAMAN shakes his rattle.)

Black robes, black magic. They are the walking pest. Wherever they go, plague go with them. Head fall off and die in longhouse. Black robes always talk about body of Jesus. They have demon in longhouse rotting away like shit making everybody sick. What kind of men are these, that say the same thing over and over and over again? They never stop talking about their Oki. What he wants. What he forbids. Never stop talking about Oki. Oki is devil. We die like flies 'cause of Oki. I think devil took big shit in Hell and Jesuits were born. The black robes, when they die, will go to the land were they eat serpents and toads all day and all night. The sooner we send them to that place, the better.

(The SHAMAN shakes his rattle. The lights fade.)

Scene Twenty-five

(In another playing area the lights fade in. BRÉBEUF is crawling on the ground.)

BRÉBEUF: Feeding on crumbs. What a feast.

(The lights fade.)

Scene Twenty-six

(In another playing area the lights fade in. BRÉBEUF and the SHAMAN enter.)

SHAMAN: May Iouskeha gnaw your bones forever, and then beat your bones with stones.

BRÉBEUF: Oh Lord, mount me backwards on a donkey and send me forth, I will gather fireflies to show us the way.

SHAMAN: When I die, bury me deep in the ground. Fifty feet deep. I want my body close to the longhouse of the demons.

BRÉBEUF: Shake! *(He shakes his rattle.)*

SHAMAN: I hope your enemies eat you like the meat of a wild beast.

BRÉBEUF: Shake! *(He shakes his rattle.)*

SHAMAN: If I could put you in a kettle. What happiness. You are an evil sorcerer. Something wrong with you.

BRÉBEUF: Shake! *(He shakes his rattle.)*

SHAMAN: When you die you will live in the sky with your demon. I will live in the ground so that a tree may grow.

BRÉBEUF: In the next life I will kill that tree.

SHAMAN: In the next life you will come back as a toad, and this tree will laugh.

(The lights fade.)

Scene Twenty-seven

(In another playing area the lights fade in. LALEMANT kneels in prayer.)

LALEMANT: If the Church said that a black rock was white I would say that rock was white and yet I would not believe the gospel if the church did not urge me to do so and yet—

(BRÉBEUF enters.)

BRÉBEUF: I have just had lunch in the forest with the Holy Mother and Jesus.

LALEMANT: Very good, Jean, very good. Did they speak?

(BRÉBEUF smiles.)

BRÉBEUF: With their eyes. Listen.

(A distant chanting of "Jesus" is heard.)

They are all praying to Jesus. They live in complete fear of Jesus.

(BRÉBEUF smiles. The lights fade.)

Scene Twenty-eight

(In another playing area the lights fade in. BRÉBEUF and ATIRONTA enter.)

ATIRONTA: No problem. You can sprinkle the death water on me anytime.

BRÉBEUF: Can I do it now?

ATIRONTA: Go ahead.

BRÉBEUF: I baptize you in the name of the Lord.

(BRÉBEUF baptizes ATIRONTA.)

ATIRONTA: See, I not die. I'm still alive.

BRÉBEUF: You are the first person that I have baptized that will live.

ATIRONTA: We know you are a powerful sorcerer. If I turn into a white man you will have many converts.

BRÉBEUF: We will call you Peter. You are the rock we will build our faith upon.

ATIRONTA: I am the rock. Look, I am still alive.

(The lights fade.)

Scene Twenty-nine

(In another playing area the lights fade in. BRÉBEUF holds up a cup.)

BRÉBEUF: This is my cup. God I love cleaning my cup. This is the cup I drink my water out of.

(The lights fade.)

Scene Thirty

(In another playing area the lights fade in. TEGANNISSORENS and JOGUES enter.)

TEGANNISSORENS: You would have better luck converting a den of bears to Christianity than us. I once killed a black robe that looked just like you. But before I killed him I tortured him good. But he wouldn't cry out. So I put my ear to his mouth. And as the fire burned his belly he made this sound.

(TEGANNISSORENS emits a barely audible gasp.)

This ear heard it. That sound is in my ear forever.

JOGUES: Did I ever tell you that once when I was with the Huron, they captured an Iroquois?

TEGANNISSORENS: He showed them how to die.

JOGUES: And they tortured him to death. But before they tortured him I started telling him about Jesus.

TEGANNISSORENS: I bet when you started talking he looked at you like this.

(TEGANNISSORENS makes a face.)

JOGUES: No, he looked at me like this.

(JOGUES makes a face.)

TEGANNISSORENS: That not Iroquois. You talk about Jesus—Iroquois put tomahawk in your head, like this.

(TEGANNISSORENS brandishes his tomahawk. The lights fade.)

Scene Thirty-one

(In another playing area the lights fade in. BRÉBEUF beats a saucepan with a spoon.)

BRÉBEUF: Children, children.

(AGONA enters.)

AGONA: Yes, Echon, you call ... What?

BRÉBEUF: Who do you love?

AGONA: Jesus.

BRÉBEUF: And does he love you?

AGONA Yes.

BRÉBEUF: How do you know he loves you?

AGONA: The book says so.

BRÉBEUF: Good. Now I will tell you the story about the stork and the fox.

AGONA: What colour was the stork?

BRÉBEUF: White. And the fox was very large.

(ATIRONTA enters.)

ATIRONTA: Echon, Iroquois are coming. We must fight.

AGONA: You are a Christian Huron. It is forbidden to fight. The book says so.

ATIRONTA: You have destroyed the spirit of my people.

(ATIRONTA exits.)

BRÉBEUF: And the stork said to the fox—

(BRÉBEUF shakes a rattle. The lights fade.)

Scene Thirty-two

(In another playing area the lights fade in. BRÉBEUF is tied to the stake. LALEMANT is tied to the stake. BRÉBEUF bawls like an ox.)

BRÉBEUF: I am an ox fit only for burden.

TEGANNISSORENS: You are going to die a thousand deaths before you die once. You are going to burn, sorcerer. Burn bright, I can tell.

(LALEMANT starts whimpering.)

BRÉBEUF: Be brave. God is with you.

TEGANNISSORENS: Oooh, this one, this one is possessed.

BRÉBEUF: God is my salvation. Leave me imp to my peace. I do not converse with devils.

TEGANNISSORENS: You will cause great strife, you die so well. Many warriors will die fighting to see who will eat your heart. You are brave, but this one, this one is a woman.

(TEGANNISSORENS holds a tomahawk against LALEMANT's neck. LALEMENT screams.)

BRÉBEUF: And the book says honour thy mother and—

(AGONA enters holding a knife.)

AGONA: And the book says many things, Echon. And the book says "Thou shalt not suffer a witch to live."

(AGONA approaches BRÉBEUF with the knife. The lights fade.)

Part Four

Radisson

Scene One

(In another playing area the lights fade in. PIERRE RADISSON, MAURICE, and LOUIS, a fur trader, stand at a bar counter.)

MAURICE: Dollard des Ormeaux. Now there was a man. A hero, with sixteen men he held off eight hundred Iroquois. Saved New France and our way of life.

LOUIS: What kind of life did he save? Go into the forest and trap beavers without a permit they put you in jail.

RADISSON: You need a note from the governor to trap beavers. What are you? A pussy willow?

MAURICE: Hey, don't say bad things about this man. He is my brother.

RADISSON: Your brother is a pussy willow.

MAURICE: You say another word I pull out your tongue. I am Maurice. You are talking to Maurice.

RADISSON: Don't talk back to me. I get my knife and cut your nuts. I buried Des Ormeaux. He was out there to get furs, not save New France.

LOUIS: You must be Radisson,

RADISSON: That's right. When I was a boy I was captured by the Iroquois. I took my torture like a man.

(MAURICE and LOUIS laugh.)

You want to see the scars? The Iroquois call me Dodcon. It means little Devil. They made me run the gauntlet and they beat me with rocks and tomahawks, knives and sharp sticks, but I run, I piss blood, but I run.

MAURICE: And then they adopt you.

RADISSON: That's right. If Mohawk ever catch you, they not adopt you. They put it up your ass forever. You cry like baby and then you not believe what they do to you. An old woman with only four teeth in her whole head, two on top, two on bottom, had face like a snake but she the big boss of tribe, and she takes me into longhouse.

(MAURICE and LOUIS laugh.)

MAURICE: And what happened then?

RADISSON: What do you think?

MAURICE: You fucked her.

RADISSON: That's right. Me, Radisson, I fuck for my life. In the longhouse under a million scalps I fuck.

(MAURICE and LOUIS laugh.)

That old hag pick up thorn bush then grab my dick and strop me down. Strop me down good. I like to see you in that situation. You cry like baby, but not me, I smile. And then I become Mohawk, and I hunt, and I go on warpath and I kill enemies.

LOUIS: I don't believe this.

RADISSON: I once scalp Frenchman look just like you. I take my knife and cut out brain and eat. I prove to my brothers I am Mohawk. Then I escape, I stab my brothers in the back and I escape. I tell you the story of my life, it make you sick.

(The lights fade.)

Scene Two

(In another playing area the lights fade in. JEAN TALON enters.)

TALON: Attention, attention, attention. This is a proclamation from Laval, bishop of New

France. Anyone who is caught selling liquor, or firewater, or whoop-up juice, or scuttywaboo, or whatever it is called to the Indians, will be hung. Do you understand? ... Bon.

(The lights fade.)

Scene Three

(In another playing area the lights fade in. LAVAL enters.)

LAVAL: We are being plagued by goblins. They are called the Iroquois. They pray to demons and speak the language of hell. The only path to paradise for the Iroquois is to be burned at the stake. It is good for their soul. We need soldiers of God to wipe them out.

(The lights fade.)

Scene Four

(In another playing area the lights fade in. The MARQUIS DE TRACY enters holding a sword and a cross.)

TRACY: I, Alexandre Prouville, The Marquis de Tracy, by order of the Knights of St. John and the Order of Malta, am Protector of the Faith. I have abandoned all desires, I have no will of my own. Whatever God wills, so be it. With this cross on my chest and this sword in my hand I will fear no evil. The enemies of the faith will be given up to the wrath of God. This land belongs to the Holy Virgin. Every tree, every blade of grass, but hobgoblins live here. If any of you men die killing them you will die a martyr's death and be assured of a place in paradise. We will smite our enemies and take their land as our inheritance. In this holy war, we are soldiers of God. Let us do our duty.

(The lights fade.)

Scene Five

(In another playing area the lights fade in. TEGANNISSORENS and TRACY enter. TRACY aims a musket at TEGANNISSORENS.)

TEGANNISSORENS: Oh Onontio. Oh Great Mountain. Give ear. I am the mouth of my nation. When I speak, I speak for all the Iroquois. There is no evil in my heart. My song is the song of peace. You have many devils dressed the same. They walk like one. They speak as loud as thunder. We are impressed. You have done us great wrongs. We have done you great wrongs. I say we should bury the hatchet. I want to be your friend. I want you to be my friend. Do you believe me?

TRACY: Yes.

TEGANNISSORENS: Then why you point thunderstick at me.

TRACY: Old habits die hard.

TEGANNISSORENS: I speak truth.

TRACY: Keep talking.

TEGANNISSORENS: I say, farewell war, farewell arms. Hello peace, hello friend. This hand has killed many white men. This hand has ripped off many dresses from many women.

TRACY: I'll cut that hand off if you say another word.

TEGANNISSORENS: Shake this hand. We will be friends.

TRACY: Keep your distance.

(TEGANNISSORENS holds up a musket.)

TEGANNISSORENS: I have thunderstick too. Let us touch thundersticks. We be friends.

(The musket of TEGANNISSORENS touches the musket of TRACY. The lights fade.)

Scene Six

(In another playing area the lights fade in. LAVAL and TRACY enter.)

LAVAL: It is the nature of things that while some men are rich, others are poor, while some men are powerful, others are powerless. Do you agree?

TRACY: That is as succinct a description of reality as I have ever heard.

LAVAL: Excellent. Now, Governor, with regard to making decisions. There are three votes. You will have one vote and I will have one vote. If we are deadlocked I will have a second vote to break the tie.

TRACY: Sounds pretty good to me.

(The lights fade.)

Scene Seven

(In another playing area the lights fade in. RADISSON enters.)

RADISSON: You not believe what it like up by the Big Bay. Eighty degrees below zero. You go for a walk your blood freeze. Your balls turn blue and you turn into snowman. And be food for caribou. Turn into plant. See this jacket. I eat a jacket just like this, last winter. By the Big Bay you don't eat. You chew and spit, chew and spit. I eat rawhide till my mouth bleed. But I like it up there.

(The lights fade.)

Scene Eight

(In another playing area the lights fade in. TALON and LOUIS enter.)

TALON: What is your name?

LOUIS: Louis.

TALON: And where were you born?

LOUIS: I was born in a barn.

TALON: I mean what town, what village?

LOUIS: That I do not know.

TALON: Does your mother know?

LOUIS: My mother, she was born in a barn too, so—

(LAVAL enters.)

TALON: This is impossible. They're all like this. This man should be living in a stall with a horse, or a pig, or a cow—

LOUIS: Should be, I do.

TALON: Men like this are legion, they are everywhere. They don't know where they were born, why they were born, when they were born.

LAVAL: Yes, we need more of them. They make good followers and Jesus loves them. The more people, the greater his love, and though they be helpmates of the devil, this wilderness needs women.

LOUIS: I have many squaws to choose from.

LAVAL: I do not mean the heathens. I mean God-fearing Catholics with one purpose in life … to multiply.

TALON: Yes, marriage will turn these louts into sensible hardworking drones.

LAVAL: I will write to the king.

(The lights fade.)

Scene Nine

(In another playing area the lights fade in. MAURICE, RADISSON, and LOUIS enter.)

MAURICE: And then I was chased by mad Indians. See, they cut my bum bad with knife. But I run fast and hard. And I starve all the time, but I see tracks in snow of wolf. And I follow, and I see body of half-eaten deer trapped in the ice, and I eat. Me Maurice, I eat.

RADISSON: Out west I saw more beavers in one day than you'll skin in your whole life.

MAURICE: Here, put this in your firewater. Make you stand up big and straight.

RADISSON: Don't make jokes about me. I got more women than you. I'm telling you something you don't know.

MAURICE: And I've done things you'll never do.

RADISSON: You don't know what this place is like. I have maps drawn by the Cree, and the Sioux.

MAURICE: The who?

RADISSON: The Sioux.

MAURICE: The who?

RADISSON: See, you don't know what you see beyond the big lakes. Beavers as big as donkeys.

MAURICE: No, no, not as big as donkeys.

RADISSON: Well, pretty big anyway.

MAURICE: How big is that?

RADISSON: Big as a small bear.

(MAURICE shakes his head.)

Hey Louis, how big are the beavers beyond the big lake?

LOUIS: As big as me.

RADISSON: See, big as a small bear. And you should see these beavers work. They work like … what can I say … they work like beavers. You should see them, working all day, working all night. Work, work, work, have a snooze, then get up and work, work work. They turn rivers into lakes. The stuff that dreams are made of.

(Pause.)

LOUIS: The girl on the farm is my dream.

RADISSON: You have been talking about the girl on the farm for ten years.

LOUIS: Yes.

RADISSON: When you first mentioned this girl on the farm, she was twelve years old. And this woman on the farm is still not married.

LOUIS: That is why I dream.

RADISSON: Why don't you marry her?

LOUIS: As you know, Pierre, I am shy.

RADISSON: There are reasons for being shy, and there are reasons for not being shy.

LOUIS: Perhaps. But I smoke my pipe and dream.

MAURICE: I have seen the girl he dreams about. I would put it to my donkey before I would put it to the one he dreams of.

LOUIS: Don't make remarks about the girl on the farm.

RADISSON: The love that never speaks dirty. A good love.

(GROSSEILLIERS enters.)

GROSSEILLIERS: Ah, radishes.

RADISSON: Ah, gooseberries.

GROSSEILLIERS: Don't talk to him, he's too ugly.

RADISSON: I know, and he's got a big mouth.

MAURICE: Look who's talking.

GROSSEILLIERS: Hey, don't fool with this man. He'll get his knife and cut your nuts.

RADISSON: That's right.

GROSSEILLIERS: Forget him.

RADISSON: I see you in the forest, I drink your blood. I don't think I like your face.

GROSSEILLIERS: Forget him. Come over here. I talked with the English. Fat fart can't pronounce my name but we can work for them.

RADISSON: I don't want to work for them.

GROSSEILLIERS: Many furs and much money if we get the beavers from the Big Bay and sell them to the English. Our brothers won't give us the shit that comes out their bum, but the English give us money.

(The lights fade.)

Scene Ten

(In another playing area the lights fade in. TALON enters.)

TALON: Mes amis, bonjour, bonjour. The lucky day has arrived. Today we celebrate the joys of Hymen and Cupid. The tall and the short, the blond and the brown, the plump and the lean are here. Messieurs. Les Filles du Roi.

(Lights up on MARIE and HÉLÈNE. The lights fade.)

Scene Eleven

(In another playing area the lights fade in. HÉLÈNE and MARIE enter with TALON.)

MARIE: They told us in France that sheep on the hoof, already roasted, walk around ready to eat. Is that true?

TALON: Yes.

HÉLÈNE: With knives and forks in their backs?

TALON: That's right.

MARIE: And that it rains gold?

TALON: Twice a month.

HÉLÈNE: What are the men like?

TALON: The men are as polite as bears.

MARIE: Are they handsome?

TALON: Some bears think so. Others, you will see.

MARIE: The world has only offered me it's butchers, bakers, and candlestick makers. The new world cannot offer me worse.

TALON: When you see these Frenchmen in the forest, you will wonder if they are Frenchmen.

MARIE: When the storm is raging, any port will do.

(The lights fade.)

Scene Twelve

(In another playing area the lights fade in. MARGUERITE BOURGEOYS enters.)

BOURGEOYS: Under my watchful eyes you will pass the time in as gormless and insipid a manner as possible. I don't want to see men climbing my ivy looking for charms. I am going to treat you all like turnips. Now, I understand you are orphans. Ha! That's a laugh.

Before I took my orders I was once a woman of the world, once. Have any of you turnips ever had a man between your legs? Ha! I thought so. I know what it's like to have delight turn to alarm. When a man loves a woman he assassinates her flesh. Now all you god-forsaken pig-eyed flirts, listen to me. I want to hear your personal history. Speak, have you had any amorous adventures.

(HÉLÈNE steps forward.)

HÉLÈNE: When I was seventeen I eloped with a man.

BOURGEOYS: Ah yes. Did you lope to an altar or to a bed? Ha! I thought so. This turnip is damaged goods. What about you? Have you had a bite taken out of you? Have you been poked? Have a pair of dark eyes played havoc with your heart? Speak, you beautiful looking idiot.

(MARIE steps forward.)

MARIE: I realized as a young girl that if I listened to prudence I would die a spinster.

BOURGEOYS: You are all going to learn that beauty in its most hideous form is truth, and you are all ugly liars. Tomorrow you will be put on display. The lucky ones will meet men with velvet coats and lavender ribbons, the unlucky ones will meet men with a different garb. But in the meantime there are rabbits to feed and dough to knead.

(BOURGEOYS smiles. The lights fade.)

Scene Thirteen

(In another playing area the lights fade in. TALON, LE BOEUF, and JACQUES BEAUPORT enter.)

TALON: Now gentlemen, you know it is against the law to remain a bachelor. Come now, one of you must be brave. They also come with a dowry of one horse, one cow, two pigs, and three chickens. And, and this is the "piece de resistance" you will be paid one hundred francs per child, and if it is a boy, an extra one hundred francs.

BEAUPORT: Are these women pretty?

TALON: No, but God loves them.

LE BOEUF: How many pigs do I get?

TALON: Two.

LE BOEUF: Two pigs, two pigs.

BEAUPORT: Why not an extra two hundred francs if it is a boy?

TALON: Pray for twins.

(The lights fade.)

Scene Fourteen

(In another playing area the lights fade in. HÉLÈNE, BOURGEOYS, and MARIE enter.)

BOURGEOYS: Speak.

HÉLÈNE: I looked for fruit on a tree that grew only flowers. I was married for eleven years to an impotent old drudge. I am still a virgin, I think.

BOURGEOYS: Speak.

MARIE: When I was a girl I married a man, or at least I thought he was a man. He wasn't. He was a monster. The He-man of Gascony.

BOURGEOYS: Personal habits.

HÉLÈNE: My husband knocked on my door many times but never set a foot inside. Knock, knock. "Who is it?" says I. "It is your husband, can I come in?" "Entrez," says I.

(HÉLÈNE repeats the above three lines with a sense of mounting anxiety and frustration until BOURGEOYS says "enough.")

BOURGEOYS: Personal habits, please.

MARIE: He would come into my room and say "Anyone who smell my breeze regret it." And I would hold my breath till the last extremity, but at last I would have to breathe his fumes. When I would gently criticize him, he would turn to me and say "Do I not put food in your mouth and now this mouth says bad things about me." And then he would sing his song. It would go like this. Doo-doo, doo-doo, doo-doo. He would sing it for hours. It drove me mad.

BOURGEOYS: Enough, enough, enough! It is a sublime joy to be lifeless and yet alive.

HÉLÈNE and MARIE: Yes it is.

BOURGEOYS: When you were sixteen.

HÉLÈNE: I wanted a philosopher.

BOURGEOYS: When you were eighteen.

MARIE: I wanted a knight in shining armor.

BOURGEOYS: When you were twenty.

HÉLÈNE: A cultivated man, a gentleman.

BOURGEOYS: When you were twenty-one.

HÉLÈNE and MARIE: A man. Any man.

BOURGEOYS: I thought so.

(The lights fade.)

Scene Fifteen

(In another playing area the lights fade in. RADISSON and LOUIS are playing a game of dice.)

RADISSON: Snake eyes. The story of my life. What are you thinking about?

LOUIS: I am thinking of getting married.

RADISSON: To the girl on the farm.

LOUIS: No, to one of the Filles du Roi.

RADISSON: No, no, that's not what you want. You don't want a woman from Paris. You want a big-limbed, big-bummed ... you want a woman who is big everywhere. Like the girl on the farm.

LOUIS: Don't make remarks about the girl on the farm.

RADISSON: You belong with me in the forest, feasting on a beast in the middle of the night. There's no life like it. In the forest you can say "I am Caesar," and there is no one to disagree with you. But you walk up to a woman and say "I am Caesar," well you just said the wrong thing at the wrong time. You come with me and we go up to the Big Bay and we look at the beavers and the icebergs. Icebergs are like naked ladies. I could look at them forever. What are you thinking about?

LOUIS: I am thinking I would like to eat mush from the skull of your grandmother.

(The lights fade.)

Scene Sixteen

(In another playing area the lights fade in. HÉLÈNE and BOURGEOYS enter.)

HÉLÈNE: As a baby eats pudding I devoured men and diamonds.

(HÉLÈNE looks up.)

Why is that man hanging naked from that tree with a stake through his heart?

BOURGEOYS: He is a suicide. His soul is howling in hell. In the morning we will burn his rotting carcass with our garbage. That's what we think of him. Only criminals commit suicide.

(The lights fade.)

Scene Seventeen

(In another playing area the lights fade in. MARIE and BEAUPORT enter.)

BEAUPORT: Ah mademoiselle, I compliment you on the length of your eyelashes.

MARIE: Merci.

BEAUPORT: Oh, and your arms are strong.

MARIE: Hmmm-hmmm. Do you own land?

BEAUPORT: Miles. And your body is voluptuous. Are you an atheist?

MARIE: Sir?

BEAUPORT: Only a pagan could have a body like this.

(BEAUPORT puts his hands on MARIE's shoulders.)

MARIE: First thing's first. What is your name?

BEAUPORT: Jacques Beauport.

MARIE: What a shame. If you were Jacques de Beauport, I would be yours.

BEAUPORT: Ah I see. But you must remember mademoiselle, if I was Jacques de Beauport, would I be yours?

(MARIE turns up her nose.)

Right, mademoiselle. It is mademoiselle Croissant, not—?

MARIE: Oui monsieur. Untouched womanhood. Fresh baked.

BEAUPORT: You don't have a husband in France?

MARIE: Non monsieur.

BEAUPORT: Are you sure?

MARIE: Oui monsieur.

BEAUPORT: It is rumored that some of these orphans are not virgins.

MARIE: Is that important to you monsieur?

BEAUPORT: No.

(MARIE looks at BEAUPORT)

MARIE: Well, Jacques, my name is Marie.

(The lights fade.)

Scene Eighteen

(In another playing area the lights fade in. HÉLÈNE and LE BOEUF enter.)

HÉLÈNE: But sir, I want to be chaste.

LE BOEUF: Very well, I will chase you.

HÉLÈNE: That's not what I mean.

LE BOEUF: What do you mean?

HÉLÈNE: Do you own land?

LE BOEUF: Yes, and I have four pigs.

HÉLÈNE: And are you a man of ambition?

LE BOEUF: I have taught my pigs to sing. If you marry me, I will teach them to dance.

HÉLÈNE: Oui. My ambition is to get milk from a bull.

LE BOEUF: Marry me and I will give it to you by the quart.

HÉLÈNE: Very well, I will marry you.

(Pause.)

Well?

LE BOEUF: Alas, I cannot.

HÉLÈNE: Why not?

LE BOEUF: Because if I marry you, you will turn me into a cuckold. And then you and your lover would find out what kind of man teaches pigs to sing.

HÉLÈNE: I think I know already.

LE BOEUF: I love you but I cannot bare the thought of being cuckolded.

HÉLÈNE: And I cannot bare the thought of cuckolding you, so, au revoir monsieur.

LE BOEUF: I knew you would say something like that. All I want is a woman who is beautiful and stupid.

(HÉLÈNE sneers.)

Because a stupid woman wouldn't cuckold me.

HÉLÈNE: No, a stupid woman wouldn't.

LE BOEUF: I know it is my destiny to wear the goat horns. But I am the maker of my own fortune and I defy my fate. So! Are you a virgin?

HÉLÈNE: Are you a virgin?

LE BOEUF: No. In France I was once married.

HÉLÈNE: Oh, I can imagine how that turned out.

LE BOEUF: Oh, what she did to me.

HÉLÈNE: Yes, it is too predictable.

LE BOEUF: Oh what she did to me.

HÉLÈNE: Yes, I can't imagine why.

LE BOEUF: Oh what she did to me. Me, Boeuf Le Boeuf, the He-man of Gascony. Each day me and my wife would wake up ...

HÉLÈNE: And then what?

LE BOEUF: And I would go merrily off to work. Singing my song. Doo-doo, doo-doo, doo-doo. And while I was at work guess what my wife was doing?

HÉLÈNE: What you were doing.

LE BOEUF: While I was doing hard work, I mean hard work, my elbows and knees were going up and down all the time. Well my wife's knees and elbows were going up and down too. The whole village. First a snicker, but I pay no mind. Then laughter, but I pay no mind. Then a remark, but I pay no mind. Then taunts, but I pay no mind. Then they put a sign around my neck, but I pay no mind. And then they put the goat horns on me. And then I lose my mind. I go berserk. I turn into mad bull and go crazy in that village. Not a house left standing in that village. I make everybody regret what they did to me and I mean everybody, except my wife. She got away. I scour France looking for her but she get away. So I came here. I didn't want to be in France, and yet I did.

HÉLÈNE: Yes, to be and not to be, at the same time. What a life.

(HÉLÈNE smiles. She fans herself. The lights fade.)

Scene Nineteen

(In another playing area the lights fade in. BOURGEOYS is holding a bouquet of flowers.)

BOURGEOYS: I like to pass my time sitting on a log, thinking about God.

(BOURGEOYS smiles.)

I love watching frogs eat flies

(The lights fade.)

Scene Twenty

(In another playing area the lights fade in. BEAUPORT enters. A HABITANT enters and falls to his knees.)

HABITANT: Oh Mr. Beauport, oh Mr. Beauport, oh Mr. Beauport. I bring you homage from the fiefdom by the river. Please accept my harvest because I am a man of faith and an honest vassal on your seigneury.

BEAUPORT: Go dance around my maypole.

HABITANT: Oh Mr. Beauport, oh Mr. Beauport, oh Mr. Beauport. I grind my grain in your mill. I bake my bread in your oven. I will continue to fish in your rivers, and harvest your land. I pledge my faith to you as I did to your father.

BEAUPORT: Enough. Go. I am going to meet my wife at the masquerade. I do not have time to talk with you. The grass is growing. Go graze.

(BEAUPORT exits.)

HABITANT: Now there is a man I would love to rob. I hope he dies in a duel over that whore of a wife.

(The HABITANT laughs. The lights fade.)

Scene Twenty-one

(In another playing area the lights fade in. MARIE and HÉLÈNE are fanning themselves.)

HÉLÈNE: Oh men are the strangest creatures. My husband, right now, is at home baptizing his pigs, he loves them so much. When I say "Are you sure you should be doing this?" He says, "Do I not put food in your mouth, and now this mouth says bad things about me?"

(MARIE's eyes dart.)

And then he says, "I am the He-man of Gascony!! You are the wife of the He-man of Gascony."

(MARIE looks alarmed.)

Is anything wrong?

MARIE: No ... not at all.

(MARIE holds a masquerade ball mask to her face.)

How do I look?

HÉLÈNE: If I was a man I would eat you.

MARIE: Yes.

(The lights fade.)

Scene Twenty-two

(In another playing area the lights fade in. TALON, BOURGEOYS, HÉLÈNE, LE BOEUF, MARIE, and BEAUPORT hold masks to their faces and dance the minuet.)

BOURGEOYS: Oh these women are mixed goods.

TALON: But good.

BEAUPORT: Madame, I compliment you on the length of your eyelashes.

LE BOEUF: I named one of my pigs Mary and the other Jesus.

MARIE: Oh these men ... ugh.

HÉLÈNE: Phew.

(The chimes are heard.)

TALON: Time to unmask. Time to unmask.

BEAUPORT: Look, it's me. It's me.

LE BOEUF: No, it's me, it's me.

BEAUPORT: And look, my beautiful wife, she is shy.

(MARIE is unmasked.)

LE BOEUF: You. The blood is in my brain I cannot speak. You.

MARIE: The same.

BEAUPORT: What is going on?

MARIE: This man married me for my money and then took everything.

LE BOEUF: This witch. This witch ruined my life, ruined my life.

BEAUPORT: Monsieur, do not point your finger at my wife.

LE BOEUF: She is my wife, I am married to her.

BEAUPORT: Non, my friend, she is married to me.

LE BOEUF: I tell you something my friend, take your hand off my wife.

HÉLÈNE: His wife.

(HÉLÈNE faints into the arms of TALON.)

BEAUPORT: She is not your wife. That is your wife.

LE BOEUF: This is my wife, but this is my wife, too.

(LE BOEUF points a finger at TALON.)

Do not kiss my wife.

BEAUPORT: We will let the lady choose.

LE BOEUF: She is not a lady.

BEAUPORT: Oh, prepare to die, Boeuf.

(The lights fade.)

Scene Twenty-three

(In another playing area the lights fade in. TALON, LE BOEUF, BEAUPORT, HÉLÈNE, and MARIE enter.)

TALON: Attention, attention, attention. I can solve our problems.

OTHERS: How?!

TALON: You are going to marry this woman.

(TALON indicates BEAUPORT and HÉLÈNE.)

LE BOEUF: What, my wife?

TALON: And you are going back to France.

LE BOEUF: What?

TALON: And you are going to come with me.

(TALON indicates MARIE.)

LE BOEUF: What, my wife? No, this would never happen in France.

TALON: But this is not France. This is Canada and the winters are cold. Bienvenue and au revoir.

(BEAUPORT admires HÉLÈNE.)

BEAUPORT: Mademoiselle, I compliment you on the length of your eyelashes.

HÉLÈNE: Oh monsieur.

LE BOEUF: Oh what she did to me.

TALON: Madame, my name is Jean de Talon.

MARIE: Enchanté, monsieur.

(The lights fade.)

Part Five

Frontenac

Scene One

(The lights fade in. TALON and MARIE enter.)

TALON: Perhaps you want to see what is in my little letter. When you see what is inside my little letter you will want to kiss and hug me. They say Count Frontenac is a man's man.

MARIE: I wonder what that means.

TALON: Wouldn't you like to find out? They say he has a knife for men and a special knife for women.

MARIE: They say, they say.

TALON: They say Count Frontenac is making peace with the Iroquois.

MARIE: And when he has done that I will give him a piece he will not get from the Iroquois.

TALON: They say Fortune is a woman.

MARIE: So they say.

TALON: And now the moment you have been waiting for. An invitation to the governor's banquet.

MARIE: Oh how can I thank you?

TALON: At the right moment, the moment that memories are made of ... whisper the word Mississippi in his ear.

MARIE: Mississippi.

TALON: Oh the way you say that word is criminal.

(The lights fade. During the darkness.)

VOICE: *(Off.)* His Excellency, the governor of New France, Count Frontenac.

(In another playing area, the lights fade in. FRONTENAC enters. TALON and MARIE "ooh" and "aah.")

FRONTENAC: Are my clothes not of the finest cut?

TALON: The finest.

FRONTENAC: Is my table not the finest in New France?

TALON: The finest.

FRONTENAC: And my new found friends?

TALON: The finest also. Governor—

FRONTENAC: You will refer to me as High and Mighty Lord.

TALON: Very well, oh High and Mighty Lord. We are honoured to be here. Let me give you this robe made from the skin of a beast that is the king of this forest empire.

(TALON puts a bearskin around FRONTENAC's shoulders.)

FRONTENAC: This will keep me warm in winter.

TALON: Oh High and Mighty Lord, this is Mademoiselle Croissant. Women like this make the winter short.

FRONTENAC: Enchanté, Mademoiselle Croissant.

MARIE: I am honoured to meet you, oh High and Mighty Lord.

(MARIE holds up a jar of honey.)

I want to give you my jar of honey. It is sweet and sticky, but spread it smooth and it will cause you much delight.

FRONTENAC: Merci, Mademoiselle Croissant. Garçon, cognac.

TALON: Cognac for our High and Mighty Lord.

FRONTENAC: To old memories and new dreams. To the fur trade, to the good life.

TALON: And to the Mississippi.

FRONTENAC: Why not.

TALON: Out by the big lakes we could make ten times what we are already making.

FRONTENAC: Yes, yes, cognac my friend.

(LAVAL enters.)

LAVAL: Repent!

FRONTENAC: Oh, what a face. Have you come to toast my good fortune, proud prelate?

LAVAL: I am Laval.

FRONTENAC: I know who you are.

LAVAL: Governor.

FRONTENAC: You will refer to me as High and Mighty Lord.

LAVAL: I certainly will not. The High and Mighty Lord I serve could turn a person like you into a turd. In fact he already has.

FRONTENAC: Your face is too repulsive to even spit on.

LAVAL: Governor, with regard to making decisions. There are three votes—

FRONTENAC: No. There is one vote and I have it.

LAVAL: The church rules here.

FRONTENAC: You think you are a secret government.

LAVAL: We are a secret government. We are in the boudoirs of kings, the cabinets of ministers, and the huts of savages. We are everywhere.

FRONTENAC: The king rules here.

LAVAL: And the pope.

FRONTENAC: You Jesuit.

LAVAL: I am not a Jesuit. I support their ideas but I am not a Jesuit.

FRONTENAC: What an interesting debate you must have with yourself.

LAVAL: I do not have debates.

FRONTENAC: And neither do I. Get out of my sight you filthy monster.

LAVAL: I accuse you of the devil's work.

FRONTENAC: I accuse you of being a hypocrite.

LAVAL: I accuse you of being a lecherous swine.

FRONTENAC: And I accuse you of perverting peoples' minds.

LAVAL: When you die you are going direct to hell. No purgatory for you.

FRONTENAC: And you are going out of this room. And do not stop at the stable for a meal.

(The lights fade.)

Scene Two

(In another playing area the lights fade in. FRONTENAC enters.)

FRONTENAC: Ottawa, Chippewa, Nipissing, Huron. Welcome children, welcome. It is right that I call you children. I am older than you. I am your father, I am as you say, your Onontio, your Great Mountain. Do not make me angry little ones, or I will take the tomahawk from your hands and stick it in your head. As you can see, I wear the hair of the dead. You have seen how quickly I built this fort. It has been built for you. You can bring your furs here. We will give you firewater for your furs. You will not get firewater in Hochelaga. You will not get firewater in Three Rivers. You will not get firewater in Quebec. You will get firewater here. Do not climb on me or I will shake. How many of you believe in Jesus. You … you … you. If you believe in Jesus we will give you thundersticks. We will give you thundersticks for furs, if you believe. Some of you are friends of the English. The English are bad. They are devils. Jesus was a Frenchman. His mother was a virgin, a nice French lady. The English killed Jesus. If you want the love of Jesus do not trade with the English. If you trade with us we will give you crucifixes, we will give you the shrine of the Virgin. You can hang your wampum on the shrine of the Virgin. Think about that. Do you understand?

(The lights fade.)

Scene Three

(In another playing area the lights fade in. LAVAL enters holding a cup and a spoon.)

LAVAL: I hate my servant. He always complains about being overworked, and of course he is not. For lunch I eat a small piece of meat … tiny, and of course a stale piece of bread. I don't have disagreements. I do not debate my decisions. In fact it is not even discussed. If anyone disagrees with me I damn them to hell. The thought of sulfur coming out of every orifice makes me smile. Ringing the bells for mass is my greatest joy. I exist only for self-annihilation. When I go to the stable with my spoon and eat the droppings of the cow, it is indeed a holy supper, by mortifying my sense of taste I come to know you. Oh Lord, it is a humbling experience. I will leave you now and meditate on my own worthlessness.

(The lights fade.)

Scene Four

(In another playing area the lights fade in. FRONTENAC and GARANGULA enter.)

FRONTENAC: Children.

GARANGULA: Brothers.

FRONTENAC: Children.

GARANGULA: No, brothers.

FRONTENAC: I am your great white father. I have adopted you in the name of the king.

(Pause. GARANGULA smiles.)

GARANGULA: Iroquois here first. We adopt you … as brother.

FRONTENAC: Am I not your protector?

GARANGULA: Dogs in red say that too. What are we to think?

(FRONTENAC sneers.)

FRONTENAC: You are blockading the Ottawa river and stopping furs from coming to Hochelaga. Why do you blockade river?

GARANGULA: That's our river.

FRONTENAC: You don't own that river.

GARANGULA: Didn't say we did. But we like that river. That good river. When we see Algonquin warrior with furs in canoe on river. We say … Hi friend … Hi neighbor. We like to see Algonquin warrior in canoe with furs on river. We not see enough of them.

FRONTENAC: I want the river free from ambush.

GARANGULA: What you want is what you want.

FRONTENAC: I know you take the furs to the English.

GARANGULA: Why you so sad? French give Indian one gew-gaw for beaver skin. English give Indian four gew-gaw for beaver skin.

FRONTENAC: It's not right.

GARANGULA: It never is.

FRONTENAC: Those beavers belong to the king of France.

GARANGULA: Those beavers belong to whoever sell them at market.

FRONTENAC: I see you are going to be difficult.

GARANGULA: I tell you something my friend. I am Garangula, chief of the Onondaga. There have been many great mountains, but only one Garangula. But I am not here to tell you about myself. I am here to sign a peace treaty. Are you?

FRONTENAC: Hmmm-hmmm.

(FRONTENAC nods his head.)

GARANGULA: But before we sign that treaty, we will plant the Tree of Peace.

(GARANGULA claps his hands. A warrior enters holding a twelve inch sapling with tiny leaves.)

This is the Tree of Peace. Plant it and water it and it will become a big beautiful tree.

FRONTENAC: I accept this tree as our tree.

(FRONTENAC and GARANGULA smile. The lights fade.)

Scene Five

(In another playing area the lights fade in. MARIE and TALON enter.)

MARIE: Oh I am so fat, so fat. I am fat like the pig that eats all the time.

TALON: A soufflé, madame.

MARIE: No, no, no.

TALON: I saw Laval laughing today.

MARIE: Oh, that means something truly awful has happened to someone. I wonder what it is. Where is the count?

TALON: He is at the fur fair. A ton of beaver has arrived. He talks with the fur traders.

MARIE: He loves them.

TALON: Cognac, dear.

MARIE: No.

TALON: You say no to cognac, you say no to life. Is my little bird not happy?

MARIE: This little bird will bite that finger if you do that again. Why are you such a pig?

TALON: It's a way of passing time.

MARIE: I once lived with a pig. It makes me sick thinking about it. It was an unbelievable experience. But this Frontenac ... I don't care if it is the rage in Paris, the next time he demands an enema, I'm going to poison him.

TALON: That is also the rage in Paris.

MARIE: It's just not romantic.

(The lights fade.)

Scene Six

(In another playing area the lights fade in. FRONTENAC enters.)

FRONTENAC: I am Frontenac, the governor! I am empowered to arrest all of you because you poach the king's furs and then sell them to the English. But I chose to look the other way. Until now. Each of you will pay me fifty per cent of your profits or I will put you in the jug for the rest of your rotten lives. Remember Perrot, governor of Montréal? He thought he was powerful. I put him in irons and sent him to live in the Bastille. Now we are agreed. Do you understand? Comprenez. All of you coureurs de bois, you runners of the woods, you work for me now.

(The lights fade.)

Scene Seven

(In another playing area the lights fade in. RADISSON and MAURICE enter.)

MAURICE: Well that's a pipeful. Are you going to work for him?

RADISSON: Do you know what I do if I ever meet Frontenac in the forest? I get a rope and I stick it up his ass and then I work it through and then I pull rope out his mouth, and then—Laval, I hate him too—then I shove rope down Laval's mouth and pull out ass, and then I pull them along ground like fish on a string. I hate them so much. I work for English again before I work for Frontenac.

(The lights fade.)

Scene Eight

(In another playing area the lights fade in. A Molière Harlequinade.)

ACTOR: And with that, we leave to your wedded care, the honorable and worthy Valère.

(In another playing area the lights fade in. FRONTENAC, MARIE, and cronies roar with laughter. The ACTOR bows.)

MARIE: Oh Molière, he is so amusing.

FRONTENAC: Bravo, bravo. Well done Captain. My regards to the barracks.

(LAVAL enters holding a crucifix.)

LAVAL: Stop, stop. This is an outrage. This is the work of Satan.

FRONTENAC: Ah, excellent. The real Tartuffe has arrived.

(LAVAL turns to the actors.)

LAVAL: Out, pig. Friend of pig, out. Leave us whore. Exit, you whore of shit.

(The actors exit. FRONTENAC applauds.)

FRONTENAC: Bravo, bishop, bravo. So now you are our entertainment. Speak.

(LAVAL holds up a proclamation.)

LAVAL: This decree signed by King Louis the Fourteenth demands that you be recalled to France, Citizen Frontenac.

FRONTENAC: You are a fool, as far as the eye can see, it is now safe for you to build churches in every forest and on every river.

LAVAL: And those churches will be built, while you are in France, Citizen Frontenac.

FRONTENAC: I am still Count Frontenac.

LAVAL: In old France perhaps, not in New France. Kiss this ring.

FRONTENAC: Kiss my ass, bishop.

(The lights fade.)

Scene Nine

(In another playing area the lights fade in. DENONVILLE and LAVAL enter. DENONVILLE kisses LAVAL's ring.)

LAVAL: Governor, will you join me for a midnight prayer?

DENONVILLE: Certainly.

LAVAL: We must pray for deliverance from demons. The Iroquois have turned all our God-loving Hurons back into pagans. Oh Lord, this tool that kneels beside me, give him words. Save us from the Iroquois.

DENONVILLE: It would be a great joy to exterminate them. In fact, we shouldn't spend our time trying to convert them to Christianity. We should just kill them, let God sort them out.

LAVAL: Exactly.

DENONVILLE: What we should do is have a special peace conference to re-affirm the peace, and when they are smoking their pipes, we arrest them and send them off to the galleys of France.

LAVAL: That's a brilliant idea.

DENONVILLE: I am sure the consequences will be favourable.

(The lights fade.)

Scene Ten

(In another playing area the lights fade in. TALON enters screaming.)

TALON: Massacre, massacre, disaster!

(MARIE enters.)

Lachine. Every man, woman and child, skinned alive and eaten.

(LAVAL enters holding a crucifix.)

LAVAL: Look at this.

(TALON screams. DENONVILLE enters.)

DENONVILLE: What has happened?

TALON: The woods are full of demons tonight. Burning, torturing, killing, looting, raping, many were taken captive. There are thousands of them and they have guns.

(Drums, screams, shrieks and laughter is heard.)

VOICE: *(Off.)* Come out, Onontio, come fight. You wanted war, come fight.

DENONVILLE: If we go into that forest it is certain death for us. If I die, who protects the women and children?

VOICE: *(Off.)* You wanted war, come fight.

TALON: When I left they were digging up the graves of my mother and father.

(TALON screams. LAVAL holds up the crucifix.)

DENONVILLE: I see fires and people at the stake. This will go on for days.

VOICE: *(Off.)* You wanted fight, come out.

(MARIE and TALON approach DENONVILLE.)

TALON: What are we to do?

LAVAL: You have seen the ways of God. Look at this and see another.

(TALON screams.)

MARIE: What are we to do?

(DENONVILLE approaches LAVAL.)

DENONVILLE: What are we to do?

(The lights fade.)

Scene Eleven

(In another playing area the lights fade in. MARIE, DENONVILLE, and TALON enter. TALON holds his head in his hands.)

DENONVILLE: I don't know what to say except I am sorry.

MARIE: You are so stupid, I am amazed you can even breathe you are so stupid.

(FRONTENAC enters.)

My hero.

TALON: Oh our High and Mighty Lord is back. My wonderful friend is back.

FRONTENAC: The Giant Fart Monster walks again. Weep you wretches. I have learned nothing, but more to the point, I have forgotten nothing. Where is Laval?

(Lights up on LAVAL.)

LAVAL: You were chastized by whips, now you will be chastized with scorpions.

FRONTENAC: Kiss this.

(FRONTENAC puts a hand on his backside.)

Are you hungry, proud prelate? There is food in here.

LAVAL: God often works his marvels through the worst of persons.

FRONTENAC: Go vegetate in misery.

LAVAL: Hearing you say that makes my heart glow.

FRONTENAC: What are you doing here?

DENONVILLE: I don't know what to say.

FRONTENAC: Neither do I. Don't you know anything? Those chiefs you sent into slavery were chiefs of the Peace. Did you not know that they would then elect chiefs of war.

DENONVILLE: I thought when we took their chiefs they would be leaderless.

FRONTENAC: The Iroquois are a nation of chiefs.

VOICE: *(Off.)* Come out Great Mountain, wherever you are. The clouds no longer hide the sun. We can see you.

FRONTENAC: That voice. I remember it well.

(FRONTENAC turns to TALON.)

Dry your tears my little friend, there is a new rage in Paris.

VOICE: *(Off.)* Come out, Onontia, before the sun cries and everyone dies.

(The lights fade.)

Scene Twelve

(In another playing area the lights fade in. FRONTENAC and GARANGULA enter.)

GARANGULA: In this world there is nothing greater than me. Nothing. I am Garangula, Chief of the Onondaga. There is nothing I value more than sex and a good meal. Nothing. There is nothing Garangula likes more than stripping, roasting, and eating Frenchmen. Nothing. The Iroquois have never been conquered in war. Never. Not once.

FRONTENAC: Get to the point.

(GARANGULA holds up a vine of weeds.)

GARANGULA: Remember this? This is the Tree of Peace. Look how beautiful it is. This is our tree. What do you think of this tree?

FRONTENAC: Get that monstrosity out of my sight.

(GARANGULA throws the tree into the shadows.)

GARANGULA: Exactly. Many moons have passed since white devil kill three chiefs.

FRONTENAC: This is ancient history. This is over eighty years ago. Too long to remember.

GARANGULA: Iroquois never forget. Iroquois never forgive. Why you so mad?

FRONTENAC: I am mad because you massacred women and children.

GARANGULA: Great Mountain, give ear. After you leave, New Great Mountain invite us to pow-wow. Smoke peace pipe. Instead steal our people. Steal our chiefs. That not Great Mountain, that ant hill. We step on ant hill. Why are you so mad? Are you mad because we step on ant hill?

FRONTENAC: My king is now at war with the English king.

(GARANGULA turns to the shadows.)

GARANGULA: Two devils now at war. This good.

(A grunt of approval from the Iroquois in the shadows.)

FRONTENAC: You are going to work for the English devil.

GARANGULA: No. We kill devils. We not work for them.

FRONTENAC: I want to attack the English, not Iroquois.

GARANGULA: Good.

FRONTENAC: I want you to watch the English attack me.

GARANGULA: Very good. While you live there will be peace between us.

(The lights fade.)

Scene Thirteen

(In another playing area the lights fade in. FRONTENAC and MARIE enter.)

FRONTENAC: You are like the rose that lives its little hour.

MARIE: Yes, I have had my half-hour in the sun. I am a rose in full-bloom.

FRONTENAC: But I am attracted to rosebuds.

MARIE: In six months I will be as square as a cube, and as red as a shrimp. I am going to give birth to a baby Frontenac.

FRONTENAC: I will pray for your soul.

MARIE: I am sure your prayers will be well received. But a good conscience outlives a good appearance.

FRONTENAC: You will not be the first sinner to be converted.

MARIE: Because I have commited one sin, must I commit them all?

FRONTENAC: No. Get your buns to a nunnery. Spring is in the air. Is there a finer season to begin a war?

(The lights fade.)

Scene Fourteen

(In another playing area the lights fade in. A scowling PRIEST sits in a chair. FRONTENAC addresses INDIANS who are standing in the shadows.)

FRONTENAC: Look at me. I am Frontenac, the Great Mountain. I am going on the Warpath. I will only be happy if I die fighting. You will only be happy if you die fighting. You are all like eagles. Does an eagle eat worms? What kind of eagle is that? An eagle eats meat, English meat. Be an eagle and our enemies will fly like geese.

(FRONTENAC holds up a glass of blood.)

See this. This is English blood.

(FRONTENAC drinks the blood.)

Delicious.

(The PRIEST shakes his head and mutters to himself.)

Now I am strong. I am going to kill the English. All of them. Even the baby English. No mercy. Earlier at feast of friendship I had wild pig between my jaws. And you all laughed. That is what I am going to do to the English. Now, I am going to teach you a new song. And when we dance the war dance we will sing this song. All of us.

(FRONTENAC looks to the shadows and the sound of drums begin. FRONTENAC raises a tomahawk and dances the war dance.)

Let us trample the English under our feet. Let us trample the English under our feet. Let us trample the English under our feet.

(The PRIEST shakes his head and mutters to himself. INDIANS enter from the shadows, singing and dancing. The lights fade.)

Scene Fifteen

(In another playing area the lights fade in. MARIE and BOURGEOYS enter.)

BOURGEOYS: You are as beautiful as an angel but as wicked as a fiend. Have you ever seen the devil?

MARIE: Yes. He looks just like you.

BOURGEOYS: You have committed black crimes.

MARIE: Non madame, dark brown, perhaps, not black.

BOURGEOYS: I am going to shave off all your hair, and I mean all of it. Then you will make a hair shirt out of it and I will give you a scourger. And then I want you to get to it.

(The lights fade.)

Scene Sixteen

(In another playing area the lights fade in. FRONTENAC enters holding scalps.)

FRONTENAC: Children, rejoice, rejoice. Let's dance around the maypole. Look, English scalps. Many scalps.

(The lights fade.)

Scene Seventeen

(In another playing area the lights fade in. An ENGLISH OFFICER and GARANGULA enter. The ENGLISH OFFICER holds up an orange.)

ENGLISH OFFICER: There is a new king on the throne in England.

GARANGULA: What exciting times we live in.

ENGLISH OFFICER: William of Orange is my king.

(The officer gives GARANGULA the orange. He peels the orange.)

I have brought you five barrels of gunpowder and fifty thundersticks. It is a gift from my king.

GARANGULA: It is a good present. Give my regards to your king.

ENGLISH OFFICER: I will. I understand you are thinking about talking peace with the French.

(GARANGULA gives the ENGLISH OFFICER half an orange.)

GARANGULA: What else am I thinking?

ENGLISH OFFICER: You are thinking that one day you will be like one of those beasts that the French tie to their ploughs.

GARANGULA: What else?

ENGLISH OFFICER: You are thinking "What the English did to the Dutch, they will now do to the French."

GARANGULA: What else?

ENGLISH OFFICER: You are thinking that if I attack Quebec, then you will attack the trading posts in the west. You are thinking about victory over your enemies. What will you tell the French?

GARANGULA: I will tell them that their children will not grow up to be Frontenacs.

(The lights fade.)

Scene Eighteen

(In another playing area the lights fade in. FRONTENAC enters.)

VOICE: *(Off.)* My commanding officer, General Phips, demands that you surrender Quebec. What have you to say?

FRONTENAC: The mouths of my cannon will speak for me. And tell your general that if he dare land I will use his head for a cannonball. Sing, my cannons, sing.

(Cannon fire. The lights fade.)

Scene Nineteen

(In another playing area the lights fade in. FRONTENAC and BOURGEOYS enter.)

BOURGEOYS: Laval put a large painting of our Saviour on the church wall. The English are like the Spanish bull, enraged. Their ships fire all their cannons at Jesus.

FRONTENAC: And the picture still stands.

BOURGEOYS: Yes, but there are many dents in the head of Jesus.

FRONTENAC: Interesting, the English are short on gun powder and we are short on cannonballs. Gather up the English balls I want to shove them down their throats.

(The lights fade.)

Scene Twenty

(In another playing area the lights fade in. The sound of cannons being fired. Then the sound of cannonballs hitting the wall. A cannonball rolls into view. BOURGEOYS enters.)

BOURGEOYS: Oop, there's another one.

(BOURGEOYS picks up the cannonball.)

Oh, this is a big one.

(The sound of a cannonball being fired. Then the sound of a cannonball hitting the wall.)

Oop, there's another one.

(The lights fade.)

Scene Twenty-one

(In another playing area the lights fade in. FRONTENAC enters.)

FRONTENAC: The English fight like women. They do not return the fire. They are out of ammunition. They are retreating. This is not a fight. The next time you want to fight a war make sure you have ammunition.

VOICE: *(Off.)* We'll be back you murderous bastards. Right is on our side.

FRONTENAC: But guns are on ours. Gentlemen, the wars with the English have begun. This is the beginning of many victories.

(The lights fade.)

Scene Twenty-two

(In another playing area the lights fade in. LAVAL and FRONTENAC enter.)

LAVAL: This war is disgusting. The Canadians have developed a great talent for boiling, baking, and roasting people alive. Disgusting.

FRONTENAC: Odious is the word.

LAVAL: When will it end?

FRONTENAC: When Quebec is the seat of a great empire. We have pushed the English back. The Giant Fart Monster walks again. You do not like the word fart, monsignor?

LAVAL: Only the Iroquois remain.

FRONTENAC: Yes, only the Iroquois and you, my love.

(The lights fade.)

Scene Twenty-three

(In another playing area the lights fade in. Two HURON WARRIORS enter, carrying FRONTENAC in a small canoe.)

FRONTENAC: I am Frontenac. I have come for your bones. Prepare to die. I have not come to break your canoes and burn your cornfields. I have come for your skin. I am here to drink your blood. I am Frontenac. I have come for your bones.

(The lights fade.)

Scene Twenty-four

(In another playing area the lights fade in. GARANGULA and FRONTENAC enter. GARANGULA holds up white wampum beads.)

GARANGULA: With this string, I make this house clean.

(GARANGULA holds up white wampum beads.)

With this string, I ease your pain because you are old and have made a long journey.

(GARANGULA holds up white wampum beads.)

With this string, I show that we remember your song of peace and the words you have spoken.

(GARANGULA holds up black wampum beads.)

With this string, I show what we think of your song. Wipe away your tears, Great Mountain, or drown. The song you sing must be beautiful to the ear, or we will frown.

FRONTENAC: Children.

GARANGULA: Brothers.

FRONTENAC: Brothers. Can you not understand me? I will crush your brain between two rocks if you defy me.

GARANGULA: Be careful it is not you between those rocks. Talking to a Frenchman is like talking to a stone. Worse, like talking to a wild stupid brute with no ears, but with big teeth. I have always kept the peace, always. To prove my point I give you two beavers and one raccoon.

FRONTENAC: I am like a cloud.

GARANGULA: Yes, sometimes you are there, sometimes you are not.

FRONTENAC: A cloud full of thunder and lightning. A big black cloud is coming toward you.

GARANGULA: Good. Our cornfields are thirsty.

FRONTENAC: Do you not understand me?

GARANGULA: The French are like dog with tail between legs. Not like man with cock facing up. If you visit our trees we will kill you for only one reason. So that your body can lie in the forest and stink forever. So that all who pass that patch of forest will lift up their nose and say "a Frenchman has been here."

(FRONTENAC holds up a peace treaty.)

FRONTENAC: I understand you cannot make a peace treaty because you are subjects of the English.

GARANGULA: Wrong. I have two eyes. One eye sees the English, one eye sees the French.

FRONTENAC: Where are your prisoners?

GARANGULA: Where are your prisoners?

FRONTENAC: I have eaten my prisoners.

GARANGULA: And I have eaten mine. We are here to discuss a peace treaty, not our meals.

(FRONTENAC holds up the peace treaty. It has a picture of a five-legged bear on it.)

FRONTENAC: This is your symbol.

(GARANGULA nods his head.)

I understand bears have four legs. This one has five.

GARANGULA: When your king sees leg number five, he will know what it is for.

FRONTENAC: We have been fools, let us be brothers.

GARANGULA: Whatever Great Fart Monster says, is.

(The lights fade.)

Scene Twenty-five

(In another playing area the lights fade in. BOURGEOYS is with MARIE and HÉLÈNE who sing as they churn butter.)

MARIE and HÉLÈNE: We are churning butter for our Lord. We are churning butter for our Lord. We are churning butter for our Lord.

BOURGEOYS: Well sisters, it's a great life.

MARIE and HÉLÈNE: Churning butter for our Lord.

BOURGEOYS: We have a convent.

MARIE and HÉLÈNE: Churning butter for our Lord.

BOURGEOYS: God's hotel is full.

MARIE and HÉLÈNE: Churning butter for our Lord.

BOURGEOYS: And we have a school.

MARIE and HÉLÈNE: Churning butter for our Lord.

BOURGEOYS: We will teach the Indians what to think.

MARIE and HÉLÈNE: Churning butter for our Lord.

BOURGEOYS: It's a great life, sisters, a great life.

MARIE and HÉLÈNE: Churning butter for our Lord. We are churning butter for our Lord.

(The lights fade.)

Scene Twenty-six

(In another playing area the lights fade in. RADISSON and MAURICE are playing cards.)

RADISSON: When I first got to Montréal, you see that mountain up there, it was a hole in the ground when I first got here. When I first got here that mountain was covered with dead trees, and those dead trees were full of dead birds, singing dead songs.

MAURICE: I thought when you first got here it was a hole in the ground.

RADISSON: That's right. The dead trees full of dead birds singing dead songs were inside the hole in the ground.

MAURICE: What happened to the dead birds?

RADISSON: They turned into grizzly bears and flew away.

MAURICE: I don't believe that one.

(MAURICE deals the cards.)

RADISSON: Hey, my friend, don't deal the cards like that.

MAURICE: Why not?

RADISSON: Everytime you deal the cards like that you win.

MAURICE: Too bad.

RADISSON: Oh then you win, my deal.

MAURICE: Give me skin.

(RADISSON gives MAURICE a beaver skin.)

RADISSON: Now give me cards. You deal like that again I break your hands. And maybe I get my knife and cut your nuts while I'm at it. The way you deal the cards prove you work for the devil.

(RADISSON deals the cards.)

MAURICE: Just don't give me the marked card.

RADISSON: Why not?

MAURICE: I don't like that card.

RADISSON: But it likes you.

(RADISSON gives MAURICE the marked card.)

MAURICE: I told you I didn't want that card.

RADISSON: Well, you got it.

MAURICE: Here give me the cards.

RADISSON: Give me skin.

(MAURICE gives RADISSON a beaver skin.)

MAURICE: You deal me that card again I break your hands. And maybe I get my knife and cut your nuts while I'm at it.

(RADISSON holds up a small bottle.)

RADISSON: Here, put a bit of this behind your ears.

MAURICE: What is it.

RADISSON: Balls and sperm of beaver crushed and mushed. It looks like runny snot but it makes me hot. It makes everyone hot. Here take a whiff.

(RADISSON holds up the bottle for MAURICE to smell. MAURICE grabs the bottle and drinks.)

You turn into woman now.

MAURICE: We'll see who turns into woman.

RADISSON: Deal.

(The lights fade.)

Scene Twenty-seven

(In another playing area the lights fade in. LAVAL and FRONTENAC enter. LAVAL makes the sign of the cross.)

LAVAL: Have you any sins to confess?

FRONTENAC: I have loved war too much and women too little. I have killed many men.

LAVAL: How many?

FRONTENAC: Hundreds. Raped many women.

LAVAL: How many?

FRONTENAC: Dozens. Debauched my life gambling and drinking.

LAVAL: For how long?

FRONTENAC: All my life. I have cheated thousands. I regret it all.

(LAVAL holds up the crucifix.)

LAVAL: Do you accept Jesus as your saviour?

FRONTENAC: Yes.

LAVAL: Then say a thousand "Our Fathers" and eight hundred "Hail Marys."

FRONTENAC: I am too tired. Say them for me.

(LAVAL starts to say the "Our Fathers.")

Oh, enough. Say them outside. Let an old man die in peace.

(LAVAL starts to exit.)

Wait. When I die I want you to cut out my heart and send it to my wife. It was not hers during my life. It will be hers during my death. That is my last request. Now farewell.

(FRONTENAC closes his eyes.)

LAVAL: Au revoir.

(LAVAL smiles. The lights fade. The end.)

The British

Part Two of the History of the Village of the Small Huts

Part One

The Plains of Abraham

Scene One

(The lights fade in. LORD AMHERST and sundry ENGLISH OFFICERS enter.)

AMHERST: Gentlemen, I have just been given a dispatch. Our good king of England, George the Second, is now at war with that fiend from France, King Louis the Fifteenth. England expects us to do our duty, and we will do it here. We will take Canada from the Frenchmen.

ENGLISH OFFICERS: Here, here.

AMHERST: The first thing we will do is get rid of the pope-loving stenchers in Acadia.

ENGLISH OFFICERS: Here, here.

AMHERST: We will send them into the wilderness, their God will show them the way.

(The lights fade.)

Scene Two

(In another playing area the lights fade in. The MARQUIS DE VAUDREUIL enters.)

VAUDREUIL: I am not a Frenchman. I was born here. When I was twelve, I was a soldier. At seventeen, a captain, in my twenties, a major. My father was the governor. He never said bad things about me. And now, I am the governor of New France. And on this day, I, Pierre de Rigaud, the Marquis de Vaudreuil, welcome the Marquis de Montcalm, to Quebec.

(VERGOR enters.)

VERGOR: Governor, governor, the general, he is arriving.

VAUDREUIL: Excellent. I will flaunt myself in his presence.

(The lights fade.)

Scene Three

(In another playing area the lights fade in. FRANÇOIS BIGOT and MONSIEUR and MADAME PEAN enter.)

MME PEAN: Oh, I am fond of all things that make life lovely.

BIGOT: I have a scratchy finger.

MONSIEUR PEAN: Sir, that is my wife you are compromising.

BIGOT: She likes my finger.

MONSIEUR PEAN: How dare you say that to me. Come swine, let us settle our affairs.

(VERGOR enters.)

VERGOR: Do not say bad things about Mr. Bigot.

MONSIEUR PEAN: Look, whoever you are, I have no quarrel with you.

BIGOT: This is Vergor.

MONSIEUR PEAN: Ah yes, I have heard of you. You are the village dullard.

VERGOR: Do not say bad things about me or I will rip off your nose and drink your blood. You say bad things about me, you say bad things about him, you say bad things about him, you say bad things about me.

MONSIEUR PEAN: This man has a vocabulary of seven words.

BIGOT: Yes, and I suggest you leave while the night is young. I am going to show her my thumb.

(MME PEAN laughs.)

MONSIEUR PEAN: Disgusting.

VERGOR: Do not say bad things—

BIGOT: Vergor, that's enough. This is not France,

Mr. Pean. This is Canada and the winters are cold. Goodnight.

(MONSIEUR PEAN exits.)

Well done Vergor, well done. I will set you up in business by collecting the harvest from the farmers as rations. Then I will give you a list of the men who have deserted, and then we will sell the harvest back to the farmers and split the profits fifty-fifty.

(VERGOR says "yes" after every statement.)

VERGOR: So that's how it's done.

BIGOT: Yes, that's how it's done, faithful servant.

(VAUDREUIL enters.)

VAUDREUIL: This way, this way.

(The MARQUIS DE MONTCALM and the CHEVALIER DE LEVIS enter.)

Ah François, this is Louis-Joseph de Gozon, the Marquis de Montcalm. And this is François-Gaston, the Chevalier de Levis. This is Bigot.

MONTCALM: Ah yes, I have heard of you.

BIGOT: And I have heard of you.

MME PEAN: I am Madame Pean.

LEVIS: Enchanté.

BIGOT: Bienvenue au Canada. Welcome to this land of beavers, bears, and barbarians.

MONTCALM: Merci.

LEVIS: You are like a beautiful flower.

MME PEAN: And you are like a little bee. Buzz-buzz here, buzz-buzz there.

MONTCALM: And now with introductions I assume safely out of the way, I must retire.

BIGOT: Excellent idea, excellent, excellent.

LEVIS: If this bee could roll around inside you and turn your juice into honey.

MONTCALM: And my quarters?

BIGOT: Your quarters are, how should I put this, less than a castle but—

MONTCALM: —better than a stable, I hope.

BIGOT: We have converted Maître Abraham's barn into a house.

MONTCALM: That's more than I expected.

MME PEAN: Perhaps you would like to have a pique-nique with me?

BIGOT: I hope you do not find this middle-class country beneath aristocrats.

MONTCALM: I'm sure I will ... find out.

VAUDREUIL: Yes.

BIGOT: Yes.

MME PEAN: Oh I will give you a big basket to play with.

LEVIS: And then can I put my jewels inside your jewel box?

MME PEAN: For safe keeping?

LEVIS: Oui.

BIGOT: Ah, chevalier, here is another person you may want to meet. This is Vergor. Vergor, say something.

VERGOR: There is too much brain in my head for me to think. I am honoured to meet you.

LEVIS: The same.

MONTCALM: Chevalier, shall we retire?

LEVIS: Yes.

MONTCALM: And now gentlemen, goodnight. Madame.

LEVIS: Madame.

BIGOT and VAUDREUIL: Goodnight.

(MONTCALM and LEVIS exit.)

VAUDREUIL: He is going to be difficult.

BIGOT: Yes.

(The lights fade.)

Scene Four

(In another playing area the lights fade in. MONTCALM enters.)

MONTCALM: What kind of world is this? The Indians pray to demons and speak the language of hell. They have dreams, fits, and cravings, and they commit the most revolting tortures. And the Canadians are just as bad. They have developed a great talent for roasting, baking, and boiling people alive. I thought the scalpings were bad but ... Look!

VOICE: *(Off.)* Cut here, and then rip off like this.

MONTCALM: Stop, stop, stop. Not in my sight, if you please. Fortunately my stomach is stronger than my heart.

(LEVIS enters.)

LEVIS: Ah there you are. You are ready to receive Pontiac?

MONTCALM: Yes.

LEVIS: Good. Now, you will have to dance the war dance with them.

MONTCALM: Oh God.

LEVIS: And sing their chants.

MONTCALM: Oh God.

LEVIS: This can go on for hours, sometimes days.

MONTCALM: Oh God.

LEVIS: But they must accept you as one of them before they will follow you. You must sing this song. "Let us trample the English under our feet. Let us trample the English under our feet."

MONTCALM: Oh God.

LEVIS: Otherwise we will have no allies against the English. Look, here he comes.

(PONTIAC enters holding a cup.)

LEVIS: This is Pontiac.

PONTIAC: Hail, Great Mountain. Oh Onontio. We thought your head would be in the clouds, but you are a little man, my father. But when I look in your eyes I see the eagle. Drink, oh Great Onontio, drink.

(PONTIAC offers the cup. MONTCALM takes the cup.)

MONTCALM: What is it?

LEVIS: It is English blood.

(MONTCALM looks disgusted.)

MONTCALM: Oh God.

LEVIS: Taste it, it's delicious.

PONTIAC: Drink, Great Father, drink.

(MONTCALM drinks. War whoops are heard.)

Very good, little mountain.

MONTCALM: And now as a token of our esteem, I give you this.

(LEVIS gives a French officer's uniform to PONTIAC.)

PONTIAC: Ah, this is good gift, good gift. Many thank-yous for this. I will wear this in the forest all the time and walk around like devil and sing "Let us trample the English under our feet." Not many words to that song, but I like that song. I sing it all the time. "Let us trample the English under our feet."

MONTCALM: Yes, let's. You must join us in this fight.

PONTIAC: We will follow Little Mountain into battle if he will sing the victory song.

MONTCALM: Oh God.

PONTIAC: Come Onontio, let us dance the war dance and sing.

(Drums and chanting.)

VOICE: *(Off.)* Let us trample the English under our feet! Let us trample the English under our feet!

PONTIAC: Come Onontio, join us.

(MONTCALM joins the dancing and singing. He dances awkardly. LEVIS gives encouragement. The dance and the chant build in ferocity. The lights fade.)

Scene Five

(In another playing area the lights fade in. AMHERST is smoking a pipe. JAMES MURRAY enters.)

MURRAY: General sir, bad news.

AMHERST: Oh no.

MURRAY: Disaster has struck Fort William Henry.

AMHERST: Oh no.

MURRAY: The fort is now in possession of the French.

AMHERST: Oh no.

MURRAY: The French, the Canadians, and the Indians also massacred the inhabitants.

AMHERST: Oh no.

MURRAY: Hundreds of British soldiers were scalped.

AMHERST: Oh no.

MURRAY: Many women were raped and murdered.

AMHERST: Oh no.

MURRAY: Children and tiny babies were roasted alive and then eaten.

AMHERST: Oh no. The bloody bastards, the bloody bastards.

(LORD TOWNSHEND enters.)

TOWNSHEND: General sir, glorious news. As of today there are less Frenchmen in the world.

AMHERST: Good.

TOWNSHEND: Fort Niagara is now in English hands.

AMHERST: Good.

TOWNSHEND: Unfortunately our troops were not able to prevent the Indians from massacring everybody.

AMHERST: Good.

TOWNSHEND: Hundreds of French and Canadians were scalped, and disemboweled.

AMHERST: Good.

TOWNSHEND: The women were gang raped and taken captive by the Indians.

AMHERST: Good.

TOWNSHEND: The Commander of Fort Niagara, a Frenchman, was put on a spit and roasted alive.

AMHERST: Good.

TOWNSHEND: Our troops are now marching on Ticonderoga.

AMHERST: Good.

(The lights fade.)

Scene Six

(In another playing area the lights fade in. VAUDREUIL and MONTCALM enter.)

MONTCALM: I am planning the defense of Carillon, or Ticonderoga, or whatever it is called.

VAUDREUIL: You will take your orders from me.

MONTCALM: I certainly will not.

VAUDREUIL: I am the governor-general of New France.

MONTCALM: And I am the commanding general.

VAUDREUIL: On the field of battle.

MONTCALM: You are like a snake.

VAUDREUIL: With a belly ache. Before the battle you will take orders from me. On the field of battle you can do what you like.

MONTCALM: But I must prepare the strategy.

VAUDREUIL: In concert with my instruction. You sneer.

(The lights fade.)

Scene Seven

(In another playing area the lights fade in. AMHERST and TOWNSHEND enter.)

AMHERST: He was tried, blooded, and found true during the slaughter at Culloden, and he is a master of amphibious warfare. His name is Wolfe.

TOWNSHEND: Wolfe. I know that name. The man is a commoner.

AMHERST: What do you think of him?

TOWNSHEND: He is not worth meeting and beating with a stick. I hold in more esteem, the cavities in my teeth.

AMHERST: Ah well, that decides it then. We'll make him the commanding officer.

(TOWNSHEND smiles.)

TOWNSHEND: Very good, Your Lordship.

(JAMES WOLFE enters.)

AMHERST: Ah, Colonel Wolfe, I take it.

WOLFE: General Amherst, I assume.

AMHERST: Sit. You come highly recommended. You kissed the ground I hope.

WOLFE: No, but I watched the others.

AMHERST: I understand the voyage was difficult.

WOLFE: Yes. My stomach has a mind of its own.

AMHERST: When you see people tortured at the stake, boiled alive, and eaten, your stomach will be mindless. You heard about the massacre at Fort William Henry, I hope.

WOLFE: Yes. The hell hounds from Canada are now led by an old fox.

AMHERST: We plan to wipe the French off the face of the map.

WOLFE: Excellent.

AMHERST: Our first assault will be Louisbourg. I want that place annihilated.

WOLFE: It will be.

AMHERST: You will lead the assault.

WOLFE: Of course.

(MURRAY enters.)

MURRAY: General sir, bad news.

AMHERST: Oh no.

MURRAY: Montcalm has defeated Abercromby at Ticonderoga.

AMHERST: That bloody bastard. Were there any scalpings?

MURRAY: Only the wounded. The men ran.

AMHERST: That bloody—

WOLFE: I think we should go to the heart of the matter and attack Quebec. The Canadian vermin should be sacked, pillaged, and repaid in cruelty.

AMHERST: I agree, but first things first. We need a victory. We will take Louisbourg.

WOLFE: With great mischief.

AMHERST: Yes, with great mischief.

(The lights fade.)

Scene Eight

(In another playing area the lights fade in. MONTCALM, MME PEAN, BIGOT, and VAUDREUIL enter.)

VAUDREUIL: Vergor, dance for us.

BIGOT: Where is that big ugly bear? Vergor, dance for us.

(VERGOR enters singing and dancing.)

VERGOR: Ticonderoga is ours, Ticonderoga is ours.

VAUDREUIL: See, he is dancing because the sun is shining, and he is happy because I am happy because you are happy.

BIGOT: Up goes the big bear's foot.

MME PEAN: Down goes the big bear's foot.

BIGOT: Up.

MME PEAN: Down.

VAUDREUIL: Look, is he not the king of this forest empire?

MONTCALM: I must inspect the fortifications.

MME PEAN: Will you stay and gamble with me?

MONTCALM: Oh madame, you are like a little flower.

MME PEAN: And you are like a little shrub. Always basking in the sun but never growing tall.

VERGOR: This bear wants honey.

BIGOT: Oh honey for a big angry bear.

MME PEAN: Will you stay and play tope et tingue with me.

MONTCALM: Ah, tope et tingue.

VAUDREUIL: Ah, it is your weak spot.

BIGOT: I will give you credit at my gaming table. Where lives are ruined with a smile.

(BIGOT laughs. The lights fade.)

Scene Nine

(In another playing area the lights fade in. Two FRENCH OFFICERS on a battlement at Louisbourg. WOLFE enters. SERGEANT FRASER stands in the shadows with the cannon.)

WOLFE: You are surrounded. Have you anything to say?

FRENCH OFFICER ONE: Rien.

WOLFE: Surrender.

FRENCH OFFICER ONE: Jamais.

WOLFE: Speak English, you frogging swine.

FRENCH OFFICER ONE: Parlez-vous anglais?

FRENCH OFFICER TWO: Oui … Moi.

FRENCH OFFICER ONE: Parlez.

FRENCH OFFICER TWO: I spit on you, you English pig. You English pig, I spit on you.

WOLFE: All right, that does it. Grease it down and load it up.

FRENCH OFFICER TWO: I fart in your face. In your face, I fart.

WOLFE: All right, that tears it. Sergeant … Fire!

(The cannon is fired. The French side groan.)

FRASER: Long live the king.

WOLFE: Sergeant, let's show these bastards the meaning of the word. Grease it up and load it down. Fire!

(The French side moans. FRENCH OFFICER ONE dies.)

Surrender.

FRENCH OFFICER TWO: Jamais.

(FRENCH OFFICER TWO rattles his saber. WOLFE rattles his saber.)

WOLFE: Ah, going to be like this about it, are you?

FRENCH OFFICER TWO: Come, show your mettle.

WOLFE: Very well, I will stab you.

(They fence. WOLFE stabs FRENCH OFFICER TWO.)

Any last words?

FRENCH OFFICER TWO: I spit on you, you English pig, I spit.

(FRENCH OFFICER TWO dies.)

WOLFE: Excellent, Louisbourg is ours. Long live the king.

(FRASER enters.)

FRASER: Long live the king.

(WOLFE points to FRENCH OFFICER TWO.)

WOLFE: This slime here. Chop it up, stuff it in the cannon, and fire it into the sea.

FRASER: Yes sir.

WOLFE: Come, gentlemen, let us take Louisbourg ... with mischief.

(FRASER roars. The lights fade.)

Scene Ten

(In another playing area the lights fade in. BIGOT and MME PEAN enter.)

BIGOT: Who has the body of a man but the mind of a runting pig?

MME PEAN: Oh, let me think. There are so many possibilities. New France is so big, so full of men.

BIGOT: Oh ma cherie, ma cherie. I have to raise fifty thousand francs for my new pleasure party. How am I going to raise it?

MME PEAN: Let's see, there are fifty thousand people in New France.

BIGOT: Oui, ma cherie.

MME PEAN: Oh, I have a brilliant idea. We should hang you publicly and then charge all the spectators one franc each.

(BIGOT laughs.)

BIGOT: Oh I love you so much.

(BISHOP BRIAND enters.)

Oh it's the bishop. "I still believe in the golden calf, the golden calf."

BRIAND: You fornicator. Do you believe in God, you sinner?

BIGOT: When I see a clock I am aware there is a clock maker.

BRIAND: But do you believe in God?

BIGOT: Yes, and his name is Mammon.

BRIAND: You fornicator.

(VAUDREUIL enters.)

VAUDREUIL: That's enough.

BRIAND: Fornicator.

BIGOT: I have no use for your blessing, I have no fear of your curse.

BRIAND: Fornicator.

VAUDREUIL: That's enough. Gentlemen, we have lost Louisbourg.

BIGOT: I'll drink to that.

BRIAND: You fornicator. The demons will be singing for our blood now.

BIGOT: The abyss is covered by a carpet of flowers. The English will not dare to step on our roses.

(MONTCALM enters. BRIAND exits.)

MONTCALM: Why am I here? Oh to be in France, at my chateau in Candiac with my wife, my chestnuts, my mulberry bushes, but instead I am in this hell hole with you.

VAUDREUIL: Show me respect, I am the governor.

MONTCALM: If I could be English for a moment I would put your head on a stick and dance round it.

VAUDREUIL: Show me respect.

MONTCALM: What a country. Rogues become rich and honest men are ruined. What were the king's engineers doing with the money. Building outhouses. There are no earthworks, no ditches, the walls are crumbling, the cannons do not face in the obvious direction.

VAUDREUIL: Mother nature is our greatest protector.

MONTCALM: If the English should ever arrive on the Plains of Abraham, God forbid, we will have to go out and meet them.

VAUDREUIL: Not necessarily.

MONTCALM: Quebec will only withstand a siege if the English attack in single file.

VAUDREUIL: I have appointed Vergor and one hundred Royal, loyal Canadians at the Anse au Foulon. They could withstand an army. The English do not have wings. They will never get up that cliff.

(The lights fade.)

Scene Eleven

(In another playing area the lights fade in. WOLFE, TOWNSHEND, and AMHERST enter.)

AMHERST: Well done Wolfe, well done. You have achieved a great victory.

WOLFE: Yes, gentlemen, a toast. To the day when British colours fly over every port and fort in North America.

TOWNSHEND: Here, here, Colonel Wolfe. So it's back to England, old chap.

WOLFE: Unfortunately, no. I had hoped to be promoted and posted in Germany where war is civilized, but I now have different orders.

AMHERST: Ah yes, Townshend, I neglected to tell you. Wolfe will be leading the attack on Quebec.

TOWNSHEND: What?

AMHERST: I hope you don't mind.

TOWNSHEND: No sir.

(WOLFE smiles. The lights fade.)

Scene Twelve

(In another playing area the lights fade in. MONTCALM and VAUDREUIL enter.)

MONTCALM: This colony is doomed. I have great fears.

VAUDREUIL: I cannot imagine the unimaginable.

MONTCALM: If only you had imagination. The English have taken Kingston, Fort Duquesnes—

(COLONEL BOUGAINVILLE enters.)

BOUGAINVILLE: Greetings from the king of France.

VAUDREUIL: What news?

MONTCALM: Are there going to be reinforcements?

BOUGAINVILLE: The king says, and I quote "When the house is on fire, one cannot occupy oneself with the stable."

MONTCALM: So, we will have to defend Canada with what we have.

BOUGAINVILLE: Yes.

MONTCALM: Oh that is bad news.

BOUGAINVILLE: No, that is the good news. The bad news is, a large fleet of ships carrying twelve thousand troops have left Portsmouth with the intention of invading Quebec.

MONTCALM: What. Why am I here?

VAUDREUIL: It doesn't matter. I will save Quebec. I will fight with a zeal, an ardour, a fury that will defy comprehension.

MONTCALM: You're a fool.

VAUDREUIL: My actions will be applaudable, you will see. Each man and woman will sing "Canada our native land shall bury us under its ruins before we surrender to the English."

MONTCALM: Sung to the tune of "We shall trample the English under our feet" no doubt.

VAUDREUIL: Do not be facetious. You always sneer at the Canadians. They will save the country, you will see.

(MONTCALM grunts.)

MONTCALM: We should fortify Quebec. The harrowing is about to begin.

(The lights fade.)

Scene Thirteen

(In another playing area the lights fade in. WOLFE enters holding a telescope. TOWNSHEND enters holding a drawing pad.)

WOLFE: So we have arrived, have we?

TOWNSHEND: Hold that pose.

WOLFE: Townshend—

TOWNSHEND: Lord Townshend, please.

WOLFE: Townshend, be a darling, and go ask the admiral if we have arrived.

TOWNSHEND: Admirals do not talk to generals, and more to the point, generals do not talk with admirals.

WOLFE: So, this is Quebec. What does that word mean?

TOWNSHEND: How should I know?

WOLFE: Anyone?

VOICE: *(Off.)* It is an Indian word, my lord. It means "the narrowing."

WOLFE: The narrowing, eh.

(WOLFE puts the telescope to his eye. TOWNSHEND continues to draw. The lights fade.)

Scene Fourteen

(In another playing area the lights fade in. FRASER enters.)

FRASER: So the recruiting sergeant said "If you fight for German George, you can dress like me." And he was dressed like I am right now. But you know what I was wearing when he said that to me ... Bunny fur. Me, a Fraser, wearing bunny fur. So I fight for German George. And I don't give a damn about anything. Now laddies, watch me close. I'm about to show you Colonel Cundum's wonderful new invention. I'm only going to put it on once, so I want you to watch me close. You know there are only three women for every hundred men, I'm trying to help you. God knows you all deserve a big pulcerous chancre on your John Thomas, and you'll get it too. But you won't be able to say I didn't try to help you. Now laddies, pass me the sheepskin.

(The lights fade.)

Scene Fifteen

(In another playing area the lights fade in. TOWNSHEND and MURRAY enter.)

TOWNSHEND: Are we here to take Quebec, or are we here to plant cabbages? Will that man never make a decision? We have had five plans of attack and not tried one.

MURRAY: Indecision and hesitation are fatal errors.

TOWNSHEND: Fatal. Criminal. We have the best army in the world.

MURRAY: Men who have been tried and found sterling.

TOWNSHEND: Officers, second to none.

MURRAY: Well said, that calls for another pipe.

TOWNSHEND: And who leads us. A general who is really a lieutenant.

MURRAY: I have to agree with you.

TOWNSHEND: The man's brain is a bladder.

MURRAY: I don't want to agree with you, but I have to agree with you.

TOWNSHEND: I should be leading this campaign.

MURRAY: No, I should be leading this campaign.

(WOLFE enters holding one of TOWNSHEND's caricatures.)

WOLFE: Fortunately our troops have been spared that fate. One can only imagine where you would lead an army.

TOWNSHEND: I would at least make a decision. Terrorizing the population with cannons and skirmishing with the Indians is a waste of time.

WOLFE: It passes the time anyway, doesn't it, you clever cartoonist.

TOWNSHEND: It is a shame I will never rise above my material.

WOLFE: As a general you make a fine cartoonist.

TOWNSHEND: And as a general you make a fine—

WOLFE: Enough. Gentlemen, I have made a decision. We will attack Montmorency.

TOWNSHEND: Montmorency, are you sure?

WOLFE: Positive, these are the details.

(The lights fade.)

Scene Sixteen

(In another playing area the lights fade in. MONTCALM and VAUDREUIL enter.)

VAUDREUIL: The best defense is a good offense.

MONTCALM: Only if you have a good offense.

VAUDREUIL: If the Frenchmen haven't the stomach for fighting, send in the Canadians.

MONTCALM: That is exactly what Wolfe wants us to do. We will hold our ground. Wolfe will come to us, we will not chase him. Beauport, the place he really wants to attack, he will attack last. He will attack somewhere around ... Montmorency.

VAUDREUIL: What about the Anse au Foulon.

MONTCALM: The enemy does not have wings.

(The lights fade.)

Scene Seventeen

(In another playing area the lights fade in. MME PEAN enters.)

MME PEAN: My husband is so lazy.

(VAUDREUIL enters.)

VAUDREUIL: Ah madame, you are like a beautiful flower.

MME PEAN: And you are like a sweet smelling weed.

VAUDREUIL: Your husband is having an affair with my wife.

MME PEAN: So.

VAUDREUIL: Does that shock you?

MME PEAN: No, it surprises me. Your wife must be very attractive.

VAUDREUIL: You must fight fire with fire. Have an affair with me.

MME PEAN: You must think I am mad. I have thrown over a husband for a lover.

VAUDREUIL: And now throw over your lover for a governor. Remember I am the Marquis de Vaudreuil. I will give you fifty thousand francs if you will be my mistress.

MME PEAN: From a lover that is too much, and from one I do not love, too little.

VAUDREUIL: How much then?

MME PEAN: I am fond of everything that makes life lovely.

VAUDREUIL: You are just like my wife, only worse. You coquette. Oh the fate of all men is truly terrible. To come from between those legs to die in those arms. What a useless existence.

MME PEAN: You wish to die in my arms.

VAUDREUIL: No, I wish to reverse my fate.

(BIGOT enters.)

Ah François, how good to see you. I have just offered Madame fifty thousand francs to be my mistress and she has refused.

BIGOT: Offer me those francs and you can have her.

(BIGOT puts out his hand.)

VAUDREUIL: Madame, to him, or to you.

(VERGOR enters.)

VERGOR: Monsieur Bigot.

BIGOT: What do you want? Get out.

MME PEAN: Give it to him.

VERGOR: Give what to me?

BIGOT: A taste of my dick if you do not get out of my sight.

VERGOR: Monsieur, I have had a taste and I am hungry for more.

BIGOT: Why are you here? What do you want?

(Pause.)

Well.

VERGOR: Now I remember … the English are attacking Montmorency.

VAUDREUIL: What! Why didn't you tell me?

VERGOR: I tried.

VAUDREUIL: Allez, get out of my way. This is serious business.

BIGOT: The money, the money.

(VAUDREUIL exits.)

One day you will hear the words "Well done faithful servant," but not today.

(The lights fade.)

Scene Eighteen

(In another playing area the lights fade in. MURRAY and FRASER enter. Offstage is heard the dying rumble of the Battle of Montmorency.)

MURRAY: How goes the battle?

FRASER: Badly, it was like running up a slippery hill to attack a firing squad. Many were killed and we had to retreat, leaving the wounded on the hill to be scalped by the bastards.

MURRAY: The bloody bastards.

FRASER: I saw it with my own eyes. Brain and hair seared from screaming mouths.

MURRAY: The bloody bastards.

FRASER: It was a nightmare, and our general has been struck down by the fever.

MURRAY: I think he had the fever before the battle.

FRASER: Yes, that thought is shared by many.

(The lights fade.)

Scene Nineteen

(In another playing area the lights fade in. WOLFE and TOWNSHEND enter.)

TOWNSHEND: It's a scandal, a scandal.

WOLFE: Stop acting like a troll.

TOWNSHEND: It's a scandal. I am going to request a parliamentary investigation. I am going to write a letter to my brother. He is a member of Parliament. He knows all about politics and victories.

WOLFE: Yes. And after you have written it, perhaps you can deliver it in person. We will put you on a fast ship and send you across the Atlantic. And then you can be what you have always wanted to be. A postman.

TOWNSHEND: How dare you talk to me that way.

WOLFE: Tell that man to retire before I lose my temper.

TOWNSHEND: This is a scandal, a scandal.

(The lights fade.)

Scene Twenty

(In another playing area the lights fade in. BIGOT, MME PEAN, and VERGOR enter laughing uproariously.)

MME PEAN: Oh, that's funny, that's funny.

BIGOT: And then I will give you brandy. And then we will put on the feedbag, and then I will be like a stallion, and you, like a hot steamy mare.

MME PEAN: Yes.

(VAUDREUIL enters.)

BIGOT: Oh look, it is the conquering hero.

VAUDREUIL: Yes it is I, your governor, fresh from the wars.

BIGOT: Look Pierre, does she not look like a Pompadour?

VAUDREUIL: War has blinded my passion. Even you look like a Pompadour.

(They roar with laughter. BOUGAINVILLE enters.)

BOUGAINVILLE: The Marquis de Montcalm sends his regrets. He will not partake in the celebration tonight. He is with his troops.

MME PEAN: And what does he do with his troops at night?

BOUGAINVILLE: Not what you do, that is for sure.

MME PEAN: How dare you say that to me. I should slap your face.

BOUGAINVILLE: And if I were a lady I would turn the other cheek.

VAUDREUIL: All right, that is enough. Enough, enough.

(BOUGAINVILLE turns to VERGOR.)

BOUGAINVILLE: What are you doing here? You should be guarding the Anse au Foulon.

VERGOR: My farmers are guarding it. The British are defeated. It is safe.

(BOUGAINVILLE shakes his head.)

VAUDREUIL: Tell your general I will give him his orders in the morning.

BOUGAINVILLE: You know the way to Montmorency.

VAUDREUIL: Yes. Goodnight.

(BOUGAINVILLE exits.)

BIGOT: That man has no sense of humour.

VAUDREUIL: No. Come my dear, let us go to the bomb shelter where the party never ends.

(MME PEAN laughs. The lights fade.)

Scene Twenty-one

(In another playing area the lights fade in. FRASER is singing.)

FRASER: "Though our clothing is changed
yet we scorn a powder puff.
so at you, ye bitches,
here's giving you hot stuff."

The man who wrote that is dead. Killed in his prime. Poor Neil Botwood. The bard of the barracks is dead meat.

VOICE: *(Off.)* We'll never sing that again.

FRASER: No, never again.

(TOWNSHEND enters.)

TOWNSHEND: These are our orders from our sick general. We are to begin the scourging. We are to liberate all the cattle we find and burn, sack, and pillage every house and farm in as gruesome and nasty a fashion as possible. Any inhabitants who do not respect neutrality are to be ... taught a lesson. And only Indians and Canadians dressed as Indians are to be scalped.

FRASER: Good. My knife has waited a long time for this moment.

TOWNSHEND: And there will be no raping or looting.

FRASER: Except in the presence of officers.

(Laughter offstage.)

TOWNSHEND: Anyone caught raping will receive three hundred lashes.

FRASER: During the last ten years I have received thirty thousand lashes. I do not fear the cat. You want to see my back?

(FRASER smiles. The lights fade. During the darkness the sounds of the sacking, burning, and pillaging are heard.)

Scene Twenty-two

(In another playing area the lights fade in: the gates of Quebec. Two habitants, PIERRE and MARIE, confront BIGOT.)

PIERRE and MARIE: Let us in. The English are eating our cattle and sheep and trying to kill us. Let us in.

BIGOT: Go fight the English.

PIERRE: No, they are dressing us up as Indians and then scalping us. Let us in.

BIGOT: Go fight the English or we'll put the Indians on you.

PIERRE and MARIE: No.

MARIE: Let me in. My father was scalped last night and they're after me.

BIGOT: Did you bring your harvest?

MARIE: I brought a sack of flour.

BIGOT: Then enter.

PIERRE: And I brought sheep.

BIGOT: Then enter.

(The lights fade.)

Scene Twenty-three

(In another playing area the lights fade in. WOLFE enters holding a bottle. TOWNSHEND and MURRAY enter.)

MURRAY: I resent that.

WOLFE: Be quiet.

TOWNSHEND: Never. Resign you swine.

MURRAY: To attack the Beauport defenses is to attack the enemy's strongest position.

WOLFE: It is also the only position where we can land our troops in sufficient numbers to properly engage the enemy.

TOWNSHEND: It is not sound.

MURRAY: I agree with General Townshend.

WOLFE: When do you not agree with General Townshend?

MURRAY: I resent that.

TOWNSHEND: I have never had such disagreeable company before in my life.

WOLFE: You should tell that to your mirror.

TOWNSHEND: This is a scandal.

WOLFE: No plan of attack against Quebec is sound. All is chance.

MURRAY: Some chances are better than others.

TOWNSHEND: If you would stop drinking goat's urine you would know that.

WOLFE: Get out of my sight. I am devising a plan of attack.

TOWNSHEND: And when you form one, we will carry it out as effectively and efficiently as possible. But it is madness to wait for winter.

WOLFE: You think I am mad.

TOWNSHEND: Think? I know you are mad.

WOLFE: Then watch your step, I may bite you.

TOWNSHEND: Don't you dare.

WOLFE: Fool. Leave me scab. Go play the flute with your friend.

MURRAY: I resent that.

TOWNSHEND: This is a scandal.

(The lights fade.)

Scene Twenty-four

(In another playing area the lights fade in. MONTCALM and LEVIS enter.)

MONTCALM: Vaudreuil's brother defends Montréal. He is an idiot.

LEVIS: Yes. Are you going to be leaving soon?

MONTCALM: Why?

LEVIS: No reason.

(MME PEAN enters.)

Well, look who it is.

MME PEAN: Buzz-buzz here, buzz-buzz there.

LEVIS: Ah, ma cherie.

MME PEAN: Oh, and you're with your little friend.

LEVIS: Yes, my little friend. And I have another little friend you may want to meet.

MME PEAN: Does this little friend want to shake my hand.

LEVIS: Oh very much.

MONTCALM: Chevalier.

LEVIS: Oui, mon général.

MONTCALM: You will go to Montréal.

LEVIS: What?

MONTCALM: You will take command.

LEVIS: When?

MONTCALM: Right now.

LEVIS: What? My apologies to Madame. Another time, another place.

(LEVIS exits.)

MME PEAN: Oh, you are so powerful.

MONTCALM: Kiss this ring.

(The lights fade.)

Scene Twenty-five

(In another playing area the lights fade in. PIERRE the habitant enters holding a sheep. FRENCH SOLDIER ONE enters.)

PIERRE: I brought my sheep here because I did not want the English to eat them.

FRENCH SOLDIER ONE: Good, because now we can eat them.

PIERRE: Non.

FRENCH SOLDIER ONE: Oui.

PIERRE: Non.

FRENCH SOLDIER ONE: Oui.

PIERRE: Non.

FRENCH SOLDIER ONE: Fermez la bouche. Allez.

PIERRE: Mes bêtes.

(FRENCH SOLDIER ONE kicks PIERRE in the backside.)

FRENCH SOLDIER ONE: Allez.

(The lights fade.)

Scene Twenty-six

(In another playing area the lights fade in. FRASER enters. He is looking up the side of a cliff.)

FRASER: Ah, ya muzzled bastards. Come down here and fight ... you dirty. Ah, this is no good. Halt! Who goes there?!

PIERRE: A friend. Look, I bring you a sheep. Eat.

FRASER: Are you a deserter?

PIERRE: Non, I mean no harm. Let me go, I know a path.

FRASER: A path.

(The lights fade.)

Scene Twenty-seven

(In another playing area the lights fade in. WOLFE, FRASER, and PIERRE enter.)

WOLFE: Tell me what I want to know or I'll saw your arm off.

(TOWNSHEND and MURRAY enter.)

TOWNSHEND: I must see Wolfe.

FRASER: The general is not seeing anyone this evening. He is deep in thought.

TOWNSHEND: There is a rumour among the troops that we attack tomorrow. Is this true?

WOLFE: Yes.

TOWNSHEND: He cannot treat me this way. I'm a brigadier-general, and the son of a lord.

MURRAY: And I'm the son of a Peer.

WOLFE: Would you kindly tell these sons of bitches that I am going to retire for the evening and I will give them the plans tomorrow.

TOWNSHEND: But we attack tonight.

WOLFE: And you will have the plans before we attack. Goodnight.

(TOWNSHEND and MURRAY exit.)

WOLFE: And what else?

PIERRE: Sometimes most of us work Vergor's farm in the daytime and sleep at night, and the others are given permission to work their own farms instead of standing guard.

WOLFE: Hmmm-hmmm. It is a steep cliff.

PIERRE: Yes.

(The lights fade.)

Scene Twenty-eight

(In another playing area the lights fade in. WOLFE and TOWNSHEND enter.)

WOLFE: The boast of heraldry, the pomp of power. and all that beauty and wealth ever gave await alike the inevitable hour. The paths of glory lead but to the grave.

TOWNSHEND: Bullocks.

WOLFE: Gentlemen, I would rather have written those lines than take Quebec, but having not written those lines I will take Quebec.

TOWNSHEND: Bullocks.

WOLFE: The action we are about to undertake is the stuff that dreams and memories are made of.

TOWNSHEND: Bullocks.

WOLFE: Gentlemen, we will give the French a fight and feel no pain tonight.

TOWNSHEND: Bullocks.

WOLFE: Monckton, you will cover the right. Burton, you the centre, and Murray, the left.

(WOLFE turns to TOWNSHEND.)

WOLFE: And you will bring up the rear.

TOWNSHEND: If this plan fails, it will be a scandal.

WOLFE: It will be a scandal if it is successful. So kindly bring up the rear. Gentlemen, we have a rendezvous with destiny.

(WOLFE turns to TOWNSHEND.)

And you have a rendezvous with the rear.

(The lights fade.)

Scene Twenty-nine

(In another playing area the lights fade in. BOUGAINVILLE and FRENCH SOLDIER ONE.)

FRENCH SOLDIER ONE: Oh my bleeding stinking feet. If we're going to chase ships why don't we have shoes that fit. Oh, if I could shove these in an Englishman's face, I would be happy.

BOUGAINVILLE: Yes, keep them away from me. I'm not an Englishman.

FRENCH SOLDIER ONE: We have chased those ships up and down, down and up.

(MME PEAN enters on a pogo stick with a horse's head.)

BOUGAINVILLE: Well look who it is.

MME PEAN: Yes look. Can a strong powerful soldier help a lady in distress?

BOUGAINVILLE: Are you a lady?

MME PEAN: Slap me and find out.

(BOUGAINVILLE smiles and pats MME PEAN's horse.)

BOUGAINVILLE: This horse is in a sweaty lather.

MME PEAN: If you were between my legs for two hours you would be in a sweaty lather too.

(BOUGAINVILLE laughs.)

BOUGAINVILLE: And why are you out on such a dark night?

MME PEAN: I am going to that house over yonder. Do you want the password?

BOUGAINVILLE: We don't use passwords in the French army. We just take what we want.

MME PEAN: Well perhaps you could take me to my house.

BOUGAINVILLE: Always glad to escort a lady.

(BOUGAINVILLE and MME PEAN exit.)

FRENCH SOLDIER ONE: Can I come too?

(The lights fade. During the darkness.)

VOICE: *(Off.)* A sail.

Scene Thirty

(In another playing area the lights fade in. FRASER enters.)

FRASER: All right lobsters, we've landed. Observe quiet. I am about to speak French like a Frenchman.

VOICE: *(Off.)* Qui vive?

FRASER: La France, et vive le roi.

VOICE: *(Off.)* A quel regiment?

FRASER: De la reine.

VOICE: *(Off.)* Laissez les passer. Ils sont nos gens avec les provisions.

FRASER: All right lobsters. Now the climb.

(The lights fade.)

Scene Thirty-one

(In another playing area the lights fade in. A HABITANT on sentry duty enters.)

HABITANT: Who goes there?

FRASER: *(Off.)* Friends. We are your relief.

HABITANT: Relief? From what?

(FRASER enters holding a sword.)

FRASER: From life.

(FRASER stabs the HABITANT.)

We're up.

(VERGOR enters.)

VERGOR: What is it? My God, run, they are here.

(VERGOR exits. WOLFE enters.)

FRASER: It is ours.

WOLFE: Excellent. Sergeant, bring that cannon up that cliff.

FRASER: Aye, aye, sir.

(WOLFE exits.)

All right you dirty dogs, you heard what he said. Bring the cannon up the cliff.

(The lights fade. During the darkness.)

VOICE: *(Off.)* Oh God, for the love of Jesus, where are the horses … Good Lord.

FRASER: *(Off.)* Shut your filthy hole!

Scene Thirty-two

(In another playing area the lights fade in. MONTCALM enters.)

MONTCALM: Where is Bougainville? Why did I send Levis to Montréal? Oh, now I remember. Oh what a night. She made my fat flesh lean. Oh the shame.

(VERGOR enters.)

VERGOR: Mon général, they are here, they are here.

MONTCALM: Who are here?

VERGOR: Les maudits Anglais.

MONTCALM: Where?

VERGOR: On the Plains of Abraham.

MONTCALM: What?

Scene Thirty-three

(On another playing area the lights fade in. WOLFE and FRASER enter.)

WOLFE: Beat drum, blow bugle, march. Take care, wheel into line. Dress. Close step. Present arms. Handle cartridge. Prime. Load. Fix bayonet. You there, sponge. Powder. Ram load, ram. Dress. Close up.

(FRASER enters.)

FRASER: Sir, the thin red line stretches half a mile. The Canadians and Indians are sniping at us from the forest.

WOLFE: How I love fighting in the rain. Reminds me of Scotland. Grey skies, is there a more beautiful colour?

FRASER: No sir.

WOLFE: Well I'm a chatty person today, aren't I. Brave soldiers, brave soldiers. Retreat is impossible. Die hard.

FRASER: We'll be victorious, don't worry about that. If the nicht be the nicht, and the lads be the lads.

WOLFE: Yes, yes, yes.

(FRASER holds up a broadsword.)

FRASER: Oh, we'll sing the old songs tonight.

(The lights fade.)

Scene Thirty-four

(In another playing area the lights fade in. MONTCALM enters on his horse—a pogo stick with horse head.)

MONTCALM: There they stand. The enemy. Where they have no right to be. We must fight before they entrench. Êtes-vous preparez, mes enfants.

VOICE: *(Off.)* Oui, mon général, oui. Vive notre général.

MONTCALM: Vive le roi.

VOICE: *(Off.)* Vive le roi.

MONTCALM: Why do I have this terrible feeling ... Allons-y!

(The lights fade. During the darkness the sound of bagpipes, drums, trumpets, war whoops, yelling—chaos.)

Scene Thirty-five

(In another playing area the lights fade in. WOLFE and FRASER enter with ENGLISH SOLDIERS. The ENGLISH SOLDIERS aim their muskets at the audience. Cannon and musket fire. WOLFE is shot in the wrist. He ties a kerchief to the wrist.)

WOLFE: Ready ... Aim ...

(WOLFE is shot in the abdomen. He puts a hand to his midriff.)

Fire!

(The roar of musket fire. The lights fade.)

Scene Thirty-six

(In another playing area the lights fade in. MONTCALM enters with FRENCH SOLDIERS. MONTCALM is wounded. Wounded FRENCH SOLDIERS curse, swear, scream, gesticulate, moan, and groan. The lights fade.)

Scene Thirty-seven

(In another playing area the lights fade in. WOLFE, FRASER, and ENGLISH SOLDIERS enter.)

WOLFE: Charge!

(WOLFE is shot in the chest. ENGLISH SOLDIERS advance.)

Hold me up.

(FRASER catches WOLFE as he is about to fall.)

FRASER: Surgeon.

WOLFE: Hold me up.

FRASER: Surgeon, surgeon, surgeon.

WOLFE: Hold me up so that my brave soldiers may not see me drop.

FRASER: Surgeon.

WOLFE: It is needless. I am finished. Do not grieve for me. I shall be happy. But tell me, how goes the battle.

(FRASER lays WOLFE on the ground.)

FRASER: Egad! Everywhere they give away. They run, see how they run.

WOLFE: Who run?

FRASER: Egad sir, the enemy. They give way.

WOLFE: Good. The day is ours. Now God be praised I will die.

(WOLFE smiles. WOLFE dies. The lights fade.)

Scene Thirty-eight

(In another playing area the lights fade in. MARIE, the habitant, enters.)

MARIE: Oh my God, my God. The marquis is killed.

(A wounded MONTCALM enters on his horse.)

MONTCALM: Yes, and Fontobonne and Senezergues are dying also.

MARIE: My God, my God. Your wounds are mortal.

MONTCALM: Do not be distressed my good friend. It is nothing. I will recover. I shall not live to see the surrender of Quebec.

(MONTCALM exits with MARIE. Offstage are the sound of wounded retreating French soldiers. VAUDREUIL enters.)

VAUDREUIL: How goes the battle?

(Two FRENCH SOLDIERS enter screaming and shrieking.)

Cheer up, I am arrived. I will rally the troops.

FRENCH SOLDIER TWO: I've got no balls, they've been shot off.

FRENCH SOLDIER THREE: Oh for the love of screaming blue shit. I have been stabbed in the bladder.

FRENCH SOLDIER TWO: I lost my legs to a cannon.

(VERGOR enters.)

VERGOR: What should we do, mon général?

FRENCH SOLDIER THREE: I've got no stomach.

VAUDREUIL: Retreat, retreat, retreat, retreat.

VERGOR: While you retreat, should I stay and fight and hold them off?

VAUDREUIL: Yes, faithful servant, yes. Retreat, retreat.

(VAUDREUIL exits with the two FRENCH SOLDIERS. FRASER enters.)

FRASER: Here's another one. Here, meet your maker.

(FRASER stabs VERGOR.)

VERGOR: Mon Dieu.

FRASER: Now, let's see what he's got.

(FRASER starts looting. TOWNSHEND enters.)

TOWNSHEND: What in bloody hell do you think you're doing?

FRASER: Just collecting souvenirs. It's a great day, sir. A night in the boats, a climb, and then a fight. A great day.

TOWNSHEND: Yes, I suppose so.

FRASER: We heard you died with our heroic general.

TOWNSHEND: How could I be dead? I was in the rear, climbing up the bloody cliff.

FRASER: Is General Murray dead?

TOWNSHEND: No, but ... I am in charge. Tell that battalion of soldiers over there to stop looting and rally over by that oak tree.

FRASER: Yes sir.

(VERGOR groans.)

TOWNSHEND: And put that man out of his misery.

FRASER: Yes sir.

(FRASER stabs VERGOR. The lights fade.)

Scene Thirty-nine

(In another playing area the lights fade in. MONTCALM is on his deathbed, with BRIAND and MME PEAN.)

BRIAND: You must sign the note of surrender.

(VAUDREUIL enters.)

VAUDREUIL: Oh dear me, dear me. What am I to do?

MONTCALM: Ah, Angélique.

VAUDREUIL: Stop looking at that woman and talk to me. I said stop looking at that woman.

MONTCALM: That woman is my wife, so be quiet.

MME PEAN: Non monsieur, I am not your wife. I am Marguerite de Pean.

MONTCALM: Ah, Angélique, in my mind I am with you.

MME PEAN: Sire, Quebec is the place to be ill.

VAUDREUIL: Oh dear me, dear me. What am I to do, what am I to do?

MONTCALM: You have three choices. Surrender. Attack. Retreat. The choice is yours.

VAUDREUIL: Oh no, who is going to help me? Who? ... who? ... who? ...

MONTCALM: Is there an owl in this room?

VAUDREUIL: It is all your fault. You have done this to me on purpose.

MONTCALM: Oh leave me. I have more important matters to deal with than the state of your corrupt, cruddy colony, and this wretched country. Get out of my sight.

VAUDREUIL: I will call a council of war and save Quebec.

(MONTCALM applauds.)

MONTCALM: Bravo, bravo.

VAUDREUIL: I will.

MONTCALM: Why not? Ah, Angélique.

VAUDREUIL: Oh, what am I to do?

(VAUDREUIL exits.)

BRIAND: You must sign this note of surrender.

(BRIAND gives MONTCALM a quill and paper.)

MONTCALM: To whom it may concern ... I am obliged to yield Quebec to your arms.

(MONTCALM sings the paper.)

Oh France.

(BRIAND takes the paper.)

What time is it?

MME PEAN: Four o'clock.

MONTCALM: Just think Angélique, right at this moment someone is trying to prevent the extinction of our race.

(MONTCALM smiles. MME PEAN smiles.)

Send in the bishop.

BRIAND: Do not worry sinner. I am with you. You are going to burn in hell forever.

(The lights fade.)

Scene Forty

(In another playing area the lights fade in. VAUDREUIL, BIGOT, and CAPTAIN RAMEZAY enter.)

VAUDREUIL: So, what would you suggest?

RAMEZAY: The garrison is poorly equipped and will never withstand a siege. And if we attack, we will be slaughtered.

VAUDREUIL: And what would you suggest?

BIGOT: We must fight, we must attack.

RAMEZAY: That is not a wise plan.

VAUDREUIL: I want to make a note here, for the record, that the Officers of France were indisposed for battle.

RAMEZAY: Wait one moment, one moment. I will rally the troops and stand in the front line and attack, if you will stand with me.

VAUDREUIL: I am the governor, not the general. My death would be an act of surrender. We will retreat so that we may fight another day. We will give up Quebec, not New France. Captain de Ramezay, I order you to hold Quebec to the last extremity before surrendering.

(BOUGAINVILLE enters.)

RAMEZAY: Well look who it is. What were you doing, picking flowers?

BOUGAINVILLE: I came as soon as I could. Better late than never.

RAMEZAY: No, unfortunately they are the same thing.

BOUGAINVILLE: Don't look at me like that.

(The lights fade.)

Scene Forty-one

(In another playing area the lights fade in. MARIE, the habitant, enters.)

MARIE: Some say he is bearing up well and that he may recover, but others say ... Look a light.

(BRIAND enters.)

Is there any word? Well?

BRIAND: Only God is immortal.

(MARIE wails.)

MARIE: What will become of us? What will become?

(Noises offstage.)

The English are coming.

BRIAND: No, no, look.

MARIE: Our army is retreating. Come back, come back.

(RAMEZAY enters.)

RAMEZAY: They are not retreating. They are running, running for their lives. The English are two miles away, you would think they were two feet behind them.

(Church bells chime.)

BRIAND: We are going to bury the marquis among the bones and skulls of our fathers.

(MARIE wails.)

RAMEZAY: Bury me with him.

BRIAND: No. You must surrender.

(The lights fade. During the darkness.)

FRASER: Let's give three cheers to our victorious dead General. James Wolfe, hero. Hip hip ...

Scene Forty-two

(In another playing area the lights fade in. TOWNSHEND and MURRAY enter.)

TOWNSHEND: Quiet. I am going to England. The people here can suck my tapioca. I have had enough. This has been the most disagreeable experience of my life. You are now commanding officer. Things seem to have devolved on you.

MURRAY: Seems that way.

FRASER: *(Off.)* Hip hip ...

TOWNSHEND: Quiet. Bon chance.

MURRAY: And bon chance to you.

(The lights fade.)

Scene Forty-three

(In another playing area the lights fade in. BIGOT and MME PEAN enter.)

BIGOT: Small pox, famine, plague, and syphilis are everywhere. My face is going to rot off.

MME PEAN: I see it is happening already.

BIGOT: I am as ugly as sin.

MME PEAN: Yes, you are.

(VAUDREUIL enters.)

VAUDREUIL: But life goes on. Surrender is not the end of everything.

BIGOT: No, and I burned the books. No one will ever know the true state of anything.

VAUDREUIL: Good, I think our future is in France.

(LEVIS enters.)

LEVIS: Yes, in the Bastille.

BIGOT: It wasn't us, we didn't do anything.

LEVIS: I know.

(The lights fade.)

Scene Forty-four

(In another playing area the lights fade in. FRASER and MARIE, the habitant, enter.)

FRASER: In Scotland I was a bare-assed Danny Boy. But I can't be a bare-assed Danny Boy in this place. I got to protect what's under my kilt. Now if I give you this will you make me some woolens.

MARIE: I won't tell you "yes," and I won't tell you "no."

FRASER: Then what are you telling me? Are you telling me "maybe?"

MARIE: I won't tell you "yes," and I won't tell you "no."

FRASER: If you make me a big wooley, I'll give you this. I swear on my dirk.

MARIE: I won't tell you—

(A NUN enters.)

FRASER: Sister of Mercy, can you find it in your heart to make this papist idolater bastard a big wooley?

(The NUN smiles and nods her head. The lights fade.)

Scene Forty-five

(In another playing area the lights fade in. LEVIS, BIGOT, and MME PEAN enter.)

LEVIS: Where is that idiot, Vergor?

BIGOT: He died a hero's death.

LEVIS: You will refer to me as High and Mighty Lord.

BIGOT: He died a hero's death, oh High and Mighty Lord.

(LEVIS turns to MME PEAN.)

LEVIS: You look so nice.

(LEVIS turns to BIGOT.)

And you look so awful.

BIGOT: You don't like my face.

MME PEAN: Oh you are so powerful.

(VAUDREUIL enters.)

LEVIS: What do you want? Get out.

VAUDREUIL: Oh High and Mighty Lord, I bring good news.

LEVIS: Speak.

VAUDREUIL: I have rallied the men. They are ready to march on Quebec.

LEVIS: Why didn't you tell me this? Allez.

(LEVIS exits.)

VAUDREUIL: He is going to be difficult.

BIGOT: Yes.

(The lights fade.)

Scene Forty-six

(In another playing area the lights fade in. FRASER and PRIVATE JENKINS enter.)

JENKINS: MeDrawd, Marchag, Marb, Cymru, Gorku, Cymru.

FRASER: And so in we came, all grin and gash, whiskers and moustache. I took this from a Frenchman.

(FRASER holds up a scalp.)

When I hit him with this.

(FRASER holds up his sword.)

I didn't mean to kill him, but his skull was thin, and he died, but I could see it in his eyes that he was born to be hanged, so I saved him from his fate.

JENKINS: Cymru, Gorku, Cymru.

FRASER: I come from a clan so old, so long in the tooth that when the great flood came, we built our own boat.

JENKINS: Cymru, Cymru.

FRASER: Shut up. I'm a Scotch man and I'm making my soup.

JENKINS: I'm praying to my dragon. I might not get another chance. Why is your face covered in blood?

FRASER: There's no blood on me. Be gone you half-wit.

JENKINS: Your face is covered in blood.

FRASER: I want no Ticonderoga stories out of you.

JENKINS: MeDrawd, Marchag.

FRASER: The bullets you hear are the ones that miss you. The one you don't hear is the one that kills you. Remember that, put your trust in cold steel.

JENKINS: Your face is covered in blood.

FRASER: Shut up. Just pray laddies that you're never captured by the Indians. I was captured once, they tied me to a stake, squatted over my face, and as they were about to brown log me to death I started singing the old songs.

(MURRAY enters.)

MURRAY: All right scum, wake up.

JENKINS: Your face is covered in blood.

MURRAY: We are going to meet the French on the Plains of Abraham. Are you ready to fight?

JENKINS: When I was young I drank the dragon's blood. The blood, the thunder in my veins has made me mad with hatred. By your grace, if you show me the enemy I will show you a man in pieces.

MURRAY: And you?

FRASER: I'm ready to sing the old songs right now, to hell with tonight.

MURRAY: In this battle we will take no prisoners.

JENKINS and FRASER: Those words are music to our ears.

FRASER: Sir, do you see any blood on me?

MURRAY: No, of course not.

JENKINS: Your face is covered in blood.

(MURRAY puts a hand to his face.)

MURRAY: Forward.

(The lights fade.)

Scene Forty-seven

(In another playing area the lights fade in. LEVIS enters.)

LEVIS: What am I going to do? Vaudreuil is a moron, and Bigot … Oh Bigot.

(MME PEAN enters.)

MME PEAN: It's white and it's following me.

LEVIS: What?

MME PEAN: My ass, monsieur.

(They laugh.)

LEVIS: Ah, my dear, you fool me again.

MME PEAN: Oh monsieur, you are so …

LEVIS: Feel this hand.

MME PEAN: Hot and sweaty.

LEVIS: Oh what am I to do?

MME PEAN: Ah, I have a brilliant idea.

LEVIS: What?

MME PEAN: You must use a *ruse de guerre.*

LEVIS: No madame, it must be *force de frappe.* But I don't have enough soldiers.

MME PEAN: Don't worry monsieur, as you have taken Quebec in your dreams, you will take it in your sleep.

LEVIS: No madame …

(VAUDREUIL and BIGOT enter.)

What do you want? Get out.

VAUDREUIL: The British are advancing.

LEVIS: Mes amis, mes enfants. We will avenge the memory of our general and take back what is ours. In this battle we take no prisoners. What say you to that?

VAUDREUIL: Vive le général.

BIGOT: Vive le général.

LEVIS: Allons-y.

(The lights fade. During the darkness: the sounds of battle.)

Scene Forty-eight

(In another playing area the lights fade in. MURRAY, FRASER, and JENKINS enter.)

MURRAY: Die hard, die hard. Colonel Drummond, is he alive?

JENKINS: Yes, but he has no face.

MURRAY: Die hard, die hard. And Captain Henderson, what does he say?

FRASER: He has been shot in the mouth and is now speechless.

MURRAY: Die hard, die hard.

(The sound of the battle becomes louder.)

I think we should withdraw.

FRASER: Retreat! Retreat!

(The lights fade.)

Scene Forty-nine

(In another playing area the lights fade in. LEVIS enters.)

LEVIS: They give way. Allez.

(The lights fade.)

Scene Fifty

(In another playing area the lights fade in. JENKINS and FRASER enter. FRASER sings 'If the Nicht be the Nicht' with a pike through him.)

FRASER: Oh God.

JENKINS: Your face is covered in blood.

FRASER: There's no blood on me.

JENKINS: Your face is covered in blood.

(MURRAY enters.)

MURRAY: Good God, what a disaster. Jesus wept, I'm going to be crucified. My brain is a bag of nails.

(The lights fade.)

Scene Fifty-one

(In another playing area the lights fade in. LEVIS and MME PEAN enter.)

MME PEAN: It's white and it's following me.

LEVIS: It's white and it's going to be inside you.

(VAUDREUIL enters.)

VAUDREUIL: Oh High and Mighty War Lord.

LEVIS: Get out of my sight.

VAUDREUIL: Oh conqueror supreme. I pull the lion's tail at the risk of your wrath but I compliment you on putting events into the hands of heaven.

LEVIS: It is all a man can do. The ship that arrives in the spring will be of more than passing interest. Let us pray it is from France.

(The lights fade.)

Scene Fifty-two

(In another playing area the lights fade in. MURRAY and JENKINS enter. MURRAY holds a telescope.)

MURRAY: A sail. I pray it's ours. I spy with my eye ... the flag of St. George. We've won, we've won. Wolfe's victory is preserved. Praise God. If I had lost this place after it being won so dearly ... I don't even want to think about it. We've won.

(The lights fade.)

Scene Fifty-three

(In another playing area the lights fade in. LEVIS and VAUDREUIL enter.)

LEVIS: We are the damned.

VAUDREUIL: What are we to do?

LEVIS: Montréal. We will make our last stand at Montréal.

VOICE: *(Off.)* The English are coming. They are advancing.

(The lights fade.)

Scene Fifty-four

(In another playing area the lights fade in. AMHERST enters.)

AMHERST: Gentlemen, we have Montréal surrounded. I want everybody in this village scalped and cut into tiny little pieces.

(MURRAY enters.)

MURRAY: Lord Amherst.

AMHERST: What?

MURRAY: A white flag.

AMHERST: What?

(LEVIS and VAUDREUIL enter.)

VAUDREUIL: We surrender.

LEVIS: But only if we are given the honours of war.

AMHERST: No honours in this war. Scalping and torture, disgusting. If you do not surrender I will personally take your scalp with this.

(AMHERST holds up a tomahawk.)

VAUDREUIL: Oh we surrender, we surrender.

LEVIS: Fungula.

(LEVIS exits.)

AMHERST: What?

(The lights fade.)

Scene Fifty-five

(In another playing area the lights fade in. PONTIAC enters.)

PONTIAC: Brethren. The French are dead meat. The dogs in red have taken Hochelaga. We have dipped our arrows in shit for no reason. We will see if these dogs in red trade like Frenchmen.

(The lights fade.)

Scene Fifty-six

(In another playing area the lights fade in. JENKINS enters.)

JENKINS: All right lads. Hip, hip …

VOICES: *(Off.)* Hooray.

JENKINS: Hip, hip …

VOICES: *(Off.)* … Hooray

JENKINS: Hip, hip …

VOICES: *(Off.)* … Hooray

(VAUDREUIL, BIGOT, MME PEAN, and MARIE enter.)

JENKINS: Right, let's lord it over them. I do not want to hear any more of this odious French. You are all, every one of you, including you, you are all His Britannic Majesty's subjects. Do I make myself clear?

(VAUDREUIL, BIGOT, MME PEAN, and MARIE grimace.)

And thank your lucky stars. From this day forth, the history of this country begins. And this victory proves God is a Protestant.

(MURRAY and BRIAND enter.)

MURRAY: That's enough. The English are gracious in victory.

(BRIAND advances down stage and envelopes the habitants in his robe.)

Gentlemen, a toast. All is well in the world tonight, and the future is bright.

(MURRAY and JENKINS smile. BRIAND and the habitants scowl. The lights fade.)

Part Two

The Conspiracy of Pontiac

Scene One

(Darkness. The beating of drums and a chant: "Hail Pontiac. Hail Pontiac, hail." The lights fade in. PONTIAC enters.)

PONTIAC: When the whiteman first came to this land, they told us they were gods. They are not gods, they are devils. They take our land, rape our women, kill our children. When the whiteman dies, he goes to a place called hell. We must send as many whitemen as we can to that place. Except the French. The French became our friends, our allies against the Iroquois. But the French are gone. Now dogs in red speak ugly voice. Speak lies. You all have grievance. Speak Blackhawk.

(BLACKHAWK, the Warrior Chief, enters wearing a white dress.)

BLACKHAWK: I am Blackhawk, the Warrior. You all know of my deeds. The English rob me of my furs. Give me this *(He indicates dress.)* instead of Thunderjuice. Dogs in red think I am woman.

(BLACKHAWK shakes his head.)

Me not woman.

(In another playing area lights up on ENGLISH OFFICER ONE is tied to a stake.)

This dog know I am not woman.

ENGLISH OFFICER ONE: Oh please don't.

BLACKHAWK: He is woman. That leg between your legs, we will roast and feed to our turtles.

(ENGLISH OFFICER ONE groans. The lights fade.)

PONTIAC: Brothers, each of you know our injustice. The French never try to change us. We change them. But the English, the English try to kill us. Many forts on many rivers now fly red flag of devil. In the winter we ask for blankets to keep us warm. They give us blankets, blankets with disease. Many women die, many children die. But what do we do? Do we fight the English? No. We fight with ourselves. We should fight paleface, man who look sick all the time, we should fight him.

(BLACKHAWK brandishes a tomahawk.)

BLACKHAWK: I hate man who look sick all the time.

PONTIAC: Dogs in red call this land Canada. Long knives call this land America. Neither. This land is our land. But white man say drink firewater, sign this, now land mine.

(BLACKHAWK brandishes the tomahawk.)

BLACKHAWK: I hate the white man.

PONTIAC: Brothers, my heart is strong and hot. Where are your fathers? They are ghosts that cry in the night. And our night is more dark than all the night before us. We must awaken and sleep no more. The Great Spirit has made us all one. We are from many tribes, but we are all brothers. My brothers, I will make it rain. Rain hell on the white man. For one hundred summers our tribes were powerful, united, strong. As a spider weaves a web we must conspire to rise up and speak the language of our nature. And if we die, then we will lay our soul on the ground, and flowers will grow where our bodies have lain. I am Pontiac. I have spoken.

(The lights fade.)

Scene Two

(In another playing area the lights fade in. ENGLISH OFFICER TWO and his WIFE enter. PONTIAC enters.)

PONTIAC: Did you like our dance?

ENGLISH OFFICER TWO: Oh it was very good. Didn't you think so, Margaret?

WIFE: Oh yes, it was very colourful. What do you call it?

PONTIAC: It's the Rain Dance.

(MARGARET laughs.)

WIFE: Oh, I hope it doesn't rain on us.

(PONTIAC smiles and holds up a lacrosse stick.)

PONTIAC: You have seen us dance. Now watch us play. As you can see, I have brought many young men with me.

WIFE: Yes, they look like they are in very good shape.

(PONTIAC grunts.)

ENGLISH OFFICER TWO: Oh, this will be marvelous. I've seen the Indians play this game. It's very violent, Margaret.

WIFE: If it's too violent, I'll close my eyes.

(The WIFE laughs. PONTIAC smiles.)

PONTIAC: Come. Bring everyone out of the fort to watch us play.

ENGLISH OFFICER TWO: Oh, this will be jolly good.

PONTIAC: Yes, it will.

(PONTIAC smiles. The lights fade. During the darkness—the sound of a massacre.)

Scene Three

(In another playing area the lights fade in. MAJOR HENRY GLADWYN and MAHOGANNE enter.)

GLADWYN: Oh my child. You are like a beautiful flower.

MAHOGANNE: Oh, I love rubbing my nose in your beard.

GLADWYN: And I love rubbing you too. What is the matter?

MAHOGANNE: Oh happy victory. I will never rub my nose in your beard again.

GLADWYN: Oh nonsense.

MAHOGANNE: No, oh I shouldn't tell you this but …

GLADWYN: What?

MAHOGANNE: Oh Pontiac.

GLADWYN: Pontiac!

MAHOGANNE: He is going to kill you.

GLADWYN: What?

MAHOGANNE: Oh I shouldn't tell you this.

GLADWYN: Tell me.

MAHOGANNE: When Pontiac comes to visit you.

GLADWYN: Tomorrow.

MAHOGANNE: Yes. He is going to hold up a wampum belt. If he holds up the red side. It is the signal to attack.

GLADWYN: Oh no.

MAHOGANNE: And if he holds up the white side, they will not attack.

GLADWYN: Why is he doing this?

MAHOGANNE: I don't think he likes the English. But if Pontiac could know you like I know you, he would like you so much.

GLADWYN: Yes.

(The lights fade.)

Scene Four

(In another playing area the lights fade in. GLADWYN, BAKER, and CAPTAIN DALYELL enter. PONTIAC, MINAVAVANA, FRANÇOIS, a fur-trader, and WARRIORS enter.)

GLADWYN: All right. Here they come. Remember the sign.

PONTIAC: Remember the sign. Hail, Great Mountain, hail.

GLADWYN: Ah Pontiac, welcome to Detroit.

PONTIAC: I bring the Calumet. Smoke, fill your cheeks with this.

GLADWYN: Ah the Peace Pipe.

(PONTIAC hands the pipe to GLADWYN. GLADWYN smokes the pipe and then hands it to DALYELL.)

PONTIAC: Now bring everyone out of the fort to watch us play.

GLADWYN: No, I don't think so.

PONTIAC: Why not?

GLADWYN: Oh you know why.

PONTIAC: I thought we were friends.

GLADWYN: So did I.

PONTIAC: Then to prove my friendship I want to give you a gift.

(PONTIAC holds up the wampum.)

GLADWYN: So this is the wampum.

PONTIAC: This is it. Wampum is of great value to us. This belt tells the story of your life.

GLADWYN: Really.

PONTIAC: I want to hold it up for my brothers so they can see your life. Now.

GLADWYN: Now!

(GLADWYN, BAKER, and DALYELL raise their swords. PONTIAC's WARRIORS raise their tomahawks.)

PONTIAC: I don't understand.

GLADWYN: I don't either, but I am.

PONTIAC: I am giving you a gift.

GLADWYN: Then give it.

(PONTIAC gives the wampum belt to GLADWYN—white side up.)

PONTIAC: The story of your life. A white snowbank.

GLADWYN: So, let's see what's on the other side. Ah ha, I thought so.

(MAHOGANNE enters.)

MAHOGANNE: Is everyone safe?

PONTIAC: I thought so.

(PONTIAC and his WARRIORS exit. The lights fade.)

Scene Five

(In another playing area the lights fade in. PONTIAC and MAHOGANNE enter. WARRIORS stand in the shadows.)

PONTIAC: As honey is sweet, this woman is beautiful. But there is a blackbird inside this maiden. A blackbird that is never quiet. A blackbird that tells the English all our plans. We will boil you alive in maple sap, and save you for the winter, and then roll you in the snow for our pleasure. Take her from my sight.

(A WARRIOR enters from the shadow and takes MOHOGANNE offstage.)

My brothers, the English know of our plans. We must speak with one voice, and be one body. I know most of you are with me. But what says Minavavana, Great Chief of the Ojibway?

(MINAVAVANA enters from the shadows.)

MINAVAVANA: I will consult the Great Turtle and see what he has to say.

PONTIAC: Very good. The words of a true chief. While he talks with his turtles I will fight the English. My brothers, we are the makers of our own fortune. We do not need to talk to turtles, or to the beavers to know it is right. We must kill the English without mercy. We are penned like pigs by English forts. We complain, we cry, but pigs in pigpen always die. Join my conspiracy and there will be many prisoners when the corn is this high. *(PONTIAC indicates the height of corn.)* We will kill all the English. No mercy. And from their scalped skulls we will grow our pumpkins. The English women, we will make them kiss all the toads in the Great Lake and then beat them to death with our bags of corn. And all the forts will be our forts. There are many scalps to be taken and much blood to drink. What mercy has the white man shown us? Speak. He has shown us the mercy of death. I will show him the same mercy, but before he dies he will know my feeling. I hate the English.

(The lights fade.)

Scene Six

(In another playing area the lights fade in: Detroit. GLADWYN and CAPTAIN CAMPBELL look up at the sky.)

GLADWYN: I don't like the look of that cloud.

CAMPBELL: Me neither. It is as black as the Hobbes. It is a bad sign. It is directly over this fort and nowhere else.

GLADWYN: And those drums, those bloody drums, never stop.

(Noises offstage. DALYELL enters with TOWNSPEOPLE.)

DALYELL: Disaster, massacre.

GLADWYN: Speak man, for God's sake, speak.

DALYELL: Many forts have fallen and what

I have seen defies telling. The torture, the horror.

GLADWYN: Tell us, for God's sake tell us.

DALYELL: The Indians captured Fort Miami, Michilimackinac and Le Boeuf with all supplies. The liquor made them mad. They poured all the whiskey into an empty canoe and then dunked their heads in, and drank till they almost drowned. Some were so drunk they just cried and weeped, but others, others turned into demons, devils from hell. The women hid their knives and tomahawks but that didn't stop them, the fiends went round gouging out eyes, biting off noses. My eyes have made me mad. And Pontiac sits like a Satan, like a great Satan in the forest surrounded by his hordes. Remember little Bobby Thompson, remember him, the drummer boy.

TOWNSPEOPLE: Yes, we rememeber little Bobby Thompson.

DALYELL: Well little Bobby Thompson started to cry when all the noses were being eaten. And a vicious hag took a knife and cut off the top of little Bobby Thompson's head, and then ripped off the scalp, and then the bastards grabbed him by the head and started eating his brains. And he was alive when they did this. I have seen people skinned alive, boiled, scalped, eaten. The flesh from your father's rump is now used as a tobacco pouch.

(A TOWNSWOMAN screams. Another WOMAN screams from offstage.)

CAMPBELL: The bastards are hurling heads over the fence.

(WOMAN enters screaming, holding a head.)

WOMAN: My husband, my husband.

GLADWYN: Unhand that head.

(A SOLDIER enters.)

CAMPBELL: Sir, an Indian approaches holding a white flag.

GLADWYN: I want him knackered.

CAMPBELL: But he holds a white flag.

(BLACKHAWK enters. He blows his nose on the white flag.)

BLACKHAWK: Greetings from Pontiac. Hail White Father. The Great Pontiac invites you to come sit on the Great Bearskin. Do not be afraid, he knows you are not a woman.

(BLACKHAWK laughs.)

GLADWYN: You impudent cur.

BLACKHAWK: Pontiac brings you a gift.

(BLACKHAWK pulls out a severed head from a burlap bag.)

Remember him.

(A TOWNSMAN screams.)

TOWNSMAN: That's my brother.

BLACKHAWK: He sits in hell without his head. But do not cry. When you go there you can give it to him.

(BLACKHAWK throws the head to the TOWNSMAN.)

As you can see Pontiac is generous with his gifts.

TOWNSMAN: Oh my poor brother.

GLADWYN: What do you want?

BLACKHAWK: Pontiac invites you to a great feast, his kettles are ready, and his fires lighted. Will you parley? You are surrounded by many warriors, many creatures of the forest await you.

GLADWYN: Captain Campbell.

(CAMPBELL steps forward.)

CAMPBELL: Sir.

GLADWYN: You know these people better than I. Try to reason with this Pontiac. Tell him this is no longer French land.

BLACKHAWK: It was never French land. It has always been our land.

GLADWYN: Look savage, we won this land fair and square.

BLACKHAWK: From whom? From Pontiac. Pontiac never loses what cannot be lost and never gives what cannot be given. Come quickly before our turtles become angry.

(The lights fade.)

Scene Seven

(In another playing area the lights fade in. CAMPBELL is tied to the stake.)

CAMPBELL: Oh God, why me?

(FRANÇOIS, the fur-trader, enters.)

FRANÇOIS: Oh this man is going to die.

CAMPBELL: I might have known you were behind all this.

FRANÇOIS: Remember the prettiest girl in New France.

CAMPBELL: I remember her well.

FRANÇOIS: Shut up, or I get my knife I cut your nuts. Oh this man is going to die. You wait until you see what I'm going to do to you.

CAMPBELL: I'll show you how to die.

(PONTIAC enters.)

FRANÇOIS: Ah, Pontiac. Look, I have a gift from the governor of Louisiana.

(FRANÇOIS holds up a bottle of perfume.)

Perfume. Make you smell so nice. And the governor asked me to tell you that the French king who was sleeping is now awake again, and is hungry. Hungry for this man's blood.

PONTIAC: Hear that, brothers. We will have allies. Like the old days.

CAMPBELL: A hogshead of hogwash on you.

FRANÇOIS: Shut up. Brothers, the French king right now is jumping up and down shouting, "Let us trample the English under our feet."

CAMPBELL: Hogwash. The war is over.

PONTIAC: Englishman, you know the French king is our father. And we promised to be his children. Englishman, you will regret that you did not fill our canoes with presents. With guns and rum, with blankets, with kettles.

(CAMPBELL groans.)

Englishman, in this forest you have the status of a squirrel. And every squirrel lives for the day it will be a feast, when it will be put in the old soup pot. Your day has come. The kettles are ready, the fires lighted.

(A SQUAW enters.)

Englishman, you see that fat squaw. She will squat on your face and then you will know something about something.

(MINAVAVANA enters holding a dead snake.)

Have you spoke with your turtle?

MINAVAVANA: Yes, he thinks it is right that we kill the English.

PONTIAC: A wiser turtle has never lived. Good.

(MINAVAVANA approaches CAMPBELL.)

MINAVAVANA: This snake is my grandfather. How dare you kill my grandfather. I will strangle you with my grandfather.

PONTIAC: We will avenge your grandfather in other ways. This one is friend, we honour him. Let us roll the plum stones to see if he lives.

(PONTIAC rolls the plum stones.)

Snake eyes.

(PONTIAC grins. The lights fade.)

Scene Eight

(In another playing area the lights fade in. Screams are heard offstage. GLADWYN and DALYELL enter.)

DALYELL: Good God, listen to that.

GLADWYN: Poor devils, poor devils.

DALYELL: What are they doing to make a man scream like that?

GLADWYN: Poor devils, poor devils.

DALYELL: There are two kinds in this world, the poor and the lucky.

GLADWYN: Oh the poor devils, poor devils.

DALYELL: Once, seven years ago, I had the great misfortune to be in Calcutta. But I was one of the lucky ones. The Thuggee put me in the Black Hole, but others were not so lucky. I saw the Thuggee hammer twenty nails into the head of my best friend. He screamed like that man is right now.

GLADWYN: Poor devils, poor devils.

DALYELL: No hope, no hope. Wait. A ship. We're saved.

GLADWYN: Oh no, look … Pontiac.

DALYELL: Turn back, go away. Go away!

(DALYELL starts waving his hands.)

GLADWYN: They're waving to us. They think we're waving to them.

DALYELL: Go away … it's a trap! Oh no. Pontiac is killing everybody.

(The lights fade.)

Scene Nine

(In another playing area the lights fade in. FRANÇOIS enters. PONTIAC enters dressed as a French officer.)

FRANÇOIS: The French king is no longer jumping up and down, Pontiac.

PONTIAC: I am like you, I am a Frenchman. The Marquis de Montcalm, do you remember him? He gave me this. The king of France is my father. I have proven to you all that my balls are big and hairy. Now prove to me that you are men, that you are Frenchmen. The corn is now this high, and this fort is still in English hands. Did I not promise you many scalps, many victories? Seventeen English forts in this land. Sixteen ça n'existe pas. Must we who make the whole earth tremble die at the hands of children? Help me lift the hatchet so that I may cut the English flesh into pieces and scatter it among the tribes. You are English, or you are French?

FRANÇOIS: I am French.

PONTIAC: If you do not help me, you are English.

FRANÇOIS: I am French.

PONTIAC: You are useless, worse, you are hopeless. Why must I fight your battles. The whole Algonquin nation. United, first time. I am making friends with your enemy, my enemy, the Iroquois, because Iroquois compared with English, are friend. Think, a tree grows only once.

(The lights fade.)

Scene Ten

(In another playing area the lights fade in. GLADWYN is sleeping. DALYELL enters and wakes him up.)

GLADWYN: What? Where am I?

DALYELL: Detroit.

GLADWYN: This is like a bloody nightmare.

DALYELL: The men are in a bad mood.

GLADWYN: Really. Well, we'll see about that.

(A SOLDIER enters.)

What's the matter with you?

SOLDIER: I want food, I want water, I want ammunition, I want booze, and I want a woman, right now. Or I'm going to mutiny. And put your head on a stick.

GLADWYN: This is like a bloody nightmare. I am going to go berserk.

(GLADWYN draws his sword and stabs the SOLDIER.)

What do you think of that?

(The SOLDIER groans. GLADWYN withdraws his sword.)

Anyone else for mutiny?

(The lights fade.)

Scene Eleven

(In another playing area the lights fade in. THAYENDANEGEA enters. PONTIAC stands in the shadows.)

THAYENDANEGEA: I am Thayendanegea. The name means "two sticks tied together for strength." Is there any man that would contest that? If there is, let him speak, so that I might hear him. Thayendanegea, Iroquois chief. I am the mouth of my nation. When I speak, I speak for all the Iroquois. I, too, have many scalps.

(THAYENDANEGEA holds up a bush of hair.)

French scalps. Pontiac, Great Chief of the Ottawa, say we are brothers, say we should kill all the English. Pontiac say we should kill all the whiteman, except the French, because the French are friends of Pontiac. The English are friends of Thayendanegea. Over a thousand moons since Frenchman kill three Iroquois chief. Iroquois never forget, Iroquois never forgive. My great, great, great father made vow. "French would never be kings of this forest." They are slaves of the English. Iroquois now kings of the forest. English give Iroquois liquor for French head.

PONTIAC: And English take Iroquois land. Seneca fight with Pontiac, why not Mohawk, Onondaga? Why you like English so much? You are like dog that barks, not like dog that bites.

THAYENDANEGEA: Thayendanegea throw this dog that bites a bone.

(PONTIAC barks.)

Pontiac kill all English, Thayendanegea not see.

(A murmur of approval from the shadows.)

But Pontiac not see when Thayendanegea kill all French.

(A murmur of unrest.)

PONTIAC: The French are the friends of Pontiac.

THAYENDANEGEA: *(Referring to himself by his Christian name.)* And the English are friends of Joseph Brant.

(PONTIAC smiles. THAYENDANEGEA smiles. The lights fade.)

Scene Twelve

(In another playing area the lights fade in. GLADWYN enters singing to himself.)

GLADWYN: I'm just singing a song, holding on, holding on.

(FRANÇOIS enters holding an old boot.)

FRANÇOIS: Here, eat. Eat.

GLADWYN: What is it?

FRANÇOIS: It's food. Eat it.

(FRANÇOIS gives GLADWYN the boot. FRANÇOIS exits.)

GLADWYN: I'm just singing a song, holding on, holding on.

(A TOWNSWOMAN enters wailing.)

There, there, it's all right, it's all right. There's nothing to cry about today, we cried yesterday, that's enough. Just singing a song, holding on, holding on. I'm so tired of this place, I wish I could go home, but the party is about to begin, but I wish I could go home anyway.

(DALYELL enters.)

DALYELL: Major Gladwyn.

GLADWYN: What do you want?

DALYELL: The men want to organize a sneak attack.

GLADWYN: Why not? You can die now, you can die later, who cares.

DALYELL: The idea is to go out at midnight with bayonets and stab and hack every damn Indian we see, if we're lucky we'll kill Pontiac, and if we're not lucky we'll run back into the fort. At least we'll do something.

GLADWYN: That's a good idea, at least do something, at least do something.

DALYELL: Sir, are you all right?

GLADWYN: Who is going to lead the attack?

DALYELL: I am.

GLADWYN: Yes, you're a good man.

DALYELL: God, listen to those drums.

GLADWYN: Yes, listen.

DALYELL: We have your permission?

(GLADWYN nods his head and sings.)

GLADWYN: Holding on, holding on.

(DALYELL exits. The lights fade.)

Scene Thirteen

(In another playing area the lights fade in. FRANÇOIS is tied to the stake.)

FRANÇOIS: Oh god.

(PONTIAC and MINAVAVANA enter.)

MINAVAVANA: Before the leaves fall the English will be here. Must the corn be so high we cannot see? We have had them surrounded for three moons but the English do not come out.

PONTIAC: That is because someone is feeding the English. I do not think my Frenchmen are Frenchmen. Frenchman, it is to you that I speak. Will you feed the English or will you fight?

FRANÇOIS: I'll fight, I'll fight.

(Noises offstage. BLACKHAWK enters.)

BLACKHAWK: Blackbird. Turtle Man. Great Pontiac, we see over one hundred English trying to sneak up on us. They not see us, but we see them.

PONTIAC: Light the fires. We must show them the place to sneak up on.

(The lights fade.)

Scene Fourteen

(In another playing area the lights fade in. DALYELL and an ENGLISH SOLDIER enter.)

DALYELL: Quiet.

(They take a few steps. Hands come out of the shadows to grab DALYELL. The ENGLISH SOLDIER screams. The lights fade.)

Scene Fifteen

(In another playing area the lights fade in.)

GLADWYN: Oh, this boot tastes good.

(A WOMAN enters.)

WOMAN: I hear they're making women eat their children.

GLADWYN: Just singing a song.

WOMAN: Are you going to do anything about it?

GLADWYN: That's it, I've had it.

(The SOLDIER enters.)

SOLDIER: Massacre, disaster.

GLADWYN: Oh Jesus.

SOLDIER: The bloody bastards ambushed us as we were sneaking up on them. It's a bloody mess out there.

(The WOMAN starts to wail.)

GLADWYN: All right that is it. We can't get out, they can't get in. We'll just sit tight. We have enough shoes to eat. We'll be fine. We'll just wait for winter, or reinforcements, whichever comes first.

(The lights fade.)

Scene Sixteen

(In another playing area the lights fade in. DALYELL is tied to the stake.)

DALYELL: Good God. Why me?

(PONTIAC enters.)

PONTIAC: Hail, Snake Eyes.

DALYELL: Please don't.

PONTIAC: English are like little sucking baby that cry all the time. Ahhhhhhh, poor sucking baby. I'm going to give you something to cry about.

DALYELL: Oh no.

(PONTIAC holds up an arrow.)

PONTIAC: I'm going to cut your fist off, and then stick this in, right up to your elbow. Then you have something to cry about. You little sucking baby.

DALYELL: Oh no.

(The lights fade.)

Scene Seventeen

(In another playing area the lights fade in. BLACKHAWK and MINAVAVANA enter.)

BLACKHAWK: With these arms we used to conquer.

(They laugh. PONTIAC enters.)

PONTIAC: It is not enough to celebrate. There are more scalps to be taken.

MINAVAVANA: We have enough scalps. The war is won.

PONTIAC: No. Detroit still stands.

MINAVAVANA: But nothing else. This is all our land now.

PONTIAC: For how long? We must fight.

MINAVAVANA: The walls are too high, and they won't give us ammunition. We must save what we have for the hunt. The winter comes quickly. Do not ask us to starve. We have drank enough blood. We are hungry.

(FRANÇOIS enters.)

FRANÇOIS: Pontiac.

MINAVAVANA: We fought for the Frenchmen and his lilies. Which is more than he did. This frog jumps. The French traders say their Great Father gave all this land to the English. François lied to you.

FRANÇOIS: Pontiac, the English are coming—in many boats.

BLACKHAWK: We must bury the hatchet and next year dig it up with this.

(BLACKHAWK holds up a tomahawk. The lights fade.)

Scene Eighteen

(In another playing area the lights fade in. GLADWYN enters.)

GLADWYN: Whoever Joshua was, I am. I will make no covenant with infidels, if the heathen is delivered to me I will destroy him utterly.

(WILLIAM JOHNSON enters.)

JOHNSON: Congratulations on a heroic defense.

GLADWYN: Thank you.

JOHNSON: What are your plans?

GLADWYN: I think for the rest of my life I will grow cabbages. And never when I leave this godforsaken country will I ever return.

JOHNSON: Pontiac sues for peace. They acknowledge King George as their new father.

GLADWYN: If you believe that, you are a fool. They have temporarily stopped for … thank God, enough Englishmen have died, and my recommendation to you is to give each Indian a ton of rum, or even better a ton of raw alcohol, each, and let them extirpate themselves in the most bilious fashion possible and be done with it. As part of the British Empire, the trees are lovely.

(The lights fade.)

Scene Nineteen

(In another playing area the lights fade in. PONTIAC, JOSEPH BRANT [formerly Thayendanegea], and JOHNSON.)

BRANT: This is Sir William Johnson. My father, the Warrageheygey.

PONTIAC: Warrageheygey. "One who fucks much."

BRANT: "One who does much."

JOHNSON: I would like to see you live the rest of your days like a happy bear.

PONTIAC: On fruits and roots. Does that make you happy? To see Pontiac eating insects.

JOHNSON: To see you drink milk and eat honey would make me happy.

PONTIAC: This bear eats meat.

JOHNSON: Will you accept King George as your father?

PONTIAC: First bark.

JOHNSON: Will you sign this peace treaty?

PONTIAC: Second bark.

JOHNSON: Will you be friends with the English?

PONTIAC: Third bark.

JOHNSON: What means this bark.

PONTIAC: I have barked three times, have I not?

JOHNSON: You have.

(PONTIAC smiles and nods his head.)

Will you sign this treaty?

PONTIAC: First bite.

(JOHNSON holds up the peace treaty.)

I cannot hear words with my eye.

JOHNSON: Sign this treaty and you will laugh and grow fat.

PONTIAC: I knew a man once, a great man named Stinking Blanket. You laugh. He was called Stinking Blanket because he was too busy killing white men to change his blanket. He was so busy. Well he was a thin man, but after talking to a white man he would come back like this.

(PONTIAC holds his hands apart.)

Fat and stout. Just stuffed with lies. Just stuffed.

JOHNSON: I am going to stuff you full of truth.

PONTIAC: As there are stars in heaven, there are as many ways to cheat.

(JOHNSON holds up a bottle.)

JOHNSON: Drink my firewater and we will make much hee-hee. Let us be one people with one king.

PONTIAC: When the sun becomes a hole in the sky. I will die before my heart goes soft. I will dip my arrows in shit forever. As you can see we have not come here with our wives. We knew you would try to steal them. The white man is so greedy. The Great Spirit once told his children that when they died they could take nothing with them. Nothing. Not their clothes, not their pipes, not their wives, not their land, nothing. But your Great Spirit must have told you something different, he must have told you that when you die you can take everything. The white man is so greedy. But I tell you something, white man. He lied to you.

JOHNSON: Drink Pontiac, drink. Let us drink until our bags are full and then listen to the grass grow.

PONTIAC: I can listen to the grass grow anytime.

JOHNSON: To lies.

PONTIAC: And truth.

JOHNSON: And peace.

PONTIAC: And war.

(The lights fade.)

Scene Twenty

(In another playing area the lights fade in. FRANÇOIS enters.)

FRANÇOIS: And the chief's short round wife jumped up and down and cried "I want to touch you, I want to touch you" and so I lowered my head that she might touch me and you know what she did ... she bit my ear off. Right off. See, no ear. You see an ear? No ear. And I tell you something it will be a snowy day in July before I show that bitch my other ear. But this ear hears that Pontiac is up to his old ways again. And when this ear hears, this body listens. I don't go in that forest. The wives of Pontiac, never turn your back.

(The lights fade.)

Scene Twenty-one

(In another playing area the lights fade in. JOHNSON enters holding a bottle. A burlap bag lays at his feet. The ASSASSIN enters.)

ASSASSIN: Uh, blackbird ... why me? Why me?

JOHNSON: Want to trade, chief?

ASSASSIN: Uh, blackbird. Give me a present.

(JOHNSON takes a rattle from the burlap bag.)

JOHNSON: Shake.

(The ASSASSIN shakes the rattle.)

ASSASSIN: Now give me something sweet.

JOHNSON: I got just the thing.

(JOHNSON gives the ASSASSIN a candy. The ASSASSIN eats the candy.)

ASSASSIN: Now, what you want to trade for my furs.

(JOHNSON pulls a kettle from the bag.)

No.

(JOHNSON pulls a pot from the bag.)

No.

(JOHNSON pulls a bottle of liquor from the bag.)

Give.

JOHNSON: Not so fast.

ASSASSIN: Give.

JOHNSON: We have to trade first. I give you firewater for furs.

ASSASSIN: Give.

JOHNSON: But not the whole bottle.

ASSASSIN: How much?

JOHNSON: Four fingers.

ASSASSIN: Four fingers for my furs.

JOHNSON: That's right. Take it or leave it.

ASSASSIN: Four fingers.

JOHNSON: The whole bottle would kill you. This is one hundred, pure firewater.

ASSASSIN: Give.

(The ASSASSIN takes the bottle, JOHSNON takes the furs. The ASSASSIN drinks.)

JOHNSON: You're almost there ... you're past.

ASSASSIN: Look, big bird in sky.

JOHNSON: Where ...? Hey that's not fair, stop, stop, you've had a lot more than four fingers. You've had ... nine fingers.

ASSASSIN: Nine fingers for my furs. That more like it. Uh blackbirds, everywhere.

JOHNSON: Would you like a barrel of whoop-up juice.

ASSASSIN: Uh, blackbird.

JOHNSON: Kill Pontiac and I will give you a barrel of this.

ASSASSIN: Taste.

(JOHNSON gives the bottle to the ASSASSIN.)

Oh, this powerful firewater.

JOHNSON: Kill Pontiac and you can bathe in it. Is it a deal?

ASSASSIN: Pontiac powerful warrior, powerful warrior. Much trouble when he die. I am a Peoria warrior. If I kill Pontiac you are looking at the last of my race.

JOHNSON: Kill Pontiac and I will give you all the thunder juice you can drink in one sitting.

ASSASSIN: That more like it. Deal.

(The lights fade.)

Scene Twenty-two

(In another playing area the lights fade in. PONTIAC enters.)

PONTIAC: Everywhere I go, blackbirds follow. Just singing that evil song, "Ha, kill the English." Just singing that evil song.

(BLACKHAWK enters with a tomahawk.)

BLACKHAWK: Look what I just dug up.

PONTIAC: Just singing that evil song.

BLACKHAWK: Not many warriors answer the call.

PONTIAC: But they will.

BLACKHAWK: Not many warriors, not many.

PONTIAC: Everytime I go for a walk in the forest.

BLACKHAWK: Blackbirds follow.

PONTIAC: When I say I will fight no more.

BLACKHAWK: The blackbirds start singing.

PONTIAC: If our men are to be killed, they are too many.

BLACKHAWK: Sing the blackbirds.

PONTIAC: If they are to fight, they are too few.

BLACKHAWK: Sing the blackbirds.

PONTIAC: Just singing that evil song.

BLACKHAWK: Kill the English.

PONTIAC: Sing the blackbirds.

(The lights fade.)

Scene Twenty-three

(In another playing area the lights fade in. PONTIAC enters. The ASSASSIN enters behind PONTIAC. The ASSASSIN stabs PONTIAC in the back. PONTIAC falls to his knees. The lights fade. Thunder and lightning.)

Scene Twenty-four

(In another playing area the lights fade in. BLACKHAWK enters holding a small bundle of clothes over his head.)

BLACKHAWK: My son: The panther coming across. The shooting star. Tecumseh.

(Thunder and lightning.)

Remember me.

(Thunder and lightning. The lights fade.)

Part Three

The Loyalists

Scene One

(The lights fade in. An ENGLISH SOLDIER holding the Union Jack enters.)

ENGLISH SOLDIER: His Excellency, the governor-general of Canada, Guy Carleton.

(The lights fade.)

Scene Two

(In another playing area the lights fade in. GUY CARLETON and COLONEL JOHN CAMPBELL enter. CAMPBELL holds a map.)

CAMPBELL: Here now is an idea of what this colony looks like. It is not finished, of course, but almost.

CARLETON: It is huge. So big, so beautiful, so hateful. There is a curse on this land. The French are hateful, the Indians are hateful, and the colonies are filled with hate and treason. Why can this wilderness not accept a king?

CAMPBELL: It can and it will.

CARLETON: I was on the plains with Wolfe and I can tell you victory is a strange beast. A French-speaking British colony.

CAMPBELL: Which brings up the delicate matter of the fur-traders in Montréal.

CARLETON: Oh them.

CAMPBELL: They want the vote.

CARLETON: I will not put the fate of sixty-thousand habitants in the hands of sixty English-speaking fanatics. The army is the law. Tell them Canada is not a democracy.

(The lights fade.)

Scene Three

(In another playing area the lights fade in. THOMAS WALKER, an English fur-trader, enters; CAMPBELL enters.)

CAMPBELL: Hear ye, hear ye! A proclamation. This land called Canada will hereafter be called Quebec.

WALKER: A French word.

CAMPBELL: That's right. This land will be called Quebec because the colonists of New England find the word Canada obnoxious and odious.

WALKER: So what?

CAMPBELL: Shut up. We are changing the name so that settlers will come here.

WALKER: They'll never come here. The winters are awful.

CAMPBELL: Shut up face! Settlers will come here because they will have no choice but to come here. All westward expansion of the colonies is hereafter prohibited.

WALKER: They'll live on top of one another before they'll come here. I'm only here because of the fur trade.

CAMPBELL: Shut up fart! When a sufficient number of settlers speaking the English tongue have arrived, democracy will be instituted.

WALKER: That could be a long time. Everyone here speaks French.

CAMPBELL: Until that time—

WALKER: I am an Englishman, I want my rights.

CAMPBELL: Which are?

WALKER: To rule.

CAMPBELL: The king rules here.

WALKER: You call him an Englishman. He can't even speak the language. Dunder und Blixen. Goot Pipple, what for you abuse me? I am here for own goot. What for you abuse me?

CAMPBELL: By God sir, you rile me.

WALKER: If his father had not married his brother's daughter, who knows.

CAMPBELL: Corporal, arrest this man.

(The lights fade.)

Scene Four

(In another playing area the lights fade in. SEIGNEUR CHARLES BONTEMPS and BISHOP BRIAND enter. They applaud. CARLETON enters.)

BONTEMPS: We are like the beaver. Happy and proud you are here.

CARLETON: Thank you for those warm hands.

BRIAND: Oh you smell so nice.

CARLETON: Thank you. Will you take tea with me?

BONTEMPS: Oh we are honoured.

CARLETON: Speak.

BRIAND: We pay our compliments to you for the Quebec Act.

CARLETON: It pleases you?

(BONTEMPS and BRIAND gasp with joy.)

And the population at large.

(BONTEMPS and BRIAND exchange looks.)

BONTEMPS: They whistle while they work.

BRIAND: They are happy, do not worry about them. They do as they are told.

CARLETON: I wish my compatriots in the thirteen colonies were half as obedient.

BONTEMPS: We have a long history with … Les Batards, I don't know what else to call them.

CARLETON: Rebels, perhaps … traitors.

BONTEMPS: Yes, I suppose you could say that.

BRIAND: Dark and desperate days are ahead. I will pray.

(The lights fade.)

Scene Five

(In another playing area the lights fade in. CAMPBELL and WALKER enter. WALKER is holding his ear.)

WALKER: Oh they cut off my ear.

CAMPBELL: Because you wouldn't listen.

WALKER: Oh there will be blood.

CAMPBELL: Such trash. These hands have never been soiled in trade.

WALKER: And these hands do not have blood on them.

CAMPBELL: Be gone. Go visit your Money God.

WALKER: Oh, there will be blood.

CAMPBELL: Corporal, arrest this man.

WALKER: What, again?

(The lights fade.)

Scene Six

(In another playing area the lights fade in. JOHN JOHNSON and CARLETON are drinking tea.)

JOHNSON: These yokels, these yahoos were liberated from French terrorism. They owe the king seventy-million English pounds. And will they pay? Not on your life, Godfrey, not on your life. And when the king exercises his God-given right, the colonials scream, nay shriek, "No taxation without representation," as if they were Englishmen.

CARLETON: They are a disgusting rabble. I hate them profoundly.

JOHNSON: And now these farmers, these rascals have organized themselves into groups, calling themselves "Sons of Liberty."

CARLETON: Sons of bitches would be more appropriate.

JOHNSON: Exactly. They tar and feather good men doing the king's duty. Three years ago in Boston, four loud-faced, foul-mouthed hooligans, ruffians of the first order found a home for a bullet.

CARLETON: Only four you say. Pity.

JOHNSON: And they called it a massacre.

CARLETON: S'blood! I'd like to show them what a massacre is.

JOHNSON: So would I, so would we all. And now rowdies dressed as Mo-hogs, have thrown good English tea into Boston harbour.

CARLETON: What kind of monsters live in this Boston?

JOHNSON: And they have the impudence, the impertinence, to call it a "tea party."

CARLETON: This is an outrage. This is intolerable.

JOHNSON: Exactly. I think our swords will soon speak.

CARLETON: Mine is on the verge of screaming.

(The lights fade.)

Scene Seven

(In another playing area the lights fade in. BONTEMPS enters.)

BONTEMPS: My name, Charles Bontemps. My wife, she sleeps here, she sleeps there. Do I care? Of course not. The other seigneurs can have her. On my land I have seigneur's rights. My tenants tremble when they see me. On their wedding day their daughters run. But not fast enough. This old goat is unstoppable. Before the conquest I did not have seigneur's rights. But Carleton, he is a great man. My vassals can go dance around my maypole forever. My eyebrows are so beautiful. A little pluck here, a little pluck there.

(In another playing area the lights fade in. BRIAND enters.)

BRIAND: The British esteem my virtue when I curtsy and nod. They are fools. You cannot pull the wool over the eyes of this black-hearted sinner. The creatures of the barnyard that live in the Palace of Versailles can go straight to hell and burn forever. I am no longer a Frenchman. I am happy to serve the King of Kings. When I am with the British I wink and smile, but when I am with you, I sneer. I am so full of pride.

(In another playing area the lights fade in. PIERRE, the habitant, enters.)

PIERRE: We have an aristocracy of morons. These lords of the land think we will be hewers of wood, drawers of water. We will be hewers of heads first. The priests think we will be slaves to the church. These priests will be a slave to my dick before I am a slave to the church. My grandfather would never accept this. When he crossed the ocean he crossed more than water. This is worse than before. The seigneurs do not speak for me, they do not speak for themselves. They speak for the English. I hate the English, but the English who say they are not English. I hate them even more.

BONTEMPS: A little pluck here.

BRIAND: A little wink there.

(The lights fade.)

Scene Eight

(In another playing area the lights fade in. CARLETON enters.)

CARLETON: The French habitants want to believe in their deity, we let them believe in it. They want to speak their language, we let them speak it. They want to own land, we let them own it. Why aren't they happy?

(BONTEMPS and BRIAND enter.)

BONTEMPS and BRIAND: They are happy.

(CARLETON holds up a portrait of George the Third.)

CARLETON: Will they believe in this as their king?

BONTEMPS: Well, they're not that happy, but they're happy.

BRIAND: In the gathering storm they will stay loyal.

CARLETON: The gathering storm. It is near, the clamour in Boston grows. The rabble scream with one voice "Give us Liberty or give us Death." Always screaming.

BONTEMPS: The words of rich landowners are cheap. They will value their estates more than their freedom and if—

BRIAND: Hellions brewing rebellion, Satan stirring the stew trying to make a revolution.

CARLETON: Don't say that word. It is a civil war.

(CARLETON holds up the portrait.)

We will win the hearts and minds of these Colonials with this. Need I say more.

BONTEMPS: No, that says it all.

CARLETON: They will love him, they will respect him, or they will die.

BRIAND: Oh well said.

(CAMPBELL enters.)

CAMPBELL: The rebels have tasted victory at Lexington. Vagabonds and ruffians have put our troops to flight at Concord.

CARLETON: What? This is an outrage. This is the greatest insult in recorded history.

CAMPBELL: And now the league of Lucifer is banging and tootling away, preparing to fight another day.

CARLETON: Gentlemen, let passion rule. Cry havoc and let slip the dogs of war.

(The lights fade.)

Scene Nine

(In another playing area the lights fade in. WALKER is holding a banner with the image of a dismembered snake and the motto "Join or Die.")

WALKER: It is ridiculous, absurd, that an island should rule a continent. It is only common sense. One honest man is worth more to society than all the crowned hoodlums that ever lived.

(CAMPBELL enters.)

CAMPBELL: You speak treason.

WALKER: Brothers, I mean cousins, if you love mankind, oppose tyranny and stand forth. Death to tyrants.

CAMPBELL: You are a traitor.

WALKER: I am an American, I speak my mind.

CAMPBELL: You are a traitor.

(WALKER holds up his ear.)

WALKER: Here talk to this, it'll listen.

CAMPBELL: Loyal habitants, do not let this man disturb your slumber. Do not be alarmed. Everything will be as ever. Sleep, sleep.

WALKER: Look no ear.

CAMPBELL: Arrest this man.

(The lights fade.)

Scene Ten

(In another playing area the lights fade in. BONTEMPS and PIERRE enter.)

BONTEMPS: Loyal habitant, listen to me.

PIERRE: Non.

BONTEMPS: I am your seigneur.

PIERRE: Non.

BONTEMPS: You censitaires belong to me.

PIERRE: Non.

BONTEMPS: Our way of life is threatened.

PIERRE: Non.

BONTEMPS: We must fight for the British.

PIERRE: Non.

BONTEMPS: Against the Yankees.

PIERRE: Non.

BONTEMPS: Fight for me and you fight for France.

PIERRE: Non.

BONTEMPS: We are now part of the British Empire.

PIERRE: Non.

BONTEMPS: We must pay homage to our benefactors.

PIERRE: Non.

BONTEMPS: As you pay homage to me.

PIERRE: Non.

(BRIAND enters.)

BONTEMPS: Speak with them.

BRIAND: Sinners, listen to me. I baptised you, I married you, I will bury you. You must listen to this man.

PIERRE: Non.

BRIAND: Quiet or you will burn in hell forever. Fornicators, you fornicators. Listen.

(Silence. The lights fade.)

Scene Eleven

(In another playing area the lights fade in. CARLETON enters.)

CARLETON: I think I shall drink tea and eat cucumber.

(CAMPBELL enters.)

CAMPBELL: Ethan Allen and his brother Heman have captured the Ticonderoga.

CARLETON: What?

CAMPBELL: General Montgomery is invading Montréal.

CARLETON: What?

CAMPBELL: It is rumoured that quite a few of the Canadians are joining the invaders.

CARLETON: What? We must fortify Quebec. The harrowing is about to begin.

(The lights fade.)

Scene Twelve

(In another playing area the lights fade in. PIERRE enters.)

PIERRE: Don't mind me, I'm just sitting here eating my fleas. I got thirty wives. In that forest I am like the woodchuck that never stops chucking. The Yankee Richard Montgomery is outside these gates. I want to see these liberators. Before I stand in the shade I will see where the sun shines.

(Offstage cheering. RICHARD MONTGOMERY enters wearing the badge "Liberty or Death.")

MONTGOMERY: Friends, mes amis, friends, brothers, fathers, uncles, what can I call you?

PIERRE: Call us people.

MONTGOMERY: People, listen to me. Give me your ears. We come not as an invading army. We come as liberators. You are free.

(MONTGOMERY holds up his "Liberty or Death" badge.)

Believe in this and you will be happy. But we must go the distance.We must go to Quebec and free the rest of this land from British tyranny. Mr. Wooster.

(CAPTAIN WOOSTER enters.)

WOOSTER: Sir.

MONTGOMERY: You will take command of Montréal. *(To someone off-stage.)* You there, you will advise my second on the nature of reality. Come my brave soldiers, the destiny of Caesar is before us.

(MONTGOMERY exits.)

WOOSTER: You there, assemble the priests and the landowners for my pleasure. I want them to meet their new master. A Yankee master.

PIERRE: Non.

(The lights fade.)

Scene Thirteen

(In another playing area the lights fade in. CARLETON enters. He stands beside a miniature rocking horse, twelve inches high, and a tiny vale of hay.)

CARLETON: All right, what have you to say you Yankee bow-wow.

(In another playing area the lights fade in. BENEDICT ARNOLD enters.)

ARNOLD: *Sibi totique.* "For self and all." I have given you the good word or my name is not Benedict Arnold. Give me liberty or give me death.

CARLETON: I don't know too much about liberty, but one step forward and I will give you death.

ARNOLD: Your king is an idiot. I can say that, you can't. Do you surrender?

CARLETON: We will surrender when this horse has eaten this hay, and not before. We will never surrender. *(He holds up a tomahawk.) Quondam his vicimus armis.*

ARNOLD: What?

CARLETON: "With these arms we used to conquer."

ARNOLD: Does that mean you surrender?

CARLETON: We will never surrender.

(The lights fade. During the darkness.)

VOICE ONE: *(Off.)* Who goes there?

VOICE TWO: *(Off.)* The great Jehovah.

Scene Fourteen

(In another playing area the lights fade in. ARNOLD enters with a canteen and rations.)

ARNOLD: I don't mind eating rotten meat. Lord knows, I've eaten a lot of rancid gristle. But this putrid piece of shit has so much salt in it, that it's uneatable. You can't keep this piece of crap in your mouth, no matter how hungry you are. *(ARNOLD takes a bite of his rations.)* And now the yellow water. *(He holds up a canteen.)* Now watch me boys. The idea is to get it into your throat before you puke. The object being to wet your tonsils.

(ARNOLD takes a drink from the canteen. The lights fade. During the darkness.)

VOICE ONE: *(Off.)* What are you doing out there? Licking each other's asses.

VOICE TWO: *(Off.)* Shut up.

Scene Fifteen

(In another playing area the lights fade in. JOSEPH BRANT and MOLLY BRANT, also a Native converted to Christianity, enter. CARLETON enters. MOLLY holds a rattle and a tree branch. MOLLY shakes the rattle at CARLETON.)

CARLETON: Joseph Brant, the Iroquois.

JOSEPH: Iroquois. A French word, means "vile viper."

CARLETON: Yes.

(MOLLY shakes the rattle.)

JOSEPH: This is my sister, Molly Brant.

(MOLLY shakes the rattle at CARLETON.)

CARLETON: Why is she shaking that rattle?

JOSEPH: She likes you.

(MOLLY shakes the rattle.)

CARLETON: Well you are like a beautiful flower.

(MOLLY shakes the ratle.)

JOSEPH: See, she likes you.

CARLETON: Well, once again, I invite you to feast on a Bostonian and to drink his blood ...

(MOLLY shakes the rattle.)

What do you say to that?

(MOLLY shakes the rattle.)

JOSEPH: In the old days, the English used to invite the Iroquois to feast on a Frenchman. Why don't you bring in a Frenchman, and we'll put him in the kettle together, right now?

CARLETON: No. The invitation is now to feast on a Bostonian and to drink his blood.

(MOLLY shakes the rattle.)

What do you say to that?

JOSEPH: In the old days I used to eat my meals with the Bostonians. Now it seems like the Bostonians are the meal.

CARLETON: That's right. Times have changed. In the past you fought for the king, will you fight for him now?

JOSEPH: We are leery to take sides because we love old England as much as we love New England. When we have internal quarrels we settle them in the longhouse.

(Musket fire and cannon fire is heard.)

CARLETON: Hear that.

JOSEPH: Ah, harsh words.

CARLETON: The English cannot be defeated.

JOSEPH: That's not what the rebels say.

CARLETON: The Iroquois are like a tree with big branches. But you will be a log in the river if you do not fight the Yankee bow-wows.

JOSEPH: We may be a log in the river if we fight the bow-wows.

CARLETON: I will drive the Yankee bow-wows from this land and together we will drive them into the sea. What do you say to that?

JOSEPH: The Yankees may drive us into the sea.

CARLETON: Upon the successful completion of the war any lands lost to you will be returned.

JOSEPH: Is that a promise?

CARLETON: The English are ever loyal. The English cannot be defeated. You must go to London and see for yourself.

JOSEPH: London in the springtime is—

CARLETON: Beautiful.

JOSEPH: You are worthy of being called an Iroquois.

CARLETON: Yes, I am.

(BRANT smiles. The lights fade.)

Scene Sixteen

(In another playing area the lights fade in. ARNOLD enters.)

ARNOLD: Without excuses for failure this army would die, expire on the spot. They complain, they whine—

(MONTGOMERY enters.)

General Richard Montgomery, I assume.

MONTGOMERY: General Benedict Arnold, I assume. How's the army.

ARNOLD: My army, if you can call it that—

MONTGOMERY: Sir, are you, or are you not in command of a large body of men, in short an army?

ARNOLD: I am in nominal command of a legalized mob of morons who will kill anything that moves, including themselves.

MONTGOMERY: Where are they?

ARNOLD: They are standing still by the big oak tree yonder. I have made a map of Quebec. Our informants have given us the precise locations of the garrisons, headquarters, and stores.

MONTGOMERY: Excellent.

ARNOLD: We must move quickly. The terms of enlistment for many of our troops expires January first. The winter has made them cranky and crotchety.

MONTGOMERY: Their morale will improve when they have sampled the creature comforts within that citadel and had their way with the fleshpots that live there. We will attack on New Year's Eve.

ARNOLD: Yes, come let us look at the map.

(The lights fade.)

Scene Seventeen

(In another playing area the lights fade in. MONTGOMERY and two AMERICAN SOLDIERS enter.)

AMERICAN SOLDIER ONE: I can't see a bloody thing, this damn bloody snowstorm.

MONTGOMERY: Good, that means the bloody-backs can't see a damn thing either.

AMERICAN SOLDIER TWO: Okay, we're through, I think.

MONTGOMERY: All right men, single file, advance.

(The lights fade.)

Scene Eighteen

(In another playing area the lights fade in. MONTGOMERY and AMERICAN SOLDIERS enter.)

MONTGOMERY: There's a house over yonder.

(In another playing area the lights fade in. CARLETON, CAMPBELL, and an ENGLISH SOLDIER enter.)

CARLETON: Light the fuses.

MONTGOMERY: Wait, a light.

(An explosion.)

Havoc, disaster, retreat. Run for your lives. Get out of my way, move or I'll kill you.

(Musket fire.)

Oh, I am killed.

CARLETON: Well done men, tea and crumpets all around.

(The lights fade.)

Scene Nineteen

(In another playing area the lights fade in. ARNOLD and AMERICAN SOLDIERS enter.)

ARNOLD: The cannon diversion has begun. Come quickly.

AMERICAN SOLDIER ONE: There are barricades in the streets.

ARNOLD: Of course. Let's see if they're manned.

(In another playing area the lights fade in. CARLETON and troops enter.)

They're manned.

(Musket fire.)

Oh, I am wounded. Oh bloody knee, speak to me. British troops are everywhere, we're trapped like rats in a shit house, damnation, retreat.

CARLETON: Forward. We will drive Benedict Arnold from this land forever.

(The lights fade.)

Scene Twenty

(In another playing area the lights fade in. PIERRE enters.)

PIERRE: The American general is a pig. He closes the church on the day the baby Jesus was born. What kind of man is that? A great tusker. *(He holds up a piece of money.)* And they used to give us this for our cows. They call it money, I call it paper. And now they don't even do that anymore. They just take our cows and laugh. And now they are arresting citizens because they say they are working for the English. These English who say they are not English—are the nightmare the priests always told us about. When I stop them from ravishing my daughters they go out and ravish my sheep. Les Batards. We should free ourselves from our liberators. Here come our conquerors.

(WOOSTER enters.)

Good morning.

WOOSTER: What are you doing here?

PIERRE: Just breathing the air.

WOOSTER: Go home and breathe it. You know you are not to assemble in the streets.

(ARNOLD enters.)

ARNOLD: To arms, to arms, the British are coming.

(ARNOLD exits.)

WOOSTER: The Twinks … Go home.

(WOOSTER exits.)

PIERRE: Look, he runs like a rat.

(CARLETON and BRIAND enter.)

BRIAND: Look, they run. Without firing a shot, they run. Shall we pursue them?

CARLETON: No. First there are traitors to be found.

BRIAND: And when you find them I will excommunicate them.

CARLETON: Are you a traitor?

PIERRE: Who me? Non, I am not a traitor, I am Pierre.

CARLETON: I invite you to eat the flesh and to drink the blood of a Bostonian. Just like the good old days. Do you remember?

PIERRE: Je me souviens.

CARLETON: Damn right you do. Will you eat and drink with me?

PIERRE: No.

CARLETON: Why not?

PIERRE: Englishmen are too salty.

CARLETON: Are you a traitor?

PIERRE: Non, I am Pierre.

(The lights fade.)

Scene Twenty-one

(In another playing area the lights fade in. JOSEPH enters holding a portrait of himself.)

JOSEPH: My brothers, I have been to London. They treated me like a God. They gave me this. *(He holds up the portrait.)* This is me. See how this face is like my face? Brothers, we have been blessed by the serpent. The English are like the cannibal giant. Always hungry, always eating. Always drinking the snake's blood. In London I visited the king of England, the Great White Father. Ha, the king of all the red dogs. He sleeps and eats all the time. That's all he does. The English think that is the mark of a great man. Ha! The king of the red dogs never speaks. A man who has a face like a mask speaks for him. He looks like this when he speaks. *(He makes a gross facial contortion.)* He looks just like a big evil manitou. But this manitou is on our side. The dogs in red are like the trees in the forest. They cannot be beaten, they are too many. And they fight for us, we must fight for us.

(The lights fade.)

Scene Twenty-two

(In another playing area, the lights fade in. CARLETON and GENERAL JOHN BURGOYNE enter.)

BURGOYNE: Born from the lusty union of Hercules and Socrates, I am the apex of mankind. As you are like an ape, I am like an angel. I am man as warrior, as poet, as lover, as everything.

CARLETON: Can you get to the point?

BURGOYNE: This messenger from the vortex brings you terrible news.

CARLETON: Can you be more succinct?

BURGOYNE: For failing to pursue the enemy you are relieved of your duties. Is that succinct enough for you?

CARLETON: And my replacement.

BURGOYNE: Yours truly, John Burgoyne.

CARLETON: Ah, gentleman Johnnie.

BURGOYNE: Mr Burgoyne, to you. I will free you from your martial responsibilites, and this man will assume your civil aspects.

(FREDERICK HALDIMAND enters.)

HALDIMAND: Frederick Haldimand, at your service.

CARLETON: A German.

BURGOYNE: Now, now, temper, grave Carleton, temper. He is a professional soldier.

CARLETON: A mercenary.

HALDIMAND: I am a German warrior in the service of my king.

BURGOYNE: You have drank the sweet juice from my cup. Do not be bitter.

CARLETON: This is outrageous.

BURGOYNE: Temper, temper.

CARLETON: Murderers rape for relaxation and nincompoops surrender.

BURGOYNE: Temper.

CARLETON: If I should ever think about taking up service for this king again, may this arm rot off and this head turn into a potato.

BURGOYNE: Temper.

CARLETON: I will leave you pair of Greeks to suck each other's bodily fluids.

BURGOYNE: Temper.

(The lights fade.)

Scene Twenty-three

(In another playing area the lights fade in. PIERRE enters holding a scroll in each hand.)

PIERRE: Lafayette says "You were born French and you cannot cease to be so."

(He snorts. He looks at the second scroll.)

Tom Paine says "Those who suffer tyranny condemn the unborn millions to slavery."

(He is about to comment, then continues reading. The lights fade.)

Scene Twenty-four

(In another playing area the lights fade in.)

VOICE ONE: *(Off.)* Bumpkins are Republicans.

VOICE TWO: *(Off.)* Sir, you are being redundant. A Republican is a bumpkin.

VOICE ONE: *(Off.)* I just said that.

(BURGOYNE enters.)

VOICE ONE and TWO: *(Off.)* To a gay spirit.

BURGOYNE: Everyone look at me. Well, we're in a jolly mood tonight. Do you see anything you haven't seen before?

VOICE ONE: *(Off.)* No.

BURGOYNE: Ooooohh! You're such a dandy. Well, I'm certainly well dressed tonight.

VOICE TWO: *(Off.)* You certainly are.

BURGOYNE: Thank you, I thought you would never notice. Gentlemen, rejoice. It is I, Gentleman Johnny, here to grace your company.

VOICE ONE: *(Off.)* Speech, speech.

BURGOYNE: It is well known that a man cares about only four things. Sleeping, eating, excreting, and reproducing himself. Gentlemen, as of this day I want to add a fifth. He also cares about victory.

(The voices cheer.)

Gentlemen, a toast. What shall we drink to?

VOICE ONE: *(Off.)* It's your toast.

BURGOYNE: Then let us drink to the sleep of reason and the birth of virgins.

VOICE TWO: *(Off.)* Why not?

VOICE ONE: *(Off.)* Gentleman Johnny's had one too many.

BURGOYNE: I heard that, I have not had enough. Gentlemen, I am going to relieve the Americans from the anxiety they have so long feared. I am going to invade them. I have a plan of infallible conquest. Rejoice, we conquer.

(The lights fade.)

Scene Twenty-five

(In another playing area the lights fade in. HALDIMAND and BONTEMPS enter.)

BONTEMPS: The peasants are now completely loyal. They have seen the light.

HALDIMAND: Yes, we have shown the rebels that it is not wise to pull the lion's tail.

(CAMPBELL enters.)

CAMPBELL: General Burgoyne has met with disaster at Saratoga.

HALDIMAND: *(To BONTEMPS.)* Do not be alarmed. Continue.

CAMPBELL: General Burgoyne marched seven thousand troops into the forest.

HALDIMAND: Yes.

CAMPBELL: None marched out.

HALDIMAND: Ach du lieber Zeit! Ach du lieber Zeit! If Burgoyne, that fop, that twink, was here, I would put my hands on my hips and shout at the top of my voice "Fool!" But do not be alarmed ... ach du lieber Zeit!

(The lights fade.)

Scene Twenty-six

(In another playing area the lights fade in. MOLLY enters holding a stick and a tomahawk.)

MOLLY: In the year with three sevens.

(MOLLY hits the stick with the tomahawk. In another playing area the lights fade in. JOHN JOHNSON and COLONEL JOHN BUTLER enter.)

BUTLER: I bring you terrible news.

JOHNSON: Speak.

BUTLER: All of your land has been confiscated by your neighbours. Your wife and children were taken to prison. Your wife was gang raped, then tarred and feathered, and then a sign was put around her neck that said "Tory Swine!"

JOHNSON: And what of my children?

BUTLER: They have been murdered.

JOHNSON: Colonel Butler.

BUTLER: Sir.

JOHNSON: You will have cause to organize a group of men in the Company of Rangers to serve with Indians. After you have organized the men, you will prepare them for a march. We are going to pay our neighbours a visit.

(MOLLY hits the stick with the tomahawk.)

MOLLY: In the year with three sevens.

BUTLER: We had occasion to meet a John Reynolds and his three brothers.

JOHNSON: Ah yes, I remember them well.

BUTLER: They were living in your house.

JOHNSON: Were they now? They were well received, I hope.

BUTLER: Very. Joseph and my son Walter gave them a real Irish reception.

(JOSEPH and WALTER BUTLER enter.)

JOSEPH: I never liked that man Reynolds.

WALTER: And I never liked his brothers. Even when I was this high, I never liked them.

JOSEPH: And when I see them in the house of the Warrageheygey, your father, my blood boil like hot mad.

WALTER: And I give them something special.

JOSEPH: Mohawk surprise. I take my knife and I cut here.

(JOSEPH indicates the abdomen.)

WALTER: And then I put my knife on the ground.

JOSEPH: And then I take my hand and I put inside and pull things out.

WALTER: They scream, they shout, but we quiet them.

JOSEPH: And then I take what was inside them and place on the branches of the trees in the forest.

WALTER: And then I make them each walk around tree.

JOSEPH: They cry, but I make them walk.

WALTER: And they walk until it is impossible to walk.

JOSEPH: And we stop, and I laugh, and they scream.

WALTER: And trees in forest look like Christmas trees.

JOSEPH: Only it not Christmas.

(MOLLY hits the stick with the tomahawk.)

MOLLY: In the year with three sevens!

JOSEPH: Now Joseph hopes that Jesus not see what these hands do. But Thayendanegea knows that Ododharho see. And Ododharho, he smile. Now my sister Molly cries all the time. I bring her a branch from a tree by the longhouse, but that makes her even more sad. Because in 1777, Mohawk own the world. And Mohawk lose it all.

(MOLLY hits stick with the tomahawk.)

MOLLY: In the year with the three sevens!

(The lights fade.)

Scene Twenty-seven

(In another playing area the lights fade in. WALTER enters.)

WALTER: The rabble made a blacklist and my name was on it. I have seen people hanged, flayed. They took my land. I was apprehended by the Committee of Public Safety and interrogated at an Inquisition. Those bastards in the name of liberty would not let me speak. "Give us liberty or give us death" cried the slaveowner. And then I was branded like a cow. *(He opens his shirt.)* "T" for tory. And as they were stirring the tar and plucking the goose, I made a timely exit.

(In another playing area, the lights fade in. A tarred and feathered LOYALIST enters.)

LOYALIST: I didn't. Bubble, bubble, bubble, bubble in the pot. The tar is boiling, it's getting really hot. Oh bubble, bubble, bubble, bubble in the pan. Stir in the feathers and tar a tory if you can.

WALTER: Shut up. I was branded like an animal. If only I could be an animal. I would tear them limb from limb.

(BUTLER enters.)

BUTLER: Walter, that's enough. We must make our oppressors tell the same story. It is a limited joy, for sure, but the oppressed cannot choose their pleasure. What has been done to us will be done to them. And if they topple the king we will help them make this land the Republic of Hell. Will you fight?

WALTER: Damn right. They got my mother and my sister in that Yankee dungeon and I know what they're doing to them. Yankees, I hate them so much. When we come the hedgehogs run. The cowards.

BUTLER: Walter, that's enough. We are going to organize an attack.

WALTER: Is it what I hope?

BUTLER: Cherry Valley.

WALTER: Oh father, you have made my day. Yankees live there. And I know them all personally.

(WALTER smiles. The lights fade.)

Scene Twenty-eight

(In another playing area the lights fade in. WALTER enters holding scalps.)

WALTER: Look, Yankee scalps. Many scalps.

(BUTLER and JOSEPH enter. WALTER holds up a head on a stick.)

This used to be my best friend. Say hello to my best friend.

JOSEPH: This man is—

WALTER: I'm Irish, Mr. Brant. I leave it at that. But don't ever look at me like that again. Or I just might cut you up into little pieces and feed you to the little birds.

BUTLER: Walter, that's enough.

WALTER: I hate them so much.

BUTLER: Now, we're going back to Johnstown.

WALTER: Yankees live there.

BUTLER: Walter.

WALTER: I'm glad we're going to Johnstown. I'm tired of chasing that fart Daniel Boone. Now there's a man I'd like to get in my hands. I'd make him suck my balls.

BUTLER: Walter.

JOSEPH: This man is—

WALTER: Viciousness is its own virtue, Mr. Brant.

(The LOYALIST enters holding a tomahawk.)

WALTER: What do you want? Get out.

BUTLER: Are you going to take that tar off?

LOYALIST: Do you have any idea how difficult it is, to get this stuff off?

BUTLER: You are bad for morale.

LOYALIST: I want to go with you to Johnstown. I got my tomahawk. Don't worry I don't stick to anything. I want to go too.

WALTER: Do you have reason to hate, my friend?

LOYALIST: No. Actually I love Yankees.

BUTLER: Take that tar off.

(The LOYALIST holds up his tomahawk.)

LOYALIST: After, after.

(The lights fade.)

Scene Twenty-nine

(In another playing area the lights fade in. JOSEPH enters.)

JOSEPH: Brothers, do not worry about the lands that have been taken from us. When the war is over they will be returned. By the great thundering water, Niagara, we will build a new birdhouse. Brothers, they have destroyed the nests, not the birds. Hungry birds rise to great heights. All our lands will be returned. The English governor said so. This ear, the ear of our nation, heard him. Brothers ... you must listen to me.

(The lights fade.)

Scene Thirty

(In another playing area the lights fade in. HALDIMAND and JOHNSON enter.)

HALDIMAND: Cornwallis has surrendered at Yorktown.

JOHNSON: The war goes badly.

HALDIMAND: The war goes like all wars.

JOHNSON: The colonies are lost.

HALDIMAND: Thirteen perhaps, but the two colonies up here, Quebec and Nova Scotia, we'll keep these.

JOHNSON: If the king would commit troops to the battle, we would win.

HALDIMAND: But the king does not commit troops to the battle.

JOHNSON: Our king is a dunderhead.

HALDIMAND: Sir, that is treason.

JOHNSON: Sir, that is truth.

(The lights fade.)

Scene Thirty-one

(In another playing area the lights fade in. HALDIMAND, CAMPBELL, and JOSEPH enter.)

CAMPBELL: With the signing of the Treaty of Paris, here is an idea of what the colony looks like.

HALDIMAND: It is huge.

CAMPBELL: It was huge. These are the thirteen colonies, this is Louisiana, this is Rupert's Land, and this of course is Canada. Guy Carleton—

HALDIMAND: Ha!

CAMPBELL: Guy Carleton has negotiated the release of the loyalists and they will soon be arriving by the thousands.

JOSEPH: In this treaty, there is no mention of my people.

HALDIMAND: That is because it is a treaty between Great Britain and the new born United States of America.

JOSEPH: The United States of America is in one word—bullshit!

CAMPBELL: Don't use that kind of language in front of the governor.

HALDIMAND: No, I am Swiss, I understand.

JOSEPH: Long time ago English guarantee our lands.

HALDIMAND: And you will now have to seek those same guarantees from the United States.

JOSEPH: The terms of this treaty show that we suffered a terrible defeat. Not so.

HALDIMAND: Britain retains Canada. I am sorry the peace has been bought.

JOSEPH: With our blood.

HALDIMAND: With the blood of many. The king loves you like a son. He is going to give you a gold medal attached to a big red ribbon.

(JOSEPH sneers.)

JOSEPH: I need land for my people.

(He points at the map.)

Here.

HALDIMAND: And you shall have it.

JOSEPH: Long knives will try to take our land down here. We will fight. We hope the English help their friends.

HALDIMAND: The English are ever loyal.

(JOSEPH grunts. The lights fade.)

Scene Thirty-two

(In another playing area the lights fade in. BONTEMPS and BRIAND enter.)

BONTEMPS: His Excellency, the governor-general of Canada, Lord Dorchester.

(BONTEMPS and BRIAND applaud. CARLETON enters.)

BRIAND: Ah, Guy Carleton.

CARLETON: Lord Dorchester to you.

BONTEMPS: Once again, we are like the beaver. Happy and proud you are here.

CARLETON: Thank you for those warm hands.

BONTEMPS: Oh you are so beautiful.

CARLETON: Thank you.

BRIAND: And you smell so nice.

CARLETON: Merci. Fee, fie, foe, fum, I smell a German bum.

(HALDIMAND enters holding a bottle of schnapps.)

HALDIMAND: While the great war raged I ate caribou and drank schnapps.

CARLETON: Ah, it is the sour kraut himself.

HALDIMAND: To Guy Carleton.

CARLETON: Lord Dorchester to you.

HALDIMAND: Will Lord Dorchester drink my schnapps?

CARLETON: No, and I will not give you even one minute of my time. You have been recalled, courtesy of yours truly.

HALDIMAND: To Guy Carleton.

CARLETON: Lord Dorchester to you.

HALDIMAND: You English ... It seems in the great scheme of things I have been given my place in the winter. I shall miss this place as much as I have missed hot sauerkraut on a summer's day.

CARLETON: And we shall miss you even less.

HALDIMAND: You English ... I am going to have my tedium rewarded. Oh the crud at the top. And I am going to be part of it.

CARLETON: But not here. Out you filthy beast. Guards.

HALDIMAND: No, I will go. Auf weider sehen.

CARLETON: And auf weider sehen to you. And when you get to London, give my regards to that twink, Gentleman Johnnie.

(HALDIMAN exits.)

Good God, I am sweating.

BONTEMPS: Oh His Lordship is sweating.

CARLETON: Enough.

BRIAND: Last night, I prayed for your soul.

CARLETON: How kind of you. Now go pray for your own.

(BRIAND exits.)

Now I will give you one minute of my time. Speak.

BONTEMPS: Oh High and Mighty Lord, can you help me? My body is covered with open festering sores. My eyesight is bad, I am going blind. Someone has stolen my underwear. I have been wearing the same clothes for three years. I am—

CARLETON: Enough. What do you want?

BONTEMPS: A position in government. Menial or major, I don't care. My wife beats me with a stick all night. My children throw stones at me. I will suck your big black boot.

CARLETON: Enough. I will give you a ... job.

BONTEMPS: Anything.

CARLETON: You will collect taxes.

BONTEMPS: Thank you High and Mighty Lord. I am a natural-born tax collector. Oh you are so beautiful.

CARLETON: Now get out.

(The lights fade.)

Scene Thirty-three

(In another playing area the lights fade in. JAMES SECORD kisses the ground.)

SECORD: On British soil again. Oh God, smell the air.

(The LOYALIST enters.)

LOYALIST: I just came from Shelbourne, Nova Scotia.

SECORD: The boomtown.

LOYALIST: That's right. Boom it's up, boom it's down. A lovely place.

SECORD: Well this ain't no boomtown.

LOYALIST: No, this is a metropolis.

SECORD: Are you being sarcastic?

LOYALIST: Have you ever thought of going to Shelbourne? You'd fit right in.

(JOHNSON enters holding a hat.)

JOHNSON: Gentlemen, time to draw your luck. Now, the waterfront lots have all been chosen by officers and sundry betters that you will come to know well. We are now offering the back lots. As you cannot judge a book by its cover you cannot judge land by the way it looks. All those who took the king's shilling prepare to take the king's land.

LOYALIST: Hold the hat high, don't let him cheat.

(SECORD picks from the hat.)

SECORD: Back lot number nine, number nine.

(The lights fade.)

Scene Thirty-four

(In another playing area the lights fade in. JOHNSON and CARLETON enter.)

CARLETON: Ah John, it has been a long time.

JOHNSON: It has. You have done very well.

CARLETON: As you seem to have.

JOHNSON: I have.

CARLETON: I will give you one minute of my time.

JOHNSON: How gracious of you.

CARLETON: Your manners are superb. At some date in the future, will you take tea with me?

JOHNSON: I would be delighted.

CARLETON: Time is passing.

JOHNSON: As you know, I own most of what is now called Upper Canada.

CARLETON: Hmmm-hmmm.

JOHNSON: Well I think I should be the lieutenant-governor.

CARLETON: That makes sense to me, but of course I don't make that decision. Unfortunately, John Graves Simcoe—

JOHNSON: Not that Queen's Ranger person?

CARLETON: Yes, him.

JOHNSON: What an outrage.

CARLETON: Yes, he is always ranting away like a teapot. Just ranting away.

JOHNSON: Oh the shame, the disgrace. I will have my revenge. Those who've conspired against me and those who've—

CARLETON: Hoove.

JOHNSON: Yes, those who've—

CARLETON: Hoove.

JOHNSON: Yes, who've.

CARLETON: Hoove.

JOHNSON: Yes, those who have … who've.

CARLETON: Hoove.

JOHNSON: Who've!

CARLETON: Hoove!

JOHNSON: Those who've—!

CARLETON: Hoove.

JOHNSON: Stop. I forget what I was trying to say. No, now I remember. Those who've—

CARLETON: It doesn't matter, John. Your English is terrible, John Graves has the positon, and you've had your one minute.

(The lights fade.)

Scene Thirty-five

(In another playing area the lights fade in. SECORD enters.)

SECORD: Some of the backwater lots are like a swamp. I was cutting down a tree this wide *(He holds his hands four feet apart.)* with a knife. I hacked away at that tree all day and finally it fell. And I sat on the stump, contemplating the joys of pulling that stump, when they arrived. Mosquitoes that big. *(He holds his hand six inches apart.)* Thousands of them, all stuck their yammers into me, pumping me for all I was worth. They would stick their horns right into an artery and then fill right up. And then they were this big and this fat. *(He holds his hands twelve inches apart.)* So full of blood they could barely fly away. So they wouldn't fly away. They'd come back for more. One mosquito, the king monster of them all, I swear, had a gallon of my blood inside him. He fixed right on my neck. He was going for the kill I could tell. He just stuck his hooves right in, and I swear he was going for the marrow. And I prayed to Jesus, give me strength, and he did, and I swatted the bastard. The sound was sickening but the bath was worse. What was once inside me was now outside me. Covered in a red sticky, sickly, prickly … Words cannot describe the way I looked or the way I felt. I thought to myself, "I'm a goner, I'm done. I am going to make one of the most disgraceful exits possible from life … In the jaws of insects."

(LAURA SECORD enters.)

LAURA: Ah, you're a blarney man.

SECORD: No mother, it's true.

LAURA: I knew you wouldn't pull that stump.

SECORD: It was 'cause of the mosquitoes.

LAURA: Agh.

SECORD: All right mother, I know what you want. You want to dance.

LAURA: Does a man like to drink until his bags are full, and then listen to the grass grow?

SECORD: You're damn right.

LAURA: Then get up and dance for me, you thug. The new lieutenant-governor is coming.

(The lights fade.)

Scene Thirty-six

(In another playing area the lights fade in. JOHN GRAVES SIMCOE and ELIZABETH SIMCOE enter.)

SIMCOE: Come along, Elizabeth.

ELIZABETH: Oh. The buttercups are so big.

SIMCOE: Tent here.

(An ENGLISH SOLDIER enters.)

You will have cause to erect a tent here. Are you capable of that?

SOLDIER: Yes sir.

SIMCOE: Then do it.

(The ENGLISH SOLDIER exits.)

By God there will be discipline. These bloody troops are so drunk on demon rum, they could hardly row the boat.

ELIZABETH: Yes, it made the journey tedious.

SIMCOE: Tedious, it made it impossible. And what if the Yankees attacked, and the men drunk?

ELIZABETH: Oh please, don't go on about the Yankees.

SIMCOE: You know how I feel about them.

ELIZABETH: Yes, please—

SIMCOE: Just hearing the word makes my blood boil in bilious black rage.

ELIZABETH: Oh you're going to go on.

SIMCOE: How many times have I told you my feelings about the Yankees.

ELIZABETH: Countless.

SIMCOE: And each time are you not convinced of the just nature of my cause.

ELIZABETH: Totally.

SIMCOE: Exactly. I was with Cornwallis in Yorktown.

ELIZABETH: Oh no.

SIMCOE: I had to wear sheep's clothing and leave in steerage, or be taken prisoner. And I knew what that was like. Have you any idea what it is like to be put in a Yankee dungeon?

ELIZABETH: It is like eating maggots and garbage and drinking excrement.

SIMCOE: That's right. That's exactly what it is like. And I was the lucky one. I lived. My regiment, the Queen's Rangers were shot and hung—

ELIZABETH: —and drawn and quartered for being traitors.

SIMCOE: And they were not traitors. They were Loyalists. The real traitors have built an empire of treason.

ELIZABETH: Oh, John, you are rabid.

SIMCOE: Oh to be. I would bite every Yankee I see. This land will be British, or there will be blood. I know the Yankee bastard will try to make this the land of the mongrel bitch. But good luck to you. A British bulldog stands in this forest, and I will pit myself against every Yankee rat, I don't care how big they are. This is a cataclysm, Elizabeth.

ELIZABETH: Oh, listen to the frogs and the owls.

SIMCOE: When I plant the flag of St. George on this soil, they will chirp and burp even louder.

ELIZABETH: Oh. How elegant. It's so beautiful here. What's this place called?

SIMCOE: The Indians call this place Toronto. But I will not refer to this place by an Indian name. I will name this place York, after the Duke of York, and to honour the occasion, we will fire a twenty-one gun salute.

ELIZABETH: Oh that will be grand.

SIMCOE: Yes it will.

(The lights fade.)

Scene Thirty-seven

(In another playing area the lights fade in. CARLETON enters, then CAMPBELL.)

CAMPBELL: Lady Dorchester entering the room.

(LADY DORCHESTER enters; CAMPBELL exits.)

CARLETON: Ah, there you are. The Prince of the Blood will be here any moment.

LADY DORCHESTER: And that woman, Madame St. Laurent.

CARLETON: Yes, Madame ... his companion.

LADY DORCHESTER: She has mud in her blood. Oh, I cannot bear the thought of being seen with her.

CARLETON: Yes.

LADY DORCHESTER: When he visits his father, he does not take his escort. When he visits his friends, he does not take his escort.

CARLETON: Yes.

LADY DORCHESTER: But when he's here, he takes his escort.

CARLETON: Yes, Canada, my love.

LADY DORCHESTER: I cannot bear to be seen with her.

CARLETON: We must all make sacrifices.

(CAMPBELL enters.)

CAMPBELL: The Duke of Kent, Prince Edward Augustus, and escort, entering the room.

LADY DORCHESTER: I am going to go berserk.

(PRINCE EDWARD and MADAME ST LAURENT enter.)

I am going to go berserk.

MME ST LAURENT: Is this rude, crude creature the Lady of the House, or the maid?

LADY DORCHESTER: So madame, I am sorry to hear that your father lost his head to the guillotine.

MME ST LAURENT: Firstly, it was not my father, it was my uncle, and secondly, I am touched by your condolence.

CARLETON: Enough, shall we dine?

LADY DORCHESTER and MME ST LAURENT: Yes.

CARLETON: Your Highness.

PRINCE: Mein schlager ist schwanger.

(The lights fade.)

Scene Thirty-eight

(In another playing area the lights fade in. ELIZABETH enters holding her diary.)

ELIZABETH: I spend my time squashing caterpillars. Perhaps I will grow peaches. It is a life of no consequence. I yearn for former times. I should have been born a Roman woman. A Spartan woman, at least an Englishman. Each day I listen to the frogs and the owls, smell the rich odour of the dung heap, and wonder to myself "Why am I here?" In the meanwhile, I live for the dance. I love setting fires and eating oranges. Watching the flames while the juice dribbles down my chin. What ecstasy. Oh the fairies have got me now. Listen to the loons.

(ELIZABETH smiles. The lights fade.)

Scene Thirty-nine

(In another playing area the lights fade in. The PRINCE and MME ST LAURENT enter wearing bibs.)

PRINCE: Well I am glad that over.

MME ST LAURENT: That was one of the most terrible experiences of my life.

PRINCE: Sitting for three hours with face like this because my father cannot speak English and so make rule of complete silence while eating why for me must be the same for. My English is implacable.

MME ST LAURENT: And now our open-minded host and hostess.

(CARLETON and LADY DORCHESTER enter.)

CARLETON: Well that was delicious.

PRINCE: Yes it was.

LADY DORCHESTER: Stop looking at me like that.

PRINCE: Sorry my face is set.

(BONTEMPS, BRIAND, and GENET enter.)

BONTEMPS: Oh sanctuary, people. Oh madame, you are so beautiful.

BRIAND: And you smell so nice.

PRINCE: Who the hell are you? I feel like I know you forever.

CARLETON: This is Charles Bontemps.

BONTEMPS: Seigneur and bon-vivant.

(CARLETON puts out his foot.)

Oh no, not here.

CARLETON: Just stretching.

PRINCE: No oom-pah here. No oom-pah, no oom-pah.

BONTEMPS: Oh High and Mighty Lord. Here is a person I want you to meet. This is Monsieur Genet.

CARLETON: Enchanté, monsieur.

GENET: Perhaps you think I am the king's brother?

CARLETON: What?

GENET: I am not "monsieur." I am Citizen Genet. Ambassador of revolutionary France.

CARLETON: What?

BONTEMPS: I don't understand. He told me he was a businessman.

GENET: I am the rage of the people.

BRIAND: Oh this is a scandal.

LADY DORCHESTER and MME ST LAURENT: I am going to go berserk.

GENET: What my Jacobin brothers have done in France is nothing to what they will do to the English. I am going to put your head on a stick.

CARLETON: When it comes to putting head on a stick, revolutionary France can teach the English nothing. What do you want?

GENET: A revolution. Heads are going to roll.

MME ST LAURENT: Oh I am going to faint.

GENET: Blood is going to drip.

CARLETON: All over you if you don't get out of my sight.

GENET: Heads are going to roll.

CARLETON: Bontemps.

BONTEMPS: I didn't know, I didn't know.

(BRIAND forces GENET to exit.)

CARLETON: Now, get out of my sight you filthy beast.

(BRIAND exits.)

He makes my flesh stink. I am so worked up. Look, I am sweating.

BONTEMPS: Oh, His Lordship is sweating.

CARLETON: The habitants are restless. I can feel it in my blood. Will they stay loyal?

BONTEMPS: Oui, High and Mighty Lord, oui.

(The lights fade.)

Scene Forty

(In another playing area the lights fade in. BONTEMPS and PIERRE enter.)

BONTEMPS: As landowner, I want a favour from you.

PIERRE: Non.

BONTEMPS: I want you to enlist in my regiment.

PIERRE: Non.

BONTEMPS: Revolutionary France must be defeated.

PIERRE: Non.

BONTEMPS: We must fight for the king of England.

PIERRE: Non.

(The lights fade.)

Scene Forty-one

(In another playing area the lights fade in. SIMCOE, ELIZABETH, and JOSEPH enter.)

SIMCOE: If the good Lord wanted us to talk and eat at the same time, he would have given us two mouths.

ELIZABETH: Well, shall we make conversation?

SIMCOE: Yes, ah Joseph, here is something that will make you smile. Did you know that the king of France got his head cut off?

ELIZABETH: Please.

SIMCOE: It is better than gossiping about lechers and misers, snobs and bootlickers.

JOSEPH: I am glad that the king of France lost his head. He caused my people great trouble.

SIMCOE: Now Joseph, you are a Christian Indian. I forbid you to glory in regicide, or some people will think you are a Republican. And you will learn that honest Englishmen hate Indian forms of government, like democracy—

JOSEPH: The king of England is like a squirrel, and I am like an acorn. He can have me anytime.

ELIZABETH: Captain Jarvis tells me that you met President Washington.

SIMCOE: Ah ha, the lizard king himself.

JOSEPH: That is right. He offered me a red ribbon and a bribe to convince my brothers to give their land to the Long Knives.

SIMCOE: He is a vile reptile. I hate him profoundly.

JOSEPH: Lord Dorchester has expressed the same sentiment.

SIMCOE: It is the only thing that we agree upon.

JOSEPH: The Long Knives will take our land now. The slaugher begins.

SIMCOE: You rest assured Joseph, that if the Yankee bastard crawls into the anus of the king, that he will get more than he bargained for. I will see to it personally.

JOSEPH: Is that a promise?

SIMCOE: Yes it is.

(A SOLDIER enters.)

SOLDIER: The American Ambassador, Mr. Squat.

(The SOLDIER exits. MR SQUAT enters.)

SQUAT: Just call me Diddley. Why shucks, I reckon my name is Diddley Squat. At your service. I'm from Virginia, I like it down there.

SIMCOE: Your credentials. Speak, I am on a very short wick.

SQUAT: My credentials are loyalty to our chief of men, George Washington. He is as wise as Socrates, and as fierce as Caesar, as patriotic as Hannibal, and as—

SIMCOE: Vile as Satan.

SQUAT: I was forewarned you would speak like this. But I am a gentleman from Virginia.

SIMCOE: Just don't pee on my carpet, you Yankee dog.

SQUAT: Well now, this dog going to bark for watermelon. It is my … pleasure to inform you that you must remove your forts from the U.S. of A. on pain of war.

SIMCOE: War! I'll give you war, I'll give you war right now.

(SIMCOE draws his sword.)

JOSEPH: Kiss my mocassins, I am Iroquois chief.

(The lights fade.)

Scene Forty-two

(In another playing area the lights fade in. ELIZABETH and LADY DORCHESTER enter.)

LADY DORCHESTER: I'm not very good at this.

ELIZABETH: And neither am I.

LADY DORCHESTER: You will of course respect my superiority.

ELIZABETH: And you will of course respect mine.

LADY DORCHESTER: My dear, I am the wife of the governor-general.

ELIZABETH: And my father was related to King Arthur.

LADY DORCHESTER: The son of Mordred, no doubt.

(MME ST LAURENT enters.)

What do you want? Get out.

MME ST LAURENT: I must speak with Mrs. Simcoe.

ELIZABETH: Lady Simcoe to you. Go away!

MME ST LAURENT: No.

(ELIZABETH and LADY DORCHESTER gasp.)

LADY DORCHESTER: If you do not leave this room I am going to go berserk.

MME ST LAURENT: Lady Simcoe, there is something wrong with your husband.

ELIZABETH: How dare you say that to me. And while we are on the topic, madame, there is something very wrong with your … friend. How you like that?

MME ST LAURENT: Your husband—

ELIZABETH: Stop talking about my husband.

LADY DORCHESTER: I am going berserk.

MME ST LAURENT: Your husband looks like he has just swallowed a porcupine. I just thought you might like to know.

(SIMCOE and CARLETON enter.)

SIMCOE: Ah, there you are.

CARLETON: Ah, there you are.

SIMCOE: Your Ladyship.

CARLETON: Your Ladyship. Too many ships in this room. All ladies, please exit.

(ELIZABETH, LADY DORCHESTER, and MME ST LAURENT exit.)

SIMCOE: You want to speak with me I believe.

CARLETON: Yes. Are you aware of what you have done?

SIMCOE: Yes.

CARLETON: We are almost in a state of war with the United States.

SIMCOE: Good.

CARLETON: You are a war just waiting to happen.

SIMCOE: Yes.

CARLETON: We must be more diplomatic with the Yankees.

SIMCOE: Yankees.

(SIMCOE draws his sword.)

CARLETON: How dare you pull that out in my presence?

SIMCOE: I go berserk when I hear that word. Berserk. Yankees.

CARLETON: Put that sword away. I do not like them either, but—

SIMCOE: But nothing. My father died at the conquest of Quebec.

CARLETON: Yes, I knew him. He was a good man. A sailor I believe.

SIMCOE: An admiral is not a sailor.

CARLETON: Well, they're all sea dogs to me.

SIMCOE: You're calling my father a sea dog. You go too far when you pull my twirlies.

CARLETON: Now, before you tie your dong in a knot, we should get something clear. Quite clear. I am the governor. You are the lieutenant-governor. The king does not want a war. Neither does the prime minister, nor the Americans, and least of all me. Only you want a war. Stop. Desist. Or the consequences for you will be disastrous. Do I make myself clear?

SIMCOE: Quite.

(The lights fade.)

Scene Forty-three

(In another playing area the lights fade in. SIMCOE and ELIZABETH enter.)

SIMCOE: Baggage here.

(A SOLDIER enters.)

You will have cause to place our baggage here. Are you capable of doing that?

SOLDIER: Yes sir.

SIMCOE: Then do it.

(The SOLDIER exits.)

ELIZABETH: Well I'm glad to be leaving and yet, oh the buttercups.

SIMCOE: Next spring we'll be drinking tea with the Maharajah of Bamboolah land, or whatever it is called.

ELIZABETH: Aye, that'll be grand.

SIMCOE: India the land of the Hindu nabob. Get a good cup of tea there. Not here, bloody Yankees, I'd rather live with Buddha or the Fuzzy-wuzzy than Yankees. Yankees.

ELIZABETH: Quiet.

SIMCOE: Next year we'll be with Cornwallis, peeling oranges, eating pomegranate, showing the polly wogs what it's all about, but I wish I could stay here.

ELIZABETH: Yes.

SIMCOE: I'd attack the Yankees. I'd bite their heads off. Dorchester, he loves them so much.

ELIZABETH: Shut up.

SIMCOE: Me and Cornwallis.

ELIZABETH: You and him forever.

SIMCOE: No, the British Empire forever. I'm just a dog blinking.

ELIZABETH: You'll look grand in a turban.

(The lights fade.)

Scene Forty-four

(In another playing area the lights fade in. CARLETON and JOSEPH enter. JOSEPH holds his portrait and a bottle.)

CARLETON: Well Simcoe left in a huff and a puff. How you like that Joseph?

JOSEPH: Yes, he made me a promise.

CARLETON: Yes, he was always ranting away like a teapot. Just ranting away. But now peace reigns supreme. Blessed be the peace makers.

JOSEPH They shall inherit everything.

CARLETON: That's right, Thayendanegea.

JOSEPH: Who?

CARLETON: With these arms we used to conquer. I am worthy of being called an Iroquois. Do you remember, Joseph?

JOSEPH: No, you are worthy of being called an English dog. Betraying the Iroquois, all the time betraying.

CARLETON: Joseph, you must learn to hold your liquor.

JOSEPH: I must learn to hold your head in my hands. You want this land so much. I should fill you up with dirt. You want this land so much.

CARLETON: Drink, Joseph. Drink will soothe your savage soul. Now Joseph, I will give you one minute of my time.

JOSEPH: If the Iroquois had known we were signing treaties with people like you … The English treat us like the cow that has been milked with both hands. Now out to pasture. And the young bulls have all been visited by the knife. The English say we own this pasture but will not give us piece of paper that says so. They give us red ribbons, blue ribbons, gold ribbons, but not piece of paper. I have learned that hatred is stronger than two sticks tied together. As Joseph, I will die happy. But as Thayendanegea, I close my eyes and think about the days of my youth, and I remember, and I wonder. I will fight no more. My own people hate me. They think I am like dogs in red. Joseph believes in God but I believe in this. *(He holds up the bottle.)* Thayendanegea believed …

CARLETON: Joseph, you've had your one minute.

JOSEPH: I close my eyes and I wonder.

(The lights fade.)

Scene Forty-five

(In another playing area the lights fade in. CARLETON enters.)

CARLETON: I am old and irritable. Completely empty of ideas. Anyone who disagrees with me, I detest. I make them suck my big black boot until they stop disagreeing. I relish authority. As Pro-Consul of the British Empire I will never give these people responsible government. It only leads to revolution. Democracy makes people insolent. Friday's children do not need the vote. Donkies, puppies, weasels, and mules were made on the fifth day. Man was made on Saturday. But the Canadians were made on Friday. They are one step up from dogs. Always jumping up from the gutter, barking away. Just barking away. They don't talk to each other here, they bark. The other day I asked the bishop if he would like some crumpet. The bishop turned to me and went "Oui." I knew that was a "yes." I love sitting fully dressed in a dark room by myself.

(He smiles. The lights fade.)

Part Four

The War of 1812

Scene One

(The sound of drums and rattles. The lights fade in. TECUMSEH and the PROPHET enter. The PROPHET lies on the ground in a seizure.)

TECUMSEH: I am the panther coming across. Born during the Hunger Moon. I am the shooting star. I am Tecumseh.

PROPHET: Hail Tecumseh, hail.

TECUMSEH: The white man takes our land, rapes our women, kills our children.

PROPHET: Hail Tecumseh, hail.

(The PROPHET comes out of his seizure.)

TECUMSEH: What says my brother, the prophet? Speak.

(The PROPHET shakes his rattle.)

PROPHET: Hear me brothers, you have witnessed my prophecies. Witness another. You ... what is my name.

TECUMSEH: You are known as the one with the open mouth.

PROPHET: That's right. The open mouth, always open. The open mouth speaks only prophecy. Do you want to hear another?

(The PROPHET cups his hand to his ear.)

I can't hear you.

TECUMSEH: Yes, Open Mouth, speak.

PROPHET: This man is this. *(He holds up a black wampum belt.)* Victory. Let's sing. "Happy am I to die in battle and not like a squaw in the wegiwa."

(Voices in the darkness sing as the PROPHET speaks.)

I have made the sun stand still, the dead rise from the grave, do not make me angry or you will know me by my other name. And that name is—

TECUMSEH: He-who-makes-a-big-noise.

PROPHET: That's right. He-who-makes-a-big-noise. Many have asked what I think of the white man. This is what I think. *(He farts.)* He-who-makes-a-big-noise has spoken.

TECUMSEH: Brother, the prophecy. Speak.

PROPHET: In three moons there will be a sign. The sun will turn red. The trees will fall. Rivers will flow backwards. Mountains will be born. When the Great Spirit speaks we will rise up. And this warrior, this man among men, will lead us. Hail, Tecumseh.

(Noises offstage.)

Long knives, long knives.

(WILLIAM HENRY HARRISON and an AMERICAN OFFICER enters.)

HARRISON: I am William Henry Harrison. I have here a contract to buy this land. It is also a peace treaty. Sell us this land.

TECUMSEH: Why not buy the clouds instead?

HARRISON: We want to buy this land.

TECUMSEH: Do you want to buy the air too?

HARRISON: Don't be ridiculous. You can't buy the air.

TECUMSEH: Then you can't buy the land. They are the same.

HARRISON: The Great Father in Washington says "If you give us this land you can then move to the land beyond the Great River and live in peace forever."

TECUMSEH: And the Great Spirit says you trespass.

HARRISON: We will give you firewater and ploughs so that you may farm the forest.

TECUMSEH: Offer us guns and cannons and we will think about it—

HARRISON: The English give you guns.

TECUMSEH: Not enough.

HARRISON: Enough to kill innocent god-fearing settlers.

PROPHET: These innocent settlers are wise in the ways of the devil.

HARRISON: Don't talk to me about the devil, gargoyle.

PROPHET: Many people have asked me what I think of the white man.

HARRISON: We know what you think of the white man. Give us this land or we will take it.

TECUMSEH: You force us to be allies of the Red Coats.

HARRISON: We will take their land too. You will see.

TECUMSEH: And you will see Long Knife, that the land is not forgiving. Now go.

(HARRISON and the AMERICAN OFFICER exit.)

You have heard the word. When the sign is given we will take back what is ours, and drive the Long Knives beyond the mountains.

PROPHET: Hail Tecumseh, hail.

(The lights fade.)

Scene Two

(In another playing area the lights fade in. GENERAL ISAAC BROCK and PARSON JOHN STRACHAN enter, drinking port.)

BROCK: This place is like a prison. Why am I here? Why am I not in Portugal with Wellington, fighting Napoleon? Instead I am in this muddy bloody place.

STRACHAN: You will glory here.

BROCK: To what end? Before whom will I promenade? My mirror. You know of my exploits. After all my victories on the continent, and what is my reward? I have been placed on a shelf in a Canadian pantry, never to be touched, never to be eaten.

STRACHAN: You will mellow when we put the maple syrup on you.

BROCK: Do not jest with me. This place is not fun.

(JOHN ROBINSON enters.)

Speak.

ROBINSON: Tecumseh has crossed into Canada with six hundred warriours.

BROCK: Excellent. When the Americans declare war, we will have allies. The Yankees want this land, but they will not get it.

(ROBINSON exits.)

Gentlemen, I am not going to be liberal about this. I hate the Yankee pig.

STRACHAN: Here, here.

BROCK: I have no use for democracy.

STRACHAN: Here, here, well said.

BROCK: I have a king.

STRACHAN: And so do we.

BROCK: That is enough for me.

STRACHAN: Us too.

BROCK: This land is part of the British Empire.

STRACHAN: Well said.

BROCK: And when the Empire calls what do we sing?

STRACHAN: Ready, aye, ready.

BROCK: Exactly.

(ROBINSON enters.)

Speak.

ROBINSON: General William Hull with a large American Force is approaching Detroit. He sends you his regards.

(ROBINSON gives BROCK a letter. BROCK reads.)

BROCK: Gentlemen, this is a declaration of war. Come, we must prepare. The game begins.

(The lights fade.)

Scene Three

(In another playing area the lights fade in. RICHARD BOERSTLER and CHAPIN, two American officers, enter.)

BOERSTLER: Hull, he looks like a man, he talks like a man, but—

CHAPIN: They say he fought like a lion in the revolution.

BOERSTLER: That was over thirty years ago. This lion is now a full grown belly bag.

CHAPIN: They say he was wounded nine times in battle.

BOERSTLER: He won't be wounded once in this one. We need a fighting machine, not an eating machine. On this expedition we have more sauce pans than guns.

CHAPIN: They say—

BOERSTLER: They say, they say. He sleeps and eats that's all you can say about him.

(Noises offstage.)

Behold, our leader.

(BOERSTLER and CHAPIN exit. GENERAL WILLIAM HULL enters with his WIFE.)

HULL: Oh, what a lovely war. It is like marching to a picnic.

HULL'S WIFE: Yes, and the scenery is lovely.

HULL: And it will get better my dear, it will get better. Spread the blankets. The sun is hot, we will stop.

(BOERSTLER enters.)

BOERSTLER: General sir, our envoy has returned from the river Thames.

HULL: Was he welcomed with open arms?

BOERSTLER: He was strangled.

HULL: Strangled?

BOERSTLER: He read your proclamation and was immedately garotted.

HULL: Good Lord.

(CHAPIN enters as BOERSTLER exits.)

CHAPIN: Michilimackinac has been taken by the English.

HULL: What?

CHAPIN: With the help of Indians.

HULL: Indians.

CHAPIN: Yes, many Indians in many canoes are now flocking to Tecumseh.

HULL: Tecumseh.

CHAPIN: Yes, he is in these woods.

HULL'S WIFE: Oh William, oh William, are we going to be massacred?

HULL: Massacred.

CHAPIN: General, calm yourself. You are surrounded by twenty-five hundred troops.

(BOERSTLER enters as CHAPIN exits.)

BOERSTLER: General, our supply columns have been ambushed by Indians.

HULL: Oh no, that was from the south.

BOERSTLER: Yes.

HULL: And the hoardes are descending from the north.

BOERSTLER: Yes. Shall we lay out the blankets?

HULL'S WIFE: Oh William, our daughters and granddaughters are here.

HULL: Stay calm.

(CHAPIN enters.)

What?

CHAPIN: General Brock and British reinforcements are advancing on our positon.

HULL: Oh no, we are surrounded. Retreat, retreat. Back to our side, to Detroit.

CHAPIN: But there are only a few hundred troops in Amherstburg.

HULL: Retreat I say, retreat. We will go back to our side of the border. Maybe they will leave us alone.

(The lights fade.)

Scene Four

(In another playing area the lights fade in. BROCK and HENRY PROCTOR stand in front of a map of Detroit.)

PROCTOR: They are well fortified, surrounded by forest, manned by twenty-five hundred troops.

BROCK: Hmm-hmmm.

PROCTOR: We have approximately four hundred troops, two hundred militia, and of course, six hundred Indians.

BROCK: Hmm-hmmm.

(Noises offstage. TECUMSEH enters carrying a leather satchel full of letters. The PROPHET enters carrying a scalp hanging from a stick.)

PROCTOR: And this is Tecumseh. And this, Tecumseh, is General Isaac Brock.

BROCK: I have heard many things about you.

TECUMSEH: And I, many things of you.

BROCK: Do you think we should attack?

TECUMSEH: Yes.

PROCTOR: No savage, this is not a forest war. Detroit is a fortified fort.

TECUMSEH: It is a mud hut with a high fence. And the Long Knives are afraid. *(He holds up the satchel.)* Read.

(BROCK takes the satchel and reads the letters.)

BROCK: This is Hull's correspondence.

TECUMSEH: Yes, now it is yours.

PROCTOR: You cannot seriously contemplate an attack on Detroit.

BROCK: My dear Proctor, I did not travel from York to here to contemplate an attack.

(TECUMSEH grunts approval. BROCK holds up letter.)

Hull is a frayed old man.

PROCTOR: But we are outnumbered three to one.

BROCK: Two and a half to one.

TECUMSEH: And the Long Knives are half-men, so it is even.

PROCTOR: There are more defenders than attackers. It is a text book mistake to attack.

BROCK: Who said anything about attack? *(PROCTOR points at TECUMSEH.)* The only thing we will attack is the Yankee imagination. We will let it run wild. We will use a "*ruse de guerre*." We will bluff them out of their fort.

TECUMSEH: Ah yes. Me and my six hundred.

BROCK: Can you make six hundred warriors sound like ten thousand.

TECUMSEH: No problem. And if it come to it. These six hundred will fight like ten thousand. We will make a great wind around this fortress. They will imagine us victorious and we will be.

BROCK: Yes, this will be an excellent divertissement. Excuse my French.

TECUMSEH: Ho. The long knife in Detroit is not a man. This is a man.

(The lights fade.)

Scene Five

(In another playing area the lights fade in. BROCK, HULL, HULL'S WIFE, BOERSTLER, CHAPIN, and MACDONELL enter.)

BROCK: You must surrender. You are outnumbered.

CHAPIN: Never.

(TECUMSEH enters.)

BROCK: The forest is crawling with ten thousand blood thirsty Indians, each with their own scalping knife. Listen to them.

(Noises offstage. HULL gasps. PROCTOR enters.)

We have five thousand British regulars, as tough as steel, battle tried, with twenty-six cannon.

HULL: Oh no, oh no, oh no.

(HULL takes a white handkerchief from his coat and blows his nose.)

BROCK: If you do not surrender we will take your grandmother, your mother, your wife, your daughters, and your granddaughters and rape the shit out of them.

(HULL waves the handkerchief.)

HULL: We surrender, we surrender.

CHAPIN: No. You fool.

BOERSTLER: You traitor.

(BOERSTLER breaks his sword.)

HULL: It is for the best. You will see. I surrender.

BOERSTLER: This is a disgrace. Surrendering without a fight. What kind of world is this?

CHAPIN: Not an American one.

BOERSTLER: That's for sure.

CHAPIN: When we meet again, there will be blood. By God there'll be blood.

(The lights fade.)

Scene Six

(In another playing area the lights fade in. BROCK and SERGEANT JAMES FITZGIBBON enter.)

BROCK: Do you remember the day I taught you to read?

FITZGIBBON: Right you did. I consider it a great achievement.

BROCK: And do you remember the day I taught you to write your own name?

FITZGIBBON: Right, you did. You taught me to write my own name in my own hand. I consider it a great achievement.

BROCK: Sergeant Fitzgibbon.

FITZGIBBON: Sir.

BROCK: You are a professional soldier.

FITZGIBBON: I am.

BROCK: And a respectable character.

FITZGIBBON: No sir. I have served you too honestly to be called a respectable character.

BROCK: Well, you take orders well.

FITZGIBBON: That I do. I am like a donkey that brays for the whip.

BROCK: Listen to me. When I am speaking you are listening. I want you to form a special unit comprised of men with bodies of iron and a bag of nails for a brain.

FITZGIBBON: Ah, you'll be needing some "bloody boys."

BROCK: That's right. I have it on good authority that in Spain they have a word called "guerilla." Excuse my French. It means "little war" and those that fight the "little war" are called "guerillas." Excuse my French. That is the kind of war we must fight. One by one, little by little, we win.

(The lights fade.)

Scene Seven

(In another playing area the lights fade in. FITZGIBBON and a RECRUIT enter.)

RECRUIT: Why are you looking at me like I am a prize winning hog?

FITZGIBBON: What's your name?

RECRUIT: John Smith.

FITZGIBBON: Do you drink?

RECRUIT: Like a Smith.

(FITZGIBBON gives the RECRUIT a bottle. The RECRUIT drinks.)

FITZGIBBON: Do you have any mental disorders?

RECRUIT: No.

FITZGIBBON: Are you sure?

RECRUIT: I hope not. Why are you looking at me like I am a—?

FITZGIBBON: Have you ever thought of joining me and my bloody boys in the bush?

RECRUIT: No. I can see that where you go, trouble goes.

FITZGIBBON: I can see it in your eyes, you were born to be hanged. When you enlisted you took the king's shilling.

RECRUIT: That's right.

FITZGIBBON: And I expect every man to earn his shilling, starting with you. I want volunteers. You, c'mon, act like you got a pair. All those who do not volunteer will regret it profoundly. Mark that word please, it means deeply. Do you know what a toothbrush is?

RECRUIT: It's like a little broom.

FITZGIBBON: That's right, it's like a little broom. How would you like to clean out the shit house with a little broom? Now do I have any volunteers.

RECRUIT: Me.

FITZGIBBON: Ah, I knew when I first met you that you were born to do great things ... Who else!

(The lights fade.)

Scene Eight

(In another playing area the lights fade in. GENERAL JOHN PREVOST and BROCK enter.)

BROCK: But we must attack the Yankee bow-wow.

PREVOST: Lord Wellington calls his troops the scum of the earth. And he sends me his rejects, anyone that does not fit in, he sends to me. What an army! I have garrisoned this country with cut-throats, knaves, lunatics, rabble of the lowest—

BROCK: Beware Governor, they say Lord Wellington's ears are as big as his nose.

PREVOST: Ah yes, Old Nosey, the Sepoy General. I know the duke well. On the playing fields of Eton we used to sit underneath the walnut tree and watch all the cheaters play cricket.

BROCK: He has come a long way. Have you?

PREVOST: Do not be impertinent. I am John Prevost. I am supremo here.

BROCK: I do not suffer superiours gladly unless they are brave, which you are not.

PREVOST: Beware Brock, these are fighting words.

BROCK: Damn right.

(BROCK slaps the cheek of PREVOST with his gloves.)

PREVOST: Pistols at dawn.

BROCK: Excellent. And I will call the distance.

PREVOST: Done.

(The lights fade.)

Scene Nine

(In another playing area the lights fade in. LAURA SECORD enters.)

LAURA: I've pigged with you for fifteen years, but I'll never pig with you again if you don't get up.

(JAMES SECORD enters.)

SECORD: Woman, stop faffing round. What's the matter with you? Is it a crime for a man to have a snooze?

LAURA: Yes. The Yankees have just invaded Queenston.

SECORD: What? How do you know this?

LAURA: While you were in there picking your fartleberries I was out there giving the pig a scrub.

SECORD: And?

LAURA: Well I saw with my own peepers, the Yankees on the Heights. Look!

SECORD: Oh my God, I better get my gun.

LAURA: Yes, you better.

(The lights fade.)

Scene Ten

(In another playing area the lights fade in. BROCK and PREVOST enter.)

PREVOST: Brock, I am the best shot in the world. I have killed six men in duels. Prepare to die.

BROCK: Hold for a moment. As you recall I get to call the distance.

PREVOST: Just make it less than twenty paces.

BROCK: Sir, I will make it less than twenty inches.

(BROCK holds up his handkerchief.)

Grab hold.

PREVOST: But we will both die.

BROCK: That is correct. Grab hold.

PREVOST: But—

BROCK: Grab hold.

(PREVOST grabs hold of the handkerchief.)

Now, cock your pistol.

PREVOST: But—

(FITZGIBBON enters.)

FITZGIBBON: The Yankees have taken Queenston Heights with four cannons.

PREVOST: Brock, I order you to discharge your duties and defend Upper Canada.

BROCK: Yes. Tell me more, but first hand me my cumberbund.

FITZGIBBON: You're wearing it.

BROCK: Then hand me my sword. A river of blood will lead to an ocean of love. Come.

(The lights fade.)

Scene Eleven

(In another playing area the lights fade in. Two AMERICAN SOLDIERS enter singing "Yankee Doodle." WINFIELD SCOTT enters.)

SCOTT: Come, let's turn the cannon this way.

(The lights fade.)

Scene Twelve

(In another playing area the lights fade in. BROCK and SECORD enter.)

BROCK: Ah, brave volunteer. Come gentlemen,

let us run up that greasy hill as fast as we can. The jaws of victory await us.

(The lights fade.)

Scene Thirteen

(In another playing area the lights fade in. SCOTT and two AMERICAN SOLDIERS enter.)

AMERICAN SOLDIER ONE: I just shot a general.

SCOTT: Are you sure?

AMERICAN SOLDIER ONE: He was dressed like a general.

VOICE: *(Off.)* Revenge the general!

SCOTT: So you did. Here they come … fire.

(The sound of gunfire, then moans and groans.)

The day is ours. Show the colours.

(The lights fade.)

Scene Fourteen

(In another playing area the lights fade in. A wounded BROCK and a wounded SECORD lie on the ground.)

BROCK: Quiet, brave volunteer.

(FITZGIBBON enters.)

FITZGIBBON: General, does it hurt?

(BROCK groans.)

Any last words?

BROCK: Give me my handkerchief.

(FITZGIBBON gives BROCK the handkerchief. BROCK blows his nose. FITZGIBBON grabs the handkerchief.)

Revenge your general.

(BROCK dies. FITZGIBBON stands up and shakes his fist.)

FITZGIBBON: It's going to be a bad day for you boyo. A bad day.

(FITZGIBBON looks at the hankerchief. The lights fade.)

Scene Fifteen

(In another playing area the lights fade in. SCOTT enters with two AMERICAN SOLDIERS.)

SCOTT: Here come the Red Coats.

AMERICAN SOLDIER ONE: We are badly outnumbered.

AMERICAN SOLDIER TWO: I'm out of ammunition.

SCOTT: Shut up. It's on the other side of the river. It's not as if we don't have it.

AMERICAN SOLDIER ONE: We killed their general.

AMERICAN SOLDIER TWO: We're going to be scalped.

(The two SOLDIERS exit.)

SCOTT: Come back … It's a cliff, you'll kill yourself.

VOICE: *(Off.)* Aiyeeee.

SCOTT: Dashed on the rocks.

(FITZGIBBON and the RECRUIT enter holding swords.)

FITZGIBBON: All right, boyo, it's a bad day for you.

SCOTT: I surrender, don't chop me up, I surrender.

FITZGIBBON: I'm going to give you a good chopping.

SCOTT: Don't chop me up, I'll give you anything you want. Cigarettes, chocolate, just don't chop me up. I'll do anything, I'll go to Washington and dig up old George and screw him, just don't chop me up.

(The RECRUIT restrains FITZGIBBON from stabbing SCOTT. The lights fade.)

Scene Sixteen

(In another playing area the lights fade in. PROCTOR and the PROPHET enter. A sign on a corral post reads "Frenchtown." Offstage are the sounds of a massacre.)

PROPHET: War is good. Many Long Knives die by the knife today.

PROCTOR: Yes, blood demands blood. At Detroit, we traded Hull for thirty British privates. Brock was ten times the worth of Hull. He is dead. The Americans will pay ten times.

(Offstage is the sound of snorting pigs.)

PROPHET: Look, pig eat Long Knives' head. Good.

PROCTOR: Let the hogs of hell go mad on human flesh. Brock is avenged.

(The lights fade.)

Scene Seventeen

(In another playing area the lights fade in. PREVOST enters.)

PREVOST: Oh the sun is shining, the robins are singing, and I am going to recommend myself for a medal. There is no point giving medals to dead people. I've been in this army twenty years. I know what it's all about. A bit of brown, someone to towel you off. I know what it's all about. I am supremo.

(GENERAL GORDON DRUMMOND enters.)

PREVOST: Ah, General Gordon Drummond.

DRUMMOND: Sir.

PREVOST: You are going to replace Commander Brock. In Upper Canada.

DRUMMOND: Sir.

PREVOST: You will fight a purely defensive war.

DRUMMOND: In Spain my troops called me "Bulldog."

PREVOST: Good. You will make an excellent watchdog.

(DRUMMOND sneers. The lights fade.)

Scene Eighteen

(In another playing area the lights fade in. BOERSTLER and CHAPIN are on the poop deck of the U.S.S. Madison.)

BOERSTLER: Look, the general, the fatman himself.

CHAPIN: Our granny has come to lead us in battle.

(GENERAL HENRY DEARBORN and MAJOR ZEBULON PIKE enter.)

PIKE: All clear for the general.

DEARBORN: Men of brave hearts, your general speaks. We are now anchored within sight of York,capital of Upper Canada. This day will give us our first victory. We outnumber the inhabitants ten to one. We cannot fail. And to make doublesure, Major Zebulon Pike is leading the attack. Pike.

(PIKE steps forward.)

PIKE: Men, brave men. The cure for seasickness is land. The capital is before us. Let us give them our vomit. Tonight we drink blood.

(A cheer from the darkness.)

We will take the British blockhouse and the blockheads that live there prisoner. Come to the boats.

(The lights fade.)

Scene Nineteen

(In another playing area the lights fade in. STRACHAN enters holding a bible.)

STRACHAN: You must become a slave to God. Know your betters and plough the fields of your masters happily. Man is born to work, like a cow is born to give milk, and a pig is born to be bacon. Every man serves God under the name of lord or worker. Do not let pride stand in the way of worshipping God. If you do, then I say unto the Lord, "Oh Lord, smite them."

(Noises offstage.)

What's all that shouting?

(LAURA SECORD enters.)

LAURA: The Yankees are here.

STRACHAN: What?

LAURA: They have landed.

STRACHAN: The fiends. Come, we must do something. Organize the militia, something.

(The lights fade.)

Scene Twenty

(In another playing area the lights fade in. PIKE and an AMERICAN SOLDIER enter.)

PIKE: The day is ours. They retreat. Forward, tonight we sleep in the arms of victory.

(CHAPIN enters.)

CHAPIN: The blockhouse is surrounded.

PIKE: Bring up the cannon.

(The AMERICAN SOLDIER exits.)

CHAPIN: The white flag is up.

PIKE: Excellent, I want the general's sword. Our first victory. Now I'll just sit on this toadstool over here and wait for them to surrender.

(A huge explosion. Blackout.)

CHAPIN: They blew up the blockhouse.

(Lights up. PIKE is mortally wounded.)

PIKE: Oh my God, I am killed by a flying pitch fork. Oh God. The glory.

(The lights fade.)

Scene Twenty-one

(In another playing area the lights fade in. DRUMMOND and FITZGIBBON enter.)

FITZGIBBON: The blockhouse is no more.

DRUMMOND: Good, now blow up the magazine, and the ship in the harbour. And blow up that building. This cruddy, muddy, bloody place is not worth the keeping. The Yankees can have it. We will save the army, and fight another day. We will retreat.

(STRACHAN enters.)

STRACHAN: You can't retreat.

DRUMMOND: I will not surrender the army.

STRACHAN: But who will negotiate the terms of surrender?

DRUMMOND: You will. Come, all is hurry and confusion.

(DRUMMOND and FITZGIBBON exit.)

VOICE: *(Off.)* Forward, revenge the general. Burn this place to the ground.

(BOESTLER and CHAPIN enter holding torches.)

STRACHAN: Do what you have to do, but please respect private property.

BOERSTLER: Out of my way preacher. There is mischief to be done.

STRACHAN: Burning homes is the work of the devil.

CHAPIN: Be careful we do not burn you, warlock. Let it burn!

(The lights fade.)

Scene Twenty-two

(In another playing area the lights fade in. DRUMMOND and FITZGIBBON enter. FITZGIBBON holds a telescope.)

DRUMMOND: Why is that creek so stony?

FITZGIBBON: They're sitting in their boats again. No! They're getting out again. No! They're sitting down again.

DRUMMOND: Well I wish they'd make up their bloody mind.

FITZGIBBON: Well, we know it's coming sometime.

DRUMMOND: Yes, why is that creek so stony?

(The lights fade.)

Scene Twenty-three

(In another playing area the lights fade in. SCOTT enters.)

SCOTT: Haw-haw, we're back. And this time we're going to shove it up the royal bum hole good. I am redeemed.

(BOERSTLER enters.)

BOERSTLER: Our troops are fast arriving.

SCOTT: Good, this time we will capture a fort and an army. I will be redeemed. I was in a limey dungeon for six months. Words cannot describe living in a belching slimepot with the creatures. Nor the way I felt. I became a figure of shame, the butt of every joke, an object of abuse. But I will redeem. I will enter Canada and leave the rest to heaven.

(A huge explosion is heard.)

BOERSTLER: They blew up the fort.

SCOTT: Again.

BOERSTLER: And the army is retreating into the woods.

SCOTT: Tarnation.

(The lights fade.)

Scene Twenty-four

(In another playing area the lights fade in. DRUMMOND and FITZGIBBON enter.)

FITZGIBBON: Our scouts tell us the Yanks are in and around Stony Creek. What do you recommend?

DRUMMOND: A bayonet attack.

FITZGIBBON: Yes, a bayonet attack.

(The lights fade.)

Scene Twenty-five

(In another playing area the lights fade in. FITZGIBBON and the RECRUIT enter.)

RECRUIT: I can't see a bloody thing.

FITZGIBBON: Shut up. We're very close. Look, the American campfires. Forward.

(The lights fade.)

Scene Twenty-six

(In another playing area the lights fade in. FITZGIBBON and the RECRUIT enter.)

FITZGIBBON: They're not here, these fires are a ruse. They're—

(The sound of musket fire.)

—in the dark. Charge.

(Various BRITISH and AMERICAN troops enter carrying bayonets and swords and fight the battle of Stony Creek. Musket fire, cannon fire, oaths, shrieks, lamentations, and screams score the battle. The BRITISH and AMERICAN troops retreat simultaneously leaving the stage littered with the wounded and the dying. The lights fade.)

Scene Twenty-seven

(In another playing area the lights fade in. SCOTT enters.)

SCOTT: I'm Winfield Scott. I'm from South Carolina. I hear you Kentucky boys think you're tough but you don't want to fight. Well you're going to fight Limeys or you're going to fight me. Isn't a man living I couldn't kick his crack. I been wounded six times. Had my belly ripped, my shoulder torn, got a gash on my back as big as a watermelon. But I don't sit around with my finger up my ditch crying. No sir. No sirree. I'm ready for number seven. I feel lucky. I flip silver dollars for long cock with you anyday, boy. I got a horse looking for a stable. Don't look at me like that. I use this foot to step on niggers, and this one Indians, but I'll use them both to step on you. Now there's work to be done. Villages to burn, men to kill, and women to service. Let's get us some possum.

(The lights fade.)

Scene Twenty-eight

(In another playing area the lights fade in. Sound of musket fire and cannons. SCOTT enters.)

SCOTT: Oh Prunella. Shot in the ass again. Oh this is the fourth time. Let's get the hell out of here.

(The lights fade.)

Scene Twenty-nine

(In another playing area the lights fade in. PREVOST and DRUMMOND enter.)

PREVOST: I am near the breaking point.

DRUMMOND: What is the problem?

PREVOST: I have a severe case of piles and am not able to sit on my horse.

DRUMMOND: Oh you poor dear. Shall we get you a carriage?

PREVOST: Not if the road is bumpy.

DRUMMOND: Oh, then how would you like to be carried into battle?

PREVOST: Preferably horizontally, by four men.

DRUMMOND: Like pall bearers?

PREVOST: That's right.

DRUMMOND: Well I think we can arrange that.

PREVOST: And it is very important that my legs be kept together, I would not want to go into battle with my legs open.

DRUMMOND: No, you certainly would not.

PREVOST: Is the morale of the troops good?

DRUMMOND: Could be better.

PREVOST: They're not complaining again, are they? What are their complaints.

DRUMMOND: Food.

PREVOST: Food! What are they eating?

DRUMMOND: Insects.

PREVOST: Insects?

DRUMMOND: But that's no reason to be concerned. They have just eaten some grasshoppers and feel quite chipper.

PREVOST: Do these men have any other complaints?

DRUMMOND: Uniforms. The men would like uniforms.

PREVOST: I don't know what I'm going to do about that.

DRUMMOND: No, you never do so—

PREVOST: Any more complaints?

DRUMMOND: Ammunition. The men would like some ammunition.

PREVOST: Ammunition! Ah, that I can solve. I am a firm believer in the use of the bayonet. It was good enough for the Duke of Marlborough, it's good enough for me.

DRUMMOND: Exactly. The men are keen to stick a piece of steel into somebody.

PREVOST: Good. Hardship makes men hard.

DRUMMOND: Yes, it does. God help the poor Yankee that falls into their hands. They would strip him naked, pig stick for hours, and then eat him.

PREVOST: Good.

(The lights fade.)

Scene Thirty

(In another playing area the lights fade in. FITZGIBBON enters.)

FITZGIBBON: I see smoke.

(The lights fade.)

Scene Thirty-one

(In another playing area the lights fade in. Two wounded AMERICAN SOLDIERS enter. AMERICAN SOLDIER TWO tries to make a stretcher out of tree branches.)

AMERICAN SOLDIER TWO: I know I shouldn't have lit that fire, but jumping Jehosephat I don't care anymore.

AMERICAN SOLDIER ONE: Me neither, I've had enough. When I enlisted the sergeant said it was for only three months and I'd be stationed in the U.S. The first month was all right, going on parade everyday, nothing wrong with that, but then the bastards put us across the border and didn't tell us. Said we were in the U. S. of A. And I got my arms shot off. Look at them, they're useless.

(AMERICAN SOLDIER ONE swings his lifeless arms.)

AMERICAN SOLDIER TWO: And some Limey shot off my legs, and for what. They're monsters.

AMERICAN SOLDIER ONE: They're not monsters, they're mansters. Mansters!

AMERICAN SOLDIER TWO: Well, I'm going home, I don't care anymore. I'm going home ... I need a bigger branch. This one won't hold me.

AMERICAN SOLDIER ONE: I'll kick one over to you.

(AMERICAN SOLDIER ONE exits.)

AMERICAN SOLDIER TWO: Jeremiah, I'm inclined to think that when we come to our lines, we just keep walking. I know that's easier said than done and you're doing the walking but—

(Noises offstage.)

Jeremiah.

(FITZGIBBON enters.)

FITZGIBBON: It's a bad day for you, boy-o. I'm the man that came up from the belly of the beast and I'm going to cut your throat from ear to ear and there's nothing you can do about it.

(FITZGIBBON brandishes his knife. The lights fade.)

Scene Thirty-two

(In another playing area the lights fade in. LAURA and JAMES SECORD enter. LAURA carries a bucket.)

SECORD: So the Yankees like our house, do they? Did you jack the bull?

LAURA: Oh, did I ever ... Look.

SECORD: Hold it up. Put a bit of that in too.

(SECORD spits into the bucket.)

VOICE: *(Off.)* Apple jack!

SECORD: Oh there they are, bellowing away.

LAURA: We'll give their bellies something to bellow about, the bunch of raping, marauding, murdering bastards ... turning us into maid and butler in our own house. My faffle juice will fill their boots with the brown water.

(The lights fade.)

Scene Thrity-three

(In another playing area the lights fade in. CHAPIN and BOERSTLER enter.)

CHAPIN: But anyway, we don't want to shoot Fitzgibbon. We want to capture him, so we can torture him, get information out of him, listen to him scream.

BOERSTLER: Yes. Where's that apple jack?

CHAPIN: Apple jack, apple jack.

(LAURA enters holding a jug.)

BOERSTLER: Ah, madam. A toast to our host. Dear lady, I want to compliment you on the excellent food you have served my table.

LAURA: My table, you mean.

BOERSTLER: Madam.

LAURA: Don't "madam" me.

BOERSTLER: I am Richard Boerstler, but my womenfolk call me Yankee Dick.

LAURA: Well Yankee Dick. I have brought you this.

(LAURA holds up the jug.)

BOERSTLER: Ah, more hooch. This Yankee gentleman is delighted.

LAURA: Is it possible to be a Yankee and a gentleman?

BOERSTLER: I am living proof.

CHAPIN: But I'm not. This Yankee gentleman couldn't give a fart about anything. Gimme.

(CHAPIN takes the jug. He drinks.)

LAURA: Be careful kind sir. Liquor loosens the tongue.

CHAPIN: It loosens more than the tongue, my dear. Here.

(CHAPIN gives the jug to BOERSTLER. He drinks.)

BOERSTLER: Ah, delightful.

CHAPIN: You've got big shoulders and I bet you've got a big pair of sweaties.

(SECORD enters holding a crutch.)

SECORD: You wouldn't be compromising my wife, would you? Laura, take a walk.

(LAURA exits.)

CHAPIN: Get back to your hole, cripple.

SECORD: I got these wounds at Queenston, you'll get yours here if you don't leave my wife alone.

CHAPIN: Shut up cripple.

SECORD: Leave my wife, or I'll blind you. My father was with the Butler's Rangers.

CHAPIN: I knew you were a blackguard. You and your cow can go to your hole.

BOERSTLER: This apple jack is mighty unusual.

SECORD: Would you like some more?

(The lights fade.)

Scene Thirty-four

(In another playing area the lights fade in. LAURA enters riding a cow.)

LAURA: Come moo-cow. We will tread the night darkly and give milk in the day.

(The lights fade.)

Scene Thirty-five

(In another playing area the lights fade in. LAURA enters.)

LAURA: This world is full of bastards. But the meanest little bastard in the world is a black fly. Drive you mad, not half-mad, all the way mad. Meanest little bastard.

VOICE: *(Off.)* Who goes there?

LAURA: It is I, Laura Secord, a farmer's daughter, young maiden, well young matron, anyway.

(FITZGIBBON enters holding a bayonet.)

FITZGIBBON: What do you wnat?

LAURA: Are you Captain Fitzgibbon?

FITZGIBBON: Yes, and I consider it a great achievement.

LAURA: Am I glad to see you. I have been jumping over creeks, climbing hills, milking this creature, in short I am too hot and bothered to remember what I'm supposed to tell you. Do you know what I'm talking about?

FITZGIBBON: No madam, but I'm sure you do.

LAURA: Americans and Canadian traitors are advancing on Beaver Dams to capture you and your bloody boys.

FITZGIBBON: Hmmm. This sounds important.

LAURA: Damn right. Move!

Scene Thirty-six

(In another playing area the lights fade in. BOERSTLER and CHAPIN enter.)

CHAPIN: When I get him, I am going to tie this around his—

BOERSTLER: Quiet. By the pricking of my thumbs, something evil this way comes.

(Offstage: musket fire, war whoops, yelling.)

CHAPIN: Ambushed. God save me Christ. Lord, we're going to be massacred.

BOERSTLER: Quiet. Take cover.

(The lights fade.)

Scene Thirty-seven

(In another playing area the lights fade in. Musket fire. FITZGIBBON enters.)

FITZGIBBON: Do you surrender?

(In another playing area the lights fade in. CHAPIN and BOERSTLER are under fire.)

CHAPIN: Oh, we're being killed like flies. Like flies.

BOERSTLER: Shut up.

FITZGIBBON: Do you surrender?

BOERSTLER: Never.

CHAPIN: Shut up.

BOERSTLER: Quiet.

FITZGIBBON: But not before we scalp you and torture you and then feed you to the wild pigs.

CHAPIN: Oh no.

BOERSTLER: Shut up.

CHAPIN: Quiet.

FITZGIBBON: Do you surrender?

BOERSTLER: We surrender. Damn, lost another one without a fight.

(The lights fade.)

Scene Thirty-eight

(In another playing area the lights fade in. LAURA and FITZGIBBON enter.)

FITZGIBBON: It was a great victory madam, a great victory. We used a *ruse de guerre*. Excuse my French. We ambushed the Americans and put them in a cross fire. They thought we were a large army, hundreds of them surrendered to forty Indians and fifty Englishmen at Beaver Dams. And we have traitors as our trophy. A great victory madam, to you.

(The lights fade.)

Scene Thirty-nine

(In another playing area the lights fade in. ROBINSON enters.)

ROBINSON: Death to immigrants and traitors. Traitors are everywhere. Scabs. Like scabs on my body. Prick my vitals. As God shall judge me. *Exitus acta probat.* Death to immigrants and traitors.

(In another playing area the lights fade in. JACOB OVERHOLSER is revealed on his knees.)

Where were you born?

OVERHOLSER: Pennsylvania.

ROBINSON: You're an American.

OVERHOLSER: Well, I was.

ROBINSON: What do you think of George Washington?

(OVERHOLSER shrugs.)

Do you think he is a swine?

(OVERHOLSER shrugs.)

Oh come now, you must have an opinion. What do you think of him?

OVERHOLSER: He was a good general.

ROBINSON: What do you think of democracy?

(OVERHOLSER shrugs.)

Speak.

OVERHOLSER: I have no opinion.

(A slight hysterical giggle from OVERHOLSER.)

ROBINSON: This is not a laughing matter.

OVERHOLSER: I'm not laughing.

ROBINSON: You are on trial for high treason. I have already convicted twelve traitors of treason. Each of whom had the insolence to sing "Yankee Doodle" in my presence. Do you know the words to that song? Sing it.

OVERHOLSER: "Yankee Doodle went to town riding on a pony ..." Everybody, where I come from everybody knows that song.

ROBINSON: Really.

OVERHOLSER: I am an ignorant farmer. I grow hay for horses. I don't know how to read or write. I came here with my wife and four children in 1810.

ROBINSON: Are you a spy?

OVERHOLSER: No. My accusers, my neighbours, never made me welcome.

ROBINSON: Your accusers are men of unquestioned loyalty.

OVERHOLSER: My accusers are not men.

ROBINSON: What do you think of King George the Third.

OVERHOLSER: King George the Third. If he is anything like you he must be the biggest jackass that ever walked the earth.

(ROBINSON smiles.)

ROBINSON: I am going to find you guilty of high treason and sentence you to be hung by the neck but not until dead. For you will be cut down while alive and your entrails taken out and burned before you. Your head will be cut off and your body divided into four quarters. After which your head and quarters will be at the king's disposal.

(The lights fade.)

Scene Forty

(In another playing area the lights fade in. The PROPHET enters wearing an American officer's jacket.)

PROPHET: Look, I am Long Knife.

(TECUMSEH enters.)

TECUMSEH: Take off those clothes, you dress in disgrace.

PROPHET: Dogs in red give me these clothes. Long Knifes come, dogs in red run.

TECUMSEH: Where is Proctor?

PROPHET: King dog run first, others follow. See dust, that Proctor.

TECUMSEH: We must stop them, we must fight. Come.

PROPHET: I stay here. The land is ours. We die. Look I am Long Knife.

TECUMSEH: You must come with me.

PROPHET: Whitemen. Pugh. Yankees just like dogs in red, and red dogs just like Yankees. Pugh.

TECUMSEH: Pugh.

PROPHET: Whitemen.

TECUMSEH: With Brock, there was a chance.

PROPHET: But with Proctor, no hope, no hope.

TECUMSEH: I will make him fight.

PROPHET: Chickenman will never fight.

(PROCTOR enters.)

PROCTOR: Ah Tecumseh.

PROPHET: Chickenman.

PROCTOR: And you. We are going to retreat.

TECUMSEH: You should be wearing petticoats, not this uniform. When will we turn and fight?

PROCTOR: You don't understand, Commodore Perry has defeated Barclay. The Great Lakes are lost.

PROPHET: Too much dust behind this man.

TECUMSEH: This is our land.

PROCTOR: And it is lost.

TECUMSEH: Unless we fight.

PROCTOR: It is a textbook mistake to fight. We have not eaten in three days, we have no ammunition.

TECUMSEH: We must fight.

PROCTOR: We will. We have no choice. But we will choose our ground.

TECUMSEH: This is our ground.

PROCTOR: Oh very well. Now if you will excuse me. I must mix haste with caution.

PROPHET: Squirrel man.

PROCTOR: You.

(PROCTOR exits.)

TECUMSEH: This land, you see. Look how beautiful it is. How like a paradise. Cowards have been here. This land is the mother of our mothers. We are home.

(Musket fire is heard.)

PROPHET: Long Knives.

(The lights fade.)

Scene Forty-one

(In another playing area the lights fade in. HARRISON enters.)

HARRISON: Remember the Raisin, remember Frenchtown? Proctor, Tecumseh, when we get hold of you we're going to skin you alive and melt you down and feed you to pigs.

VOICE: *(Off.)* Sir, we have captured two farmers.

HARRISON: Bring them to me. I want them to meet their new master. A Yankee master.

(The lights fade.)

Scene Forty-two

(In another playing area the lights fade in. HARRISON enters with three AMERICAN SOLDIERS.)

AMERICAN SOLDIER THREE: General Harrison, yonder is the enemy.

HARRISON: Very well, brave lads. Your commander requests twenty men to ride into glory.

AMERICAN SOLDIERS: I'll go, I'll go, I'll go.

HARRISON: The purpose of this ride is to attract the enemy fire. When the enemy is reloading our cavalry will attack full force. Do I have any volunteers. Remember Frenchtown ... Remember the Raisin.

AMERICAN SOLDIERS: I'll go. And me. And me. And me. And me too.

HARRISON: Well done lads, well done. And to the rest of you, I will give a silver dollar to the man that brings me the head of Henry Proctor on a stick.

(The AMERICAN SOLDIERS cheer. The lights fade.)

Scene Forty-three

(In another playing area the lights fade in. PROCTOR enters running.)

PROCTOR: It's a cavalry attack. Run, run. The men have broken. The men run, but the Indians are still skirmishing. Sound the retreat.

(The lights fade.)

Scene Forty-four

(In another playing area the lights fade in. Three AMERICAN SOLDIERS enter. TECUMSEH enters holding a tomahawk. They fight. TECUMSEH kills the AMERICAN SOLDIERS.)

TECUMSEH: I am Tecumseh.

(The lights fade.)

Scene Forty-five

(In another playing area the lights fade in. PROCTOR enters, pursued by HARRISON.)

PROCTOR: Run for it.

HARRISON: I want your head.

PROCTOR: Run for it.

HARRISON: I want your head.

(The lights fade.)

Scene Forty-six

(In another playing area the lights fade in. TECUMSEH enters.)

TECUMSEH: I have killed eighteen men today. Look no scalps. Am I not a great warrior?

(Three AMERICAN SOLDIERS enter carrying bayonets.)

I am ...

(The AMERICAN SOLDIERS stab TECUMSEH. TECUMSEH dies. The lights fade.)

Scene Forty-seven

(In another playing area the lights fade in. A wounded AMERICAN SOLDIER enters.)

AMERICAN SOLDIER: Help me.

(The PROPHET enters holding a tomahawk.)

PROPHET: Happy am I to die in battle and not like ... Harrison run. All white dogs run. Happy am I. My brother is dead, but Proctor, he lives. What a world.

(The PROPHET hits the soldier with the tomahawk. The lights fade.)

Scene Forty-eight

(In another playing area the lights fade in. PROCTOR and PREVOST enter.)

PROCTOR: Sir.

PREVOST: Ah, Colonel Proctor. I am going to court martial you for losing the Battle of the Thames.

PROCTOR: But sir.

PREVOST: No buts about it. You're finished, no buts about it. You're through. I'm going to rub your nose in it, Proctor. Rub your nose in it, Proctor.

PROCTOR: But I didn't have any provisions, ammunition.

PREVOST: No excuses in this world, Proctor. Dismissed.

PROCTOR: But—

PREVOST: Dismissed.

(PROCTOR exits.)

Oh I just love mashing people.

(The lights fade.)

Scene Forty-nine

(In another playing area the lights fade in. CHARLES DE SALABERRY enters.)

SALABERRY: I am generous to my friends, but brutal too. I dish it out good. My men respond to me as High and Mighty Lord or I start dishing up. I make them do what my heart desires. Anyone that disagrees with me can climb on this. *(Indicating his groin.)* I am impossible to please. I am tough but fair. That's what the fools think, anyway. Oh my soldiers, what would I do without them. They love me so much.

Around the campfire they sing their little songs. I make them sing this one. They love me so much. "Here's our colonel, with Satan in his soul. He'll be the death of us all. There is no beast of prey that can stand in his way. And no matter how far you seek, our colonel is, as they say, 'C'est magnifique'."

As I rouge my lips I say to myself will it be *ruse de guerre* or *force de frappe*. I toy with my emotions as if they were a little plaything, as if they were a little chipmunk that I could strangle with my big greasy fingers. I know the names of all my troops by heart. The names of the donkeys, too.

In the heat of battle I give my troops courage. I say to them "If you do not kill Les Batards I will go back to Montréal and fuck your mother." That puts a smile on their face. I dance on the tree stump in victory. In full glory I dance. People don't know what to admire more. My courage or my virtue. My admirers can go straight to hell. I am a hero. I am Charles de Salaberry. The hero of Chateauguay.

(PREVOST enters.)

PREVOST: I am going to take credit for your victory. What have you to say to that?

SALABERRY: Climb.

PREVOST: What?

SALABERRY: Climb.

PREVOST: What are you saying to me?

SALABERRY: Climb. You will give me a medal with a big red ribbon or I will cut you in half with this. *(He draws his sword.)* In battle I am swift and bold. I ask for no quarter, and of course, I give none. In this army, all I want is rank and honour.

PREVOST: You will get rank, and perhaps honour.

SALABERRY: No, rank and honour.

PREVOST: And I repeat, rank and perhaps honour.

SALABERRY: My victory at Chateauguay was like Thermopylae. With three hundred I held off seven thousand. I am like Leonidas.

PREVOST: So what. I am supremo here.

SALABERRY: Before each duel I walk like this. *(He walks about the stage.)* With a smile on my face I flaunt my power.

PREVOST: General Drummond.

SALABERRY: Perhaps you don't like the colour of my eyes?

PREVOST: General Drummond.

SALABERRY: Or perhaps you think my nose is too big for my face?

PREVOST: General Drummond.

(DRUMMOND enters.)

DRUMMOND: Sir.

PREVOST: Is the Chevalier de Salaberry's medal ready?

DRUMMOND: Medal?

PREVOST: Yes.

(The lights fade.)

Scene Fifty

(In another playing area the lights fade in. SCOTT and an AMERICAN SOLDIER enter.)

AMERICAN SOLDIER: I didn't sign to fight on foreign soil. I haven't seen my wife in six months. Feed me, pay me, give me clothes for winter. I'm in the militia, not the army.

SCOTT: Shut up. If you say another word, I will barf in your mouth. I am your commander. Respect me.

AMERICAN SOLDIER: I want to go home, my six months are up.

SCOTT: If you go, we'll have to abandon this fort.

AMERICAN SOLDIER: Good I hate this place.

SCOTT: Oh, then go home.

(JOSEPH WILLCOCKS enters.)

WILLCOCKS: No. My home village is ripe for burning. And it's just over that hill.

SCOTT: What's it called?

WILLCOCKS: Newark.

SCOTT: Newark! Didn't they used to call that place Butlersburg.

WILLCOCKS: Damn right, they did.

SCOTT: Burn it to the ground.

WILLCOCKS: Hee-haw!

(The lights fade.)

Scene Fifty-one

(In another playing area the lights fade in. WILLCOCKS and AMERICAN SOLDIERS enter holding torches. LAURA enters.)

LAURA: Willcocks, you traitor.

WILLCOCKS: A tory sow speaks.

LAURA: You used to live here.

WILLCOCKS: And after we have burned this tory village to the ground, you will be able to say you used to live here too.

(WILLCOCKS and the AMERICAN SOLDIERS laugh.)

Burn her house.

LAURA: You'll hang for this.

WILLCOCKS: And her hut too.

LAURA: Not my chickenhouse.

WILLCOCKS: Don't worry, we won't burn your tory chickens, we'll eat them.

(WILLCOCKS and the AMERICAN SOLDIERS laugh.)

LAURA: Willcocks, you scummy cock.

WILLCOCKS: Hey, watch we don't put you in the pot.

LAURA: You may as well, I'll die in the winter without my chickens. They're all I have. What kind of war is this?

WILLCOCKS: This war is like all wars. Ugly and stupid. Now get out of my way.

(WILLCOCKS and the AMERICAN SOLDIERS exit.)

LAURA: Yankee swine, Yankee swine, Yankee swine.

(The lights fade. During the darkness the chant of "Yankee swine" is augmented by cries, shrieks, and curses, until it becomes inaudible and is replaced by a chant of "Limey swine.")

Scene Fifty-two

(In another playing area the lights fade in. FITZGIBBON and the RECRUIT enter.)

FITZGIBBON: Let that be a lesson to you. Burn our villages, we'll burn yours.

(FITZGIBBON laughs. The lights fade.)

Scene Fifty-three

(In another playing area the lights fade in. SCOTT enters.)

SCOTT: Raise the Stars and Stripes and strike up "I'm a Yankee Doodle Dandy." It is I, Winfield Scott, conqueror of countries, shatterer of dreams, wooer of war, on this bloody soil again.

(An AMERICAN SOLDIER enters.)

AMERICAN SOLDIER: General, the fort is ours. The British await you at Chippewa.

SCOTT: Then we will not keep them waiting.

(The lights fade.)

Scene Fifty-four

(In another playing area the lights fade in. Two British soldiers—the RECRUIT and PRIVATE THOMAS—are playing cards)

THOMAS: Three years ago I was happily rotting away in jail.

RECRUIT: Now you're rotting away here.

THOMAS: I thought I was leaving hell.

RECRUIT: But you were only entering.

THOMAS: I didn't want to get killed in Spain.

RECRUIT: No point in doing that.

THOMAS: So they sent me to the icebox.

RECRUIT: And here you are.

THOMAS: The first day the sergeant didn't like the look of me.

RECRUIT: So he beat the brown out of you. In this devil's game I assume ace takes precedence over king.

THOMAS: That's right, and threes are bigger than deuces.

RECRUIT: How civilized. Are you going to shuffle the cards?

THOMAS: No.

RECRUIT: Oh yes you are. I know we are playing for trifles but if I lose my jock strap I lose one of the necessities of life.

THOMAS: Shut your gob or I'll give you a taste of my cobb.

RECRUIT: If you're not quiet I'll give you a ball and chain to play with.

VOICE: *(Off.)* To arms!

THOMAS: Oh Jesus, born for a bullet.

(The lights fade.)

Scene Fifty-five

(In another playing area the lights fade in. SCOTT enters.)

SCOTT: I am filled with grief and shame. In short, I am mortified. I am mortified to be alive. I want to see discipline. Or I will put you in chains and whip you without mercy. Some of you Kentucky boys like to do things ass backwards, in fact you're proud of it. Any man that comes at me ass backwards walks into my July surprise. I'll give you a taste of "old glory." I am War Pig Supreme. I am the revolution incarnate. I got worlds to conquer. People exist to be kicked or kissed. What do men want in life? Nothing, 'cept a good kick in the ass. Kick a man in the ass, he's happy. I kick you into ecstasy. My grand-daddy was killed at Culloden. Any of you Kentucky boys know what that means? That means I got a grudge to settle. And when I'm angry, I'm dirty. When I catch an Englishman, you know what I do? I hang him by his thumbs on a tree branch. Then lean into him and say, "I'm gonna stab you in the belly, gonna stab you in the belly. Watch you die slow. In agony. Gonna stab you in the belly. Gonna stab you in the belly. *(He laughs.)* Gonna stab you in the belly."

(The lights fade.)

Scene Fifty-six

(In another playing area the lights fade in. The RECRUIT enters.)

RECRUIT: Flee, flee, flee! The Yankees have taken Fort Erie!

(The lights fade.)

Scene Fifty-seven

(In another playing area the lights fade in. SECORD and LAURA enter.)

LAURA: This world is full of bastards.

SECORD: Don't start. I just put my sap inside you. Be happy.

LAURA: Full of bastards.

SECORD: Don't start. We got to get out of here. They're rounding people up as if they were stray pigs, and then treating them like idiots, and then throwing red herrings at them.

LAURA: Full of bastards.

SECORD: Don't start.

(The lights fade.)

Scene Fifty-eight

(In another playing area the lights fade in. The RECRUIT and THOMAS enter holding torches.)

THOMAS: Oh look ... ants having a war.

RECRUIT: Ah yes, red ants killing black ants. Black ants killing red ants.

THOMAS: I wonder if they know what they are doing?

RECRUIT: Not a clue. Look. *(He stamps his foot on the ground.)* They think God has arrived.

THOMAS: Now the red ants will win.

(FITZGIBBON enters.)

FITZGIBBON: Corporal, stop lollygagging. Have you found the passage?

RECRUIT: Yes, this is Lundy's farm. A lane is over there.

FITZGIBBON: Good. We will wheel the troops into line. Be quick.

(FITZGIBBON exits.)

THOMAS: What a calamity you have wrought on these poor ants. Berserkness is everywhere. I wonder if they have generals.

(The RECRUIT nods his head.)

RECRUIT: Just like ours.

(The lights fade. During the darkness.)

VOICE ONE: Lundy's Lane is just over here, boys.

VOICE TWO: I can't see a bloody thing.

VOICE THREE: I can't see a bloody thing either.

VOICE FOUR: Me neither.

VOICE FIVE: Who goes there?

VOICE ONE: A friend.

VOICE FIVE: What kind of friend?

VOICE ONE: From the eighty-ninth.

VOICE FOUR: From the eighty-ninth? Who are you?

VOICE TWO: Who are you?

(The lights fade. FITZGIBBON and SCOTT are revealed.)

FITZGIBBON: Yankees.

SCOTT: Brits. Do you surrender?

FITZGIBBON: We're too ignorant to know what the word means.

SCOTT: Do you surrender?

FITZGIBBON: How is the word spelled.

SCOTT: "S "... as in swine, "U" ... as in usurper, "R" ... as in rat, another "R" ... as in—

FITZGIBBON: Hold on, too many letters.

SCOTT: Charge!

(Various BRITISH and AMERICAN TROOPS enter to fight the battle of Lundy's Lane. During the battle LAURA walks through the melee.)

LAURA: Fitzgibbon, have you seen my husband?

FITZGIBBON: He's over there, madam.

(The battle continues. FITZGIBBON kills AMERICAN SOLDIERS. SCOTT kills BRITISH SOLDIERS. FITZGIBBON and SCOTT find each other.)

Well boy-o, it's a bad day for you.

SCOTT: Tarnation. I'm gonna hang you by your thumbs, boy, and stab you in the belly.

(They fight. FITZGIBBON stabs SCOTT.)

Oh, he stabbed me in the belly. He stabbed me in the belly.

(DRUMMOND enters.)

DRUMMOND: There are no more reinforcements. We must give way. Sound the alarm.

SCOTT: Let's get the hell out of here.

(The lights fade.)

Scene Fifty-nine

(In another playing area the lights fade in. DRUMMOND and STRACHAN enter.)

DRUMMOND: We are about to begin the seige of Fort Erie. Chaplain, have you completed that sermon?

STRACHAN: I have. Brave soldiers, love your enemies.

DRUMMOND: No, no, no. We are going into battle. It is going to be bloody, very bloody, very bloody.

STRACHAN: Oh sorry. Ah, I have it. Brave soldiers, kill your enemies, only cowards go to hell.

DRUMMOND: That's more like it.

(STRACHAN exits. FITZGIBBON enters.)

FITZGIBBON: Faggots march. Faggots halt. Sir, all faggots accounted for.

VOICE: *(Off.)* Stop calling me that.

FITZGIBBON: Quiet, fag.

DRUMMOND: Have you put the new recruits through their drill?

FITZGIBBON: I have.

DRUMMOND: Listen. Do you hear it? A little robin singing his beautiful song.

FITZGIBBON: Yes, I think I do.

DRUMMOND: Are you ready for combat?

FITZGIBBON: I got my bayonet.

DRUMMOND: Are the men ready?

FITZGIBBON: Are the men ready?

DRUMMOND: Well, are they?

FITZGIBBON: Scum! Are you ready?

VOICES: *(Off.)* Ready, aye, ready.

DRUMMOND: We will march in full battle formation then rotate to our left and perform a full frontal assault on their cannon, then we will rotate to our right and attack the barricades. Any questions, impressions, opinions? Good. You have your orders.

(DRUMMOND exits.)

FITZGIBBON: That we do. We who are about to rotate, salute you.

(FITZGIBBON salutes. The lights fade.)

Scene Sixty

(In another playing area the lights fade in. FITZGIBBON and the RECRUIT enter.)

FITZGIBBON: Come my brave lads, there are teeth to march into.

(A loud explosion.)

See how they smile.

(Moans and groans from the shadows. The lights fade.)

Scene Sixty-one

(In another playing area the lights fade in. DRUMMOND and FITZGIBBON enter.)

DRUMMOND: Rotate, rotate, rotate!

FITZGIBBON: Sir, do you want me to rotate to my left, or to my right?

DRUMMOND: Full circle.

(DRUMMOND exits. FITZGIBBON rotates full circle.)

FITZGIBBON: What the hell am I doing?

(The lights fade.)

Scene Sixty-two

(In another playing area the lights fade in. DRUMMOND and FITZGIBBON enter.)

DRUMMOND: And what happened to Colonel Shrapnel?

FITZGIBBON: When the bomb burst, so did his body.

DRUMMOND: I always knew the man had guts.

FITZGIBBON: Now everybody knows.

DRUMMOND: Why is your hair standing on end?

FITZGIBBON: No particular reason.

DRUMMOND: Oh, woe is woe. If I could have, if yesterday I could have known what I know now.

FITZGIBBON: Yes.

DRUMMOND: Sound the retreat. We will let winter win this victory for us. And what they abandon, we will take as the spoils.

(The lights fade.)

Scene Sixty-three

(In another playing area the lights fade in. THOMAS and the wounded RECRUIT enter.)

THOMAS: Ah it's a great life. After this war is over I'm heading home. I think I'll form a company and be the head of it.

(The RECRUIT slowly raises his left leg.)

RECRUIT: What is this that rises from the deep and rears a head so ugly it must look to me for comfort? It is my toe. It is still mine.

(The RECRUIT laughs. FITZGIBBON enters.)

FITZGIBBON: How goes it?

RECRUIT: Well. I have lost one foot, but I have another.

FITZGIBBON: And how is Private Thomas?

RECRUIT: He has no arms, no legs.

FITZGIBBON: Has he got a head?

RECRUIT: Yes.

FITZGIBBON: Then he'll eat.

RECRUIT: Hear that head, you'll eat.

FITZGIBBON: Have you heard the news? Napolean has abdicated. Lord Wellington's troops have burned Washington and Baltimore.

RECRUIT: Off. This leg, off.

FITZGIBBON: The geography of this war is changing.

RECRUIT: Off, now.

FITZGIBBON: But old asshole supremo didn't do anything. Marched his troops into Plattsburg, and then marched them back again. Without firing a shot. It's a scandal, a disgrace.

RECRUIT: Off.

FITZGIBBON: God, what would we do without old asshole.

RECRUIT: Off.

FITZGIBBON: You are going to die of your wounds. There is no point.

RECRUIT: Off!

(The lights fade.)

Scene Sixty-four

(In another playing area the lights fade in. PREVOST and DRUMMOND enter.)

PREVOST: How dare you say that to me. I am the commanding officer. I am the governor-general. I am everything. I lead the invasion of the United States. Me, not you, me. Do I make that clear?

DRUMMOND: You are as we used to say in India ... nimmukwallah. You are an absolute nincompoop.

PREVOST: Respect my superiority.

DRUMMOND: I do not suffer superiors gladly unless they are brave, which you are not.

PREVOST: I learned all my lessons on the playing fields of Eton.

DRUMMOND: Watching the cheaters play cricket.

PREVOST: The battle was a near run thing.

DRUMMOND: What battle? You call going on parade a battle.

PREVOST: It was a near run thing.

DRUMMOND: Everything is a near run thing with you. Eating your food, it's a near run thing.

PREVOST: How dare you say that to me.

DRUMMOND: You are going to be court-martialed.

PREVOST: It's all over but the roaring. The war is over.

DRUMMOND: For you, definitely.

(The lights fade.)

Scene Sixty-five

(In another playing area the lights fade in. FITZGIBBON and the RECRUIT enter. The RECRUIT has only one leg.)

FITZGIBBON: Polish my boots. I'm going on parade. Hop to it.

(The RECRUIT polishes FITZGIBBON's boot.)

I could stay in the army and catch farts all my life, or retire on half-pay and be a pillar of society.

RECRUIT: Caterpillar, you mean.

FITZGIBBON: What's the matter boy-o? Did you put it in the sheep shit instead of the sheepskin?

RECRUIT: Can I crack wise?

FITZGIBBON: Go ahead.

RECRUIT: Did General Brock ever ask you to have a bath with him?

FITZGIBBON: No. But once I had the great privilege of seeing him blow his nose on this handkerchief. *(FITZGIBBON holds up the handkerchief.)* My lucky charm.

(FITZGIBBON looks at the handkerchief.)

RECRUIT: Can I touch it?

FITZGIBBON: Just polish my boots, you bacon-faced weasel.

(The lights fade.)

Scene Sixty-six

(In another playing area the lights fade in. SECORD enters holding a bottle.)

SECORD: As I was going up the road I met my sister Ann, I cut her throat and sucked her blood, and let her body stand. Ah, they don't write them like that anymore.

(LAURA enters.)

LAURA: I knew it, shit-faced again.

SECORD: Quiet woman, there's a rumour, the war is over.

LAURA: Only a rumour.

SECORD: Aye, but a good one.

LAURA: I knew it.

SECORD: Quiet or I'll put it out on the table.

LAURA: Go ahead, and I'll get my rolling pin and roll it out good. I thought you gave up the grape.

SECORD: So did I. But my misfortune began when I spied a full bottle with no cork. It started with a whiff, that gave rise to a snort, that lead to a drink, that gave way to a guzzle. And here I am.

LAURA: Shit-faced.

SECORD: Completely. As I was going up the road I met my …

(The lights fade.)

Scene Sixty-seven

(In another playing area the lights fade in. The PROPHET enters holding a bottle.)

PROPHET: Magic Oki live inside this bottle. In peace time sons bury their fathers. In time of war fathers bury their sons. I will fight no more. *(He looks inside the bottle.)* Remember me.

(The lights fade.)

Scene Sixty-eight

(In another playing area the lights fade in. ROBINSON, DRUMMOND, and STRACHAN enter.)

ROBINSON, DRUMMOND, and STRACHAN: The war is over!

ROBINSON: The news is glorious.

STRACHAN: Yes, the headlines are excellent.

DRUMMOND: And the details are superb. Feast.

(DRUMMOND gives the peace treaty to STRACHAN.)

STRACHAN: Gentlemen, nothing has changed. Everything is as it was. Are these not glorious words?

DRUMMOND: Keep massaging our ears.

STRACHAN: Let us hope the treaties they sign with us are more honourable than the ones they sign with the Indians.

DRUMMOND: Oh for sure, it will be.

STRACHAN: The Americans have annexed the Indian Territories of Michigan, Illinois, and Ohio. They will not want our land.

DRUMMOND: Yes, and now with our borders safely defined we will rule this wilderness with an iron fist.

STRACHAN: And woe to the man who becomes a scab on the body politic.

ROBINSON: Here, here.

STRACHAN: From this day forth we say to hell with democracy. This country will grow, and one day become a truly great colony. Let us drink a toast. To the British flag, to the Bitish king, to the British way.

ROBINSON: Here, here.

STRACHAN: Gentlemen, to the war.

ROBINSON and DRUMMOND: To the war!

(They drink. The lights fade. The end.)

THE MACKENZIE-PAPINEAU REBELLION

PART THREE OF THE HISTORY OF THE VILLAGE OF THE SMALL HUTS

Act One

Scene One

(Two playing areas: stage right is Upper Canada; stage left is Lower Canada. The lights fade in stage right.)

VOICE: *(Off.)* His Excellency, the lieutenant-governor of Upper Canada, Sir John Colborne entering the room.

(SIR JOHN COLBORNE enters. The lights fade in stage left.)

His Excellency, the lieutenant-governor of Lower Canada, The Earl of Gosford entering the room.

(The EARL OF GOSFORD enters.)

COLBORNE: I am tyrant here.

GOSFORD: I know what is best.

COLBORNE: In this country only brutes go to Parliament.

GOSFORD: Parliament is proof that democracy is government by morons for idiots.

COLBORNE: Representatives of the mob are too stupid and vicious to make decisions about anything.

GOSFORD: Let alone how they want to be governed.

COLBORNE: The mob.

GOSFORD: The mob is a mass of insane depravity.

COLBORNE: A midden of lusts, vanities, unwholesome thoughts …

GOSFORD: … perversions, lies, envies, jealousies, cruelties …

COLBORNE: … stupidities, and this mass of berserk immorality …

GOSFORD: … is asked to choose a leader.

COLBORNE: It is the stuff that nightmares are made of.

GOSFORD: And they always choose the wrong person.

COLBORNE: They elect monsters to lead them.

GOSFORD: I hate the mob.

COLBORNE: I am tyrant here.

GOSFORD: I know what is best.

(The lights fade.)

Scene Two

(In other playing areas the lights fade in. WILLIAM LYON MACKENZIE and LOUIS-JOSEPH PAPINEAU enter.)

MACKENZIE: I am William Lyon Mackenzie. I exist to defy tyrants.

PAPINEAU: I am Papineau, the orator. The great orator.

MACKENZIE: Read your *Colonial Advocate.* These are our grievances. Top of the list: The Family Compact.

PAPINEAU: This government is a stench in my nostril. Acadia, America, Ireland, Canada. England will be judged on those four words.

MACKENZIE: The Family Compact control everything in this colony, everything.

PAPINEAU: The English say we are in defiance of their rule. We are in defence of our rights.

MACKENZIE: We demand electoral reform.

PAPINEAU: Defence not defiance.

MACKENZIE: And I say to you in this election.

Don't vote tory, they cannot be held accountable. Vote reform.

PAPINEAU: Agitate, agitate, agitate.

(The lights fade.)

Scene Three

(In another playing area the lights fade in. SAM LOUNT and ANTHONY ANDERSON enter.)

ANDERSON: Well let me tell you what you'll find in York: mud, mosquitoes, and snobs. Snobs for no reason which is intolerable. That's what you'll find in York.

LOUNT: I hear old MacDonald lost his farm to the Canada Company.

ANDERSON: I don't doubt it. The mean-spirited, shit-faced bastards.

LOUNT: There is no hope.

ANDERSON: No hope, no hope.

(Noises offstage.)

MACKENZIE: *(Off.)* Whoa Nellie, whoa. Sugar and new shoes for you.

(MACKENZIE enters.)

MACKENZIE: Are you a blacksmith?

LOUNT: Is the king of England a German?

MACKENZIE: Ah good. My horse has—

LOUNT: Ah yes, I see you riding this way, I see you riding that way.

MACKENZIE: The name's—

LOUNT: I know who you are. The name's Lount, but call me Sam.

ANDERSON: And my name's Anthony, but you can call me Mr. Anderson.

MACKENZIE: Well Sam, Mr. Anderson. What do you think of the Family Compact?

ANDERSON: Is it bigger than a snuff box?

MACKENZIE: No, it only seems that way. Read this.

(MACKENZIE holds up a newspaper.)

LOUNT: "Down with Parson Strachan."

ANDERSON: "To Hell with the Family Compact."

LOUNT: Now that's what I call a headline.

(The lights fade.)

Scene Four

(In another playing area the lights fade in. IGNACE BOURGET, PIERRE, and JEAN-OLIVIER CHENIER enter.)

BOURGET: Feast and multiply. You there, fornicator. When you make babies, who is watching?

PIERRE: Jesus.

BOURGET: That's right. And while he is watching, what is he doing?

PIERRE: Smiling.

BOURGET: That's right. And why is he smiling?

PIERRE: Because he loves us.

BOURGET: That's right. You there, Jean, fornicator and tête de cochon. When you and your wife make noises that you thought were not humanly possible, who is watching?

CHENIER: Jesus. He pulls up the roof and has a peek.

BOURGET: That's right. And while he is watching, what is he doing?

CHENIER: He's pulling himself good.

BOURGET: You fornicator.

CHENIER: Jesus pulls for everybody. He loves us so much.

BOURGET: You fornicator.

(The lights fade.)

Scene Five

(In another playing area the lights fade in. MACKENZIE and CHARLES FRENCH enter.)

MACKENZIE: Apprentice. I pay you two shillings a week, do I not?

FRENCH: That you do.

MACKENZIE: I expect an honest day's work for my money. I think you're dogging it, and if you dog it much longer you'll take it like a dog. Do I make myself clear? *(He snorts.)* Typeset this.

(MACKENZIE gives FRENCH a piece of paper.)

FRENCH: Oh, Mr. Mackenzie, if you print this, it will be a hot time in the old shithouse tonight.

MACKENZIE: That's right. It's going up in chunks.

(The lights fade.)

Scene Six

(In another playing area the lights fade in. PAPINEAU enters.)

PAPINEAU: I can conform to this society and feel like a wretched failure, or I can change society and be the man that I am. Man is naturally good, society is naturally evil, and yet man cannot exist without society, therefore man is naturally evil. Society is the original sin.

(PIERRE enters.)

What do you want? Get out.

PIERRE: Oh High and Mighty Lord. I come to pay homage. Please accept my humble—

PAPINEAU: Yes, yes.

PIERRE: My grandfather served your grandfather, my father served your father, and I serve you.

PAPINEAU: Yes, yes.

PIERRE: I will continue to fish in your rivers, harvest your lands, cut your meat.

PAPINEAU: Yes, yes.

PIERRE: Is there anything more I can do for you?

PAPINEAU: Yes, get out. No, stay. Polish my shoe.

(PIERRE starts to polish PAPINEAU's shoe.)

PIERRE: Aristotle says that some are born for slavery and others for dominion.

PAPINEAU: And he was correct in that those born *in* slavery are born *for* slavery, and slaves in bondage lose everything, even the desire to escape from their bondage. That's enough.

PIERRE: Thank you, High and Mighty Lord.

(LOUIS LAFONTAINE enters.)

LAFONTAINE: Who is this person?

PAPINEAU: This is my slave. Out, slave. Monsieur Lafontaine, the social contract as it stands is such that the English say "I make an agreement with you entirely at your expense and entirely for my benefit, and I shall observe it as long as I please."

LAFONTAINE: Yes, that is the situation, yes.

PAPINEAU: Well that is going to change. There is a difference between subduing a multitude and ruling a society.

LAFONTAINE: Yes, there is.

PAPINEAU: Well, I believe in the "just society."

LAFONTAINE: So do I.

PAPINEAU: And so will we all.

(The lights fade.)

Scene Seven

(In another playing area the lights fade in. MACKENZIE enters.)

MACKENZIE: The Family Compact is a beast from the dark ages. A primeval monster. Cut off the head of the hideous father, and its son will rear its repulsive face. Destroy that ghastly visage and you have the gruesome appearance of its brother. How do you slay such a brute? Easy, you stab it in the heart. But this grotesque monstrosity has no heart. Instead it has a money bag that beats and thumps like thunder. And the heartstrings of this bag are held by the appointed advisors to the governor. They must be replaced by elected representatives. They must be held accountable to the people.

(JOHN STRACHAN enters.)

MACKENZIE: Well look who it is. Parson Strachan. *(Pronouncing it "Strackan.")*

STRACHAN: Strachan. *(Pronouncing it "Strawn.")* You'll never be a gentleman.

MACKENZIE: Aye, but I'll be an honest man. And one honest man is worth more than all the crowned hoodlums—

STRACHAN: You're a strunting Yankee.

MACKENZIE: And you're a strutting parrot. The Family Compact is a vile nest of unclean birds.

STRACHAN: Print that and see what happens. I dare you.

(The lights fade.)

Scene Eight

(In another playing area the lights fade in. PAPINEAU, LAFONTAINE, and CHARLES BONTEMPS enter.)

BONTEMPS: Hey Louis, it is I, Charles Bontemps, seigneur and bon vivant, and your best friend, in this room with you. Cognac for your best friend.

PAPINEAU: Garçon. Fetch.

(LAFONTAINE gets the cognac.)

I hear your wife—

BONTEMPS: Ah, my wife. She sleeps here, she sleeps there. Do I care? I don't care. The other seigneurs can have her.

PAPINEAU: That's good to know.

BONTEMPS: Because on my seigneury I have seigneur's rights. The daughters of my censitaires run fast, but not fast enough. This old goat is unstoppable. And who is your little friend?

PAPINEAU: This is Monsieur Lafontaine.

BONTEMPS: Enchanté, monsieur. Do you have a sister?

PAPINEAU: She looks just like him.

BONTEMPS: You should introduce me to her.

LAFONTAINE: Here, pour it yourself.

(LAFONTAINE exits.)

BONTEMPS: What? Come back.

PAPINEAU: Forget him. You say no to cognac, you say no to life. Drink.

(BONTEMPS and PAPINEAU drink. The lights fade.)

Scene Nine

(In another playing area the lights fade in. MACNAB, JOHN ROBINSON, and STRACHAN enter.)

STRACHAN: When I first came here I was a Presbyterian. But I didn't cross the ocean to suck my thumb. So I became an Anglican. I think God is terrific. He helps those who help themselves. What the church don't own, I own. I am no penny pincher. The Clergy Reserves are for the Church of England. I don't care what anyone says. The Methodists can go holy roll themselves to hell. Whatever I believe is right. And who is there to disagree?

ROBINSON: Governor Colborne.

STRACHAN: In this world all swans are white. Our governor, like the others before him, will see things clearly, or I'll be bound.

MACNAB: I'm going to make a big hat with the name MacNab on it, so everybody will know who I am. Pig my sow is all I'm going to say, pig my sow.

(COLBORNE enters.)

COLBORNE: My order of superiority is not being respected in this room.

ROBINSON: Oh terribly sorry.

COLBORNE: Accepted. I insist on proper protocol.

STRACHAN: Very well.

(ROBINSON, STRACHAN, and MACNAB bow.)

COLBORNE: The British Empire demands sacrifice and discipline. I, of course, have made the supreme sacrifice. This arm is a piece of wood. Lost it in the Pensular Campaign in Spain with Wellington.

ROBINSON: Tell us about Waterloo again.

COLBORNE: Waterloo, Waterloo. A momentous battle.

ROBINSON: You are too modest.

COLBORNE: I will never forget the sound of the horses. My calvary routed Napoleon's Imperial Guard. I was awarded honours by everyone. In this world you earn the accolade of scum.

STRACHAN: The curses also.

(JUNIOR enters holding a newspaper.)

JUNIOR: Aaaaaagh! Read this.

ROBINSON: It's that detestable cur, Mackenzie again.

STRACHAN: He's called us a "Vile nest of unclean birds." Oh his destruction is to be devoutly prayed for.

ROBINSON: And his printing press.

STRACHAN: Mackenzie's out of town.

COLBORNE: What they need is a good taste of the lash.

STRACHAN: He is a rabble rouser of the first order, a foul-mouthed low life, I hate him profoundly. Who will remove this pebble from my shoe?

JUNIOR: Sir.

(The lights fade.)

Scene Ten

(In another playing area the lights fade in. PAPINEAU enters.)

PAPINEAU: I grasp nothing and yet see everything. I live a life of self-adulation. It is not enough. We will be master in our own house.

(MADAME PAPINEAU enters.)

MME PAPINEAU: Infamata, you should have been a priest.

PAPINEAU: Mother please.

MME PAPINEAU: Bringing you into this world broke my body. Watching you grow broke my heart. Infamata. Do you remember when you were a boy, I used to beat you.

PAPINEAU: I remember.

MME PAPINEAU: The memory of New France is burning in my loins. Burning. Confess your sins, sinner.

PAPINEAU: With each beating I loved you more.

MME PAPINEAU: You will receive no mercy from me, sinner.

PAPINEAU: When I was a youth, a single castle was the limit of my ambition. But now I want more.

MME PAPINEAU: Kiss this ring, sinner.

PAPINEAU: Oh mother, oh mother.

(LAFONTAINE enters.)

LAFONTAINE: I hope I am not interrupting. Madame, my deepest respect. I am like a blade of grass and you are like the sun.

MME PAPINEAU: Beware of this one Louis, beware of this one.

LAFONTAINE: Your mother is quite the—

PAPINEAU: Great woman.

LAFONTAINE: Yes.

PAPINEAU: What do you want?

LAFONTAINE: The governor has agreed to see us, at last.

PAPINEAU: Come, let us go up the mountain. It is from mountain tops that one sees things clearly.

MME PAPINEAU: Carry a cross.

(The lights fade.)

Scene Eleven

(In another playing area the lights fade in. MRS MACKENZIE enters knitting.)

MRS MACKENZIE: Oh I glory in doing a yard and a half a day. Just glory in it.

(Noises offstage. FRENCH enters.)

FRENCH: Oh Mother Mackenzie, your son's printing press, they're destroying it.

MRS MACKENZIE: Stop them.

(FRENCH exits.)

You're a bunch of savages.

(JUNIOR enters.)

JUNIOR: We are the sons of nobility.

MRS MACKENZIE: You're a bunch of louts.

JUNIOR: Quiet you belligerent bitch or we'll piss in your mouth.

MRS MACKENZIE: Hoodlums and bullies. I'll take my broom and sweep you into the ditch. You pieces of dirt.

JUNIOR: Let's throw it in the river.

MRS MACKENZIE: You mean the lake, don't you?

JUNIOR: That's right, the lake.

MRS MACKENZIE: You morons, you idiots.

JUNIOR: Down to the lake.

(The lights fade.)

Scene Twelve

(In another playing area the lights fade in. MACKENZIE, MRS MACKENZIE, and FRENCH enter.)

MRS MACKENZIE: And they threw it into the lake. Little Johnny here tried to stop them but he's awful wee and they broke his head.

FRENCH: They broke my head.

MACKENZIE: They'll pay, the bastards, they'll pay, they'll pay.

(The lights fade.)

Scene Thirteen

(In another playing area the lights fade in. JAMES FITZGIBBON, STRACHAN, ROBINSON, and JUNIOR enter.)

FITZGIBBON: The court has found your sons guilty of destroying Mackenzie's press.

STRACHAN: I want the judge removed.

ROBINSON: He will be.

FITZGIBBON: You have to pay the fine. *(He holds up a money bag.)* I have solicited donations.

STRACHAN: This is like giving money to the devil.

JUNIOR: Oh Dad, are they going to put me in jail, oh Dad.

ROBINSON: We'll keep our fine young men out of jail.

(ROBINSON and STRACHAN put money in the bag. The lights fade.)

Scene Fourteen

(In another playing area the lights fade in. MACKENZIE and LOUNT enter. MACKENZIE holds up the money bag.)

LOUNT: To William Lyon Mackenzie. Six hundred and twenty-five pounds. Woo-hoo!

MACKENZIE: Aye, we're going to twirl their curlies good. And here's our chief witness.

(A cheer. FRENCH steps forward.)

Three cheers for Charles French.

(They cheer. In another playing area the lights fade in. ROBINSON and POWNALL, the bully, enter.)

ROBINSON: See that man. I want you to fix him good.

POWNALL: With my tongs?

(POWNALL holds up his tongs.)

ROBINSON: Yes, with your tongs.

(FRENCH holds up a bottle.)

FRENCH: I feel like I have actually done something.

MACKENZIE: You have.

ROBINSON: You have.

(The lights fade.)

Scene Fifteen

(In another playing area the lights fade in. GOSFORD, PAPINEAU, and LAFONTAINE enter.)

GOSFORD: As a member of the elected Assembly—

PAPINEAU: As Speaker of the Assembly.

GOSFORD: Whatever. You have no power to make laws but you can give forth advice.

PAPINEAU: Then stand back. I am about to give forth. Since the beginning you have tried to destroy us. You interfere with our quality of life. A little clique—

GOSFORD: Château Clique, I believe, is the term you use behind my back.

PAPINEAU: Château Clique is the term I use to your face. A small group of Englishmen and insanely afraid collaborators control all business.

LAFONTAINE: French Canadien businessmen are excluded from the joys of exploitation.

PAPINEAU: Quiet puppy. Instead we are exploited. The constitution of Lower Canada gives equal rights to French and English subjects. We outnumber the English ten to one.

GOSFORD: This place was conquered by British arms, is ruled by a British king, and governed by British men. All stout and true. We are trying to create an aristocracy here. You don't fit in, it's that simple.

LAFONTAINE: We are like insects.

PAPINEAU: The British governor is so happy with the way we live he wants us to stop reproducing ourselves.

GOSFORD: Correct.

PAPINEAU: Such arrogance. You will regret that. The treasury will become fat. No bills will be paid. The taxes of the habitants will not support you and your Château Clique. You can go to hell.

(The lights fade.)

Scene Sixteen

(In another playing area the lights fade in. MACKENZIE and MRS MACKENZIE enter.)

MRS MACKENZIE: Oh the fairies are singing

tonight, tonight. The fairies are singing tonight.

MACKENZIE: Mother that's enough.

(A gunshot, offstage.)

Thundering lizards, is there no peace in this village?

(FRENCH enters.)

FRENCH: I just shot a man, he was trying to kill me with his tongs.

(The SHERIFF enters.)

SHERIFF: All right laddie, you're under arrest for murder. I got my bullwhip. Make a move if you want a taste.

MACKENZIE: Thundering lizards.

(The lights fade.)

Scene Seventeen

(In another playing area the lights fade in. ROBINSON enters.)

ROBINSON: Has the jury reached a verdict?

VOICE: *(Off.)* We have your honour. We find the defendant not guilty.

(In another playing area the lights fade in. FRENCH and MACKENZIE celebrate.)

ROBINSON: I find that verdict completely unacceptable. I find the defendant guilty of murder. I sentence you to be hanged by the neck until dead, after which you will be drawn and quartered.

FRENCH: Well Mr. Mackenzie. I came to the new world to find riotous living. It looks like I found it.

MACKENZIE: So the game heats up. Well to hell with them Charlie. I'm going to run for Parliament.

(The lights fade.)

Scene Eighteen

(In another playing area the lights fade in. PAPINEAU and LAFONTAINE enter.)

PAPINEAU: I believe we can change the political system without changing the social structure.

LAFONTAINE: What kind of revolution is that?

PAPINEAU: Our revolution will be conducted with the blessing of the church, otherwise everything we do will be for the benefit of the English.

LAFONTAINE: If we wait for the blessing of the church we will have beards down to our knees.

PAPINEAU: We will make the Republic. A republic of landowners.

LAFONTAINE: You are like the old regime, before the English.

PAPINEAU: Is that not preferable to the English?

LAFONTAINE: Anything is preferable to the English.

PAPINEAU: The clergy and the seigneurs will save the country.

LAFONTAINE: Enslave the country is more like it.

PAPINEAU: You must resign yourself to the inconvenience.

(The lights fade.)

Scene Nineteen

(In another playing area the lights fade in. MACKENZIE and MRS MACKENZIE enter.)

MACKENZIE: We came to this country in steerage. Steerage. Have you any idea what that is like? Squashed like a sardine in a rat-infested, slimy floating hole somewhere in the ocean. Constantly squished by horrible foul-mouthed smelly people, and their barfing babies, and the swearing sailors, and the crying mothers, and in the middle of that, a man, a crazy man, completely deranged would play the bagpipes.

(MRS MACKENZIE mimics the sound of bagpipes.)

And the creatures would dance, every shape and size imaginable would flit and flart, and the man on the pipes.

(MRS MACKENZIE mimics the sound of bagpipes.)

And the wind would howl, the ship would roll, and the waves beat like thunder, and the people would scream, and a maniac would shriek the last rites, and then the storm would stop and there would be silence. And then …

(MRS MACKENZIE mimics the sound of bagpipes.)

And it would begin again. It went on for seven weeks. It almost drove me mad.

(The lights fade.)

Scene Twenty

(In another playing area the lights fade in. PAPINEAU, LAFONTAINE, GOSFORD, MOFFAT, and BOURGET enter.)

GOSFORD: How dare you say that to me. I am an aristocrat.

LAFONTAINE: Our governor considers himself an aristocrat.

PAPINEAU: That means he will do anything to maintain his right to be a congenital idiot.

LAFONTAINE: Anything ... murder, fraud.

PAPINEAU: The dictionary of the crimes of man begins with "A." "A" for aristocrat.

GOSFORD: What's your game, ducky, what's your game?

MOFFAT: Off to putney on a pig are you?

GOSFORD: The king can do no wrong.

PAPINEAU: Neither can an idiot or an insane person.

LAFONTAINE: Government has the right to exist only by the consent of the governed.

MOFFAT: To be Frenchified is a fate worse than death.

GOSFORD: This is Canada, and we do not speak French in Montréal or Quebec.

LAFONTAINE: Non, you do not speak French in Montréal or Quebec.

MOFFAT: You are a conquered people, speak English.

PAPINEAU: If the conquered people speak the language of the conqueror, why don't the English speak the language of William the Conqueror?

GOSFORD: It's completely different.

LAFONTAINE: Is it? As Canadiens we are deemed aliens in our own country.

MOFFAT: This is not a country, this is a colony.

PAPINEAU: La Nation Canadienne.

GOSFORD: Must be crushed.

LAFONTAINE: We are superior to the English in every way.

PAPINEAU: In the way we dress.

LAFONTAINE: In the way we cook our food.

PAPINEAU: In the way we walk.

LAFONTAINE: In the way we copulate.

PAPINEAU: You sneer, ask any woman.

MOFFAT: I'm ready for a civil war.

PAPINEAU: Écoute, monsieur.

GOSFORD: How dare you use those words, Mr. Papineau.

PAPINEAU: Monsieur, s'il vous plâit.

GOSFORD: I will make this one concession for the sake of civility. It is my way, or it is the doorway.

PAPINEAU: I know you have a brain as big as a pea, but—

MOFFAT: I'm ready for a civil war.

PAPINEAU: And so are we, mon ami, so are we.

(The lights fade.)

Scene Twenty-one

(In another playing area the lights fade in. ROBERT BALDWIN and JOHN ROLPH enter.)

ROLPH: I understand you are running for election in York.

BALDWIN: Correct. I am putting my honour to the test.

ROLPH: Good luck. He who receives the laurels will be lucky.

BALDWIN: He who receives the laurels will be honourable. My father is the most honourable man in the world.

ROLPH: And you are his worthy son, the Honourable Robert Baldwin. And one day you will be the Right-honourable.

BALDWIN: Perhaps, but not if my honour is impugned. Anyone who impugns my honour commits a crime against humanity. Not only must it not be impugned, it must not seem to be impugned. Never forget that, Mr. Rolph.

ROLPH: Call me John.

BALDWIN: I would never presume such familiarity.

ROLPH: We've known each other for ten years, we are law partners.

BALDWIN: Mr. Rolph, in my eyes your honour is suspect.

ROLPH: What?

BALDWIN: The Family Compact are ugly trolls and Mackenzie is the hobgoblin of Upper Canada, and you speak with both sides.

ROLPH: But not with affection.

BALDWIN: It is dishonourable. I love you as much as I love my cousin, but your association with them indirectly associates me with them, and that impugns my honour.

ROLPH: I am terribly sorry.

BALDWIN: Very well, I forgive you, if you cease and desist.

ROLPH: I will.

BALDWIN: Kiss this cheek, shake this hand, now turn around and walk out that door.

(ROLPH exits. The lights fade.)

Scene Twenty-two

(In another playing area the lights fade in. ANDERSON, DUNCAN ALLEN, ROLPH, and STRACHAN enter.)

STRACHAN: Now who ya voting for, Dunc?

ANDERSON: Ya gotta vote Mackenzie.

STRACHAN: Here's a few shillings for the wife.

ROLPH: Listen closely to the Honourable Doctor Robert.

(LOUNT enters.)

LOUNT: Quiet, you hogwallows, quiet. This is the Candidates' Debate.

(MACKENZIE, BALDWIN, and ROBINSON enter.)

MACKENZIE: We will have no Family Compacters here. Go home. Your daughter is having her fudge compacted by an Irishman. Go home and watch.

ROBINSON: Disgraceful.

STRACHAN: For shame.

MACKENZIE: Friend of pig, out.

STRACHAN: It's a free country.

(ROBINSON exits.)

LOUNT: Mr. Mackenzie will speak first.

MACKENZIE: My honourable friend, willing.

BALDWIN: Of course, speak first.

MACKENZIE: This is my black list. Top of the list: Robert Baldwin.

BALDWIN: I have never …

MACKENZIE: He is not a true reformer. Vote for him and you vote for the Family Compact.

BALDWIN: I have never in my life.

MACKENZIE: He married his cousin.

BALDWIN: This is outrageous.

MACKENZIE: Act like you got a pair or go home and count your money.

BALDWIN: Disgraceful.

MACKENZIE: Those hands been counting money all their life.

BALDWIN: This is beneath contempt. Goodbye.

(BALDWIN exits.)

MACKENZIE: Who ya voting for?

ANDERSON: Mackenzie.

MACKENZIE: Damn right you are. Do you like being the Family Compact's bumfodder? Answer me straight. You like it?

ALLEN: I never thought about it actually.

MACKENZIE: Well think about it. What's your name?

STRACHAN: Don't tell him.

ALLEN: I don't know.

MACKENZIE: I think you're lying, but I'll try you again. Who was your father?

STRACHAN: Don't tell him.

ALLEN: I don't know.

MACKENZIE: Now you're telling the truth, you bastard. You been smelling big cheesers all your life and now you think it's air. It's not. Wake up. I have it on good authority that the Family Compact fornicate with farm animals. What do you think of that?

ALLEN: Never thought about it actually.

MACKENZIE: Well think about it. And while you're thinking about it. Vote for Mackenzie, you bastard.

STRACHAN: A radical dog.

MACKENZIE: Upstart choir boy.

STRACHAN: Filthy liar.

MACKENZIE: Tory pig. Dirty son of a bitch.

STRACHAN: Dirty son of a bitch.

(MACKENZIE baas like a sheep, STRACHAN barks like a dog. The lights fade.)

Scene Twenty-three

(In another playing area the lights fade in. LAFONTAINE, BONTEMPS, and BOURGET enter.)

LAFONTAINE: Priest and vendu, I salute you. Monsieur Papineau feels it is important that we become good friends.

BONTEMPS: Your eyes are too close together. We can never be friends.

BOURGET: God thinks you are in league with the devil.

LAFONTAINE: He told you this personally.

BONTEMPS: Are you loyal to the king of England?

LAFONTAINE: Kings drink blood from human skulls. I exist to drink blood from the skulls of kings.

BOURGET: It is better to have no opinion than a bad one. Tête de cochon.

LAFONTAINE: Bow down to your idols when you say that, priest.

BOURGET: You fornicator.

LAFONTAINE: The fables of hell exist only in your mind, priest. I am not interested in the feeble-minded superstitions of ignorant people. I am going to eat mush from the skull of your grandmother, vendu.

(PAPINEAU enters.)

PAPINEAU: Ah gentlemen, I see you are becoming acquainted.

BOURGET: Your protégé, dear cousin, is vile and vicious.

PAPINEAU: You must respect this man.

LAFONTAINE: Non.

PAPINEAU: You must listen to this man.

BOURGET: Never.

LAFONTAINE: The revolution is like God. It is everywhere without being anywhere. First the revolution, then the Republic.

PAPINEAU: Non, first the Republic, then the revolution. We are all patriotes.

LAFONTAINE: A patriote is a man who will kill for the Republic.

PAPINEAU: Non, a patriote is a man who will defend his country.

BOURGET: And the church?

PAPINEAU: And the church.

BONTEMPS: And seigneurs' rights too?

PAPINEAU: And seigneurs' rights too.

BOURGET: Do you believe in God?

LAFONTAINE: Give me Greek gods. I believe in gods that copulate and fart. That is something I can believe in.

(LAFONTAINE exits.)

PAPINEAU: He is young, but he is learning.

BOURGET: Your little friend disgusts me. He has come straight from the anus of the devil. I am going to inform my mother.

PAPINEAU: Non, don't do that. She will inform my mother.

BOURGET: I will pray for your soul, Louis.

(BOURGET exits.)

PAPINEAU: And Charles, what do you think?

BONTEMPS: Your little friend disgusts me. He has no respect. If he is your friend, we cannot be friends.

PAPINEAU: But.

BONTEMPS: Au revoir, Louis.

(BONTEMPS exits.)

PAPINEAU: Sacre bleu. What am I going to do now?

(The lights fade.)

Scene Twenty-four

(In another playing area the lights fade in. STRACHAN and MACKENZIE enter. They stand in the shadows. ALLEN enters holding a club.)

ALLEN: My name is Duncan Allen.

STRACHAN: Who ya voting for, Dunc?

ALLEN: I am going to vote and I have this club.

STRACHAN: All right Dunc, who ya voting for?

ALLEN: I vote for Mr. Mackenzie.

STRACHAN: You Yankee-loving traitor bastard. You piece of—

(ALLEN steps forward and brandishes the club.)

ALLEN: Get away from me, I've just voted.

(ALLEN exits. ROBINSON enters.)

ROBINSON: My name is John Beverley Robinson. On this day I am going to vote, and I have this club.

MACKENZIE: Stick it up your ass sideways, you tory-loving bastard.

ROBINSON: I vote tory.

MACKENZIE: Ram it up.

(The lights fade.)

Scene Twenty-five

(In another playing area the lights fade in. MACKENZIE enters being carried by LOUNT and ANDERSON.)

LOUNT: A great victory, a great victory.

MACKENZIE: Boys, lads, it's going to be a hot time in the old Assembly House tonight.

(LOUNT and ANDERSON cheer.)

To hell with the Family Compact!

(The lights fade.)

Scene Twenty-six

(In another playing area the lights fade in. CHENIER and PIERRE enter.)

CHENIER: To the St. Jean-Baptiste Society. And all things French.

PIERRE: To Fraternity.

CHENIER: Liberty.

PIERRE: Equality.

CHENIER: For seventy-five years we hide underground. In our own country, we hide underground. And now there is no place to hide.

PIERRE: The English are trying to destroy us. We need action.

CHENIER: That's right. The English life in this country is like a great fancy dance at the governor's Château. Is your life like that?

PIERRE: No, it is like a wrestling match in the shithouse.

CHENIER: That's right. I have been arrested and thrown in the jug three times for contempt, sedition. Do I care? I don't care.

(PAPINEAU enters wearing the Étoffe de Pays.)

PAPINEAU: Patriotes, we must have order. We must organize, we must agitate. Citizens, we will no longer wear English homespun. We will dress like this, wearing the Étoffe de Pays.

PIERRE: Everyone's going to dress like me.

PAPINEAU: That's right. How do I look?

PIERRE: You look like a farmer.

PAPINEAU: Good. Our uniform. Patriotes. America, Acadia, Ireland, Canada. England will be judged on those four words.

(PIERRE and CHENIER applaud.)

In the beginning this island was called Hochelaga.

PIERRE: My great grandfather was with Maisonneuve. He will agree with this man.

PAPINEAU: Pierre, please. We took it from the Iroquois.

CHENIER: With the gun.

PAPINEAU: And called it Montréal.

CHENIER: That's right.

PIERRE: That's right.

PAPINEAU: The English took it from us.

CHENIER: With the gun.

PAPINEAU: Jean, please. But not fair and square.

PIERRE: Non.

PAPINEAU: We will win it back.

CHENIER: With the gun.

PAPINEAU: Non, with reason, with logic.

CHENIER: It will come to blows or it will come to nothing.

PAPINEAU: The time for speeches is over. There is no turning back. Let joy reign supreme. The revolution begins. Now, let's sing our song.

(PAPINEAU begins to sing the "Marseillaise".)

Sing.

(The lights fade.)

Scene Twenty-seven

(In another playing area the lights fade in. STRACHAN enters.)

STRACHAN: Now you louts, pay attention. When I am speaking, you are listening. His Lordship, John Colborne, the war hero, is coming to supper. You are going to learn some manners, or I'll be bound. First, don't tuck your napkin under your chin, put it on your lap. And eat from the side of the spoon, not the end. It's too awkward. No gurgling when eating soup. Don't bite your bread off, break it off. And don't eat food off the point of a knife. All of you will be like your fathers. *(He brandishes a strap.)* Without exception. You are being groomed to be a member of the ruling class. Now, you will pick up that slice of lemon in front of you, and proceed to suck that lemon dry without wincing, like so.

(STRACHAN puts a slice of lemon in his mouth and sucks. The lights fade.)

Scene Twenty-eight

(In another playing area the lights fade in. STRACHAN, ROBINSON, MACNAB, FITZGIBBON, MACKENZIE, LOUNT, and ANDERSON enter.)

ROBINSON: Order, order. The House recognizes the Honourable Member from York.

MACKENZIE: Mr. Speaker, does the House know that election officials can be bribed? Why are government contractors making so much money building the Welland Canal? Why is the best land kept idle for the Clergy Reserves?

STRACHAN: For shame, for shame.

MACKENZIE: Exactly. I demand electoral reform. The majority of this House represents twenty per cent of the population. *(He points a finger at MACNAB.)* That honourable member there, was elected by thirty votes, I was elected by over a thousand voters and yet his thirty voters have one representative equal to the one thousand in York.

ROBINSON: The honourable member represents a larger area than you.

MACKENZIE: That is not populated by people. Whom is he representing? Bullfrogs, trees?

ROBINSON: The member from York is out of order.

MACKENZIE: I demand electoral reform.

STRACHAN: Oh he is black magic. Turn him out. To hell with the law. Turn him out I say.

(The lights fade.)

Scene Twenty-nine

(In another playing area the lights fade in. MACKENZIE enters holding a book.)

MACKENZIE: I have been elected five times. And each time expelled from the legislature. There is no truth in this colony. One cannot speak the injustice that is everywhere. There is no hope. But we'll give it one more try. This book of grievances. I'm going to send them to England.

(The lights fade.)

Scene Thirty

(In another playing area the lights fade in. STRACHAN, ROBINSON, and COLBORNE enter.)

COLBORNE: Now Famillians, gather 'round. As you well know I am leaving my post as lieutenant-governor of Upper Canada to become military commander of Lower Canada.

(STRACHAN and ROBINSON applaud.)

Thank you. Rebellion and treason is in the air, but this hand holds the sword. As my replacement, I give you, Sir Francis Bondhead.

(SIR FRANCIS BONDHEAD enters.)

BONDHEAD: Good evening, good evening, good evening.

STRACHAN: Oh, Your Lordship.

ROBINSON: Your Excellency.

STRACHAN: Your Worship.

ROBINSON: Your Majesty.

COLBORNE: Goodbye.

(No one takes any notice of COLBORNE.)

BONDHEAD: Very good, stop. You must obey all my commands. Stand up and smile. I am going to inspect you. You elegant smelly people. I think I am going to like you.

(ROBINSON and STRACHAN line up. MACNAB enters.)

BONDHEAD: And who are you?

MACNAB: The name's MacNab.

BONDHEAD: I think I fancy you.

(The lights fade.)

Scene Thirty-one

(In another playing area the lights fade in. LAFONTAINE and PAPINEAU enter.)

LAFONTAINE: What do we do if the English make us take a loyalty oath?

PAPINEAU: When the oath is a crime, perjury is a virtue.

(GOSFORD and COLBORNE enter.)

GOSFORD: Attention, attention. I want to introduce to you the new military commander of Lower Canada, Sir John Colborne.

COLBORNE: Well, Mr. Papineau, they say you are quite a radical.

PAPINEAU: They say, they say. I admire Robespierre, but I detest blood. And now mesdames, if you will excuse us.

COLBORNE: Now you seigneurs, listen to me. I am going to impart some English wisdom. If you want to get along, you go along.

(COLBORNE holds up a small Union Jack.)

Now let me explain the meaning of this flag. The blue stands for the royalness of the sceptred isle.

PAPINEAU: You mean the tears of the oppressed.

COLBORNE: The red stands for courage.

PAPINEAU: The blood of many massacres.

COLBORNE: The white stands for honour.

PAPINEAU: The honour of devils.

COLBORNE: Mr. Papineau.

PAPINEAU: Monsieur, s'il vous plaît.

COLBORNE: We have tried to win you over but you insist on being independent. I shouldn't say this, but I would like to see our fine soldiers copulate with these French Canadian women, make them produce babies, send those babies to England, raise them as Englishmen, then bring them back, and let them be Canadians. But unfortunately, we cannot do that, so we are doing the next best thing.

PAPINEAU: You are ignorant and gross.

GOSFORD: See Johnny, what I have to deal with?

PAPINEAU: Le petit roi speaks.

COLBORNE: I see it clearly. Louis-Joseph, le Premier.

PAPINEAU: At your service.

GOSFORD: See what I have to deal with? He gives me the piacres. Every morning when I wake up, I put on my trousers and say to myself, "What can I do for these marvelous Canadians, to make their life happier?"

PAPINEAU: Die.

GOSFORD: What?

COLBORNE: I see it clearly.

(The lights fade.)

Scene Thirty-two

(In another playing area the lights fade in. LOUNT enters.)

LOUNT: Ah, it's a glorious day for calling the wife. A glorious day. Wife, wife, wife!

(SARAH LOUNT enters.)

SARAH: You're a horrible man, Sam Lount, a horrible man.

LOUNT: Quiet, wife.

SARAH: Own up to your failure as a man and as a human being. Own up to it.

LOUNT: Never. Mr. Mackenzie is having a political meeting. I'm going to it.

SARAH: When is Mr. Mackenzie not having a political meeting?

LOUNT: Quiet wife. So I'll be home late.

SARAH: You just come home sober.

LOUNT: You won't miss me.

SARAH: When I'm slopping the hogs I'll think about you. Don't worry about it Sam Lount.

LOUNT: You're an awful woman. I don't know why I married you.

SARAH: I do.

LOUNT: Ah.

(LOUNT exits.)

SARAH: Own up to it. You're going to get yourself killed, Sam Lount.

(The lights fade.)

Scene Thirty-three

(In another playing area the lights fade in. GOSFORD and COLBORNE enter.)

COLBORNE: If you had to wrestle with a bear—

GOSFORD: I would never wrestle with a bear, under any circumstances.

COLBORNE: But if you had no choice, except the bear could be a full-grown grizzily, or a little baby cub. Which would you choose?

GOSFORD: Well, if I had to choose, I would be guided by my sense of English fair play, and all that, and choose the big, ugly, full-grown bear and leave the cub to people like you.

COLBORNE: It is only a matter of time before they rebel.

GOSFORD: Yes, I suppose. Political ideas horrify me.

COLBORNE: It is in our interest to exasperate them into a premature revolt and then crush them.

GOSFORD: Yes, I suppose. Politics for me is giving perks, recieving perks. This is horrifying.

COLBORNE: This is carrot and stick. We will move the beast forward.

(The lights fade.)

Scene Thirty-four

(In another playing area the lights fade in. MACKENZIE and BONDHEAD enter.)

MACKENZIE: Good lord. We send them our grievances, and look what they send us. Good lord.

BONDHEAD: So you are Mackenzie.

MACKENZIE: I am.

BONDHEAD: Who is your tailor? You must belong to the industrial classes.

MACKENZIE: That's right. The beaver is our God.

(BONDHEAD holds up the book of grievances.)

BONDHEAD: In England I was given this. Your grievances. Very unimaginative.

MACKENZIE: How about this one? We demand cheaper tea and an end to the monopoly of the British East India Company. Cheaper tea, get the message. We demand—

BONDHEAD: Stop garbling. I received this with pleasure and I give this back to you, with pleasure. From this day forth I will dress down and speak in homilies. Good day.

MACKENZIE: Good lord, what have we here?

(The lights fade.)

Scene Thirty-five

(In another playing area the lights fade in. LAFONTAINE and PAPINEAU enter.)

LAFONTAINE: Every time we go to a restaurant, I pay the bill. For seven years, I pay the bill.

PAPINEAU: I thought you had become used to it.

LAFONTAINE: No.

PAPINEAU: There are more important things to discuss than who pays for the wine. Are there not?

LAFONTAINE: Yes.

PAPINEAU: Now, we are going to suspend the government.

LAFONTAINE: Welcome to the sheepfold.

PAPINEAU: Monsieur Lafontaine, in order to be a good guest you do not dispute politics or the choice of wine with the host.

LAFONTAINE: Is flattery a vice or a virtue?

PAPINEAU: In young people it is a virtue. You play the coquette too often, monsieur.

LAFONTAINE: Not often enough it seems.

MME PAPINEAU: *(Off.)* Louis. Louis.

LAFONTAINE: God is calling you.

(MME PAPINEAU enters.)

MME PAPINEAU: An imp from hell is here to see you.

(MACKENZIE enters.)

MACKENZIE: Ah, Mr. Papineau, I presume. I am William Lyon Mackenzie.

PAPINEAU: Mother, we are going to discuss politics.

MME PAPINEAU: Infamata.

(MME PAPINEAU exits.)

MACKENZIE: What a charming woman.

PAPINEAU: Yes.

MACKENZIE: Does the thought of committing high treason scare you? Answer me straight.

PAPINEAU: What I think and what I do, are the same. I am suspending the government.

MACKENZIE: Aye, that's a grand tune. Music to my ears. Makes me want to dance and shout. And who is this fine fellow who sneers like a gargoyle?

PAPINEAU: This is Mr. Lafontaine.

LAFONTAINE: Prove your credentials. I am a revolutionary.

MACKENZIE: Well, a twit anyway.

PAPINEAU: Quiet puppy. The struggle for freedom—

MACKENZIE: Freedom, oh blessed word.

PAPINEAU: And the liberty of the people—

MACKENZIE: Liberty of the people, oh divine sentiment.

PAPINEAU: Requires men to do men's work. Go fetch the wine. Now.

(LAFONTAINE exits.)

I believe that those who suffer tyranny condemn the unborn millions to slavery.

MACKENZIE: Exactly. Sooner or later, what is up goes down, and what is down goes up, and the sooner the better.

PAPINEAU: I am organizing my militia at St. Charles and St. Denis.

MACKENZIE: And I've got men training too. The cork is going to fly. There's no debate about it.

(LAFONTAINE enters holding a bottle of wine.)

PAPINEAU: Yes, let us prepare to drink.

(The lights fade.)

Scene Thirty-six

(In another playing area the lights fade in. BONDHEAD, STRACHAN, MACNAB, ROBINSON, and FITZGIBBON enter.)

BONDHEAD: Now gentlemen.

FITZGIBBON: Sir, there is something you should know about Mackenzie.

BONDHEAD: Gentlemen.

FITZGIBBON: He's in Lower Canada talking to Papineau about revolution.

BONDHEAD: MacNab.

MACNAB: Quiet, you dog.

BONDHEAD: The Princess Victoria is now queen. A lass sits on the throne. It will be a gay revelry. The words of the little princess when she held the sceptre were "I shall be good." Is that not charming? Oh, if I could be a cushion on that throne. The sights, the smells, the wonder, the joy. Long live the queen.

STRACHAN, MACNAB, ROBINSON, and FITZGIBBON: Long live the queen.

MACNAB: Quiet, you dog.

BONDHEAD: Not a cloud on the horizon.

STRACHAN: Except Mackenzie.

BONDHEAD: Oh him.

ROBINSON: We throw him out but he keeps getting elected.

BONDHEAD: Which proves that democracy is government by low lifes for low lifes. Reformers, radicals, republicans. They're all the same to me. In the next election I will lead the elite against the rabble.

STRACHAN: Oh Mr. Bondhead, if you only would.

(The lights fade.)

Scene Thirty-seven

(In another playing area the lights fade in. LAFONTAINE and BONTEMPS enter.)

LAFONTAINE: Papineau. He puts on such "noble airs". The way he behaves, you'd think he was Champlain.

BONTEMPS: His father was a barrel-maker.

LAFONTAINE: We are led by the nouveau-riche. Ha! The nouveau-riche who do not spend their own money.

BONTEMPS: That's right. My family goes back to Champlain. We know things he doesn't. Papineau is committing political suicide. He is finished. If I was you I would put distance between yourself and Papineau. Big foot is going to come down.

LAFONTAINE: But he has great support in the countryside.

BONTEMPS: Big foot is going to come down.

(The lights fade.)

Scene Thirty-eight

(In another playing area the lights fade in. BONDHEAD and MACNAB enter. MACNAB holds a club.)

BONDHEAD: Vote with your blood. Vote tory, and you vote for this. *(He holds up a Union Jack.)* Vote for Reform, and you vote for this. *(He holds up an American flag.)* The flag of traitors. Do your duty, God save the queen. If we quarrel with England we quarrel with bread and butter. You there, what have you to say?

MACNAB: I was born here but I know home is over the ocean.

BONDHEAD: Damn right it is. Do your duty. God save the queen. Vote tory and God save the queen.

MACNAB: God save the queen!

(MACKENZIE enters singing.)

MACKENZIE: God save the rights of man, God save the rights of man, God save the rights. We demand a secret ballot.

BONDHEAD: Nonsense. A man must be man enough to stand in a circle in plain view of everyone and announce his choice in a loud voice.

MACKENZIE: But there is all kinds of intimidation.

BONDHEAD: Only for the disloyal.

MACKENZIE: You're a deceitful despot. A toad swallower if ever I met one.

BONDHEAD: MacNab.

(MACNAB kicks MACKENZIE.)

MACKENZIE: Oh, he kicked me in the bladder.

BONDHEAD: Oh, MacNab.

(The lights fade.)

Scene Thirty-nine

(In another playing area the lights fade in. The SHERIFF enters holding his whip. ALLEN enters.)

SHERIFF: I'm the Sheriff. And you will respect me or you will die. Who you voting for?

ALLEN: Mackenzie.

SHERIFF: Not here.

ALLEN: But I can't vote anywhere else.

SHERIFF: Not my problem. Vote here, it will cost you an eye.

(The SHERIFF cracks the whip. The lights fade.)

Scene Forty

(In another playing area the lights fade in. BONDHEAD, STRACHAN, and ROBINSON enter.)

STRACHAN: To a great victory.

BONDHEAD: Yes, it wasn't exactly according to Hoyle, was it? But it was a great victory. We have smashed the rebels. Driven them underground. Oh everything is good now.

STRACHAN: What is our first order of business?

BONDHEAD: We will pass the Everlasting Salaries Bill.

STRACHAN: Oh very good show.

BONDHEAD: Any objections? I thought not.

(The lights fade.)

Scene Forty-one

(In another playing area the lights fade in. MACKENZIE enters.)

MACKENZIE: It's a fraud, a cheat. Oh ye false Canadians. Tories, pensioners, placemen, profligates, Orangemen, churchmen, spies, informers, brokers, gamblers, parasites, and knaves of every description. Allow me to congratulate you. Never was a vagabond race more prosperous. Never did successful villainy rejoice in brighter visions of the future than ye may indulge. You may plunder and rob with impunity. Your feet are on the people's necks. They are transformed into tame, cringing slaves ready to be trampled on. Erect your juggernaut. The people are ready to be sacrificed under the wheels of the idol.

(LOUNT and ANDERSON enter holding a furled banner.)

There is only one question. What is to be done? The Family Compact has to go. There is no debate about it. They have to go. But how? In an election. That's good for an amusing laugh, isn't it. We are going to remove the

Queen's representative in an election. That's very funny. Then how?

LOUNT: You're not thinking of force of arms, I hope.

MACKENZIE: That's exactly what I'm thinking.

(ANDERSON and LOUNT unfurl the banner. The words "Off to a Good Beginning" are revealed on the banner.)

LOUNT: Off to a good beginning.

MACKENZIE: And a bad end to the Family Compact.

(The lights fade.)

Scene Forty-two

(In another playing area the lights fade in. CHENIER enters.)

CHENIER: My horses are as big as dogs. My pig is that big. Big enough for one sandwich. I eat pea soup.

(PAPINEAU and PIERRE enter.)

PAPINEAU: Patriotes, agitate, agitate, agitate. Citizen, believe in the Republic.

PIERRE: With yourself as president?

PAPINEAU: Silence. Or I will make you sing my name in a high shrill voice. We will be masters in our own house.

PIERRE: And you will be Louis-Joseph, le Premier.

PAPINEAU: Sing my name.

PIERRE: Papineau.

PAPINEAU: Higher.

PIERRE: Papineau.

PAPINEAU: Higher.

PIERRE: Papineau.

PAPINEAU: Enough. Get my bags.

(PIERRE exits.)

We must organize, boycott, withdraw, suspend, agitate! I want you to elect your own representatives. I want you to elect your own military officers. Mes amis, this is a truly great day. I proclaim the Republic and the rights of man.

(BONTEMPS enters.)

BONTEMPS: Peasants, listen to me.

PAPINEAU: Non.

BONTEMPS: I am your seigneur and your justice of the peace.

PAPINEAU: Speak to this man.

CHENIER: You have been unelected. You don't represent us.

BONTEMPS: By what authority?

CHENIER: By authority of Jean-Olivier Chenier. Allez, monsieur.

(BONTEMPS exits.)

PAPINEAU: I declare you to be a man. The revolution has begun. We are arresting the bureaucrats. Agitate, agitate, agitate.

(The lights fade.)

Scene Forty-three

(In another playing area the lights fade in. MACKENZIE and ROLPH enter.)

ROLPH: This is an unprincipled government. Free elections are a farce in this country. Well, I can smile and be a villain. Scoundrels deserve their fate.

MACKENZIE: That they do.

ROLPH: I graduated as a doctor and as a lawyer from Cambridge University.

MACKENZIE: I know.

ROLPH: I have no future here.

MACKENZIE: None of us do.

ROLPH: No prospects.

MACKENZIE: None.

ROLPH: If you are not intermarried with this group—

MACKENZIE: A fate worse than death.

ROLPH: —you have no possibilities.

MACKENZIE: That's right. What are your political desires?

ROLPH: You make it sound like I should be under arrest. To change the government.

MACKENZIE: How does president of the Republic of Upper Canada sound to you? I want to seize control and make you governor or president, I don't care.

ROLPH: Interesting. How many fighting men do you have?

MACKENZIE: Thousands.

ROLPH: What is the feeling in the countryside?

MACKENZIE: United, determined, ready for action.

ROLPH: I will give my support. But I cannot reveal it publicly. I can't sign anything.

MACKENZIE: You're a natural born politician.

ROLPH: Treason is never successful. When it is, none call it treason.

MACKENZIE: Does committing high treason scare you?

ROLPH: But I want proof of your support.

MACKENZIE: Proof.

ROLPH: The names of your supporters in a book.

MACKENZIE: I've done that already. Here.

(MACKENZIE gives ROLPH a book.)

ROLPH: Now to be successful, we must first seize the arms at city hall.

MACKENZIE: Exactly.

ROLPH: And proclaim a provisional government.

MACKENZIE: Exactly, Mr. President.

(The lights fade.)

Scene Forty-four

(In another playing area the lights fade in. LAFONTAINE enters.)

LAFONTAINE: Papineau, he makes me sick. He wants me to be a little Papineau. If I am going to be a Papineau, I will be a big Papineau. He is in for a surprise. Success in this country is contemptible. It is like being a monkey on a stick. If the monkey climbs to the top of the stick, it is patted on the head, given a peanut, and told "You are a success." Well we are the makers of our own fortune. This monkey wants bananas, and this monkey is going to get bananas.

(The lights fade.)

Scene Forty-five

(In another playing area the lights fade in. BALDWIN enters holding a book of poetry.)

BALDWIN: Oh I love reading poetry in the forest. "Can man be free if woman be a slave." Ohhh.

(ROLPH enters.)

ROLPH: Ah, there you are. Come we must talk politics.

(BALDWIN groans.)

I have spoken with Mackenzie. He has a very interesting plan.

BALDWIN: Oh Camilla, he is such a troll. I don't care what his plan is. He makes me sick. And you are a fool to talk with him. He is mad, bad, and dangerous to know. A radical, Mr. Rolph.

ROLPH: Really.

BALDWIN: Mr. Rolph, much is concealed from me, but I see enough to know that I do not see everything. Violence is a blindfolded demon.

ROLPH: But what other course is there?

BALDWIN: There is the course I am following.

ROLPH: Which is?

BALDWIN: It is only logical that the political reforms in England be applied to the colonies. After all, the rights of Englishmen are the rights of Englishmen, whether in England or in Canada. I am lobbying the Colonial Secretary. Oh very well, what did Mackenzie say?

ROLPH: Nothing.

(The lights fade.)

Scene Forty-six

(In another playing area the lights fade in. BOURGET, COLBORNE, GOSFORD, MOFFAT, and LAFONTAINE enter.)

GOSFORD: I know what Duckey's game is.

MOFFAT: Everyone is complaining.

GOSFORD: I know what Duckey's game is.

MOFFAT: My brothers, my sons, my cousins, my uncles, my in-laws, my friends. Everyone.

GOSFORD: Oh I know how you feel. I am down to my last ten crates of claret. But I know what Duckey's game is.

BOURGET: Papineau is stirring up all kinds of trouble.

LAFONTAINE: Papineau is lost and must be sacrificed.

BOURGET: He is in league with the devil.

LAFONTAINE: Trust me.

GOSFORD: Get away from me.

BOURGET: Everywhere I go, the peasants call me pig. I'm tired of being called pig.

LAFONTAINE: I can form a government.

GOSFORD: Get away.

BOURGET: And infidels are stealing money from the church to finance the work of Satan.

VOICES: *(Off.)* Down with Colborne, long live Papineau!

COLBORNE: Such insolence.

VOICES: *(Off.)* Down with Colborne, long live Papineau!

COLBORNE: I think we will need more troops.

BOURGET: Yes, more troops.

(The lights fade.)

Scene Forty-seven

(In another playing area the lights fade in. GENERAL CHARLES GORE and COLONEL GEORGE WETHERALL enter.)

WETHERALL: When I was seven years old, I was an officer. A lieutenant.

GORE: So what. I served in the Peninsular Campaign. I was with Wellington at the sack of Badajoz.

WETHERALL: I, of course, was the conqueror of Java. Oh the glory.

GORE: I pull rank on you there. I fought at the battle of Waterloo. I saw Sir John's arm fly through the air.

(COLBORNE enters.)

COLBORNE: General Gore, Colonel Wetherall.

GORE: Sir.

WETHERALL: Sir.

COLBORNE: Papineau and these French bastards are calling themselves the "Sons of Liberty."

GORE: Sons of bitches would be more like it.

COLBORNE: Exactly. We must arrest Papineau and his band of ruffians.

GORE: Will do.

(The lights fade.)

Scene Forty-eight

(In another playing area the lights fade in. PAPINEAU and PIERRE enter.)

PAPINEAU: When I proclaimed the rights of man, I meant to say with special rights for the seigneurs and clergy.

PIERRE: Well you should have said that. The rights of man is one thing. The rights of man with special rights for others is something else.

PAPINEAU: I do not have time to discuss the fine points of politics with you.

PIERRE: Fine points!

PAPINEAU: Your job is to fight.

PIERRE: Fight ... for you.

PAPINEAU: We will be masters in our own house.

PIERRE: And I will be a servant.

PAPINEAU: You are a servant. Pick up my bags.

(LAFONTAINE enters.)

LAFONTAINE: Louis, the English are coming to arrest you.

PAPINEAU: Allez, to St. Denis.

(PIERRE exits.)

You dress like a patriote but—

LAFONTAINE: I do not think the time is right for an uprising.

PAPINEAU: He said in his nightgown while filling his waterbottle.

LAFONTAINE: Someone has to be between you and the English. You are old enough to be my father. I have my life and my political future ahead of me.

PAPINEAU: You sell-out, you betrayer, you stinkpot.

LAFONTAINE: I will be a voice of conciliation.

PAPINEAU: You stencher.

LAFONTAINE: I wish you all the best.

PAPINEAU: I wish you all the worst.

(The lights fade.)

Scene Forty-nine

(In another playing area the lights fade in. GOSFORD and COLBORNE enter.)

COLBORNE: The bloody bastard escaped our clutches and is now fomenting rebellion in St. Charles and St. Denis.

GOSFORD: Papineau gives me the piacres.

COLBORNE: We will perform a simultaneous

assault on their two centres of power. General Gore will attack St. Denis. And Colonel Wetherall will attack St. Charles. We will break the back of this rebellion.

GOSFORD: Oh whatever you think is best.

(The lights fade.)

Scene Fifty

(In another playing area the lights fade in. LOUNT, SARAH, and MR and MRS O'TOOLE are dancing a square dance. MACKENZIE enters.)

MACKENZIE: Canadians, brave Canadians, loyal Canadians. Bow to your partner, bow to your friend. Put on your smile before this ends. Do you love freedom, I know you do. Who'd deny it, would you, would you? Down with the butcher, down with the baker, down with Her Majesty's candlestick maker. Do you hate oppression, I know you do. Who'd deny it, would you, would you? We all work and we all toil. The Family Compact says we're disloyal. A Reformer disloyal?

OTHERS: Never!

MACKENZIE: We're all loyal to Her Majesty. Pick up your guns and march with me. We're all loyal to Her Majesty. Pick up your guns and march with me.

(The lights fade.)

Scene Fifty-one

(In another playing area the lights fade in. BONDHEAD enters.)

BONDHEAD: I get up at eight, breakfast at nine, and kill flies until ten. Then I write letters till eleven. Then I murder flies without the smallest mercy until twelve. Then I snack until one, and then I nap until four. And then I bathe until five, and then I change clothes until six, and then I'm ready for dinner. I live for dindins. Oh, I'm in love with my vegetables.

(FITZGIBBON enters.)

FITZGIBBON: I have just seen all the troops marching out of Toronto.

BONDHEAD: I have sent all the troops to Lower Canada.

FITZGIBBON: What?

BONDHEAD: Lower Canada is about to be involved in an insurrection and the military commander needs them, so I have sent them, and that is all there is to it.

FITZGIBBON: But I have seen Mackenzie and his men drilling parade square. Parade square routine.

BONDHEAD: Oh you spoil my day.

FITZGIBBON: Beware danger.

BONDHEAD: If MacNab's militia cannot defend the province then the sooner it is lost the better.

FITZGIBBON: Fool.

BONDHEAD: I have had quite enough of you.

FITZGIBBON: Fool.

BONDHEAD: Expand your vocabulary.

FITZGIBBON: You fool.

BONDHEAD: You will regret that Mr. Fitzgibbon.

(The lights fade.)

Scene Fifty-two

(In another playing area the lights fade in. PAPINEAU and PIERRE enter.)

PAPINEAU: What is our motto?

PIERRE: Death to the wealthy.

PAPINEAU: No.

PIERRE: Everyone is equal.

PAPINEAU: No.

PIERRE: What is it then?

PAPINEAU: Down with fur hats. Down with the Château Clique.

PIERRE: Down with fur hats. Down with the Château Clique.

PAPINEAU: What is the philosophy of the British Empire?

PIERRE: No mercy for the weak and the tiny.

PAPINEAU: What kind of philosophy is that?

PIERRE: That is slavery.

PAPINEAU: My friends, this is a truly great day. I proclaim the Republic and the rights of man.

PIERRE: With special rights for others, don't forget that.

PAPINEAU: Silence. Draw up your wills and man the barricades.

PIERRE: To the barricades.

(The lights fade.)

Scene Fifty-three

(In another playing area the lights fade in. COLBORNE and COLONEL JOCK WEIR enter.)

COLBORNE: Colonel Wetherall has not arrived at his assignation point. You must tell General Gore at St. Denis to delay his attack for one day. Can you deliver this important message behind enemy lines?

WEIR: You don't give a man's work to a milksop. And they don't call me Jock Weir for nothing. You want something done, give it to Jocko.

(The lights fade.)

Scene Fifty-four

(In another playing area the lights fade in. WEIR enters humming the words "Where am I?" to the tune of "Scotland the Brave"—he stops.)

WEIR: Where am I?

(WEIR stands motionless, listening. Hands come out of the shadows and grab him. The lights fade.)

Scene Fifty-five

(In another playing area the lights fade in. GORE enters.)

GORE: God, smell the air.

(A SERGEANT-MAJOR enters.)

SERGEANT-MAJOR: Sir, the rebels await you at St. Denis.

GORE: Excellent. Men, I fought with Wellington at Waterloo. To the memory of the forty-third.

SERGEANT-MAJOR: To the memory of the forty-third.

GORE: Advance.

(The lights fade.)

Scene Fifty-six

(In another playing area the lights fade in. PAPINEAU enters.)

PAPINEAU: St. Denis is the patron saint of France. And I will end up like St. Denis, holding my head in my hands if I do not leave. I am the head of the revolution. And my followers are the hands and feet. If I am killed I abort the revolution. But the wine is poured, it is fitting that I drink it.

(Noises offstage. PIERRE enters with WEIR, plus two PATRIOTES.)

PIERRE: Look, a prisoner.

PAPINEAU: What is your name?

WEIR: My name is Jock Weir. I am a Colonel with Her Majesty's army. That is all I am going to tell you. This is war, rebellion, and you are traitors.

PAPINEAU: Would you like some wine?

WEIR: No. I will not drink with rebels.

PAPINEAU: Put this dog in a dungeon.

PIERRE: Non, we have no place to jail him.

WEIR: Know also that it is my duty to try and escape.

(PIERRE points a gun at WEIR's head.)

PAPINEAU: Go ahead.

WEIR: Well, not when you are looking.

PAPINEAU: You are going to come to a bad end my friend. I can tell.

PIERRE: The English are coming, the English are coming. Here they come.

PAPINEAU: Les Batards. To arms.

(GORE and five ENGLISH SOLDIERS enter. They attack PAPINEAU and the PATRIOTES.)

Have faith.

GORE: They're picking us off like flies.

PAPINEAU: The sublime and the ridiculous are related.

GORE: By bang there will be bang, by bang.

PAPINEAU: Have faith.

PIERRE: Get out of my way, I am trying to kill the English.

GORE: By bang there will be bang, by bang.

WEIR: I want to see the soldiers. I want to see the soldiers.

PIERRE: Come back here.

WEIR: I want to see the soldiers.

(PIERRE and two PATRIOTES stab WEIR.)

Oh God, I'm Jocko, I'm Jock-ah.

GORE: They've killed Jock Weir.

SOLDIERS: They've killed Jock Weir.

GORE: At them, lads.

(The fighting continues.)

We are going to lose our cannon. We are going to have to retreat and leave behind our cannon. Oh God, blast me to pieces. The disgrace. Retreat, retreat, retreat.

(GORE and the ENGLISH SOLDIERS exit.)

PAPINEAU: They are retreating. Praise the saints.

PIERRE: No, Praise the patriotes.

PAPINEAU: Praise the patriotes. Now I must fly to St. Charles. Pick up my bags.

(The lights fade.)

Scene Fifty-seven

(In another playing area the lights fade in. COLBORNE, WETHERALL, and GORE enter.)

COLBORNE: In India we used to call people like you Nimmuckwallah.

WETHERALL: Nimmuckwallah.

COLBORNE: Hereafter you will be the officer's tea boy.

WETHERALL: I like mine with a slice of lemon.

COLBORNE: You have shamed the service.

WETHERALL: Leaving your gun in the field.

GORE: I regained it.

COLBORNE: Tea boy, quiet.

WETHERALL: A rank amateur, I knew it.

COLBORNE: Well St. Charles will pay for this disgrace to English arms. Pay with blood. General Wetherall.

WETHERALL: Sir.

COLBORNE: You will lead the attack on St. Charles. Colonel Gore, you will assist.

WETHERALL: *(To GORE.)* You will bring up the rear.

(The lights fade.)

Scene Fifty-eight

(In another playing area the lights fade in. PIERRE and PAPINEAU enter.)

PIERRE: Come, mighty God, you know the words.

PAPINEAU: Yes, so this is St. Charles. Oh look at that brute strangling a chicken. How quaint. I will inspire him. Patriotes. You are fighting to be slaves. Stop. Be slaves.

PIERRE: I don't think you should say that.

PAPINEAU: No. Don't listen to me. No, listen to me. Patriotes. To hell with Queen Victoria. To hell with the czar of Russia. To hell with them all. The old world will give no more monarchies to the new world. The new world will give Republics to the old. That's more like it. First the Republic, then the revolution.

PIERRE: First the Republic, then the revolution.

(The lights fade.)

Scene Fifty-nine

(In another playing area the lights fade in. MACKENZIE enters holding a book.)

MACKENZIE: We have the names of fifteen hundred men in this book. Volunteers all, who will rise up on the appointed day if armed. The time to strike is now. Fort Henry is empty, and all troops are in Lower Canada. Four thousand rifles stand guarded by one soldier. We could not have a better chance than now. One short hour can deliver us. Gentlemen, we must whisper our alarms and prepare for December seventh. The day of reckoning.

(The lights fade.)

Act Two

Scene One

(The lights fade in. PAPINEAU enters.)

PAPINEAU: I am Papineau. I control the people. What the people think, I speak. I am the people. They are mine. They do what I wish. Like a little plaything, they obey.

(Two PATRIOTES enter.)

PATRIOTES: Long live Louis-Joseph, le Premier, Louis-Joseph, le Premier.

PAPINEAU: Patriotes. The earth is thirsty for the blood of our oppressors. No mercy for the slave owners. What mercy have they shown us? They have shown us the mercy of death. We will show them the same mercy. But before they die, they will know my feeling. I hate the English.

(The PATRIOTES cheer.)

PATRIOTES: Louis-Joseph, le Premier. Long live Papineau.

PAPINEAU: We must rise up and speak the language of our nature. At St. Charles, we are ready.

PATRIOTES: Long live Papineau, long live Louis-Joseph.

(PAPINEAU smiles. The lights fade.)

Scene Two

(In another playing area the lights fade in. BONDHEAD, ROBINSON, ROLPH, and FITZGIBBON enter. FITZGIBBON holds a newspaper.)

BONDHEAD: Your information about rebellion is at best second-hand, if not third-hand.

ROLPH: If not fourth-hand.

FITZGIBBON: Would you like it first-hand? How once in the great war I led a small band of men against great odds to great victory.

ROLPH: Old memories die hard.

BONDHEAD: I will fight the rebels on my ground, not their ground.

ROLPH: Exactly.

FITZGIBBON: You are going to wait until they arrive in your bedroom.

BONDHEAD: How dare you say that to me?

ROLPH: How dare you say that to the governor?

FITZGIBBON: Read.

BONDHEAD: No.

FITZGIBBON: Independence, revolution.

BONDHEAD: Go away.

FITZGIBBON: I have seen men ready to march on Toronto.

ROLPH: An over active imagination.

ROBINSON: I'd like to see them try. They're all wind.

FITZGIBBON: I have seen over five hundred with pikes.

BONDHEAD: Oh pugh.

ROLPH: Yes, pugh.

FITZGIBBON: The rebels are gathering at Montgomery's Tavern.

BONDHEAD: Pugh.

FITZGIBBON: I have never seen a bigger idiot in my life.

ROBINSON: The governor is upset. You spoil his day.

ROLPH: You spoil his day.

FITZGIBBON: You must arrest Mackenzie for

high treason. They are going to attack on December seventh.

BONDHEAD: Oh very well, arrest Mackenzie for high treason.

(ROLPH exits. The lights fade.)

Scene Three

(In another playing area the lights fade in. ANDERSON enters singing "Old MacDonald Had a Farm." ROLPH enters.)

ROLPH: Is Mackenzie here?

ANDERSON: No.

ROLPH: We must move the uprising up three days to December the fourth.

ANDERSON: What is this? I just heard about the first date yesterday.

ROLPH: Well, it's been moved up. The militia is being organized. A warrant for high treason has been issued for Mackenzie. Tell him there is a warrant for his arrest. Go, go now.

(The lights fade.)

Scene Four

(In another playing area the lights fade in. The sound of musket fire. PAPINEAU and two PATRIOTES enter.)

PAPINEAU: I feel like a blade of grass.

PATRIOTES: You are hungry.

PAPINEAU: No, I am not hungry.

(The PATRIOTES fire their muskets.)

I fear St. Charles will not be like St. Denis. The situation is grim. There are no reinforcements. Each man has only four bullets.

PATRIOTE TWO: That's it. I'm out of bullets.

PATRIOTE ONE: And I have one left, should I fire it?

PAPINEAU: Non, we surrender, we surrender.

(SERGEANT-MAJOR and two ENGLISH SOLDIERS rush in with bayonets.)

SERGEANT-MAJOR: It's going to be a bad day for you, boy-o.

(WETHERALL enters.)

WETHERALL: No prisoners.

(The ENGLISH SOLDIERS stab the PATRIOTES repeatedly.)

PATRIOTES: We surrender. *(Stab.)* You bastard. *(Stab.)* I should have shot ya. *(Stab.)* You bastard.

(The PATRIOTES die.)

WETHERALL: Now that bunch over there, stab them. And then burn this village to the ground.

(A wailing HABITANT enters.)

Priest.

(BOURGET enters.)

Speak to them

BOURGET: Peasants, learn your lessons. If you rebel against authority you become criminals in the eyes of God. These patriotes are in league with the devil. I excommunicate them and refuse to have them buried in consecrated ground.

WETHERALL: Crucify.

BOURGET: Yes, crucify them, upside down, in front of their families.

WETHERALL: Long live ...

BOURGET: Long live the queen of England.

WETHERALL: Loyalty ...

BOURGET: Loyalty, obedience—

HABITANT: Mangez la merde.

BOURGET: Who said that? The language of hell will not save your soul.

HABITANT: Priests are black pigs.

BOURGET: How dare you say that, you fornicator. I refuse the last rites, and may your soul be damned in hell.

HABITANT: Black pigs.

(The lights fade.)

Scene Five

(In another playing area the lights fade in. PAPINEAU enters.)

PAPINEAU: These murderers. With these actions I place a curse on the English forever. Les maudits Anglais. The fucking English.

(The lights fade.)

Scene Six

(In another playing area the lights fade in. MACKENZIE and ANDERSON enter.)

MACKENZIE: Who advanced the date of the resistance?

ANDERSON: Rolph told me to tell you, and I told my hired hand to tell you or Lount, but he met Lount's nephew instead, and Lount's nephew told everybody.

(LOUNT enters.)

LOUNT: That's right. I heard it from the milk man. So much for secrecy.

MACKENZIE: Good God, thundering lizards, leaping dogs. What are we going to do?

LOUNT: We're going on the fourth instead of the seventh.

MACKENZIE: Good God.

ANDERSON: I think it's a foolhardy venture and I think we should call the whole thing off.

(Noises offstage.)

LOUNT: There's my men. They're here.

(LOUNTS exits.)

MACKENZIE: You there, barkeep. Feed these men. Prepare hot meals.

VOICE: *(Off.)* Who pays?

MACKENZIE: You are trying to throttle the revolution. This makes you a traitor. Don't turn your back on me.

(MACKENZIE exits. Offstage he harangues the men.)

ANDERSON: There he goes again, having a fit. Oup, there he goes again. He flipped his wig again.

(MACKENZIE enters adjusting his wig followed by ALLEN.)

Oup, here he comes.

MACKENZIE: Give me men with a piece of steel between their legs.

ALLEN: That's exactly where we don't want it.

MACKENZIE: And we'll win the revolution.

ALLEN: We'll win the revolution if you would only shut up.

MACKENZIE: Never.

ALLEN: Then I'm going home. I marched forty miles through shit to get here. And what's here? Nothing. No food, no guns, no men, nothing. Except him, and he never stops shouting.

MACKENZIE: Because you will not follow orders.

ALLEN: This is like the bloody army. I don't take orders from you. I'll take orders from Anderson or Lount, or somebody that knows what they are doing. But not you. Where's Lount?

(LOUNT enters.)

LOUNT: Easy boys, stand easy. Don't listen to him. He doesn't know what he's saying. He's not responsible for his actions.

(MACKENZIE takes his wig and throws it in the air.)

ANDERSON: Oup, there he goes again.

MACKENZIE: By thundering Christ there's a price on my head for high treason. I'll hang.

ALLEN: Well I'm not going to hang with you.

MACKENZIE: Get out on sentry duty.

(ANDERSON exits.)

ALLEN: There are sentries out there.

MACKENZIE: I mean downtown. Go reconnoitre Toronto.

ALLEN: You go reconnoitre Toronto, I'm hungry.

(Sound of gunshots.)

MACKENZIE: What's that?

(ANDERSON enters.)

ANDERSON: The landowner Moodie has been shot.

ALLEN: Jesus, Jesus.

ANDERSON: Two of his friends escaped to warn the governor.

ALLEN: Jesus.

MACKENZIE: Blood, blood is on my hands. Hot bubbling blood, we have shed blood. The faint hearted can leave.

LOUNT: Where are you going Dunc?

ALLEN: Get out of my way.

(ALLEN exits.)

MACKENZIE: There is no turning back now. We must attack, now!

(The lights fade.)

Scene Seven

(In another playing area the lights fade in. BONDHEAD enters.)

BONDHEAD: Well la de da. In my bed chamber with my taffeta nightgown. I walk like this. I flaunt my power. We'll have no strange birds here. On the Pampas I used to ride my ponies like this. Building up a big sweaty lather. Not a cloud on the horizon. Except Fitzgibbon. That super-annuated war hero. I'd like to put his head on my bedpost and stick pins in it. It is like being pestered by a goblin. He spoils my day. But then there is MacNab. Oh he is a delight. He makes my day. I feel like a misanthrope who needs affection.

(Noises offstage.)

FITZGIBBON: *(Off.)* I must see him.

VOICE: *(Off.)* His Lordship gave strict—

FITZGIBBON: *(Off.)* Oh to hell with Your Lordship, I must see him.

(FITZGIBBON enters.)

BONDHEAD: Oh.

FITZGIBBON: The more I see him, the more I see why they're coming for him.

BONDHEAD: Oh.

FITZGIBBON: Shut up. Colonel Moodie has been shot. Killed.

(BONDHEAD screams.)

Oh for the love of … Do I have your permission to assemble volunteers to fight in your defence? Jesus.

BONDHEAD: Yes.

FITZGIBBON: What'd you say?

BONDHEAD: I said yes. And someone fetch MacNab. I must have him here with me.

(The lights fade.)

Scene Eight

(In another playing area the lights fade in. MACKENZIE and ANDERSON enter.)

MACKENZIE: Can't see a bloody—

ANDERSON: Quiet. Footsteps. Who goes there?

(ROBINSON enters.)

ROBINSON: Your humble trout.

ANDERSON: Hands up.

ROBINSON: I don't understand.

MACKENZIE: A tory doesn't understand. I proclaim the Republic of Upper Canada. You are our prisoner.

ANDERSON: Higher.

(ROBINSON puts his hands up.)

Are you armed?

ROBINSON: No.

ANDERSON: Well I'm going to search you.

MACKENZIE: No, Anthony, because he is a gentleman. We will not search him because we are respectable revolutionaries. Where there is justice, there is dignity.

ROBINSON: How sporting of you.

ANDERSON: March.

(ANDERSON and ROBINSON exit.)

MACKENZIE: We've got a big fat tory prisoner. Off to a good beginning.

(Offstage: The sound of a gunshot.)

ANDERSON: *(Off.)* Oh, he shot me.

(ROBINSON enters holding a pistol.)

ROBINSON: I just killed Anderson.

MACKENZIE: Ah, you lying bastard.

(ROBINSON exits. MACKENZIE draws his pistol and misfires at ROBINSON.)

God save me Christ, how do these things work?

(The lights fade.)

Scene Nine

(In another playing area the lights fade in. BONDHEAD and ROLPH enter.)

BONDHEAD: A man has been killed. I am horrified, just horrified.

(FITZGIBBON enters in uniform with medals. He draws his sword.)

FITZGIBBON: So they want a republic, eh?

(BONDHEAD groans. FITZGIBBON laughs. ROBINSON enters.)

ROBINSON: Murder, murder, there's rebels afoot. Armed. I just killed a man.

BONDHEAD: I am horrified.

FITZGIBBON: We must organize resistance.

BONDHEAD: I am terrified, completely terrified. MacNab, where is he?

FITZGIBBON: But first we must buy time. We must send men under a flag of truce to parley.

BONDHEAD: Oh yes, loyal men, only loyal men.

FITZGIBBON: But someone the rebels can talk with. Rolph.

BONDHEAD: Rolph, oh yes Rolph. Will you represent me to the rebels?

ROLPH: I am ever loyal.

(The lights fade.)

Scene Ten

(In another playing area the lights fade in. MACKENZIE and LOUNT enter.)

MACKENZIE: Hot bubbling blood is on my hands.

LOUNT: Anthony Anderson was a good man.

MACKENZIE: Hot bubbling blood, he did not die in vain. Hot bubbling.

(O'TOOLE enters.)

Who are you?

O'TOOLE: The names's O'Toole, and O'Toole's hungry.

MACKENZIE: Montgomery, feed these men. That man will not fish nor cut bait.

LOUNT: God what a world.

O'TOOLE: I'm hungry.

MACKENZIE: Did you come to eat or fight?

O'TOOLE: Both.

MACKENZIE: And you will do both. Fight, then eat.

O'TOOLE: No, eat, then fight.

MACKENZIE: I am your commander in chief. Follow me.

(MACKENZIE exits. O'TOOLE and LOUNT stand motionless. MACKENZIE re-enters.)

O'TOOLE: Useless. We've been gammoned, I'm going home.

(O'TOOLE exits.)

MACKENZIE: Come back here, you'll fight the Family Compact or you'll fight me.

(MACKENZIE exits.)

LOUNT: A white flag.

(LOUNT exits. ROLPH and BALDWIN enter holding a flag of truce.)

BALDWIN: I cannot believe I am doing this.

ROLPH: I cannot believe I am doing this either.

BALDWIN: Representing the trolls to the goblin. My honour is irreparably scarred.

ROLPH: It is in our interest to be seen to be supporters of the government, for the moment.

BALDWIN: What?

ROLPH: Nothing.

(MACKENZIE, LOUNT, and O'TOOLE enter.)

MACKENZIE: They're surrendering, what did I tell you? They surrender. You!

ROLPH: This is a flag of truce.

MACKENZIE: You!

ROLPH: I am empowered by the government to ask what it is you want.

MACKENZIE: Are you now? Tell the governor we want independence and a convention to arrange the details, in writing, in one hour.

ROLPH: I shall relay the message to the governor. After you.

(BALDWIN exits.)

Proceed. Press forward. What are you waiting for? The time to strike is now. It is now or never.

(ROLPH exits.)

LOUNT: I thought Rolph was on our side.

MACKENZIE: He is.

LOUNT: Then why is he representing the governor?

MACKENZIE: He's spying on him. Now get up off your belly. We are going to attack.

LOUNT: Well, it's been a good life. I enjoyed breathing.

MACKENZIE: Come quickly.

(The lights fade.)

Scene Eleven

(In another playing area the lights fade in. CHENIER and PATRIOTES THREE and FOUR enter.)

CHENIER: At St. Eustache, we are ready.

PATRIOTES: God help the English we meet.

CHENIER: Do what you like, I shall fight, and if I am killed, well, I shall kill before dying.

PATRIOTES: God help the English we meet.

CHENIER: The dead are hopeless, but we are alive. Living in a grave, you can bury me now or you can bury me later. It doesn't matter. We are going to change our fortune.

PATRIOTES: The English are coming, the English are coming!

CHENIER: We must fight, we must prepare.

PATRIOTES: But we have no guns.

CHENIER: Don't worry. Some will get killed and you can take their arms. Allez, get in, get in.

(CHENIER beats the PATRIOTES with his sword.)

Into the church, into the church.

(The lights fade.)

Scene Twelve

(In another playing area the lights fade in. COLBORNE and BONTEMPS enter.)

COLBORNE: The clouds. How invincible. All powerful, all knowing.

BONTEMPS: Bang me with a hammer.

COLBORNE: You are my faithful hound. Stand behind your master.

BONTEMPS: Yes, High and Mighty Lord.

(WETHERALL enters.)

WETHERALL: The rebels await you at St. Eustache.

COLBORNE: St. Eustache? What is the meaning of that?

WETHERALL: Haven't the slightest.

BONTEMPS: It is named after a great French warrior who was roasted alive after seeing the crucifixion in the antlers of a stag.

COLBORNE: How interesting.

WETHERALL: We have the rebels surrounded, inside a church. We are now in the process of burning that church down.

COLBORNE: Excellent, General Wetherall.

(Two ENGLISH SOLDIERS enter.)

WETHERALL: Remember Jock Weir.

ENGLISH SOLDIERS: Remember Jock Weir.

WETHERALL: Fix bayonets. No prisoners.

ENGLISH SOLDIERS: Jock-o, Jock-o, Jock-o.

COLBORNE: Splendid.

(The lights fade.)

Scene Thirteen

(In another playing area the lights fade in. PATRIOTES THREE and FOUR enter.)

PATRIOTE THREE: Have faith sinner. Jesus was a sans culotte.

(CHENIER enters.)

CHENIER: We're being roasted like rats. We have to leave the church. Get out. Through the windows, through the doors, through whatever you can get through, get out.

(The lights fade.)

Scene Fourteen

(In another playing area the lights fade in. CHENIER and PATRIOTES THREE and FOUR enter.)

CHENIER: Thank God, we're out of there.

(Three BRITISH SOLDIERS enter holding bayonets.)

Oh no, remember St. Eustache.

(The SOLDIERS stab CHENIER and the PATRIOTES. WETHERALL and SERGEANT-MAJOR enter.)

WETHERALL: Excellent.

SERGEANT-MAJOR: Uh oh, he smells blood. He's going to go into a frenzy.

WETHERALL: Sergeant-major.

SERGEANT-MAJOR: Sir.

WETHERALL: We are going to show these French bastards the horrors of war. Those men over there, give them a good chopping.

SERGEANT-MAJOR: Chopping time.

WETHERALL: Burn that church. And those flesh pots, rape them. And those old hags over there, strip them naked, I want to see them dance in the snow. And then burn this village to the ground.

(Little PIERRE enters at the point of a bayonet.)

You there, French boy. Tell them what you have seen. Tell them about the British army.

LITTLE PIERRE: I will.

WETHERALL: And count yourself lucky, French boy. Count your lucky stars. Now get out of here.

(Offstage: Screams, shrieks, and groans. BONTEMPS enters. A wounded CHENIER groans.)

CHENIER: Help me.

(BONTEMPS points at CHENIER.)

BONTEMPS: That is Chenier, the leader of the rebels.

WETHERALL: I'm going to cut out his heart. But first, hold out his hands.

(SERGEANT-MAJOR holds out CHENIER's hands. WETHERALL raises the swords over his head—the sword descends.)

CHENIER: No!

(The lights fade.)

Scene Fifteen

(In another playing area the lights fade in. COLBORNE, WETHERALL, and GORE enter. WETHERALL holds up a heart pierced by a sword.)

WETHERALL: Behold, the heart of a traitor.

COLBORNE: General Wetherall.

WETHERALL: Sir.

COLBORNE: Well done. I am recommending you for a citation.

WETHERALL: My mother will be very proud. St. Eustache and St. Benoit have been sacked, pillaged, burned, destroyed. Not a twig left standing.

COLBORNE: Excellent, first class, capital. The rebellion in Lower Canada is crushed.

(The lights fade.)

Scene Sixteen

(In another playing area the lights fade in. The sound of a bell ringing. BONDHEAD and FITZGIBBON enter.)

BONDHEAD: Listen. They're saying, "Mur-der, mur-der, murder!"

FITZGIBBON: He's in good shape.

BONDHEAD: Murder!

(ROLPH enters.)

FITZGIBBON: What does Mackenzie say?

ROLPH: He says he wants independence and a convention to arrange the details. You have one hour to make your decision and it must be in writing.

BONDHEAD: Oh pugh. I could never agree, never, not in writing, never.

FITZGIBBON: I have men doing picket on Yonge Street. If there's any shooting, we'll know soon.

ROLPH: Now, I will retire to my quarters.

(ROLPH exits.)

BONDHEAD: We've done all we can. MacNab, if only he was here.

(The lights fade.)

Scene Seventeen

(In another playing area the lights fade in. The SHERIFF enters.)

SHERIFF: Now men, the governor is not giving in to the rebels. We are the first line of defence. Let's stand behind that fence and wait.

(The lights fade.)

Scene Eighteen

(In another playing area the lights fade in. MACKENZIE, LOUNT, O'TOOLE, and others enter holding cudgels.)

MACKENZIE: Well here we are at Yonge and Eglinton. Let's walk.

(O'TOOLE holds up his cudgel.)

O'TOOLE: Look at this.

MACKENZIE: The men up front got the guns.

O'TOOLE: And I got this. I'm going to attack the governor with this. I'd rather take out my John Thomas and attack him with that, than attack him with this.

MACKENZIE: Well here we are at Yonge and Bloor. Keep marching.

LOUNT: Oh I am going to die. I know it.

MACKENZIE: Shut up. Well here's MacGill Street. Keep walking. The Sheriff.

VOICE: *(Off.)* All right boys, fire.

(A deafening roar of gunshots. MACKENZIE, LOUNT, O'TOOLE, and supporters stampede.)

MACKENZIE: Stop, stop, you cowards. Stop.

(MACKENZIE and LOUNT are swept along with the stampede. They exit. The lights fade.)

Scene Nineteen

(In another playing area the lights fade in. BONDHEAD and FITZGIBBON enter.)

BONDHEAD: Oh MacNab, where are you?

(Noises offstage. MACNAB enters. BONDHEAD jumps up and down.)

MacNab, MacNab, MacNab, oh MacNab. You're here, you're here.

(BONDHEAD embraces MACNAB.)

MACNAB: Easy my lord, easy. Now what's all this about a rebellion?

BONDHEAD: Oh rebels are rebelling. You must lead the troops against them.

FITZGIBBON: What about me?

MACNAB: I take rank here.

BONDHEAD: Oh MacNab.

FITZGIBBON: I'll tell you something about war, laddie. When you were loading the cannon with your father, I was in the forest cutting men's throats with my bare hands. Your Lordship here could have his neck wrung like a chicken if we fail.

MACNAB: We will lead the troops together.

BONDHEAD: Oh MacNab.

(The lights fade.)

Scene Twenty

(In another playing area the lights fade in. MACKENZIE, LOUNT, O'TOOLE, and a REFORMER enter.)

REFORMER: Oh Mr. Mackenzie, I am wounded.

MACKENZIE: Well a coward anyway.

O'TOOLE: You are useless, except for talking and flipping your wig, calling a wounded man a coward. You should be shot. Useless. If there was an election between Bondhead and you, I'd vote for Bondhead. Useless.

LOUNT: Mr. Mackenzie, say something to inspire the men.

MACKENZIE: Canadians, brave Canadians, loyal Canadians. You are outnumbered two to one. God help you.

O'TOOLE: Thank you for those inspiring words. Useless.

(Offstage: The sound of gunshots.)

LOUNT: And so it begins.

REFORMER: Here come the Family Compact.

LOUNT: And so it begins.

(The lights fade.)

Scene Twenty-one

(In another playing area the lights fade in. BONDHEAD and MACNAB enter.)

BONDHEAD: Look at the way that man runs.

(FITZGIBBON enters.)

FITZGIBBON: The rebels are in full retreat.

BONDHEAD: Oh everything is going to be good now.

(The lights fade.)

Scene Twenty-two

(In another playing area the lights fade in. MACKENZIE, LOUNT, and others are in a stampede. MACKENZIE carries the book of names. MACKENZIE drops the book. They exit. BONDHEAD, FITZGIBBON, and MACNAB enter. MACNAB picks up the book.)

FITZGIBBON: After them.

(FITZGIBBON exits.)

MACNAB: Traitors. Names of traitors.

BONDHEAD: Oh let me see.

(FITZGIBBON enters.)

FITZGIBBON: Mackenzie has escaped but we captured Lount.

BONDHEAD: Oh I want his head on a stick. I will offer one thousand pounds for Mackenzie's head. And I want everyone to wear a pink ribbon on their arms, anyone who doesn't wear a pink ribbon is a traitor.

(The lights fade.)

Scene Twenty-three

(In another playing area the lights fade in. PAPINEAU and CHARLES HINDENLANG enter.)

PAPINEAU: Who are you?

HINDENLANG: I am Charles Hindenlang. A soldier and a warrior with the Frères Chasseurs.

PAPINEAU: Ah, the Brother Hunters.

HINDENLANG: Death is nothing to a Frenchman. Nothing. What kind of man do you think deserts from the French army?

PAPINEAU: It must be the nearest thing to a wild beast imaginable.

HINDENLANG: I laugh at pain.

PAPINEAU: So we have come to this have we? A hired ruffian. A soldier of fortune.

HINDENLANG: I make my living fighting. You make your living talking. I have the blood of Charlemagne in these veins.

PAPINEAU: Such bravado.

HINDENLANG: The more French the more beautiful.

(MME PAPINEAU enters.)

PAPINEAU: Hindenlang, the Frenchman.

MME PAPINEAU: Beware of this one, Louis.

HINDENLANG: My father was a Prussian but my mother was made from the earth of France.

PAPINEAU: Dirty muck.

HINDENLANG: We are going to attack.

PAPINEAU: That is a rash mistake. I think we should sue for peace. I only wanted constitutional reform, anyway. This rebellion is so revolting.

HINDENLANG: We must attack, we must invade.

PAPINEAU: We need support from the United States government.

HINDENLANG: We can't wait for them. I have here this Declaration of Independence. We are going to abolish seigneur's rights.

MME PAPINEAU: Infamata.

PAPINEAU: I will never support this declaration.

HINDENLANG: What will you support?

PAPINEAU: I will not support anything. I will not lead, I will not follow. I am what I am. I will go into exile with my mother. I will go to France. Where is my servant? Where are my bags?

(The lights fade.)

Scene Twenty-four

(In another playing area the lights fade in. MACKENZIE and MRS MACKENZIE enter. Offstage: The croaking of frogs.)

MRS MACKENZIE: Oh listen to the frogs.

MACKENZIE: Oh, I know how you feel.

(STRACHAN enters holding a torch.)

STRACHAN: Mackenzie, when we get hold of you we're going to skin you alive and melt you down for soap. I want that reward. Mackenzie, when we get hold of you.

(The lights fade.)

Scene Twenty-five

(In another playing area the lights fade in. BONDHEAD, STRACHAN, and ROLPH enter. BONDHEAD holds the book.)

BONDHEAD: Now we are going to arrest all the traitors. Shall we start with "A" and work our way through?

STRACHAN: Why not?

(ROLPH exits.)

BONDHEAD: Abercrombie.

STRACHAN: Oh to hell with the P's and Q's. Let's get to the R's. Rolph.

BONDHEAD: What? A traitor in my bosom, a vile viper ready to strike. Is there no one I can trust? I want his head, I want his head.

(FITZGIBBON enters.)

FITZGIBBON: Mackenzie has escaped to Buffalo.

BONDHEAD: I want his head.

(The lights fade.)

Scene Twenty-six

(In another playing area the lights fade in. The SHERIFF enters singing and cracking his bullwhip.)

SHERIFF: They call me the bullpup. Who will fight the bullpup? No one. They call me the bullpup.

(ROLPH enters holding a suitcase.)

Where are you going?

ROLPH: Just going on a little trip.

SHERIFF: It must be important.

ROLPH: It is.

SHERIFF: In time of rebellion a man doesn't take a little trip.

ROLPH: This one does, excuse me.

(ROLPH exits.)

SHERIFF: They call me the bullpup.

(The lights fade.)

Scene Twenty-seven

(In another playing area the lights fade in. COLBORNE and LAFONTAINE enter.)

COLBORNE: Is you name Louiss Hipplolightee Lafontaine?

LAFONTAINE: Non, monsieur. It is Louis-Hippolyte Lafontaine.

COLBORNE: Close enough. You are under arrest for high treason.

LAFONTAINE: Pourquoi?

COLBORNE: What?

LAFONTAINE: Pourquoi?

COLBORNE: Speak white.

LAFONTAINE: Parlez blanc?

COLBORNE: Come with me.

(LAFONTAINE utters a stream of curses en Français.)

Guards.

(The lights fade.)

Scene Twenty-eight

(In another playing area the lights fade in. MACKENZIE enters.)

MACKENZIE: Citizens of Buffalo. Lend me your ears. We are going to liberate the Canadas. Labourers will leave their jobs, mechanics their counters, magistrates their duties, husbands their families, children their parents, and Christians their churches. All for the glorious cause. Liberate the Canadas. Now I need volunteers. Oh you sons of Liberty, come join us on Navy Island. We have the steamer Caroline ready to take you there. You there, will you join us.

(ROLPH enters.)

ROLPH: You, there you are.

MACKENZIE: Gentlemen, the president of the Republic of Upper Canada, John Rolph.

ROLPH: Don't listen to him. He has ruined me. Men have died in vain.

MACKENZIE: They did not die in vain. Hot bubbling blood is on my hands.

ROLPH: You are mad, completely mad.

MACKENZIE: Is the love of madness freedom?

ROLPH: What?

MACKENZIE: Will you lead us?

ROLPH: The Honourable Robert was right. I am a fool.

MACKENZIE: Well, a coward anyway. Does the thought of committing high treason scare you?

ROLPH: No. But invading Canada with you does.

MACKENZIE: The blood of fine men is on my hands.

ROLPH: You are a blundering idiot, a blathering. I am ruined, destroyed, finished.

MACKENZIE: Hot bubbling blood.

(ROLPH exits.)

How does president of the Republic of Upper Canada sound to you?

(The lights fade.)

Scene Twenty-nine

(In another playing area the lights fade in. STRACHAN and LOUNT enter.)

STRACHAN: Now Lount—

LOUNT: Mr. Lount to you, parson.

STRACHAN: Give us the names of Mackenzie's—

LOUNT: Mr. Mackenzie to you, parson.

STRACHAN: Do you repent your transgressions?

LOUNT: No. Mr. Mackenzie was a great man, and he did the right thing, only it didn't work out like it should have.

STRACHAN: Give us the names of your friends and you'll go free.

LOUNT: You'll get no names from me, parson.

STRACHAN: Then it's death for you.

(In another playing area the lights fade in. ROBINSON enters.)

ROBINSON: I sentence you to be hung by the neck until dead.

LOUNT: The mean-spirited …

(In another playing area the lights fade in. BONDHEAD and SARAH enter.)

SARAH: Oh, Mr. Bondhead, if you could find it in your heart some mercy.

BONDHEAD: Madam, a thousand times, no. He had the bad taste to rebel against me. He is going to hang and then off to the vivisectionist.

LOUNT: The mean-spirited …. Those who die in a great cause never fail. The prospect of eternity makes me smile.

(The lights fade.)

Scene Thirty

(In another playing area the lights fade in. FITZGIBBON enters. ROBINSON laughs.)

FITZGIBBON: Disgraceful.

VOICE ONE: *(Off.)* We'll kill your children, bitch, if you don't tell us where your husband is.

VOICE TWO: *(Off.)* Take your hands off my wife.

VOICE THREE: *(Off.)* Your name was in the book and you'll pay.

FITZGIBBON: Disgraceful. If I'd have known you were going to behave like this, I'd have let the rebels win.

(ROBINSON laughs. The lights fade.)

Scene Thirty-one

(In another playing area the lights fade in. BONDHEAD, STRACHAN, and MACNAB enter.)

STRACHAN: Oh, we're on top good now.

MACNAB: Did you see Mrs. Lount? "Oh please don't hurt my husband." *(He laughs.)* Oh, she's a fine looking woman.

(ROBINSON enters.)

ROBINSON: Mackenzie and his ruffians have just taken over Navy Island, just above Niagara Falls.

MACNAB: And they got a steamer running a ferry service between that island and the United States.

BONDHEAD: I have asked the Americans to extradite Mackenzie but they refuse. Oh I feel like declaring war on them.

STRACHAN: Oh, Mr. Bondhead if only you would.

BONDHEAD: Mackenzie, I must have him.

MACNAB: You will.

(FITZGIBBON enters.)

ROBINSON: Well look who it is. We're going to give you a medal with a big blue ribbon.

FITZGIBBON: Stick it. What you are doing to these people—

STRACHAN: Is justice.

FITZGIBBON: Is a disgrace.

STRACHAN: I would pervert the prophets if it served my purpose. This is politics with a capital "P."

FITZGIBBON: To the Family Compact, all flesh is pork. One less snout to feed means more for me.

STRACHAN: That's right, Mr. Fitzgibbon. A still hog eats the most.

FITZGIBBON: God what a world.

STRACHAN: Yes, what a world.

FITZGIBBON: I have served you people for twenty-five years. It has been a donkey's joy. Well no more, good day.

MACNAB: Good riddance.

STRACHAN: Oh, we're on top good now.

(The lights fade.)

Scene Thirty-two

(In another playing area the lights fade in. MACNAB enters holding a torch.)

MACNAB: All right, laddies, there's the steamer, the Caroline. We are going to cut it loose and then burn it. Smuggle my pork, this will put me on top good. Smuggle my pork, I say.

(The lights fade.)

Scene Thirty-three

(In another playing area the lights fade in. MACKENZIE enters holding a quill and paper. MRS MACKENZIE enters holding a pot.)

MRS MACKENZIE: Ah wee Willie, I've made you some broth from rocks. Drink it down now.

MACKENZIE: Stop your nattering mother. I'm writing the Declaration of Independence.

MRS MACKENZIE: Drink it down now.

MACKENZIE: Oh mother, Navy Island would be a dreary place without you and your broth.

MRS MACKENZIE: You're my bonnie bairn. What's that sound? It sounds like thunder.

MACKENZIE: Aye Mother, it's Niagara Falls. One of the wonders of the world.

MRS MACKENZIE: Oh glory be.

(RENSELLAER and BILL JOHNSTON enter.)

RENSELLAER: I'm here, I'm here. Let the banners fly and the bugles blow. This uniform was good enough for my father so it's good enough for me.

JOHNSTON: Let's make a fire.

MACKENZIE: Oh liberty, what crimes—

RENSELLAER: Did anyone bring the ammunition?

MACKENZIE: Ah, no hope. We have to plan things.

RENSELLAER: There is a plan. We are going to invade and I am going to take over. I will be boss.

MACKENZIE: Good God.

JOHNSTON: And I'm an admiral. Admiral Bill Johnston.

MACKENZIE: A pirate. Leaping goats and jumping monkeys. What are we going to do?

RENSELLAER: We are going to conquer the world and I will be king.

MACKENZIE: Oh God.

(An ALAMO MAN enters holding a bottle.)

JOHNSTON: What's that you got there?

ALAMO MAN: This is tequila.

JOHNSTON: That sounds like booze.

ALAMO MAN: This is scorpion juice. They make this out of scorpions. You drink this, you'll see God.

JOHNSTON: Gimme that.

MACKENZIE: I am with bandits and drunkards.

(JOHNSTON takes the bottle from the ALAMO MAN.)

ALAMO MAN: You want to know what God looks like? It looks like a lizard eating a grass hopper.

MACKENZIE: Pagan.

JOHNSTON: Look, there's a fire floating on the river. Look!

RENSELLAER: Good ... that's the Caroline. The steamer.

ALAMO MAN: It's heading for the falls like a fourth of July.

JOHNSTON: And away she goes.

MACKENZIE: This is beautiful. Now we have no communicaitons and no more supplies. This is beautiful.

RENSELLAER: I think we are going to retire.

ALAMO MAN: We're not going to invade. That's first blood, first blood.

RENSELLAER: I have changed my mind. We are going to retire in order.

MACKENZIE: Ignominious.

RENSELLAER: Quiet. We came to liberate the Canadas.

MACKENZIE: But we didn't fire a shot.

RENSELLAER: But we retreated with honour.

(RENSELLAER exits.)

ALAMO MAN: Did we come here to invade or did we come here to invade?

(ALAMO MAN exits.)

MACKENZIE: Ignominious.

JOHNSTON: Quiet you fat little fart.

MACKENZIE: I'm not fat. You're completely insensible. You should be in a nut house.

JOHNSTON: I am.

(JOHNSTON exits.)

MACKENZIE: I feel like I've gone to hell.

(The lights fade.)

Scene Thirty-four

(In another playing area the lights fade in. BONDHEAD and ROBINSON enter.)

BONDHEAD: Oh MacNab has sunk the Caroline. Three cheers for MacNab.

ROBINSON: The Americans are in an uproar.

BONDHEAD: Let them roar.

ROBINSON: No, you don't understand. During the sinking of the Caroline some Americans were killed.

BONDHEAD: So?

ROBINSON: So it is being interpreted as a hostile act.

BONDHEAD: Good. It is.

ROBINSON: Many Americans are forming groups with the intention of invading. They are so exasperated.

BONDHEAD: Good. Exasperated men become enraged men, and enraged men become dead men. Pour it on. I am feeling omnipotent.

(MACNAB enters holding a letter.)

Oh MacNab, the hero of the Caroline.

(MACNAB gives BONDHEAD the letter. BONDHEAD reads the letter.)

ROBINSON: The Americans are forming themselves into hunter lodges. They are skirmishing here and there. They are planning to invade.

BONDHEAD: I am reading this letter from the colonial secretary. Oh no. Oh my God, Lord Durham has been appointed governor-general of the Canadas. Why?!

(The lights fade.)

Scene Thirty-five

(In another playing area the lights fade in. COLBORNE and GOSFORD enter.)

COLBORNE: Well Archibald, the British government has suspended the constitution of the colony and appointed a new governor-general, Lord Durham.

GOSFORD: I don't care. I have been recalled and I am glad. This place is a pill.

COLBORNE: Well I am in charge now. That will make the wife smile.

(The lights fade.)

Scene Thirty-six

(In another playing area the lights fade in. ROBINSON enters.)

ROBINSON: I love hangings. I like to see the feet kicking. And the tongue bulging out, blue, a bright blue, that's the detail that appeals to me.

(STRACHAN enters holding a proclamation.)

STRACHAN: Quiet, you, quiet. We have a new governor.

ROBINSON: They say he is a radical whig.

STRACHAN: Proud and ill-tempered.

ROBINSON: I hope he doesn't insult us.

STRACHAN: I hear he beats his servants.

ROBINSON: I hope he doesn't beat us.

STRACHAN: Quiet, you, quiet. They call him Radical Jack. Well, he'll do my bidding or I'll be bound. Like the others he will see things clearly, or I'll be bound.

(The lights fade.)

Scene Thirty-seven

(In another playing area the lights fade in. BONDHEAD, ROBINSON, STRACHAN, and MACNAB enter.)

BONDHEAD: Oh, he's marvelous. He's a real lord. He's not a lord like you're a lord. He's a real lord. His sense of etiquette is going to make you feel like a savage, and he's going to make you feel like a wild beast. But he's going to take a fancy to you.

(COLBORNE enters.)

COLBORNE: His Excellency, the governor-general of the Canadas, Lord Durham.

(LORD DURHAM enters.)

STRACHAN: Your Excellency, Your Worship, Your Majesty.

DURHAM: Enough. I understand you are the Legislative Council.

COLBORNE: As you well know, His Lordship is making an inquiry into the cause of the rebellion.

DURHAM: In order to create tranquility, I am on my own authority, by executive decree, declaring an amnesty for all the political prisoners except the leaders who will be banished to

Bermuda and Australia. Now, Sir Francis, I understand we are almost in a state of war with the United States.

BONDHEAD: It wasn't me. It was him. MacNab, oh MacNab. I am betrayed again.

MACNAB: I was only doing what I thought was best.

DURHAM: I shudder to think of you at your worst. The beast can leave the room.

BONDHEAD: That means go.

(MACNAB exits.)

DURHAM: You are dismissed.

STRACHAN: That means go.

(BONDHEAD exits.)

DURHAM: Send in the American ambassador.

STRACHAN: Oh wait till you see him. He is such a beast.

COLBORNE: The American ambassador, Mr. Squat.

(SQUAT enters.)

SQUAT: Just call me Diddley. I am a man of some education. When spoken to, I speak. To whom is we talking to.

COLBORNE: This is Lord Durham.

SQUAT: Pleased to make your pleasure, sir. Mighty pleased.

DURHAM: How do you do?

SQUAT: Oh, I do very well, very well indeed, sir.

DURHAM: I understand that the American government has some misgivings with regard to the sinking of the Caroline.

SQUAT: I would not use a verb like "misgiving."

DURHAM: Noun.

SQUAT: I would not use a noun like "misgiving" to express our feelings about the massacre of an American citizen. We is plenty pissed-off, plenty. We will use this as a pretext for war unless we receive an abject apology, abject.

DURHAM: You have an amazing similarity to Andrew Jackson.

SQUAT: Why thank you, sir. I pride myself on that man. Pride myself.

DURHAM: Let's drink a toast to Andrew Jackson.

SQUAT: Now you're talking. And fireworks too.

(DURHAM looks at COLBORNE.)

COLBORNE: I will arrange for fireworks.

DURHAM: I think we can work this out.

SQUAT: I think so.

COLBORNE: Get along, little doggie.

(SQUAT exits.)

DURHAM: Now, Parson Strachan.

STRACHAN: Bishop Strachan.

DURHAM: I know the Archbishop of Canterbury, personally. That is a bishop.

STRACHAN: Very rich, very rude.

DURHAM: Send in Mr. Baldwin.

(BALDWIN enters.)

What do Canadians want?

BALDWIN: I am not going to defend the actions of Mr. Mackenzie.

DURHAM: What a relief.

BALDWIN: But if political reform is not instituted, men of milder persuasion than Mr. Mackenzie will become more radical than Mr. Mackenzie. We desire the same form of government as the mother country. Is that too much to ask?

DURHAM: No.

STRACHAN: You Republican.

BALDWIN: Do you think I am a Republican?

DURHAM: I would not, what is the word, impugn your honour?

BALDWIN: Exactly.

DURHAM: Gentlemen, I am going to recommend to the Home Office the union of the Canadas.

STRACHAN: No.

DURHAM: And the application of the concept of responsible government.

STRACHAN: No.

DURHAM: To Upper and Lower Canada.

STRACHAN: No.

DURHAM: There is nothing worse in this world than a pampered priest.

STRACHAN: Very rich, very rude.

DURHAM: Quiet, you overstuffed lout. Your lot in life is to lick and loathe the hand that holds the sword. Your lot in life is not to wield the sword. Is that clear?

STRACHAN: Your Excellency. We are only trying to preserve a wee bit of England in this forest.

DURHAM: And while you are doing that, you will make sure that the inhabitants have the rights of Englishmen. And one of those rights, is now the vote.

STRACHAN: Responsible government will give power to rascals.

DURHAM: Perhaps, but perhaps not. What kind of backwater is this place? Have you not heard of democracy?

STRACHAN: That's a Yankee word. I go berserk when I hear that word, berserk. This country will become a truly great colony, or I'll be bound.

DURHAM: Yes, it will, and you will.

(The lights fade.)

Scene Thirty-eight

(In another playing area the lights fade in. PAPINEAU, PIERRE, and MME PAPINEAU enter.)

PAPINEAU: Rousseau, Lamennais, Lamartine, I have read them all. But life is not what I have read about.

PIERRE: No it is not.

PAPINEAU: Come dear slave, let us drink a glass in praise of folly.

MME PAPINEAU: Infamata.

PAPINEAU: You and I, with dear maman, are going to France, to live in exile.

MME PAPINEAU: Infamata.

PAPINEAU: But one day we will return.

PIERRE: That will be a good day for France.

PAPINEAU: Pick up my bags and sing my name. En avant.

(The lights fade.)

Scene Thirty-nine

(In another playing area the lights fade in. MACKENZIE enters wearing handcuffs.)

MACKENZIE: Is the love of freedom madness? Does the love of freedom make you a criminal? I have been convicted of violating the neutrality laws of the United States. Eighteen months in the hoose-gow. Thundering lizards.

(The lights fade.)

Scene Forty

(In another playing area the lights fade in. DURHAM enters.)

DURHAM: My first impressions of Canada, you ask? What a mess. Two of everything in this colony. Two races, two languages, two religions. Two of everything. Well, the philosopher-king has come to solve your problems. When I came here I expected to find a dispute between the people and the executive. Instead I found two nations warring in the bosom of a single state. The struggle is a racial one. The national feud. The French must be assimilated. As an amoeba eats bacteria, the English must eat the French.

(The lights fade.)

Scene Forty-one

(In another playing area the lights fade in. LAFONTAINE enters.)

LAFONTAINE: I highly recommend living in a dungeon. One has time for contemplation. Society is the biggest prison ever invented. I am a drone. Droning on.

(COLBORNE enters.)

COLBORNE: His Lordship will now see you.

LAFONTAINE: At last. I'm talking to myself already.

(DURHAM enters.)

DURHAM: I will give you one minute of my time.

LAFONTAINE: I understand you are going to recommend the union of the Canadas.

DURHAM: That is correct. The union of the Canadas and an eventual confederation of the provinces is to be desired.

LAFONTAINE: The union of the Canadas will guarantee the extinction of the French-Canadien race.

DURHAM: Correct. The French must be assimilated.

LAFONTAINE: Non.

DURHAM: This province will be British. What happens here must benefit the mother country.

LAFONTAINE: But—

DURHAM: But no but. These Canadiens compared to the Irish peasants are quite well off.

LAFONTAINE: But the Irish peasants are made to live like wild beasts. Worse. Our grievances are genuine. An amnesty for the political prisoners—

COLBORNE: One minute.

DURHAM: Good day.

(DURHAM and COLBORNE exit.)

LAFONTAINE: The more I see of men, the more I admire dogs.

(The lights fade.)

Scene Forty-two

(In another playing area the lights fade in. LAFONTAINE and BALDWIN enter. They each hold a copy of DURHAM's report.)

VOICE: *(Off.)* All hail the act of union!

BALDWIN: It says here that Upper Canada will now be called Canada West.

LAFONTAINE: And Lower Canada will be called Canada East.

BALDWIN: This changes everything.

LAFONTAINE: What changes but remains the same.

BALDWIN: Now there will be real reform.

LAFONTAINE: This is a lie, a cheat. This is imperialism.

BALDWIN: Oh you black pigs at the trough of despotism. Drink deep, while you can.

LAFONTAINE: But God in his mercy leaves hope for the oppressed.

BALDWIN: This changes everything.

LAFONTAINE: Even though man is born in a stable, he is not a cow.

BALDWIN: And as dirt defies a queen.

LAFONTAINE: We will rule our rulers.

BALDWIN: Together.

(LAFONTAINE and BALDWIN turn toward each other. The lights fade. The end.)

Confederation and Riel

Part Four of The History of the Village of the Small Huts

Act One

Scene One

(In two separate playing areas the lights fade in. GEORGE BROWN and GEORGE-ÉTIENNE CARTIER enter.)

BROWN: My name is George Brown.

CARTIER: I am George-Étienne Cartier.

(BROWN holds up a copy of The Globe. *The headline reads "1864.")*

BROWN: I founded this political journal twenty years ago. In this colony one must declare where one stands or others will declare it for you.

CARTIER: Jacques Cartier was my great, great, great, great grandfather. He discovered this country. That means I own this country. If anyone doesn't think so I will take my knife and peel them like an apple.

BROWN: I represent a majority of the elected representatives of Upper Canada, Canada West if you like.

CARTIER: I control Lower Canada, Canada East s'il vous plaît. What I say goes or there's hell to pay.

(In another playing area the lights fade in. JOHN A. MACDONALD enters.)

MACDONALD: Big George, Little George. We have had four governments in the last two years, based on an Upper Canada majority with a Lower Canada minority, or a Lower Canada majority with an Upper Canada minority. Deadlock. Hopeless. In order to govern properly you need two simultaneous majorities in Upper and Lower Canada. We've all been prime minister. We've all served in cabinet. They are having a revolution in Mexico, a civil war in the United States, and will this flea circus called Parliament discuss important matters such as military defence, intercolonial communication? Will they discuss that? Of course not. They would rather call each other dogs that eat their own vomit. They would rather insult each other. Heap abuse on each other. Petty squabblers.

BROWN: I hate you so much you French Catholic Papist bastard.

CARTIER: Suck this you English turd.

BROWN: One day I am going to be prime minister, again.

CARTIER: You haven't got a hope in hell.

BROWN: The purpose of the Act of Union was to assimilate the French.

CARTIER: Well it didn't work out that way, did it?

BROWN: Upper Canada demands justice. Representation by population, I'll say it again. Representation by population.

CARTIER: That's what we said in 1840 but people like you laughed.

BROWN: It is criminal that five Englishmen are equal to four Frenchmen. We outnumber you by two hundred and fifty thousand and yet we have the same number of seats.

CARTIER: I care for the rights of this quarter of a million Englishmen like I care for the rights of a quarter million codfish. You make me sick.

BROWN: This can't go on. I'll say it again, representation by population.

MACDONALD: The Canadas or Canada.

CARTIER: The rights of Lower Canada will be respected.

BROWN: Rep. by pop. I say, rep. by pop.

MACDONALD: The question is, "What is to be done?" What is to be done, indeed.

(MACDONALD smiles. The lights fade.)

Scene Two

(In another playing area the lights fade in. LOUIS RIEL and MRS RIEL enter holding a buffalo skin.)

MRS RIEL: The voice of God told me to marry your father.

RIEL: Yes, the voice of God. How sweet to the ear.

MRS RIEL: I wanted to be a nun, or failing that, vegetate like a plant, ferment in my own juice. I wanted to be like a dry leaf, but Mother Mary in her wisdom did not drain me of my sap. What is going to become of you?

RIEL: God will decide.

MRS RIEL: Louis, make your mother's heart sing. Become a religious.

RIEL: A religious what?

MRS RIEL: Just a religious.

RIEL: There, one buffalo skin.

MRS RIEL: A skin for a skin.

RIEL: All that a buffalo hath will he give for his life.

MRS RIEL: Too late for this one though. Pull.

(The lights fade.)

Scene Three

(In another playing area the lights fade in. MACDONALD enters holding a bottle.)

MACDONALD: That which is easy to secure is difficult to maintain. But that which is difficult to secure is easy to maintain.

VOICE: *(Off.)* Opium.

MACDONALD: George-ÉTIENNE Cartier and I, are co-prime ministers, associate prime ministers. But one day I will be prime minister with no co-this, or associate-that about it. And when I am prime minister I will make the provinces fractions of a unit instead of units of a multiple.

VOICE: *(Off.)* Opium.

MACDONALD: Parliament is power. Parliament can do anything except make a man into a woman. But he who controls Parliament can make men act like women. That makes me smack my lips.

VOICE: *(Off.)* Opium.

MACDONALD: Just the wife. Pay no attention.

VOICE: *(Off.)* Opium.

MACDONALD: I am going to love her till the day she dies.

VOICE: *(Off.)* Opium.

MACDONALD: Do you drink?

VOICE: *(Off.)* Opium.

(The lights fade.)

Scene Four

(The lights fade in. BISHOP TACHÉ and RIEL enter.)

BISHOP TACHÉ: In this sign thou shalt conquer.

RIEL: *In hoc signo vinces.*

BISHOP TACHÉ: Blessed is he that cometh in the name of the Lord.

RIEL: *Benedictus qui venit in nomine dominii.*

BISHOP TACHÉ: Very good Louis, very good. You are a brilliant student. Beyond praise, in fact. Now Louis, people have great expectations. You are the future of your people.

RIEL: Yes.

BISHOP TACHÉ: That appeals to you, does it? The road to hell is paved with the sin of pride, Louis, remember that.

RIEL: Yes, always.

BISHOP TACHÉ: Hold my hand. We are going to send you to the College de Montréal, the Sulpician Seminary. And when you come back, you will be Louis Riel, Métis priest. The first. The Church's dream come true. Be proud.

RIEL: Yes.

(BISHOP TACHÉ smiles. The lights fade.)

Scene Five

(In two playing areas the lights fade in. CARTIER and MADAME CUVILLIER enter. BROWN enters.)

CARTIER: My great, great, great—

MME CUVILLIER: You have told me this a thousand times. Tell me something new.

BROWN: I am a Presbyterian. That means I spend every waking moment justifying my existence.

CARTIER: Oh my friend Jean.

MME CUVILLIER: Oh him.

CARTIER: He is not like the others, he has heart. When I do things, he looks the other way, he understands me. Me and Jean, prime ministers together.

MME CUVILLIER: You love him so much.

(BROWN holds up The Globe.*)*

BROWN: I have no wife, this is my life.

CARTIER: I am in love with power.

MME CUVILLIER: And therefore you are in love with me.

BROWN: When I came to this country, I did not come as a Scotsman.

CARTIER: Call me Jacques.

MME CUVILLIER: Would you like a drink, Jacques?

BROWN: But as a British free man.

MME CUVILLIER: Or do you have to go home to your wife?

CARTIER: Do you want to talk about Hortense?

MME CUVILLIER: Non.

BROWN: A British free man is what I am.

MME CUVILLIER: Cognac, Jacques?

CARTIER: My kidneys are killing me.

BROWN: But I am not an ex-slave.

MME CUVILLIER: You say no to cognac you say no to life.

BROWN: I am a Canadian.

CARTIER: What the hell, on the rocks.

(The lights fade.)

Scene Six

(In another playing area the lights fade in. RIEL and BISHOP IGNACE BOURGET enter.)

BOURGET: You are enjoying your stay in Montréal?

RIEL: Very.

BOURGET: Your studies are going well?

RIEL: Very.

BOURGET: Excellent. Expiate.

RIEL: I am filled with avarice and lust. I am lazy and stupid. Envious and ignorant.

(BOURGET smiles.)

And I am vain, oh so vain.

(The lights fade.)

Scene Seven

(In another playing area the lights fade in. BROWN and CARTIER enter.)

BROWN: God in all his goodness gave us freedom of the kirk.

CARTIER: What? Speak English.

BROWN: The church. I believe in a school system based on the teachings of the Bible.

CARTIER: So do I.

BROWN: Not the commandments of popes.

CARTIER: Heretic.

BROWN: Popes! I reach for my gun when I hear that word. The subject who is truly loyal to the chief magistrate will neither advise nor submit to arbitrary matters.

CARTIER: Shut the mouth up.

BROWN: Quiet you screeching wretch.

CARTIER: You pompous ass.

(MACDONALD enters.)

MACDONALD: Ah gentlemen, gentlemen. Renewing old friendships I see.

CARTIER: Oui.

BROWN: How can you support this man?

CARTIER: Don't worry Big George, Lower Canada will look after the rights of Upper Canada.

BROWN: Upper Canada demands divorce from Lower Canada.

CARTIER: Monsieur Brun.

BROWN: Mr. Brown.

CARTIER: I have always advocated the principle of responsible government, but—

BROWN: Because I am a slave to the railroads I have abandoned all my principles.

CARTIER: We got the majority, call in the members. Put it to a vote.

MACDONALD: This cannot go on. A coalition is to be desired. Big George, come here.

(MACDONALD whispers into BROWN's ear.)

CARTIER: The rights of the French minority must be protected. The rights of the Catholic Church must be protected.

MACDONALD: Little Georges, come here.

(MACDONALD whispers into CARTIER's ear.)

BROWN: Constitutional reform will be inititated in order to establish the principle of representation by population, and to squash the French.

MACDONALD: So we are agreed. You will consent to a coalition, to a great coalition.

BROWN and CARTIER: Yes. Oui.

MACDONALD: Excellent, just excellent.

(The lights fade.)

Scene Eight

(In another playing area the lights fade in. BOURGET and RIEL enter.)

BOURGET: Everyone look at me. Students. This is our prize pupil. Can a man be more pure than his maker?

RIEL: Non.

BOURGET: Did the clay say to him that fashioned it, "What are you making?"

RIEL: If the clay came from Manitoba, you better believe it.

BOURGET: This Indian boy has such a sense of humour. Well Indian boy, you have a mission in life. Your people are as sheep that have no shepherd. You are the elect. You have been chosen. You have a mission, fulfill it. Right, Indian boy.

RIEL: Yes.

(The lights fade.)

Scene Nine

(In another playing area the lights fade in. MACDONALD and NARCISSE BELLEAU enter.)

BELLEAU: Narcisse Belleau reporting.

MACDONALD: I have three questions. I do not want you to answer any of them. If offered a position in cabinet, would you accept it? Or would you demand a definite offer before giving a definite answer? And if the definite answer proved to be "No," would you be prepared to treat the offer as never having been made?

BELLEAU: I think my answer to question number one will answer all three. If offered a position in cabinet I would accept it.

MACDONALD: I have nothing to offer you. Such presumption on your part. Get out.

(BELLEAU exits.)

Cabinet-making, one of the joys of life.

(The lights fade.)

Scene Ten

(In another playing area the lights fade in. D'ARCY McGEE, CARTIER, MACDONALD, ALEXANDRE GALT, and ÉTIENNE TACHÉ enter.)

CARTIER: Cognac? You say no to cognac, you say no to life.

McGEE: What a world. In this world whores are called mistresses, bribes are called contributions, and traitors are called free-thinkers.

MACDONALD: Galt, we want to form a confederation based on the federal principle.

McGEE: When one's country is in danger, indifference is a crime.

MACDONALD: What do you think of that?

McGEE: Only the infamous are neutral.

CARTIER: When he goes on like this I can't tell if he is drunk or sober.

MACDONALD and CARTIER: So ... so?

GALT: I believe that if a principle when taken to logical extremes is bad, then the principle is bad.

MACDONALD: Yes, it is always bad to shave your head when all you wanted was a haircut.

TACHÉ: I'm a Canadian, I admit it.

MACDONALD: Excuse me.

MACDONALD and CARTIER: Be gentle, be brutal.

MACDONALD: Now Mr. McGee.

McGEE: They call me D'Arcy for a reason.

CARTIER: Enchanté, monsieur.

MACDONALD: They say you are a Liberal. Which goes to prove that just because a man is called a Liberal doesn't mean he believes in liberalism.

CARTIER: Have you met my dear friend, Étienne Taché? This is a Canadian, the real thing.

TACHÉ: Yes, I am a Canadian, I admit it.

McGEE: That term implies nationhood.

MACDONALD: Correct.

McGEE: We all venerate our mother countries too dearly to be a nation.

MACDONALD: Oh you're in top form McGee. So, it is going well?

CARTIER: It is, yes.

(BROWN enters holding a key.)

BROWN: Now, I have locked the door. No one can leave. We are going to agree on certain constitutional principles or I will know the reason why. I am the voice of Upper Canada.

GALT: Now if you ask for my opinion …

MACDONALD: Who's asking?

GALT: Well. I think the Province of Canada should divide into two sections, each governing itself in local matters in tandem with a general legislature for matters of national interest.

MACDONALD: Who asked for your opinion?

GALT: All seems obvious to me. And furthermore a confederacy of all the British North American colonies is desired.

MACDONALD: Galt.

BROWN: When I hear the word confederacy I think of negro slavery. What kind of confederacy do you have in mind?

MACDONALD: A strong central government is indispensible to success, we must be careful to avoid the mistakes of the United States.

GALT: I will only enter the government if my plan is adopted.

MACDONALD: Galt.

CARTIER: The rights of the minority must be protected.

MACDONALD: And they will be. The rich are always fewer in number than the poor. Now this great coalition is going to need a leader.

BROWN: You'll never be prime minister.

MACDONALD: And neither will you.

(MACDONALD points at CARTIER, McGEE, and then GALT.)

BROWN: That screeching wretch hasn't got a hope in hell. I don't think so, I don't think so.

TACHÉ: I'm a Canadian, I admit it.

McGEE: A Canadian nation cannot exist where there is no independent Canadian state, call us Canadians and we will smile for no reason, call us cattle and we will smile knowingly.

MACDONALD: Hey you, Taché.

TACHÉ: Are there bees making honey here?

MACDONALD: How would you like to be prime minister?

TACHÉ: What?

(MACDONALD, BROWN, and CARTIER confer.)

MACDONALD: How would you like to be prime minister.

TACHÉ: What?

(The lights fade.)

Scene Eleven

(In another playing area the lights fade in. RIEL and BOURGET enter.)

RIEL: One question Your Eminence?

BOURGET: Speak child.

RIEL: The forbidden books by Voltaire, Montaigne, Lamartine …

BOURGET: Don't mention those names in my presence.

RIEL: Why can't I read them?

BOURGET: Because they are in league with the devil, Louis.

RIEL: But they are free-thinkers, aren't they?

BOURGET: Who has planted this demon seed within you? Answer me?

RIEL: Just gossip in the washroom.

BOURGET: And that's where it should stay. There is only one love. Him!

RIEL: Oh yes Him, the most beautiful man in the world.

BOURGET: We exist for only one reason. To serve him.

RIEL: Master, master.

BOURGET: You have a mission. You are the elect. The chosen. Is that understood?

RIEL: Yes.

BOURGET: Good.

(The lights fade.)

Scene Twelve

(In another playing area the lights fade in. MACDONALD and LORD MONCK enter.)

MACDONALD: Your Excellency, there is a rumour that British troops are going to be removed from Canadian soil. As you are no doubt aware, our good neighbour, to the south, has tied his dong in a knot and is unable to untie it.

MONCK: You are referring to the American Civil War?

MACDONALD: Yes.

MONCK: Our government is officially neutral. Although we would like to see the Confederacy win, we are not supporting them.

MACDONALD: And that is why the Americans by attacking us, attack you. The responsibility for defending Canada from the United States is the responsibility of Great Britain.

MONCK: As you are no doubt aware, there is great talk in London that some of our colonies are an expensive burden.

MACDONALD: Protect us from the Americans.

MONCK: Protect yourselves from the Americans. What is the matter with you people? You demand the privileges of independence without accepting the responsibility. Now I understand we are going to see the American asmbassador.

MACDONALD: That is correct, Your Excellency. Mr. Sammy …

(MISTER SAMMY enters.)

SAMMY: Just call me Sam. How you doing, John A.?

MACDONALD: This is the governor-general of the Province of Canada, Lord Monck.

SAMMY: Nice to meet you Lord.

MONCK: How do you do?

SAMMY: Oh I do very well, very well indeed, sir.

MACDONALD: You have a message you wish to communicate to His Excellency.

SAMMY: That is correct, sir. Now we, in Washington, are hearing rumours that you are going to confederate, or federate, or do something up here. Maybe you haven't noticed. We don't like confederacies.

MACDONALD: Perhaps you prefer the Kingdom of Canada.

SAMMY: No, that one makes us feel powerful mean. Powerful mean, John A.

MACDONALD: Keep your shirt on. The Dominion of Canada is the choice.

SAMMY: Just what makes you think we will recognize the government of this Dominion of Canada?

MONCK: You will have no choice but to recognize that government.

SAMMY: Lordy, lordy, my, my. The dead come alive.

MONCK: British arms will protect the sovereignty of this country.

SAMMY: My, my, you make me feel warm and juicy. Now I am going to give to you the facts of life. We just freed our slaves, and a lot of white boys got killed freeing those slaves. So you know what that means?

MONCK: One can only guess.

SAMMY: That's right, you guess right. That means we want new ones. And you Canadians, or whatever you call yourselves look natural born.

MACDONALD: Mr. Sammy.

SAMMY: Don't give me mouth when I want ear.

MACDONALD: Entre nous.

SAMMY: Ah, speaking like a Frenchie. You know what we would do if we had Frenchies. We'd cornhole 'em just so we could watch them walk funny.

MACDONALD: Our neighbour.

MONCK: Good lord.

SAMMY: Is that all you can say?

MONCK: No. Guards, guards! British arms will protect the sovereignty of this country.

(The lights fade.)

Scene Thirteen

(In another playing area the lights fade in. RIEL and BOURGET enter.)

RIEL: I have been here six years. I cannot go seven. My father has died.

BOURGET: There is only one father, Louis.

RIEL: And my father is sitting in his lap. I am going to leave the seminary.

BOURGET: Perhaps God does not want you to be a priest. Perhaps he has other plans for you.

RIEL: Yes.

(The lights fade.)

Scene Fourteen

(In another playing area the lights fade in. BROWN, McGEE, CARTIER, TACHÉ and GALT enter.)

BROWN: Where the hell is he? It's three o'clock. He's three hours late.

GALT: Now I'm a portly man.

McGEE: Patriotism rejects prefixes Mr. Cartier. French-Canadians, English-Canadians, Irish-Canadians. There are only Canadians.

CARTIER: The will for self-determination is ignored at the peril of the ruling authority.

McGEE: Yes.

CARTIER: We demand a certain independence. Quebec demands a certain independence. Like Ireland demands a certain independence from England.

McGEE: The history of Irish independence, Mr. Cartier, will be written in blood. Don't forget that. There are only Canadians, or there are traitors.

CARTIER: Some patriots are traitors.

McGEE: They have a saying in Ireland, Mr. Cartier. One living patriot is worth a churchyard of dead ones.

CARTIER: You sound like Lord Durham.

GALT: Now I'm a portly man.

BROWN: Where the hell is he? He's over three hours late.

(MACDONALD enters.)

MACDONALD: Don't stand up.

BROWN: You're drunk.

TACHÉ: Listen, I hear the sound of bees. Are there bees making honey here?

MACDONALD: Dead bees don't make honey.

BROWN: It is an humiliation to be in the same room with you. You bilious, vile, unclean beast. You bunkum-talking cormorant. You mass of putridity. You make me feel like I have been cutting up a dead dog all day. You are like an excrescence that cannot be got rid of.

MACDONALD: Quiet.

BROWN: Never. The elected representatives of Nova Scotia, New Brunswick, Prince Edward Island, are meeting in Charlottetown to discuss maritime union.

MACDONALD: So.

BROWN: So we must go to Charlottetown.

CARTIER: What's the matter?

MACDONALD: I fear that by persuading others we will convince ourselves.

GALT: Now I'm a portly man.

MACDONALD: Portly. You're a whole harbour.

BROWN: We must go to Charlottetown.

MACDONALD: We will.

(The lights fade.)

Scene Fifteen

(The lights fade in: The railing of the S.S. Victoria. A life preserver is attached to the railing. The sound of seagulls. MACDONALD, BROWN, and CARTIER enter.)

MACDONALD: Four million of us under one paternal government. Is there anything nobler in life?

BROWN: Confederation will try to neutralize sectional feelings while constantly perpetuating those feelings. Do you see anything wrong with that?

CARTIER: Non.

MACDONALD: I don't see a welcoming committee.

CARTIER: Wait, there's a man in a rowboat.

MACDONALD: I say bum-boater, what's the price of a shellfish?

(JAMES POPE enters in a rowboat.)

POPE: I'm not a fisherman. I'm your welcoming committee. Welcome to Charlottetown. Sorry there is no one else to meet you, but there is a circus in town, and all the maritime delegates have gone to see the dancing bears.

MACDONALD: So, they want to see dancing bears, do they?

(MACDONALD, CARTIER, and BROWN smile. The lights fade.)

Scene Sixteen

(In another playing area the lights fade in. CHARLES TUPPER, SAMUEL TILLEY, GEORGE COLE, and JOSEPH HOWE enter.)

TUPPER: They've all gone to the circus, wasting their time.

TILLEY: When they could be fishing.

COLE: And discussing maritime union.

HOWE: This is just one piece of botheration after another.

COLE: Look, Mr. Howe, the problem with maritime union is this: We have three provinces and therefore three legislatures.

TUPPER: After maritime union we will have one province and one legislature.

TILLEY: We hate that with passion.

HOWE: Then why discuss it?

COLE: There's nothing else to do, Mr. Howe.

TUPPER: We could discuss that or be silent.

TILLEY: Silence is hateful.

COLE: Could always go fishing.

TUPPER: Cut down a tree maybe.

TILLEY: But the real reason we discuss it, Mr. Howe, is because our appointed lieutenant-governor demands that we discuss it.

(POPE enters.)

POPE: Masters, masters. The delegates from the Province of Canada have arrived.

TUPPER: Excellent, just excellent.

COLE: I think we'll adjourn, Mr. Howe.

HOWE: Just one piece of botheration after another.

(The lights fade.)

Scene Seventeen

(In another playing area the lights fade in. RUDOLPHE LAFLAMME and RIEL enter.)

LAFLAMME: I am Rodolphe Laflamme. Welcome to the Institut-Canadien, monsieur …

RIEL: Riel.

LAFLAMME: Excuse me, Monsieur Riel. Confederation is bullshit, long live the Republic!

VOICE: *(Off.)* Confederation is bullshit, long live the Republic.

LAFLAMME: I have to remind them every now and then. You look like you just got out of jail.

RIEL: I have just spent six years at the College de Montréal.

LAFLAMME: Same thing. But we don't care what the church says. You can think here.

RIEL: Bishop Bourget says you are anti-clerical.

LAFLAMME: Really, I can't imagine why. Bourget. Bourget fornicates with farm animals and swabs his dick with honey. You're lucky to be out of there. Popes, bishops, kings, queens. The world is rotten with them. You can think here. We don't care what the church says. Where are you from, Monsieur Riel?

RIEL: Manitoba.

LAFLAMME: Well you won't find any buffalo here.

RIEL: You won't find any buffalo there, either.

LAFLAMME: That's right. Because of the English. They eat all the buffalo. They'll eat you next. Oh, les maudits Anglais. The fucking English. What is the philosophy of the English? No mercy for the weak and the tiny. To hell with the English. You will like it here. We will give you books to read, educate you, you are one of us. Your first name is …

RIEL: Louis.

LAFLAMME: Enchanté Louis.

(The lights fade.)

Scene Eighteen

(In another playing area the lights fade in. MACDONALD and CARTIER enter.)

MACDONALD: If I can get them off the champagne and into the brandy, we'll get the deal signed.

CARTIER: Don't you worry. We going to hustle these gars out of their underwear. Here they come. Oh mes amis, mes amis. I love you so much.

(CARTIER exits. COLE enters.)

MACDONALD: You there, come here. And who are you?

COLE: My name is George Cole.

MACDONALD: Really. A world full of Georges. How marvelous. And where were you born?

COLE: In Prince Edward Island.

MACDONALD: Really. How would you like to sit on my knee? Here drink this.

(COLE sits on MACDONALD's knee. MACDONALD gives COLE a brandy bottle.)

Hmmm. You've got a soft neck.

COLE: Oh that feels nice.

MACDONALD: And you have a fine set of ribs too.

COLE: Oh Mr. Macdonald, I like you, but if you put your hand where I think you're going to put it, you'll have to marry me.

MACDONALD: That's the idea.

COLE: Mr. Macdonald, that's not funny.

(CARTIER enters.)

CARTIER: Come here, I show you what funny is. First I sing like this. "Vous-etes trés belle et aprés la dernière nuit, tu es trés belle." And then I dance like this. And then I drink champagne, and then I kiss. Kiss for love.

COLE: These two are power mad. Mad for it they are, mad for it.

(COLE exits.)

CARTIER: You and me, Jean. Prime ministers together.

MACDONALD: Sing that crazy French song.

CARTIER: Oh Canada, mon pays, mon amour.

(CARTIER exits. TUPPER and TILLEY enter.)

TUPPER: The name's Charles Tupper.

TILLEY: The name's Samuel Tilley.

TUPPER: He's from New Brunswick.

TILLEY: He's from Nova Scotia.

TUPPER and TILLEY: What are you offering us?

MACDONALD: Galt.

GALT: The general government will assume all debts, and provide revenue to the provinces based on size of population.

MACDONALD: McGee.

McGEE: In unity there is strength. Our intercolonial defence will be improved. Our friends to the south will be less likely to invade us.

MACDONALD: Cartier.

CARTIER: And we'll give you a railroad connecting Montréal to St. John to Halifax.

MACDONALD: And this proposal has the full support of the colonial secretary?

TUPPER: We won't quarrel over the skin till we've killed the bear.

MACDONALD: Exactly.

TILLEY: I'm baffled, just baffled.

TUPPER: When shall we meet again?

MACDONALD: In Quebec for the Quebec Conference.

TILLEY: Just baffled.

(HOWE enters.)

HOWE: Just one big piece of botheration. Just one big piece.

(The lights fade.)

Scene Nineteen

(In another playing area the lights fade in. LAFLAMME and RIEL enter.)

LAFLAMME: To possess gold. Or to conquer those that possess gold. Which is more honourable? Think about that. You can think here. Right, Louis?

RIEL: Yes.

(The lights fade.)

Scene Twenty

(In another playing area the lights fade in. MACDONALD, CARTIER, CARTER, COLE, TUPPER, TILLEY, and GALT enter.)

CARTER: Now, the people of Newfoundland were not invited to the first conference.

MACDONALD: So.

CARTER: So we are P.O.-ed. P.O-ed bad.

MACDONALD: But you have been invited to this one.

CARTER: Well as far as we're concerned, don't bother.

MACDONALD: Then get out of here.

(CARTER exits.)

COLE: P.E.I. objects.

CARTIER: But we're going to give you a ferry boat.

COLE: Prince Edward Island objects. You buy the island or you shove it.

CARTIER: Shove it.

COLE: Then P.E.I. is shoving off.

(COLE exits.)

TILLEY: If we can't agree on confederation let's at least agree on a customs union.

TUPPER: Why?

TILLEY: Because going from New Brunswick to Nova Scotia is like going to a different country.

TUPPER: Damn right it is, and it'll stay that way.

(BROWN enters.)

BROWN: What did you say to Mr. Potato Head? He is a firm supporter of reciprocity.

GALT: Mr. Brown, as finance minister, I have given the matter great consideration and cognition. Fiscal independence is important. I think free trade is wicked, wicked, wicked!

MACDONALD: Defence is the issue. We are isolated and defenceless. We need a strong central government that speaks with one loud voice.

(MONCK enters.)

MONCK: I have received word that Confederate agents have attacked St. Albans and have been pursued across the border by Union troops.

MACDONALD: Gentlemen, armed American troops have just crossed our border. Not much we can do about it, is there? Defence is the issue.

(The fathers of confederation echo everything MACDONALD says.)

Whereas the Provinces of Canada, Nova Scotia, and New Brunswick have expressed their desire to be federally united into one dominion under the crown of Great Britain and Ireland with a constitution similar in principle to that of the United Kingdom. And whereas such a Union would conduce to the welfare of the provinces and promote the interests of the British Empire. And whereas—

(HOWE enters.)

HOWE: This is just one big piece of botheration. Just one big piece.

(The lights fade.)

Scene Twenty-one

(In another playing area the lights fade in. CARTIER and LAFLAMME enter.)

LAFLAMME: Mes amis, we are going to debate the pros and cons of confederation. We seek to delay this act of confederation not to frustrate the purposes of a majority of our countrymen, but to prevent their being surprised against their will, into a political change which however obnoxious and oppressive to them it might prove to be, cannot be reversed.

CARTIER: Hey Laflamme, suck this.

LAFLAMME: So much for rational debate.

CARTIER: Mes amis, patriotes. In '37, with Papineau, I took up the gun against the English. Did you?

LAFLAMME: I was a boy.

CARTIER: So was I.

LAFLAMME: Oh vous tête de cochon.

(CARTIER and LAFLAMME exchange French curses.)

CARTIER: Bourget.

(BOURGET enters.)

BOURGET: I damn you to hell.

LAFLAMME: Oh sacre.

BOURGET: Burn in hell, infidel, burn. I damn this man to hell.

(LAFLAMME exits. CARTIER and BOURGET shake hands.)

CARTIER: That's how it's done.

(The lights fade.)

Scene Twenty-two

(In another playing area the lights fade in. HOWE and TUPPER enter.)

HOWE: So you signed it, did you, Mr. Tupper?

TUPPER: I did, Mr. Howe.

HOWE: We are going to lose control of the customs revenue.

TUPPER: We will receive compensation. The federal government will give back to the provinces on a per capita basis, eighty cents.

HOWE: Sold to the Canadians at eighty cents a head. Ignominious. Sold for the price of a sheepskin. I love it, I love it.

(The lights fade.)

Scene Twenty-three

(In another playing area the lights fade in. MONCK and MACDONALD, CARTIER and BROWN enter.)

MONCK: I object to the usage of the word confederation. A confederation is a political entity based on a union of independent, sovereign states. These resolutions are not the resolutions of a confederation. This is a federation.

MACDONALD: I know. But we are calling it a confederation. This is Canada.

MONCK: This is hypocrisy.

MACDONALD: Well, yes, but that notwithstanding, we need royal assent for this.

MONCK: These proposals set in motion a legislative union based on a strong central government.

CARTIER: With provincial legislatures.

MACDONALD: Yes, it is hoped that these provincial legislatures will become essentially glorified municipal councils.

CARTIER: Like hell we do.

MACDONALD: I am sure the colonial secretary will approve.

MONCK: I am sure he will, but is it right?

MACDONALD: It is this, or anarchy.

(BELLEAU enters holding an earhorn.)

BELLEAU: Excusez-moi, s'il vous plaît. Old Taché has died. This is all that is left.

MACDONALD: I think Cartier should be prime minister.

BROWN: That screeching wretch will never be prime minister. I should be prime minister.

MACDONALD: Under no circumstances. I should be prime minister.

BROWN: No way. Never.

MONCK: What's your name?

BELLEAU: Narcisse Belleau, Member of the provincial Parliament of Canada, reporting.

MONCK: How would you like to be prime minister?

BELLEAU: I like. Prime Minister Belleau, boss of all bosses.

BROWN: Quiet, you ass-licking son of a bitch.

MACDONALD: On your way out close the door.

(BELLEAU exits.)

Really beginning to hate you George.

BROWN: Really beginning to hate you, John A.

(The lights fade.)

Scene Twenty-four

(In another playing area the lights fade in. MACDONALD, CARTIER, BROWN, BELLEAU, and COLONEL GARNET WOLSELEY enter.)

BROWN: While in London we will have the privilege of seeing great English lords living in patriarchal splendour, in their own hereditary halls.

BELLEAU: I can't wait.

CARTIER: The thought of going to London makes my bowels swell with joy.

BELLEAU: Me too.

(TUPPER enters.)

TUPPER: The bloody Fenians are attacking Nova Scotia. We got Fenians in the morning, Fenians in the evening.

MACDONALD: Colonel Garnet Wolseley here will defend Nova Soctia from the Warriors of Ireland.

TUPPER: The fiends of Ireland would be more like it.

WOLSELEY: Gentlemen, I am a paragon of imperialism. The Bolgie will be stepped on firmly, flatly, and—

MACDONALD: Finally.

WOLSELEY: Yes.

MACDONALD: So you see Charles, the advantages of union?

TUPPER: Yes, but the people of Nova Scotia are all wearing black armbands. I do not think I will do well in the next election.

MACDONALD: Aye, but where there's money, there's votes.

TUPPER: And Joseph Howe is leading a delegation to London to have Nova Scotia secede from the union.

MACDONALD: Don't worry about Mr. Howe. I will see that the colonial secretary steps on him firmly, flatly, and—

WOLSELEY: Finally.

MACDONALD: Yes.

(MONCK enters.)

MONCK: So, you are off to London with your constitution. In London you will be accorded a great honour. After Royal Assent you will be given the privilege of kissing hands.

ALL: Oh kissing hands.

MONCK: Bon voyage.

(The lights fade.)

Scene Twenty-five

(In another playing area the lights fade in. GALT, MACDONALD, TUPPER, and CARTIER enter. QUEEN VICTORIA enters holding out her hands. GALT, MACDONALD, TUPPER, and CARTIER kiss her hands.

GALT: Oh you are so beautiful.

MACDONALD: So kind.

CARTIER: Love you so much.

TUPPER: Oh, just luscious.

ALL: Thank you, thank you. Oh Your Majesty.

(The lights fade.)

Scene Twenty-six

(In another playing area the lights fade in. RIEL awakens from a nightmare. The lights fade in. BROWN enters holding The Globe.*)*

BROWN: We hail the birthday of a new nationality. A United British America, with its four millions of people, takes its place this day among the nations of the world.

(The lights fade.)

Scene Twenty-seven

(In another playing area the lights fade in. MACDONALD, LADY AGNES MACDONALD, CARTIER, and TUPPER enter waving Union Jacks.)

MACDONALD: What does the British North America Act mean? It means we are a self-governing colony within the British Empire. We made it.

TUPPER: It's Confederation Day, July 1st. To wives and sweethearts, may they never meet.

(MONCK enters.)

MONCK: For your devotion and distinguished service you are created Knight Commander of the Bath, and you are now entitled to be addressed as Sir John A. Macdonald.

MACDONALD: Thank you.

MONCK: And hence your new wife will be referred to as Lady Macdonald.

LADY MACDONALD: I am flattered but I leave my speech making to my husband who I am proud to think makes very big ones.

TUPPER and CARTIER: What about us?

MONCK: You of course will be Commanders of the Bath.

TUPPER: But not Knight Commander?

CARTIER: What an insult. He can be called "sir," but we can't.

MACDONALD: Now gentlemen, these honours and decorations are just toys.

MONCK: Toys! With such toys we govern men.

CARTIER: Exactly. Oh you pig, you pig. Ten years ago when we began our partnership, you had it made. You had that big nose and me. Now you've just got that big nose.

MONCK: And furthermore, I have recommended

to the colonial secretary that Sir John A. Macdonald form the first government of the Dominion of Canada.

CARTIER: Oh you pig, you pig. Good day, sir.

(CARTIER exits. HOWE enters holding a baby-like puppet with the words Canada Confederation.)

HOWE: Let us assume this baby is the Canadian confederation incarnate. What do I think of this incarnation?

(HOWE goes into a frenzy. He strangles the baby and pulls its head off.)

I'll strangle the life out of the bitch if I get the chance, strangle the life. You are just one big piece of botheration. Just one big piece.

MACDONALD: Shake this hand, Mr. Howe.

HOWE: Yes.

MACDONALD: I have learned to be a good judge of character. I'm going to buy you off.

HOWE: No you're not.

MACDONALD: Oh but I am. I'm going to buy you off. And there's nothing you can do about it.

HOWE: What are you offering?

MACDONALD: I'll make you customs collector for Fisheries.

HOWE: I'll take it.

MACDONALD: Good. Get out.

(HOWE exits.)

Confederation. Ontario and Quebec were divorced from each other; New Brunswick joined out of fright; Nova Scotia was coerced; British Columbia and Prince Edward Island will be bought. The state of the union.

(BROWN, EDWARD BLAKE, ALEXANDER MACKENZIE and WILLIAM McDOUGALL enter.)

MACKENZIE: Well, look who it is. George Brown and his Brownies.

BROWN: This is William McDougall, this is Edward Blake, and this is Alexander Mackenzie. I want them to be part of the coalition cabinet.

MACDONALD: Why do you use the term coalition cabinet?

BROWN: I see.

MACDONALD: Coalitions come, coalitions go, Mr. Brown.

BROWN: I resign.

MACDONALD: You're fired. And take your Brownies with you. Except McDougall, I want him.

BROWN: William, this is the Family Compact with a red nose and nothing more.

MACKENZIE: William, are you a true reformer, or are you a true reformer?

BLAKE: Always choose right over wrong, good over bad, but the choice is yours.

McDOUGALL: It is an honour to make your acquaintance, Mr. Macdonald.

BLAKE: How rude.

BROWN: I'll have you read out of the Reform Party, McDougall.

McDOUGALL: Out, out.

BROWN: I will devote my life to *The Globe.* In this country journalism governs.

(BROWN, MACKENZIE, and BLAKE exit.)

MACDONALD: I move that the first business of the Dominion be to annex the Northwest Territories.

McDOUGALL: Hallejulah.

MACDONALD: A toast. The experiment in politics begins.

(The lights fade.)

Scene Twenty-eight

(In another playing area the lights fade in. RIEL, MRS RIEL, LÉPINE, and NORBERT enter.)

MRS RIEL: So you are back, but not as a priest.

RIEL: But as a man.

MRS RIEL: Well man, big changes have happened here. Big changes.

(SCHULTZ enters.)

Welcome back to Red River.

LÉPINE and NORBERT: Yes welcome back, Louis.

SCHULTZ: Canada wants you. Canada first, become part of Canada.

RIEL: Things have changed.

MRS RIEL: In the old days we were infested with grasshoppers. Now this.

SCHULTZ: Confederation or annihilation.

MRS RIEL: Famine, drought, plague, grasshoppers. 1867, not a good year Louis.

RIEL: The day of the locust.

MRS RIEL: That's right Moses. Mark my words, not a good year.

SCHULTZ: Confederation or annihilation.

MRS RIEL: Not a good year.

(The lights fade.)

Scene Twenty-nine

(In another playing area the lights fade in. CARTIER enters.)

CARTIER: Each night before I go to sleep I clasp my hands like this and say my prayers. I pray that in my dreams I will be visited by angels bearing aphrodisiacs. But is that what comes to visit me? Not on your life. Goblins and gonnorhea. I wake up screaming "There is no justice for a Catholic." Tortured and tormented, there is no rest for the wicked.

(MACDONALD enters.)

MACDONALD: My little friend is not happy.

CARTIER: Oh don't bother. I demand my rights. Oh Canada, ma merde, ma haine.

MACDONALD: Now before you tie your dong in a knot, I have some news for you. You are going to be given a baronetcy that will entitle you to be addressed as "sir." It is a higher honour than I have received.

CARTIER: That's better.

MACDONALD: Now cheer up and sing me that crazy French song.

CARTIER: Oh Canada, mon pays, mon amour.

(The lights fade.)

Scene Thirty

(In another playing area the lights fade in. BLAKE and MACKENZIE enter.)

BLAKE: What do you think of McDougall? Crossing the floor to John A., the corruptionist himself.

MACDONALD: I hold in more esteem the cavities in my teeth.

BLAKE: Me too.

(BROWN enters.)

BROWN: Gentlemen, I am resigning as leader of the Liberal Party.

BLAKE: But—

BROWN: But no but, Blake. Since my marriage my life is wife and baby. Oh wife and baby.

BLAKE: Such rapture.

BROWN: Mr. Mackenzie, I think you should lead the Party.

BLAKE: But—

MACKENZIE: But no but, Blake.

(The lights fade.)

Scene Thirty-one

(In another playing area the lights fade in. MACDONALD, CARTIER, and McDOUGALL enter.)

CARTIER: And with that riposte I concluded the deal.

(CARTIER holds up a document.)

All of Rupert's Land belongs to the Dominion of Canada. The Hudson Bay authority will be transferred to imperial authority, and then one month later transferred to Canadian authority.

MACDONALD: Good. Seems quite straight forward. Congratulaions. That's worth a belt.

(MACDONALD holds up a bottle.)

To the good life.

CARTIER: And now all we need to do is take possession of it.

MACDONALD: You there, McDougall, how would you like to be lieutenant-governor of Rupert's Land?

McDOUGALL: Oh, I would be beyond honoured.

MACDONALD: Done.

CARTIER: See how it is done. You do nice things for him, he does nice things for you.

MACDONALD: Yes.

CARTIER: Should we inform the Hudson Bay governor at Red River of the transfer of power?

McDOUGALL: When I proclaim myself lieutenant-governor he will be so informed.

CARTIER: And the inhabitants of Red River?

McDOUGALL: Don't bother, they will do as they are told.

(The lights fade.)

Scene Thirty-two

(In another playing area the lights fade in. RIEL and MRS RIEL enter. NORBERT and LÉPINE enter holding a proclamation.)

LÉPINE and NORBERT: What is it? I don't know.

RIEL: It's a proclamation.

NORBERT: How do you know this?

LÉPINE: Quiet. This man knows how to read and write, speak and think, do you?

NORBERT: I know how to speak.

LÉPINE: Then shut up if that's all you know how to do. What's it say?

RIEL: It says the Hudson's Bay Company has sold all this land to Canada.

NORBERT: What does that mean?

(McDOUGALL, THOMAS SCOTT, SCHULTZ, and COLONEL CHARLES BOULTON enter.)

McDOUGALL: It means I claim all this land for Canada.

SCHULTZ: And it means jobs, the best kind of jobs. Government jobs.

SCOTT: And it means land, we're going to take your land.

SCHULTZ: All of it.

SCOTT: We're going to turn this country into one big Ontario.

RIEL: Like hell you are.

NORBERT: I was born here.

LÉPINE: My mother and father were born here.

NORBERT: My grandmother and grandfather were born here.

LÉPINE: My great grandmother and great grandfather were born here.

RIEL: And their ancestors were born here.

SCOTT: But they're not Canadians.

RIEL: Then what the hell is a Canadian?

SCOTT: A Canadian is an Englishman who lives in a colony.

SCHULTZ: You're nothing.

RIEL: If you're an Englishman, and you arrive right off the boat, five years later you're a Canadian. But if you've been here hundreds of years, you're nothing, and if you've been here thousands of years, you're less than nothing, you're an animal.

LÉPINE and NORBERT: Well to hell with that.

RIEL: We must organize or we must perish. We must form a government. A government that speaks with your voice.

LÉPINE and NORBERT: That's right.

RIEL: You there.

McDOUGALL: Who is it that speaks to the queen's emissary with such contemptible familiarity?

RIEL: The people of Manitoba.

McDOUGALL: The people of what?

RIEL: Who are you?

McDOUGALL: I am William McDougall, lieutenant-governor of the Northwest Territories. I am here to annex this territory.

RIEL: I assume that means the people that live here also. We wish to negotiate the rights of the Métis and other inhabitants of this colony.

McDOUGALL: You insolent, impertinent, impudent half-breed. I will not negotiate with you.

RIEL: Then who will you negotiate with?

McDOUGALL: I will negotiate with no one.

RIEL: Then you can turn around and head that way, monsieur.

McDOUGALL: You just do as you are told.

RIEL: Why?

McDOUGALL: Because I say so.

RIEL: You have no constituency here. Allez, monsieur, go!

(NORBERT and LÉPINE raise their rifles.)

McDOUGALL: Outrageous.

RIEL: On to Fort Garry.

(The lights fade.)

Scene Thirty-three

(In another playing area the lights fade in. MACDONALD is on his knees, his head in a bucket. LADY MACDONALD enters holding a bucket.)

LADY MACDONALD: My life is comprised of small wifely triumphs. He won't stop drinking, but he is clean.

MACDONALD: Agnes, one here too.

LADY MACDONALD: Yes.

(MACDONALD puts his head in LADY MACDONALD's bucket.)

MACDONALD: I don't know what I'd do without you.

LADY MACDONALD: I do. This house is too political. I was in the kitchen cutting my turnips and the flies formed into two lines facing each other, just like Parliament.

(CARTIER enters.)

CARTIER: William McDougall has just been expelled from the Red River, and Louis Riel has taken over Fort Garry.

(MACDONALD gives a blank stare. Then he puts his head in the bucket. The lights fade.)

Scene Thirty-four

(In two separate playing areas the lights fade in. RIEL, NORBERT, LEPIN, and DONOGHUE enter the first; SCOTT and SCHULTZ enter the second.)

RIEL: The fort is ours. That flag is proof that we are a nation.

SCOTT: The bloody bastards have taken over Fort Garry.

SCHULTZ: It'll be a snowy day in July when a good stout Orangeman takes orders from a French-Catholic son of a bitch like Riel.

RIEL: The Hudson's Bay Company no longer rules here. We do.

DONOGHUE: I have the Hudson's Bay funds.

RIEL: Then you will be treasurer.

(BOULTON enters the second playing area.)

BOULTON: I am Charles Boulton.

DONOGHUE: The name's Donoghue. I am with the Fianna Erin.

BOULTON: I am authorized to organize men to resist the rebellion.

RIEL: A Fenian.

DONOGHUE: As the day is bright.

BOULTON: I am looking for brave loyal men, real he-men.

DONOGHUE: What you have done is very interesting.

SCHULTZ: You're looking at one.

SCOTT: And me too, I'm a he-man too.

DONOGHUE: I am filled with admiration. You have formed a government. Now act like a government. You must send delegates to Ottawa.

(BISHOP TACHÉ enters the first playing area.)

RIEL: Father, would you represent the provisional government to Ottawa?

BISHOP TACHÉ: I would be honoured, you are a dream come true.

(BISHOP TACHÉ exits.)

BOULTON: Give these rebels a taste of iron fist.

SCOTT: Iron fist.

(LÉPINE enters the first playing area.)

LÉPINE: The strangers are organizing an attack.

BOULTON: Can we use your house as a command station.

SCHULTZ: Is a pig born to be bacon?

DONOGHUE: Never trust an Orangeman.

BOULTON: Excellent, we'll turn your home into a fort.

RIEL: What does every revolution fear the most?

LÉPINE: Starvation.

DONOGHUE: Being defeated.

RIEL: Exactly.

SCHULTZ: Fort Schultz, we'll call it. Fort Schultz.

LÉPINE: The strangers are organizing an attack.

RIEL: We must beware the counter-revolution.

SCOTT: It's July 12th all over again.

RIEL: Come, before the revolution goes backwards, come.

(RIEL, DONOGHUE, NORBERT, LÉPINE, and MRS RIEL attack SCHULTZ, SCOTT, and BOULTON. BOULTON exits.)

SCHULTZ: It's Riel and the Métis.

SCOTT: They have us surrounded.

LÉPINE: Surrender, we have you surrounded.

SCHULTZ: Oh my God, we're trapped like rats in a shithouse.

SCOTT: And our glorious hero, the Conservator of the Peace. Where is he?

SCHULTZ: He left.

SCOTT: In a hurry.

LÉPINE: You may think your house is a fort. It's not. You have fifteen minutes to surrender, at which point your story is over.

SCOTT: What are we going to do?

SCHULTZ: I'm a brave man, not a stupid man.

SCOTT: This sounds like surrender.

VOICE: *(Off.)* Fourteen minutes.

SCHULTZ: We surrender, we surrender.

(The lights fade.)

Scene Thirty-five

(In another playing area the lights fade in. MACDONALD, CARTIER, and BISHOP TACHÉ enter.)

CARTIER: Here is the man. He can solve all your problems.

MACDONALD: Tell Mr. Taché that *if* the Hudson's Bay government is restored there *may be* a possibility of a general amnesty after which it is quite possible that I will negotiate with delegates of Mr. Riel's provisional government.

(MACDONALD exits.)

CARTIER: The prime minister says if the Hudson's Bay government is restored there will be a general amnesty and then negotiations with delegates of Monsieur Riel's provisional government.

BISHOP TACHÉ: Oh merveilleuse, merveilleuse.

(The lights fade.)

Scene Thirty-six

(In another playing area the lights fade in. SCHULTZ and SCOTT are seen through the bars of a prison window.)

SCOTT: They made me eat buffalo shit and they made jokes about the hair on Queen Victoria's legs.

SCHULTZ: It's coming.

SCOTT: Oh Riel, I want him alone in a room, no rules.

SCHULTZ: It's coming, there.

(The bar comes loose.)

They don't make jails like they used to.

SCOTT: You should know.

SCHULTZ: I'm going to go to Ottawa for help.

SCOTT: Very good, just snow-shoe right out of here.

SCHULTZ: That's right, but I know where Riel is.

SCOTT: Where?

SCHULTZ: With his mother.

SCOTT: Of course, why didn't I think of that? Oh Riel, we've got to get Riel.

SCHULTZ: Now let's get out of here.

(The lights fade.)

Scene Thirty-seven

(In another playing area the lights fade in. RIEL enters.)

RIEL: Norbert, where are you?

(NORBERT jumps out from the shadows. RIEL shouts.)

NORBERT: I was hiding in the bushes.

RIEL: Oh, you scared me.

NORBERT: I was hiding in the bushes and you didn't see me. You didn't see me.

RIEL: No, I didn't. Norbert, do you remember when we used to play hide and seek?

NORBERT: Do I remember.

(NORBERT covers his eyes with his hands.)

RIEL: Well, how would you like to play I spy the devil. There are bad men planning to attack me.

NORBERT: I'll hide and seek them.

RIEL: Yes, see them but don't be seen by them. That's the game.

NORBERT: That's the game.

(The lights fade.)

Scene Thirty-eight

(In another playing area the lights fade in. DONALD SMITH enters.)

SMITH: I started working for the Hudson Bay, counting rat skins in some foul, smelly hole that defies description. After five years of that,

I was promoted to counting beaver skins in some foul, smelly hole that defies description. Now I own the company.

(MACDONALD enters.)

MACDONALD: Now Donald Smith, chief factor of the Hudson Bay Company, listen to me. You are going to represent me to these half-breeds. Promise them anything. Bribes, gifts, amnesties, liquor, whatever. Just keep them talking till spring. Then we're going to send the troops in. And then—well lordy, lordy, what happens then you don't want to know about.

SMITH: I'm the owner of the Hudson Bay, John A.

MACDONALD: I know, chief factor. Now here's how I want you to negotiate.

(The lights fade.)

Scene Thirty-nine

(In another playing area the lights fade in. SCOTT enters with his hands around MRS RIEL's neck.)

SCOTT: You'll tell me where that son of a bitch is or I'll scalp you.

(BOULTON enters with NORBERT.)

NORBERT: Not fair.

BOULTON: I caught a spy.

NORBERT: No, I was playing hide and seek, not fair.

SCOTT: I remember this one. This will learn you for making jokes about the hair on Queen Victoria's legs.

(SCOTT kills NORBERT with a hatchet.)

MRS RIEL: Maniac.

SCOTT: First blood, first blood.

MRS RIEL: Maniac.

SCOTT: I'm a Protestant, I'm a Protestant. Now we are going to attack Fort Garry.

(The lights fade.)

Scene Forty

(In another playing area the lights fade in. RIEL and SMITH enter.)

RIEL: These are our demands. Are you, as commissioner, able to guarantee one single article on this list?

SMITH: While I might have power in regard to some of the articles, to assure you, so far as assurance can be given to anything which has not yet occurred, I could not, at the same time, do so equally in regard to the whole.

RIEL: Can you guarantee one single article on this list?

SMITH: I believe that the nature of my commission is such that I can give assurances, full assurances, so far as any guarantee can be given, that the government of the Dominion would so place the right guarantee before Parliament that it would be granted.

RIEL: I think the Canadian government has not given you the power to negotiate in good faith.

SMITH: That is your opinion.

RIEL: No, Monsieur Smith. It is not an unformed impression. It is a fact. You speak and say nothing.

(Noises offstage.)

What are your credentials? What are your instructions from the government of Canada? Are you empowered to negotiate a deal?

SMITH: I can't tell you "yes" and I can't tell you "no."

RIEL: Then what can you tell me?

(Noises offstage. LÉPINE enters.)

LÉPINE: We've captured fifty English.

RIEL: Friends of yours. Bring them in.

(A MÉTIS enters with BOULTON and SCOTT under guard)

LÉPINE: Here are our prisoners.

RIEL: Who is the leader?

BOULTON: I am.

RIEL: For trying to overthrow the government, prepare to die at twelve o'clock.

BOULTON: Very well.

(SCOTT gasps.)

RIEL: Put that dog in a dungeon.

MÉTIS: Mush, mush.

(MÉTIS, BOULTON, SCOTT, and LÉPINE exit.)

SMITH: If you kill that man you will irreparably

damage your position. Acts of murder beget acts of murder.

RIEL: And if I spare his life?

SMITH: I will reveal my credentials and instructions from the government of Canada.

RIEL: He is spared.

SMITH: I am empowered to offer an amnesty.

RIEL: Hmmm-hmmm.

SMITH: And to recognize your provisional government.

RIEL: Hmmm-hmmm.

SMITH: And …

(The lights fade.)

Scene Forty-one

(In another playing area the lights fade in. SCOTT, MÉTIS, and LÉPINE enter.)

SCOTT: I'm a Protestant, I'm a Protestant. They said they were going to kill him and now he's been reprieved. You haven't got the guts to kill a man. You haven't got the balls. I'm a Protestant, I'm a Protestant.

LÉPINE: Shut up, you moron.

SCOTT: Methusaleh was the oldest man that ever lived but he died before his father.

LÉPINE: You will respect me or you will die.

SCOTT: I'll never respect you, you French Catholic pope-loving bastard. You Jesuit monstrosity. I'm a Protestant. I'm superior to you in every way, you devil-worshipping pervert.

LÉPINE: Oh this man is going to die.

SCOTT: Last night there were four Marys, and tonight there'll be but three because Jesus was a Protestant.

(DONOGHUE enters.)

I'm a Protestant.

DONOGHUE: Well fling me to the ground and curse me with impotence. Can I believe my eyes? A Protestant where he belongs. In his own little zoo.

LÉPINE: Go get Riel.

(MÉTIS exits.)

SCOTT: Ulster forever you Fenian bastard.

DONOGHUE: You are going to die like a toad on the road to Belfast.

SCOTT: You will call me "sir."

DONOGHUE: Where I come from, the only people called "sir," are Protestants on horseback carrying guns.

SCOTT: I'm a Protestant.

DONOGHUE: But you ain't on horseback, and you ain't carrying a gun.

SCOTT: Save us from popery, brass coins, and wooden shoes.

DONOGHUE: Stinking Billy can't save you now.

SCOTT: The British Empire began with the conquest of Ireland.

DONOGHUE: And it'll end with the liberation of Ireland.

SCOTT: Ireland will never be free 'cause it's English to the bone.

DONOGHUE: Up the Republic and fuck the begrudgers.

(RIEL enters.)

RIEL: What justification is there for killing him?

DONOGHUE: Six centuries of Irish misery. Pretty protty going to die tonight. You have to make an example of him or the other prisoners will end up being just like him. You have to show that the provisional government has authority, respect. If you won't do it for the Métis nation, then do it for Ireland. The fact that he lives corrupts the life experience for all of us. He's an Orange Gillie.

(MRS RIEL and MÉTIS enter.)

MRS RIEL: That's the one. He's the one that killed Norbert. Maniac.

LÉPINE: Norbert, he killed Norbert.

RIEL: Very well. He will die.

DONOGHUE: You have just crossed the Rubicon. You will remember this day for the rest of your life.

RIEL: Let the dye be cast.

(The lights fade.)

Scene Forty-two

(In another playing area the lights fade in. RIEL, LÉPINE, two MÉTIS, SCOTT, and DONOGHUE enter.)

RIEL: Ready.

SCOTT: You haven't got the guts.

RIEL: Aim.

SCOTT: You haven't got the guts.

RIEL: Fire.

(LÉPINE and the two MÉTIS shoot SCOTT.)

SCOTT: Guts.

(SMITH enters.)

SMITH: You have irreparably damaged your position.

(LÉPINE points a pistol at SCOTT's head.)

LÉPINE: For Norbert.

(The lights fade.)

Scene Forty-three

(In another playing area the lights fade in. MACDONALD, CARTIER, BROWN, and SCHULTZ enter. SCHULTZ holds up a Globe *headline, "French Half-Breeds Kill White Man.")*

SCHULTZ: Says it all, doesn't it? Would this newspaper lie to you?

CARTIER: Damn right it would.

SCHULTZ: The blood of Ulster cries vengeance. A Loyal Orangeman from Ontario has been fouly murdered by Louis Riel. The Red River colony and the Northwest Territories belong to Ontario. Whosoever disagrees with me I repudiate as a Canadian. I repeat, repudiate. Fenian flags are flying. Bastards are speaking French, praying to popes. We want this country to be one big Ontario.

CARTIER: Like hell we do.

SCHULTZ: Send in the army. Send in the army!!

(The lights fade.)

Scene Forty-four

(In another playing area the lights fade in. RIEL and MRS RIEL enter.)

RIEL: Mother, I'm going to sell the cow.

MRS RIEL: Why?

RIEL: Don't disagree with me.

MRS RIEL: What's the matter with you?

RIEL: I need a new suit.

MRS RIEL: Why?

RIEL: I want to look nice.

MRS RIEL: Why?

RIEL: I want to look powerful.

MRS RIEL: Why?

RIEL: I am a man of some importance.

MRS RIEL: I know, so?

RIEL: So I want to look like it.

MRS RIEL: Power corrupts, Louis. God puts down one only so he can set up another. Remember that.

RIEL: Yes.

(The lights fade.)

Scene Forty-five

(In another playing area the lights fade in. WOLSELEY enters flapping his arms.)

WOLSELEY: Just exercising. I spend every waking moment doing something. I love war. I have waited too long for this. From ensign to colonel in five years. Then I came to Canada. Nine years in this backwater and I'm still a colonel. And I love war. Well this campaign will make me Sir Garnet. I remember fighting the slopeheads in China. They're all heathens, and they're all insane. I took pleasure killing them. And now the French bastards in this country. I don't understand why they are allowed to live. Just exercising.

(The lights fade.)

Scene Forty-six

(In another playing area the lights fade in. RIEL, BISHOP TACHÉ, DONOGHUE, and LÉPINE enter. RIEL is holding the BNA *Act.)*

BISHOP TACHÉ: You are wearing a suit.

RIEL: Yes.

BISHOP TACHÉ: It doesn't fit properly.

RIEL: But it will.

DONOGHUE: Damn right it will.

RIEL: Any word on the amnesty?

BISHOP TACHÉ: Not yet. But it was promised.

DONOGHUE: It's time to frost the ass of the English. Call Manitoba the Republic of Rupert's Land. That'll frost them.

RIEL: That will frost more than the English.

DONOGHUE: Then let's annex ourselves to the United States. We can become the 39th state.

RIEL: No. We will become a province. The aspirations of the Métis people go beyond—

DONOGHUE: It is annexation or annihilation. I have friends in high places. Men you want to meet.

RIEL: Mr. Donoghue, I am beginning to have my doubts that you have the interests of the Métis people at heart.

DONOGHUE: Erin Go Bragh.

BISHOP TACHÉ: This ear heard it, Louis, "amnesty," this ear heard it.

RIEL: I think you should go back from whence you came. Give my regards to Washington.

LÉPINE: You heard him. Move.

(DONOGHUE exits.)

BISHOP TACHÉ: You're lucky to be rid of him. Wherever he goes, disaster goes too. Now Louis, listen. They want you to send delegates to Ottawa.

(RIEL holds up the BNA Act.)

RIEL: This is like a dream unfolding. We are going to use this against them. We will negotiate the terms of entry of Manitoba into confederation. Take a letter.

BISHOP TACHÉ: Yes, oh great one.

RIEL: To Sir John A. Macdonald, prime minister of Canada. As you are no doubt aware ...

(The lights fade.)

Scene Forty-seven

(In another playing area the lights fade in. MACDONALD enters holding a letter. BERNARD enters.)

MACDONALD: Signed Louis Riel. We will incorporate this territory as the Province of Manitoba and accede to these demands. Send in Wolseley.

(BERNARD exits.)

We will also assert our military authority. Métis and Fenians, a devil's brew.

(WOLSELEY enters.)

Garnet Wolseley.

WOLSELEY: The one and only.

MACDONALD: Here is the situation. The Americans wish to annex the Northwest Territories.

WOLSELEY: You would think they were imperialists.

MACDONALD: They are.

WOLSELEY: There is only one imperialism worth the word and that is British imperialism. American imperialism is piracy.

MACDONALD: Yes. We must make a show of force to show that this territory is—

WOLSELEY: British.

MACDONALD: Exactly.

(The lights fade.)

Scene Forty-eight

(In another playing area the lights fade in. RIEL and LÉPINE enter.)

LÉPINE: Louis, armed troops are marching toward us.

RIEL: I must wait for the government's response to the terms of entry of Manitoba into Confederation.

LÉPINE: I think this is the response. We gotta go. Now.

RIEL: I don't know where I'm going.

LÉPINE: But you're very well dressed. Come.

(The lights fade.)

Scene Forty-nine

(In another playing area the lights fade in. WOLSELEY enters.)

WOLSELEY: Halt. God blimey, what a backwater. First we go by train to Collingwood. Then by steamer to Sault Ste. Marie. Then we walk sixty miles. Then it's back in the steamer. Then get off the steamer and walk a hundred miles ... then back in the row boats, then in canoe, hacking our way through the forest, forty-seven portages. Bloody portages. And then there's Kakabeka. Kakabeka. My backside goes ping when I hear that word. Kakabeka. But at last we are here.

(SMITH enters.)

SMITH: Colonel Wolseley, welcome to Winnipeg. I have bribed, sweet-talked, and threatened everyone. They are defenceless. Forward.

(The lights fade.)

Scene Fifty

(In another playing area the lights fade in. WOLSELEY, SCHULTZ, SMITH, and BOULTON enter.)

SMITH: The men are looking very rag tag.

WOLSELEY: That is acceptable. After all, we don't put on our good clothes to butcher hogs, do we?

SCHULTZ: They've all fled.

WOLSELEY: Blast. That cemetery over there, dig up the graves and scatter the bones. We'll show these half-breeds what we think of them. You there, Pea-souper, come here, I said come here.

(A SOLDIER and LÉPINE enter.)

SOLDIER: We caught this one trying to escape.

LÉPINE: I wasn't trying to escape.

SCHULTZ: I'm a Protestant.

(SCHULTZ assaults LÉPINE.)

WOLSELEY: Well this is a pip, a real pip. Mr. Smith you are now the temporary lieutenant-governor.

SMITH: A thousand pounds for the head of Louis Riel.

LÉPINE: To hell with this, I'm going to Saskatchewan. God.

(The lights fade.)

Scene Fifty-one

(In another playing area the lights fade in. RIEL enters holding a bible.)

RIEL: I am like unto David, the saviour of my nation. And there arose a new king, oh Lord, I am a stranger in a strange land. I am an exile. I feel inspired.

(LÉPINE enters.)

LÉPINE: That's good, because they are beating everybody up in Winnipeg.

RIEL: Well this Canada, these Canadians, have not seen the last of me.

LÉPINE: They say they are going to have elections.

RIEL: Yes, to be one of the elect. The battle is only beginning.

(RIEL smiles. The lights fade.)

Scene Fifty-two

(In another playing area the lights fade in. MACDONALD, SMITH, WOLSELEY, and CARTIER enter.)

MACDONALD: Beginning. Well done Colonel Wolseley.

WOLSELEY: They ran, not a shot fired in anger.

MACDONALD: To the little colony that grew. Off to a good beginning.

(They laugh. The lights fade.)

Act Two

Scene One

(The lights fade in. MACKENZIE enters.)

MACKENZIE: Will you take the pledge? Why did God make wheat? God made wheat so we could eat? Not make whisky. Why did God make the grape?

VOICE: *(Off.)* So we could make wine.

MACKENZIE: That man is going to burn in hell. Behold.

(A theatrical family enters: FATHER, MOTHER, DAUGHTER, and SON.)

A happy family. Sweetness and light.

(The family act out MACKENZIE's description.)

And then the demon rum enters. The father drinks, oh how he drinks. Then he beats the wife, swears at the children. The wife in despair drinks the demon rum, and then the most foul debaucheries are committed. And yet, take away this. And you have this. A happy family. Will you take the pledge?

(The lights fade.)

Scene Two

(In another playing area the lights fade in. MACDONALD and CARTIER enter.)

CARTIER: And then I said to Amor de Cosmos …

MACDONALD: Make a long story short.

CARTIER: I have negotiated the terms for British Columbia's entry into confederation.

MACDONALD: And …?

CARTIER: Toot toot. The key condition is that we build a great railroad to connect them to the rest of the country.

MACDONALD: The little colony that grew.

(BISHOP TACHÉ enters.)

BISHOP TACHÉ: The Métis have been forced to leave Manitoba, forced to leave their wives and children. I can see the larger problems are of no interest, perhaps the smaller ones are. The amnesty.

MACDONALD: What amnesty?

BISHOP TACHÉ: For Monsieur Riel.

CARTIER: In '37 with Papineau I took up the gun. I was a rebel.

BISHOP TACHÉ: And you were given an amnesty.

CARTIER: That is what political careers are made of. Good day Monsieur Taché

BISHOP TACHÉ: But this ear, this ear.

CARTIER: Good day.

(BISHOP TACHÉ exits.)

MACDONALD: The little colony that grew and grew and grew.

(GALT enters.)

GALT: Getting bigger all the time.

MACDONALD: You should know, Galt. If they want a railroad, we'll give them a railroad. Do it. All right Galt, spill your guts.

GALT: We need money for the election.

MACDONALD: Oh you're in top form Galt.

GALT: The opposition has two dollars for our one. And this railroad is going to cost money too.

MACDONALD: Galt.

CARTIER: I know how we can kill two birds, I know how we can kill two birds.

(The lights fade.)

Scene Three

(In another playing area the lights fade in. SMITH, a MÉTISSE, and SCHULTZ enter.)

SMITH: Now we are going to have elections. Two MPs for Manitoba. Since I am the landlord of the Northwest Territories, I, of course, will be one. But the other, who will it be?

MÉTISSE: Riel.

SMITH: If Riel sets foot in this country he will be arrested.

SCHULTZ: He'll be shot.

MÉTISSE: We'll elect him anyway.

(The lights fade.)

Scene Four

(In another playing area the lights fade in. MACDONALD, CARTIER, and HUGH ALLAN enter.)

ALLAN: My name is Hugh Allan. My motto is "What's good for me is good for everybody."

MACDONALD: Would you like a drink from the bottle that likes to sit beside my arm? Mr. Cartier tells me that you have one hundred and sixty thousand dollars available for a campaign donation.

ALLAN: Maybe I do.

MACDONALD: One hundred and sixty thousand dollars. Fifty thousand, sixty thousand votes. Voting day means money day. Move 'em in, move 'em out.

ALLAN: If I give you one hundred and sixty thousand dollars, what do I receive?

MACDONALD: The power of government will be exercised by making you president of Canada's first railway.

CARTIER: You will be president of the CPR. And of course my law firm will handle all legal aspects of the company. You make a little here, you make a little there. Why not?

ALLAN: Exactly.

MACDONALD: Bought and sold. Let's drink to that.

(The lights fade.)

Scene Five

(In another playing area the lights fade in. SMITH and ALLAN enter.)

ALLAN: I'm going to be rich, rich. It's what young men dream about, Donald, what young men dream about.

SMITH: You are already rich.

ALLAN: I'm going to be richer. The richer the bitcher. I got the CPR contract in my hand. There it is.

(ALLAN holds up a piece of paper.)

Waiter, garçon, boy, boy! Champagne and caviar, toot, toot, now, toot, toot.

SMITH: And how did you secure this contract?

ALLAN: I bribed the prime minister. I got the proof in my safe. I got Sir John's big knackers in my hands and I can smell them anytime I want. Toot, toot.

(The lights fade.)

Scene Six

(In another playing area the lights fade in. Various MEN enter. MAN ONE holds a bottle and money bills.)

MAN ONE: Who ya voting for? Macdonald right? Drink this. Here you, take one of these. You're voting Macdonald right?

MAN TWO: Right.

(MACDONALD enters.)

MAN ONE: It is a shame that a good man can only vote once.

MACDONALD: Yes it is. But a good man on a fast horse can vote six times. I remember you. How's your father and your pretty daughter?

MAN THREE: He's getting older and she's getting prettier.

MACDONALD: That's what we like to hear.

(MACKENZIE and BLAKE enter.)

MACKENZIE: I can stoop to small talk too. You there, I remember you. How's your mother?

MAN THREE: She's still dead.

MACKENZIE: I'm sorry to hear that.

MAN THREE: You were sorry the last time too.

BLAKE: Pitiful.

MACKENZIE: Thanks Blake.

(The lights fade.)

Scene Seven

(In another playing area the lights fade in. SMITH enters.)

SMITH: Stand fast, Craigellachie, stand fast. I think only good thoughts. Good thoughts give me inner happiness. My good thought for the day. How can I off Hugh Allan and get the CPR contract for myself? That's my good thought for the day. Thirty years in Labrador makes a man dream about power. Power. Stand fast, Craigellachie, stand fast.

(The lights fade.)

Scene Eight

(In another playing area the lights fade in. MACDONALD and CARTIER enter.)

CARTIER: We need more money.

MACDONALD: Oh balderdash.

CARTIER: We need more money.

MACDONALD: This campaign is making me sick.

CARTIER: We are going to lose the election. We need more money.

MACDONALD: And you make me sick.

CARTIER: Money.

MACDONALD: I am so depressed. Boy, send a telegram. To Hugh Allan. "I must have another ten thousand dollars. Do not fail me. Answer today. Signed John A."

VOICE: *(Off.)* I'll send it right off.

MACDONALD: You do that. That should solve a problem.

(The lights fade.)

Scene Nine

(In various playing areas the lights fade in. Two MEN are holding MACDONALD.)

MEN: To a great victory, John A. To a great victory.

(RIEL and LÉPINE enter.)

RIEL: Hiding in a haystack, I celebrate my victory. M.P. for Provencher.

(SMITH and a CLERK enter.)

SMITH: I understand you are the senior clerk at Mr. Hugh Allan's office.

CLERK: I am, sir.

(SCHULTZ enters.)

SCHULTZ: Riel, when we find you, we're going to kill you. You may have won the election but you'll never take your seat.

MEN: To a great victory, John A. To a great victory.

(MACKENZIE and BLAKE enter.)

BLAKE: You're finished.

MACKENZIE: Thanks Blake.

RIEL: I have faith in democracy.

LÉPINE: If this is democracy, I'm going to Saskatchewan.

SMITH: How would you like to make five thousand dollars?

(SMITH holds up a wad of money.)

CLERK: Five thousand dollars. And what would you want me to do for this five thousand dollars.

MEN: To a great victory, John A. To a great victory.

SCHULTZ: Riel, when we find you, we're going to kill you.

LÉPINE: There's buffalo out there.

BLAKE: You're finished.

MACKENZIE: Thanks Blake.

SMITH: There is a telegram in Mr Allan's safe that needs to see the light of day. Discretion is assured.

RIEL: Men use their reason only to outdo the beasts at being beastly.

MEN: To a great victory, John A. To a great victory.

(The lights fade.)

Scene Ten

(In another playing area the lights fade in. BLAKE and MACKENZIE enter.)

BLAKE: It's a cheat, a fraud, a lie! They bought the election.

MACKENZIE: I know Blake. But we can't prove it.

(SMITH enters.)

Ah, Mr. Smith. This is Mr. Blake. My trusty lieutenant.

BLAKE: And future leader.

MACKENZIE: But not now. The future is tomorrow.

BLAKE: And tomorrow.

SMITH: Gentlemen, I have something that you may find interesting. This pertains to the most recent election.

(SMITH gives MACKENZIE a file folder. BLAKE grabs it out of MACKENZIE's hands.)

MACKENZIE: Really Blake.

(BLAKE looks inside the file folder. BLAKE gasps.)

SMITH: From an anonymous friend.

BLAKE: Mr. Speaker.

MACKENZIE: Mr. Speaker.

(The lights fade.)

Scene Eleven

(In another playing area the lights fade in. MACDONALD and ALLAN enter.)

MACDONALD: You didn't destroy the telegram.

ALLAN: I never destroy anything that involves a financial transaction. Especially when it involves giving out money. I keep my records straight.

MACDONALD: Of everything.

ALLAN: Everything.

MACDONALD: I recall one hundred and sixty thousand dollars or thereabouts.

ALLAN: I gave the Conservative party four hundred thousand dollars.

MACDONALD: I beg to differ with your figures. We initially agreed upon—

ALLAN: I have signed receipts.

MACDONALD: Signed receipts.

ALLAN: Damn right. I'm a businessman not a fool. If I am going to speculate in a risky venture you can bet every drop you drink that I am going to cover my hairy ass. I secured two hundred thousand dollars from my friends in the United States.

MACDONALD: All signed for.

ALLAN: Of course.

MACDONALD: It will look like I am in the employ of the Americans.

ALLAN: Not my problem. I learned early the importance of getting a pound for a penny, and I got your pound in my hand, and I'm going to squeeze.

(ALLAN shows MACDONALD a piece of paper.)

MACDONALD: Who signed for this?

ALLAN: Your friend Cartier.

MACDONALD: Fool, the first rule, fool.

(The lights fade.)

Scene Twelve

(In another playing area the lights fade in. CARTIER and MACDONALD enter.)

CARTIER: I've got a kidney as big as a pumpkin. I am full of black piss.

MACDONALD: I never begrudged you taking money.

CARTIER: You never begrudged me anything. I appreciate it.

MACDONALD: Why did you put it in writing?

CARTIER: The syphilis was attacking my brain. I was out of my mind. I'm not responsible for my actions anymore.

MACDONALD: You must have needed it for something important.

CARTIER: Oh yes.

(CARTIER smiles.)

MACDONALD: Oh, what am I going to do?

CARTIER: Face up to it. My story is over, yours is ending.

MACDONALD: Because of you.

CARTIER: Let an old crook die in peace.

MACDONALD: Give me your hand.

(MACDONALD grabs hold of CARTIER's hand.)

CARTIER: Don't squeeze it off. I am going to visit His Infernalness. Oh God, the black hole is coming.

MACDONALD: What am I going to do?

(The lights fade.)

Scene Thirteen

(In another playing area the lights fade in. MACDONALD and BERNARD enter with the dead body of CARTIER.)

MACDONALD: Is it in?

BERNARD: It's in.

MACDONALD: Now give me the pen and paper.

(MACDONALD puts the pen in CARTIER's hand. SMITH enters.)

SMITH: What are you doing?

MACDONALD: He's signing a confession.

SMITH: But he's dead.

BERNARD: We've just put a fly inside his mouth.

MACDONALD: So it was signed while there was life inside him. Come on Georges.

SMITH: No, John A.

MACDONALD: Dead men tell no tales. It wasn't me, it was him. Him!

SMITH: I have no idea where they received it but they have a telegram with your request for ten thousand dollars, to be sent to you immediately.

MACDONALD: It's a plot, it's a plot.

SMITH: Mackenzie and Blake are already calling it the Pacific scandal.

MACDONALD: Calumnies, libels, lies. I'll stonewall it, they'll never get it. These hands are clean.

(LADY MACDONALD enters.)

LADY MACDONALD: Let's see them.

MACDONALD: Ah Agnes, how pleasant to see you.

LADY MACDONALD: Where's this finger been?

MACDONALD: Oh stop.

LADY MACDONALD: I just came by to remind you about the garden party with the Smiths. They are putting on promenade their Pekingese dogs, and they have a giant chihuahua that they have named in your honour. Sir John A. they call him.

MACDONALD: How delightful.

LADY MACDONALD: Are things going well today?

MACDONALD: Just the usual.

LADY MACDONALD: Till later.

MACDONALD: Till then.

(LADY MACDONALD exits.)

Jesus wept. What am I going to do?

SMITH: You're going to have to resign.

MACDONALD: No. Never.

SMITH: It will be a brutal session in the house.

MACDONALD: As long as the ranks are loyal, Donald, as long as.

(The lights fade.)

Scene Fourteen

(In another playing area the lights fade in. MACDONALD, SMITH, BLAKE, MACKENZIE, and others, including the SPEAKER of the House, enter.)

MACDONALD: I am going to appoint a Royal Commission …

(Groans.)

To investigate.

(Groans.)

These charges that have been levelled against me.

(Groans.)

BLAKE: The accused gets to investigate and prosecute himself.

MACKENZIE: What kind of government is this?

MACDONALD: This is an honest government.

(Groans.)

MACKENZIE: Mr. Speaker, Mr. Speaker. I have this telegram. Quote: "Send me another ten thousand dollars. Do not fail me. Answer today."

BLAKE: Now I ask you, who would perpetrate such a dastardly deed?

MACDONALD: Shut up.

BLAKE: You just spoke the language of hell. I feel violated. You have violated my person.

MACDONALD: Shut up.

MACKENZIE: Has the prime minister been drinking?

MACDONALD: Shut up.

BLAKE: Did the prime minister take a bribe?

MACDONALD: What I did, I did for the good of the country.

BLAKE: Are you saying that you took a bribe for the good of the country?

MACDONALD: These hands are clean.

MACKENZIE: But is the rest of you?

MACDONALD: Pot calling kettle.

MACKENZIE: Kettle calling pot.

BLAKE: I think we should move for a vote of non-confidence.

MACKENZIE: Thanks Blake.

SMITH: Mr. Speaker.

SPEAKER: The House recognizes the member for Winnipeg.

SMITH: Mr. Speaker, before the House votes on an issue of confidence in the government, I wish to make a few remarks. Parliament should be incorruptible, clean, and pure. Only honourable men should be members of Parliament. This dishonourable man has made this house an unclean house.

MACDONALD: You stencher, you stinkpot, I should slap your chops, slap your chops. I could lick you any day, Smith. Lick you any day.

BELLEAU: I am going to lose my seat because of you.

MACDONALD: You deserve to lose your seat.

BELLEAU: All my hopes and dreams, destroyed because of you.

MACDONALD: I could lick you any day, Smith. Lick you any day.

(The lights fade.)

Scene Fifteen

(In another playing area the lights fade in. BLAKE, MACKENZIE, and SMITH enter. BLAKE holds a bottle of champagne.)

BLAKE: To the new prime minister of Canada, Alexander Mackenzie.

MACKENZIE: The demon juice will never touch my lips.

BLAKE: Speech.

MACKENZIE: I promise to do an honest job for an honest day's wage.

BLAKE: To an honest man.

MACKENZIE: Because there is no sand in me. I am clear grit.

BLAKE: Clear grit. Down with Macdonald and the Conservative party means down with organized hypocrisy. This is a great day, Alexander Mackenzie.

MACKENZIE: Call me Sandy.

BLAKE: Sandy it is.

(ALLAN enters holding the CPR contract.)

ALLAN: Am I still the president of the Canadian Pacific Railroad?

MACKENZIE: What railroad? The beast can leave the room.

(BLAKE takes the CPR contract from ALLAN. ALLAN exits. SMITH enters.)

SMITH: Mr. Mackenzie.

MACKENZIE: Mr. Smith.

SMITH: I represent a syndicate that wants to secure the CPR contract.

MACKENZIE: I will leave the railway as a national legacy to this country. No private company will own same.

SMITH: I found this suitcase of money on the doorstep.

MACKENZIE: Hard granite grinds true if it's "clear grit," Mr. Smith.

SMITH: And what the hell does that mean?

MACKENZIE: That means get out of this office.

SMITH: If you no touch me, I'll nay touch you, but if you claw me I'll claw you.

MACKENZIE: Wheresoever the carcass is, there will the eagles be gathered together.

SMITH: Aye.

BLAKE: How rude.

(The lights fade.)

Scene Sixteen

(In another playing area the lights fade in. RIEL and LAFLAMME enter.)

LAFLAMME: The member for Provencher, Manitoba is going to sign in.

RIEL: What form of government is this? If they can't bribe the voters, they try to intimidate them. And if they can't intimidate them, they try to stop them from voting. This is an election?

LAFLAMME: The member for Provencher, Manitoba is going to sign in.

RIEL: And if you win, they threaten to kill you if you take your seat. This is democracy?

LAFLAMME: The member for Provencher, Manitoba is going to sign in.

RIEL: The member for Provencher, Manitoba has signed in.

LAFLAMME: Good, now come quickly.

(BLAKE and MACKENZIE enter.)

BLAKE: If you take your seat, you rotten bastard, we'll kill you. This is Thomas Scott country, Frenchman.

RIEL: You. Demon go change your shape.

BLAKE: I am going to put a price on your head. Ten thousand dollars for the head of Louis Riel.

(RIEL has an emotional breakdown.)

LAFLAMME: Come, I know a place.

(The lights fade.)

Scene Seventeen

(In another playing area the lights fade in. BLAKE and MACKENZIE enter.)

BLAKE: These policies are going to create bad relations with the United States, exhibit disloyalty to the British Empire, and ruin this country.

MACKENZIE: Blake, I haven't got time for this.

BLAKE: What do you have time for? You have time to destroy the external and internal worlds as we understand them, but no time to discuss the error of your ways.

MACKENZIE: Blake, I haven't got time for this.

BLAKE: We are trying to give the people decent, honest government. Decent government. Can people ask for more?

MACKENZIE: That's enough Blake.

(In another playing area the lights fade in. SMITH enters.)

SMITH: Just thinking good thoughts. My good thoughts for the day. What can I do to get rid of these two?

(The lights fade.)

BLAKE: Administering this country is a soul-destroying experience.

MACKENZIE: We all make sacrifices, Blake.

BLAKE: No one values my intellect and integrity here.

MACKENZIE: If you say so, Blake.

BLAKE: I find that when I am arguing with someone, I notice that my finely drawn distinctions are not appreciated. I feel insults keenly. I suspect that you secretly do not approve of me.

MACKENZIE: That's right, Blake.

BLAKE: Then you earn my contempt. You earn it.

MACKENZIE: Thanks Blake.

BLAKE: This colony aspires to nationhood.

MACKENZIE: That's right, Blake.

BLAKE: Very well then. I am beginning to have my doubts about the importance of the imperial connection. What do you think about that? That gets your attention.

MACKENZIE: What do you want, Blake?

BLAKE: That gets your attention, Sandy.

MACKENZIE: Call me Alex.

BLAKE: That gets your attention, Alexander.

MACKENZIE: Mr. Mackenzie to you.

BLAKE: Oh, how rude. I resign.

MACKENZIE: Blake!

BLAKE: I resign.

(The lights fade.)

Scene Eighteen

(In another playing area the lights fade in. MACDONALD enters with the champagne bottle.)

MACDONALD: "Get thee glass eyes and like a scurvy politician seem to see the things thou dost not." Impotent and useless I continue. I owe money to everybody. What would a man do without his debts? My debts are my little darlings. I would expire on the spot without them. Debts are like flies. They disappear and then new ones arrive. Politicians have to live. You make a little here, lose a little there, then make a whopping fortune, then lose a little, why not, then make the score of all scores, then lose a little, what the hell. Is that a crime? What's done is done. There is no use crying over spilt milk. Life is just one piece of bunkum after another. Bunkum. Master of the grand bunkum. Bunkum good. Bunkum till they can't stand it anymore. Then bunkum again. Bunkum good.

(LADY MACDONALD enters.)

LADY MACDONALD: John, what is the matter?

MACDONALD: Just the raving of a drunk. Go back to sleep.

LADY MACDONALD: Only if you will stop talking to yourself.

MACDONALD: Never.

LADY MACDONALD: Oh my anxious wifely heart pains me so.

MACDONALD: It's a cheat, a fraud, a lie. I'll not be cheated. I'll not be cheated. I'll not be cheated.

(The lights fade.)

Scene Nineteen

(In another playing area the lights fade in. RIEL and LÉPINE enter.)

RIEL: I am envious and ignorant, vain and stupid, corrupt and decadent.

LÉPINE: Doctor Barnabé.

(DOCTOR BARNABÉ and EVELINA enter.)

BARNABÉ: I am Doctor Barnabé.

LÉPINE: My friend is seriously disturbed.

BARNABÉ: And this is my lovely daughter, Evelina.

(RIEL looks at EVELINA.)

RIEL: I think I want to smile.

EVELINA: Then you should smile.

BARNABÉ: We'll take care of him. Come.

RIEL: Where are you taking me?

LÉPINE: Don't worry, Louis.

BARNABÉ: Come.

(The lights fade.)

Scene Twenty

(In another playing area MACDONALD and BERNARD enter.)

MACDONALD: But the national policy, the high tariff, will protect Canadian manufacturers.

BERNARD: They like the policy but they will not contribute to the campaign. You are a tainted man, John A.

(SMITH enters.)

MACDONALD: You.

SMITH: I'm a Hudson Bay man, Mr. Macdonald. How much do you want to be prime minister? I want that contract.

MACDONALD: Show me what you found on the doorstep.

(The lights fade.)

Scene Twenty-one

(In another playing area the lights fade in. BARNABÉ and EVELINA enter.)

RIEL: *(Off.)* I have been named David, David, David.

BARNABÉ: And how is our guest?

EVELINA: Oh he gets happier every day. In fact he's about to burst. Look.

(RIEL enters with his face covered by a handkerchief.)

RIEL: I am so happy. I don't want anyone to see how happy I am. I am so happy.

EVELINA: Let's see how happy he is.

(EVELINA take the handkerchief away from RIEL's face. RIEL is revealed to be beaming grotesquely. EVELINA laughs.)

RIEL: Everyone's looking at me. Why? Stop looking at me. Stop looking at me.

EVELINA: We're not looking at you.

RIEL: Stop looking at me. I hear voices.

EVELINA: He hears voices.

RIEL: I am a prophet.

EVELINA: He is a prophet.

RIEL: I have a mission.

EVELINA: He has a mission.

RIEL: Gaganagagaga..

(The lights fade.)

Scene Twenty-two

(In another playing area the lights fade in. BARNABÉ, EVELINA, RIEL, and a NUN enter.)

BARNABÉ: This man is seriously ill. He is speaking in tongues. He likes to refer to himself as David.

NUN: I am happy to see you, Mr. David.

RIEL: Why do you call me that? I am Louis Riel.

NUN: Sure.

RIEL: I am.

NUN: Come with me.

RIEL: Where are you taking me?

EVELINA: I will write you, I promise.

NUN: Come.

(The lights fade.)

Scene Twenty-three

(In another playing area the lights fade in: a political picnic. MACDONALD and five MEN and WOMEN enter.)

MEN: Oh I am stuffed. I have eaten ham, turkey, beef.

MACDONALD: Spread the blankets and keep eating. There's more where that came from. It's a picnic, keep eating.

WOMEN: How can you afford all this?

MACDONALD: This is only a taste of what the national policy will bring us.

MEN: Are you going to make a speech?

MACDONALD: Have to look at the crowd first. Oh look at them eat, they're getting a speech.

(MACKENZIE enters.)

MACKENZIE: Oh you poor decent hardworking sods. Listen to me, I am the truthsayer.

MACDONALD: Parties for votes equal votes for party.

MACKENZIE: John A. MacDonald's national policy is the corn laws all over again.

MACDONALD: The national policy: Canada for Canadians.

MACKENZIE: It is protectionism, pure and simple.

MACDONALD: Free trade is evil.

MACKENZIE: Protectionism is evil.

MACDONALD: We will protect our industry with tariffs.

MACKENZIE: Protectionism is designed to raise the price of the working man's crust while increasing the power and wealth of the few and mighty.

MACDONALD: We will not be trampled upon and ridden over as we have been in the past by the capitalists of a foreign country.

MEN: We'll be ridden over by capitalists of this country.

MACDONALD: You're on the mark tonight, sir.

MACKENZIE: We are going to change that. We are going to initiate free trade with the United States.

MEN: We'll all be thrown out of work, you dog.

MACDONALD: A fair day's wage for a fair day's work. Think about that while you're eating your shoo-fly pie.

MACKENZIE: And we are going to make it against the law to drink liquor in this country.

MEN: Fuck off.

MACKENZIE: The story of liquor in this country is all over.

MEN: All over for you, you mean.

MACDONALD: The story of liquor is just beginning.

MACKENZIE: In the next election everyone will take the pledge.

MEN: Like hell we will.

MACKENZIE: Woe unto him who giveth his neighbour drink.

MEN: Woe unto you.

MACKENZIE: It's me or John A. the bag man himself.

MACDONALD: Do you prefer Alexander Mackenzie sober, or John A. drunk?

MACKENZIE: Think about that, that quietens you.

MEN: We're thinking.

MACDONALD: He isn't long for this world.

(The MEN move toward MACDONALD. BLAKE enters.)

BLAKE: Pitiful.

MACKENZIE: Thanks Blake.

(The lights fade.)

Scene Twenty-four

(In another playing area the lights fade in. RIEL enters.)

RIEL: A constitutional debate with the government of Canada. I could do that in my sleep, Lord. Challenge me, put me to the test. I dare you. Do with me what thou wilt. I am your tool, your instrument. Sharpen me like a pencil. At least point me in the right direction.

(The NUN enters holding a letter.)

Nun, I'm in love. Did you hear that, in love.

NUN: I have this letter for you. Do you want me to read it to you?

RIEL: I want to kill you so much.

NUN: It is from Mademoiselle Evelina Barnabé. Do you know this woman?

RIEL: I'm in love with her. I want to kill you so much.

(The NUN opens the letter.)

NUN: Dearest beloved.

RIEL: Oh sublime sentiment.

NUN: I am alone in my bedroom thinking about you.

RIEL: Cock-a-doodle-doo.

NUN: That's enough. You control yourself. I am in love with your goodness.

RIEL: She's in love with my goodness. Turn it into rapture.

NUN: Quiet. I won't read this section to you.

RIEL: I love the way you read letters to me. I want to kill you so much. I want to kill you so much.

NUN: And it ends with "And so I cannot see you ever again."

RIEL: What! She's in love with my goodness and can't ever see me again. Why?

NUN: Go to sleep.

RIEL: What are you doing?

NUN: I'm taking away your bible.

RIEL: No.

NUN: Because it makes you insane.

RIEL: No. Beat me with clubs, whack me till I'm black and blue but don't take away my bible. She took my bible. Give that to me. God wrote that. Give it to me.

NUN: No, because it makes you insane.

RIEL: Don't talk to me about sanity, you devil's bitch. Give me a hair shirt and a scourger and I'll show you why they were invented, sister.

NUN: Quiet, you evil crazy person. Quiet.

RIEL: The bishops, the priests, the nuns! They work for the English.

NUN: Quiet, you evil crazy person. Quiet.

RIEL: Jesus, Jesus, oh Jesus.

(RIEL bellows like a bull.)

NUN: Quiet.

RIEL: Corruption is everywhere. You have sold your soul to the devil for no reason, you evil crazy woman.

NUN: Quiet.

(The NUN beats RIEL with a club.)

RIEL: Jesus, Jesus, oh Jesus.

(The lights fade.)

Scene Twenty-five

(In another playing area the lights fade in. BLAKE and MACKENZIE enter.)

MACKENZIE: We gave them honest, decent government.

BLAKE: And we were trounced for our efforts. Humiliated. You had your nose rubbed in it.

MACKENZIE: That's enough Blake.

BLAKE: Had your nose rubbed in it.

MACKENZIE: Thanks Blake.

BLAKE: You're finished, I'm taking over.

MACKENZIE: Good luck Blake.

(The lights fade.)

Scene Twenty-six

(In another playing area the lights fade in. The NUN and RIEL enter.)

NUN: We are discharging you from this hospital.

RIEL: Nut house, you mean.

NUN: You have been here two years.

RIEL: How time flies.

NUN: I want to give you some good advice.

RIEL: That's a first.

NUN: Live a quiet life.

RIEL: After two years with you?

NUN: Live outdoors.

RIEL: Like a beast.

NUN: And avoid people that disturb you.

RIEL: Starting with you. Sign me out, sister, sign me out. I think I'll go to Nebraska, Lord. I'll become a farmer. I think I'll grow carrots, yes, carrots. And after they're grown, I'll wash them four times a day. Because I want clean carrots.

NUN: Sign this.

RIEL: On second thought, Lord, I think I'll go to Montana and hunt buffalo. Yes, hunt buffalo.

(The lights fade.)

Scene Twenty-seven

(In another playing area the lights fade in. MACDONALD, TUPPER, TILLEY, GALT, et al. enter.)

MACDONALD: *(A la Gilbert and Sullivan.)* I am the nation's chief MP. The ruler of the whole country—whose praise Great Britain loudly chants.

CHORUS: And we are his toadies and his grateful sycophants.

MACDONALD: And they are my toadies and my grateful sycophants.

CHORUS: And we are his toadies and his grateful sycophants, his grateful sycophants!!

(SMITH enters.)

SMITH: Right.

(SMITH holds the CPR contract.)

Now here is what we want. We want a subsidy of twenty-five million dollars. Plus twenty-five million acres, plus possession and complete ownership of everything that has been built to date. An absolute railway monopoly in western Canada for twenty years. Exemption from taxation on all property, plus the right to set tariffs at whatever rate we see fit.

MACDONALD: Done.

(The lights fade.)

Scene Twenty-eight

(In another playing area the lights fade in. A MAN enters with surveyor chains. LÉPINE, and a MÉTIS and MÉTISSE enter.)

MAN: Over to the left, now the right.

LÉPINE: Here we go again. We need someone who can read and write, speak and think. We need Riel.

(The lights fade.)

Scene Twenty-nine

(In another playing area the lights fade in. MACDONALD and SMITH enter. MACDONALD drinks from a bottle.)

SMITH: Now the land in the northwest. It's covered in Indians and Métis. It's no use to us.

MACDONALD: We will give the Métis title to their land by issuing scrip and then you'll buy it back for pennies.

SMITH: Aye. But what about the Indians? You're not thinking of giving them money.

MACDONALD: No, they'd just drink it.

SMITH: Then what are you thinking about.

(COLONEL CROZIER enters.)

CROZIER: Colonel Crozier of the Northwest Mounted Police reporting.

MACDONALD: Extinguish the native land claims to their land, by any means, starve them into submission. Tell them Queen Victoria is eating all the buffalo and if they sign the treaty, she will stop eating them.

CROZIER: Thy will be done.

(The lights fade.)

Scene Thirty

(In another playing area the lights fade in. BIG BEAR and WANDERING SPIRIT enter.)

WANDERING SPIRIT: I am Wandering Spirit. I have killed thirteen warriors. But none in the last five years. Because of this man. But I say to this man, more buffalo and less white dogs and this is a better world.

BIG BEAR: Listen the grasshoppers are singing.

(CROZIER and SERGEANT PRESTON enter.)

CROZIER: You must be Big Bear.

BIG BEAR: No, I am hungry bear.

CROZIER: All right Big Bear, you've made your point.

BIG BEAR: Point!

CROZIER: This is a present from Queen Victoria.

BIG BEAR: What is it?

CROZIER: It's a treaty.

BIG BEAR: Why do I feel a rope around my neck?

WANDERING SPIRIT: We have many grievances. When the women are hungry and the children cry, men turn into rattlesnakes. Remember that, white dog.

BIG BEAR: I am surrounded by rattlers, always rattling. They have their reasons.

CROZIER: Sign this treaty.

BIG BEAR: Not as long as there are buffalo.

WANDERING SPIRIT: That is what we call Shaganappi. Get it away from us. When we want to catch a fox, we set a trap and scatter meat all around the trap. Then we knock the fox on the head.

CROZIER: What the hell does that mean?

BIG BEAR: Let me make it simple. We want no bait. If your chief wants this land so much he should come here like a man and ask for it. This is our land. It isn't a piece of pemmican to be cut off and given in little pieces back to us. It's our mother.

CROZIER: You two are bad Indians.

WANDERING SPIRIT: Agh.

BIG BEAR: No point talking to you.

CROZIER: Sergeant Preston.

(CROZIER and PRESTON exit.)

BIG BEAR: Listen, the grasshoppers are singing.

WANDERING SPIRIT: Your life is the buffalo hunt, your life is the buffalo hunt.

BIG BEAR: Yes, but listen closely. For as long as the buffalo last you will not sign that treaty, for as long as the buffalo last.

(The lights fade.)

Scene Thirty-one

(In another playing area the lights fade in. MACDONALD, SMITH, BLAKE, MACKENZIE, SPEAKER, and others enter.)

SPEAKER: Order, order.

BLAKE: Mr. Speaker, Mr. Speaker.

SPEAKER: The House recognizes the member for West Durham.

BLAKE: The prime minister continues to build his monument to infamy. It will be a snowy day in July when the CPR gets another penny from this House. The CPR is a fiasco. It is the story of corruption, bribes, gifts! Gifts! Gifts of money, gifts of land. And loans! The loans, I hate the loans. Interest-free loans, non-repayable loans. The loans are so crooked. The government says to that man "We will give you everything and half as much again, and then you will own it. We will make you landlords of the northwest." All I ask is justice, or I will become, against my better nature, permanently irritable. Permanently irritable.

MACDONALD: This is hog shearing, Mr. Blake.

BLAKE: Lots of crying but no wool.

MACDONALD: Correct, Mr. Blake.

BLAKE: Then I say to the government: God damn the CPR.

(SMITH laughs. The lights fade.)

Scene Thirty-two

(In another playing area the lights fade in. BIG BEAR enters.)

BIG BEAR: All I want is peace. They want to give me piece all right. A piece of land as big as my ass, just big enough to sit on, and then I'm not supposed to move, and then they want to shove a piece of pig in my face and say, "Eat." I have spent my entire life wandering this land. I have spent my entire life eating buffalo, and now I am supposed to eat pig. I don't think so.

(WANDERING SPIRIT and CROZIER enter.)

WANDERING SPIRIT: We are starving, we have no choice.

CROZIER: Sign this treaty.

WANDERING SPIRIT: Listen to your people.

CROZIER: Listen.

WANDERING SPIRIT: The women and children.

CROZIER: Listen. Listen to them.

BIG BEAR: If we sign this treaty we will regret it forever.

WANDERING SPIRIT: If we don't sign this treaty we will die of starvation. The buffalo are gone.

CROZIER: The horses are gone.

BIG BEAR: And now we are gone.

(BIG BEAR signs the treaty. The lights fade.)

Scene Thirty-three

(In another playing area the lights fade in. MACDONALD enters.)

MACDONALD: In this country, in order to become master of the better sort of people you have to become a slave to the worst. The nature of politics.

(SMITH enters holding a piece of paper.)

The population of Ontario has increased and I have to add four seats.

SMITH: Good, I have four candidates in my pocket, solid Company men, but three of them just got out of jail and the other one couldn't win an election paying whores in a whorehouse.

MACDONALD: Not to worry. It is the government's preogative to draw the electoral boundaries. This riding here. I'll shape it like this. That way I'll hive the grits, and turn this one area here into two tory ridings, and then this one ...

(The lights fade.)

Scene Thirty-four

(In another playing area the lights fade in. GABRIEL DUMONT enters.)

DUMONT: I'm Gabriel Dumont, the leader of the hunt. The people of Batoche know that I'm the boss. I am Gabriel Dumont, president of the Métis Buffalo Hunters Association. I know six languages but I speak English the best.

(LÉPINE enters.)

LÉPINE: Gabriel, the surveyors are coming. They want to take our land. What should we do?

DUMONT: We should shoot them. You all came from the Red River fourteen years ago. The same story.

LÉPINE: That's right. We send our petitions to the government, we may as well throw them in the river.

DUMONT: What can we do?

LÉPINE: We need Riel, we need Riel.

DUMONT: I remember him. Where is he?

LÉPINE: He is teaching school in Montana.

DUMONT: I will go and get him.

LÉPINE: I will go too.

(The lights fade.)

Scene Thirty-five

(In another playing area the lights fade in. RIEL enters with a watering can.)

RIEL: Oh the little things of life are truly great. Teaching the little babies the alphabet, so they can read the gospel. Growing carrots. Oh the little things of life are truly great. Oh you will grow up big and strong, don't worry.

(DUMONT enters.)

DUMONT: Is your name Louis Riel?

RIEL: And who is asking, monsieur?

DUMONT: My name is Gabriel Dumont.

RIEL: Gabriel.

DUMONT: I have come on a mission.

RIEL: Mission.

DUMONT: From my people, your people, in the Saskatchewan.

RIEL: My people. I see a cross.

DUMONT: Where?

RIEL: In the sky. In flames coming toward me.

DUMONT: How big is it?

RIEL: Big enough to crucify us all, Gabriel, big enough to crucify us all.

(RIEL smiles.)

DUMONT: Yes.

(The lights fade.)

Scene Thirty-six

(In another playing area the lights fade in. MACDONALD and SMITH enter.)

MACDONALD: What's the matter? Not making your fast bucks fast enough?

SMITH: Labour costs are out of control. A dollar a day is not enough they say.

MACDONALD: I can get you all the cheap labour you want.

SMITH: Who would work for less than a dollar a day?

MACDONALD: The Chinese. Seventy-five cents a head. Move them in, move 'em out.

SMITH: But they're heathens, and they're lazy.

MACDONALD: They may be heathens but they are not lazy. If they can build the Great Wall of China, they can build the railroad.

SMITH: Yes.

(The lights fade.)

Scene Thirty-seven

(In another playing area the lights fade in. BIG BEAR enters. A railway MAN enters.)

MAN: Coolies, over here. We're going to put this railway right through that teepee. And then a big iron horse is going to come whipping down this track.

BIG BEAR: Iron monster you mean.

MAN: Right through that teepee.

BIG BEAR: I know you have no brains, but you do have ears.

MAN: Whatever you say is going to go in this ear and then out this one.

BIG BEAR: Then go like a breeding buffalo. I hate the government. But I hate the CPR even more. We don't ride on the railroad. The railroad rides on us.

(The lights fade.)

Scene Thirty-eight

(In another playing area the lights fade in. DUMONT, RIEL, LÉPINE, and MÉTISSE enter.)

DUMONT: This is the matron of our clan.

MÉTISSE: On behalf of all the people, I welcome you to Batoche. You are like an angel that God has sent to earth to help his people.

RIEL: Thank you.

VOICES: *(Off.)* Riel, Riel, Riel!

RIEL: I remember you all from the Red River. Red River. Fourteen years ago. Fourteen. I am back.

VOICES: *(Off.)* Riel, Riel, Riel!

RIEL: We will petition the government with our grievances.

VOICES: *(Off.)* Riel, Riel, Riel!

(The lights fade.)

Scene Thirty-nine

(In another playing area the lights fade in. MACDONALD and BERNARD enter.)

BERNARD: Riel is back.

MACDONALD: I'm trying to sober up. Do you mind?

BERNARD: He is in Saskatchewan organizing the Métis.

MACDONALD: Riel is a poor man. A poor man can be bought cheaply. Offer him three thousand dollars. Let's see if he takes it.

(The lights fade.)

Scene Forty

(In another playing area the lights fade in. RIEL, LÉPINE, DUMONT, and ANDRÉ, a priest, enter.)

ANDRÉ: Louis, you are showing great wisdom by taking this money.

RIEL: Three thousand dollars is a lot of money. But I don't accept bribes, even if it comes from the prime minister. Every time we send the government a petition, they send police. We're saying help us, and they send police. I denounce this government as thieves and liars. I want you to sign this oath. It reads "We pledge ourselves to do everything we can do to save our souls by living a holy life, and to save our country from a wicked government." That is your name, put your mark there.

(DUMONT puts his mark on the paper.)

LÉPINE: Which is my name?

DUMONT: I don't know, that one.

LÉPINE: How do you know?

DUMONT: I don't know.

RIEL: It is that one. I want your permission to give a mass in your church for my brethren.

ANDRÉ: Permission is refused.

RIEL: Then no permission is needed.

ANDRÉ: I protest.

RIEL: You are such a Protestant.

ANDRÉ: How dare you say that.

RIEL: I want all priests put under surveillance. Especially him. He is like a gargoyle sitting on a lettuce leaf.

DUMONT: Yes he is.

RIEL: They are all in league with the devil. They have formed their own confederation. I see snakes. We will form a provisional government. We will call the government the …

LÉPINE and DUMONT: Government.

RIEL: Non. We will call it the Exovedate.

ANDRÉ: Heretic.

(LÉPINE forces ANDRÉ offstage.)

RIEL: From out of the flock comes the shepherd. And I am he as you are me.

(The lights fade.)

Scene Forty-one

(In another playing area the lights fade in. MACDONALD and SMITH enter.)

SMITH: We need another twenty million dollars.

MACDONALD: If I give the CPR another twenty million dollars, I am going to have to make some budget reductions.

SMITH: A man's got to do what a man's got to do.

MACDONALD: We'll start with my portfolio.

SMITH:Why not?

MACDONALD: The Indian affairs budget. I'll cut it in half from three hundred thousand to—

SMITH: Zero.

MACDONALD: To one hundred and fifty thousand dollars.

SMITH: Very good, more cuts.

MACDONALD: I can't think of any, but we'll start with that one.

SMITH: Very good, more cuts.

(The lights fade.)

Scene Forty-two

(In another playing area the lights fade in. CROZIER and PRESTON enter. CROZIER is holding a telegram.)

CROZIER: Gentlemen of the Northwest Mounted Police. I have been given this order. We are going to mobilize our forces against Riel and the half-breed. Let us do our duty. God save the queen.

PRESTON: God save the queen.

(The lights fade.)

Scene Forty-three

(In another playing area the lights fade in. BIG BEAR, WANDERING SPIRIT, DELANEY, and QUINN enter.)

DELANEY: All you Indians look at me. I am the farming instructor.

BIG BEAR: I have come for my food.

QUINN: Pay attention you red rotten bastards.

DELANEY: This is a shovel.

BIG BEAR: My people are starving. When the government took our land they said my people would be provided for.

DELANEY: This is how you use a shovel. Like this, and then you do this. And then you can plant your peas and potatoes.

BIG BEAR: Give us back the prairies and we will not ask for food.

QUINN: If you're hungry you should learn to eat grass.

DELANEY: Now let's see you do it.

WANDERING SPIRIT: I hate this. I was a great warrior, and a great buffalo hunter, and an outstanding horse thief.

QUINN: Go on, graze.

WANDERING SPIRIT: What more was there to life? And now I do this. Dig, dig, dig.

QUINN: If you were dying of thirst I wouldn't give you the sweat off my balls.

BIG BEAR: I am hungry.

QUINN: That by the way is government policy.

WANDERING SPIRIT: I know, white dog, I know.

DELANEY: No work, no rations.

BIG BEAR: That's all they ever say. No work, no rations. I am getting thinner and you are getting fatter.

WANDERING SPIRIT: Why?

DELANEY: Foot on shovel and push. You impudent lazy Indian.

WANDERING SPIRIT: That's it.

(WANDERING SPIRIT hits DELANEY with the shovel.)

BIG BEAR: No.

(The lights fade.)

Scene Forty-four

(In another playing area the light fade in. BIG BEAR and WANDERING SPIRIT enter.)

BIG BEAR: If we can create one large reserve out of all the reserves.

WANDERING SPIRIT: I hate all the white dogs.

(CROZIER, PRESTON, and DELANEY enter.)

But these ones, I hate them even more than it is possible to hate.

DELANEY: That is the man.

CROZIER: You are under arrest for assaulting a white man.

BIG BEAR: The Northwest Mounted Police, all they do is starve us to death, beat us up, and name forts after themselves.

WANDERING SPIRIT: I hate the police.

PRESTON: Come with me. I am going to put you in jail.

WANDERING SPIRIT: White dog.

BIG BEAR: If I had my choice. One big reserve, one big reserve.

(The lights fade.)

Scene Forty-five

(In another playing area the lights fade in. MACDONALD and SMITH enter.)

SMITH: The CPR is bankrupt.

MACDONALD: Again.

SMITH: We need another sixty million dollars.

MACDONALD: I just got you twenty.

SMITH: We need sixty more.

MACDONALD: What are you doing with it?

SMITH: I have a deep appreciation of what life can be, John A. We need sixty more.

MACDONALD: Can't get it.

SMITH: You have to.

MACDONALD: Blake is leading a filibuster against the CPR.

SMITH: We get the money from the government or it's off to the penitentiary.

MACDONALD: Can't be done. If we go into bankruptcy we will have to auction off everything, equipment, engines, steel, land, and forfeit everything we have invested. What are we going to do?

SMITH: Think.

MACDONALD: We need a miracle.

(SMITH snorts. The lights fade.)

Scene Forty-six

(In another playing area the lights fade in. A TRADER enters. RIEL, DUMONT, LÉPINE, and MÉTIS enter. RIEL holds a crucifix.)

LÉPINE: Who is boss here?

TRADER: I am.

RIEL: Non, monsieur, I am. Take the guns. Riel wants ma-te-Riel.

LÉPINE: Funny, eh?

TRADER: If you say so.

LÉPINE: I don't like your face. Come with me.

(MÉTIS, LÉPINE, TRADER, and DUMONT exit. RIEL turns to the crucifix.)

RIEL: Don't worry. If we succeed in our rebellion we will pay for them. If we do not succeed the government of Canada will pay for them.

(DUMONT enters.)

DUMONT: Ah, Prophet, awake and sing. The Mounted Police have been seen at Duck Lake.

RIEL: Stop them, stop them.

DUMONT: Wait, I have a plan.

(DUMONT exits. The lights fade.)

Scene Forty-seven

(In another playing area the lights fade in. CROZIER, PRESTON, and MOUNTIE, a Northwest Mounted Police officer, enter.)

CROZIER: What's that lake called?

RIEL: *(Off.)* Oh, Lord, please get angry with the Mounted Police.

PRESTON: Duck Lake.

RIEL: *(Off.)* Give them hemorrhoids.

CROZIER: Look, Métis.

RIEL: *(Off.)* They deserve it. Oh get angry with them.

(DUMONT, ISIDORE, and MÉTIS enter.)

DUMONT: Isidore, will you carry this flag of truce and parley with the police?

ISIDORE: Oui. Look it is me. I am holding a white flag. I come to parley.

(PRESTON shoots ISIDORE.)

CROZIER: Very good, you'll get a medal for that.

DUMONT: The bastards, they shot him. My brother, the bastards.

(RIEL enters holding a crucifix.)

RIEL: In the name of the Son, the Father, and the Holy Ghost. Reply to that. Fire!

(DUMONT and MÉTIS fire their rifles.)

PRESTON: They're picking us off like flies. Like flies.

CROZIER: Oh belch.

MÉTIS: There's one that looks like he is only eighteen years old.

(DUMONT fires his rifle.)

DUMONT: Won't live to be nineteen.

MÉTIS: And look, there's one eight hundred miles away.

(DUMONT fires.)

DUMONT: Should have been nine hundred.

MOUNTIE: They're picking us off like flies.

CROZIER: Oh belch. Retreat, retreat.

(CROZIER and MOUNTIE exit.)

DUMONT: Now we will kill them like buffalo.

RIEL: Stop, stop.

DUMONT: But my brother has been killed.

RIEL: I will pray for his resurrection. On your knees and give thanks.

(DUMONT and MÉTIS fall to their knees.)

Our Father.

OTHERS: Our Father.

(The lights fade.)

Scene Forty-eight

(In another playing area the lights fade in. MACDONALD and SMITH enter.)

MACDONALD: Oblivionville is my kind of town, my kind of town.

SMITH: The CPR is bankrupt.

MACDONALD: I know what it's like to be dead.

SMITH: We need another sixty million.

MACDONALD: Can't be done.

SMITH: Everything I have worked for, schemed for, stolen, purloined, is going to be lost.

MACDONALD: There, there.

SMITH: My bank, my businesses, my mansions. I will be a pauper.

MACDONALD: Oblivionville is my kind of town.

SMITH: This is a disaster.

MACDONALD: This is the end. Public funds lost, debts unpaid, the promises to British Columbia broken, a continent lost. Only an act of God can save us.

SMITH: If the CPR falls today, the government of Canada falls tomorrow.

MACDONALD: Oblivionville is my kind of town.

SMITH: The sheriff is going to come knocking at my door and put me in jail.

MACDONALD: Oh you poor little baby. Come here.

(MACDONALD hits SMITH on the back.)

Burp baby burp. C'mon burp.

SMITH: I am facing financial ruin.

MACDONALD: Burp.

SMITH: I will be reduced to living in a shack.

MACDONALD: Burp.

SMITH: A shack.

MACDONALD: You deserve better.

(BERNARD enters.)

BERNARD: There have been shots fired at Duck Lake.

(MACDONALD jumps up.)

MACDONALD: A national emergency, a national emergency! I know how we can get the money. I know how we can get the money.

(The lights fade.)

Scene Forty-nine

(In another playing area the lights fade in. RIEL, DUMONT, and LÉPINE enter.)

RIEL: God has given us a great victory over the Mounted Police. Rise up, children, rise up. England must be destroyed. France must be destroyed. Canada must be destroyed. Especially Canada. The pope must be destroyed. Yes, the pope. I decree a new order. A new dream. I will give Quebec to the Prussians. They deserve it. They deserve each other. The Irish can have Ontario, if they want it. The Hungarians and the Bavarians can have British Columbia. And the Jews, will get a piece of the country too. I will give the whole world a piece of the cake. Read this. I wrote it in buffalo blood, so it's important. This is the Constitution of the Métis Republic of Saskatchewan.

(The lights fade.)

Scene Fifty

(In another playing area the lights fade in. BLAKE, MACKENZIE, and WILFRID LAURIER enter.)

LAURIER: A national emergency. That is how they secured the funds for the CPR. Politics, there is no honour.

BLAKE: I am now permanently irritable, Mr. Laurier. Permanently irritable. Everything bothers me. Everything. Everything gives me a headache. Ottawa, what crimes are committed in your name? What crimes? Canada, the word, just the word. This undertaking is insane.

LAURIER: You should know, Monsieur.

BLAKE: The CPR is building the railroad, but the government is paying for it, but the CPR is going to own it. Insane. I detest my position as leader of the Liberal party. Absolutely detest it. But I am irreplaceable, right, Wilfrid?

LAURIER: I believe in the sunny way.

BLAKE: I think I am going to resign.

LAURIER: Every man should do what he thinks he should do.

BLAKE: Who could replace me?

LAURIER: Let's make a list starting with "A," Blake.

BLAKE: You!

LAURIER: No "A."

(The lights fade.)

Scene Fifty-one

(In another playing area the lights fade in. BIG BEAR and WANDERING SPIRIT enter.)

WANDERING SPIRIT: And though our enemies be as powerful as the sun, and as numerous as the stars, we will defend our homes.

BIG BEAR: Now the whirlwind is unleashed. I hate the government. Their well of promises has become a fountain of blood.

WANDERING SPIRIT: You are no longer the band leader. I am.

BIG BEAR: But I fear more for the captives at the hands of young warriors. For their destruction will be our destruction. To defeat the white man, you must act like the white man.

(BIG BEAR shakes his head.)

WANDERING SPIRIT: I am now the band leader.

(The lights fade.)

Scene Fifty-two

(In another playing area the lights fade in. DELANEY enters.)

DELANEY: I'm a settler. All I want to do is live peaceably in my habitation. I built this habitation from the ground up. These hands, oh Lord, these hands work so hard. My little shack on the prairie. I love it so much. Home, my home. My little shack proves there's a place for me in this world. Good feeling. Makes me proud. Canadian, whatever the hell that is, I am.

(QUINN enters looking at the Eaton's catalogue.)

QUINN: Look at the pair on this one. I'll stick her up my ass later.

(MISERABLE MAN and BAD ARROW enter.)

Well look who it is. It's Miserable Man and Bad Arrow.

MISERABLE MAN: That's right, white dog.

QUINN: Do you want to smell the cork or what? April Fool Day, today.

BAD ARROW: Big lie day.

(The sound of a coyote.)

MISERABLE MAN: Coyote.

QUINN: What's he saying?

MISERABLE MAN: You don't want to know. Oh Coyote.

(WANDERING SPIRIT enters.)

QUINN: The high and mighty himself.

WANDERING SPIRIT: Round up all the other white dogs. You are our prisoners. We are taking this food.

QUINN: No work, no rations.

WANDERING SPIRIT: No speak, no death.

(WANDERING SPIRIT points a gun at QUINN.)

You are known as the man who always says "No." Well I am going to hear you say "Yes."

QUINN: No you're not. I'll take no shilley from an Indian.

WANDERING SPIRIT: You are coming with us.

QUINN: No I'm not.

WANDERING SPIRIT: Yes you are.

(WANDERING SPIRIT poins a gun at QUINN.)

QUINN: No I'm not.

(WANDERING SPIRIT shoots QUINN.)

WANDERING SPIRIT: Kill all the white dogs.

BAD ARROW: The priests too.

WANDERING SPIRIT: Especially them. And him, stuff grass in his mouth.

(The lights fade.)

Scene Fifty-three

(In another playing area the lights fade in. FREDERICK MIDDLETON and a SOLDIER enter. The sound of train whistles.)

MIDDLETON: Success is a matter of marching. When they see us, they will run. These half-breeds may kill me but they do not scare me. I remember when I was in India putting down the mutiny of '57. Fighting the Thuggee, I was twice recommended for the Victoria Cross. But was I awarded the Cross? Of course not. They don't give the Victoria Cross to people like me. I was retired on half pay and after begging on my knees for a commission I was sent to Canada. The Siberia of the British Empire.

(BOULTON enters.)

BOULTON: Sir.

MIDDLETON: What, yes what.

BOULTON: The troops are embarked.

MIDDLETON: Excellent. Then we're off.

(The sound of a train whistle.)

VOICE: *(Off.)* All aboard.

(The lights fade.)

Scene Fifty-four

(In another playing area the lights fade in. ANDRÉ and RIEL enter.)

ANDRÉ: These heresies may be acceptable to Protestants, but not to good, God-fearing Catholics.

RIEL: The pope is completely corrupt, rotten to the core.

ANDRÉ: And I repeat, these heresies may be acceptable to Protestants, but not to good God-fearing Catholics.

(Music.)

RIEL: At Frog Lake, Wandering Spirit has risen up. They have killed two priests.

(Music ends.)

Excellent, just excellent. This is only the beginning, priest, only the beginning.

(DUMONT enters with LÉPINE and MÉTIS.)

DUMONT: I have seen Middleton's troops at Fish Creek. I want to treat them like Buffalo. I want to shoot the invaders.

RIEL: Oh very well, shoot the invaders. Only the beginning, priest.

DUMONT: En avant.

(MIDDLETON, BOULTON, and SOLDIERS enter.)

MIDDLETON: Follow me lads.

DUMONT: Let's get them.

(The Battle of Fish Creek. DUMONT kills three SOLDIERS, he shoots one, he stabs one, he strangles one.)

MIDDLETON: Retreat, retreat.

(MIDDLETON, BOULTON, and SOLDIERS exit.)

DUMONT: To a great victory at Fish Creek. To a great victory at Fish Creek.

(DUMONT exits.)

RIEL: This is like a dream unfolding. I am Louis "David" Riel. Prophet, infallible pontiff, and priest-king. The Holy See will be transferred from Rome to St. Boniface. My hometown. We're going to build St. Peter's cathedral in St. Boniface. Oh you lucky St. Bonifacians. Why do Manitobans have all the luck? As priest-king the first thing I will do is destroy Ontario. Ontario is going up in flames. I can't wait.

(Offstage: a loud uproar.)

What's all that shouting?

(DUMONT and LÉPINE enter.)

DUMONT: A cow has given birth to a calf.

RIEL: That is an important omen. Describe the calf to me.

DUMONT: It is beautiful to the eye.

RIEL: Yes, tell me more.

DUMONT: Its shape and colour is perfect.

RIEL: Yes.

DUMONT: But there is one defect.

RIEL: I knew it, yes.

DUMONT: Its testicles are coming out its ears.

RIEL: I knew it, I knew it. Not a good sign, not a good sign.

LÉPINE: That is one of the worst signs.

DUMONT: Quiet. The prophet is about to speak. Speak prophet.

RIEL: Batoche, oh Batoche. Because you have abandoned God. God abandons you.

(The sound of thunder. The lights fade.)

Scene Fifty-five

(In another playing area the lights fade in. MIDDLETON, BOULTON, and SOLDIERS enter.)

MIDDLETON: Stand easy. Colonel Boulton, what is the problem?

BOULTON: I don't know how to saddle my horse.

SOLDIER ONE: Listen to that.

MIDDLETON: Learn.

SOLDIER TWO: Said the pot to the kettle.

MIDDLETON: Men, we are going to attack.

BOULTON: On to Batoche. Get into your ox carts and on to Batoche.

(The lights fade.)

Scene Fifty-six

(In another playing area the lights fade in. MIDDLETON, BOULTON, and SOLDIERS enter.)

MIDDLETON: Forward.

SOLDIER ONE: We're always fighting with the sun in our eyes. With this general, always with the sun in our eyes.

(DUMONT, MÉTIS, LÉPINE, and RIEL enter.)

MÉTIS: You are a better shot than me.

DUMONT: Yes.

MÉTIS: Kill.

(MÉTIS gives his gun to DUMONT. DUMONT fires the gun. SOLDIER THREE dies.)

DUMONT: One less dog in this world.

MIDDLETON: We are going to retreat.

SOLDIER ONE: Jesus, let's fire a few shots anyway.

MIDDLETON: I have never lost a battle.

SOLDIER ONE: Never won one either.

LÉPINE: Here, you are a better shot than me.

SOLDIER TWO: Bring up the Gatling gun.

(DUMONT fires. SOLDIER TWO dies.)

MIDDLETON: I'm not in favour of this. Innovation leads to corruption. If cold British steel was good enough for the Duke of Wellington, it's good enough for me.

(BOULTON enters with the Gatling gun.)

When the bullets go pugh, pugh, pugh. It is ridiculous to drop to one's feet. If you hear it it means it missed you. It's the one you don't hear, that's the one that kills you.

(Sound of a gunshot. MIDDLETON drops to his knees.)

I heard it.

(A MAN enters with blood on forehead.)

He didn't.

(RIEL gives LÉPINE the crucifix. RIEL steps forward with arms outstretched like Christ. DUMONT, LÉPINE, and MÉTIS become inspired. They fight with vigour.)

MIDDLETON: Retreat, retreat.

SOLDIER ONE: Oh God.

(They exit.)

DUMONT: They are retreating.

RIEL: Praise God. Praise God.

(The lights fade.)

Scene Fifty-seven

(In another playing area the lights fade in. RIEL, DUMONT, and LÉPINE enter.)

RIEL: Batoche, oh Batoche. Have you confessed your sins?

LÉPINE: This is just like going to church, only seven days a week. I think he is touched in the head.

DUMONT: He talks to God all day. Can you do that?

LÉPINE: No.

DUMONT: Then shut up.

(LÉPINE exits.)

You should eat.

RIEL: No. When I sleep the angels feed me.

(LÉPINE enters.)

LÉPINE: The invaders are here.

RIEL: Yes. I have seen the battle already.

DUMONT: And …

RIEL: Christ is leading us to the cross. He wants to repay us for our labours. Batoche. Oh Batoche.

(The lights fade.)

Scene Fifty-eight

(In another playing area the lights fade in. SOLDIER ONE enters.)

MIDDLETON: *(Off.)* The enemy of course was soundly defeated.

SOLDIER ONE: That's why we retreated. The very model of a modern major general.

(SOLDIER TWO and SOLDIER THREE enter.)

SOLDIER TWO: Where is General Teapot?

SOLDIER ONE: He's pottering about somewhere.

(BOULTON enters.)

BOULTON: He was pottering about somewhere, but now he's wandered off somewhere.

SOLDIER ONE: We don't know where he is.

SOLDIER THREE: And we don't care.

SOLDIER TWO: I think these half-breeds are out of ammunition. Let's charge them. To corned beef and glory.

ALL: To corned beef and glory.

(The SOLDIERS charge off.)

BOULTON: I don't know if the general will like—

(BOULTON is knocked to the ground. Hand to hand combat between the MÉTIS and the SOLDIERS. MIDDLETON enters.)

The great Am I himself is here. Just got up from his snooze.

MIDDLETON: What's all that shouting?

BOULTON: It's all over but the roaring, General.

MIDDLETON: Who told them to attack? Why didn't they tell me?

(The MÉTIS retreat. The lights fade.)

Scene Fifty-nine

(In another playing area the lights fade in. MIDDLETON, SOLDIER ONE, and SOLDIER TWO enter.)

SOLDIER ONE: Look, that house is full of furs.

MIDDLETON: Put them in my tent. I want no looting! Now, I am going to go on parade.

(LÉPINE enters at the point of a bayonet.)

You there. I am going to deprive you of all your civil rights.

LÉPINE: Thanks.

MIDDLETON: You there.

(The lights fade.)

Scene Sixty

(In another playing area the lights fade in. DUMONT and RIEL enter.)

DUMONT: We are defeated.

RIEL: I want to mortify myself. I'm not even going to sit comfortably. I'm going to sit like this. Everything is pain and punishment now.

DUMONT: Come we must escape.

RIEL: No. I submit. I surrender. God wills it.

(The lights fade.)

Scene Sixty-one

(In another playing area the lights fade in. SOLDIER ONE enters.)

SOLDIER ONE: When I first came out here, I was a finicky eater. But now I will eat what no dog will touch. Just scoff your pork without a fork. Just bolt the vile stuff down.

(MIDDLETON and BOULTON enter.)

MIDDLETON: Batoche is ours.

SOLDIER ONE: And we also secured a great victory at Frenchman's Butte. We suffered no casualties and annihilated one Indian.

MIDDLETON: How did that happen?

SOLDIER ONE: An Indian came out holding a white flag.

MIDDLETON: And ...

BOULTON: We shot him.

MIDDLETON: Very good. You'll get a big medal for that.

(BOULTON exits.)

SOLDIER ONE: Look, Big Bear is surrendering.

MIDDLETON: I have not come to debate with a savage. If he does not do as I say I will kill all the women and children in his village.

(BIG BEAR and WANDERING SPIRIT enter.)

BIG BEAR: Anybody got anything to eat?

MIDDLETON: Put that man in chains.

BIG BEAR: Ah, General Middlebum.

MIDDLETON: Shoot him, shoot him.

BIG BEAR: All I wanted was to be as free as my namesake.

MIDDLETON: Put that man in a dungeon.

WANDERING SPIRIT: I am so filled with hate, I am destroyed.

(BIG BEAR and WANDERING SPIRIT exit. RIEL enters.)

RIEL: I am looking for General Middleton.

MIDDLETON: Ah, the head muckamuck himself.

RIEL: I surrender, God wills it.

MIDDLETON: Ball and chain for this one. Arrest him.

(The lights fade.)

Scene Sixty-two

(In another playing area the lights fade in. RIEL, JUDGE, DEFENCE ATTORNEY, PROSECUTOR, and a SOLDIER enter.)

JUDGE: Louis Riel, you stand charged on oath before me for maliciously and traitorously attempting to subvert and destroy the constitution and government of this realm contrary to the duty of your allegaince to Our Lady the Queen, her crown and dignity.

RIEL: I protest.

DEFENCE ATTORNEY: Quiet.

RIEL: No.

DEFENCE ATTORNEY: You're insane.

RIEL: No, I'm not. Your Honour, I want to discuss the grievances of the Métis people against this government.

JUDGE: You are on trial for high treason. We are trying to decide if you led an armed revolt against your sovereign.

RIEL: I did.

DEFENCE ATTORNEY: Because he is insane.

RIEL: No. Because there are legitimate grievances against this government that would not be redressed unless—

PROSECUTOR: Your Honour, this man is on trial not the government of Canada.

JUDGE: Exactly. I think we'll pass sentence.

RIEL: What kind of trial is this?

JUDGE: Louis Riel.

RIEL: What!

JUDGE: I find you guilty of high treason and

sentence you to be hanged by the neck until dead. May God have mercy on your soul.

RIEL: The same.

JUDGE: Out, out.

(The SOLDIER takes RIEL away.)

Send in the Indians.

(BIG BEAR enters.)

Big Bear.

BIG BEAR: I know I'm ugly but I did nothing.

JUDGE: We're going to put you behind bars.

BIG BEAR: I prefer that to the reserve.

JUDGE: Three years of hard labour. All the rest of you Indians, I sentence you all to death.

BIG BEAR: Somebody dig a big hole.

(The lights fade.)

Scene Sixty-three

(In another playing area the lights fade in. MACDONALD, SMITH, SCHULTZ, and LAFLAMME enter.)

LAFLAMME: He must be given a pardon.

SCHULTZ: He must hang.

SMITH: God works in strange ways, John A. The CPR should build a monument to Louis Riel, a monument.

SCHULTZ: With a scaffold on top. Orange Ontario demands that he hang.

MACDONALD: Abide by me and I will make you lieutenant-governor of Manitoba.

LAFLAMME: I protest the legalized murder of Monsieur Riel. He is insane.

MACDONALD: Is he?

LAFLAMME: Your William Shakespeare once said—

MACDONALD: Don't quote the bard to me, Mr. Pecksniff. Some men should be destroyed for the good of others.

LAFLAMME: Weep no more, Ontario. You will get your blood.

MACDONALD: And though every dog in Quebec may bark, he'll hang, he'll hang.

(The lights fade.)

Scene Sixty-four

(In another playing area the lights fade in. MACKENZIE, BLAKE, and LAURIER enter.)

LAURIER: Had I been born on the banks of the Saskatchewan, I myself would have shouldered a musket.

BLAKE: Mr. Laurier, really.

LAURIER: We should censure the government.

BLAKE: Said Caesar.

LAURIER: With this execution, the Conservative party is finished.

BLAKE: I'm on to you.

LAURIER: All that is required is a leader.

BLAKE: Don't get on my wick, Wilfrid, don't get on my wick.

MACKENZIE: Blake, resign.

(LAURIER smiles. The lights fade.)

Scene Sixty-five

(In another playing area the lights fade in. Tableau vivant: the famous photograph of Craigellachie depicting the completion of the CPR. SMITH hammers the last spike.)

OTHERS: Missed.

(SMITH hits the last spike.)

Hurrah.

(SMITH smiles. The lights fade.)

Scene Sixty-six

(In another playing area the lights fade in. RIEL and MRS RIEL enter. MRS RIEL holds a pair of red moccasins.)

RIEL: Though I am sentenced to death, the government is in greater danger.

(MRS RIEL gives RIEL the red moccasins.)

MRS RIEL: Put those on your feet and remember.

RIEL: I will. It is a bad cause that asks for mercy. Those who die in a great cause never fail. The prospect of eternity makes me smile.

(The lights fade.)

Scene Sixty-seven

(In another playing area the lights fade in. There is the sound of a trap door, then a pair of feet wearing red moccasins kicking in the air. The lights fade.)

Scene Sixty-eight

(In another playing area the lights fade in. Tableau vivant: the CPR train moving across the stage carrying SMITH and VAN HORNE. In another playing area the lights fade in. MACDONALD is sitting on the shoulders of a farmer and a labourer. MACDONALD holds a Union Jack with the words "The old flag, the old policy, the old leader.")

MACDONALD: A British subject I was born, a British subject I will die.

(MACDONALD smiles. The lights fade. The end.)

Laurier

Part Five of The History of the Village of the Small Huts

Act One

Scene One

(The lights fade in. An old white-haired WILFRID LAURIER, at age seventy, enters. The sound of a church bell.)

LAURIER: I remember.

(The sound of a piano sonata. The lights fade.)

Scene Two

(In another playing area the lights fade in. Madame Gauthier's boarding house, 1864. ZOE LAFONTAINE is playing the piano. LAURIER, at age twenty-three, enters.)

LAURIER: You play very beautifully.

ZOE: Merci, monsieur. My mother is upstairs dying and I am down here singing.

(ZOE plays the piano.)

I am a poor girl, but I can plant roses.

LAURIER: Are you happy?

ZOE: Only on Thursdays, monsieur.

LAURIER: Do you believe in Jesus?

ZOE: This is like a catechism.

LAURIER: I studied to be a priest.

ZOE: I believe you, monsieur.

LAURIER: Call me Wilfrid.

ZOE: Never.

LAURIER: No really. That's my name. Look, my birth certificate.

(LAURIER shows ZOE a piece of paper.)

ZOE: Henri Charles Wilfrid Laurier. Well Henri.

LAURIER: Call me Wilfrid. How many men have you met called Wilfrid?

ZOE: None, monsieur.

LAURIER: Right. But look, they don't even spell it right. Some ignorant priest, worse than the English. They can't do anything right. They spell it "ferd." Wilferd. Not Fred, or Frid, but Ferd. Can you imagine anyone called Ferd?

ZOE: No, Wilfrid.

LAURIER: What's your name?

ZOE: Zoe, monsieur. Zoe Lafontaine.

LAURIER: Enchanté, mademoiselle.

ZOE: Enchanté, Ferd.

(ZOE smiles. The lights fade.)

Scene Three

(In another playing area the lights fade in. BISHOP IGNACE BOURGET enters.)

BOURGET: To be Canadien you must be French. You must be French-speaking. And of course, you must be Catholic. There is no debate or discussion about it. It is divine truth. God wills it.

(BOURGET smiles. The lights fade.)

Scene Four

(In another playing area the lights fade in: Madame Gauthier's boarding house. LAURIER and ZOE enter.)

LAURIER: And of course our landlady, old Mrs. Gauthier was an old friend of my mother.

ZOE: She is an old friend of my mother too. In fact she is an old friend of all mothers.

(Noises offstage.)

LAURIER: Oh speak of the devil.

(MADAME GAUTHIER enters.)

MME GAUTHIER: I found a penny, I found a penny, I found a penny.

ZOE: What are you going to do with it?

MME GAUTHIER: I'm going to give it to my priest.

LAURIER: Oh what a fanatic.

MME GAUTHIER: How is your old mother?

ZOE: Dying.

MME GAUTHIER: Of what?

ZOE: Consumption.

MME GAUTHIER: Don't be ashamed of it. God kills the good ones only because he wants to talk to them. Don't be ashamed. His mother died of it. His sister, too. And he's going to die of it unless he gets married.

LAURIER: Oh madame, please. I have a weak chest, but a strong heart.

MME GAUTHIER: I am going to make you some soup.

LAURIER: It's obscene the way you say that word.

MME GAUTHIER: A bowl of woman's broth.

LAURIER: Makes me big and strong.

MME GAUTHIER: For a reason. How old are you?

LAURIER: Twenty-three.

MME GAUTHIER: What are you waiting for?

LAURIER: Spring.

MME GAUTHIER: That's what you said last year.

(MME GAUTHIER gestures to ZOE to move closer to LAURIER.)

I'm going to make you some soup.

(MME GAUTHIER exits. LAURIER and ZOE look at each other. The lights fade.)

Scene Five

(In another playing area the lights fade in. BOURGET enters.)

BOURGET: I am ultra montane. I believe in the church supreme. Religious, social, political, spiritual, cultural. The pope supreme. My allegiance is to Rome, not to France. Government is by divine right or it is nothing.

(The lights fade.)

Scene Six

(In another playing area the lights fade in: Madame Gauthier's boarding house. LAURIER enters. MME GAUTHIER and ZOE enter. ZOE weeps.)

MME GAUTHIER: Only God is immortal. God wills it. So be it. Her mother is dead.

LAURIER: Oh I am terribly sorry to hear that. You must be very distressed.

ZOE: Oh please.

MME GAUTHIER: We're going to the funeral, Wilfrid.

LAURIER: I'll come with you.

ZOE: You don't have to.

LAURIER: I want to.

(MME GAUTHIER nods her head. The lights fade.)

Scene Seven

(In another playing area the lights fade in. BOURGET and LOUIS RIEL enter.)

BOURGET: You have been here almost six years, Indian boy.

RIEL: Yes.

BOURGET: What does it mean if we lose our language?

RIEL: It means we lose our faith?

BOURGET: And what does it mean if we lose our faith?

RIEL: It means we burn in hell forever with the English, with sulphur coming out of every orifice.

BOURGET: You have a mission in life. Your people are as sheep that have no shepherd. You are the elect. You have been chosen. One day, you will be Louis Riel, Métis priest. The first. The Church's dream come true. You have a mission, Indian boy. Fulfill it.

RIEL: Yes.

(The lights fade.)

Scene Eight

(In another playing area the lights fade in. LAURIER enters. He is practising his smile in front of a mirror.)

LAURIER: How do you do?

(LAURIER smiles and extends his hand.)

How do you do?

(He smiles and extends his hand.)

How do you do?

(ZOE enters.)

ZOE: Very well, Henri.

LAURIER: I am just practising.

ZOE: It makes perfect.

LAURIER: It is a big night for me tonight. I am graduating from McGill University, Faculty of Law. First in my class, of course.

ZOE: So, you are going to be a lawyer.

LAURIER: Yes. I love law, truth, beauty, justice. All of it. I am an individual. No one is like me. I call myself Wilfrid because no one else is called Wilfrid. I dress like this because no one dresses like this. I walk like this because no one walks like this. I talk like this because no one talks like this. I am unique. I am an individual. No one is like me. How do you do?

(LAURIER extends his hand and smiles. The lights fade.)

Scene Nine

(In another playing area the lights fade in. There is a sign with the words "Rodolphe Laflamme, Lawyer." It is 1864. RUDOLPHE LAFLAMME and LAURIER enter. LAFLAMME holds a piece of paper.)

LAFLAMME: Very impressive Monsieur Laurier, very impressive. So you wish to study the articles of law?

LAURIER: Yes.

LAFLAMME: Where are you from, monsieur?

LAURIER: St. Lin.

LAFLAMME: Ah, twenty miles from St. Eustache. Remember the patriotes, Monsieur Laurier.

LAURIER: Always.

LAFLAMME: Prove your credentials, monsieur.

LAURIER: My father was a patriote, my mother was a patriote, even the cat was a patriote.

LAFLAMME: Oh bravo, Wilfy.

LAURIER: You are with the Institut-Canadien?

LAFLAMME: I am.

LAURIER: And with the Parti rouge?

LAFLAMME: Oui. I am as red as red can be. There is no pink in me. I am with the party of Papineau. Have you ever met the great man?

LAURIER: Non.

LAFLAMME: Oh you must meet him. He is rouge de rouge.

LAFLAMME: He is addressing the Institut-Canadien tonight. You must come.

LAURIER: Can I bring a friend, Monsieur Laflamme?

LAFLAMME: Call me Rodolphe.

LAURIER: How do you do?

(The lights fade.)

Scene Ten

(In another playing area the lights fade in. LOUIS-JOSEPH PAPINEAU enters.)

PAPINEAU: Mes amis. Canadiens. Écoutez. The confederation scheme is a stench in my nostril. It allows the English colonies to escape the future. Annexation to the United States. It will happen sooner or later, but that is not why we are opposed to it. We are opposed to it because it will be the tomb of the French race and the ruin of Lower Canada. What do we have in common with the English colonies? Origin, religion, language, aspirations? Non. We have nothing in common with the English colonies except our servitude to Great Britain. We share the honour of the colonial yoke. Nothing more. We do not care a fig for the English colonies. Nova Scotia, Prince Edward Island, New Brunswick, or Newfoundland. We have the same relationship with them as with Australia. We are colonies of England. That is all. The only difference is the distance. Australia's is greater, ours is lesser.

(LAURIER, ZOE, LAFLAMME, ERIC DORION, and JOSEPH GUIBORD enter.)

LAURIER: That was an excellent speech, just excellent.

PAPINEAU: Merci, monsieur.

LAURIER: You're my hero.

PAPINEAU: That's nice. Have you met my protégé, Eric Dorion?

DORION: I am enfant terrible.

LAURIER: How do you do? Excellent.

DORION: And who is your beautiful friend?

LAURIER: Oh, this is Zoe Lafontaine.

DORION: Cognac, mademoiselle?

ZOE: Non.

DORION: You say no to cognac, you say no to life.

LAFLAMME: I think we should appeal to the Privy Council in London for better terms.

PAPINEAU: Non, everytime we appeal to London we perpetuate our colonial status.

DORION: Drink.

LAURIER: I think—

PAPINEAU: The confederation scheme is a stench in my nostril. If you don't go in you won't have to go out. Simple.

LAFLAMME: Oh you are rouge de rouge.

PAPINEAU: Don't pull my tail.

LAFLAMME: Oh rouge de rouge. And what does little enfant terrible think?

DORION: I think, we are already attached by the belly to Upper Canada. And now they want to tie our feet to New Brunswick and Nova Scotia, and our arms over our head to Newfoundland and Prince Edward Island. What kind of Parliament is that? One Canadien and five Englishmen. We're dead.

LAFLAMME: And what does little Wilfy think?

PAPINEAU: Who cares? The revolution will not be made by parlour room revolutionaries. You puppies.

(PAPINEAU exits.)

LAURIER: One should never meet one's hero.

LAFLAMME: Don't cry, he's like that to everybody.

LAURIER: I love my country more than ideas about my country.

LAFLAMME: Oh bravo, Wilfy.

GUIBORD: I am Hpesoj Drobiug.

ZOE: A Ukrainian?

GUIBORD: Non. That is Joseph Guibord, backwards. I can think.

ZOE: If he can think, carrots and turnips can think also.

GUIBORD: It's a printer's joke.

DORION: Ah, I see you are experiencing the tittle-tattle that passes for conversation in this backwater.

ZOE: Yes.

LAFLAMME: I think priests are pimps, nuns are prostitutes and God is an asshole.

GUIBORD: You know many people think you are anti-clerical.

LAFLAMME: Really. I can't imagine why.

LAURIER: These are my friends.

(ZOE rolls her eyes. The lights fade.)

Scene Eleven

(In another playing area the lights fade in. BOURGET and RIEL enter.)

BOURGET: Why were we conquered by the English?

RIEL: Because we denied God.

BOURGET: On the Plains of Abraham. We denied God. God destroyed the nation. This province is a gift of providence. The imps of hell will be banished. The people of this land will return to the faith of Brébeuf or God will destroy them. The Church will provide the greatest victory a nation can achieve. We will conquer our conquerors.

(The lights fade.)

Scene Twelve

(In another playing area the lights fade in. LAURIER enters reading Aesop's fables. ZOE enters.)

ZOE: Always reading a book.

LAURIER: Yes.

(DORION enters.)

DORION: You look so beautiful, you smell so nice, and your hair is lovely too.

ZOE: This is my new friend, Eric.

LAURIER: Yes, we've met.

DORION: Well shall we go?

LAURIER: Where are you going?

ZOE: Out, monsieur bookreader, out!

(ZOE and DORION exit. MME GAUTHIER enters.)

MME GAUTHIER: You're going to lose that girl.

(The lights fade.)

Scene Thirteen

(In another playing area the lights fade in. RIEL and BOURGET enter.)

RIEL: I have been here six years, I cannot go seven. My father has died.

BOURGET: There is only one father, Louis.

RIEL: And my father is sitting in his lap. I am going to leave the seminary.

BOURGET: Perhaps God does not want you to be a priest. Perhaps he has other plans for you.

RIEL: Yes.

(The lights fade.)

Scene Fourteen

(In another playing area the lights fade in: The Institut-Canadien. LAFLAMME and RIEL enter.)

LAFLAMME: Confederation is bullshit! Long live the Republic! Confederation is bullshit! Long live the Republic!

VOICES: *(Off.)* Confederation is bullshit! Long live the Republic!

LAFLAMME: I have to remind them every now and then. You look like you just got out of jail.

RIEL: I have spent six years at the College de Montréal.

LAFLAMME: Same thing. But we don't care what the Church says. You can think here.

RIEL: Monsieur Laflamme.

LAFLAMME: Call me Rodolphe.

RIEL: Bishop Bourget says you are anti-clerical.

LAFLAMME: Really, I can't imagine why. Bourget. You're lucky to be out of there. Popes, bishops, kings, queens. The world is rotten with them.

(Noises offstage.)

Come monsieur, join us. We are debating the confederation scheme.

(The lights fade.)

Scene Fifteen

(In another playing area the lights fade in. DORION, LAURIER, and GUIBORD enter.)

GUIBORD: It's going to be a federation.

DORION: Non.

LAURIER: Non, not at all. I agree with Monsieur Dorion. It's going to be a federation and a confederation at the same time.

DORION: It's a compromise.

LAURIER: A compromise between George Brown and his Protestant reformers and Cartier and the conservative clerical bunch.

DORION: It won't work.

GUIBORD: And who does it benefit?

LAURIER: More to the point. What does it benefit? The Grand Trunk Railroad.

DORION: That's right. There's a railway in it, mark my words. Half the cabinet are directors of the Grand Trunk Railway: the solicitor-general, the receiver general, the inspector.

LAURIER: Private enterprise with public monies. That's confederation.

DORION: It's a swindle.

LAURIER: Eric, calm yourself.

GUIBORD: What does the Church gain by supporting confederation?

LAURIER: Power. Pure power.

DORION: That's right.

(LAFLAMME and RIEL enter.)

LAFLAMME: Watch and learn. And what does little Wilfy think?

LAURIER: The confederation I advocate is a real confederation. A union of independent sovereign states. But John A. Macdonald says you must take the whole measure or no part of it. No amendments are possible. We want a real confederation. We have no desire to create a new nationality.

RIEL: That's right.

(The lights fade.)

Scene Sixteen

(In another playing area the lights fade in. LAURIER enters reading Madame Bovary*. ZOE enters.)*

ZOE: Always reading a book.

LAURIER: Yes.

ZOE: What do you think of Eric Dorion? The enfant terrible.

LAURIER: You should read this. You'd like it. She kills herself with rat poison.

ZOE: Why?

LAURIER: That is for you to find out.

(LAURIER gives the book to ZOE. The lights fade.)

Scene Seventeen

(In another playing area the lights fade in. BOURGET and FRANÇOIS LA FLECHE enter.)

BOURGET: These books are forbidden. Nowhere in the world will the syllabus of errors be more fully accepted than the province of Quebec. I declare war on rationalism, liberalism, socialism, communism, and modern civilization.

LA FLECHE: And there are members of the Institut-Canadien that are not French and not Catholic. English Protestants are members and worse. Women. Women. Women! Imagine women reading Voltaire.

(BOURGET makes the sign of the cross.)

BOURGET: They are heretics, apostates, socialists. The Insitut-Canadien wants to satanize the good men and women of this province. Antichrist. These books are censored. We will burn them and excommunicate the readers.

(The lights fade.)

Scene Eighteen

(In another playing area the lights fade in. LAURIER enters. ZOE enters holding up the book.)

LAURIER: And, and, and …

ZOE: Satan wrote this.

LAURIER: Yes, it's been banned by the Church.

ZOE: I'm glad. Writing about a woman like that. Having affairs with random abandon.

LAURIER: It happens.

ZOE: In life perhaps, but not in books. Here.

(The lights fade.)

Scene Nineteen

(In another playing area the lights fade in: The Institut-Canadien. LAURIER and GUIBORD enter.)

LAURIER: What is love, Joseph? Is it two pigs in a trough having a go at each other, or is it the desire for immortality?

GUIBORD: Both.

LAURIER: Joseph, think.

GUIBORD: I am, I can. I can think.

(LAFLAMME enters.)

LAFLAMME: Mesdames, mes amis. Écoute. Tonight we will not discuss the confederation scheme.

(GUIBORD applauds.)

But we will discuss it tomorrow. Tonight, Monsieur Wilfrid Laurier will give his lecture on the following topic: "Is the present system of education defective?"

LAURIER: There is more to education than "Our father who art in heaven" and the catechism.

(BOURGET enters.)

BOURGET: Stop. Anyone who reads books on the Index …

(BOURGET holds up a thick book.)

Books banned by Pope Pius the Ninth … will be excommunicated and denied the sacraments. In the name of God, the Holy Spirit, and Jesus Christ I declare this to be so.

LAURIER: And in the name of Liberty I declare the right of freedom of expression.

BOURGET: When God turned Lucifer into Satan he revealed his feelings toward Liberals.

LAURIER: Hell is red with the flesh of roasting priests, bishop.

BOURGET: You are the high priest of the Liberal religion.

LAURIER: You have your prayers. I have my books.

GUIBORD: Just bury me with my books.

BOURGET: And if you read them you will be excommunicated, shunned and avoided by all good Catholics. And when you die you and the Parti rouge can visit His Infernalness and burn in hell forever.

(BOURGET exits.)

LAFLAMME: He is proof that there are Catholics and then there are Jesuits.

LAURIER: Yes. And there are Jesuits and then there is Bourget.

LAFLAMME: Oh Bourget.

GUIBORD: Oh Bourget.

LAURIER: He is supernaturally ugly.

GUIBORD: With a voice from the grave.

LAFLAMME: He poses the central question.

LAURIER: Was he born or was he made? We are fighting the infamous thing. Intolerance. With the Church. It is war.

GUIBORD and LAFLAMME: War.

(The lights fade.)

Scene Twenty

(In another playing area the lights fade in. LAURIER enters. ZOE enters holding a book, Flaubert's Sentimental Education.*)*

ZOE: Monsieur, for your birthday. A gift.

(ZOE gives LAURIER the book.)

LAURIER: Oh thank you, thank you, this is a difficult book to get.

ZOE: Actually, I like him as a writer. I don't think the Church should ban his work.

LAURIER: There is hope for you.

(LAURIER opens the book.)

ZOE: He reads it right away.

(MME GAUTHIER enters holding a little cake with a big candle.)

MME GAUTHIER: Here's your cake. Eat it all, Wilfrid. Happy birthday to you. We wanted to put twenty-six candles on it but we only had one, so there it is. Now make a wish.

(LAURIER looks at ZOE. He blows out the candle and looks at ZOE again. The lights fade.)

Scene Twenty-one

(In another playing area the lights fade in. LAFLAMME and RIEL enter. RIEL holds a book.)

LAFLAMME: Wilfy. That book is proscribed by the Church. If you read it you will be excommunicated. I can recite it by heart. Oh Wilfy. Bourget has excommunicated all members of the Institut-Canadien. He has placed the mark of Cain upon us. It is a mark of honour. We are outcasts. In this province anyone who has not been excommunicated is not worth anything. Oh Wilfy.

(LAURIER enters.)

LAURIER: Yes.

LAFLAMME: This is Louis Riel. He will be working as the office boy. I am preparing for the confederation debates with John A. Macdonald's lackey George-Étienne Cartier. I am too busy to deal with him. Outline our protocols to him.

LAURIER: Monsieur Laflamme likes his coffee with extra cream.

(LAFLAMME exits.)

You are Métis?

RIEL: Yes.

LAURIER: You are descended from our coureurs de bois.

RIEL: That's right, that's me. The runners of the woods are now the runners of the plains.

LAURIER: Well, Monsieur Laflamme will have you running. Are you taking an interest in the confederation debates?

RIEL: Very much.

LAURIER: For, or against?

RIEL: Against.

LAURIER: Perhaps you would like to come to our demonstration against the beast.

RIEL: Very much. Fight the beast.

LAURIER: Yes.

(The lights fade.)

Scene Twenty-two

(In another playing area the lights fade in. LAURIER and ZOE enter. DORION enters holding a placard with the words "Down with Confederation. Long live the Republic." GEORGE-ÉTIENNE CARTIER and LAFLAMME enter.)

CARTIER: Confederation allows us the opportunity to create a new nation. We will create a federation that is Catholic and Protestant, English and French, Irish and Scottish.

LAFLAMME: I demand to speak.

CARTIER: Shall we be content to maintain a mere provincial existence when by combining together we could become a great nation? A nation that can take it's place among the nations of the world.

LAFLAMME: I demand to speak.

CARTIER: That is the opportunity that confederation gives to us. We should take it.

LAFLAMME: I demand to speak. Mes amis. Canadiens. Écoutez. We seek to delay this act of confederation not to frustrate the purposes of a majority of our countrymen, but to prevent their being surprised against their will, or without their consent, into a political change which, however obnoxious and oppressive to them it might prove to be, cannot be reversed.

CARTIER: Mes amis, patriotes. In '37 with Papineau, I took up the gun against the English.

LAFLAMME: So much for rational debate.

CARTIER: Did you?

LAFLAMME: I was a boy.

CARTIER: So was I.

LAFLAMME: Oh you—

CARTIER: Bourget.

(BOURGET enters.)

BOURGET: I damn you to hell. Burn in hell, infidel. Burn. I damn that man to hell.

(LAFLAMME exits. CARTIER and BOURGET shake hands.)

CARTIER: That's how it's done.

LAURIER: That's how it's done.

(The lights fade.)

Scene Twenty-three

(In another playing area the lights fade in. LAURIER and GUIBORD enter. LAURIER writes a letter.)

GUIBORD: We are the vice-presidents of the Institut-Canadien. Me and you. You and me. The lawyers are the sawyers, they saw the law.

LAURIER: Enough Joseph.

GUIBORD: Lawyers. What ring of hell do you think they're consigned too?

LAURIER: The third I believe.

GUIBORD: Lawyers. It is unbelievable what lawyers will do for money. Unbelievable. If you pay a lawyer enough he will say anything. Anything. You're a lawyer, aren't you?

LAURIER: Joseph.

GUIBORD: You're a lawyer.

LAURIER: I believe that the source of all good is knowledge, and that the source of all evil is ignorance.

GUIBORD: If I paid you a million dollars would you say the source of all good is ignorance and the source of all evil is knowledge?

LAURIER: Non. But a priest would say that for nothing. Voila. C'est finis. A letter to the pope protesting the "Undue Influence" of the Church in politics. This is the beginning of the end.

(The lights fade.)

Scene Twenty-four

(In another playing area the lights fade in. LAURIER, LAFLAMME, and ZOE enter. LAURIER reads Le Défricheur.*)*

LAFLAMME: Bourget is now frothing mad. You are a marked man.

(DORION enters.)

DORION: He is my protégé. He is under my protection.

LAFLAMME: Good, he will need it.

LAURIER: Ah, the member of Parliament for Drummond-Athabaskaville.

DORION: That's right. Have you ever been to Athabaskaville?

LAURIER: No.

DORION: Oh you should go there. It's a great place. No English live there.

LAFLAMME: You should meet his brother Antoine-Aimé. He is big in the Parti rouge.

LAURIER: I'd like to meet him.

DORION: I bet you would. I tell you what. Give me your woman for the night and I'll introduce you to him.

LAURIER: What?

DORION: Only joking. I am enfant terrible.

ZOE: You are too old to be enfant terrible.

DORION: Perhaps. But not too old to be enfant.

LAURIER: Monsieur, you are talking to my wife, I mean bride-to-be.

DORION: Well excuse me.

ZOE: Are you proposing to me?

LAURIER: Yes. You are a witness.

(DORION has a heart attack.)

LAURIER and ZOE: Oh what a face.

(DORION falls to the ground. The lights fade.)

Scene Twenty-five

(In another playing area the lights fade in: a funeral. LAURIER, GUIBORD, ZOE, and ANTOINE-AIMÉ DORION enter. They look at the floor.)

LAURIER: The soul of our nation is in that hole.

GUIBORD: I feel like jumping in.

LAURIER: Don't.

GUIBORD: I was joking.

ANTOINE: Ah mon frère, mon frère, mon frère.

(LAURIER whispers in ANTOINE's ear.)

Ah, so you are the young Wilfrid. My brother spoke of you. Poor enfant terrible. Oh enfant terrible. The Parti rouge will need someone to step into his shoes. Perhaps you. Oh mon frère.

(LAFLAMME enters holding a proclamation.)

LAFLAMME: Read and weep. They ratified this in London on March 29th. They have set July 1st as Canada Day.

LAURIER: They can't do that. We demand a referendum, a plebiscite, call it what you will, at least an election.

LAFLAMME: Read.

(LAURIER puts a handkerchief to his mouth and coughs blood.)

LAURIER: We must protest, we must organize. We must protest.

(BOURGET enters.)

BOURGET: Who are you to reject constitutionally and legitimately accomplished facts?

(BOURGET holds up the BNA Act.)

Those opposed to this constitution take the path of anarchy, treason, revolt. They take the path to hell. You will respect this new constitution that is given to you as the expression of the supreme will of God himself.

(The sound of thunder. The lights fade.)

Scene Twenty-six

(In another playing area the lights fade in. The sound of rain. LAURIER, LAFLAMME, RIEL, and GUIBORD enter. They watch fireworks. LAURIER holds a blood spattered handkerchief.)

LAFLAMME: July 1st, 1867. It's all over but the fireworks. John A. Macdonald announced that the first business of the Dominion of Canada would be to annex the Northwest Territories. Get right to it.

RIEL: I think I will go back to Manitoba. My people will need me.

(RIEL exits.)

LAURIER: Cartier we can fight, but Bourget poses the question.

(LAURIER coughs.)

LAFLAMME: You are ill.

GUIBORD: Sick in the head.

LAFLAMME: Joseph.

GUIBORD: I know for a fact he is sick in the head. He got married. Why?

LAURIER: I have no idea. We hate for no reason. We love for no reason too.

GUIBORD: Do you love her?

LAURIER: Truth does not have to be spoken in order for it to be apparent.

GUIBORD: What an intellectual.

LAFLAMME: Yes, this intellectual is going to represent the Parti rouge in Athabaskaville.

GUIBORD: A career in politics.

(ZOE enters holding a suitcase.)

ZOE: How are you?

(LAURIER nods his head.)

GUIBORD: You must be very happy?

LAURIER: Take care of your health. If you die they will bury you in unconsecrated ground.

LAFLAMME: If at all.

GUIBORD: Tend to your own gardens, messieurs.

ZOE: We will.

(LAURIER and ZOE exit. The lights fade.)

Scene Twenty-seven

(In another playing area the lights fade in: Athabaskaville. LAURIER and ZOE enter. JOSEPH LAVERGNE enters.)

LAVERGNE: Welcome to Athabaskaville. I am Joseph Lavergne, your welcoming committee. Your reputation Monsieur Laurier precedes you. I know you are rouge de rouge. We will fight the good fight. And this must be the wife. How are you?

ZOE: Very good.

LAVERGNE: I'll have a wife one day, God willing.

ZOE: Oh I love it here, love it. I can grow roses and lettuce and radishes too. Oh I will become a big roly-poly one here.

LAVERGNE: Wait till you see what the priests are like here.

LAURIER: Yes.

(The lights fade.)

Scene Twenty-eight

(In another playing area the lights fade in. GUIBORD, DOCTOR, and BOURGET enter.)

BOURGET: Recant. You'll be damned if you don't.

GUIBORD: I'll be damned if I do.

BOURGET: On his deathbed, even the antichrist Voltaire recanted.

GUIBORD: Jesuits will say anything. Even shameless lies.

BOURGET: Confess your sins.

GUIBORD: Get out of my life.

BOURGET: He is possessed by a powerful demon. Out demon, Out. Out.

DOCTOR: He's dead.

BOURGET: Excellent. He is being judged right now. An unrepentant sinner. This one is going straight to hell. We will bury him in the ground that we bury the unbaptized bastards.

(The lights fade.)

Scene Twenty-nine

(In another playing area the lights fade in. LAFLAMME and LAURIER enter.)

LAFLAMME: His corpse is rotting in a coffin, unburied. Rotting at the Institut-Canadien. But we're going to bury him if we have to go right to the Vatican, we're going to bury him.

LAURIER: Because he fought for the right to read, he is denied the right to be buried. Everything that fat priest holds dear I will destroy.

(The lights fade.)

Scene Thirty

(In another playing area the lights fade in. JEAN and JACQUES, two habitants, enter. They look at a posted bulletin.)

JEAN: What's that one say?

JACQUES: France has collapsed. The Prussians are in Paris.

JEAN: Oh the English are bad, but the Germans.

(LAURIER and LAVERGNE enter.)

LAURIER: How would you like to be my partner-in-law?

LAVERGNE: I feel like breaking into song.

LAURIER: Does that mean yes?

LAVERGNE: Yes.

LAURIER: Excellent.

JEAN: And what about that one?

JACQUES: Louis Riel and the Métis have formed a government in Manitoba.

LAVERGNE: They are all peasants here, all of them. But they love life.

LAURIER: What do they think of the Church?

LAVERGNE: It depends if the church is full of priests or not.

JACQUES: Fucking priest.

LAURIER: Monsieur please, your language.

JACQUES: Monsieur, you are new here. You will find out that there are priests and then there are fucking priests. Wait till you meet the fucking priest that lives here. Speak of the devil.

(LA FLECHE enters.)

LA FLECHE: Peasants, listen. We are inaugurating the Progamme catholique. It is your duty to vote only for those who are willing to conform entirely with the teachings of the Church.

LAURIER: Bourget.

LA FLECHE: If you have a choice between two Conservatives, vote for the one that subscribes to the Programme.

LAURIER: A theocracy.

LA FLECHE: Between a Conservative and a Liberal, vote Conservative. Between a Conservative who rejects the Programme and a Liberal, abstain.

LAURIER: Bourget.

(LA FLECHE smiles at LAURIER. LAURIER smiles at LA FLECHE.)

LA FLECHE: Furthermore.

(The lights fade.)

Scene Thirty-one

(In another playing area the lights fade in. LAURIER, ZOE, LAVERGNE, and LAFLAMME enter. ZOE spoon feeds LAURIER.)

LAFLAMME: John A. Macdonald got caught with his hand in the till and resigned.

ZOE: Open.

LAFLAMME: The Ontario Reform party and the clear grits, or whatever they call themselves. and our Parti rouge have been asked by the governor-general to form a government. Obviously they cannot, so there is going to be an election. The Conservatives will be annihilated.

ZOE: Open.

LAFLAMME: This riding was represented by the enfant terrible. The brother of the enfant has given his blessing to your candidacy. You are the chosen one. We have the organization, the campaign workers, and more important, the money and the muscle.

LAVERGNE: And I have canvassed the riding. It is no contest.

ZOE: Open.

LAFLAMME: You see, a fait accompli. If you run, you win.

LAVERGNE: And don't worry about the firm of Laurier and Lavergne.

ZOE: Open.

LAFLAMME: You'll have to jump on a stump and talk about this, talk about that.

LAURIER: Yes. I love Liberty more than my country.

LAFLAMME: And as long as you don't say things like that, it'll be a walk. Put you in Ottawa and fight the bastards.

LAURIER: In the name of Liberty.

LAFLAMME: Why not? Yes, in the name of Liberty. Well?

(LAURIER looks at ZOE. ZOE nods her head.)

LAURIER: Done.

LAFLAMME: All right.

LAVERGNE: All right.

ZOE: Open.

(The lights fade.)

Scene Thirty-two

(In another playing area the lights fade in. LAURIER, ALEXANDER MACKENZIE, and EDWARD BLAKE enter. BLAKE holds a bottle of champagne.)

BLAKE: To the new prime minister of Canada, Alexander Mackenzie.

MACKENZIE: The demon juice will never touch my lips.

BLAKE: Speech.

MACKENZIE: I promise to do an honest job for an honest day's wage.

BLAKE: To an honest man.

MACKENZIE: Because there is no sand in me. I am clear grit.

BLAKE: Clear grit. Down with John A. Macdonald and the Conservative party means down with organized hypocrisy. This is a great day Alexander Mackenzie.

MACKENZIE: Call me Sandy.

BLAKE: Sandy it is.

MACKENZIE: And now I will meet the members of my caucus.

BLAKE: This is young Wilfrid Laurier. The member for Drummond-Athabaska.

LAURIER: How do you do?

MACKENZIE: I have heard of you. The young rouge who likes to fight priests and bishops.

LAURIER: Hopefully I will not become an old rouge fighting priests and bishops.

MACKENZIE: This is Edward Blake, my trusted lieutenant.

BLAKE: And future leader.

MACKENZIE: But not now.

(LAURIER smiles.)

BLAKE: Yes. And this is …

(The lights fade.)

Scene Thirty-three

(In another playing area the lights fade in. LAURIER and ZOE enter. LAURIER reads a book.)

ZOE: I had a dream about you last night. I went to kiss you, and seven snakes came out of your mouth. Bit me here, here, here, here, here, and here, and here too. I liked it better when you were just a lawyer in Athabaska, not in Ottawa. Don't like Ottawa. I want to move back to Athabaskaville.

(LAURIER looks up from his book.)

LAURIER: What?

(The lights fade.)

Scene Thirty-four

(In another playing area the lights fade in. LAURIER, MACKENZIE, and BLAKE enter.)

BLAKE: Administering this country is a soul-destroying experience.

MACKENZIE: We all make sacrifices, Blake.

BLAKE: This colony aspires to nationhood.

MACKENZIE: That's right, Blake.

BLAKE: Very well then. I am beginning to have my doubts about the importance of the imperial connection. What do you think of that? That gets your attention.

MACKENZIE: What do you want, Blake?

BLAKE: That gets your attention, Sandy.

MACKENZIE: Call me Alex.

BLAKE: That gets your attention, Alexander.

MACKENZIE: Mr. Mackenzie to you.

BLAKE: Oh how rude. I resign.

MACKENZIE: Blake.

BLAKE: I resign.

MACKENZIE: Blake.

(BLAKE exits. The lights fade.)

Scene Thirty-five

(In another playing area the lights fade in. ZOE enters.)

ZOE: Just give me good fertilizer, Jacques, just give me good fertilizer.

VOICE: *(Off.)* I'll give you good fertilizer.

(LAURIER enters.)

ZOE: You're back. I'm so happy. I'm growing roses for my Moses. A rose for your thoughts.

(ZOE holds up a rose.)

LAURIER: Blake and Mackenzie are crazy.

ZOE: Put your finger inside.

LAURIER: Show me a rose and I see thorns.

ZOE: Feel it. Hot and sweaty.

LAURIER: A tremendous opportunity is developing in Ottawa. Tremendous.

ZOE: Oh I am so happy I do not want to think.

LAURIER: Do you see any gray hairs?

ZOE: Do I see any brown ones would be more like it. Here's one.

(The lights fade.)

Scene Thirty-six

(In another playing area the lights fade in. LAURIER, MACKENZIE, and BLAKE enter.)

BLAKE: I resign, again.

MACKENZIE: Blake, how many times have you resigned from my cabinet?

BLAKE: Twice.

MACKENZIE: I will not forgive you thrice. Now, Riel has been elected again in Provencher.

LAURIER: Provencher.

MACKENZIE: We keep refusing him his seat but they keep electing him.

BLAKE: And now he has signed the Rolls of Parliament. A fugitive from justice is a member of Parliament.

LAURIER: Yes, the choice of all criminals. Parliament or jail.

MACKENZIE: Mr. Laurier, really.

BLAKE: Call the police, Mr. Prime Minister.

MACKENZIE: No Blake, we do not want to apprehend Mr. Riel. He could say many things that are best left unsaid. We just wish he would go away, but he won't.

BLAKE: So arrest him.

MACKENZIE: Blake.

(LAURIER smiles. The lights fade.)

Scene Thirty-seven

(In another playing area the lights fade in. LAURIER and LAVERGNE enter.)

LAVERGNE: I feel like bursting into song.

LAURIER: Why?

LAVERGNE: I have met the most beautiful, wonderful woman.

LAURIER: Nothing is what it seems.

(LAFLAMME enters.)

LAFLAMME: The man of the hour is going to visit us. The founder of Manitoba, the hero of the Red River rebellion, the one and only, Louis Riel. Remember him?

LAURIER: Oh yes.

LAFLAMME: But we cannot tell anyone he is coming.

LAURIER: Because?

LAFLAMME: Because there is a warrant for his arrest for the murder of Thomas Scott, the Orangeman. He is a fugitive from justice. We are giving him shelter. He is coming to your picnic.

LAVERGNE: Oh can I bring Emilie.

LAURIER: Is she a Liberal?

LAVERGNE: Oh, rouge de rouge and sophisticated too. She has just returned from ten years in Paris.

LAURIER: Yes, show her how the other half lives.

LAVERGNE: Oh, Emilie Barthe, she stole my heart.

(LAVERGNE exits.)

LAFLAMME: Lavergne in love. What a squalid story that will be.

(LAURIER laughs. The lights fade.)

Scene Thirty-eight

(In another playing area the lights fade in: A political picnic. LAURIER and LAFLAMME enter.)

LAFLAMME: Ah, I see our guest of honour is arriving. Now, two things not to discuss with him. Politics and religion.

LAURIER: The only things worth discussing.

(RIEL enters.)

LAFLAMME: Louis, Louis, Louis. How good to see you. Do you remember young Wilfrid?

RIEL: Yes, I once saw you speak at the Institut-Canadien. It changed my life forever.

LAURIER: You have changed.

RIEL: So have you. I was a boy, now I am a man.

LAFLAMME: How is your love life?

RIEL: The love of my life is fighting the English. This criminal government says I am a criminal. The English, they want to turn this country into one big Ontario. I was born here. My mother and father were born here. My grandmother and grandfather were born here. My great grandmother and great grandfather were born here. And their ancestors were born here. But they're not Canadians. Then what the hell is a Canadian?

LAURIER: Good question.

RIEL: If you're an Englishman and you arrive right off the boat, five years later you're a Canadian. But if you've been here hundreds of years, you're nothing. And if you've been here thousands of years, you're less than nothing, you're an animal. Well to hell with that.

LAURIER: Exactly.

RIEL: What form of government is this? If they can't bribe the voters, they intimidate them, they try to stop them from voting. That's an election. And if you win, they threaten to kill you if you take your seat. That is democracy.

LAURIER: I don't think so.

ZOE: Would you like to see my lilies?

RIEL: Yes.

ZOE: They have huge pistils, huge.

(RIEL and ZOE exit.)

LAFLAMME: Oh you are rouge de rouge.

LAURIER: The genuine article. When he speaks I realize I have changed.

LAFLAMME: You are now a Liberal, you are no longer rouge.

LAURIER: Yes.

(LAVERGNE enters.)

LAVERGNE: Her hand. It is the only part of her body she will give to me.

(EMILIE enters.)

I am obsessed with her hand. I want to hold it, kiss it, slap my face with it. Put it in my mouth. Stand on it. Oh here she comes, here she comes, here she comes. I am going to make her my wife, god willing. Emilie. Oh Emilie.

EMILIE: Ah Joseph, how lovely it is to see you again.

LAVERGNE: Yes. I want you to meet my dearest, closest friend. Wilfrid Laurier. Miss Emilie Barthe. Miss Emilie Barthe, Wilfrid Laurier.

LAURIER: Enchanté, mademoiselle.

EMILIE: Enchanté, monsieur. So. You are a politician?

(ZOE enters.)

LAFLAMME: Oh yes, he is a politician. He is a politician to end all politicians.

LAVERGNE: And I am his law partner.

ZOE: And I am his wife.

(The lights fade.)

Scene Thirty-nine

(In another playing area the lights fade in. EMILIE enters.)

EMILIE: I live in a democracy but I cannot vote. I live in a society that hates the extraordinary woman. As Flaubert says, "To be bourgeois is to be mean spirited." This country is so bourgeois. It is full of ideophobes. I hate them. If I could make myself into a man I would settle my account with society in the tried and true manner. Alas, I cannot. But Caesar can change all that.

(The lights fade.)

Scene Forty

(In another playing area the lights fade in. MACKENZIE enters.)

MACKENZIE: I'm praying to you, Jesus, I'm praying. We are trying to give the people decent, honest government. Decent government. Can people ask for more? In the next election we are going to prohibit the sale of the demon rum.

BLAKE: What?

(DONALD SMITH enters holding a suitcase.)

SMITH: Mr. Mackenzie.

MACKENZIE: Mr. Smith.

SMITH: I represent a syndicate that wants to secure the CPR contract.

MACKENZIE: I will leave the railway as a national legacy to this country. No private company will own same.

SMITH: I found this suitcase full of money on the doorstep.

MACKENZIE: Hard granite grinds true if it's clear grit, Mr. Smith.

SMITH: What does that mean?

MACKENZIE: That means get out of this office.

(LAURIER enters and applauds. SMITH looks at LAURIER. The lights fade.)

Scene Forty-one

(In another playing area the lights fade in. ZOE and EMILIE enter looking at a picture book. LAURIER and LAVERGNE enter.)

LAURIER: There is going to be an election and Mackenzie is going to run on a temperance plank. The prohibition of alcohol.

LAVERGNE: Who is going to vote for that?

LAURIER: Exactly. Especially in this province.

LAURIER: But we will hold our own. Look at them. Pretty as a picture.

LAVERGNE: She is going to marry me.

LAURIER: Congratulations, Joseph.

LAVERGNE: I want you to be my best man.

LAURIER: I am honoured.

EMILIE: Oh that one brings back memories. I love to travel. I have been to London, Paris,

Berlin, Rome, Athens. Oh Athens. Have you ever travelled?

ZOE: We've been to Rimouski.

EMILIE: Oh Rimouski. What is that place like?

ZOE: It's like Montréal.

EMILIE: Really, or is Montréal like Rimouski, only bigger?

ZOE: Oh yes, definitely bigger.

(LAURIER clears his throat.)

EMILIE: Ah, the member of Parliament. I am going to form a salon combining the agreeable and the useful for you.

LAVERGNE: And me too?

EMILIE: And you too.

ZOE: And I can play the piano.

EMILIE: Yes, you can play the piano.

(EMILIE smiles. The lights fade.)

Scene Forty-two

(In another playing area the lights fade in. BOURGET and JOSEPH ISRAEL TARTE enter. TARTE holds a newspaper.)

TARTE: The date for the election has been set. September 17th, 1878.

BOURGET: Laurier is the high priest of the Liberal religion.

TARTE: He is difficult. He is a man of principle. We must make him feel disgust with public life. Leave it to me. Lie, lie, lie, and lie again. Something will stick. I can't wait to get at him. In this election even the dead will vote bleu.

BOURGET: I will pray for his failure.

TARTE: Prayers don't win elections, priest.

(The lights fade.)

Scene Forty-three

(In another playing area the lights fade in: The 1878 election. LAURIER enters. JEAN, JACQUES, and TARTE enter.)

LAURIER: To be an enemy of the Liberal party is to be an enemy of Liberty. To be Liberal is to believe in Liberty, tolerance.

TARTE: Don't listen to him. He is a friend of Guibord. A friend of excommunicated devils.

LAURIER: Tolerance is knowing that one is not always right.

TARTE: Everywhere he goes his friends renounce their faith and become Protestants. The Church wonders if you convert them.

LAURIER: I think the Church converts them.

TARTE: How can you believe this man? His private life is a disgrace. He does not baptize his children.

LAURIER: I don't have any children. Who are you?

TARTE: I am a Catholic Conservative. A castor, a hardworking beaver. Always working for the pope and God in that order.

LAURIER: What a fanatic!

TARTE: Are you a good Catholic?

LAURIER: Can a Liberal be a good Catholic?

TARTE: Non.

LAURIER: Bourget says when we are born, we are born as criminals. He is wrong. My friends, listen.

(BOURGET enters.)

BOURGET: I will not allow the antichrist to speak. He is a serpent in paradise. Vote for the Liberals and you will go to hell. Vote for the Conservatives and you will go to heaven.

LAURIER: Bourget.

(The lights fade.)

Scene Forty-four

(In another playing area the lights fade in. LAFLAMME and LAVERGNE enter.)

LAVERGNE: Twenty-four votes, twenty-four votes.

LAFLAMME: He squeaked in.

LAVERGNE: Bourget is trying to destroy the Parti rouge.

LAFLAMME: There is no trying about it, he has destroyed it. Wilfy and a handful of others, that is the Parti rouge.

LAVERGNE: How did Mackenzie do in Upper Canada?

LAFLAMME: Don't ask. John A. Macdonald is back in power.

(LAURIER enters.)

LAURIER: Gentlemen, we are no longer members of the Parti rouge. We are Liberals. We must remember the words of the master. That which is difficult to secure is easy to maintain. When we come into power we will come into it forever. Mark my words.

(The lights fade.)

Scene Forty-five

(In another playing area the lights fade in. LAURIER, MACKENZIE, and BLAKE enter.)

MACKENZIE: We gave them honest, decent government.

BLAKE: And we were trounced for our efforts. Humiliated. You had your nose rubbed in it.

MACKENZIE: That's enough Blake. I have lost the confidence of the country and confidence in myself.

LAURIER: And you have lost the confidence of the party.

MACKENZIE: Would the Liberal party kick a man when he is down?

LAURIER: They are lining up.

(BLAKE smiles.)

MACKENZIE: Blake.

(The lights fade.)

Scene Forty-six

(In another playing area the lights fade in. LAURIER and EMILIE enter.)

LAURIER: I am the Quebec lieutenant for Edward Blake.

EMILIE: All lieutenants want to be generals. And all generals should wear gloves.

(EMILIE holds up a pair of white gloves.)

One day you will be a great man. Perhaps a cabinet minister, who knows, perhaps a prime minister. Time and table manners will tell. Now let's pretend, I love to pretend, that you are having tea with a big stone-faced Englishman. You hold your cup like this.

(The lights fade.)

Scene Forty-seven

(In another playing area the lights fade in: Parliament. The SPEAKER of the House, LAURIER, and BLAKE enter. LAURIER hands BLAKE his books and fills his glass.)

SPEAKER: The House recognizes the member for West Durham.

BLAKE: Mr. Speaker, Mr. Speaker. The CPR is a fiasco. It is the story of corruption, bribes, gifts. Gifts! Gifts of money, gifts of land, and loans. The loans, I hate the loans. Interest free loans, non-repayable loans. The loans are so crooked. The CPR is a story of corruption. The government says to this syndicate "We will give you everything and half as much again, and then you will own it. We will make you landlords of the northwest." Well I say to the government: God damn the CPR.

(The lights fade.)

Scene Forty-eight

(In another playing area the lights fade in. LAURIER and EMILIE enter.)

EMILIE: In the end everything warm becomes cold, everything fast becomes slow. Love is not immoral. Society is. My conscience is not subject to the decisions of priests, or men. Is yours?

LAURIER: No.

EMILIE: I am a Liberal. I do not mind sharing you with your wife.

(The lights fade.)

Scene Forty-nine

(In another playing area the lights fade in. LAURIER and ZOE enter.)

ZOE: You were with her for twelve hours.

LAURIER: We were talking. Do you dispute that?

ZOE: No. I am sure you talked. What else did you do?

LAURIER: You were not present therefore you have no right to make insinuations.

ZOE: I hate you so much. I gave you fresh vegetables. What a waste. Go read a book.

(LAURIER picks up a book and reads. In another playing area the lights fade in. LAVERGNE and EMILIE enter.)

LAVERGNE: Infidelity is a weakness, but duplicity is a vice.

EMILIE: Joseph, do not play the intellectual with me.

LAVERGNE: Are you having an affair with my best friend?

EMILIE: Joseph, please.

LAVERGNE: The peasants in the village …

EMILIE: Oh yes, the peasants. They say this, they say that. Who has time to listen? You. You and your useless life have all the time in the world. When an angel falls in love with an angel, do they copulate, fornicate, rut? Of course not. That is too vulgar. Your good friend, who admires you greatly, is not like you, Joseph. You are a man and the thoughts of a man are like those of a beast. But your friend is a pure spirit.

LAVERGNE: Enough. Are you having an affair with my best friend?

EMILIE: Joseph.

(EMILIE turns to LAVERGNE. The lights fade.)

ZOE: Put your hand here.

LAURIER: I'm reading. Don't look at me like that. You know that I think life is an experience of the mind and reality is a figment of the imagination. It's elementary Plato, don't argue with me.

ZOE: There's more to life than that, Ferd.

LAURIER: Don't call me that. Don't you ever call me that.

(The lights fade.)

Scene Fifty

(In another playing area the lights fade in. JOHN A. MACDONALD is glad handing tories. In another playing area the lights fade in. LAURIER and BLAKE enter.)

BLAKE: Look. The corruptionist at work.

LAURIER: It is amazing how he manages men. Amazing.

BLAKE: A suitcase full of money will do wonders.

LAURIER: He keeps the Jesuits from Quebec and the Orange Lodge from Ontario united in one party. Only he can do that. The Conservative party is a house of cards. After him, the deluge.

BLAKE: After him, me. A hard rain is going to fall, Wilfrid, a hard rain.

LAURIER: Yes.

(The lights fade.)

Scene Fifty-one

(In another playing area the lights fade in. LAURIER and LAFLAMME enter. ZOE and LAVERGNE enter.)

LAFLAMME: Great news. Bourget is dead.

LAURIER: That is proof that God exists.

LAFLAMME: One less priest makes a better world, but a bishop.

LAURIER: As you know I do not drink. But tonight we will have champagne. Great things are now possible.

(ZOE makes the sign of the cross.)

What do you think you' re doing? Don't you ever do that again. If you must pray to gods, pray to Greek gods. Gods that fart and belch.

ZOE: Joseph has something to tell you.

LAVERGNE: We're going to have a baby.

LAURIER: We, Joseph?

LAVERGNE: Emilie is going to have a baby.

LAURIER: Congratulations Joseph. Well done.

LAVERGNE: Yes.

(The lights fade.)

Scene Fifty-two

(In another playing area the lights fade in. LAURIER, BLAKE, and MACKENZIE enter.)

BLAKE: I am now permanently irritable. Permanently irritable. Everything bothers me. Everything. I crave for books like he craves for naked women.

MACKENZIE: That's a good one Blake.

BLAKE: I detest my position as leader of the Liberal party. Absolutely detest it. But I am irreplaceable. Right, Wilfrid?

LAURIER: Yes, Blake.

BLAKE: I think I am going to resign.

LAURIER: Every man should do what he thinks he should do.

BLAKE: Who could replace me?

LAURIER: Make a list starting with "A," Blake.

BLAKE: You.

MACKENZIE: No "A."

(The lights fade.)

Scene Fifty-three

(In another playing area the lights fade in. LAURIER and ZOE enter. EMILIE and LAVERGNE enter. EMILIE holds a baby.)

LAURIER: What have you named him?

JOSEPH: Armand.

LAURIER: Armand. Armand Lavergne. Gou-gou, gou-gou.

EMILIE: Ah, he bit you.

LAVERGNE: He doesn't like you.

LAURIER: Yes. He will know how to dance before he knows how to walk. He looks just like you.

LAVERGNE: Really?

LAURIER: Yes. Little Armand.

(LAURIER smiles. The lights fade.)

Act Two

Scene One

(In another playing area the lights fade in. LAURIER, ZOE, EMILIE, LAVERGNE, and ARMAND, at age five, enter. ARMAND holds a toy tomahawk.)

EMILIE: Look he is walking. Walking.

LAVERGNE: He looks just like you. He dresses just like you too.

EMILIE: And what do you think of Uncle Wilfrid?

LAVERGNE: He's not your uncle, he's your father's friend.

EMILIE: And your mother's too.

ARMAND: I want to kill you so much.

ZOE: His first words.

ARMAND: I want to kill you so much.

EMILIE: I don't know where he picks it up.

(LAURIER looks at LAVERGNE. ARMAND hits LAURIER in the knee with the tomahawk.)

LAURIER: Very good, Armand.

LAVERGNE: Isn't he cute?

LAURIER: Yes.

(The lights fade.)

Scene Two

(In another playing area the lights fade in. JOHN THOMPSON and MACDONALD enter.)

THOMPSON: Riel is back.

MACDONALD: I'm trying to sober up. Do you mind?

THOMPSON: He is in Saskatchewan, organizing the Métis.

MACDONALD: Riel is a poor man. A poor man can be bought cheaply. Offer him three thousand dollars. Let's see what he does.

(The lights fade.)

Scene Three

(In another playing area the lights fade in. LAURIER and EMILIE enter reading newspapers. ARMAND enters.)

LAURIER: "Riel forms Métis Government at Batoche."

EMILIE: "Mounties Attacked at Duck Lake: Twelve Dead, Twenty-five Wounded."

LAURIER: "The Rebellion in the Northwest is in Full Swing." Oh he's getting bigger.

(Black out. The lights fade in. LAURIER and EMILIE enter reading newspapers. ARMAND enters.)

EMILIE: "Cree Uprising at Frog Lake." "Fish Creek Massacre."

LAURIER: "Fall of Batoche, Riel Surrenders."

ARMAND: He's my hero.

LAURIER: The game begins.

(The lights fade.)

Scene Four

(In another playing area the lights fade in. MACDONALD, DALTON McCARTHY and MACKENZIE BOWELL enter.)

BOWELL: King Billy's got a rope and we're going to hang the pope on the green grassy slope of the Boyne.

McCARTHY: I'm a Protestant. I'm a Protestant.

BOWELL: Do the right thing, John A. Do the right thing or blow me tight.

MACDONALD: Bowell, I wouldn't blow you tight if you were the last Orangeman in this country.

McCARTHY: In 1870 Riel killed an Orangeman. The Lodge wants to see him dancing at the end of a rope.

BOWELL: I am the Grand Master of the Orange Lodge and whatever I say goes. The reason you're prime minister is because of people like me.

McCARTHY: It'll be a snowy day in July when good stout Orangemen respect French Catholic sons of bitches like Louis Riel. Wake up John A., you're talking to Dalton McCarthy your brother-in-law.

BOWELL: We don't give a damn about the dogs in Quebec. They can bark and howl all night. Do them good.

McCARTHY: Riel has got to swing or the seats you'll get in Ontario you'll be able to count on your left-hand.

BOWELL: He must swing.

MACDONALD: Weep no more Ontario. You'll get your blood. Though every dog in Quebec may bark. He'll hang, he'll hang.

(The lights fade.)

Scene Five

(In another playing area the lights fade in: Parliament. The SPEAKER and LAURIER enter.)

SPEAKER: The House recognizes the member for Drummond-Athabaska.

LAURIER: Blood, blood, blood. Prisons, scaffolds, widows, orphans, destitution, ruin! These are the words that describe the administration of this government. I appeal now to any friend of Liberty in this house and I ask, when subjects of Her Majesty have been petitioning for years for their rights and those rights have not only been ignored but have been denied, and when those men take their lives in their hands and rebel, will any man in the House say that the criminals, if criminals there were in this rebellion, are not those who fought and bled and died, but the men who sit on those treasury benches? What is hateful is not rebellion. It is the despotism which induces rebellion. What is hateful are not rebels, but the men who, having the enjoyment of power, do not discharge the duties of power. Those men who when asked for a loaf give a stone. It would dishonour the name of government to call by that name those who govern us. The name they deserve is that of organized rapine and pillage.

(The lights fade.)

Scene Six

(In another playing area the lights fade in. LAURIER and ZOE enter. Offstage: noises, shouts, shrieks, lamentations.)

VOICES: *(Off.)* Down with Macdonald. Down with the Conservatives.

ZOE: Listen to that.

MERCIER: *(Off.)* Louis Riel, our brother is dead. Sir John A. Macdonald murdered him. He died on the scaffold like the patriotes of 1837.

LAURIER: Riel is dead. Long live Riel.

MERCIER: *(Off.)* From now on there are no more Conservatives. There are no more Liberals. There are only patriotes and traitors. There are no political parties, just a people.

LAURIER: Music.

MERCIER: *(Off.)* We must unite.

LAURIER: The Conservative party is finished.

MERCIER: *(Off.)* We must form the Parti nationale and overthrow this wicked, criminal government.

ZOE: Listen to that.

LAURIER: Yes.

(The lights fade.)

Scene Seven

(In another playing area the lights fade in. LAURIER, BLAKE, and MACKENZIE enter.)

BLAKE: I voted in favour of the execution of Louis Riel.

MACKENZIE: So did I.

BLAKE: But you're dead.

MACKENZIE: So are you Blake. You just won't lay down. The Liberal party is finished in Quebec because of you.

(LAURIER enters.)

BLAKE: Mr. Laurier you voted against the execution.

LAURIER: Had I been born on the banks of the Saskatchewan, I myself would have shouldered a musket.

BLAKE: Mr. Laurier, really.

LAURIER: We should censure the government.

BLAKE: Said Caesar.

LAURIER: With this execution the Conservative party is finished.

BLAKE: I'm on to you.

LAURIER: All that is required is a leader.

BLAKE: Don't get on my wick, Wilfrid, don't get on my wick.

MACKENZIE: Blake, resign.

(The lights fade.)

Scene Eight

(In another playing area the lights fade in. LAURIER and EMILIE enter.)

EMILIE: I live my life through you.

LAURIER: Non, I live my life through you.

EMILIE: I am just a piece of underwear.

LAURIER: Non, I am just a piece of underwear.

(ARMAND enters.)

ARMAND: Mama, Mama.

(ARMAND puts his arms around EMILIE's knees.)

LAURIER: It's all right, Armand. I'm not trying to steal your mother.

ARMAND: Daddy's crying again. He's crying again.

LAURIER: I must go.

EMILIE: To her?

LAURIER: You can't be jealous of my wife. Please tell me that. Please.

EMILIE: Go. At midnight think of me.

(ARMAND growls.)

LAURIER: Armand.

(The lights fade.)

Scene Nine

(In another playing area the lights fade in. BLAKE enters.)

BLAKE: Gentlemen, if I can call you that. I don't know why, but ... Gentlemen, I am going to resign. Why are the monkeys mumbling? We need a new leader. There is only one possible choice.

VOICE ONE: *(Off.)* Haggart ... Mills ... Mulock.

VOICE TWO: *(Off.)* Cartwright.

BLAKE: Oh not them, anyone but them. They are idiots of incomparable incompetence.

VOICE TWO: *(Off.)* Then who?

BLAKE: Hmmm. Laurier.

(LAURIER enters.)

Laurier is my choice. He is the only choice. No one else. You'll keep my seat warm for me. Won't you, Wilf?

LAURIER: Yes Blake.

(The lights fade.)

Scene Ten

(In another playing area the lights fade in. LAVERGNE and EMILIE enter. ARMAND enters.)

ARMAND: Oh, daddy's crying again.

EMILIE: We move to Ottawa, or it's the bottom of the lake for me.

LAVERGNE: I want to kill you so much.

EMILIE: I've made you cry. I feel better.

LAVERGNE: I want to kill you so much.

EMILIE: It's Ottawa, or the bottom of the lake.

(The lights fade.)

Scene Eleven

(In another playing area the lights fade in: Emilie's salon. LAVERGNE and LAURIER enter.)

LAURIER: Look, free trade has been the central policy of the Liberal party since the days of Confederation. George Brown supported it. Alexander Mackenzie supported it. Edward Blake supported it. And I support it. What can John A. Macdonald do in the next election?

We are going to reduce the level of tariffs between the United States and Canada. We will be able to sell our wheat to a market of fifty millions, buy manufactured goods more cheaply. It is a depression. Free trade will be relief. It's the winning strategy. What can he do? What can he do?

(The lights fade.)

Scene Twelve

(In another playing area the lights fade in. A MAN enters holding a banner with the famous image "The old man, the old flag, the old policy." MACDONALD enters.)

MACDONALD: Mr. Laurier and the Liberal party want free trade with the United States. It is veiled treason. Free trade leads to commercial union. Commercial union leads to political union. Only a fool would disagree. As for myself, my course is clear. A British subject I was born. A British subject I will die.

(The lights fade.)

Scene Thirteen

(In another playing area the lights fade in. LAURIER and LAVERGNE enter. LAVERGNE holds a newspaper that reads "Macdonald Majority.")

LAVERGNE: John A. Macdonald has formed another majority government.

LAURIER: What a shame. Commercial Union with the United States will divorce Canada from the English motherland. For twenty years we will never mention free trade with the United States, but one day. We can forget about beating Sir John while he is alive. But after him, the deluge. And now Joseph, if you will permit it. I am going to talk with your wife.

(LAVERGNE nods his head. The lights fade.)

Scene Fourteen

(In another playing area the lights fade in. LAURIER enters reading Aesop's fables. EMILIE and ARMAND enter.)

EMILIE: Look at him, sitting in the bushes. He thinks we do not see him. I will speak to him.

(EMILIE exits.)

ARMAND: Tell me a story.

LAURIER: One day the sun and the wind saw a traveller. The wind bragged that it could make the traveller take off his coat. The sun smiled and said "Let's see you do it." So the wind huffed and puffed and blew up a terrible wind. But the man would not take off his coat. In fact he buttoned it up. An angry wind turned to the sun and said "It can't be done." The sun smiled and said "Watch this." And the sun began to shine. The traveller began to sweat. He unbuttoned his coat and then took it off. And the sun turned to the wind and said "See. The sunny way." Yes, the sunny way.

ARMAND: And … so.

LAURIER: So learn from this.

ARMAND: I hate that one. Tell me the one about the fox.

(LAURIER turns a page.)

LAURIER: A fox saw some grapes …

(The lights fade.)

Scene Fifteen

(In another playing area the lights fade in. MACDONALD, THOMPSON, BOWELL, J..J. ABBOTT, and CHARLES TUPPER enter.)

MACDONALD: Scandals, disasters, catastrophes. But these hands are clean. It's all bunkum. Bunkum. Bunkum good. Bunkum till they can't stand it. And then bunkum again. Bunkum good.

(MACDONALD has a heart attack.)

ALL: What a face.

THOMPSON: Doctor Tupper.

(TUPPER puts his head to MACDONALD's chest.)

TUPPER: Heart attack. What we have here is a dead prime minister.

(They all look at each other. LAURIER enters.)

LAURIER: The ugly mask has been lifted. The hideous face will now reveal itself.

(LAURIER exits.)

BOWELL: Now I'll be prime minister.

TUPPER: You'll never be prime minister.

BOWELL: As grand master of the Orange Lodge, I demand—

THOMPSON: If I may say a word.

BOWELL: Shut up you Catholic son of a bitch, papist bastard.

THOMPSON: Really Mr. Bowell.

TUPPER: Gentlemen, gentlemen.

BOWELL: Go back to London, High Commissioner.

THOMPSON: You lecherous pig.

BOWELL: One of us is going to be prime minister.

TUPPER: It won't be you.

THOMPSON: Abbott.

TUPPER: J.J.

ABBOTT: Yes?

THOMPSON: Perhaps you should be prime minister.

ABBOTT: Yes, perhaps.

(The lights fade.)

Scene Sixteen

(In another playing area the lights fade in. ABBOTT and THOMPSON enter.)

ABBOTT: I hate politics and everything that goes with it. The notoriety, public meetings, public speeches, caucuses.

THOMPSON: Work.

ABBOTT: But I am prime minister because I am not particularly obnoxious to anyone.

THOMPSON: Work.

ABBOTT: My administration.

THOMPSON: Work.

ABBOTT: The world is vain and ridiculous. Grotesque and stupid. And everyone who lives in this world is vain and ridiculous, grotesque and stupid. Therefore I will look at everyone I meet with a face like this.

(ABBOTT makes a face.)

THOMPSON: You will be so popular.

(ABBOTT makes a face then has a heart attack.)

What a face.

(ABBOTT falls to the ground. The lights fade.)

Scene Seventeen

(In another playing area the lights fade in. THOMPSON and BOWELL enter.)

THOMPSON: I am now prime minister.

BOWELL: But I am watching you.

THOMPSON: My cabinet, they're all crooks. Stupid and lazy. Work! Work, I love it. First order of business. The Manitoba Schools Crisis. The Catholic minority in Manitoba has appealed to the federal government to over rule the provincial legislation diminishing their rights. I will appeal to the Supreme Court whether or not the federal government has the right to veto provincial legislation. I know the answer already, but when in difficulty temporize, temporize, temporize. Work, I love it. Work!

(THOMPSON has a heart attack.)

BOWELL: What a face.

(THOMPSON falls to the ground. The lights fade.)

Scene Eighteen

(In another playing area the lights fade in. LAURIER and EMILIE enter.)

EMILIE: Mackenzie Bowell is now prime minister.

LAURIER: This is an interesting way of changing the guard. After Bowell, the deluge. How many times have I said that about this band of plotters and schemers and conspirators whose bond of union is the cement of office?

EMILIE: Bowell is among a den of lions.

LAURIER: Yes.

(The lights fade.)

Scene Nineteen

(In another playing area the lights fade in. BOWELL and TUPPER enter.)

TUPPER: Will the grand master of the Orange Lodge defy the Orangemen of Ontario?

BOWELL: The Privy Council has ruled that the federal government has the right to veto provincial legislation. So I have to protect the rights of the French Catholics.

TUPPER: An Orangeman is going to contribute to the spread of Catholicism.

BOWELL: I don't want to.

TUPPER: Then don't.

BOWELL: But I have to.

TUPPER: Why?

BOWELL: The Constitution.

TUPPER: How are you going to administer these schools if the province fails to co-operate?

BOWELL: I have no idea.

TUPPER: Resign you swine. If you do not stand aside half your cabinet will resign.

BOWELL: That nest of vipers. That nest of traitors. That nest.

TUPPER: Resign.

(The lights fade.)

Scene Twenty

(In another playing area the lights fade in. LAURIER writes a letter. In another playing area the lights fade in. EMILIE reads the letter.)

LAURIER: Dear Emilie, This country is a world unto itself. The question of separate schools is not an issue at all. It is a question of the constitution of the country, that all rights guaranteed under it be sacredly guarded. Within this wide dominion one third of the population are Roman Catholics. Are we to create in the minds of one third of the people of this dominion the sentiment that a Roman Catholic cannot obtain the same just consideration that he would if he were a Protestant?

And yet, Canada is constituted of provinces. If a majority of the population of a province do not want a certain legislation it cannot be forced on them by any government, federal or provincial. Or government becomes a tyranny. A world unto itself.

Love, W.L. P.S. …

(The lights fade.)

Scene Twenty-one

(In another playing area the lights fade in. LAURIER and ZOE enter.)

LAURIER: Lord and Lady Aberdeen arrived in Canada today. Lord Aberdeen is the governor-general. There will be a reception to greet them. You will have to go.

ZOE: I want to stay right here.

LAURIER: Zoe.

ZOE: Right here.

LAURIER: Zoe.

(The lights fade.)

Scene Twenty-two

(In another playing area the lights fade in. LORD and LADY ABERDEEN and TUPPER enter.)

TUPPER: I am now prime minister of Canada. I demand an election, Lord Aberdeen.

LORD and LADY ABERDEEN: Ooooooh!

TUPPER: I demand an election you miserable excuse for a nincompoop, I demand an election.

LORD ABERDEEN: Mr Tupper, we—!

TUPPER: We—

LORD ABERDEEN: I—!

TUPPER: I.

LADY ABERDEEN: Mr. Tupper, we think Mr. Laurier should be prime minister.

TUPPER: What? You are interfering in the internal affairs of this country. Stop. You are not worth meeting and beating with a stick.

LORD ABERDEEN: Oh frothing mad. Down with Tupperdom.

TUPPER: I demand an election.

(A BUTLER enters.)

BUTLER: Monsieur et Madame Laurier and consort. entering the room.

(LAURIER enters with ZOE and EMILIE on each arm.)

LAURIER: Relax, relax.

LADY ABERDEEN: Well Ab, young Mr. Laurier looks promising.

LORD ABERDEEN: Very.

LADY ABERDEEN: Ah, the leader of the opposition.

LAURIER: How do you do?

LADY ABERDEEN: This is my gentle Johnny.

LAURIER: And this is my wife.

LADY ABERDEEN: And this is your little friend?

LAURIER: Yes.

LADY ABERDEEN: It is so good to see a Liberal in this tory land. The tories in this land are frothing mad.

LORD ABERDEEN: Frothing mad.

LADY ABERDEEN: Mr. Gladstone sends his regards.

LORD ABERDEEN: We have secret instructions, Mr. Laurier, oh secret instructions.

LADY ABERDEEN: Mr. Tupper!

TUPPER: I love pinching royal bums. Love it.

LAURIER: Welcome to Canada.

(The lights fade.)

Scene Twenty-three

(In another playing area the lights fade in. LADY ABERDEEN, EMILIE, and ZOE enter. EMILIE and ZOE hold a banner with the words "National Council of Women.")

LADY ABERDEEN: How can we best describe a woman's mission? Can we not best describe it as mothering? In one way or another. Not all women are called upon to mother children. But we are all called upon to mother the reform of society.

EMILIE: Here, here.

(The lights fade.)

Scene Twenty-four

(In another playing area the lights fade in. LAURIER and SMITH enter.)

LAURIER: To possess gold, or to conquer those that possess gold. Which is more honourable? You own the Hudson Bay Company, the CPR, and the Bank of Montreal too. You are the lord of West Mount but no one calls you lord. What is it you really want? Money? Power? Women? What is it you really want, Lord Strathcona? In the next election support the Liberal party and you will be a Peer of the Realm. Support the Conservative party and you'll be Donald Smith. It is with such toys that men are governed.

(The lights fade.)

Scene Twenty-five

(In another playing area the lights fade in. LAURIER, EMILIE, and LAVERGNE enter.)

EMILIE: It's election night in Canada. Who will the electors vote for?

LAURIER: All the Canadiens in Quebec will vote for me because I am one of them. And all the Orangemen in Ontario will vote for me because I will not overrule the provincial legislation in Manitoba.

EMILIE: Meanwhile there is Charles Tupper upholding the constitution of the country.

LAURIER: No one will vote for him in Quebec. And none of the Orangemen will vote for him either.

EMILIE: And then you become prime minister.

LAURIER: In this election we change the nature of the constitution. Macdonald's vision of Canada, one big central government that makes all the decisions about everything, dies. And the beauty of it all is that the electorate are not aware that they are radically altering the constitution of this country. They are completely oblivious, therefore there is harmony.

EMILIE: Brilliant.

LAURIER: The electors. And what do they do? They all moo together.

EMILIE: Brilliant.

LAURIER: Turn out the lights I feel like dancing.

EMILIE: It's brilliant.

LAURIER: What do you think of that, Joseph?

LAVERGNE: Brilliant.

(ARMAND enters.)

ARMAND: No it's not. It's completely corrupt and decadent. Rotten to the core. Only an imperialist would think like that. There are real people out there. They will lose their culture, religion, language. All of it.

LAURIER: It is democracy, Armand. It is the tyranny of the majority.

ARMAND: You just keep your imperialist bloodsucking hands off Manitoba.

LAURIER: Exactly. By keeping my blood-sucking hands off Manitoba I set the precedent for all federal governments to keep their bloodsucking hands off all provinces. Including Quebec.

ARMAND: You dictator.

LAURIER: Armand.

(The lights fade.)

Scene Twenty-six

(In another playing area the lights fade in. LORD ABERDEEN and ZOE enter.)

LORD ABERDEEN: Congratulations, Mme. Laurier. Your husband has annihilated the Conservative party. You must be very happy?

ZOE: I was happier in Athabaskaville.

LORD ABERDEEN: Ah, I see the buffet is on.

(The lights fade.)

Scene Twenty-seven

(In another playing area the lights fade in. LAURIER, EMILIE, LAVERGNE, ARMAND, CLIFFORD SIFTON, and HENRI BOURASSA enter.)

EMILIE: To the new prime minister of Canada. Wilfrid Laurier. Hip hip …

SIFTON and BOURASSA: Hooray.

LAURIER: Merci, messieurs, merci. Behind my white hair, together, we will march forward. And now I will meet the members of my caucus.

EMILIE: You know him.

LAURIER: Of course.

EMILIE: This is the member for Labelle, Henri Bourassa.

LAURIER: Ah yes, the grandson of the great Papineau.

EMILIE: And this is the member for St. Boniface in Manitoba, Clifford Sifton.

LAURIER: Ah yes, the voice of the west. Do you know each other?

BOURASSA: How do you do?

SIFTON: How do you do? That man carries a knife in his boot for me.

BOURASSA: I hate that racist pig.

LAURIER: With the support of these two I will control the destiny of this country.

(The lights fade.)

Scene Twenty-eight

(In another playing area the lights fade in. LORD ABERDEEN enters.)

LORD ABERDEEN: The wife is in the other room with her lover. She has banned me from watching them. But I can listen.

(The lights fade.)

Scene Twenty-nine

(In another playing area the lights fade in. LAURIER and ZOE enter. ZOE knits.)

LAURIER: Oh the sunny way. I am like the sun. Shine on despite everything.

ZOE: Because you're perfect.

LAURIER: The members of my caucus, with notable exceptions, are incompetent.

ZOE: Because you're perfect.

LAURIER: Therefore I will make the Liberal premiers of Ontario, New Brunswick, and Nova Scotia senators and put them in my cabinet. It is a move that will not make me popular but it will make me powerful.

ZOE: You're perfect.

LAURIER: The rational manipulation of power makes the state into a work of art.

ZOE: You're perfect.

LAURIER: And Clifford Sifton, I will make him minister of the Interior, in charge of immigration. And Henri Bourassa, I will make him my protégé. I will groom him. And one day the grandson of Louis-Joseph Papineau will be prime minister of Canada. The grandson will fulfill the destiny of the grandfather. Is that not justice?.

ZOE: You're perfect. Don't you ever get tired of that word?

LAURIER: I never use that word.

ZOE: Because you're perfect.

LAURIER: Emilie is having her salon tonight. You'll have to go?

ZOE: And that thing will be there.

LAURIER: Thing.

ZOE: Their son.

LAURIER: Ah yes, their son. What a joy he is. Little Armand. Wear something nice.

(The lights fade.)

Scene Thirty

(In another playing area the lights fade in. EMILIE, LAVERGNE, BOURASSA, and ARMAND enter.)

ARMAND: Let me tell you about my family tree. In 1642 François Lavergne, note the name, came to Montréal with Maisonneuve. He married Virginie Terrebonne and Pierre Lavergne, note the name, was born.

LAVERGNE: Which reminds me of an amusing story.

EMILIE: Oh the amusing story. I have heard it a hundred times.

LAVERGNE: But they have not. It was the first of July.

EMILIE: Oh what a date.

LAVERGNE: It is like all dates, it has no importance.

EMILIE: Then why mention it?

LAVERGNE: It was the summer of 1880.

ARMAND: I wasn't even born.

EMILIE: You weren't even a glimmer in his eye.

LAVERGNE: I was in the prime of my manhood.

EMILIE: And how is my big baby boy.

ARMAND: Mother.

(LAURIER and ZOE enter.)

ZOE: I am going blind.

EMILIE: Ah the reason for our existence.

LAURIER: It is Joseph and Emilie.

EMILIE: How good to see you.

LAURIER: How do you do?

LAVERGNE: I want to thank you for making me a judge.

LAURIER: What are friends for, Joseph. Get me a drink.

(LAVERGNE exits.)

EMILIE: Don't be shy.

LAURIER: Ah, little Armand.

EMILIE: He is a philosopher.

LAURIER: Really. Say something philosophical.

ARMAND: It is good to be alive.

LAURIER: And bad to be dead.

ARMAND: No better.

LAURIER: And what is best?

ARMAND: Never to have been born.

LAURIER: You call that philosophy?

ZOE: Don't mind him. He's like that to everybody.

(BOURASSA exits.)

EMILIE: Lord and Lady Aberdeen.

(LORD and LADY ABERDEEN enter.)

LORD ABERDEEN: We have been recalled by Westminster, Mr. Laurier.

LADY ABERDEEN: We are going to be replaced by a genuine imperialist.

LORD ABERDEEN: Lord Minto.

LADY ABERDEEN: Beware, Monsieur Laurier, beware.

(The lights fade.)

Scene Thirty-one

(In another playing area the lights fade in. LAURIER and ZOE enter.)

ZOE: This dress doesn't fit properly.

LAURIER: Engage the services of a seamstress. Emilie can recommend a dozen.

ZOE: I prefer my nimble fingers.

LAURIER: Does your dress?

ZOE: Don't criticize my nimble fingers. You criticize everything else. But don't criticize my fingers.

(A SERVANT enters.)

SERVANT: His Excellency, the governor-general of Canada, Lord Minto, entering the room.

(LORD MINTO enters.)

MINTO: Mr. Laurier.

LAURIER: Monsieur, s'il vous plaît.

MINTO: How a Frenchman became Prime minister of a British colony is beyond me, but—

LAURIER: Monsieur, one third of the population of this country are descendents of the French race.

MINTO: Canada is not a country. It is a colony. It is a cornerstone of the British Empire. All your predecessors were aware of this. You will toe the line or you will go. Now, I bring good tidings for you and whoever this—

LAURIER: That is my wife.

MINTO: This is an invitation from Her Britannic Majesty, the Empress of the British Empire, Queen Victoria, to attend her Diamond Jubilee. You will be accorded that rare privilege. The kissing of hands. Oh you lucky one.

(MINTO gives the invitation to LAURIER.)

LAURIER: We are going to England.

(The lights fade.)

Scene Thirty-two

(In another playing area the lights fade in. LAURIER, ZOE, EMILIE, LAVERGNE, BOURASSA, and ARMAND enter.)

ARMAND: He's coming, he's coming.

EMILIE: He is now a knight of the British Empire. Your uncle Wilfrid has been knighted.

LAVERGNE: He's not your uncle.

EMILIE: He's going to tell us about Queen Victoria's Diamond Jubilee.

BOURASSA: 1837 to 1897. Sixty years of imperialism. When she came to the throne my grandfather and the patriotes were in rebellion.

(LAURIER and ZOE enter.)

LAURIER: And now sixty years later a Canadien is prime minister.

EMILIE: Tell us about it.

LAURIER: The sole purpose of the jubilee was to impress. I don't think the pope could do it in a superior manner. I have never seen so many conquered races on parade in my life. I was standing beside a man from Borneo with a bone through his nose holding a shrunken head. And I thought to myself "I am just like him."

EMILIE: But you were given pride of place and a knighthood too.

LAURIER: I am Sir Muckamuck. These honours and decorations are just toys.

BOURASSA: But Sir Wilfrid, it is with such toys that men are governed.

LAURIER: Yes.

(The lights fade.)

Scene Thirty-three

(In another playing area the lights fade in. MINTO enters.)

MINTO: If one wants to be happy. Be a soldier. Bayonet ready. Charge. Sudden death or victory. The joy of annihilation—one's own or someone else's. There's no life like it. Oh, we're going off to war, going to fight the Boer. Going to fight the Boers over gold and diamonds. Better than fighting over nutmeg.

(LAURIER enters.)

MINTO: Mr. Laurier.

LAURIER: Monsieur, s'il vous plaît.

MINTO: Mr. Laurier, as a Frenchman you cannot possibly possess British instincts.

LAURIER: Je ne suis pas Français. Je suis Canadien.

MINTO: What?

LAURIER: I am not French. I am Canadian.

MINTO: You make my imperialist heart beat enormously fast. Great Britain has declared war on the Boers in South Africa The colonial secretary would like a spontaneous contribution from the government of this colony. We want the colonies to suppress the rebellious colony. Canada as the eldest daughter of the empire will show the way.

LAURIER: The Boer War is a British affair. It has nothing to do with Canada.

MINTO: It has everything to do with Canada. Canada is the belly button of the British Empire. The future of Canada is the future of the British Empire. When the Empire falls, Canada falls.

LAURIER: The Boer War does not imperil the British Empire and the defence of Canada is not at stake. And yet you want troops.

MINTO: It is imperialism, Sir Wilfrid.

LAURIER: It certainly is.

(LAURIER exits.)

MINTO: How a Frenchman became prime minister of a British colony is beyond me.

(The lights fade.)

Scene Thirty-four

(In another playing area the lights fade in. LAURIER and BOURASSA enter. ARMAND enters.)

LAURIER: Listen to me. We are sending eight thousand volunteers to South Africa.

BOURASSA: The Boer War means nothing in this country.

LAURIER: There is no precedent for Canadian involvement.

BOURASSA: The precedent, sir, is the accomplished fact.

LAURIER: Sending volunteers does not compromise the country.

BOURASSA: What business do we have in Africa?

LAURIER: The majority of Canadians desire it.

BOURASSA: What the Boers in South Africa want, that is what we want.

LAURIER: Imperialism is everywhere.

BOURASSA: We are the Boers of North America.

LAURIER: The English are having their Boer War. The Americans are having their Spanish-American War. Choose your imperialism.

BOURASSA: Choose neither.

LAURIER: Then it will be chosen for you.

BOURASSA: We want to be independent.

LAURIER: We can be a satellite of London or a satellite of Washington.

BOURASSA: We want to be independent.

LAURIER: The greater the distance, the greater the freedom.

BOURASSA: He is a devious imperialist.

LAURIER: If there were only Canadiens in Confederation I would not hesitate for an instant.

BOURASSA: Devious.

LAURIER: But the idea is not yet ripe enough for the English population.

BOURASSA: This is only the beginning of our involvement in England's wars of imperialism.

LAURIER: We must have their support.

BOURASSA: First volunteers.

LAURIER: Otherwise we will put the two races in conflict.

BOURASSA: Then conscripted volunteers.

LAURIER: And instead of hastening change, we will put it back.

BOURASSA: And then conscripted.

LAURIER: Racial harmony is everything.

BOURASSA: He is a devious imperialist.

LAURIER: Trust me.

BOURASSA: He takes no account of Quebec's opinions.

LAURIER: Quebec has no opinions, it only has sentiments.

BOURASSA: From this day forth I will only contest elections as an independent.

(BOURASSA exits.)

ARMAND: He is a great man, a great man.

LAURIER: If I was twenty I would cheer him also. But I am not twenty.

ARMAND: I am.

LAURIER: Armand.

(The lights fade.)

Scene Thirty-five

(In another playing area the lights fade in: a picnic. LAURIER, ZOE, EMILIE, and LAVERGNE enter.)

LAURIER: The English, of course, have great admiration for the Hindu view of society.

ZOE: Oh the mosquitoes are enormous this year.

LAURIER: Whatever station of life you are born into, you will die in that station.

(ARMAND enters.)

ARMAND: Vive les Boers, mortes aux Anglais.

EMILIE: Quiet you nasty thing. Armand, I love you, but I am not tyrannized by my opinions. I change them all the time.

ARMAND: I am enfant terrible.

LAURIER: Non, just enfant.

ARMAND: Call me Kruger.

LAURIER: Never.

ARMAND: Then call me Mueller.

LAURIER: What?

ARMAND: I would rather be a Dutchman than a Canadien. I want to throw all the English into the St. Lawrence. All of them.

(BOURASSA and SIFTON enter.)

SIFTON: You might not be fighting in this one. But you will fight in the next one.

BOURASSA: Like hell we will. We, Canadiens, have no interest in fighting wars of imperialism.

LAURIER: Getting acquainted I see.

BOURASSA: Yes.

SIFTON: Yes.

BOURASSA: Armand.

ARMAND: Vive les Boers, mortes aux Anglais.

(BOURASSA and ARMAND exit.)

EMILIE: Joseph, do something. Wilfrid. Joseph.

LAVERGNE: The mosquitoes are enormous this year.

(LAVERGNE exits as MINTO enters.)

MINTO: Mr. Laurier I have recently received terrible news. The mother of us all, Queen Victoria has died.

SIFTON: What? … Oh no.

MINTO: Mr Sifton, stiff upper. Bloody rot is what I say. In these trying times we must show that we are men. The queen is dead. Long live the king. King Edward the Seventh. Bloody rot.

(The lights fade.)

Scene Thirty-six

(In another playing area the lights fade in. TUPPER and ROBERT BORDEN enter.)

TUPPER: I am resigning as leader of the Conservative party. That makes you smile. I can't see it on your face, but I know you're smiling. Show me your smile and I'll show you this.

(TUPPER holds up his fist.)

My young partner-in-law, Robert Borden, will be the new leader of the Conservative party. Any objections? I thought not. Robert.

(BORDEN steps forward.)

Your new leader. Tupperdom lives. Long live Tupperdom.

(The lights fade.)

Scene Thirty-seven

(In other playing areas the lights fade in. LAURIER, EMILIE, BOURASSA, LAVERGNE, SIFTON, MINTO, and ZOE enter. The lights evoke seven whispering heads. ARMAND enters.)

ARMAND: And finally, in 1849 Georges Lavergne married Brigitte Beauchamp. And Joseph Lavergne, my father was born. And then in 1878 Joseph Lavergne married Emilie Barthe. And two years later I was born. Me! I am the son of Joseph Lavergne. I am the son of all those Lavergnes.

LAURIER: He's not my son, he's not my son.

EMILIE: Poor little bastard, poor little bastard.

BOURASSA: His father is Laurier, his father is Laurier.

LAVERGNE: He's not my son, he's not my son.

SIFTON: He doesn't look like him, he doesn't look like him.

MINTO: He's a bastard, he's a bastard.

ZOE: He ruined my life.

(The lights fade.)

Scene Thirty-eight

(In another playing area the lights fade in: cabinet. LAURIER, SIFTON, and WILLIAM MULOCK enter.)

MULOCK: Here are the signed, undated letters of resignation from the cabinet.

(MULOCK gives LAURIER a sheath of papers.)

We have them all, except Mr. Sifton.

(SIFTON gives LAURIER a piece of paper.)

LAURIER: Excellent. This administration is wracked with wine, women and graft.

MULOCK: We could reform that.

LAURIER: Reforms are for oppositions. It is the business of government to stay in office.

(LAURIER holds up a piece of paper.)

I want this question framed in such a manner that the answer is irrelevant. Can you do that?

MULOCK: Certainly.

LAURIER: Good. The negotiations on the Alaska boundary dispute did not go well.

SIFTON: That is the understatement of the century. How can you negotiate with someone when everytime you raise a point that someone says "I'm going to get ugly"? How do you negotiate with someone like that?

LAURIER: With a big stick.

SIFTON: Yes.

LAURIER: But unfortunately our American friends are holding the big stick.

SIFTON: It has been a formative experience. You will not get fair dealing from the Americans. It doesn't matter what it is. A formative experience.

(The lights fade.)

Scene Thirty-nine

(In another playing area the lights fade in. LAURIER and ARMAND enter.)

ARMAND: And therefore I believe in biological nationalism. The superiority of the French race. The superiority of French blood over all others.

(LAURIER looks at an ant hill.)

LAURIER: Do you think those red ants are superior to those black ants? Or perhaps those black ants think they are superior to the red ants?

(LAURIER steps on the ant hill.)

Who cares, Armand? Only someone with the intellect of an insect would support the concept of biological nationalism.

ARMAND: You're a genuine imperialist. A sincere imperialist. You're a traitor to your race.

LAURIER: If you see the point of view of another, does that make you a traitor to your own people.

ARMAND: Yes.

LAURIER: Racial prejudice is finished in this country. I don't care what the Church says. I don't care what the English say.

(BOURASSA enters.)

BOURASSA: This Papineau has married a Papineau. I have married my cousin. The blood is pure. I am pure blood Canadien.

ARMAND: My hero.

BOURASSA: He is my protégé.

LAURIER: Non he is my protégé.

BOURASSA: He is under my protection.

LAURIER: Non, he is under my protection. Armand.

(The lights fade.)

Scene Forty

(In another playing area the lights fade in. LAURIER and ZOE enter. ZOE knits.)

LAURIER: The sovereignty of the individual is the beginning and the end of society. What do you think of that?

(ZOE looks at LAURIER. ZOE goes back to knitting.)

Nationalism is barbarism. It makes men intolerant of the rights and interests of others, except those who espouse the same nationalism. A refuge of the backward and the ignorant. A vile concept. Supporters of nationalism will destroy the liberty and independence of any people not of their race or language. Complete conformity. No differences can be tolerated. The Nation-State. I detest the whole concept. I detest even the idea. I detest even the impulse of the idea. Racial nationalism. Religious nationalism. It doesn't matter what it is. It all ends in a nightmare. What do you think of that?

(ZOE looks at LAURIER. ZOE is about to speak but does not. She goes back to her knitting.)

LAURIER: That's quite the sock you're knitting.

ZOE: It was supposed to be a toque but it turned into this.

LAURIER: But nationalism is unavoidable. We live in an age when each nationality will have it's own state and each state will have it's own nationality. And each state will include the whole nationality and nothing but the nationality. So what is one to do? The obvious. Create a new nationality. A unique nationality. A twentieth century nationality. A political nationality. A nationality that is not based on race or religion. Zoe, look at me. I will make this country a multi-national state that believes in ... Liberty. Oh Liberty. What do you think of that?

ZOE: If the cap fits, wear it.

(ZOE throws the knitting at LAURIER. ZOE exits. The lights fade.)

Scene Forty-one

(In another playing area the lights fade in. SIFTON and IVAN, an immigrant, enter.)

SIFTON: I am going to give you the facts of life immigrant boy. You came to this country in a CPR ship, you arrived at a CPR port, you got on a CPR train, so you could farm CPR land and grow CPR wheat that we can put in CPR elevators, and then in CPR grain cars and sell in CPR stores. This country, immigrant boy, is one big CPR.

(SIFTON exits.)

IVAN: Just like Russia.

(The lights fade.)

Scene Forty-two

(In another playing area the lights fade in. MINTO enters.)

MINTO: Oh the dear, dear queen.

VOICE: *(Off.)* Telegram for Lord Minto.

(A hand gives MINTO a telegram.)

MINTO: At last, I am the new viceroy of India. And my brother-in-law, Earl Grey, is going to be my replacement. Excellent. Canada, and now India, the jewels of the British Empire. The thought of leaving this place gives me pleasure.

(The lights fade.)

Scene Forty-three

(In another playing area the lights fade in. SIFTON, ARMAND, and BOURASSA enter. ARMAND repeats the last two words that BOURASSA speaks.)

SIFTON: The Ivans of this world are arriving by the thousands. Success. We are going to turn the territory of Assiniboia into the provinces of Saskatchewan and Alberta.

BOURASSA: We want only immigrants of good quality.

SIFTON: I think a stalwart peasant in a sheepskin coat, born of the soil, whose forefathers have been farmers for ten generations, with a stout wife and a half dozen children is good quality.

BOURASSA: I oppose immigration unless they are French. If you must bring strangers to this country bring them from Belgium or France. But these strangers who don't speak French, who don't even speak English. Wherever they go trouble goes. They bring only crime and anarchy. They have contributed nothing to the building of this country.

SIFTON: But they will.

BOURASSA: They are scum. Scum, scum. The scum of the world are coming to this country. They are going to destroy the Canadien way of life. We want to create a bilingual nation from sea to sea.

SIFTON: Over my dead body. I reject the bicultural compact in it's entirety.

BOURASSA: Immigrants whose tongue is neither French nor English will destroy the dream of a bilingual nation.

SIFTON: You got it. There's nothing you can do about it either.

BOURASSA: The question is the legal rights of Roman Catholics.

SIFTON: I am opposed to giving Catholics educational privileges. Privileges will be transferred into rights.

BOURASSA: Rights, are rights, are rights.

SIFTON: Quiet you screeching wretch.

(LAURIER enters.)

LAURIER: Not this again.

SIFTON: Yes, this again.

BOURASSA: Yes, this again. I want the French language on an equal footing with the English language.

LAURIER: One day that will happen.

BOURASSA: The battle is right now. Not fifty years from now. Not one hundred years from now. Right now. Manitoba is gone. Saskatchewan and Alberta are going.

SIFTON: Gone?

BOURASSA: How can you work with this man?

LAURIER: We cannot impose an educational system that the majority of people will resent. It's elementary democracy.

BOURASSA: We want a homeland that belongs to us. And not to outsiders. We want a country.

We will have a country. We will have what has been withheld from us. Power, freedom.

SIFTON: That man carries a knife in his boot for me.

BOURASSA: I will no longer work in federal politics. Only provincial politics. I resign, again.

LAURIER: I regret your departure. We need men like you at Ottawa, though I would not want two.

(The lights fade.)

Scene Forty-four

(In another playing area the lights fade in. LAURIER and EMILIE enter.)

LAURIER: Henri Bourassa. I knew his grandfather. Knowing his grandfather I understand the grandson. And knowing the grandson I understand the grandfather. He's an hermaphrodite. A castor rouge. A disgusting monstrosity. A reactionary religious conservative and a secular revolutionary radical all rolled into one. A political hermaphrodite. Hermaphrodites. They're everywhere.

(LAVERGNE enters.)

LAVERGNE: Excuse me.

(LAVERGNE exits. The lights fade.)

Scene Forty-five

(In another playing area the lights fade in. BOURASSA and ARMAND enter. ARMAND holds a placard with the words "Nationalist League of Quebec.")

BOURASSA: The French-Canadien race has a special mission to fulfill on this continent and should, to that end, maintain it's character distinct from that of other races.

I regret everytime I go back to my province to find developing the feeling that Canada is not for all Canadians. We are bound to come to the conclusion that Quebec is our only country because we have no liberty elsewhere.

This is the manifesto of the Nationalist league. For Canada, we want autonomy from Great Britian that is compatible with the colonial bond. For the Canadian provinces, we want autonomy from the federal power that is compatible with the federal bond.

VOICE: *(Off.)* Shut up you son-of-a-bitch separatist bastard.

BOURASSA: Ah, the elegance and eloquence of the English language. We also demand the fiscal independence of this country from the British Empire and the United States of America.

VOICE: *(Off.)* Shut your filthy hole.

BOURASSA: I love the way the English debate.

(LAURIER enters.)

ARMAND: Down with Laurier.

(ARMAND holds up a fleur de lis.)

LAURIER: Armand.

ARMAND: From this day forward I will no longer speak English. Everything you hold dear I will destroy.

LAURIER: Armand.

(The lights fade.)

Scene Forty-six

(In another playing area the lights fade in. LAURIER and EMILIE enter.)

EMILIE: I don't see what you are complaining about. He is just like you.

LAURIER: Non, he is just like you.

EMILIE: Love is an infernal experience. You yourself support freedom of expression.

LAURIER: He must stop. The innuendo is embarrassing.

EMILIE: He is enfant terrible. I can do nothing with him.

LAURIER: Then I can do nothing with you.

EMILIE: You said that just like a lizard.

LAURIER: Yes.

(The lights fade.)

Scene Forty-seven

(In another playing area the lights fade in. LAURIER and ZOE enter.)

LAURIER: Of all the dreams, the dreams of the past are the worst because they are impossible to realize. Even the most improbable future may succeed but the past will never succeed again. It is the great advantage of being a new nation. It cannot fall in love with it's own past.

It belongs entirely to the present and the future. Liberty allows us to create everything from the beginning. Political customs, laws, motherland. Everything comes from Liberty. Every true and good idea, from whatever land, or whatever tongue is ours. Liberty. What good fortune.

(The lights fade.)

Scene Forty-eight

(In another playing area the lights fade in. LAURIER enters.)

LAURIER: To be and not to be; that is the question. The answer too. We have become a nation without breaking the colonial tie.

(BOURASSA enters.)

BOURASSA: The two races will never get along.

LAURIER: I think it is possible that the descendants of Normandy and the desendants of the Norman invasion can get along. I may not live to see it but it is possible.

BOURASSA: We want to be independent. We will be independent. I remember.

LAURIER: I recognize the position in which our race has been placed by the battle which was fought on the Plains of Abraham. You forget this state of things. You affect to believe that a small French Republic or monarchy, I hardly know what you want, should be established on the banks of the St. Lawrence. You speak like a slave who would break his bonds, if he dared but who does not do so because he is a coward. For my part I believe myself to be a free man.

BOURASSA: And I do not. We owe nothing to England and we shall separate from her when the majority so wishes. Without remorse, and without tears.

(The lights fade.)

Scene Forty-nine

(In another playing area the lights fade in. EARL GREY, LAURIER, BORDEN, and a BUTLER enter.)

GREY: Gentlemen, to the race that is infallibly destined to control the civilization of the world. To Anglo-Saxondom.

BORDEN: Here, here.

GREY: And imperialism.

BORDEN: To imperialism.

GREY: You don't drink.

LAURIER: I don't drink alcohol.

GREY: Put water in his glass.

LAURIER: I am not thirsty.

GREY: Sir Wilfrid, Germany is in the process of overtaking England in shipbuilding. By 1912 Germany and England will have an equal number of Dreadnoughts. British supremacy on the high seas will be over. We want a spontaneous contribution of Dreadnoughts or money for Dreadnoughts from the colony.

LAURIER: I will consider the matter. This is very good.

(The lights fade.)

Scene Fifty

(In another playing area the lights fade in. BOURASSA and ARMAND enter. ARMAND has taped an "X" over his mouth and he holds a pencil and paper.)

BOURASSA: He has formed a navy in order to receive another decoration, another title. We will be involved in all of England's wars. Mark my words. We will be slaves of the English. The next step will be conscription. He is a devious imperialist. From this moment I dedicate myself to the downfall of Le Grand Wilfy. And so do you.

(The lights fade.)

Scene Fifty-one

(In another playing area the lights fade in. LAURIER enters.)

LAURIER: The imperial bonds must be weakened. They lead only to war. Free trade with the United States will weaken if not sever those bonds. Our American friends have many fine qualities. But what they have, they keep, and what they have not, they want.

This country has always been ruled by an imperial master. But we have never chosen our master. The time has come.

(The lights fade.)

Scene Fifty-two

(In another playing area the lights fade in. BORDEN and BOURASSA enter. BOURASSA holds a copy of Le Devoir*.)*

BOURASSA: In this election it is our duty to destroy Wilfrid Laurier.

BORDEN: Free trade with the United States will destroy our British heritage.

BOURASSA: Do your duty.

BORDEN: It is the treason that barters our birthright for Yankee gold.

BOURASSA: He is a devious imperialist.

BORDEN: It is her own soul that Canada risks today.

BOURASSA: Devious.

BORDEN: No truck nor trade with the Yankees.

(The lights fade.)

Scene Fifty-three

(In another playing area the lights fade in. LAURIER enters.)

LAURIER: In Quebec I am branded a jingo and an imperialist. In Ontario I am attacked as a separatist and an anti-imperialist. I am neither. I am a Canadian. First, last, and always. A Canadian.

(ARMAND enters.)

They cheer for me but they do not vote for me.

ARMAND: You lost.

LAURIER: The ideal is to work, to content oneself with little, to lose without bitterness, to grow old without regret.

ARMAND: You lost, you lost.

LAURIER: Armand.

(The lights fade.)

Scene Fifty-four

(In another playing area the lights fade in. LAURIER and ZOE enter. ZOE plays the piano.)

ZOE: Remember this?

LAURIER: Yes.

ZOE: I never know what you mean when you say that.

LAURIER: I remember. You play very beautifully.

ZOE: Merci, monsieur.

(The lights fade. The end.)

The Great War

Part Six of The History of the Village of the Small Huts

Act One

Scene One

(The lights fade in. LAURA and SIR ROBERT BORDEN enter. They play golf.)

LAURA: Fore.

(BORDEN swings a golf club.)

Slice, little boy.

BORDEN: Blast.

LAURA: You always do that.

BORDEN: That's why you yell fore. Are you all right? Sorry about that. All right Laura, show me how it's done.

LAURA: Oh little boy.

BORDEN: Just inner spirits escaping.

LAURA: See a doctor.

BORDEN: I have, there is nothing they can do.

(LAURA tees up her ball. ARTHUR MEIGHEN enters.)

MEIGHEN: Mr. Borden, Mr. Borden.

LAURA: Look who it is. It's Arthur Meighen.

MEIGHEN: Ah, Sir Robert.

BORDEN: What?

MEIGHEN: The heir to the Austro-Hungarian throne, Arch Duke Franz Ferdinand, has been assassinated at Sarajevo.

BORDEN: Yes … and …

MEIGHEN: This may be of some importance.

BORDEN: Don't bend your arm, Laura, keep it straight.

LAURA: You do it your way, I'll do it my way.

MEIGHEN: Sir Robert.

BORDEN: Blast. Can't a man play golf in this country?

MEIGHEN: Any man can play golf but only the prime minister can conduct affairs of state. I have the cables from the foreign office and I have taken the liberty of summoning your cabinet to Ottawa.

BORDEN: You would do that.

MEIGHEN: Yes.

(LAURA swings her golf club.)

BORDEN: Oh good show.

MEIGHEN: Sir Robert.

(The lights fade.)

Scene Two

(In another playing area the lights fade in. A FATHER and his son, DAVID enter. FATHER is wringing the neck of a chicken.)

FATHER: See, that's how it's done. That's how it's done. That's how it's done. See, and then you do this. See, that's how it's done. Now let's see you do it. Go on, I'm watching.

(Offstage: the sound of chicken cackling. DAVID exits. Offstage: the sound of chicken squawking.)

No, no, no, no, no! Come here.

(DAVID enters.)

Hand.

(DAVID puts out his hand. FATHER slaps his hand.)

Do it right or don't do it at all. Do you understand? Then do it. Now!

DAVID: I'll do it.

(DAVID exits.)

FATHER: He's big but he's learning.

(The lights fade.)

Scene Three

(In another playing area the lights fade in. ROBERT and his friends, STEPHEN and EDITH, enter. They are having a picnic. STEPHEN reads a newspaper. ROBERT holds a book of poetry titled Vitae Lampada.*)*

ROBERT: "The sand of the desert is sodden red—Red with the wreck of a square that broke; The Gatling's jammed and the colonel dead, And the regiment blind with dust and smoke; The river of death has brimmed his banks, And England's far, and Honour a name; But the voice of a schoolboy rallies the ranks: 'Play up! play up! and play the game!' " Isn't that wonderful.

EDITH: Oh yes, Robert.

STEPHEN: Oh yes.

EDITH: Kipling is so exquisite.

ROBERT: It's not Kipling you silly thing. It's Newbolt. Henry Newbolt.

STEPHEN: Yes.

ROBERT: But would you like to hear Kipling, Edith? I have some.

STEPHEN: Why not?

ROBERT: Oh Stephen, you and your rugby scores.

EDITH: Oh rugby.

STEPHEN: It's the only thing they print in this paper that is true.

ROBERT: Soldiers of the queen.

(STEPHEN reveals the newspaper headline "Austria Declares War On Serbia." The lights fade.)

Scene Four

(In another playing area the lights fade in. An old woman, MARTHA, is knitting. Offstage: the sound of a train.)

MARTHA: The night train. Oh it makes my heart beat fast. The night train.

(JOHN enters.)

JOHN: Mum, there's a raccoon outside killing a cat. He's going to spend all night killing that cat. Why do they do that?

MARTHA: Animals are so cruel. They're not like us. That raccoon reminds me of your father.

JOHN: I'm going to get my gun, mum. And kill that raccoon.

MARTHA: Ah, you're my man now, aren't ya, John? Aren't ya? Aren't ya? Aren't ya?

JOHN: Mum.

(The lights fade.)

Scene Five

(In another playing area the lights fade in. The DUCHESS OF CONNAUGHT enters.)

DUCHESS: Ich schmicke mir die lippen und meine augenbraue ans pflucken und dann, bin ich schoen.

(A SERVANT enters.)

SERVANT: His Excellency, the governor-general of Canada, the Duke of Connaught, entering the room.

(The DUKE OF CONNAUGHT enters holding a photo album. The SERVANT exits.)

DUCHESS: Must you do that?

DUKE: Yes. I must.

DUCHESS: Oh look, you have spoiled my face. Schweinhund.

DUKE: Such language. What would mother say? Look, the mother of us all. Queen Victoria, my mother. Look, King of England, look, Czar of Russia, look, Emperor of Germany. All grandsons of mother. And I am their uncle. Correct?

(The DUCHESS nods her head.)

Otto Schlippenschloppen came to see you today. I sent him away. I have made sure he never comes again. That makes the eyes of the Duchess shine. Do you understand me?

DUCHESS: Ja.

DUKE: Gut.

(The lights fade.)

Scene Six

(In another playing area the lights fade in. SIR WILFRID LAURIER, ARMAND LAVERGNE, and HENRI BOURASSA enter. BOURASSA holds Le Devoir*, ARMAND holds a teapot, and LAURIER holds a teacup.)*

ARMAND: The great Sir Wilfrid Laurier is no longer prime minister because of me and my

Nationalistes from Quebec. Moi. Moi. I did that. Me! Armand Lavergne!

LAURIER: And Robert Borden is now prime minister. Does that make you happy?

ARMAND: Live out your days in bitterness, old man.

LAURIER: Is there any more sugar?

ARMAND: Non, no more sugar. The great Henri Bourassa is going to speak.

BOURASSA: The Balkan powderkeg has exploded. The citizens of the Balkans are like us. Victims of imperialism.

LAURIER: Nationalism leads only to the vortex of militarism. It is a blight on mankind. It is a midden, based only on feuds and vendettas.

BOURASSA: What do you know about the Balkans?

LAURIER: Only what I read in the newspapers, Henri. Sometimes events that happen are never reported, while events that never happened are headlines.

ARMAND: The world is passing you by, old man.

LAURIER: Is there any more sugar?

(The lights fade.)

Scene Seven

(In another playing area the lights fade in. BORDEN and MEIGHEN enter.)

BORDEN: Jesus God mercy save me.

MEIGHEN: See a doctor.

BORDEN: Why am I an imperialist? I am an imperialist because I refuse to be a colonial. The British Empire is the greatest empire in the history of civilization What is life? Life is the struggle for existence. Then war is inevitable. Therefore life is war. The British Empire is not an accident. It is destiny. Twenty-five per cent of the world is under the protection of the Empire. It is our duty to defend the Empire. War is not an aberration. It occurs too frequently to be an aberration. Social evolution depends upon war. The British Empire is a beehive. We, Canadians, are the drones of empire.

(The lights fade.)

Scene Eight

(In another playing area the lights fade in. NELLIE McCLUNG enters.)

NELLIE: The subjugation of women is not based on a rational thought. It is based on an irrational feeling. And therefore cannot be refuted by logical argument. Since the twilight of civilization women have been in bondage to men because they lack the muscular strength of men. Therefore might is right. A physical fact has become a legal right. Those who were forced into obedience are now legally bound to it.

(BORDEN and MEIGHEN enter.)

MEIGHEN: Lovely speech, lovely. It was so … You!

NELLIE: The legal subordination of one sex to the other is wrong and must be changed. I advocate that it be replaced by a concept of equality.

BORDEN: What is she doing here? She should be with the wives.

NELLIE: I am nobody's wife. I am Nellie McClung.

BORDEN: A suffragette.

NELLIE: I'm a suffragist.

BORDEN: Suffering Christ, what is that?

NELLIE: Women want the vote and they want it now. V-O-T-E. What's that spell?

MEIGHEN: In Great Britain the suffragettes are considered armed and dangerous.

NELLIE: What's that spell?

MEIGHEN: I'll handle this.

NELLIE: Vote. When do we want it? N-O-W. Now.

MEIGHEN: You whore, you bitch, you prostitute.

NELLIE: Ah, the voice of our masters.

MEIGHEN: Go home, go home. Go home and make supper now.

NELLIE: The slaves are in revolt.

BORDEN: Police, police, police.

(The lights fade.)

Scene Nine

(In another playing area the lights fade in. FATHER and his son, DAVID, are fly fishing. DAVID holds a newspaper with the headline "Russia Declares War on Austria.")

FATHER: Watch. See. That's how it's done. That's how it's done. Hey, don't turn away when I'm speaking. What do you see on the old river bank?

DAVID: Flopping trout.

FATHER: That's right. Flopping trout. Pay attention. That won't help you. The only thing that's good for is wrapping fish. See, that's how it's done.

DAVID: That's how it's done.

(The lights fade.)

Scene Ten

(In another playing area the lights fade in. ROBERT, STEPHEN, and EDITH enter.)

EDITH: Why must we always come to these dreadful cemeteries?

ROBERT: I find them inspiring. Everyone here has been touched by God.

STEPHEN: And besides, what better place for a picnic? The grass is so green.

ROBERT: Exactly. Look! The words of the stone cutter. "He was a good husband and a good Christian." That's what they'll say about me one day.

EDITH: But will it be true?

ROBERT: Hopefully. The only words I believe are those carved in stone.

STEPHEN: There's going to be a war. I feel it. I feel it.

(ROBERT and EDITH look at STEPHEN. The lights fade.)

Scene Eleven

(In another playing area the lights fade in. FATHER and DAVID enter. DAVID polishes a boot.)

FATHER: It's a long way to Tipperary. It's a long way to go. It's a long way to Tipperary, to the sweetest girl I know. Ah yes, they don't write them like that anymore. There's going to be a war. Are you going to do me proud and sign up? You came out of your mother's treasure box and it killed her, killed her dead right there. But you're my son.

DAVID: Father.

FATHER: Did I ever show you these?

(FATHER holds up a box of medals.)

DAVID: A thousand times.

FATHER: Look at this one.

DAVID: It's shiny.

FATHER: Got this in the Boer War. I strangled a big Boer with my bare hands, strangled the life out of him and they gave me a medal. For queen and empire … did my duty. Now it's your turn … king and empire.

DAVID: If there's a war, I'll enlist.

FATHER: Give your dad a big kiss.

DAVID: Get your hands off me.

FATHER: You're a man now. Oh it's a long way to Tipperary.

(The lights fade.)

Scene Twelve

(In another playing area the lights fade in. BORDEN, MEIGHEN, the DUKE OF CONNAUGHT, and a BUTLER enter.)

DUKE: Oh these alliances, these alliances.

MEIGHEN: Russia has come to the defence of Serbia and declared war on Austria. Germany has come to the defence of Austria and declared war on Russia.

DUKE: It's a family quarrel, just a family quarrel. Willie is a bully and Nickie is an idiot.

MEIGHEN: Now, the king of England, George the Fifth—

DUKE: He's my nephew.

MEIGHEN: —is very alarmed that the emperor of Germany, Kaiser Wilhelm—

DUKE: He's my nephew.

MEIGHEN: —and the czar of Russia.

DUKE: He's my nephew.

MEIGHEN: —will not withdraw their ultimatums. The fear is that Russia will invoke it's alliance with France.

DUKE: That's who they should be fighting.

MEIGHEN: At which point, if Germany declares

war on France, France will invoke its alliance with England.

DUKE: Nicky and Willie should be fighting France, not each other.

MEIGHEN: And if England declares war, we are at war. It's very complicated, complex, and confusing.

DUKE: It's a family quarrel.

BORDEN: Yes. Send for the minister of Militia, Sam Hughes.

MEIGHEN: Oh not him.

DUKE: Oh not him.

BUTLER: Mr. Hughes, this way.

(SAM HUGHES enters as the BUTLER exits.)

MEIGHEN: Mr. Hughes, The prime minister desires to know the state of the armed forces.

HUGHES: We have a standing army of three thousand but our militia forces exceed seventy-five thousand.

MEIGHEN: Mr. Hughes, Germany and the Austro-Hungarian Empire have an army of fourteen million men.

HUGHES: If it comes to it, seventy-five thousand Canadians ought to be able to handle it.

(The BUTLER enters with a telegram.)

BUTLER: Urgent telegram for the governor-general of Canada.

(The BUTLER gives the telegram to the DUKE.)

DUKE: Ah, my nephew.

BORDEN: Which one?

DUKE: England has declared war on Germany.

MEIGHEN: Therefore Canada is now at war with Germany.

BORDEN: Gentlemen, a toast. To king and empire.

MEIGHEN: To king and empire.

HUGHES: God be praised. There is no going back now. It's going to a be a great war, a glorious war, a war to end all wars. It's going to be like the Boer war only bigger.

DUKE: The Canadian army must be modelled upon the British army. I will show the way by creating a regiment that I will name after my lovely daughter, Princess Patricia.

MEIGHEN: We must make the announcement.

BORDEN: Yes.

(The lights fade.)

Scene Thirteen

(In another playing area the lights fade in. BORDEN enters. Offstage: cheering.)

BORDEN: We are going to war to maintain the honour and integrity of the British Empire. No effort or sacrifice is too great. There will be no conscription, freely and voluntarily the manhood of Canada stands ready to fight beyond the seas.

(HUGHES enters.)

HUGHES: That means we want volunteers. We want a half million volunteers. Do your duty. Join your country's army. God save the king.

VOICES: *(Off.)* God save the king.

(The lights fade.)

Scene Fourteen

(In another playing area the lights fade in. A RECRUITER enters.)

RECRUITER: Do your duty, join your country's army. We'll give you a dollar a day and a free trip to Europe. But you must be at least five-foot-three and between the ages of eighteen and forty-five.

(ROBERT, STEPHEN, DAVID, and JOHN enter.)

ALL: I want to enlist. Me too.

(RECRUITER hands out papers.)

JOHN: I hope the war doesn't end before we get there.

STEPHEN: My fear too.

DAVID: I want to get in on the fun.

ROBERT: Me too.

(They exit. The lights fade.)

Scene Fifteen

(In another playing area the lights fade in. NELLIE enters holding an umbrella.)

NELLIE: What do women think of this war? Not that it matters, of course. The Great War is masculine society in crisis. The blaring bands, the marching feet, the laughing, the bragging.

For what? For war. Men, they love it. God does not make war. Men make war. And therefore when enough people say it shall not be, it cannot be. This will not happen until women are allowed to vote. When we have the vote we will ban war.

(The lights fade.)

Scene Sixteen

(In another playing area the lights fade in. LAURIER, BOURASSA, and ARMAND enter. BOURASSA holds Le Devoir *with the headline "C'est la guerre.")*

BOURASSA: This is imperialism. This will lead to conscription.

LAURIER: They are all volunteers. They want to go. Let them go.

BOURASSA: First volunteers, then volunteers by coercion, then conscription. You mark my words.

ARMAND: My hero.

LAURIER: Armand.

BOURASSA: The proper duty for Canadian troops is the defence of Canada.

LAURIER: The defeat of England and France would be a disaster for the world, for Canada, for the province of Quebec, especially for the French Canadians.

BOURASSA: Our only enemy is militarism.

ARMAND: I will not fight for England.

LAURIER: Then fight for France.

BOURASSA: We owe France less than we owe England and we owe England nothing.

ARMAND: My hero.

LAURIER: Armand.

(The lights fade.)

Scene Seventeen

(In another playing area the lights fade in. BORDEN and MEIGHEN enter. MEIGHEN reads from a document.)

MEIGHEN: "The governor in council—"

BORDEN: That's me.

MEIGHEN: Yes.

MEIGHEN: "The governor in council shall have power to do and authorize such acts and things, and to make from time to time such orders and regulations, as he may by reason of the existence of real or apprehended war, invasion or insurrection deem necessary for the security, defence, peace, order and welfare of Canada."

As you can see, the War Measures Act is of a blanket nature. We have omitted no power the government may need. And it gets better "And for greater certainty, but not so as to restrict the foregoing terms, it is hereby declared … "

(The lights fade.)

Scene Eighteen

(In another playing area the lights fade in. ROBERT, STEPHEN, and EDITH enter.)

EDITH: My two lieutenants.

STEPHEN: Oh honey lamb.

EDITH: Oh hon. Always smiling, except this one. The gloomy one.

ROBERT: You married him.

EDITH: Yes.

STEPHEN: We wanted you to be the first to know.

ROBERT: You mean the last.

EDITH: We thought you knew.

ROBERT: I always thought—

EDITH: You thought what?

ROBERT: That you and I.

EDITH: Stephen is so handsome and so … sensitive. I mean look at this face. There really was no choice.

ROBERT: Yes.

(STEPHEN smiles.)

Would you like to hear some Kipling? I have some.

EDITH: Why not?

(ROBERT opens a book of poetry.)

ROBERT: The female of the species is more deadly than the male.

(The lights fade.)

Scene Nineteen

(In another playing area the lights fade in. MARTHA and JOHN enter.)

MARTHA: Johnny, Johnny. Have you heard what the Germans are doing to the priests of Belgium? They go into all the churches and into the steeples and take down all the church bells. And then they take all the clappers out of the bells and tie all the priests inside the bells. And then they put the bells back into the steeples. And the Germans, they ring those bells and the priests go.

(MARTHA moves her head from side to side and makes bell sounds.)

JOHN: I can't wait to get at them, Mum. Can't wait.

(The lights fade.)

Scene Twenty

(In another playing area the lights fade in. EDITH enters.)

EDITH: It's not fair being a girl. The boys can be soldiers and we have to be nurses. All the brave young men of Canada are going to army training camp at Valcartier. Including Robert and my dear honey lamb Stephen. I will write letters and learn to roll bandages.

(The lights fade.)

Scene Twenty-one

(In another playing area the lights fade in: recruits leaving by train. The train enters. ARTHUR CURRIE is in the engine room and DAVID, JOHN, STEPHEN, and ROBERT are in the coach. RUSSELL BOYLE is in the caboose.)

JOHN: Goodbye Mum.

DAVID: Goodbye Father.

STEPHEN: Goodbye Edith.

ROBERT: Goodbye Canada.

BOYLE: What the hell are you looking at?

(The train exits. The lights fade.)

Scene Twenty-two

(In another playing area the lights fade in. CURRIE enters holding a jam can.)

CURRIE: Welcome to Valcartier, Quebec. I am Lieutenant-Colonel Arthur Currie. I am going to command the Second Brigade when it is formed. See this jam can? This is a grenade. It is filled with nails, screws, washers, rusty bits of iron, broken glass, and a half-pound of explosive. Now what you do is you light the fuse and when it burns halfway down you throw it. Never take your eye off the fuse. Sometimes it burns fast sometimes it doesn't. Remember, halfway down. If it ever burns all the way down and you're holding it … God help you. Your chums too. Now, who here has played baseball?

(The lights fade.)

Scene Twenty-three

(In another playing area the lights fade in. HUGHES, ROBERT, and STEPHEN enter.)

HUGHES: This is the Canadian army. We want no butt fuckers in the Canadian army. Therefore no priests.

ROBERT: But they're Anglicans.

HUGHES: A priest is a priest. This is the Canadian army. The men in the Canadian army are Canadians. The equipment too. And that includes the guns, and the bullets. All of it. One hundred percent Canadian. Not ninety-nine and a half, one hundred. Right Captain?

STEPHEN: I'm a lieutenant.

HUGHES: You're a captain now. Carry on. I'm in a frenzy.

(HUGHES exits.)

STEPHEN: Well, I'm a captain now.

ROBERT: Well it's all going your way.

STEPHEN: Yes. Salute me.

(ROBERT salutes.)

Elbow higher.

(STEPHEN exits.)

ROBERT: What an army.

(The lights fade.)

Scene Twenty-four

(In another playing area the lights fade in. HUGHES enters holding the MacAdam shovel. STEPHEN enters.)

HUGHES: Miss MacAdam, my secretary designed this. She was the sweetest little screw I ever had. It's a shield and a shovel all rolled into one. You see, you can dig your trench with it and you can protect your face with it.

See it's got a peephole. So you can see through it. I want twenty-five thousand of these. Now! Next!

(CURRIE enters holding the Ross rifle.)

CURRIE: This rifle is very poorly designed. The first shot is all right but the shell stays in the bore and you have to extract it like this.

HUGHES: Then put a bayonet on it and do some pig-sticking.

CURRIE: If under attack by the enemy and rapid firing is called for, that could be a problem.

HUGHES: The troops will fight like Billy be damned. Oh, the Ross rifle! My pride and joy. The rifle of the future. Pink a bastard at two hundred yards with this, pink him good.

CURRIE: It's a good hunting rifle—for sharp shooters only.

HUGHES: The British army uses the Lee-Enfield, we use the Ross rifle. Look at it. Load it up and go to war with it. I get the shakes when I think about firing this baby. We got one hundred thousand of them. Three-oh-three calibre. Put a hole in a man this big. It's a great rifle—my pride and joy.

CURRIE: But it jams.

(The lights fade.)

Scene Twenty-five

(In another playing area the lights fade in.)

VOICE: *(Off.)* We are Sam Hughes' army, we cannot fight, we cannot shoot. Oh what use are we!

(The DUKE and DUCHESS enter.)

DUKE: Ah, it's a great day for the British Empire. The colonies want to contribute, but we will pick and choose. Pick and choose. And what does German wife say?

DUCHESS: Look at them, colonials on parade. Marching off to fight Germany.

DUKE: A loyal colony, pick and choose.

DUCHESS: Danke schoen, Canada, danke schoen.

(The lights fade.)

Scene Twenty-six

(In another playing area the lights fade in. JOHN is writing a letter.)

JOHN: *(Off.)* Dear Mother, This is your dearest Johnny writing. It rained ninety days out of one hundred and twenty days at Salisbury Plain. Drainage was poor. But that is all behind us because now we are in France. Do not fear for me, Mother, because I am khaki-clad and mighty glad.

(Lights up on a boxcar with the sign "8 Horses or 40 Men." BOYLE and DAVID enter.)

DAVID: Captain Boyle.

BOYLE: No, I've had it, these louts.

(BOYLE takes off his jacket and throws it on the ground. SOLDIERS SIX and SEVEN enter.)

Now I'm the same as you fellows. I'm just an ordinary private as far as you're concerned. There were four men on that boat who said they'd like to punch the hell out of me. Now, I invite you four men, if you have the guts, to come over here and we'll have it out right here. C'mon, act like you got a pair, I know you don't.

(CURRIE enters.)

CURRIE: Attention. Our commanding officer, General Edwin Alderson.

(GENERAL EDWIN ALDERSON enters.)

ALDERSON: Welcome to France, brave Empire troops. Welcome to France. Here we do things in the British way. You do not know our ways. But you will. You are going to the front line at the western front. This way.

CURRIE: Right turn. Get in there.

JOHN: Jesus. We're going to the front in a cattle car.

CURRIE: At the left. Quick! March!

BOYLE: What the hell are you looking at?

DAVID: Soldiers on the hoof. Move 'em in, move 'em out.

SOLDIER SEVEN: This is a cattle car.

SOLDIER SIX: We're going to the front in a cattle car.

CURRIE: Get in there.

(The lights fade.)

Scene Twenty-seven

(In another playing area the lights fade in: a sign, "Ypres." Sound of a bird singing. DAVID, JOHN, and SOLDIER ONE enter.)

DAVID: So this is Yipes.

SOLDIER ONE: It's not called "Yipes." It's called "Ypres" [Pronounced "eep."]

DAVID: Eep!

SOLDIER ONE: Eep!

DAVID: Then why don't they spell it "peep" without the "p"?

JOHN: Because it's a French word.

DAVID: God, I'm going to die at some unpronounceable French name.

(A BRITISH SOLDIER enters.)

BRITISH SOLDIER: It's the bloody Canadians from the Canadas. They come three thousand miles to fight the Hun. Now laddies, first rule in the trench is keep to the right. And keep your head down, and watch out for the snipers, they're deadly.

JOHN: What's this place called?

BRITISH SOLDIER: Wipers.

DAVID: Listen, a bird singing. What kind of a bird is it?

SOLDIER ONE: It's a pigeon singing its little heart out.

DAVID: No.

JOHN: A robin.

SOLDIER ONE: It's a nightingale.

DAVID: No, it's a lark. There are larks here.

(CURRIE enters.)

CURRIE: The Ypres Salient is the only part of Belgium that is not occupied by the Germans. It is imperative that we hold it for symbolic reasons. Now you will be attacked on three sides. Our orders are to hold the trench at all costs. If we lose a trench we are to regain it by counter-attack immediately.

(The lights fade.)

Scene Twenty-eight

(In another playing area the lights fade in. STEPHEN, DAVID, JOHN, and SOLDIERS ONE and FOUR enter.)

STEPHEN: All the greats have fought here. Caesar fought here. Napoleon fought here and now I am fighting here.

DAVID: What are you doing?

JOHN: Just counting the clouds.

DAVID: I don't like the look of that cloud.

JOHN: Ah, what a nice breeze.

DAVID: Look.

JOHN: Oh yes, what a funny one that is.

DAVID: It's coming right over here.

JOHN: I've never seen a cloud like that.

(Traces of yellow-green fog enter. The SOLDIERS sniff the air.)

STEPHEN: Gas!

SOLDIERS: Gas!

(Yellow-green fog enters. The SOLDIERS are choking, swearing, spitting, dying.)

STEPHEN: The Germans are coming.

(The SOLDIERS fire at advancing GERMAN SOLDIERS.)

The Germans are coming.

(GERMAN SOLDIER ONE enters and is shot.)

The Germans are coming.

(The Ross rifle jams.)

The Germans are coming.

(GERMAN SOLDIERS TWO and SIX enter. GERMAN SOLDIER SIX stabs SOLDIER ONE. STEPHEN shoots GERMAN SOLDIER SIX. GERMAN SOLDIER SIX exits. SOLDIER ONE exits. GERMAN SOLDIER TWO reloads his rifle. DAVID hits GERMAN SOLDIER TWO with his rifle butt.

GERMAN SOLDIER SIX enters. GERMAN SOLDIER SIX aims his rifle at DAVID. SOLDIER FOUR stabs GERMAN SOLDIER SIX with his bayonet. GERMAN SOLDIER SIX exits. GERMAN SOLDIER TWO enters. GERMAN SOLDIER TWO aims his rifle at SOLDIER FOUR. STEPHEN shoots GERMAN SOLDIER TWO.

GERMAN SOLDIERS ONE and THREE enter. GERMAN SOLDIER ONE stabs STEPHEN. SOLDIER FOUR stabs GERMAN SOLDIER ONE. STEPHEN shoots GERMAN SOLDIER ONE. GERMAN SOLDIER THREE attacks DAVID. DAVID disarms GERMAN

SOLDIER THREE. They grapple. GERMAN SOLDIER THREE puts his hands around DAVID's neck. SOLDIER FOUR stabs GERMAN SOLDIER THREE. STEPHEN picks up a field telephone.)

Colonel Currie, Colonel Currie. Gas attack. We did not take the worst of it. On our left two French divisions have retreated. Our left flank is now completely exposed. Send men to reinforce our left flank. Quickly. Here they come again.

(The lights fade.)

Scene Twenty-nine

(In another playing area the lights fade in. BOYLE, STEPHEN, and SOLDIERS TWO, FIVE and SIX enter.)

BOYLE: We are your reinforcements. Where is the left flank?

STEPHEN: Forget the left flank. I want you to attack here, Kitchener's Wood. We are under fierce assault. Now. Do it.

(The lights fade.)

Scene Thirty

(Darkness. BOYLE and SOLDIERS TWO, FIVE, and SIX enter. Flares. BOYLE and SOLDIERS are revealed.)

BOYLE: No!

(Machine gun fire. SOLDIERS TWO and FIVE are shot, BOYLE and SOLDIER SIX flee. The lights fade.)

Scene Thirty-one

(Darkness. BOYLE and SOLDIER SIX enter.)

BOYLE: Where the hell are we?

SOLDIER SIX: I have a map.

BOYLE: Let's see it.

(BOYLE turns on a flashlight. Four GERMAN SOLDIERS are revealed in the background.)

Jesus.

(BOYLE is shot. Hand to hand combat lit by flares and starlight. The lights fade.)

Scene Thirty-two

(In another playing area the lights fade in. SOLDIER TWO enters coughing and groaning. STEPHEN and CURRIE enter.)

STEPHEN: Our assault on Kitchener's Wood was a failure.

CURRIE: You mean a disaster. They were supposed to reinforce the trench.

STEPHEN: We were under counter-attack. I ordered them to assault Kitchener's Wood.

CURRIE: You are in no position to give orders.

STEPHEN: Anyway the French have retreated, it's a rout. Bloody poison gas, bloody poison gas.

(ROBERT enters.)

ROBERT: They are using chlorine gas.

CURRIE: How do you know?

ROBERT: I studied chemistry at the University of Toronto.

STEPHEN: So what?

ROBERT: So it's chlorine gas.

CURRIE: So what can we do about it?

ROBERT: Chlorine can be rendered quite harmless by nitrogen. If we can soak a cloth in nitrogen …

STEPHEN: Where are we going to get nitrogen?

ROBERT: Urine. That is pure nitrogen. If the men soak a rag in urine and wrap it around their mouth, they'll live, the eyes will water but they'll live.

CURRIE: Do it.

(CURRIE exits. The lights fade.)

Scene Thirty-three

(In another playing area the lights fade in. JOHN and DAVID enter. CURRIE enters with a field telephone.)

CURRIE: Hello … hello … hello.

DAVID: Just do it. Then wrap it around your face like this. See, that's how it's done.

JOHN: I'm out, can you.

DAVID: Here it comes. For fuck sakes it's not going to kill you. Just do it. Don't think about it. Don't talk about it. Just do it. Here they come.

(Gas attack. GERMAN SOLDIERS TWO, SIX, and SEVEN enter. DAVID shoots GERMAN SOLDIER TWO, then DAVID's gun jams. GERMAN SOLDIER TWO exits. DAVID and GERMAN SOLDIER SEVEN have bayonet fight. JOHN and GERMAN SOLDIER SIX have bayonet fight. GERMAN SOLDIERS SIX and SEVEN are killed. The Canadian SOLDIERS cheer.)

CURRIE: We are holding the Ypres Salient. Barely hanging on. Are there reinforcements? Can you hear me? Are there reinforcements? Hello, hello, hello? God-damned machines. Here they come again.

(The lights fade.)

Scene Thirty-four

(In another playing area the lights fade in. BORDEN enters.)

BORDEN: Blast, Jesus, God, mercy, save me. I am a ponderous ponderant. We took ten times the casualties in three days that we took during three years of the Boer War. The battle of the Ypres Salient—in one word: Disaster. Disaster, disaster!

(BORDEN holds up a newspaper headline: "Ypres Gas Attack, 7000 Casualties.")

This war is the suicide of civilization. I must do something. I must visit them. My brave Canadians. And give them … my condolences. Yes, my condolences.

(The lights fade.)

Scene Thirty-five

(In another playing area the lights fade in. CURRIE and ALDERSON enter. ALDERSON sticks pins in a map of the Ypres Salient. Blindfolded and gassed SOLDIERS FOUR, SIX, and SEVEN enter.)

CURRIE: We held it.

ALDERSON: Congratulations. Now we will go on the attack. Here. Attack, attack, attack. Casualties be damned. Attack, you have your orders, attack.

CURRIE: But you are asking—

ALDERSON: Asking?

CURRIE: You are commanding men to attack machine guns.

ALDERSON: The machine gun is an over rated weapon. Attack.

CURRIE: This map is wrong. It is upside down. We are supposed to attack based on this.

ALDERSON: Then attack here, here, and here.

CURRIE: We have to take out the machine guns. It is pointless to attack machine guns.

ALDERSON: You have your orders.

(ALDERSON exits.)

CURRIE: When I first met him I knew he was dead all ready. But when he said that, I knew the worms had got into his brain.

(The lights fade.)

Scene Thirty-six

(In another playing area the lights fade in. SOLDIER SEVEN enters shrieking and groaning. DAVID and JOHN enter eating hardtack. FREDERICK SCOTT, a chaplain, enters.)

SCOTT: I am here to administer the last rites.

DAVID: I have only two questions. Who discovered Ypres and why?

JOHN: They make this out of cement. It makes the teeth really sharp so you can bite them to death when this jams.

(DAVID holds up the Ross rifle.)

DAVID: This thing is useless. If you attach your bayonet and fire it, your bayonet falls off and the shell sticks in the bolt and you have to do this to get your shell out.

JOHN: Stupid thing. It's all right for hunting rabbits. Take your time, make your shot, take your time, change your shot. But for rapid fire …

DAVID: It's hopeless. I want to get me something that works. Get me one of those Lee-Enfields. There's a lot of dead Tommies out there. I wouldn't hunt rabbits with this stupid thing let alone go into battle with it.

JOHN: Get me one too … I'll go with you.

(DAVID and JOHN exit. The sound of a death rattle for SOLDIER SEVEN.)

SCOTT: Bless you my son. Amen.

(The lights fade.)

Scene Thirty-seven

(In another playing area the lights fade in. CURRIE and BORDEN enter.)

CURRIE: This way Mr. Prime Minister, this way.

BORDEN: So this is the western front. It looks very ... very.

CURRIE: And over there we have the German lines.

BORDEN: It looks very ... very ...

CURRIE: Formidable.

BORDEN: Yes.

(ALDERSON enters.)

Who is that?

CURRIE: That is our commanding officer. He's got to go. He spends all his time watering his stupid plants.

ALDERSON: Oh there are poppies here. Poppies.

CURRIE: And when the men should be laying barbed wire and reinforcing the trench, he has them building tennis courts so that he can play badminton. Badminton on a tennis court.

BORDEN: Really?

CURRIE: And he orders men to attack machine guns. It is beyond mindless, it is brainless. The casualties are unbelievable.

BORDEN: Really?

CURRIE: General Alderson.

ALDERSON: What?

CURRIE: This is the prime minister of Canada.

ALDERSON: That means you must be a politician.

BORDEN: Well, yes.

ALDERSON: Politicians are wrecking the war. They are not worth meeting and beating with a stick. Stay away from me.

CURRIE: He's got to go.

BORDEN: Definitely.

(The lights fade.)

Scene Thirty-eight

(In another playing area the lights fade in. Wounded SOLDIERS FOUR and SIX with bandaged faces enter. BORDEN enters.)

BORDEN: I am going back to Canada tomorrow but before I go I want to offer you my condolences. How are you?

(SOLDIER SIX groans.)

What?

(Groan.)

I didn't quite catch that.

(Groan.)

Come again.

(Groan.)

What?

(Groan.)

Yes, well, carry on.

(SOLDIER SIX groans. BORDEN moves to SOLDIER FOUR.)

And how are you?

(SOLDIER FOUR groans.)

What?

(Groan.)

I didn't quite catch that.

(Groan.)

Come again.

(Groan.)

What?

(SOLDIER FOUR groans. BORDEN farts in the face of SOLDIER FOUR.)

Sorry about that. Gas attack.

(SOLDIER FOUR groans. The lights fade.)

Scene Thirty-nine

(In another playing area the lights fade in. BOURASSA and ARMAND enter. ARMAND holds up a placard: "The Nationalist League of Quebec." In another playing area the lights fade in. HUGHES enters.)

HUGHES: Do your duty.

BOURASSA: We will not participate in wars of imperialism.

HUGHES: Enlist now.

BOURASSA: Our duty is not to the British Empire.

HUGHES: When England calls what do we say?

BOURASSA: Our duty is only to Canada.

HUGHES: Ready, aye, ready.

BOURASSA: Do your duty.

HUGHES: We're fighting for the supremacy of the British Empire for God's sake.

BOURASSA: Defend Canada, not imperialism.

HUGHES: Your chums are fighting, why aren't you.

BOURASSA: Do your duty.

HUGHES: Do your duty.

(The lights fade.)

Scene Forty

(In another playing area the lights fade in. BORDEN and the DUKE enter.)

BORDEN: As you know I am not given to overstatement.

DUKE: Yes, yes.

BORDEN: I regret to inform you that your wife is making outrageous statements. Outrageous.

DUKE: The Duchess is a strong-willed woman.

BORDEN: "Death to the king of England" and "Long live the kaiser" will not do. And gloating over Canadian casualties is completely unacceptable. She must be quieted. She must. There is already a great—

HUGHES: *(Off.)* I know he's in there, I know he's in there.

MEIGHEN: *(Off.)* Mr. Hughes, you can't go in.

HUGHES: *(Off.)* I want all enemy aliens arrested. Starting with his wife. She is a Hun, a spy for the kaiser.

MEIGHEN: *(Off.)* You are speaking about the head of state, you fool.

HUGHES: *(Off.)* It is outrageous that the head of state is a German. I want his wife arrested for high treason.

DUKE: That man is completely insane.

HUGHES: *(Off.)* His wife is a traitor.

DUKE: How dare he say that.

MEIGHEN: *(Off.)* Out beast. Now! This way.

DUKE: Dunderhead.

BORDEN: You see? She must be quieted. She must.

DUKE: Yes.

(The lights fade.)

Scene Forty-one

(In another playing area the lights fade in: Mt. Sorrel. SOLDIERS FOUR and SEVEN enter wearing gas masks. They listen to the shells landing. SOLDIER FOUR holds up a bible.)

SOLDIER FOUR: This once stopped a bullet.

(SOLDIER SEVEN holds up a deck of cards.)

SOLDIER SEVEN: So did this.

SOLDIER FOUR: Deal.

(SOLDIER SEVEN deals the cards. SOLDIER FIVE enters.)

SOLDIER FIVE: Can I play?

SOLDIER SEVEN: Have you got any money?

SOLDIER FIVE: Yes.

(The other SOLDIERS look at each other.)

SOLDIER FIVE: Let's play crazy eights.

SOLDIER SEVEN: Get out of here.

(The SOLDIERS listen to the shells landing. SOLDIER FIVE ducks.)

Don't be a pussy willow. When the cannon's fired and you hear the whistle, it means it's going somewhere. It's the one you don't hear. That's the one that kills you.

(An explosion.)

SOLDIER FOUR: That's a five-point-nine.

(An explosion.)

SOLDIER SEVEN: A seventy-five.

(An explosion.)

SOLDIER FOUR: There goes a Minenwurfer.

(SOLDIER FOUR and SEVEN duck.)

SOLDIER SEVEN: Down. Down. Minenwurfers. They're the worst.

SOLDIER FOUR: It goes like this *(He circulates his hands)* and then it explodes. And God help you.

SOLDIER SEVEN: You can be in a dugout underground and a piece of Minenwurfer will come right down, turn right, then turn left, then bang, right in the old face.

SOLDIER FOUR: They're the worst.

SOLDIER FIVE: Minenwurfer.

(The sound of a pick and shovel. The SOLDIERS listen.)

SOLDIER FOUR: Listen, the Hun at work. Underneath us. Mines. The bastards want to blow us up.

SOLDIER SEVEN: It's all right, it's when they stop, that's when you worry. Deal!

(The lights fade.)

Scene Forty-two

(In another playing area the lights fade in. CURRIE enters writing a letter.)

CURRIE: *(Off.)* Dear Mrs. Hagarty. Words cannot express—

(Offstage: a loud explosion.)

What the hell was that?

(The lights fade.)

Scene Forty-three

(In another playing area the lights fade in. The DUKE and DUCHESS enter.)

DUCHESS: Kaiser und Kaiserin sind sehr glücklich, so viele Kanadier für England gestauben sind, es ist ein gröss tag fur Deutschland. *[Translation: Emperor and Empress are very happy, so many Canadians die for English, it is a great day for Germany.]*

(The DUKE holds up a bottle.)

DUKE: Look what I have for you. Your favourite. Schnapps.

DUCHESS: Schnapps.

DUKE: Yes, dwink it, dwink all of it.

DUCHESS: I will. I will dwink it all.

DUKE: Excellent.

(The lights fade.)

Scene Forty-four

(In another playing area the lights fade in. BORDEN and MEIGHEN enter. They eat supper.)

BORDEN: Mr. Hughes does whatever he wants to do.

MEIGHEN: Where he goes, disaster goes.

BORDEN: He does not inform anyone, just does it.

MEIGHEN: He has to go. Notwithstanding his personality, he is completely corrupt. Patronage in excelsius, the worst excesses imaginable. He has to go. The Ministry of Defence is a disaster. Mr. Hughes contracts with his friends for inedible food, defective rifles, and shells with no powder. Mr. Hughes and his friends are traitors.

BORDEN: I am not calling them traitors. But they could not act any differently if they were traitors.

MEIGHEN: Exactly. He must resign, he must.

BORDEN: Yes.

(The lights fade.)

Scene Forty-five

(In another playing area the lights fade in. HUGHES, MEIGHEN, and BORDEN enter.)

HUGHES: Why are the sons-of-bitches always trying to get me? Why?

MEIGHEN: Mr. Hughes, here is your resignation. Sign same.

(MEIGHEN holds up a piece of paper.)

HUGHES: Look at him, look at him. He's like a little girl. This is how you treat a loyal campaign worker.

MEIGHEN: Mr. Hughes, this government can no longer support your conduct. Sign.

HUGHES: Look at him, look at him. He's like a little girl, a little girl.

MEIGHEN: Citizen Hughes, a minister of the Crown serves at the pleasure of the prime minister. Sign. Now!

(HUGHES signs the piece of paper.)

This way.

BORDEN: Very good.

HUGHES: Look at him.

MEIGHEN: On your way out close the door.

BORDEN: Very good.

(The lights fade.)

Scene Forty-six

(In another playing area the lights fade in. The DUKE and DUCHESS enter.)

DUKE: Look, Schnapps.

DUCHESS: I feel ill.

DUKE: Look, Schnapps.

(The DUKE holds up a bottle.)

DUCHESS: No, I can't.

DUKE: You must. I know you love it so much. Here, we won't use a glass. Drink it like this.

(The DUKE puts the bottle to the lips of the DUCHESS.)

DUCHESS: No, no, no.

DUKE: Yes, yes, yes. Drink it like this.

(The lights fade.)

Scene Forty-seven

(In another playing area the lights fade in. JULIAN BYNG enters.)

BYNG: Politics, politics, everything is politics, even in wartime. Why am I sent to command the Canadians? I don't know any Canadians and I don't want to. What kind of stunt is this?

(The lights fade.)

Scene Forty-eight

(In another playing area the lights fade in. The DUKE and DUCHESS enter.)

DUKE: We are returning to England. Wave goodbye, Duchess. Auf Wiedersehen, Canada, auf Wiedersehen.

(The lights fade.)

Scene Forty-nine

(In another playing area the lights fade in. CURRIE enters. DAVID, JOHN, and SOLDIER SEVEN enter. BYNG enters.)

CURRIE: Attention. The new commander of the Canadian Expeditionary Force. Sir Julian Byng.

BYNG: Greetings brave Empire troops, greetings. In this war preparation is everything. We will have to use our shovels. You there. Do you know what a shovel is?

DAVID: Yes.

BYNG: Yes what?

DAVID: Yes, sir.

BYNG: What is it?

DAVID: It's a ...

BYNG: You don't know what a shovel is, do you?

DAVID: It's a thing, for digging.

BYNG: Describe it. What does a shovel look like?

DAVID: It's like a stick with a cup attached to it.

BYNG: Fuzzy thinking, fuzzy thinking.

(BYNG holds up a shovel.)

This is a shovel. Notice that it is a spade like instrument consisting of a broad blade of metal attached to a handle and it is used for raising and removing quantities of earth. That is a shovel. A cup attached to a stick. Fuzzy thinking.

DAVID: If he says another word I am going to lose my mind.

BYNG: Do you know how to use a shovel? I said, do you know how to use a shovel?

DAVID: Yes, sir.

BYNG: Then use it. You there. What is the population of Regina?

JOHN: I have no idea.

BYNG: How do you expect to succeed in this world if you don't know things like that.

JOHN: You're right. I am going to be a complete failure.

BYNG: You there.

(ROBERT enters.)

ROBERT: Urgent message for General Byng.

(ROBERT gives BYNG a piece of paper.)

BYNG: Gentlemen. We have orders to leave Ypres.

CURRIE: Thank God. Ypres is a death trap.

BYNG: We are going to take the offensive at the Somme.

CURRIE: Excellent. Anything is better than sitting in a trench waiting for a bullet.

BYNG: Yes. Now it is approximately eighty miles from Ypres to the Somme.

CURRIE: Now let me see. Thirty inches a step, one hundred and forty steps a minute. We can be there in twenty hours.

BYNG: We leave in fifteen minutes. Dismissed.

(The SOLDIERS march out. BYNG and CURRIE march out. The lights fade. End of Act One.)

Act Two

Scene One

(The lights fade in. CURRIE and BYNG enter.)

BYNG: In thirty seconds we begin the greatest battle to be fought since the beginning of civilization.

CURRIE: Tea?

BYNG: Please, I will subject the world to my will. I am just a tool for Him. Let the battle of the Somme begin.

(Offstage: The distant thunder of cannons. The lights fade.)

Scene Two

(In another playing area the lights fade in. CURRIE and SOLDIERS TWO, FOUR, FIVE, SIX, and SEVEN enter.)

CURRIE: We're going over the top.

SOLDIERS: All right.

CURRIE: The Canadian battalions will lead the assault. We are the spearhead of the British Empire. What an honour. Company about turn.

(CURRIE looks at his watch and blows a whistle. The SOLDIERS go over the top. The lights fade.)

Scene Three

(In another playing area the lights fade in. DAVID, JOHN, and SOLDIERS TWO, FOUR, and FIVE enter. CURRIE enters holding a piece of paper.)

CURRIE: Private Adams ... Private Adams. Private Anderson.

DAVID: Here.

CURRIE: Private Applegate ... Private Applegate. Private Baker ... Private Baker. Private Barkley.

JOHN: Here.

CURRIE: Private Blackwood ... Private Blackwood.

(The lights fade. The lights fade up.)

Private Zablonsky ... Private Zablonsky. Private Zachary ... Private Zachary.

(BYNG enters.)

Company, attention. All men accounted for.

BYNG: Excellent. One more time. Over the top. And this time with feeling.

CURRIE: This is madness.

BYNG: You have your orders.

(BYNG exits.)

CURRIE: Company, at the ready.

(CURRIE blows a whistle. The lights fade.)

Scene Four

(In another playing area the lights fade in. JOHN, DAVID, and SOLDIERS TWO, SIX, and SEVEN are caught on a belt of barbed wire shouting, shrieking, moaning, and groaning.)

DAVID: Look at them, just waiting. Why don't they fire?

JOHN: They will.

(JOHN frees DAVID from the barbed wire.)

SOLDIER SEVEN: Help me, someone help me.

SOLDIER SIX: I want to go home, I want to go home.

SOLDIER TWO: I want to see my mother.

DAVID: Bastards.

(Machine gun fire. The SOLDIERS fall dead onto the barbed wire.)

I'm hit.

JOHN: It's just a graze.

(The lights fade.)

Scene Five

(In another playing area the lights fade in. CURRIE enters.)

CURRIE: All of them dead. Or wounded. Fallen like flies. The Battle of the Somme: the great fuck up.

(The lights fade.)

Scene Six

(In another playing area the lights fade in. BORDEN reads a newspaper headline: "Disaster at the Somme.")

BORDEN: This is outrageous. If I want to find out what is happening I have to read this. The editors of this paper are congenital liars. The British war office will not tell me anything. Except that they need more troops.

(The lights fade.)

Scene Seven

(In another playing area the lights fade in: Shadow play from within a tent. LLOYD GEORGE and SIR DOUGLAS HAIG discuss the war. A SENTRY enters.)

GEORGE: *(Voice over.)* You are a complete nincompoop.

HAIG: *(Voice over.)* Fool.

GEORGE: *(Voice over.)* Pillock.

HAIG: *(Voice over.)* Swine.

SENTRY: Who goes there?

VOICE ONE: *(Off.)* First Royal Marines.

SENTRY: Pass First Royal Marines. All's well.

HAIG: *(Voice over.)* Our troops are completely expendable. They will be dead next week, or the week after.

SENTRY: Who goes there?

VOICE TWO: *(Off.)* Who wants to know?

SENTRY: Pass Canadians. All's well.

HAIG: *(Voice over.)* This is a war of attrition. And the purpose of a war of attrition is to pass the time. Ah yes, passing the time. I live for war.

GEORGE: *(Voice over.)* Nincompoop.

SENTRY: Advance and be recognized.

(CURRIE enters.)

CURRIE: Lieutenant-general Arthur Currie of the First Canadian to see Sir Douglas Haig, commander of the British Expeditionary Force.

SENTRY: He is with the prime minister of Great Britain, Lloyd George, discussing the war. He is not to be disturbed.

HAIG: *(Voice over.)* If we attack we lose one hundred and fifty thousand, if we do not attack we lose fifty thousand. So we attack. What are a one hundred thousand men? You have no idea of what it is like.

GEORGE: *(Voice over.)* Neither do you? The only way we can win this war is if you command the German army otherwise there is no hope.

HAIG: *(Voice over.)* Fool. Swine.

GEORGE: *(Voice over.)* Pillock.

CURRIE: God save us from these buggers.

(The lights fade.)

Scene Eight

(In another playing area the lights fade in. SOLDIERS FOUR and SIX, carrying DAVID on a stretcher, enter. A NURSE enters.)

DAVID: The wounded were like flopping trout, flopping trout.

SOLDIER SIX: This man has been shocked out of his senses.

DAVID: You look like an angel.

NURSE: I have to take your name.

DAVID: Am I in heaven?

NURSE: No, dear boy.

DAVID: Then I have something to look forward to.

NURSE: What is your name?

DAVID: I have no idea.

NURSE: Where are you from?

(CURRIE enters.)

DAVID: No idea.

NURSE: How old are you?

DAVID: No idea.

NURSE: What battalion are you with?

DAVID: No idea.

CURRIE: He's with the Tenth. He's a private.

(The lights fade.)

Scene Nine

(In another playing area the lights fade in. ROBERT and STEPHEN enter. STEPHEN holds a package, and reads a letter. STEPHEN laughs.)

STEPHEN: Edith sends her love.

ROBERT: Right.

STEPHEN: Oh, what a woman. How thoughtful.

ROBERT: Ha.

(STEPHEN holds up a bottle of cognac.)

STEPHEN: It is ridiculous that we are not friends.

ROBERT: Friends?

STEPHEN: I mean like before.

ROBERT: Well?

STEPHEN: I propose that we let bygones be bygones. Play up, play the game. The best man won.

ROBERT: Oh really?

STEPHEN: I'm sorry, I shouldn't say that. What do you say? Like old times.

(STEPHEN offers the bottle to ROBERT.)

ROBERT: I don't drink.

STEPHEN: For a rainy day.

ROBERT: Well … why not?

STEPHEN: That's the spirit.

(STEPHEN smiles. The lights fade.)

Scene Ten

(In another playing area the lights fade in. JOHN and SOLDIER TWO push and pull a one-ton shell on a trolley.)

SOLDIER TWO: Oh it's a big gun that fires a bullet like this.

JOHN: That's right, pull.

(In another playing area the lights fade in. STEPHEN and DAVID enter.)

STEPHEN: Welcome back, Private. Glad to see you have recovered.

SOLDIER TWO: Push, push, push.

JOHN: Pull, pull, pull.

(STEPHEN wears a steel helmet.)

STEPHEN: See, you have to wear this.

DAVID: You look like a Chinaman.

JOHN: No he doesn't. He looks like a mushroom.

DAVID: I'm not wearing it.

STEPHEN: Yes you are. I know your head is bullet proof but you have to wear it. Listen.

(STEPHEN taps the helmet.)

See. Steel.

DAVID: I'm not wearing it.

STEPHEN: That's an order.

(STEPHEN gives helmet to DAVID. DAVID puts helmet on. The lights fade.)

Scene Eleven

(In another playing area the lights fade in: an artillery bombardment. DAVID, DWAYNE, and JOHN enter. They try to talk but no words are audible. In another playing area the lights fade in. ROBERT enters with a cognac bottle. He takes a drink. He spits it out. The bombardment stops.)

DAVID: I can't hear you!

JOHN: I want—!

(The bombardment begins again. The bombardment stops.)

DWAYNE: I'm from Nova Scotia.

(The lights fade.)

Scene Twelve

(In another playing area the lights fade in. DAVID and DWAYNE enter. DAVID digs a trench.)

DAVID: Just digging my grave. The Canadian army, I love it. They give you a shovel and then tell you to dig your grave. Stand in it. And wait for a bullet. Love it.

(STEPHEN and JOHN enter.)

JOHN: Why are we here?

STEPHEN: Only dullards and dolts do not understand why we are here.

JOHN: Why are we here?

STEPHEN: We're here because we're here. Do you dispute that we are here?

JOHN: No, I want to know why.

STEPHEN: We're here because we're here. Tomorrow we'll be there because we're there.

(STEPHEN exits.)

DAVID: The wisdom of our commanding officer.

JOHN: I can't believe it, I volunteered for this. I'm eighteen, I've never been with a woman, but I've killed a lot of ... It's not right. I should do it at least once before I die.

(CURRIE enters with a megaphone.)

CURRIE: All those in the reserve trench are going on leave for two days. All those in the reserve trench are going on leave for two days.

(The lights fade.)

Scene Thirteen

(In another playing area the lights fade in. DAVID and JOHN are dancing. ROBERT enters holding a cognac bottle. SOLDIER TWO sings "Mademoiselle From Armentières." Offstage: the sound of people fornicating.)

SOLDIER TWO: Mademoiselle from Armentières, parley-vous? Mademoiselle from Armentières, parley-vous? Mademoiselle from Armentières, she hasn't been kissed in forty a year, inky dinky parley-vous.

ROBERT: Listen to that.

DAVID: Hello, hello, hello. How would you like to drink some beer with me?

ROBERT: Perkins, listen to that. You see, Perkins ... isn't that beautiful? That's what love is all about.

(STEPHEN enters.)

STEPHEN: I must have words with you.

ROBERT: I did not come here to talk.

STEPHEN: I must have words with you.

ROBERT: Oh look at that.

STEPHEN: Come let's go over here. We won't be a distraction.

ROBERT: Take your hands off me.

STEPHEN: What are you doing here?

ROBERT: Look. I don't care. I go to bars. Drink Cognac. I'll dance with anybody. Even men. I don't care.

DAVID: Hello, hello, hello. How would you like to drink some beer with me?

STEPHEN: What would they say in Toronto?

ROBERT: You and that face.

(ROBERT whispers in STEPHEN's ear.)

STEPHEN: How dare you say bad things about the finest piece of womanhood—

ROBERT: That money can buy.

STEPHEN: How dare you say that? I should slap your face.

(A BELGIAN WHORE enters.)

WHORE: Next! Who's next? Soldiers, soldiers, soldiers. Oh you big brave Canadians. Why you so big and brave? I'm man crazy. Are you a man, I'm man crazy.

ROBERT: I think she means you.

WHORE: Are you big and brave?

ROBERT: He is, but I am bigger and braver. Besides he is married.

WHORE: Oh I love married men.

ROBERT: He'll give you fifty cents, I'll give you that and cognac.

(ROBERT takes out the flask of cognac.)

Look.

WHORE: Oh, they make that out of big grapes.

ROBERT: Sniff it.

STEPHEN: Disgusting.

(STEPHEN exits. CURRIE enters.)

CURRIE: Back to the front, back to the front. Now.

(The lights fade.)

Scene Fourteen

(In another playing area the lights fade in: back at the Somme. There are two signs, "Death Valley" and "Casualty Corner." DAVID and SOLDIER TWO enter. An artillery bombardment. They try to talk. No words are audible. SOLDIER TWO holds his stomach. The artillery bombardment stops.)

DAVID: I can't hear you, I can't—

SOLDIER TWO: It won't go back in.

DAVID: Let me see. Jesus.

(The artillery bombardment starts again. The lights fade.)

Scene Fifteen

VOICE: *(Off.)* Mail call!

(In another playing area the lights fade in. JOHN, DAVID, and DWAYNE enter. JOHN reads a letter. DAVID is killing lice.)

DWAYNE: Dear John, I am marrying your best friend Charlie. I thought you might like to know.

JOHN: Shut up. It's from my mother.

DWAYNE: Dear Johnnie, you're not really my son.

JOHN: Look you.

(DWAYNE holds up a postcard.)

DWAYNE: Look at this.

JOHN: Get that away from me.

DWAYNE: Look.

JOHN: That's disgusting.

DAVID: Let me have a look.

(DAVID looks at the postcard and laughs.)

JOHN: It's disgusting. It's a picture of a woman being defiled. Defiled.

DWAYNE: I got it in Paris.

DAVID: See these seam squirrels. Now what you do is, you kill the big ones first and then the little ones die of grief.

JOHN: Like hell they do.

(Offstage: yelling.)

DAVID: Trench raid. Huns!

(OTTO SCHLIPPENSCHLOPPEN and GERMAN SOLDIERS TWO and SIX enter. They bayonet DWAYNE. DAVID exits. The GERMAN SOLDIERS confront JOHN.)

OTTO: Fraulein.

(The GERMANS smile and laugh.)

JOHN: Mother.

(The lights fade.)

Scene Sixteen

(In another playing area the lights fade in. CURRIE enters.)

CURRIE: Have you ever wondered how sausages are made? Welcome to the sausage factory.

(DAVID enters.)

DAVID: We were overrun by Huns. Private MacGregor was killed and Private Perkins was captured, I think.

CURRIE: And the trench.

DAVID: They took it.

CURRIE: You let them take my trench? We must counter-attack immediately.

(The lights fade.)

Scene Seventeen

(In another playing area the lights fade in: the crucified body of JOHN. STEPHEN, DAVID, and SOLDIERS TWO and SIX enter. CURRIE enters.)

DAVID: Look at that. Son of a bitch.

STEPHEN: Crucified him.

DAVID: They left a note.

(The SOLDIERS read the note.)

The filthy swine.

SOLDIER TWO: Filthy swine.

SOLDIER SIX: Filthy swine.

STEPHEN: The filthy swine.

CURRIE: Right.

(They look at each other.)

ALL: Right.

(BYNG enters.)

BYNG: What is the count?

CURRIE: Twenty-five thousand casualties ... and counting.

BYNG: Thank God we are out of here. We have orders to move to the Arras area, to a place called Vimy.

CURRIE: Vimy.

BYNG: Yes. While we were being annihilated here, the French were being annihilated there. We have orders to take the ridge at Easter.

CURRIE: Vimy Ridge.

BYNG: Cut him down.

(BYNG exits. CURRIE salutes. STEPHEN and SOLDIERS TWO and SIX look at the ground.

DAVID sits at the feet of JOHN. Tableaux: The crucified Canadian. The lights fade.)

VOICE: *(Off.)* Company by the left.

(Sound of marching feet.)

Company halt. Fall out.

Scene Eighteen

(In another playing area the lights fade in. ROBERT and STEPHEN enter.)

ROBERT: And even though you are in the Slough of Despond, do not despair, for this is only the beginning of your sorrow. Let me drink your sweat, I am thirsty.

STEPHEN: What is the matter with you?

ROBERT: Don't you see … we're all living the Passion.

(DAVID and SOLDIER TWO enter.)

Don't you see … look at that soldier. Wearing his crown of thorns and bearing his cross and carrying his pack of sin wherever he goes. It's perfect.

STEPHEN: Look at it. Vimy Ridge.

ROBERT: A monument to Satan. Giant Despair lives there. Giant Despair.

STEPHEN: Come, we're going to meet him.

(The lights fade.)

Scene Nineteen

(In another playing area the lights fade in. ANDREW McNAUGHTON and artillery crew enter. STEPHEN holds a stop watch. SOLDIER SIX holds binoculars. SOLDIERS TWO and FIVE load the cannon and adjust the gun levers.)

McNAUGHTON: Fire.

(A deafening roar.)

Missed. Wind?

STEPHEN: Fifteen knots, north by northwest.

SOLDIER SIX: Twenty yards to the left.

McNAUGHTON: Angle.

SOLDIER FIVE: Fifty-fifteen.

McNAUGHTON: One degree elevation. Left hand down a bit. Again. Fire.

(A deafening roar.)

Wind.

STEPHEN: Fifteen knots north by northwest.

SOLDIER SIX: Target. Destroyed.

McNAUGHTON: Excellent, excellent.

(CURRIE and BYNG enter.)

CURRIE: Colonel Andrew McNaughton, Sir Julian Byng.

McNAUGHTON: Sir.

BYNG: Things are going well, I hope. We go in two weeks.

McNAUGHTON: Ready when you are, sir. We will take out all the German guns, all of them. By using my techniques of sound ranging and flash spotting in tandem with aerial reconnaissance, I am able to pinpoint within five yards each German gun.

BYNG: Yes, yes, yes. May I?

(BYNG looks through the binoculars.)

I can see German soldiers on top of the ridge. Can you see them?

(McNAUGHTON looks through the binoculars.)

McNAUGHTON: Yes. I can see them. On April ninth they are dead men.

BYNG: Very good, carry on.

CURRIE: Tell me more about this sound ranging and flash potting.

McNAUGHTON: Flash spotting.

(The lights fade.)

Scene Twenty

(In another playing area the lights fade in: a big map of Vimy Ridge. BYNG and CURRIE enter.)

BYNG: We shall attack here, here, and here.

CURRIE: Before we attack, we need reconnaissance.

BYNG: This is reconnaissance.

CURRIE: I mean intelligence.

BYNG: This will give us our intelligence.

CURRIE: Your trench raids are too large. They are costing us five hundred casualties a week.

BYNG: Are the Canadians losing their go?

CURRIE: The Canadians are not losing their go. In fact the men like trench raids. It keeps them on their toes. But before we send a thousand men into a hail of bullets we need to know where the pill boxes are, and the machine guns, and the barbed wire, so that we can avoid them or even destroy them. And we can only get this intelligence from prisoners. German prisoners. A few small groups should do it, say twelve to fifteen men per group.

BYNG: Oh very well, form your small groups, take your prisoners. And then, we shall attack here, here, and here.

(The lights fade.)

Scene Twenty-one

(In another playing area the lights fade in. SOLDIERS TWO, FOUR, and SEVEN are in the trench. Vimy Ridge is in the background. FREDERICK SCOTT, a chaplain, enters.)

SCOTT: It's a great day for Canada, boys, a great day. It's a great day for Canada, boys, a great day.

DAVID: Father, I have never been baptised.

SCOTT: You're a bastard.

DAVID: I am.

SCOTT: God be praised. Even the heathens are fighting for Christ. Let's pray.

DAVID: You pray for me.

SCOTT: No. Pray.

DAVID: Oh, very well. Oh God, when we go over the top, make sure someone else is killed, not me.

SCOTT: What kind of prayer is that?

DAVID: Oh God, give me the strength to do my duty.

SCOTT: That's more like it. Remember all women love a brave man.

DAVID: Yes. That's what I want to be. A brave man.

SCOTT: It's a great day for Canada, boys, a great day.

DAVID: I'm going to carve me a Hun.

(CURRIE enters with a megaphone.)

CURRIE: Trench raid, trench raid. We want a prisoner.

DAVID: Prisoner.

(The lights fade.)

Scene Twenty-two

(In another playing area the lights fade in. SOLDIER TWO and DAVID enter.)

SOLDIER TWO: Did you get one?

DAVID: No, I didn't.

(SOLDIER FOUR enters with a GERMAN PRISONER.)

GERMAN PRISONER: Gnade, gnade.

SOLDIER FOUR: This way. Hands down. Down! We got a prisoner.

GERMAN PRISONER: Bitte mach das nicht.

DAVID: A prisoner.

GERMAN PRISONER: Freund, Freund.

(DAVID holds up a bayonet.)

DAVID: See this Fritzie boy? Know what I'm going to do with this? I'm going to cut the top of your head off.

SOLDIER FOUR: He doesn't understand what you're saying.

DAVID: He understands what I'm saying. I'm going to cut the top of your head off.

SOLDIER TWO: None of that.

(CURRIE and STEPHEN enter.)

CURRIE: No you're not. Attention I want information out of him. Attention.

STEPHEN: Achtung.

CURRIE: Has it come to this, that soldiers of the German army no longer respect authority?

STEPHEN: Hast du kein Respekt für ein General, deutsche Soldaten?

GERMAN PRISONER: Ja, Herr Kommandant.

STEPHEN: Ist es so gekommen dass die deutschen Soldaten kein respect für Authoritat haben?

GERMAN PRISONER: Es tut mir leid, Herr Kommandant.

STEPHEN: He says he is sorry.

CURRIE: Ask him about the locations of the pillboxes, the machine gun nests and the barbed wire.

STEPHEN: Sagen uns die Niederlassung von die Pilleboxen, die Machinengewehren, und die Stracheldraht.

GERMAN PRISONER: Here ist ein plan. Machinengewehren sind hier und hier und hier.

(The lights fade.)

Scene Twenty-three

(In another playing area the lights fade in. CURRIE, BYNG, and STEPHEN are looking at a model of Vimy Ridge.)

CURRIE: This is a model of Vimy Ridge. Here are the German gun positions. Here are the trenches. The pill boxes, the barbed wire.

BYNG: Yes, yes, yes.

STEPHEN: It's like an ant hill full of Huns.

BYNG: Yes. Now. Hopefully we have learned the lessons of the Somme. What not to do.

CURRIE: Yes.

BYNG: Now, a thousand cannons will sound at dawn. Two hundred and fifty thousand artillery shells will be fired. We will use a creeping barrage. One hundred yards every three minutes.

CURRIE: Yes.

BYNG: A curtain of hot steel will protect the men. They shall go over the top like a railroad train on the exact time or they will be annihilated. If they move too quickly they will be killed by their own artillery shells. Too slowly and they will be killed by German machine guns.

CURRIE: Yes, yes, yes. We will pay the price in artillery shells, not in human lives.

BYNG: Now for the last five months we have rehearsed and practised, we have pigged together like men. And now we are ready to do it. Correct?

CURRIE: Correct. Gentlemen, shall we synchronize our watches?

STEPHEN: Yes.

BYNG: Yes.

CURRIE: Yes. In five seconds it will be 15:30 hours plus thirty seconds.

STEPHEN: I have 15:30 plus thirty-two seconds.

CURRIE: Correct it.

STEPHEN: Yes, yes, yes.

(The lights fade.)

Scene Twenty-four

(In another playing area the lights fade in. Music: Siegfried's "Funeral March." DAVID and SOLDIERS TWO, FOUR, and SIX are in the trench. STEPHEN enters.)

STEPHEN: Ten, nine, eight, seven, six, five, four, three, two, one.

(Dawn breaks.)

Now, now, now.

(The SOLDIERS go over the top. The deafening roar of a thousand cannons. The lights fade.)

Scene Twenty-five

(In another playing area the lights fade in. A German machine gun crew enters, GERMAN SOLDIERS ONE and THREE. CANADIAN SOLDIERS enter stage right and assault the machine gun crew. SOLDIERS TWO and SIX are killed. Desperate hand to hand fighting. GERMAN SOLDIERS are bayonetted. STEPHEN waves DAVID and SOLDIER FOUR forward. The lights fade.)

Scene Twenty-six

(In another playing area the lights fade in. DAVID and SOLDIER FOUR enter. SOLDIER FOUR indicates a German dugout. DAVID throws a hand grenade into the dugout. DAVID and SOLDIER FOUR celebrate. STEPHEN enters.)

STEPHEN: What the hell do you think you're doing?

SOLDIER FOUR: Just looking for souvenirs.

STEPHEN: Take those bodies over there and make a wall. You! Get over there on sentry duty. Now!

(The lights fade.)

Scene Twenty-seven

(In another playing area the lights fade in. BORDEN, LAURA, and MEIGHEN enter.)

BORDEN: A great victory, a great victory.

LAURA: The casualties, the casualties.

BORDEN: The British couldn't do it. The French couldn't do it. But the Canadians could. Dance with me.

LAURA: The casualties, the casualties.

MEIGHEN: During March and April at Vimy Ridge we sustained twenty thousand casualties, during that same period ten thousand enlisted. Two casualties for every man that enlists. There is only one solution.

LAURA: End the war.

BORDEN: No. Anything but that.

MEIGHEN: Conscription.

BORDEN: No. Anything but that.

MEIGHEN: If it goes on for a year we won't have an army.

LAURA: What kind of war is this? This is not like the Boer War.

MEIGHEN: No. This is real war.

BORDEN: How many have enlisted to date?

MEIGHEN: Five hundred thousand.

BORDEN: That was our target.

MEIGHEN: Yes, but we need more. Another one hundred thousand should do it.

BORDEN: Yes.

(The lights fade.)

Scene Twenty-eight

(In another playing area the lights fade in. DAVID enters.)

DAVID: When you're out in No-Man's Land you have no idea what you are stepping on. A piece of mud. A dead mule. A man's face. After a while, it doesn't matter. The war is awful, but it wouldn't be so bad if you could sleep. But you can't, so you can never wake up. It makes you crazy.

(DAVID smiles. The lights fade.)

Scene Twenty-nine

(In another playing area the lights fade in. BYNG and CURRIE enter.)

BYNG: Well Sir Arthur, our victory at Vimy Ridge has captured the imagination. You are now a Knight of the British Empire. My congratulations, you lucky Canuck.

CURRIE: And you are now Lord Byng of Vimy, you lucky Englishman you, sir.

BYNG: I have been promoted to command the Third Army. I shall recommend to the war office that you assume the command of the Canadian Corps.

CURRIE: Thank you, sir. The men would like you to make a speech before you go.

BYNG: No. I couldn't possibly. I should be overcome by my emotions.

CURRIE: Another time.

BYNG: Another place.

(The lights fade.)

Scene Thirty

(In another playing area the lights fade in. CURRIE, ROBERT, and SOLDIER SEVEN enter.)

ROBERT: The men are suffering from trench foot. You! Show the general what trench foot looks like.

(SOLDIER SEVEN shows his foot.)

See, a big stinky green foot with no toes.

CURRIE: How did that happen?

SOLDIER SEVEN: Standing in freezing cold, and wet all the time.

ROBERT: It's like frost bite.

SOLDIER SEVEN: It's a blighty for me.

CURRIE: Is there any cure for this?

SOLDIER SEVEN: No.

ROBERT: Whale oil. If the troops swab their feet in whale oil every twenty-four hours, that'll prevent it.

(A COURIER enters.)

CURRIE: Do it. Any man who doesn't will be court martialled.

(The COURIER gives a letter to CURRIE.)

SOLDIER SEVEN: It's a blighty for me.

ROBERT: We're going to chop off both your feet.

SOLDIER SEVEN: Good. Anything is better than this.

CURRIE: We have new orders. We are going to a place called Passchendaele.

ROBERT: Passchendaele.

(The lights fade.)

Scene Thirty-one

(In another playing area the lights fade in: a sign, "This Was Ypres." DAVID and SOLDIERS TWO and FOUR enter. DAVID holds out his hand.)

DAVID: It's going to rain.

SOLDIER TWO: Thank god.

SOLDIER FOUR: The heat is unbelievable.

DAVID: What is this place?

SOLDIER TWO: This is Passchendaele.

SOLDIER FOUR: What a beautiful name.

DAVID: I've been here before, I know it. I've been here.

SOLDIER FOUR: There's a French word for that feeling.

DAVID: Wait a minute. This is Yipes. Yipes.

SOLDIER TWO: Yipes. I'm going to die here. Shake this hand. I'm going to die.

DAVID: Yipes.

(The lights fade.)

Scene Thirty-two

(In another playing area the lights fade in. DAVID and SOLDIER TWO enter. An artillery barrage is underway. The barrage stops.)

DAVID: I can't hear you, I can't—

SOLDIER TWO: It won't go back in.

DAVID: Let me see. Jesus.

(SOLDIER FOUR enters.)

SOLDIER FOUR: Gas!

(DAVID looks at the audience. The lights fade.)

Scene Thirty-three

(In another playing area the lights fade in. BORDEN and MEIGHEN enter.)

MEIGHEN: So, Mr. Prime Minister. An election in war time on conscription. What an opportunity for a smashing victory, smashing! We must not lose, we cannot lose. What an opportunity to grind Laurier and the French into the ground, forever. We must form a union government. All the English speaking members of the Liberal party will join it. Put all the English against the French. That's for starters. Then we'll give the vote to all the female relatives of the soldiers.

BORDEN: Give women the vote?

MEIGHEN: Only in this election. We'll give the vote to the mothers, the daughters, and the wives.

BORDEN: What about the sisters?

MEIGHEN: Yes sisters too, and the cousins. Then, we'll disenfranchise all the immigrants who have arrived in this country in the last fifteen years. Then we will …

(The lights fade.)

Scene Thirty-four

(In another playing area the lights fade in: The Election Campaign. An hysterical uproar, men enter with posters. BORDEN enters.)

BORDEN: Vote union government! A vote for Laurier is a vote for the Hun. Do your duty. When the Empire calls, what do we say? Ready, aye, ready. Put the French in the trench. Vote for conscription. Vote union government!

(In another playing area the lights fade in. MEIGHEN, BORDEN, and others are celebrating.)

MEIGHEN: We took seventy-five percent of the seats in Parliament. Seventy-five percent. Now, that's what I call a victory. Now we will invoke the War Measures Act and put Quebec under martial law.

(The lights fade.)

Scene Thirty-five

(In another playing area the lights fade in. BOURASSA and ARMAND enter. ARMAND holds a poster with the words "The Nationalist League of Quebec." YVETTE and LITTLE PIERRE enter.)

BOURASSA: Conscription is the triumph of militarism under its most dangerous and stupid form. Canada has done enough. Two million French Canadians are opposed en masse to conscription. Can two million French Canadians be wrong? You cannot do this without the consent of the people.

ARMAND: If the conscription law is enforced, Canadians have only one choice. To die in

Europe or to die in Canada. I will go to jail or be hanged or shot before I accept it.

CROWD: *(Off.)* A bas Borden. Vive la révolution. A bas Borden. Vive la révolution.

BOURASSA: The French Canadians are the most Canadian of all the Canadians. We are the real Canadians. I prefer Canada to the British Empire, therefore I am the most hated man in Canada. Do I care? I don't care.

ARMAND: Fight. Resist.

BOURASSA: Agitate, agitate, agitate.

(SOLDIERS ONE and THREE enter. There is an uproar.)

VOICE: *(Off.)* Vive la révolution! A bas Borden!

SOLDIER ONE: We're taking the boy.

SOLDIER THREE: If you won't die in the trench, you'll die here.

SOLDIER ONE: We're taking the boy.

PIERRE: Non, non. Maman, je veux aller.

SOLDIER ONE: What?

YVETTE: He wants to go.

SOLDIER THREE: This way.

(The lights fade.)

Scene Thirty-six

(In another playing area the lights fade in. LAURIER, ARMAND, and BOURASSA enter.)

ARMAND: They killed four protesters and wounded over fifty. And now they're coming for me.

LAURIER: What do you plan to do?

ARMAND: Head for the hills.

(Offstage: sound of gunfire.)

LAURIER: Very good Armand.

(ARMAND exits.)

BOURASSA: And for my part, I wash my hands of politics. From this moment I will devote my life only to the interests of religion. No more politics.

LAURIER: Very good Henri, very good.

(BOURASSA exits.)

LAURIER: Le Canada, c'est finis, c'est finis.

(The lights fade.)

Scene Thirty-seven

(In another playing area the lights fade in. ROBERT and STEPHEN enter.)

STEPHEN: I woke up and I saw a black cat looking at me.

ROBERT: Are you superstitious?

STEPHEN: Black cat.

ROBERT: Maybe it was a rat.

STEPHEN: Black cat.

ROBERT: A cat. Well it must have been as big as a tiger 'cause the rats are like this.

STEPHEN: Black cat.

ROBERT: Well you're a tender plant.

STEPHEN: What are those red lights?

ROBERT: Those aren't lights. They're rats' eyes.

STEPHEN: Rats' eyes. Always looking at you.

(A rat walks across the top of the trench.)

ROBERT: Look at the size of that one? How many soldiers do you think he's eaten.

STEPHEN: Rats' eyes.

(The lights fade.)

Scene Thirty-eight

(In another playing area the lights fade in. SOLDIERS TWO and FOUR enter. They swab each other's feet.)

SOLDIER TWO: All right, now you do me.

(DAVID enters covered in caked mud.)

I know where you been.

DAVID: No-Man's Land. I'm a walking talking shit-stick now. The mud. It's like brown glue. Take a step and you're in up to your knee. Take another step and you're up to your nuts in it. It's like a sea of mud. And walking those bloody planks. If you fall into a shell hole you're a dead man. Drown in the mud and the blood. It's unbelievable attacking with our ladders. Put the ladder down, then run across it, pick it up and put it down and run across. Certain death.

SOLDIER TWO: Yeah.

(The lights fade.)

Scene Thirty-nine

(In another playing area the lights fade in. STEPHEN is being eaten by rats. The lights fade.)

Scene Forty

(In another playing area the lights fade in. STEPHEN wakes from a nightmare.)

STEPHEN: No.

(ROBERT enters.)

ROBERT: Anything wrong?

STEPHEN: No.

ROBERT: Having the nightmare again?

STEPHEN: Yes.

ROBERT: Well now that you're up you may as well stay up. We go over the top in an hour. For king and what not. Once more into the mud. Why not?

STEPHEN: Yes.

(The lights fade.)

Scene Forty-one

(Darkness. Mutterings and curses are heard. A flare. STEPHEN and SOLDIERS ONE, THREE, and FOUR are revealed. They are up to their knees in mud.)

STEPHEN: Forward.

SOLDIER ONE: I'm stuck.

SOLDIER THREE: I can't move.

SOLDIER FOUR: Neither can I.

STEPHEN: Oh my God.

(Sound of machine gun fire. STEPHEN and the SOLDIERS fall. The lights fade.)

Scene Forty-two

(In another playing area the lights fade in. ROBERT enters.)

ROBERT: Where is he? … It's been more than a hour … oh.

(DAVID enters.)

DAVID: We found Captain Ramsay.

ROBERT: Thank Christ that lives in a tree. He's alive.

DAVID: Yes, but …

ROBERT: But what … but what … but what?

DAVID: He has no face.

(The lights fade.)

Scene Forty-three

(In another playing area the lights fade in. A NURSE, STEPHEN, and TWO PATIENTS enter. STEPHEN's face is bandaged like the Invisible Man. ROBERT enters.)

ROBERT: Stephen.

NURSE: You're all going home, back to Canada.

PATIENT ONE: Yes, but I'm finished as a man.

ROBERT: Stephen.

PATIENT TWO: Whose hand has been familiar with my privates? That's what I want to know.

ROBERT: Stephen.

STEPHEN: Robert.

ROBERT: Oh Stephen, it's so good to see you.

STEPHEN: It's good to see you.

ROBERT: How are you?

STEPHEN: I'm fine. I'm glad you asked.

ROBERT: The Canadians have taken Passchendaele.

STEPHEN: That's good, that makes me real happy.

ROBERT: I'm a captain now.

STEPHEN: That's good, that makes me real happy.

ROBERT: I brought you this.

(ROBERT holds up a bottle of cognac.)

STEPHEN: I don't want it.

ROBERT: You say no to cognac, you say no to life.

NURSE: Your friend will have to leave now.

STEPHEN: Why?

NURSE: We're going to take your bandages off.

(The lights fade.)

Scene Forty-four

(In another playing area the lights fade in. DAVID and a YANK enter. ROBERT enters and drinks from the cognac bottle.)

YANK: The Yanks have arrived, let's celebrate. Over there, over there. Send the word, send the word. Over there, that the Yanks are coming, the Yanks are coming.

DAVID: You know, there's a Canadian version of that song.

YANK: No there isn't.

DAVID: Yes there is.

YANK: No there isn't.

DAVID: Yes there is.

YANK: Let's hear it.

(YANK plays the piano.)

DAVID: They're coming over, they're coming over, and they won't get there till it's over, over there, but the Yanks are coming.

YANK: No. That's not how it goes.

DAVID: Yes it does.

YANK: No it doesn't.

DAVID: Yes.

YANK: No.

(They fight.)

ROBERT: Play up, play up, and play the game.

(ROBERT drinks. The lights fade.)

Scene Forty-five

(In another playing area the lights fade in. BORDEN and LAURA enter. They read letters.)

BORDEN: Who are these people? This one cannot even write a sentence.

LAURA: Conscription is not popular.

BORDEN: Here's another one. It begins "All bastards must die." And then it describes in intimate detail what he would do to my body with a small knife. Why a small knife? Why not a large knife?

LAURA: Here's one. It begins "Death to imperial swine."

BORDEN: It should be "imperialist swine."

LAURA: Yes it should. It says "I'm mighty handy with an axe and I've gutted a lot of pigs in my time so when I get hold of a big tusker like you I'll know what to do. I'll make a sausage out of you."

BORDEN: Who are these people? Here's one.

(The lights fade.)

Scene Forty-six

(In another playing area the lights fade in. CURRIE and ROBERT enter.)

CURRIE: Russia has collapsed. All German troops on the eastern front are now on the western front. The German offensive has pushed the British Expeditionary Force back fifty miles. We are going to spearhead the counter-attack at Amiens. We will have the usual artillery fire for a shield plus a new weapon. The tank.

(The lights fade.)

Scene Forty-seven

(In another playing area the lights fade in. STEPHEN and EDITH enter. STEPHEN has a handkerchief taped to his face. His eyes and mouth are visible.)

EDITH: You're home. Oh I am so happy, I don't want to think. It is so good to see you.

STEPHEN: It is so good to see you.

EDITH: My hero.

(The lights fade.)

Scene Forty-eight

(In another playing area the lights fade in: assault on the Hindenburg Line. There is a deafening roar. A tank enters stage right. It moves across the stage. It exits stage left. CURRIE, ROBERT, DAVID, and SOLDIERS ONE and FOUR follow the tank. The lights fade.)

Scene Forty-nine

(In another playing area the lights fade in. A wounded German officer, OTTO, enters. DAVID and CURRIE enter. ROBERT and SOLDIERS ONE and FOUR enter.)

DAVID: Here he is.

CURRIE: Amiens is ours.

OTTO: You are the officer commanding?

CURRIE: I am.

OTTO: I am Colonel Otto Schlippenschloppen, Prussian Guards. They are all gone. They knew the Canadians were coming and they left me here. German army ran from brave Canadians and left me here bleeding.

CURRIE: Send two platoons into the village and stay alert.

(ROBERT and SOLDIERS ONE and FOUR exit.)

Are your wounds serious? Perhaps I can help?

OTTO: No. I once visited your country. I caught many trout at Banff.

(Offstage: sound of machine gun fire and screams. ROBERT enters.)

DAVID: A trap, we walked into a massacre.

OTTO: Deutschewitz, deutschewitz.

CURRIE: Send the tank in.

ROBERT: Tank forward.

(The tank enters.)

CURRIE: Shoot that dog.

OTTO: Deutschland.

(DAVID shoots OTTO.)

DAVID: Goodnight, Hun.

(The lights fade.)

Scene Fifty

(In another playing area the lights fade in. CURRIE enters.)

CURRIE: Great victory for the B.E.F. Great victory for Britain. This is outrageous. British troops did not take Amiens. The Canadians did. But nowhere in this article does it say the word Canadian, and this is a Canadian newspaper. Never Canadian troops. It's always British forces supported by Dominion troops or Empire troops. We're not Empire troops. We're Canadians. This is outrageous.

(The lights fade.)

Scene Fifty-one

(In another playing area the lights fade in. STEPHEN and EDITH enter. There is the sound of birds singing.)

EDITH: More victories, more victories.

STEPHEN: Always victories in the newspapers, Edith.

EDITH: Yes, hon.

STEPHEN: Don't call me that.

EDITH: There are larks here. Larks.

(STEPHEN takes out a revolver and shoots a bird. Offstage a bird falls to the ground. EDITH and STEPHEN watch the bird fall.)

Would you like some potatoes? I mashed them.

STEPHEN: Yes.

EDITH: Stephen. It's going to be just like it used to be.

STEPHEN: Yes.

(The lights fade.)

Scene Fifty-two

(In another playing area the lights fade in. CURRIE and ROBERT enter.)

ROBERT: The men are taking a terrible shellacking. Terrible.

CURRIE: That's the way I like to see my soldiers. All mud and blood.

(DAVID enters.)

DAVID: They are surrendering in the thousands. The Germans are surrendering in the thousands.

CURRIE: They have lost the will to fight. They have lost the will to fight. On to Mons.

ROBERT: Does that mean you want us to go forward?

CURRIE: Does my bum get bigger everyday?

ROBERT: Forward.

(The lights fade.)

Scene Fifty-three

(In another playing area the lights fade in. STEPHEN enters with a revolver.)

EDITH: *(Off.)* Hon, hon, the news is wonderful. The Canadians have taken Mons. Hon, hon.

STEPHEN: Don't call me that.

(STEPHEN pulls the trigger.)

EDITH: *(Off.)* Hon.

(The lights fade.)

Scene Fifty-four

(In another playing area the lights fade in. BORDEN and a DOCTOR enter.)

BORDEN: We have eight percent of the entire population of this country in the trench. Can they ask for more? The British Empire asks for more. Always want more. Ready, aye, ready. Curse the phrase.

DOCTOR: There is nothing medically wrong with you, Mr. Prime Minister.

BORDEN: Boils, welts. I feel like a wart with a scab on it.

(A SERVANT enters.)

SERVANT: Telegram for the prime minister.

BORDEN: Read it to me.

SERVANT: The government of Germany is negotiating the terms of an armistice.

BORDEN: What?

SERVANT: The government of Germany is negotiating the terms of an armistice.

BORDEN: Give it here.

(BORDEN grabs the telegram.)

The government of Germany is negotiating the terms of an armistice.

(The lights fade.)

Scene Fifty-five

(In another playing area the lights fade in. ROBERT and DAVID enter. ROBERT looks at his watch. CURRIE enters.)

CURRIE: Mons is ours. Here August 1914, the British Expeditionary Force suffered it's first defeat of the Great War. And now on November eleventh, 1918, Mons is regained by the Canadian Expeditionary Force. The armies of Britain are redeemed. We'll see how they write that one up. At eleven a.m., the war is over. I do not drink, but tonight we will have champagne. Time.

ROBERT: 10:59 a.m. All quiet on the western front.

CURRIE: Listen to that silence.

(CURRIE exits.)

DAVID: When the war is over, I am going to go back to Moosomin and raise little bunny rabbits and give them all the carrots they can eat. Raise little kind nice creatures that don't hurt anybody. That's what I'm going to do.

(SOLDIER FOUR enters.)

SOLDIER FOUR: Look, a little German boy, looks like he's fifteen years old.

DAVID: Where?

SOLDIER FOUR: There.

(DAVID fires his rifle.)

DAVID: Won't be sixteen. Have no fear the God of War is here.

(A shot is heard.)

Son of a bitch. If anyone is going to fire the last shot in the Great War, it's me. Take your time, change your shot. Take your time, make your shot.

(DAVID fires his rifle.)

ROBERT: Five ... four ... three ... two ... one. The war is over.

ALL: The war is over!

(A shot is heard. DAVID falls to the ground.)

ROBERT: He's dead.

(In another playing area the lights fade in. CURRIE and BYNG enter.)

BYNG: The British Empire has won the Great War. Well done, brave Empire troops, well done.

CURRIE: Mons is ours.

BYNG: Yes. Truly excellent. The British army will take the salute. We are going on parade. Colonials in the rear.

CURRIE: Very good.

(BYNG exits.)

ROBERT: The river of death has brimmed his banks, and England's far, and Honour a name.

CURRIE: Bloody bull, is what I say. Bloody bull.

ROBERT: But the voice of a schoolboy rallies the ranks "Play up! Play up! and play the game!"

CURRIE: Bloody bull.

(The lights fade.)

Scene Fifty-six

(In another playing area the lights fade in. BORDEN and LAURA enter playing golf.)

BORDEN: You know, old girl.

LAURA: Yes, little boy.

BORDEN: In the Great War Canada suffered fifty-nine thousand dead and almost one hundred and seventy thousand wounded, and the British army would not let the Canadian Expeditionary Force take the salute at the end of the war.

LAURA: Yes, little boy.

BORDEN: I am beginning to feel more and more that in the end, and perhaps sooner than later, Canada must assume full sovereignty.

LAURA: Yes, little boy.

BORDEN: I feel like I must resign or die.

LAURA: Yes, little boy.

BORDEN: Now that the war is over Canada will take it's place among the League of Nations. I will see to that personally.

LAURA: Yes, little boy.

(The lights fade. The end.)

THE LIFE AND TIMES OF MACKENZIE KING

PART SEVEN OF THE HISTORY OF THE VILLAGE OF THE SMALL HUTS

Act One

Scene One

(The lights fade in. A GARGOYLE is guarding a gravestone with the words "Isabel Grace Mackenzie King. Born 1843. Died 1917." MACKENZIE KING enters holding a wreath. He places the wreath at the gravestone.)

KING: *(Voice over.)* Mother died today. Now I am alone. But I am not alone. Oh no. Oh Mother.

(KING smiles. The GARGOYLE comes to life. The lights fade.)

Scene Two

(In another playing area the lights fade in. MOLLY enters dressed as a munitions worker. She reads a telegram.)

MOLLY: *(Voice over.)* Dear Mrs. Macpherson, We regret to inform you that Private John Macpherson was killed in action at Amiens, France on August 8th, 1918.

(MOLLY looks up from the telegram. The sound of a factory whistle. The lights fade.)

Scene Three

(In another playing area the lights fade in. VINCE and JOE, soldiers at the western front, enter. SERGEANT COPPING enters.)

COPPING: One of these days I'm going to ream you out and rub your nose in it.

VINCE: And one of these days when the war is over, I'm going to meet you and you're not going to have those stripes on your arm.

COPPING: Is that a threat, or a promise?

JOE: They say the armistice is going to be signed on November 11th at 11 a.m.

VINCE: They say, they say.

JOE: Look, a little German boy. He looks like he's only fifteen years old.

VINCE: Where?

JOE: There.

(VINCE aims and fires his rifle.)

VINCE: He won't be sixteen.

(COLONEL THOMPSON enters.)

COPPING: Colonel Thompson. Stand to.

THOMPSON: Boys, men I should say. The war is over.

(The soldiers cheer.)

JOE: I'm alive.

(COPPING and VINCE look at each other. The lights fade.)

Scene Four

(In another playing area the lights fade in. ROBERT BORDEN and ARTHUR MEIGHEN enter.)

BORDEN: The Great War to end all wars is over. The world is now a happy place. The troops are coming home. Now it is back to normal.

MEIGHEN: Three cheers for Prime Minister Sir Robert Borden.

BORDEN: Mr. Meighen, we must be modest in our jubilation.

MEIGHEN: Oh such modesty. Three cheers and a tiger for the prime minister.

BORDEN: Mr. Meighen, really. Such exuberance. I am going to go to France to negotiate the terms of surrender at the Versailles Peace Conference. You, Mr. Meighen will become the acting prime minister.

(BORDEN exits.)

MEIGHEN: At last. I am in charge.

(The lights fade.)

Scene Five

(In another playing area the lights fade in. KING enters. KING looks at a portrait of his mother.)

KING: I was always an "A" student, always. U of T, University of Chicago, Harvard. Always an "A", always. Wasn't I? Oh Mother, what am I going to do? You used to tell me.

I can work for John D. Rockefeller or Andrew Carnegie. What does it mean? I hear you. It means I am Mr. Establishment. Tell Granddad, I made it. But the primrose path does not lead to greatness, great wealth, yes, but not greatness. I am a tool of divine providence. My mission is to be prime minister. The work of my grandfather continues. I hear you. I hear you. I hear you.

(The lights fade.)

Scene Six

(In another playing area the lights fade in. MOLLY and ALFRED ANDREWS enter. MOLLY holds a pink slip.)

MOLLY: But Mr. Andrews—

ANDREWS: I'm sorry, Miss, but we have to let you go. The men are returning from the war and they will want jobs.

MOLLY: But—

ANDREWS: No buts. A woman's place is in the home. You'll find another man.

MOLLY: But—

ANDREWS: This way. Next.

(The sound of a factory whistle. The lights fade.)

Scene Seven

(In another playing area the lights fade in. ROBERT RUSSELL, FRED DIXON, and FRANK ZANETH enter. They hold placards with the words "An 8 hour day.")

RUSSELL: Over the last five years the cost of living has increased by eighty percent, but our wages only by eighteen percent.

DIXON and ZANETH: One big union.

DIXON: Work and starve, or strike for a living wage. That is the issue.

ZANETH and RUSSELL: O.B.U.

ZANETH: During the Great War the government demanded sacrifice. The war is over. The sacrifice continues. Except for the profiteers.

RUSSELL and DIXON: One big union!!

RUSSELL: We want to organize by industry not by craft.

DIXON and ZANETH: O.B.U.

DIXON: We want to live in a worker's paradise.

ZANETH and RUSSELL: O.B.U.

ZANETH: The capitalist bastards who run this place think workers are the biggest joke in the world.

RUSSELL and DIXON: O.B.U.

DIXON: All the capitalists stick together, well all the workers are going to stick together.

ZANETH and RUSSELL: O.B.U.

RUSSELL: Injustice to one is injustice to all. All for one and one for all.

DIXON and ZANETH: O.B.U. O.B.U. O.B.U.

(The lights fade.)

Scene Eight

(In another playing area the lights fade in. KING and MRS BLEANEY, a fortune-teller, enter.)

MRS BLEANEY: When the small depart, the great approach.

KING: What does that mean? Tell me more, the rest of it. Speak. Out with it.

MRS BLEANEY: When Laurier dies, you will have the prize. When Laurier dies, you will have the prize. It is the design of the creator …

KING: Design of the creator. If that does not mean destiny then I know not the meaning of the word.

MRS BLEANEY: … that you will be prime minister.

KING: I knew it, I knew it. The destiny of my grandfather is mine.

MRS BLEANEY: Yes.

(MRS BLEANEY laughs.)

KING: But how can I be sure? How do you know this?

MRS BLEANEY: Mother knows, mother knows, mother knows.

KING: Mother.

(The lights fade.)

Scene Nine

(In another playing area the lights fade in. VINCE and JOE enter.)

VINCE: Oh Winnipeg, good to be back.

JOE: The trains they come, the trains they go, but I go on forever.

VINCE: Well first things first. The first thing I'm going to do, get a drink, then a job.

(RUSSELL enters.)

RUSSELL: You'll get neither, welcome back.

VINCE: I got a chest full of medals.

RUSSELL: There's a pawn shop over there. It's against the law to have a beer!!

JOE: What kind of crap hole is this place?

RUSSELL: It's Prohibition.

(SID enters holding a brown bag.)

SID: Hey, soldier. You want to buy some hooch? This is real whisky, the genuine article. Real firewater, guaranteed to take the top of your head off. Want a shot?

(SID gives the bag to JOE. JOE takes a drink.)

Now is that smooth or is that smooth?

VINCE: What the hell is this? This is poison. This is rot gut.

SID: It's Prohibition, best you'll get. You can't drink in this country. Where you been?

VINCE: Here, ram it.

SID: You ever change your mind you come see me at the Blind Owl. Hey, soldier.

(SID exits. The lights fade.)

Scene Ten

(In another playing area the lights fade in. The GARGOYLE enters.)

GARGOYLE: Who's the prettiest girl in the world? Who's the prettiest girl in the world?

(MOTHER enters.)

MOTHER: Oh Willie, Willie, Wee Willie. I'm alive, I'm alive, I'm alive! I'm alive Willie Boy, I'm alive!!

(Blackout. In another playing area the lights fade in. KING is revealed waking from a nightmare.)

KING: No!

(The lights fade.)

Scene Eleven

(In another playing area the lights fade in. ZANETH is addressing SID, RUSSELL, VINCE, and JOE.)

ZANETH: Comrades. The capitalist system cannot be reconstructed or reformed for the benefit of the workers, therefore it must be destroyed. Capitalism is exploitation. You cannot reform exploitation. Exploitation is exploitation. Truth! Oh Truth!! Here read this. Read this, read this.

(ZANETH hands out pamphlets.)

VINCE: You shouldn't be reading that.

ZANETH: It's a free country. Isn't it? Here read this. Comrades, listen to this.

(ZANETH exits.)

VINCE: Bloody communist. Winnipeg is very different.

JOE: Very.

(The lights fade.)

Scene Twelve

(In another playing area the lights fade in. SIR WILFRID LAURIER enters.)

LAURIER: I am Sir Wilfrid Laurier. I am very old and very tired. Le Canada, c'est finis. Et moi aussi, c'est finis.

(LAURIER gasps and then dies. KING is revealed standing behind LAURIER.)

KING: I am a man of Destiny. God wills it. So be it.

(The lights fade.)

Scene Thirteen

(In another playing area the lights fade in. MOLLY enters. She looks at mannequins. SID enters.)

SID: You like that dress?

MOLLY: Yes.

SID: Bet you look real nice in a dress like that.

MOLLY: Yes.

SID: When's the last time you ate a meal?

MOLLY: Are you a nice man?

SID: Am I a nice man, she says. What's your name?

MOLLY: Molly.

(The lights fade.)

Scene Fourteen

(In another playing area the lights fade in. KING enters.)

KING: If it be the work of men it will come to naught. But if it be the work of God it cannot be overthrown.

(MEN TWO and SIX enter carrying a coffin.)

The pallbearers are all candidates for the leadership. They carry Laurier to the grave. They all betrayed him in 1917, all of them. But I did not. I was loyal. I will assist the inevitable in the right direction.

(The lights fade.)

Scene Fifteen

(In another playing area the lights fade in. SID and a CROOKED COP enter.)

SID: Now, this is the marked money.

CROOKED COP: That's the marked money.

SID: All right, now I'll slip it into her purse. And then you arrest her for prostitution. She's a good girl, she won't know whether to shit or go blind. Now don't take her to the station, get her to call me.

CROOKED COP: And then you come in like a white knight and persuade me not to arrest her and you're a hero.

SID: That's right, you got it.

CROOKED COP: You must really want her bad.

SID: I love her.

CROOKED COP: I can't imagine what you would do if you hated her.

SID: If I hate somebody you don't want to know what I do.

(SID gives the CROOKED COP an envelope.)

Here.

CROOKED COP: All donations greatly appreciated.

(The lights fade.)

Scene Sixteen

(In another playing area the lights fade in. MOLLY and SID enter.)

MOLLY: I'm not a prostitute.

SID: I know.

MOLLY: And that police officer is crazy.

SID: Some of these cops are just a pest.

MOLLY: And he pulled that money out of my purse. I don't know how it got there. You have to believe me.

SID: I do. Don't worry about it. I worked it out, I got connections. C'mon, we're out of here. Pretend it didn't happen. Here.

(SID holds up a ring.)

MOLLY: A diamond.

SID: As big as the Rockies.

(MOLLY puts her head on SID's shoulder.)

MOLLY: Oh Sid.

(SID smiles. The lights fade.)

Scene Seventeen

(In another playing area the lights fade in. JAMES SHAVER WOODSWORTH enters.)

WOODSWORTH: I preach the Social Gospel, or my name is not James Shaver Woodsworth. Capitalism was invented by Satan to exploit and enslave humanity. Work and wages. The philosophy of slavery. Believe in socialism and you will receive pie in the sky when you die, and a better life now.

I preach the Social Gospel. Yes I do. There are two kinds of men in this world. Men who have and men who have not. In Canada there are those who produce everything and possess nothing, and those who produce nothing and possess everything. There are those who live and do not work, and those who work and do not live. This must change. Profits or human welfare. Which shall prevail?

(The lights fade.)

Scene Eighteen

(In another playing area the lights fade in. SID and MOLLY enter. MOLLY is dressed as a flapper.)

SID: You look real nice in that dress, real nice. Look at this. That's called money. I'll buy you anything you want. Clothes, food, you name it, you got it. Treat you like a queen. Like a queen. And you're going to treat me like a king. Right? Right? Right?

MOLLY: Yes.

(The lights fade.)

Scene Nineteen

(In another playing area the lights fade in: The Winnipeg Trades and Labour Council. ZANETH and RUSSELL enter.)

ZANETH: Comrade Robert Russell will now speak.

RUSSELL: Thank you, Comrade Zaneth. Anyone who calls me by my Christian slave name will die. I have no name, I am comrade. You! What is my name?

ZANETH: Comrade will speak.

RUSSELL: The capitalists that run this country like a private company will not recognize the concept of collective bargaining. Therefore we have taken a poll of our membership with regard to their willingness to engage in a general sympathetic strike. The results of our poll are twenty to one for a general strike.

ZANETH: Is that decisive or is that decisive?

RUSSELL: I hereby call a general strike for May 15th, 1919.

ZANETH and RUSSELL: O.B.U. O.B.U. O.B.U.

(The lights fade.)

Scene Twenty

(In another playing area the lights fade in. ANDREWS enters.)

ANDREWS: Everything is closed. Everyone is on strike. Union and non-union. Thirty-five thousand workers are on strike. No mail, no streetcars, no taxis, no newspapers, no telegrams, no telephones, no janitor service, no elevators, no barbers, no gasoline, no milk, no bread, no meat, no nothing! Winnipeg is on strike.

(The lights fade.)

Scene Twenty-one

(In another playing area the lights fade in. RUSSELL, VINCE, and JOE enter.)

RUSSELL: Great War veterans. Support the Winnipeg General Strike. This strike is a peaceful protest against low wages and the obstinate rejection of collective bargaining. Now, the police have voted to go on strike but we request that they stay on the job to prevent disorder. The bread delivery and milkmen have voted to go on strike but we request that they maintain their deliveries. We want to inconvenience the public not starve invalids and infants. That means the Strike Committee has decided to keep men at work. These "Special Permit" cards give assurance that the operators are not scabbing on the strikers, but are acting in co-operation with them. There will be no parades or mass demonstrations. We want no public disturbances. If public disturbances occur the strike will be broken by force. We know that. We must stand firm for the sake of labour elsewhere. Our demands are just and cannot be denied.

(THOMPSON enters.)

THOMPSON: Boys, men I should say. Don't support the strikers. Support the Citizens Committee of One Thousand. Now men, I was your commanding officer in the trenches of Flanders and France.

VINCE: But you're not our commanding officer now, are you, scab?

JOE: You were scabby in France and you're still scabby. We're clean, clean, clean.

VINCE: Scab, scab!

JOE: Scabby, you're scabby, you're still scabby.

VINCE: We're with the strikers.

(VINCE and JOE throw THOMPSON out.)

JOE: I'm tired of pricks saying "Do this, do that. You can't do this, you can't do that. Now we're going to bleed you, now we're going to starve you, now we're going to fuck you." I'm tired of the pricks. Tired! And I come back to Winnipeg and the place is crawling with the pricks. Crawling with the magotty-fagotty, I hate them. I'm with the workers. I don't give a damn.

VINCE: Right.

(ZANETH and RUSSELL enter.)

RUSSELL: Great War veterans, support the general strike.

ZANETH: Let's talk about something important.

VINCE: Such as?

ZANETH: The violent overthrow of this government.

(An INFORMER enters.)

INFORMER: O.B.U. O.B.U. O.B.U. I am with the Industrial Workers of the World, the IWW.

ZANETH: Let's see if you know the IWW handshake.

(ZANETH and the INFORMER shake hands.)

That's the IWW handshake alright. Let's see your card.

(The INFORMER holds up a red card.)

That's the IWW card all right. How long you been with the IWW?

RUSSELL: Who is Eugene Debs?

INFORMER: Who?

RUSSELL: Eugene Debs.

INFORMER: You got me, who is he?

RUSSELL: He's the founder of the IWW, you fool.

INFORMER: Workers of the world unite.

RUSSELL: Out.

INFORMER: O ... B ... U.

ZANETH: Out.

(The INFORMER exits.)

RUSSELL: Bloody informers.

ZANETH: Bloody informers.

(The lights fade.)

Scene Twenty-two

(In another playing area the lights fade in. MEIGHEN and ANDREWS enter.)

ANDREWS: Thousands of veterans from the Great War are in Winnipeg, and they're all socialists.

MEIGHEN: This is not a strike. This is a revolution. These strikers are a seditious conspiracy.

ANDREWS: What arguments shall we use against them?

MEIGHEN: Arguments? Why argue when you can wave the flag?

ANDREWS: Right. When you have nothing to say, shout.

MEIGHEN: Exactly. Are the police reliable?

ANDREWS: They are not on strike.

MEIGHEN: But would they go on strike, or more to the point, would they suppress a strike?

ANDREWS: I don't think so. They are union men.

MEIGHEN: Union men. Then they must be dismissed. Then we must form "Special Police." Men whose only loyalty is to this government and constituted authority.

ANDREWS: In other words, goons.

MEIGHEN: Yes. Goons.

(The lights fade.)

Scene Twenty-three

VINCE: *(Off.)* Are we downhearted?

STRIKERS: *(Off.)* No.

(In another playing area the lights fade in. VINCE, JOE, JUDY, ZANETH, and STRIKER ONE enter holding placards.)

Down with profiteers! Deport all capitalists! We are thirty-five thousand against one thousand! We fought the Hun over there! We fight the Hun everywhere!

VINCE: Are we downhearted?

JOE: No.

VINCE: The Citizens Committee of One Thousand is hiding behind the flag.

JOE: The citizens committee of a thousand boodlers more like it.

VINCE: The profiteers.

JOE: The bastards.

VINCE: Are we downhearted?

JOE: No.

(COPPING and GOONS TWO and EIGHT enters carrying clubs. They wear armbands that read "Special Police.")

COPPING: Fee Fi Fo Fum. I was born of woman's bum. Fee Fi Fo Fum. I was born of woman's bum.

STRIKERS: Goons!

(GOONS and STRIKERS fight during which VINCE and COPPING fight.)

VINCE: Look who it is.

COPPING: Still got my stripes.

VINCE: But you haven't got the army, so those stripes won't help you.

(VINCE knocks COPPING to the ground.)

Here, lets see how you like it.

(VINCE beats COPPING with a club. ZANETH hits VINCE with a placard. ZANETH exits. VINCE recovers from his beating.)

How do you like it?

(VINCE beats COPPING.)

JUDY: Are you hurt?

JOE: No.

JUDY: Come with me, we fix you up.

(The lights fade.)

Scene Twenty-four

(In another playing area the lights fade in. MEIGHEN and ANDREWS enter.)

MEIGHEN: These bolshevik bohunks, these scurrilous dogs, these scabrous hounds. We should deport them.

ANDREWS: They are Canadian citizens.

MEIGHEN: So what?! We will amend the Immigration Act. As it stands, anyone who is not a Canadian citizen and who commits a seditious offence can be deported. We will amend the act to read "any person who commits a seditious offence can be deported." Then citizenship would not mean anything. Then we could deport anybody.

ANDREWS: What about the ones born here?

MEIGHEN: Yes, them. Something special for them. Prison is too good for them. Something truly vile. But first things first. We will amend the act and have the Northwest Mounted Police arrest all the strike leaders.

(The lights fade.)

Scene Twenty-five

(In another playing area the lights fade in. RUSSELL, JOE, and JUDY enter. They stamp pamphlets. The sound of three knocks on the door.)

JOE: Are you expecting anyone?

RUSSELL: It's three o'clock in the morning. Who could it be?

(The sound of three knocks on the door.)

Who is it?

(The sound of a door being broken down.)

Out! Out the back way, that way.

(JOE and JUDY exit. MOUNTIE ONE and ZANETH enter with guns drawn.)

MOUNTIE ONE: You are charged with conspiracy to bring into hatred and contempt the government of Canada and promoting a Soviet system of government.

RUSSELL: What?

ZANETH: I charge you with seditious conspiracy.

RUSSELL: Why?

(ZANETH reveals himself as a Northwest Mounted Police officer.)

You!

ZANETH: That man is a communist.

RUSSELL: You informer, you turncoat.

MOUNTIE ONE: This way.

(MOUNTIE ONE and RUSSELL exit. MEIGHEN enters.)

ZANETH: We've arrested Robert Russell the leader of the strike.

MEIGHEN: Excellent, Commander Zaneth. Now get the telegraph offices open and get the streetcars running.

(The lights fade.)

Scene Twenty-six

(In another playing area the lights fade in. JOE and JUDY wake VINCE from a sound sleep.)

JOE: Vince, wake up. They've arrested Russell and the other strike leaders.

VINCE: What?

JOE: They've put them in Stony Mountain Prison.

VINCE: That's bullshit.

JOE: And the mayor has read the Riot Act and banned noisy demonstrations and parades.

VINCE: He has, has he? Then we will protest the arrest of the strike leaders by having a silent parade.

(The lights fade.)

Scene Twenty-seven

(In another playing area the lights fade in: The Silent Parade, June 21, 1991. VINCE, JOE, JUDY, and WOODSWORTH enter. They parade across the stage in complete silence. The clip-clop of horses' hooves is heard

MOUNTIES ONE and SEVEN enter on horseback holding clubs and baseball bats. They charge into the parade swinging their clubs. VINCE and JOE chase MOUNTIE ONE away. MOUNTIE SEVEN is unhorsed and disarmed of his club. JOE holds MOUNTIE SEVEN, while VINCE hits him on the head with his own club.)

VINCE: Here, how do you like it?

(VINCE beats up MOUNTIE SEVEN. There is a cheer. A streetcar enters. The streetcar DRIVER rings his bell.)

DRIVER: Move, or I will run you down.

VINCE and JOE: Right!

(VINCE and JOE and other STRIKERS overturn the streetcar. The STRIKERS cheer. MOUNTIE ONE and ZANETH enter with revolvers drawn. They shoot the strikers. Panic, screams, and shouts. VINCE, JOE, and JUDY exit.)

WOODSWORTH: Woe unto them, woe unto them.

ZANETH: No. Woe unto you. I arrest you for seditious libel.

WOODSWORTH: Oh woe unto you. If the prophet Isaiah were alive he would be prosecuted for seditious conspiracy and he only wanted to build the new Jerusalem.

MOUNTIE ONE: This way.

(WOODSWORTH and MOUNTIE ONE exit.)

ZANETH: Now, call in the army! Winnipeg is now under martial law.

(The lights fade.)

Scene Twenty-eight

(In another playing area the lights fade in. VINCE and JOE enter.)

VINCE: How's Judy?

JOE: When she gets out of the hospital I'm going to marry that girl.

(A SOLDIER and a tank enter, patrolling.)

SOLDIER: You there. I'm going to deprive you of all your civil rights.

VINCE: I spent four years fighting the Hun, only to find out the Hun runs Canada.

SOLDIER: You there. I'm going to deprive you of all your civil rights.

JOE: Thanks.

VINCE: God, I need a drink. And I know where to get one. The Blind Owl.

SOLDIER: You there. I'm going to deprive you of all your civil rights.

(The lights fade.)

Scene Twenty-nine

(In another playing area the lights fade in: The Blind Owl. SAM BRONFMAN, MOLLY, and a Chicago GANGSTER enter. The GANGSTER holds a Chicago newspaper.)

BRONFMAN: *(A la Al Jolson.)* Is everybody happy?

MOLLY: I lost my love in the war. And after the war, I lost my job. Now I don't care about anything. Hey Sam, are you a nice man?

BRONFMAN: No, but he is.

MOLLY: Are you a nice man? I only like nice men.

(The GANGSTER gives BRONFMAN the newspaper. VINCE and JOE enter.)

VINCE: Who's the brainshark here?

JOE: You are.

VINCE: That's right.

BRONFMAN: It says here, the Volstead Act has

been approved by both Houses of Congress in the U.S. Prohibition in America. Gewalt.

JOE: Whisky.

VINCE: Now.

BRONFMAN: Keep your shirt on big guy.

(BRONFMAN pours drinks. VINCE and JOE drink.)

JOE: Now that's smooth.

VINCE: Like hell it is.

JOE: That's whisky.

VINCE: Like hell it is. They call it whisky, but what is it?

MOLLY: You want some hooch?

VINCE: Sure.

(MOLLY takes a flask from her garter belt.)

That's not all I want.

MOLLY: It's all your getting.

BRONFMAN: Look, liquor is like anything. You make your money in wholesale. Sell by the quart, the pint, fuck it. Sell it wholesale. You want liquor, we'll give you liquor. Is everybody happy?

(SID enters.)

MOLLY: Are you a nice man?

VINCE: Yes.

MOLLY: He's not.

SID: What are you looking at, you dirty rat? I said, what are you looking at?

VINCE: Just talking to the lady.

SID: She's not a lady. Are you, babe?

MOLLY: Dance with me.

SID: I don't dance.

MOLLY: How about you?

SID: Sit down.

BRONFMAN: Sid.

JOE: We just came for a drink, remember?

BRONFMAN: Sid, it's bad for business.

VINCE: Tough guy, he's got a gun so he's a tough guy.

JOE: We just came for a drink, remember?

VINCE: Tough guy.

BRONFMAN: Is everybody happy?

(JOE and VINCE exit. MOLLY dances by herself. SID smiles. The lights fade.)

VOICE: *(Off.)* I place the name of William Lyon Mackenzie King in nomination for the leadership of the Liberal party.

Scene Thirty

(In another playing area the light fade in. KING and JACQUES BUREAU enter.)

BUREAU: They haven't got a chance. In the Great War, when the issue was conscription your rivals abandoned Laurier but you stayed true. The only one who speaks English who stayed true was you. You! Those son of a bitch bastards are finished in the Liberal party. Finished. Les Canadien-Français never forget and never forgive. Son of a bitch bastards. I don't speak English but I know the words. Son of a bitch bastards. You want it. You got it. We voted as a block and we voted for you.

(Offstage: a cheer. A FRENCH-CANADIEN enters.)

FRENCH-CANADIEN: You won, on the third ballot, you won.

BUREAU: Congratulations Mr. Leader of the Liberal party. Mr. Leader of the Opposition. Congratulations.

KING: Thank you, Jacques. I owe it all to you ... and you too.

BUREAU: That's right. You owe me. Me! Jacques Bureau. You owe.

KING: Yes.

(Offstage: a chant of "King, King, King." The lights fade.)

Scene Thirty-one

(In another playing area the lights fade in. BRONFMAN, SID, and MOLLY enter.)

BRONFMAN: I've got warehouses and boozoriums in every little town in Canada.

SID: You and all these little whistlehoots.

BRONFMAN: As long as the train stops, that's all that matters. There are provincial laws and federal laws and they are completely different and both in effect at the same time. Federalism, I love it. The law says you can ship booze from one province to another province. That's legal. But you can't ship it from one town to another town in the same province. That's illegal. That's the law, it's nuts, but it's the law. Fine. We're in the exporting business.

SID: I'm with you, and you're with me.

(BRONFMAN, SID, and MOLLY exit. VINCE and JOE enter.)

VINCE: Why she's with a mug like that I'll never know.

JOE: Yeah, well the little guy, he's got the booze. The big guy, they say he's making a fortune running it into Chicago.

VINCE: They say, they say. Why she's with a mug like that I'll never know.

JOE: Watch out for him. He's mean.

VINCE: I'm not scared of him. I know the type. He's got big arms and walks like this so he thinks he's tough. We'll see. We'll see.

JOE: And the customs men are all on the take. All of them.

VINCE: The honest dollar died with Prohibition. Everyone's making the big money. Everyone.

JOE: Except us.

VINCE: Yeah.

(The lights fade.)

Scene Thirty-two

(In another playing area the lights fade in. BORDEN and MEIGHEN enter.)

BORDEN: Piles, pus, and pyorrhoea. My body is covered with boils and cuts, warts and scabs. I suffer from every malady known to man. I negotiated the terms of peace and now I am finished. I cannot go on. I must resign. I do not see the need for a leadership convention. Behold, Arthur Meighen. He is the new leader of the Conservative party. Goodbye.

(BORDEN exits. MEIGHEN smiles. The lights fade.)

Scene Thirty-three

(In another playing area the lights fade in. KING and JOAN PATTESON enter.)

JOAN: I could not but help see that you are moving in.

KING: Yes. I'm batching it as they say.

(GODFROY PATTESON enters.)

GODFROY: Bitching it you mean.

JOAN: Ah, this is my husband. As you can see he has a head like a billiard ball.

GODFROY: So you are our new neighbour. I am Godfroy Patteson.

KING: Mackenzie King at your service.

GODFROY: He was looking at you when he said that.

JOAN: Don't pay any attention to what God-forbid says. No one else does. I am—

GODFROY: My wife.

JOAN: No, you are not your wife. Alas, I am. I am Joan. Joan Patteson. Oh you have big fat stubby fingers. Beethoven had big fat stubby fingers. Do you play the piano?

KING: Yes, in fact, I do.

JOAN: Oh, you must play for us, sometime in the afternoon, when it's raining.

KING: Yes. I would be delighted.

JOAN: Oh, God-forbid, did you hear that? He would be delighted.

GODFROY: He was looking at you when he said that.

KING: You remind me of someone.

JOAN: Oh God-forbid, did you hear that? I remind him of someone.

GODFROY: Yes.

(The lights fade.)

Scene Thirty-four

(In another playing area the lights fade in. KING and MEIGHEN enter. A SERVANT enters.)

SERVANT: The governor-general of Canada, Lord Byng, and Lady Byng entering the room.

(LORD and LADY BYNG enter.)

LORD BYNG: Oh Memsahib, Memsahib.

LADY BYNG: First Canada, then India.

LORD BYNG: Yes. You are looking at Byng in his kingdom.

LADY BYNG: No. Byng in his Byng-dom.

LORD BYNG: Yes.

LADY BYNG: Well, shall we meet the trolls of your Byng-dom?

LORD BYNG: Yes.

MEIGHEN: Your Excellency.

LORD BYNG: How do you do? My wife.

MEIGHEN: Oh, Mrs. Byng, how nice to meet you.

LADY BYNG: You will address the wife of Lord Byng as Lady Byng.

MEIGHEN: Oh I am terribly sorry. Welcome to Canada.

LORD BYNG: I've never done anything like this you know, and I expect I'll make mistakes. During the Great War I made some mistakes in France, but when I did, the Canadians always pulled me out of the hole. That's what I'm counting on here.

MEIGHEN: Yes. Your Excellency, I wish to dissolve Parliament and hold an election.

LORD BYNG: Granted.

MEIGHEN: Excellent, excellent. And this vile little toad, is the leader of the opposition.

LORD BYNG: Ah yes. Are you related to the Mackenzie of the Mackenzie-Papineau Rebellion?

KING: I am. He was my grandfather.

LORD BYNG: *(With false naivete.)* I am simple boy. So you have the blood of a radical in you.

KING: Are you biased toward the Conservatives?

LORD BYNG: You expect me to answer that?

KING: Yes.

LORD BYNG: The governor-general should be an obvious person. Obvious means "goes without saying," therefore I am going without saying.

MEIGHEN: Wait till I get him in an election. Can't wait, can't wait.

(The lights fade.)

Scene Thirty-five

(In another playing area the lights fade in: the election of 1921. MEIGHEN enters.)

MEIGHEN: The French Canadians did not like it when I imposed conscription during the Great War. Too bad. The Westmount crowd did not like it when I nationalized the Grand Trunk Railroad. Too bad. Labour did not like it when I crushed the Winnipeg General Strike. Too bad. The farmers did not like it when I imposed a high tariff. Too bad. I believe in only one thing. The national policy of Sir John A. Macdonald. Vote for me and it is back to normal. Normalcy, the old ways, the tried and true.

(In another playing area the lights fade in. KING enters.)

KING: Fate has chosen him to be my opponent. If I cannot win an election against him, I cannot win an election against anybody.

(KING smiles. The lights fade.)

Scene Thirty-six

(In another playing area the lights fade in. VINCE and JOE enter.)

VINCE: I spent four years in a stinking smelly hole. The next hole I spend time in is going to be hot and tight.

JOE: You and that broad.

VINCE: I'm going to take his woman and his business. See what he does then.

JOE: Oh I don't like the sound of that.

VINCE: Hey little Joe, it's go, go, go. What can stop us?

JOE: Oh there's going to be bad trouble.

VINCE: You said it. I spent six months at Passchendaele. That little prick doesn't scare me. All right, here it comes, the night train. Woo, woo, the night train.

(VINCE and JOE put on masks. They hold revolvers. SID, driving a truck carrying barrels of booze, enters.)

VINCE: Stick 'em up. Get out. Now!

(SID gets out of the truck.)

JOE: You can die now, you can die later! It's up to you!

SID: I want no trouble.

VINCE: He wants no trouble he says. Get his gun. Now, start walking. That way.

(SID exits. VINCE and JOE take off their masks.)

We're in business.

(VINCE and JOE get into the truck. The lights fade.)

Scene Thirty-seven

(In another playing area the lights fade in. KING and JOAN enter. They stand beside a giant Carlson-Stromberg radio. Music is heard, the "Charleston." Static is heard. JOAN twiddles a dial. Music is heard, the "Charleston.")

KING: It's incredible, what is it?

JOAN: It's an invention. They call it radio.

KING: It's incredible. How do they do it? It's like a spirit, speaking.

JOAN: Yes it is, Mr. King.

KING: Call me Rex. My friends call me Rex.

JOAN: Well Rex, you have beautiful eyes.

RADIO: This is the CBC. The final results of the 1921 election are Liberals 117, Conservatives 50, and Progressives 64. Mackenzie King is now prime minister of Canada!

JOAN: Rex, oh Rex. Congratulations Mr. Prime Minister.

RADIO: Also elected, James Shaver Woodsworth, the first socialist member of Parliament.

KING: I feel like dancing a jig. Music, music, music. Turn out the lights I feel like dancing.

(JOAN twiddles a dial. Music plays. BUREAU enters.)

BUREAU: Every Quebec seat, every Quebec seat voted Liberal. Did I tell you or did I tell you?

KING: You did, you did. Now Jacques, with regard to your position on the committee of the Privy Council.

BUREAU: The what?

KING: The cabinet.

BUREAU: I want to be Minister of Customs.

KING: Done.

(The lights fade.)

Scene Thirty-eight

(In another playing area the lights fade in. VINCE and MOLLY are dancing. SID and BRONFMAN enter.)

SID: Someone's hi-jacking all my booze.

BRONFMAN: That's not my problem.

SID: Can you give me a shipment on credit?

BRONFMAN: Get out of here. See the man dancing with your woman. He pays cash.

SID: Right, right.

(The lights fade.)

Scene Thirty-nine

(In another playing area the lights fade in. The GARGOYLE enters holding a gravestone. KING enters.)

KING: The first thing we are going to do is ban hereditary titles. I hear you. No more Sir Robert Bordens, no more Sir Arthur Meighens, no more "Sir" anything. I hear you. We are going to make this colony a nation. I hear you.

(A REPORTER from the Globe and Mail *enters. He holds a newspaper with the headline "Chanak Crisis—Britain Wants Troops.")*

REPORTER: Are you going to be sending Canadian troops to Turkey?

KING: What?

(REPORTER holds up the newspaper.)

If the government of Great Britain desires troops I am sure they will inform the Canadian government. Now, if you will excuse me.

REPORTER: But are you going to send troops?

KING: We do not conduct our foreign policy via the newspaper. Canada thinks in terms of peace. Europe thinks in terms of war. We live in a fire-proof house far from inflammable materials. Now if you will excuse me.

(The lights fade.)

Scene Forty

(In another playing area the lights fade in. MOLLY and SID enter.)

SID: That dirty rat ... that dirty rat ... that dirty—

MOLLY: I've given up trying to have a conversation with you.

SID: I talk when I want to.

MOLLY: Why bother? All you ever say is "That dirty rat, that dirty rat." and if he's in the same room with you it's "This dirty rat, this dirty rat." And if he's right in front of you—your favourite. "You dirty rat. You did this to me. You did that to me. You dirty rat."

SID: Shut up.

(The lights fade.)

Scene Forty-one

(In another playing area the lights fade in. KING, LORD BYNG, and MEIGHEN enter.)

LORD BYNG: Mr. Prime Minister, this is the third request for a commitment of troops to be sent to Armenia.

KING: And this is the third time I have told you that Parliament will decide. We have no business in Turkey, or Armenia, or anywhere.

(MEIGHEN holds a map.)

LORD BYNG: Who controls the straits of the Dardanelles controls that narrow passage separating Europe from Asia and connecting the Black Sea with the Mediterranean. This question is all important in Great Britain.

KING: I'm sure it is.

LORD BYNG: The Turks want it.

KING: It is part of Turkey.

MEIGHEN: It is part of the British Empire.

LORD BYNG: Will Canada stand by the British Empire?

KING: Parliament will decide.

LORD BYNG: *(To MEIGHEN.)* He is going to be difficult. The leader of the opposition thinks troops should be sent.

KING: In matters of the empire Mr. Meighen is more loyal than the king.

MEIGHEN: When Britain's message came we should have said "Ready, aye, ready. We stand by you."

KING: No. Steady, aye, steady.

(The lights fade.)

Scene Forty-two

(In another playing area the lights fade in. BRONFMAN, VINCE, and MOLLY enter.)

BRONFMAN: Don't worry about the frogs. I know how to handle them. Bloody frenchies. They're all on the take—all of them. And wait till you meet Jacques Bureau. Wait till you meet this son of a bitch. He's so crooked.

VINCE: How crooked is he?

BRONFMAN: He's as crooked as my dick. He's so crooked. He's so crooked he'd put his mother in a whorehouse and call it business. But I know how to handle him.

(BRONFMAN exits.)

MOLLY: He's a dirty rat.

VINCE: No, he's my boss and he's going to make me rich.

(The lights fade.)

Scene Forty-three

(In another playing area the lights fade in. BUREAU enters.)

BUREAU: I take a little here, I take a little there, I take a little everywhere. The economy of this country is based on fish, furs, wood, and liquor.

(BRONFMAN enters holding a suitcase.)

Sam, what can I do for you?

BRONFMAN: Jacques, I found this suitcase full of money on your doorstep. What shall I do with it?

BUREAU: Give it to me. I'll try to find the owner.

BRONFMAN: Very good.

BUREAU: What can I do for you?

BRONFMAN: I have a barge carrying forty tonnes that I do not want bothered by Customs.

BUREAU: Bisaillon.

(JOSEPH BISAILLON enters.)

Joseph Bisaillon, what is your name?

BISAILLON: Joseph Bisaillon, monsieur.

BUREAU: And what is your job, Monsieur Bisaillon?

BISAILLON: I am the Chief of Customs at the port of Montréal.

BUREAU: When the barge carrying forty tonnes of liquor comes down the river from the west, what are you doing?

BISAILLON: I am looking east, monsieur.

BUREAU: Very good, Joseph, very good.

(The lights fade.)

Scene Forty-four

(In another playing area the lights fade in: King and Canadian Autonomy, 1924. KING is standing in front of the Red Ensign and the

Red Ensign with crest. MEIGHEN and BYNG enter.)

KING: This is our new flag.

MEIGHEN: Where's the Union Jack?

KING: Right there, where it always is.

MEIGHEN: What's this?

KING: A crest of Canadian provinces.

MEIGHEN: Get it off, get it off, get it off. Look at it.

LORD BYNG: He's got to go.

MEIGHEN: Definitely.

(The lights fade.)

Scene Forty-five

(In another playing area the lights fade in. KING and JOAN enter.)

KING: I am afraid that if I speak I will go mad. I am filled with fear. I have terrible dreams, terrible. I am exhausted, I don't like to sleep. Sometimes I feel like you are reading my mind.

JOAN: What you need is a … dog.

KING: A dog?

JOAN: Yes.

KING: A dog.

JOAN: Godling!

(GODFROY enters.)

GODFROY: You called?

JOAN: The dog.

(GODFROY exits.)

KING: A dog, you know, my mother would not let me have a dog.

JOAN: Oh you poor boy.

KING: She said dogs reminded her of the hounds of hell. A dog. What kind of dog?

(GODFROY enters holding Pat the dog [a puppet].)

JOAN: Look Rex, look.

KING: An Irish terrier. How did you know?

JOAN: His name is Pat.

KING: Pat. What a good name for a dog. Pat. He's shy.

JOAN: Yes, he is.

(The lights fade.)

Scene Forty-six

(In another playing area the lights fade in. VINCE and JOE enter. JOE does the accounts. VINCE paces.)

JOE: It's raining.

VINCE: Yeah. She's coming over.

JOE: Again.

VINCE: Yeah. You got a problem with that?

JOE: Yeah, I got a problem with that.

VINCE: What's your problem?

JOE: This is a business, not a whorehouse. It's an office for God's sake. We work here. It's a business.

VINCE: I tell you something, when I get a broad in the sack it's business. Serious business.

(Sound offstage.)

Oh, here she comes.

(MOLLY enters.)

MOLLY: I'm living with a beast.

VINCE: He doesn't know how to treat a woman. I know how to treat a woman.

MOLLY: Vince.

VINCE: I'm going to do you in one-tenth the time it takes to do nothing. I'm going to make you wish you'd never been born.

MOLLY: Sid makes me feel like that.

VINCE: I mean in a good way. Now get in there and get your clothes off. Where you going?

(JOE exits.)

It's raining.

MOLLY: Vince.

(The lights fade.)

Scene Forty-seven

(In another playing area the lights fade in. KING holds up Pat.)

KING: The spirit of my mother is inside you. You are my only friend. Oh Pat. I love you. You are loyal, kind, honest, honest! You should be prime minister. Not me. You! I'm not worthy. Oh Pat, Pat, Pat. You have changed my life. You, yes, you. It's mad but it's true. I can't live without you. Oh Pat. I can't imagine living my life dogless. Life without a dog is incomprehensible. I declare my love for this creature. Oh Pat.

(BUREAU enters.)

BUREAU: They're on to me, they're after me. They know everything, the graft, the bribes.

KING: Yes, I have heard rumours.

BUREAU: You've heard rumours. If they arrest me I spill my guts on your table. All my guts about the Liberal party in the upcoming election.

KING: You want something?

BUREAU: The Senate. Sanctuary.

KING: What would you do to be a senator?

BUREAU: Anything.

KING: Get down on your belly and crawl around this room like a lizard.

(BUREAU crawls around.)

Now bark like a dog.

(BUREAU barks like a dog.)

Now …

(The lights fade.)

Scene Forty-eight

(In another playing area the lights fade in. KING and BYNG enter. A BUTLER serves tea.)

LORD BYNG: Tories one hundred and sixteen, Liberals ninety-nine. Congratulations, you lost the election. Now, you have three possibilities. The first is dissolution and another election. The second is that Mr. Meighen having the largest group should be called on to form a government. The third is that you should continue. The dignified thing to do is the second possibility.

KING: Mr. Meighen cannot form a government. The Progressives will never support him. The only possibility is a Liberal-Progressive coalition. Parliament will decide.

LORD BYNG: Tea?

KING: Please. I am constitutionally entitled to meet the new House of Commons as prime minister and await its verdict. Do you dispute that?

LORD BYNG: No. But you lost the election.

KING: Parliament will decide.

LORD BYNG: Mr. Meighen must first be given a chance to show whether or not he is able to govern.

KING: It seems the governors-general coming out from Britain always side with the tory party.

LORD BYNG: How can I be biased? I am a sort of umpire.

KING: The governor-general is not entitled to have views but to accept or reject the advice of his ministers.

LORD BYNG: I think you should resign. That is my opinion.

KING: Keep your uninformed impressions to yourself.

LORD BYNG: I had a very unpleasant dream about you last night. More tea?

KING: Please.

(The lights fade.)

Scene Forty-nine

(In another playing area the lights fade in. MEIGHEN and R. B. BENNETT enter.)

MEIGHEN: Mr. Bennett, I see myself as a milk-white hind on the lawn of politics. And Mr. King is like a wild boar from hell. We must bring this government down, we must.

BENNETT: There are rumours of corruption in the Customs department.

MEIGHEN: Really?

BENNETT: We have evidence connecting ministers and senior civil servants with smugglers and bootleggers.

MEIGHEN: Really?

(The lights fade.)

Scene Fifty

(In another playing area the lights fade in: Parliament. KING, BUREAU, MEIGHEN, RICHARD BEDFORD BENNETT, and the SPEAKER of the House enter.)

MEIGHEN: Mr. Speaker, Mr. Speaker.

SPEAKER: The House recognizes the member for Portage la Prairie.

MEIGHEN: Mr. Speaker, I accuse this government of condoning debauchery and corruption in the Customs department. I have evidence that shows beyond all doubt that the government encouraged, and profited from smuggling on a monstrous scale.

This government has broken every law of this land. The Public Treasury has been defrauded of large sums of money in unpaid customs duties and excise taxes.

With this evidence I censure this government and this prime minister in particular.

(An uproar. The lights fade on all characters except KING.)

KING: What am I going to do?

(The lights fade.)

Scene Fifty-one

(In another playing area the lights fade in. KING and JOAN enter.)

JOAN: This is Miss Etta Wriedt, the spiritualist.

(JOAN exits. ETTA WRIEDT enter.)

ETTA: Gnik Retsim tsilautirips a ma I.

KING: What?

ETTA: I am a spiritualist, Mr. King. I believe that the souls animating the frames of all individuals have previously hob-nobbed in a pre-natal sphere.

KING: That is not an original idea.

ETTA: I also believe that the after-death state and the pre-birth state are the same.

KING: This is elementary Plato. Get on with it.

ETTA: Is there anyone you would like to contact who has not yet been born?

KING: No.

ETTA: Is there anyone you would like to contact who has left this earthly plane and resides in the spiritual bardo we all come from and will go to?

KING: Yes.

ETTA: Give me your hand. You want to speak with your mother.

KING: Yes.

ETTA: You want to speak with her now.

KING: Yes.

ETTA: This way.

(The lights fade.)

Scene Fifty-two

(In another playing area the lights fade in. MEIGHEN and BENNETT enter. Offstage: the sounds of hoots and catcalls, derisive laughter, cheers "Point of order," "Bravo," loud applause, crude invective.)

MEIGHEN: Listen. Parliament in action. Democracy. We are going to censure the government.

BENNETT: We've got him, we've got him. We've got him.

MEIGHEN: And we're going to stick it to him good.

BENNETT: Yes.

(The lights fade.)

Scene Fifty-three

(In another playing area the lights fade in: a seance. KING and ETTA enter. ETTA uses a crystal ball and speaks in tongues.)

KING: Yes, yes, I see. Tell me more. I understand, I understand.

ETTA: Here comes the mother.

(A vision of MOTHER appears.)

MOTHER: The tories destroyed your grandfather. You must destroy them, Willie, destroy them utterly. You have a mission. You must regain the honour of your name.

KING: I will.

MOTHER: You are special. There is a score to settle with the tories. And you will settle it. Won't you, won't you, won't you?

KING: Yes, yes … but how?

MOTHER: Listen. You never listen.

KING: I'm listening.

MOTHER: You must resign without handing over power to the tories.

KING: Yes.

MOTHER: You must get Byng to accept your letter of resignation. It is of paramount importance that he accept the letter. Any government formed by Arthur Meighen will be unconstitutional. Remember Willie, when the small depart the great approach.

KING: Yes.

MOTHER: And then …

(The lights fade.)

Scene Fifty-four

(In another playing area the lights fade in. KING and LORD BYNG enter.)

LORD BYNG: I represent the king of Canada.

KING: Correct. But you are not the king of Canada.

LORD BYNG: My dear.

KING: Do not patronize me. I demand a dissolution of Parliament.

LORD BYNG: Parliament will decide, Mr. Prime Minister. The country has an absolute right to the judgement of Parliament on a motion censuring the government for misconduct. No prime minister can deny the country that right. The Crown alone can protect this right. You bloody queer.

KING: I can't believe you called me that.

LORD BYNG: You bloody queer. Do you believe it now?

KING: How dare you call me that. It is your duty to accept the prime minister's advice.

LORD BYNG: It is my duty to keep you to your word and let Parliament decide.

KING: The governor-general will not accept the advice of his first minister.

LORD BYNG: Correct.

(KING hands LORD BYNG an envelope.)

KING: My resignation.

LORD BYNG: Send for Mr. Meighen.

(MEIGHEN enters.)

Mr. Meighen—

MEIGHEN: I will form a government.

LORD BYNG: I was about to offer you the opportunity.

MEIGHEN: I will form a government. I can't wait, I can't wait.

KING: This government is unconstitutional.

MEIGHEN: Look at him. The fool. The wretch. The specious nonsense that comes out his mouth. The wretch.

KING: Unconstitutional. Unconsta—unconsta—

MEIGHEN: Look at him. He's frothing at the mouth Throw a fit you miserable wretch.

KING: Unconsta—

(The lights fade.)

Scene Fifty-five

(In another playing area the lights fade in. MOLLY and SID enter.)

SID: That dirty rat, that dirty rat.

MOLLY: You're completely insane.

SID: That dirty rat. I'm going to get that guy. I made you a whore and now you are a whore.

MOLLY: What do you mean made me a whore?

SID: Remember that cop that busted you for being a prosty, I set that up, I loved you so much. I'm going to get that guy. I got everything, you got nothing. I'm going to get that guy.

MOLLY: You stink.

SID: I'm going to get that guy.

MOLLY: You stink.

SID: I'm going to get that guy.

MOLLY: You really stink.

(The lights fade.)

Scene Fifty-six

(In another playing area the lights fade in. MEIGHEN and BENNETT enter.)

BENNETT: You lost a vote of confidence in the House.

MEIGHEN: Very well. I will ask the governor-general for dissolution of the House and request another election.

BENNETT: Very good.

(The lights fade.)

Scene Fifty-seven

(In another playing area the lights fade in: the election of 1926. KING and MEIGHEN enter.)

KING: The issue is responsible government. The governor-general rejected the advice of an undefeated prime minister and gave government to another man. Lord Byng is a tory. The prejudices of a British governor have nullified our constitution. We are no longer a self-governing dominion. Autonomy is the issue. In the name of my grandfather, Arthur Meighen has created a dictatorship. Down with dictatorship. Down with tyranny.

MEIGHEN: Whenever Mr. King is out of power, the constitution is in danger. Mackenzie King is ridiculous. He tried to escape the censure of Parliament by concocting this ridiculous constitutional issue as a smoke screen to conceal his own corruption. Vote for clean government.

(The lights fade.)

Scene Fifty-eight

(In another playing area the lights fade in. MEIGHEN and BENNETT enter.)

BENNETT: Mackenzie King has formed a majority government.

MEIGHEN: He is a despicable charlatan.

BENNETT: A majority government.

MEIGHEN: There is a screw loose, of such magnitude that I no longer believe in democracy. My race is run. I resign.

(BENNETT smiles.)

R.B. Bennett. You are the new leader of the Conservative party.

BENNETT: Yes I am. I am too busy to speak with you. On your way out close the door. I am worried about the stock market. Worried, very worried, very worried. I am going to sell all my stocks. All of them. Why are you still here?

(The lights fade.)

Scene Fifty-nine

(In another playing area the lights fade in. KING and JOAN enter.)

JOAN: A complete triumph. The Conservatives have been trounced. A majority government And Arthur Meighen has resigned.

KING: I am guided by spirits. People always wonder why I am elected. The fools. Fools. I'll say it at the top of my voice. Fools! I am guided by spirits.

JOAN: What time is it?

KING: It's boom time, boom time! Ba-ba-boom time! We're in the money time!

JOAN: Oh you're being magnificent.

KING: Buy now pay later time! Ba-ba-boom time!

JOAN: Oh you're magnificent.

KING: I am in my power.

JOAN: Bravo, bravo.

(The lights fade.)

VOICE: *(Off.)* Nail his feet to the floor.

Scene Sixty

(In another playing area the lights fade in. VINCE and SID enter. SID holds a burlap bag. The bag moves every now and then. VINCE screams.)

SID: What do you think of that, tough guy? You dirty rat.

(VINCE groans.)

What do you think of that, you dirty rat?

(VINCE groans.)

Remember you once almost jumped out of your skin when I said dirty rat? Remember? I remember. Well, guess what I got in the bag? Guess?

(The bag moves.)

A rat. A great big one. And I'm going to put it on your face. What do you think of that?

(VINCE groans. SID puts the burlap bag over VINCE'S head. VINCE screams. The lights fade.)

Scene Sixty-one

(In another playing area the lights fade in: The Stock Market Crash, 1929. STOCKBROKERS are throwing ticker tape in the air. BENNETT enters.)

BENNETT: Will you buy this?

STOCKBROKER ONE: It's a spike, a spike, a spike.

STOCKBROKER TWO: I'm ruined, ruined.

STOCKBROKER ONE: My stock has dropped five hundred points in one hour. An hour ago each of my shares was worth thirty dollars now they are worth four cents.

STOCKBROKER TWO: Consider yourself lucky. At least they are worth something. Mine are worth nothing. Nothing!

BENNETT: Will you buy this?

STOCKBROKER ONE: Get out of here.

(The lights fade.)

Scene Sixty-two

(In another playing area the lights fade in. SID enters wearing a tuxedo.)

SID: Oh I'm putting on my top hat, tying up my white tie, brushing off my tails. I'm doing up my shirt front, putting in my shirt studs, polishing my nails. Oh I'm so happy I don't even know the words.

(MOLLY enters. She stabs SID with her nail-file. SID falls to the ground.)

MOLLY: You stink.

(The lights fade.)

Scene Sixty-three

(In another playing area the lights fade in. KING enters with a watering-can. A Carlson-Stromberg radio is centre stage.)

KING: Oh the delights of the pastoral life.

RADIO: *(Voice over.)* Good evening this is the CBC. October 29th, 1929. Black Tuesday. That's what stockbrokers are calling it. The greatest stock market crash in history occurred today. Some experts are forecasting financial disaster on a world scale.

(The lights fade.)

Act Two

Scene One

(In another playing area the lights fade in: Parliament. KING, ERNEST LAPOINTE, BENNETT, HARRY STEVENS, and the SPEAKER enter.)

BENNETT: Mr. Speaker, Mr. Speaker. The provinces need unemployment relief.

KING: The only way to deal with unemployment relief is with unemployment insurance. Unemployment relief is a provincial responsibility. It is not a federal responsibility. If provinces need money for unemployment relief they should raise taxes.

BENNETT: The provinces need federal money.

KING: The provinces that are governed by tories, I would not give them a five-cent piece.

BENNETT: Shame.

KING: I repeat, I will not give tory provincial governments a five-cent piece

BENNETT: Resign.

(The lights fade.)

Scene Two

(In another playing area the lights fade in. JOE, JUDY, his wife, and their DAUGHTER enter. JOE holds a cocker spaniel.)

JOE: Our neighbours are so poor they can no longer afford to feed their pet. They thought you might like to have it.

DAUGHTER: Oh boy.

(JOE gives her the dog.)

Oh I love this dog, Dad, I love this dog. I love this dog. I'm going to call him ... Blackie. Oh Blackie, Blackie, Blackie.

(JOE smiles. The lights fade.)

Scene Three

(In another playing area the lights fade in. KING enters.)

KING: I am an ignorant man, so ignorant I cannot make a decision about anything. I am so ignorant. But people have no idea, if they did ... oooh. But when in difficulty temporize, temporize, temporize.

(LAPOINTE enters.)

Ah, Monsieur Lapointe.

LAPOINTE: In every town and city thousands of men are eating in soup kitchens.

KING: I hear you.

LAPOINTE: The ranks of the unemployed are increasing by ten thousand a week.

KING: I hear you.

LAPOINTE: The Saskatchewan and the prairie provinces have been afflicted with drought.

KING: I hear you.

LAPOINTE: And locusts.

KING: I hear you.

LAPOINTE: The St. Lawrence river is flowing backwards.

KING: I hear you.

LAPOINTE: Louis Riel has come back from the dead and is waiting to see you.

KING: Send him right in.

(The lights fade.)

Scene Four

(In another playing area the lights fade in. BENNETT enters. Behind him is a banner, "Elect a Conservative Government and Re-

lieve Unemployment." BENNETT speaks into radio microphones.)

BENNETT: My fellow Canadians, the prime minister is mean-spirited and evil. He does not care about your problems. He would not give a nickel to help the unemployed. Not a five-cent piece. He said it himself. I will end unemployment or perish in the attempt. I will use tariffs to blast a way into the markets that have been closed to you. Unemployment is not of local importance, it is not of provincial importance, it is of national importance! I will blast my way into the markets of the world. Blast my way. And we will have jobs, jobs, jobs!

(The lights fade.)

Scene Five

(In another playing area the lights fade in. There is a Carlson-Stromberg radio. KING and JOAN enter.)

KING: Mother said I was going to win the election.

RADIO: This is the CBC. Here are the election results of 1930. Tories one hundred and thirty-seven, Liberals ninety-one. Richard Bedford Bennett is the new prime minister.

KING: Now that intolerable despot is prime minister.

JOAN: There, there, little boy.

KING: Mother lied to me. She said I would win the election.

JOAN: There, there, it's for the best, you'll see.

KING: Oh mother.

(GODFROY enters.)

GODFROY: Would you like the Ouija board now?

KING: I hate the Ouija board.

JOAN: He hates the Ouija board. Out!

(GODFROY exits.)

KING: Look, look, a picture of her.

JOAN: The old woman herself.

KING: Have you ever seen a sweeter, more beautiful expression. Look at that face. She has the face of a young girl, don't you think? Look at that hair.

JOAN: She looks like the queen of the fairies.

KING: Yes. Queen of the fairies. Exactly. And I am the son.

JOAN: Yes, Wee Willie.

KING: Oh mother.

JOAN: Wee Willie, Wee Willie.

(The lights fade.)

Scene Six

(In another playing area the lights fade in. BENNETT enters.)

BENNETT: Jobs, jobs, jobs. I'm a whore. I'll say anything. But when the election is over, take off the mask. I am now the minister of External Affairs, the minister of Finance, and, of course, the prime minister. Any doubt in your mind who calls the shots? Any doubt? I make it simple. It is my way or the doorway. I am a capitalist. I am an imperialist and proud of it. If you are not a capitalist or an imperialist I will make it so your life is not worth living in this country. I will see to it personally. I am lord and master of this country. First thing we are going to do is reinstitute hereditary titles. Starting with me. I am now Sir Richard Bedford Bennett

(The lights fade.)

Scene Seven

(In another playing area the lights fade in. JOE and JUDY enter. DAUGHTER with her dog enters.)

JOE: I got laid off.

JUDY: Oh Joe.

JOE: Don't worry. I've got two arms and two legs and with you beside me, two heads. We'll get through.

JUDY: She says when she grows up, she wants to marry it.

DAUGHTER: Oh Blackie.

(The lights fade.)

Scene Eight

(In another playing area the lights fade in. BENNETT and STEVENS enter.)

STEVENS: Oh Mr. Bennett, Mr. Bennett.

BENNETT: What?

STEVENS: The ranks of the unemployed are increasing by twenty thousand a week.

BENNETT: So what? Low interest rates and a high dollar are much more important to business than the unemployed.

STEVENS: Wheat prices have fallen by fifty percent.

BENNETT: Not good, not good.

STEVENS: The drought on the prairie provinces has now reached biblical proportions.

BENNETT: Very bad, very bad.

STEVENS: The banks are losing confidence in wheat farmers

BENNETT: Don't like it, don't like it

(The lights fade.)

Scene Nine

(In another playing area the lights fade in: a dream. The GARGOYLE and MOTHER are dancing. KING enters.)

MOTHER: We're going to make love like dogs.

GARGOYLE: We're going to make love like dogs.

MOTHER: I want you to larrup it into me.

GARGOYLE: I'm going to larrup it into you.

MOTHER: Dog love. Fornicate. Copulate. Rut!

GARGOYLE: Dog love. Fornicate. Copulate. Rut!

MOTHER: Oh yes. Dog love, dog love, dog love.

GARGOYLE: Oh yes. Dog love, dog love, dog love.

(Blackout.)

KING: *(Voice over.)* No! No!

(Lights up. Pat is licking KING's face.)

No … Oh Pat, Pat. We were having a bad dream.

(The lights fade.)

Scene Ten

(In another playing area the lights fade in. JOE, FOREMAN, ED, and JOHN enter.)

FOREMAN: It's bullwork. Ten cents an hour. Can you do it?

JOE: Ten cents an hour. The minimum wage is thirty-five cents an hour.

FOREMAN: If you don't want the job, they'll take it.

(FOREMAN points at ED and JOHN.)

ED and JOHN: I'll take it, I'll take it.

JOE: I'll take it.

(The lights fade.)

Scene Eleven

(In another playing area the lights fade in. KING and GODFROY enter.)

KING: What is keeping her?

GODFROY: I have told you, she is dressing. I am supposed to entertain you. At the stroke of midnight she enters, I leave. I leave, she enters. Work it which way you will.

KING: I can't tell you how much I appreciate your generous spirit. You are kind and good.

GODFROY: Scotch?

KING: No. What is keeping her?

GODFROY: She is dressing. She has a surprise for you.

(The chimes of midnight: twelve gongs. GODFROY exits. JOAN enters dressed as Mackenzie King's mother.)

KING: You look like a … dream.

JOAN: I'm alive Willie Boy, I'm alive.

KING: You look just … luscious. Luscious.

JOAN: Wee Willie, Wee Willie

KING: Oh yes, oh yes, oh yes.

(They embrace. The lights fade.)

Scene Twelve

(In another playing area the lights fade in: Parliament. KING, LAPOINTE, BENNETT, STEVENS, and the SPEAKER enter.)

KING: We need unemployment insurance.

BENNETT: This government is committed to a balanced budget. People are destitute because of wasteful living and unwise investments. Unemployment insurance will undermine capitalism. The economy is sound. Work or be deported.

KING: We need unemployment insurance.

BENNETT: I put my faith in corporate Canada.

Our problems will be solved by keeping the tariff high and the deficit low.

KING: We need unemployment insurance, now!

BENNETT: Unemployment insurance goes far beyond milking the old cow dry. That is biting off the teats. Where will it end?

KING: Before the stock market crash unemployment was at two percent, now it is thirty-six percent.

BENNETT: Unemployment is the primary responsibility of the municipality, and secondly, that of the province. Ottawa can do nothing. No government with which I am associated will ever establish a system of unemployment insurance. I have spoken.

KING: Resign.

(The lights fade.)

Scene Thirteen

(In another playing area the lights fade in. JOE and JUDY enter.)

JOE: They closed the mill today, just like that.

(JOE snaps his fingers.)

Laid everybody off, just like that.

(JOE snaps his fingers.)

JUDY: What are we going to do?

JOE: I don't know. I've looked for another job. There are no jobs. You said you were going to look for a job. Did you have any luck? Well did you?

JUDY: No. We'll get by.

JOE: Might have to go on the dole.

JUDY: Oh no, not charity. Anything but that. Not charity.

JOE: I'll look for another job, but … there are no jobs

(JOE exits. The lights fade.)

Scene Fourteen

(In another playing area the lights fade in. BENNETT and two SECRETARIES enter.)

BENNETT: All government decisions are now by Order-in-Council.

One: No more immigration. Not one foreigner is to be allowed to enter this country.

Two: Our economic priority will be a balanced budget, lower interest rates, and a stable dollar.

Three: We will ban the Communist party, annihilate the red menace.

Four: We will raise the tariff by fifty percent on … butter, eggs, wheat, bread, oats, sundry edibles … clothes, what else? … Paper products, yes paper products, especially toilet paper, and forks and knives too.

Five …

(The lights fade.)

Scene Fifteen

(In another playing area the lights fade in. JOE, JUDY, and their DAUGHTER enter. The DAUGHTER wears a dress made out of flour sacks.)

DAUGHTER: They're always laughing at me 'cause of my dress.

JOE: You look nice.

JUDY: You can't go to school naked.

DAUGHTER: But I can't wear this.

JUDY: We don't have any money.

DAUGHTER: Get a job.

JUDY: How dare you say that to your father.

DAUGHTER: Oh, oh.

JUDY: Don't flounce.

(DAUGHTER exits.)

Come back here. You little flounce.

JOE: She used to be friendly but now she is mean and niggardly. Might have to go on the dole.

JUDY: No, anything but that. Anything.

(The lights fade.)

Scene Sixteen

(In another playing area the lights fade in. KING enters with a diary.)

KING: What evil thoughts did I think today? I suffer from brain fatigue. I hate to sleep.

(KING holds up the diary.)

A record of my sins. Last night I had a dream. I was a deer in the forest. A giant stag with big antlers. King of the forest is what the trees called me. I was running through the forest chased by wolves, and laughing at them in my deer-like way.

And then, I got my antlers caught in the trees, the branches of the trees held my antlers, and I couldn't move, and I could hear the wolves getting closer and closer, howling and growling, breaking the bush, getting closer and closer, and then ... Mother appears and saves me, and the sun is shining.

I suffer from brain fatigue. I hate to sleep.

(The lights fade.)

Scene Seventeen

(In another playing area the lights fade in. JOE, JUDY, and their DAUGHTER enter. The sound of a dog barking.)

JOE: Shut up, shut up. Shut up, or I'll wring your nuts. He's eating us out of house and home and he never shuts up. Don't look at me like that. There's no work.

JUDY: And there's no food.

(The sound of a dog barking.)

DAUGHTER: And Blackie's hungry too.

JOE: Yes.

DAUGHTER: Oh Blackie.

(DAUGHTER exits. The sound of a dog barking. JOE and JUDY look at each other. The lights fade.)

Scene Eighteen

(In another playing area the lights fade in. BENNETT enters.)

BENNETT: How do you get a belly like this, you ask? I eat six meals a day. You don't get a belly like this eating three. For breakfast I have eleven eggs and two pounds of bacon, and a loaf of bread. That gets me started. Oh bacon, bacon. Bacon, God I love it. Love it, love it, love it, love it. I can't imagine a world without bacon.

(The lights fade.)

Scene Nineteen

(In another playing area the lights fade in. JUDY and DAUGHTER enter. JOE enters holding a bag wrapped in butcher paper.)

DAUGHTER: Blackie, Blackie, where are you? Where is he?

JUDY: Muffin.

DAUGHTER: What?

JUDY: I have some terrible news. Blackie ran away.

DAUGHTER: Oh no.

JUDY: I took Blackie out on a leash for a walk. And he saw some dogs running in a pack and he ran after them barking all the way. I wasn't strong enough to hold him, wasn't strong enough. He ran away. Don't cry. He's with the other dogs now. He'll be happy. We'll get another one one day.

DAUGHTER: It's not the same.

(The lights fade.)

Scene Twenty

(In another playing area the lights fade in. KING and Pat enter. KING holds a frying pan.)

KING: Oh Pat, you're king here. And you are going to eat like a king. Look Pat, look. Your favourite. Steak and pork chops. The steak is medium rare and the pork chops are well done. Eat it all, Pat, eat it all.

(The lights fade.)

Scene Twenty-one

(In another playing area the lights fade in. JOE, JUDY, and their DAUGHTER are eating.)

JOE: Jesus that's good. Meat, meat, oh meat.

JUDY: Yes.

JOE: Jesus that's good. Meat, meat, oh meat.

JUDY: Yes.

JOE: Jesus that's good. Meat, meat, oh meat.

JUDY: Yes.

JOE: How is it, Muffin?

DAUGHTER: Oh it's good, it's good, it's good.

(They eat. The lights fade.)

Scene Twenty-two

(In another playing area the lights fade in. BENNETT is reading letters from distraught citizens.)

BENNETT: If you want to know who is responsible for all this debt look at yourself in the mirror when you are shaving. There are people who say let's spend more money, well and good, but where is the money coming from? Where is the spirit of our pioneers who tilled our soil and worked in your forests? Did they go to the government whenever they wanted anything? They did not ask government to be a wet nurse to every derelict.

(In another playing area the lights fade in.)

KING: He is a dog of a man. A brute. A dog!

(The lights fade.)

Scene Twenty-three

(In another playing area the lights fade in. JOE and JUDY enter.)

JOE: Might have no choice. Might have to go on the dole. We got to eat.

(DAUGHTER enters.)

JUDY: Muffin, what's the matter?

DAUGHTER: My friend Shirley talked to her friend Joanie whose father owns the butcher shop and she said that Daddy walked into the butcher shop with Blackie and walked out with a big bag and no Blackie. Is that true?

JUDY: Muffin.

DAUGHTER: You ate Blackie, you ate Blackie, you ate Blackie. You ate Blackie, you ate Blackie, you ate Blackie. You ate—

JOE: You had some too.

(The DAUGHTER grimaces. The lights fade.)

Scene Twenty-four

(In another playing area the lights fade in. KING enters.)

KING: R. B. Bennett is a blatherskate, a rotten blatherskate. A blathering blatherskate. A monster. No … he's not a monster. He's a manster! A manster!

(The lights fade.)

Scene Twenty-five

(In another playing area the lights fade in: The Boulevard of Broken Dreams. JOE enters, he walks past and witnesses the following scenes. In another playing area the lights fade in. A MOTHER and family are being evicted by a LANDLORD.)

LANDLORD: If you can't pay your rent you're out. You know that better than me.

MOTHER: Oh please don't.

LANDLORD: And for the money you owe me, I'm going to auction your furniture and your clothes.

MOTHER: Oh please don't.

(In another playing area the lights fade in. A COMMUNIST enters holding a banner with the hammer and sickle.)

COMMUNIST: Workers of the world, unite! Cast off your chains, you have everything to gain. The proletariat will inherit the earth.

(A MOUNTIE with a club enters. He beats the COMMUNIST. In another playing area the lights fade in: Hoboville. HOBOES ONE and TWO enter. HOBO TWO wears a placard "I'm starving feed me.")

HOBO ONE: Now, here comes a live one. Now, when you're panhandling you make a face like this and say "Can you spare a dime, mister?"

(He makes a face.)

Sometimes they'll kick you if you make a face like that, but sometimes it works.

HOBO TWO: Can you spare a dime, mister?

(In another playing area the lights fade in. MEN dancing in a conga line enter.)

LEADER: What's our slogan?

MEN: When do we eat?

LEADER: What's our slogan?

MEN: When do we eat?

LEADER: Relief, relief, relief, we want relief.

MEN: Relief, relief, relief, we want relief.

LEADER: Relief, relief, relief, we want relief.

MEN: Relief, relief, relief, we want relief.

(They exit.)

Scene Twenty-six

(In another playing area the lights fade in. There is a sign, "Welfare Office." The MEN and WOMEN of the snake parade are standing in a line. JOE joins the end of the line. MEN enter and line up behind JOE.)

VOICE: *(Off.)* Next!

(MAN ONE exits.)

JOE: Always lining up. What happened to me shouldn't happen to Hitler. But it did. I ate my daughter's pet.

ALL: *(Repeated down the line.)* Don't push.

JOE: So don't push

VOICE: *(Off.)* Next!

(MAN TWO exits.)

MAN THREE: I was a gambler. I sold the wife's wedding ring, but not the wife. Unlike others I know.

WOMAN FIVE: What do you mean by that?

MAN FOUR: What have you been doing?

MAN THREE: Picking dandelions.

MAN FOUR: Picking your nuggets you mean.

MAN FIVE: Gold nuggets.

MAN THREE: I don't think so.

VOICE: *(Off.)* Next!

(MAN THREE exits.)

WOMAN FIVE: R. B. Bennett, The "R" stands for Richard. What's the "B" stand for?

JOE: Buggerall is what it stands for. Richard Buggerall Bennett.

WOMAN FIVE: In the States they got FDR and the New Deal.

MAN SIX: What have we got?

JOE: We got Buggerall Bennett, is what we got.

MAN FIVE: Buggerall.

MAN SEVEN: This government is a disgrace to the human race.

MAN FOUR: It's got to be changed.

VOICE: *(Off.)* Next!

(MAN FOUR exits.)

WOMAN FIVE: R. B. Bennett and Mackenzie King, they came out of the same pea pod. Send it back to the great farmer in the sky. Grow better ones.

JOE: R.B. is going to hell, and if he doesn't go to hell, then there is no hell.

(A COMMUNIST enters distributing the Communist Manifesto.*)*

MAN SEVEN: Anyone who distributes that is either a communist or RCMP. Get out of here.

VOICE: *(Off.)* Next!

(WOMAN FIVE exits.)

MAN SIX: I fell in love, got married, had a kid, the depression hit, and the cow died. Me and a billion of these grasshoppers lived on the farm. Look at it. It can eat but cannot be eaten.

VOICE: *(Off.)* Next!

(MAN SIX exits.)

MAN EIGHT: I was a hat maker, but nobody would buy my hats so I got thrown out on the street. But I got the nicest hat in the store.

MAN NINE: Shut up.

MAN SEVEN: What's my story you ask? I'll tell you. Wine, women, and song. Booze, broads, and music.

JOE: Who asked you?

VOICE: *(Off.)* Next!

(MAN SEVEN exits.)

ALL: *(Repeated down the line.)* Don't push.

JOE: Don't push. It is a crime to be poor in this country.

ALL: *(Down the line.)* Yes.

VOICE: *(Off.)* Next!

(JOE exits. The line moves forward. The lights fade.)

Scene Twenty-seven

(In another playing area the lights fade in. JOE and the WELFARE MAN enter. A line of MEN stand behind JOE.)

MAN SEVEN: Thank you.

WELFARE MAN: Now get out.

(MAN SEVEN exits.)

Next. Now, Mr. Joe Slom …

JOE: Slomkovsky.

WELFARE MAN: Whatever your name is. Is that a Russian name?

JOE: I was born in Canada.

WELFARE MAN: Now Joe Slow, listen to me. You cannot be seen to be getting anything or people will become resentful, therefore you will not get anything except bare subsistence. We do not subsidize luxury living. Your telephone will be disconnected.

JOE: Good, I hate it.

WELFARE MAN: Swear on this bible that you are destitute.

JOE: I am destitute.

WELFARE MAN: Swear on this bible that no family members, parents, brothers, sisters, uncles, aunts, cousins, will help you.

JOE: No one will help me.

WELFARE MAN: Swear on this bible that all information in this application is true.

JOE: All information is true.

WELFARE MAN: Tomorrow I will come to your dwelling, or your place of abode, or home, or whatever you call it, to inspect you and your family.

JOE: Thank you

WELFARE MAN: Now get out.

(JOE exits.)

Next.

(MAN EIGHT steps forward.)

You again.

(The lights fade.)

Scene Twenty-eight

(In another playing area the lights fade in. WOODSWORTH enters in front of a banner, "Co-operative Commonwealth Federation.")

WOODSWORTH: This is the end of the road for capitalism. Is it a crime to be poor in this country? No. Among such misery it is a crime to be rich. The profit motive is evil. Life in hell is a society based on greed. Capitalism is greed in its most grotesque form. Greedy idiots decide what is good and what is bad. We pay the consequences. Children do not die because God decides they should die. They die because of bad milk

No CCF government will rest until it has eradicated capitalism and put into operation the full programme of socialized planning which will lead to the establishment in Canada of the Co-operative Commonwealth.

(The lights fade.)

Scene Twenty-nine

(In another playing area the lights fade in. BENNETT enters.)

BENNETT: What do they offer you for dumping you in the mud? Socialism. Communism. Dictatorship. I ask every man and woman to put the iron heel of ruthlessness against a thing of that kind. Stamp out socialism with an iron heel ruthlessly! I am now "Iron Heel" Bennett.

(The lights fade.)

Scene Thirty

(In another playing area the lights fade in. JOE, JUDY, and their DAUGHTER enter.)

JOE: "Iron Heel" Bennett wants to be Mussolini. Shall we let him?

JUDY: Look at him. Your father, the breadwinner.

DAUGHTER: You ate Blackie.

JUDY: And his starving family. Useless. I could have married a stick and been better off.

DAUGHTER: You ate Blackie.

(The sound of three knocks at the door. JOE exits. JOE and the WELFARE MAN enter.)

WELFARE MAN: I am with the Welfare Department. I am here to inspect you and the premises. Is this your kid?

JUDY: This is our daughter.

WELFARE MAN: How old are you?

DAUGHTER: What's it to you?

WELFARE MAN: You are impertinent and impudent. Answer my question.

DAUGHTER: I'm eleven … and a half

WELFARE MAN: You will answer all my questions or you will not receive your three dollars per week. Do you understand?

JUDY: Yes.

JOE: Is that three dollars a week each?

WELFARE MAN: No. Each household gets three dollars a week. If there's one of you, you get three dollars. If there's three of you, you get three dollars. If there's twelve of you, you get three dollars. Three dollars. Now you are a charity case. The first thing I want to look at is your underwear. We don't want our charity cases wearing frilly knickers.

JOE: This way.

(The lights fade.)

Scene Thirty-one

(In another playing area the lights fade in. BENNETT and ANDREW McNAUGHTON enter.)

BENNETT: General McNaughton.

McNAUGHTON: Call me Andy.

BENNETT: Never. Now, what is your plan?

McNAUGHTON: Each city has a hobo jungle, a breeding ground of revolution. We must take the hoboes away from the city. We must build relief camps in the middle of nowhere. Pay them twenty cents a day and subject them to military law.

BENNETT: Yes.

McNAUGHTON: I will supervise these camps personally.

BENNETT: Yes.

(The lights fade.)

Scene Thirty-two

(In another playing area the lights fade in. JOE, JUDY, and their DAUGHTER enter.)

JUDY: Three dollars a week. Not enough. All we can buy are lentils and carrots.

JOE: I need meat.

DAUGHTER: Oh don't we know it. You turned Blackie into beef.

JOE: Muffin.

DAUGHTER: Now I know why you call me that. We're just food. I'm just a piece of food in a flour sack. If I wasn't here, we would all be better off.

JOE: Three dollars a week if there are three of us. Three dollars a week if there are two of us. I'm going to go to a relief camp.

(JOE exits.)

JUDY: Joe.

(The lights fade.)

Scene Thirty-three

(In another playing area the lights fade in. KING and Pat enter.)

KING: Relief camps. Concentration camps in Canada. They are doing the same thing in Nazi Germany, Pat. Where will it all end, Pat? Where?

(The lights fade.)

Scene Thirty-four

(In another playing area the lights fade in: a relief camp. JOE, ALAN, MIKE, and JOHN enter dressed like convicts. McNAUGHTON enters.)

McNAUGHTON: Men, welcome to the relief camp. Here you are going to learn the skills of the worker and develop your physique. See those rocks over there? We are going to move those rocks from there to there. Then we will move them from there back to there. Any questions?

JOE: Yes.

McNAUGHTON: I didn't hear that. You are under military law here. You are free to leave at anytime. But if you leave you and your families will not be eligible for welfare. We give no support to slackers or cowards. Now let's begin.

(JOE and others pick up rocks and carry them.)

Quiet. No talking.

(JOE and the others drop their rocks. Then JOE and the others pick up their rocks.)

Quiet. No talking.

(JOE and the others carry their rocks.)

Quiet. No talking.

(JOE and the others drop their rocks. Then JOE and the others pick up their rocks.)

Quiet. No talking. No slacking, keep working.

(The lights fade.)

Scene Thirty-five

(In another playing area the lights fade in. BENNETT, talking to himself, enters.)

BENNETT: Now we have two hundred thousand men working. Good. But what are they doing? Keeping busy. They are too exhausted to think about overthrowing the government. What do you think of that? I like it. I don't. How about you? I agree.

(In another playing area the lights fade in. KING enters.)

KING: Look at him, he's having a cabinet meeting.

BENNETT: Why don't they do something productive? Such as? They could build the Trans-Canada Highway. The CPR wouldn't like it. So what. I can't believe my ears. What's good for the CPR is good for Canada. Is it? What do you think? I agree. Me too. We have a railway, we don't need a highway. Exactly.

(The lights fade.)

Scene Thirty-six

(In another playing area the lights fade in. JOE and MEN enter. They play craps.)

JOE: Snake Eyes. The story of my life.

(MAN SIX holds a bible while praying.)

MAN SIX: Satan is alive and well and living in Ottawa. I believe in the Bible, the whole Bible, and nothing but the Bible. Oh God.

JOE: I don't believe in God anymore. I don't believe in anything. I don't even believe that I don't believe.

MAN SIX: Satan is alive and well and living in Ottawa. I believe in the Bible, the whole Bible, and nothing but the Bible. Oh God.

JOE: Look at him, praying to his god.

MAN: Satan is alive and well and living in Ottawa. I believe in the Bible, the whole Bible, and nothing but the Bible. Oh God.

(McNAUGHTON enters.)

McNAUGHTON: Quiet. No talking. Give me that. No dice.

(McNAUGHTON takes the dice.)

Give me that.

MAN SIX: Oh no, don't take my bible. He took my bible.

(McNAUGHTON takes the bible.)

Satan is alive and well and living here. I believe in the Bible, the whole Bible, and nothing but the Bible. Oh God.

McNAUGHTON: No talking. Quiet. Go to sleep.

JOE: Then turn out the lights.

McNAUGHTON: No talking.

MAN SIX: Satan is alive and well and living here!!

(The lights fade.)

Scene Thirty-seven

(In another playing area the lights fade in. JUDY, DAUGHTER, and WELFARE MAN enter.)

WELFARE MAN: I am with the Welfare Department. I am here to inspect you and the premises. Is this your kid?

JUDY: This is my daughter.

WELFARE MAN: How old are you?

DAUGHTER: What's it to you?

WELFARE MAN: I been here before. Your man ran away, I see. Have you got one under the bed?

JUDY: Muffin go into the other room.

(DAUGHTER exits.)

WELFARE MAN: You will answer all my questions or you will not receive your three dollars per week.

JUDY: Yes.

WELFARE MAN: You are a mighty fine looking woman. Lip smacking fine. Kind of skinny but a nice set of pins. You welfare bitches give me such an itch. I will come see you at ten o'clock tomorrow night. Make sure the kid's asleep.

JUDY: Get out. Now!

WELFARE MAN: You won't get your money.

JUDY: Out now and don't you ever come back here.

(The lights fade.)

Scene Thirty-eight

(In another playing area the lights fade in. JOE and two RELIEF CAMP WORKERS play Jew's harps. McNAUGHTON enters.)

McNAUGHTON: Quiet. No music. Give me that. Give me that.

(McNAUGHTON takes Jew's harps from the RELIEF CAMP WORKERS.)

Give me that.

JOE: I have nothing.

(McNAUGHTON exits. JOE pulls out his harp and plays. McNAUGHTON enters.)

McNAUGHTON: Give me that.

(JOE knocks McNAUGHTON to the ground.)

JOE: I can stand it no more. We're going to get our clothes and get out of here. We're going to talk to the fat boy in Ottawa. On to Ottawa. On to Ottawa!

(JOE and others exit. The lights fade.)

Scene Thirty-nine

(In another playing area the lights fade in. JUDY is sewing frantically. Her DAUGHTER enters.)

DAUGHTER: I'm hungry.

JUDY: I have to do this, Muffin. I have to make twelve of these a day or they won't pay me. I'm sorry I can't stop.

DAUGHTER: I'm hungry.

JUDY: There are some string beans in the fridge.

DAUGHTER: I want something that tastes good.

JUDY: Eat it with a slice of bread. That's good, that tastes good. I'll just finish this and I'll cook it for you. I'll cook it for you. I'll just finish this and I'll cook it for you. I'll just finish this, I'll just finish this, I'll just finish this, I'll just finish this.

(JUDY sews frantically. The lights fade.)

Scene Forty

(In another playing area the lights fade in. JOE and others hop a freight train.)

JOE: On to Ottawa!

(In two other playing areas. The lights fade in. BENNETT and McNAUGHTON enter.)

McNAUGHTON: The rabble have walked out of the relief camps and are now on their way to Ottawa.

BENNETT: They're coming for me, they're coming for me. I knew it, I knew it. Call out the army, call out the RCMP, call out the police.

McNAUGHTON: We will. The "On to Ottawa" trek is approaching Regina.

BENNETT: They must be stopped there. Stop them at Regina. Give them a taste of the iron heel.

McNAUGHTON: Yes

(The lights fade.)

Scene Forty-one

(The sound of a train on the rails and train whistles. In another playing area the lights fade in. JOE, a HOBO, and MEN SIX and SEVEN are on the roof of a freight car. The HOBO points at the audience. MAN SIX prays.)

HOBO: Look.

JOE: Nice looking couple.

(HOBO waves his hand.)

HOBO: See, they always wave back. Sitting on top of a box car you realize what a great country this is. Beautiful. God lives here.

(JOE waves his hand.)

JOE: Tunnel.

(JOE, HOBO, and MAN SEVEN duck. MAN SIX does not. The lights fade. Darkness. The lights fade in. MAN SIX is missing.)

He is with God now.

(The sound of the train slowing down.)

MAN SEVEN: What is this God forsaken place?

JOE: This is Regina. Every cop in the world lives here. They all live here.

(The train stops.)

Let's go.

(The lights fade.)

Scene Forty-two

(In another playing area the lights fade in. BENNETT and MCNAUGHTON enter.)

BENNETT: These trekkers are a distinct menace to peace, order, and good government. I want all the leaders arrested, now.

McNAUGHTON: Yes

(The lights fade.)

Scene Forty-three

(In another playing area the lights fade in: The Regina Riot.)

LOUDSPEAKER VOICE: *(Off.)* Citizens of Regina. The "On to Ottawa" trek needs funds ...

(JOE, HOBO, and MAN SEVEN are having a picnic. MAN SEVEN plays a guitar.)

JOE: How about "When Mountie's Eyes are Smiling"?

MAN SEVEN: I know it.

ALL: When Mountie's eyes are happy, You know somebody's dead, 'Cause when Mountie's eyes are happy, He's broke some strikers head. When Mountie's eyes are smiling, You know someone's in jail. When Mountie's eyes are smiling, it's cause he'll never get bail.

JOE: I know one. This is a Polish folk song. called "Poland is not yet dead."

LOUDSPEAKER VOICE: *(Off.)* Citizens of Regina, the "On to Ottawa" trek needs funds ...

(The sound a police whistle.)

JOE: What's that? What—

(MOUNTIES FOUR, FIVE, and EIGHT enter with clubs. They beat JOE and his friends. JOE and the HOBO exit. MAN SEVEN moans and groans.)

MAN SEVEN: Mercy, mercy.

MOUNTIE ONE: Now here's what you do with him. You start on the ankles and work toward the head. Like this.

(MOUNTIE ONE beats MAN SEVEN as if he were playing a xylophone.)

And when you get to the head, you do this. See, that really hurts.

(MOUNTIE TWO copies the actions of MOUNTIE ONE.)

Harder, harder, you're too gentle.

MAN SEVEN: Murder, murder.

MOUNTIE TWO: Why don't we just shoot him and be done with it?

MOUNTIE ONE: No, no. No violence.

(JOE and the HOBO enter holding clubs.)

JOE: Come on, you yellow legged sons of bitches. I'm going to kill you all.

(JOE and the HOBO beat up the two MOUNTIES. The MOUNTIES exit. JOE and the HOBO help MAN SEVEN. MOUNTIE ONE enters with a gun drawn. The sound of gunshots. The HOBO and MAN SEVEN are hit by bullets and fall to the ground. MOUNTIE ONE arrests JOE.)

MOUNTIE ONE: This way.

(JOE and MOUNTIE ONE exit. The lights fade.)

Scene Forty-four

(In another playing area the lights fade in. KING enters.)

KING: We were having one of our little state dinners when news of Regina arrived. I said "Were I a man of means I would certainly do something for these unfortunate men." Joan whispered to me. "Rex, you have the body of a man but the mind of a rotweiler." Oh Joan.

(The lights fade.)

Scene Forty-five

(In another playing area the lights fade in. JUDY and her DAUGHTER enter. JUDY sews.)

JUDY: How was school today?

DAUGHTER: Stupid. Everyone at school is stupid, even the teachers.

JUDY: Well at least you're learning

DAUGHTER: Yes. Learning. Oh I'm learning.

JUDY: One day you're going to be a big beautiful girl and meet a nice man.

DAUGHTER: I hope he's not like Daddy. I'd be really mad if he's like Daddy. Where is he?

(JUDY stops sewing. The lights fade.)

Scene Forty-six

(In another playing area the lights fade in. JOE and two MOUNTIES enter.)

MOUNTIE ONE: Having been convicted of a criminal offence under Section 98 of the Criminal Code, you have no rights. You are no longer a person in the eyes of the law.

JOE: I am a political prisoner. My only crime is opposition to those in power.

(MOUNTIE ONE holds up a leather strap.)

MOUNTIE ONE: Anyone who steps out of line gets a good whacking with this.

JOE: Go on, grovel to your master, you lackey.

MOUNTIE ONE: Put him down.

(MOUNTIE TWO forces JOE to the ground.)

MOUNTIE ONE: We're going to put you in with the scum of the earth. You won't last a week.

JOE: We'll see, we'll see.

(The lights fade.)

Scene Forty-seven

(In another playing area the lights fade in. KING is writing a speech.)

KING: No "five-cent piece" speech in this election. No sir. Now lets see. No sharp turn of phrase here. Oh here's one ... "I am ruthlessly committed to helping Canadians through this crisis." But perhaps not ... "I am ruthlessly committed." Take it out, just in case. "I am committed." Yes, that's more like it. No adjectives, and no adverbs. I declare war on adverbs. Just nouns. I defy anyone to remember what I say. Just drone on for hours, drone on.

(The lights fade.)

Scene Forty-eight

(In another playing area the lights fade in: the election of 1935. BENNETT enters holding placard "I can do better." KING enters holding a placard "King or chaos.")

BENNETT: My fellow Canadians, I love you.

KING: Down with the rich intolerant despot. I will get rid of the relief camps and Section 98 of the Criminal Code.

BENNETT: The old order is gone. It will not return. I will inaugurate the Employment and Social Insurance Act. I will institute the eight-hour day, and the forty-eight-hour week. I can do better if you will back my fresh plans.

KING: The rot and gush that comes out of him is unbelievable. Unction and what not. Such a demagogue. He will say anything, anything.

BENNETT: Pillock!

KING: And so unctuous, unctuous hypocrite!

BENNETT: Swine!

KING: Mountebank.

BENNETT: Fool.

KING: Blatherskate.

(The lights fade.)

Scene Forty-nine

(In another playing area the lights fade in. BENNETT enters.)

RADIO: *(Voice over.)* This is the CBC. Here are the 1935 election results. Liberals, one hundred and seventy-one; Conservatives, thirty-nine; CCF, seven. Mackenzie King is now the prime minister of Canada.

BENNETT: The results of this election remind me that recorded history has shown that there was only one Christian and he was crucified. So be it. I resign from the Conservative party, I am emigrating to England to live out my final days. And I place a curse on this land and on the people that live on this land.

(The lights fade.)

Scene Fifty

(In another playing area the lights fade in: Parliament. KING, LAPOINTE, WOODSWORTH, MIKE, the CCFer, and the SPEAKER enter.)

KING: When Canadians voted for me they did not vote for chaos. They voted for order, and I will give them order.

WOODSWORTH: Mr. Speaker.

SPEAKER: The House recognizes the Member from Winnipeg.

WOODSWORTH: There are one point three million people on relief. People have an inalienable right to food, clothing, and shelter at the expense of the state.

KING: Only if they work. The federal treasury must be protected. The financial problem is obvious. Unemployment relief is the major cause of federal deficits. We will reduce unemployment relief by twenty-five percent. That is what we will do. I have spoken.

WOODSWORTH: This is R. B. Bennett all over again.

(The lights fade.)

Scene Fifty-one

(In another playing area the lights fade in. KING enters holding Pat.)

KING: Food riots in Vancouver, Calgary, Winnipeg, Montreal, Toronto. Where will it all end, Pat. Where? But no food riots in Nazi Germany, Pat. No sir. Hitler is just like me. All he wants is peace, order, and good government. What do you think of that? Cat got your tongue, Pat? Not talkative, are you? Last night I had a dream about Hitler. We were holding hands and smiling, watching the sun rise. He is going to be an important man, Pat. Perhaps as important as me. I am going to meet with him. What do you think of that?

(Pat growls.)

Pat.

(The lights fade.)

Scene Fifty-two

(In another playing area the lights fade in. JUDY and her DAUGHTER enter. MOUNTIE ONE enters.)

JUDY: Come on you little flounce or I'll give you a good smacking. A good smacking is what you need. *(To MOUNTIE ONE.)* Is Joe Slomkovski here? I am his wife.

MOUNTIE ONE: The shit stick's got a wife? Jesus, now I've heard everything.

DAUGHTER: Why do you call him that?

MOUNTIE ONE: When you see him you'll know why. He craps on the floor and then rubs it all over himself and what's left he throws at you. And when he gets tired of that he barfs up his lunch and then throws that at you. Feeding the slob is a nightmare.

JUDY: Can we see him?

MOUNTIE ONE: This way.

(The lights fade.)

Scene Fifty-three

(In another playing area the lights fade in. JOE, covered in excrement, enters. Two CONVICTS enter. JUDY and her DAUGHTER enter.)

JOE: Welcome to hell. Murderers are king here, but no one comes near me.

JUDY: Look at you.

JOE: I am with the scum of the earth. Fine.

JUDY: Look at you.

JOE: The prisoners are bad but the guards are worse.

JUDY: Look your daughter.

DAUGHTER: You ate Blackie.

JOE: I ate Blackie.

JUDY: We have good news. You are going to be released from prison. The law jailing you has been repealed.

JOE: Kiss me and you too. Goodbye boys.

(The lights fade.)

Scene Fifty-four

(In another playing area the lights fade in. KING enters with Pat.)

RADIO: *(Voice over.)* "I have found it impossible to carry the heavy burden of responsibility and to discharge my duties as king as I would wish to do without the help and support of the woman I love. I therefore quit altogether public affairs and lay down my burden."

KING: King Edward the Eighth has abdicated. The king is dead. Long live the king. George the Sixth is now king of England. Do you know what that means, Pat? It means I will be going to England for the coronation. And after the coronation guess who I am going to see?

(Pat growls.)

Pat.

(The lights fade.)

Scene Fifty-five

(In another playing area the lights fade in. JOE and JUDY enter. The radio is playing.)

RADIO: *(Voice over.)* This is Mackenzie King speaking. Your prime minister.

JOE: Our prime minister

RADIO: Europe is a maelstrom of strife and we are being drawn into the vortex that is none of our creation.

JOE: Shut up.

(JOE turns the radio off.)

JUDY: I read somewhere that grandsons are just like their grandfathers.

JOE: Not that one. I tell you something, Wifey, I didn't fight in the Great War so I could live like this, that's for damn sure. Fascists, they're everywhere. R. B. Bennett and his Fascist regime. And now Mackenzie King and his Fascist regime. And now the Fascists are trying to take over Spain. It's a disgrace to the human race.

JUDY: You always say that.

JOE: 'Cause it's true.

JUDY: So what are you going to do about it, besides nothing?

JOE: I am going to get me a gun and go to Spain and kill me a Fascist. That's what I am going to do. Kill me a Fascist.

JUDY: You don't have to go to Spain to do that.

JOE: That's true. But I want to go to a country where the population do not support the sons of bitches. That sounds like Spain to me.

DAUGHTER: Do you mind, I am trying to sleep.

JOE: Muffin.

(The lights fade.)

Scene Fifty-six

(In another playing area the lights fade in: Mackenzie King meets Hitler at a Banquet. KING, JOACHIM RIBBENTROP, and JOSEPH GOEBBELS enter.)

RIBBENTROP: You know, once I was in Canada. At Banff. Have you ever been to Banff?

KING: No when I take a vacation I go to Florida.

RIBBENTROP: I was not there for a vacation. King. You know, in German, "king" means "führer."

KING: Really?

RIBBENTROP: You have a great deal in common. You were born in Berlin, Ontario. And now you are in Berlin, Germany.

GOEBBELS: Do you have an interest in the occult?

KING: No.

GOEBBELS: Der Führer has a great interest in the occult.

KING: Really?

RIBBENTROP: Yes. He is deeply religious. He does not smoke, or drink, or eat meat.

KING: He must be a very gentle man.

RIBBENTROP: Oh serenely gentle.

GOEBBELS: Serenely gentle. Die Reichmeister von Deutschland. Der Führer eintrete in der Raum.

(HITLER enters. RIBBENTROP and GOEBBELS jump up.)

RIBBENTROP: Heil Hitler.

GOEBBELS: Heil Hitler.

(RIBBENTROP gestures to KING to stand up. KING stands up.)

RIBBENTROP: Das ist der Ministerpräsident von Kanada.

HITLER: Ah Kanada, Zauberwort, Kanada, zauberwort. Ist er so dumm wie er ausschaut? *[Is he as dull as he looks.]*

RIBBENTROP: Ja. The Führer says you are a great man.

KING: Really?

HITLER: Mein Kampf ist dein Kampf.

RIBBENTROP: My struggle is your struggle.

KING: Yes, yes it is. Tell him that Canadians are more like the German people than the English or the French.

RIBBENTROP: Er sagt dass die Kanadier sind mehr gleich von die Deutschen als die Engländer oder die Franzozen.

KING: We do not let Jews in our country. We ban them from Canada.

RIBBENTROP: Er sagt dass die Juden sind verboten in Kanada.

(HITLER shakes KING's hand.)

He is honoured to meet you.

(RIBBENTROP snaps his fingers. A NAZI enters holding a framed photograph of HITLER.)

A gift from der Führer.

KING: Oh thank you. I will put this beside the picture of my mother. It is a special place for me.

RIBBENTROP: Er sagt das er es neben ein Bild von seiner Mutter setzen.

HITLER: Ist das nicht fein? *[Isn't that nice.]* Zahlen ihn. *[Tell him.]*

RIBBENTROP: We are building special recreation camps. We will name one after Canada. We will call it Kanadahausen.

KING: I cannot tell you how happy I am. I ... I feel at home here. Perhaps one day you will come and visit Canada.

RIBBENTROP: Perhaps one day we will.

(The NAZIS laugh. The lights fade.)

Scene Fifty-seven

(In another playing area the lights fade in. JOE, a VOLUNTEER, and an INSTRUCTOR enter. Behind them is a banner, "The Mackenzie-Papineau Battalion.")

INSTRUCTOR: Comrades. We are forming the Mackenzie-Papineau Battalion as part of the Abraham Lincoln Brigade to fight in Spain. We are the Mac-Paps. We are named in honour of the great reformer, William Lyon Mackenzie, and the great patriote, Louis-Joseph Papineau.

Now, the Canadian government refuses to recognize or support the Loyalist side in Spain. They support Franco, Hitler, Mussolini. We support the people in their fight against fascism. Therefore we are subversives.

The great reformer is turning in his grave. But we will put him back to sleep. As you can see I am not used to giving speeches. Rise up, Canadians, rise up.

Now, we have to make our own way to Spain. Secretly. We are all Communists here. And if you are not a Communist you soon will be. Why is brown bread superior to white bread?

VOLUNTEER: Brown bread is superior to white bread because workers eat brown bread.

INSTRUCTOR: Why is brown bread—

JOE: I eat brown bread because I cannot afford to eat white bread.

INSTRUCTOR: What did Marx say in 1848 about bourgeois individualism?

JOE: Couldn't give a damn.

INSTRUCTOR: Have you memorized the "Communist Manifesto"?

JOE: Haven't even read it.

INSTRUCTOR: You are one of the lumpen. I don't know if we can send you. You are not orthodox.

JOE: I tell you something, pal. In the Great War I fought at Ypres, the Somme, Vimy Ridge, Passchendaele, Amiens, Mons, and the likes of you did not. I'm joining the Mac-Paps to kill Fascists not talk to them about communism.

INSTRUCTOR: All right.

(The lights fade.)

Scene Fifty-eight

(In another playing area the lights fade in. KING enters.)

KING: Last night I had a dream. Me and Hitler were standing beside a lake watching the sunrise. We were kissing and hugging, just being friendly, and then snakes started coming out of his head. What can it mean?

(The lights fade.)

Scene Fifty-nine

(In another playing area the lights fade in: Spain. JOE, the INSTRUCTOR, and the VOLUNTEER enter. They look at a map.)

JOE: Now the River Ebro is over here. This is the Fascist stronghold at the river. This is our final destination. We should create a diversion over here and then sneak up on them over here.

INSTRUCTOR: We should charge straight ahead shouting "Rise up Canadians, rise up."

JOE: No, we die for sure if we do that.

(A Spanish PEASANT with no arms enters.)

PEASANT: Me cortaron los brazos. Me cortaron los brazos. Y lo que le hicieron a mi mujer usted no lo qui ere saber. *[They cut off my arms, they cut off my arms. And what they did to my wife you don't want to know. I am scared to death.]*

JOE: Where are the Fascists? Donde estan los Fascistas?

PEASANT: Los Fascistas estan por aha y por aqui tambien. *[The Fascists are here and here and here.]*

JOE: Gracias, amigo. Come on, let's go.

(In another playing area the lights fade in. TWO FASCISTS, one with a machine gun, enter. JOE, the INSTRUCTOR, and the VOLUNTEER sneak up on them. The INSTRUCTOR jumps up.)

INSTRUCTOR: Rise up, Canadians, rise—

(The INSTRUCTOR is shot. JOE and the VOLUNTEER attack the FASCISTS. JOE stabs FASCIST ONE.)

JOE: Die Fascist, die. Muerta Fascista.

(JOE strangles FASCIST TWO.)

Come on, on to the River Ebro.

(The lights fade.)

Scene Sixty

(In another playing area the lights fade in. JUDY is revealed sewing.)

JUDY: Dear Mrs. Slomkovski, Your husband Joseph was killed at the River Ebro on July 14th, 1937. Dear Mrs. Slomkovski, Your husband Joseph was killed at the River Ebro on July 14th, 1937.

(The lights fade.)

Scene Sixty-one

(In another playing area the lights fade in: a seance. KING and ETTA enter. ETTA speaks in tongues.)

KING: I want to speak with my mother. I want to speak with my mother.

(ETTA speaks in tongues.)

ETTA: Here comes the mother.

(An image of MOTHER is conjured up.)

MOTHER: Adolf Hitler is a monster, Willie, a monster. Don't believe anything Hitler says, Willie.

KING: She doesn't like him.

MOTHER: Oh he's a cunt, Willie, a cunt.

KING: Mother!

MOTHER: Where he goes disaster goes. He is war and death. You want proof, Willie?

KING: Yes.

MOTHER: Gaze into the crystal ball Willie. Oh Willie, gaze into the ball.

(KING looks into a crystal ball to see the future. He sees World War II.

The sound of marching feet, stuka dive bombers, artillery, bombs, "Achtung," "Sieg heil," shrieking, and screaming for fifteen seconds.

KING looks up from the crystal ball—a look of horror. The lights fade. The end.)

WORLD WAR II

PART EIGHT OF
THE HISTORY OF THE
VILLAGE OF THE SMALL HUTS

Act One

Scene One

(The lights fade in. MACKENZIE KING and MRS BLEANEY, a fortune-teller, enter.)

KING: Do you know who I am?

MRS BLEANEY: You are Mackenzie King, prime minister of Canada.

KING: How did you know that?

MRS BLEANEY: I know everything.

KING: Can you foretell the future?

MRS BLEANEY: As accurately as you remember the past I see the future.

KING: Currently, as we speak, Adolf Hitler, Benito Mussolini, and Neville Chamberlain are meeting in Munich.

MRS BLEANEY: Ah yes, I see it clearly.

KING: What is the result of that meeting?

MRS BLEANEY: See it clearly.

(In another playing area the lights fade in. HITLER, MUSSOLINI, and CHAMBERLAIN enter. They are signing a document.)

MRS BLEANEY: I see three men signing something.

KING: Is it the peace treaty?

MRS BLEANEY: Yes.

KING: Oh blessed be the peacemakers.

MRS BLEANEY: One of them is speaking.

CHAMBERLAIN: We will have peace in our time.

(The lights fade on HITLER, MUSSOLINI, and CHAMBERLAIN.)

KING: Oh blessed be the peacemakers. Appease the brutal beast and you will have peace.

MRS BLEANEY: I see clouds and darkness.

(The lights fade.)

Scene Two

(In another playing area the lights fade in: a farmhouse. JOHNNIE and MOTHER enter.)

MOTHER: Oh look at that sunrise, Johnnie.

JOHN: It's setting, Mum.

MOTHER: Sunrise, sunset, all the same to me. Oh it's a good life. Now did you pull Nellie's tits like I showed you?

JOHN: Yes.

MOTHER: Oh we'll have milk in the morning.

JOHN: Have it now if you want.

MOTHER: No no, listen. Do you hear it?

JOHN: I hear it.

MOTHER: The grasshoppers are singing their little song. They're just like us, Johnnie, just like us. They like to sing their little song. And so do we, don't we. Let's sing our little song. Oh I love the maple syrup tree, I love the maple syrup tree. Because the maple syrup tree is so in love with me, oh! Sing it.

JOHN: Oh I love the maple syrup tree.

(The lights fade.)

Scene Three

(In another playing area the lights fade in: a restaurant sign: "Eat Fish." JAMES RALSTON and C. D. HOWE enter. RALSTON reads a newspaper. HOWE holds a menu.)

HOWE: The roast beef looks good.

RALSTON: This is a disgrace. First Hitler marches into the Rhineland, then he annexes

Austria, and now Great Britain and France have given him a third of Czechoslovakia.

HOWE: He'll go for the rest of it. Mark my words.

RALSTON: He has to be stopped. It's terrible what they're doing to Jews in Europe.

HOWE: Horrible.

RALSTON: Disgusting.

HOWE: Disgraceful.

(A WAITER enters.)

WAITER: And what would you like to order?

(HOWE points at the sign.)

RALSTON: I don't pay attention to advertising. I'll try the salmon.

HOWE: Trout for me.

WAITER: Very good.

(The lights fade.)

Scene Four

(In another playing area the lights fade in. KING and Pat, the dog, enter.)

KING: It says here, Pat, that the prime minister of Great Britain, Neville Chamberlain, has drawn a line in the sand. If Germany attacks Poland, Great Britain will come to the assistance of Poland. I am horrified. He is abandoning the process of appeasement. I am horrified, horrified! Why can't Europe do what we do? What's the matter with them? If only they could resolve differences in Europe the way Canada and the United States resolve differences. For instance, when the United States says it wants something done. We do it. Then we have peace. A lot of peace. Blessed be the peacemakers.

(Pat barks. The lights fade.)

Scene Five

(In another playing area the lights fade in. JOE, ROSE, and MUFFIN enter. ROSE holds a toaster.)

MUFFIN: Get a job.

JOE: There are no jobs. I've told you that a thousand times.

ROSE: Can you fix this?

JOE: Fix it yourself.

ROSE: Come on, be a man.

JOE: No, I've had it.

MUFFIN: Fix it. It doesn't work. It burns the toast on one side but not the other. Fix it.

JOE: Give it to me.

(ROSE gives JOE the toaster.)

Don't ever do this when it's plugged in. Otherwise you'll electrocute yourself.

MUFFIN: Fix it.

JOE: Muffin.

(The lights fade.)

Scene Six

(In another playing area the lights fade in. KING enters with a Ouija board.)

KING: Oh these alliances, these alliances. Hitler has formed an alliance with Stalin. Something big is going to happen in Europe. Something big. Oh, Laurier was so right, so right. Nationalism leads only to the vortex of militarism. It is a blight on mankind, a midden based on feuds and vendettas. Oh these alliances, these alliances.

(The lights fade.)

Scene Seven

(In another playing area the lights fade in. HOWE and RALSTON enter.)

RALSTON: Well C. D., it looks like it is going to pop in a big way.

HOWE: It does Colonel Ralston, it does.

RALSTON: And we'll do it right this time, do it right. Put the French in the trench.

HOWE: Yes, war is profits. War is big business. War will make this country a great industrial nation or my name is not C. D. Howe.

RALSTON: Know that I will conscript all the men for the army. It'll be difficult but I'll get it done. I always get my way, always.

HOWE: If you conscript all the men for the army I'll have to conscript all the women for industry.

RALSTON: Yes, a nation at war.

HOWE: Yes.

(A WAITER enters holding a telephone.)

WAITER: Telephone for Colonel Ralston.

(The WAITER gives the telephone to RALSTON.)

RALSTON: Colonel James Ralston speaking … yes … yes. Hallejulah. Germany has invaded Poland.

HOWE: Oh getting closer, getting closer. As sure as night follows day the depression is going to end.

RALSTON: Happy days are here again.

(The lights fade.)

Scene Eight

(In another playing area the lights fade in. KING and ERNEST LAPOINTE enter.)

LAPOINTE: If there is a war and conscription is imposed, I, Ernest Lapointe, will resign as Minister of Justice. And you know what that means. You have been in power for many years because of Quebec.

KING: Tell me something I don't know.

LAPOINTE: If there is a war le Canadien-Français will not fight for England, will not fight for France, le Canadien-Français will fight for only one thing. His land. Only if Canada is invaded will we fight.

KING: You want to tell me something.

LAPOINTE: If what happened in the last war happens in this one …

KING: Conscription.

LAPOINTE: Yes. If les Anglais march into Quebec and start shooting people because they won't fight for the Union Jack, it will be the end of Canada, I guarantee it.

KING: There will be no conscription. World War Two will be a good war. A war fought only by those who want to fight it.

(KING puts a rose in LAPOINTE's lapel.)

LAPOINTE: That's what they said about the first one. There will only be conscription over my dead body.

KING: Yes.

(RALSTON enters.)

RALSTON: It's a fact. Britain has declared war on Germany. It is time to issue a declaration of war. When Britain is at war, Canada is at war.

KING: In 1914 when King George the Fifth declared war on Germany we were automatically at war.

RALSTON: You betcha.

KING: But now, in 1939 when King George the Sixth declares war on Germany, we are not automatically at war.

RALSTON: What?

KING: Colonel Ralston, Canada is an autonomous self-governing colony.

(KING puts a rose in RALSTON's lapel.)

RALSTON: Still a colony. "Ready, aye, ready" then, "ready, aye, ready" now.

KING: Parliament will decide.

RALSTON: The motherland is calling. The majority of Canadians want to go to war.

LAPOINTE: Not this Canadien, monsieur.

RALSTON: I can feel it, feel it in my blood. You must issue the declaration of war or there will be a revolution.

KING: We are going to think about it … for a week. Ah yes. A week of peace. Peace, blessed word.

(The lights fade.)

Scene Nine

(In another playing area the lights fade in. JOE and ROSE enter. A radio is heard.)

RADIO: We interrupt our programming to bring you this important announcement. In Parliament today, the prime minister of Canada, Mackenzie King, declared that a state of war now exists between the German Reich and the Dominion of Canada as and from the tenth day of September, 1939.

JOE: Oh there's going to be a war.

ROSE: Oh good. I hope you join up and die in it.

JOE: Come here.

(ROSE holds up a frying pan.)

ROSE: Come near me Joe Porter and I'll brain you. I've had it with you. So I tell you something, you join, or I swear one night when you're snoring I'll kill you with this, I swear it.

MUFFIN: *(Off.)* Mum.

ROSE: Oh! Go on drink your hooch! It's all

you're good for. I thought I married a man. Ha! I married this. *(Indicating the frying pan.)*

(ROSE exits.)

JOE: I'm gonna sign up.

(The lights fade.)

Scene Ten

(In another playing area the lights fade in. RALSTON and a CLERK enter.)

CLERK: Colonel Ralston, General Andrew McNaughton to see you.

RALSTON: Send him in.

(The CLERK exits as ANDREW McNAUGHTON and HENRY CRERAR enter.)

Sit.

McNAUGHTON: There is no chair.

RALSTON: Then stand. I'm a man's man. I proved that in the Great War and I'll prove it in this one, I served in the infantry, I was wounded three times.

McNAUGHTON: Well, you know what they say. In all wars there are gunners and there are targets.

RALSTON: Infantry wins wars.

McNAUGHTON: Artillery wins wars.

RALSTON: As Minister of National Defence I represent the government of Canada. You will take all your orders from me, General.

McNAUGHTON: Certainly, Colonel. This is my chief of staff, Henry Crerar.

CRERAR: Call me Harry.

RALSTON: Never. General McNaughton, what is the state of the armed forces?

McNAUGHTON: Harry?

CRERAR: The permanent force numbers four thousand.

McNAUGHTON: And we have two tanks. I plan to make weapon development a priority. We will spare human lives by arming and equipping the troops in a first rate manner.

RALSTON: Yes, yes. General McNaughton, you will have cause to mobilize an army to fight in Europe at the side of British arms. The army will be comprised of volunteers. There will be no conscription until I authorize it. Is that understood, General?

McNAUGHTON: Certainly, Colonel.

(The lights fade.)

Scene Eleven

(In another playing area the lights fade in. KING enters.)

KING: I have declared war on Germany. Now I will declare the War Measures Act in Canada. I will ban the Canadian Nazi party. And the Canadian Communist party. And groups. Anyone who meets in groups will be banned. And everyone of German ancestry will be interned. Yes, interned. And we will arrest all the Fascists. All of them. And that includes the secret Fascists. Especially them. They're the worst. And then …

(The lights fade.)

Scene Twelve

(In another playing area the lights fade in. ROSE and MUFFIN enter.)

ROSE: Stand still … Anything interesting happen today?

MUFFIN: No … Well the Mounties came and arrested the neighbours.

ROSE: The Smiths?

MUFFIN: The Mounties said they were Schmidts. You should have heard them. They were yelling at the top of their voices "We're Austrians, we're Austrians." Didn't do them any good.

ROSE: They should have said they were Canadians.

MUFFIN: That wouldn't help them.

ROSE: That's terrible.

MUFFIN: Yes.

(The lights fade.)

Scene Thirteen

(In another playing area the lights fade in. There is a small maple tree. JOHN and MOTHER enter.)

JOHN: It's September. We won't get any sap out of the tree until spring.

MOTHER: I know, I know. Here it is, Johnnie,

here it is. My pride and joy. When it grows up to be big and strong, I'm going to get all the sap out of it. All of it. Right till the last drip-drop. Put it in my bucket.

JOHN: Yes.

MOTHER: What's the matter?

JOHN: I'm signing up.

MOTHER: Oh no, don't leave me.

JOHN: I'm going.

MOTHER: Your father got killed in the last one and you'll get killed in this one. I know it, I know it.

JOHN: I'm going.

MOTHER: Oh Johnnie.

(The lights fade.)

Scene Fourteen

(In another playing area the lights fade in. ROSE and MUFFIN enter a cinema. MUFFIN eats popcorn.)

ANNOUNCER: *(Off.)* Before our feature presentation be sure to visit our refreshment stand and buy your popcorn, candy bars, hot dogs, and refreshments.

(Trumpet fanfare.)

The NFB presents "Canada Carries On." Women are needed to make bombs. Jobs, job, jobs for women. Jobs for everybody. Support the war effort. The men are fighting. What are you doing? Put the Hun on the run. Do your bit. Women are needed to make bombs.

(ROSE exits.)

And now our feature presentation starring …

(The lights fade.)

Scene Fifteen

(In another playing area the lights fade in. JOHN, JOE, and a SOLDIER enter. McNAUGHTON and HAMILTON ROBERTS enter.)

ROBERTS: Attention.

McNAUGHTON: Welcome to Valcartier, men, welcome to Valcartier. I am General McNaughton. Thank you for signing up. This is Colonel Hamilton Roberts. He will be in charge of your training.

McNAUGHTON: What's your name?

JOE: Porter, Joe Porter.

McNAUGHTON: How's it going with you?

JOE: It's good, it's good.

McNAUGHTON: What's your name?

JOHN: John Shereski.

ROBERTS: Is that a German name?

JOHN: It's Canadian.

McNAUGHTON: Where you from son?

JOHN: Winnipeg, Manitoba.

McNAUGHTON: I'm from Moosomin, Saskatchewan.

JOHN: We're practically neighbours.

McNAUGHTON: How are they treating you?

JOHN: No complaints, sir.

McNAUGHTON: Any questions I can answer?

JOHN: Have you ever been shot?

ROBERTS: Private.

McNAUGHTON: It's all right. Once. Sniper. The Great War.

JOHN: What's it like being shot?

McNAUGHTON: Get a fish hook, one of the big ones for catching muskie. Like this.

(McNAUGHTON holds up a large fish hook.)

And dig the hook into your cheek, all the way, hook it deep, right to the thread, and then rip it out. That would be a flesh wound. Make sure this one puts the feed bag on. I want him to be big and strong when we get to England.

(McNAUGHTON exits.)

ROBERTS: All right, laddies. We have a lot of work to do. By the left. March.

(The lights fade.)

Scene Sixteen

(In another playing area the lights fade in. McNAUGHTON and ROBERTS enter. CRERAR and RALSTON enter.)

McNAUGHTON: Colonel Roberts. How are the men, Hamilton?

ROBERTS: The quality is equal to the quantity. Excellent. The men are very spruce, very spruce.

McNAUGHTON: The men look like they are in

good shape and well drilled. Well done Hamilton. One day Harry, Colonel Roberts here, will replace one of us.

(RALSTON and CRERAR laugh.)

Sixty thousand volunteers in one month. Not bad, not bad.

(McNAUGHTON and ROBERTS exit.)

RALSTON: God I hate him.

CRERAR: Our beloved general does not believe in the Imperial army.

RALSTON: No.

CRERAR: He believes in the Canadian army. So do I, of course, but I also believe in the Imperial army.

RALSTON: Really?

CRERAR: Yes.

(The lights fade.)

Scene Seventeen

(In another playing area the lights fade in. ROSE enters.)

VOICE: *(Off.)* Get a leg on. Don't you know there's a war on?

(FRED, the foreman, enters.)

FRED: You'll be making tanks. You will be paid six dollars a day. You're going to do a good job 'cause I'm going to show you. This way, Miss.

(The lights fade.)

Scene Eighteen

(In another playing area the lights fade in. McNAUGHTON, CRERAR, and SOLDIERS enter.)

McNAUGHTON: I will now embark with First Canadian Division to England. You will stay in Canada as Chief of Staff. Don't let Ralston bully you. He's a bully, don't let him bully.

CRERAR: Don't worry, Andy. I am going to wrap him 'round my finger.

(The sound of a ship's whistle.)

McNAUGHTON: Well, we're off. Forward.

(McNAUGHTON and SOLDIERS exit.)

CRERAR: Now I'm in charge. Me!

(The lights fade.)

Scene Nineteen

(In another playing area the lights fade in. KING and Pat enter.)

KING: Oh Pat, You're a saint, aren't you?

(Pat nods his head.)

A saint cannot lie. Is my mother inside you?

(Pat nods his head.)

I knew it. Are other divine spirits inside you?

(Pat nods his head.)

Are you the incarnation of Jesus Christ our Saviour?

(Pat nods his head.)

Oh Pat, I worship you as a living god. Do you know why we are fighting this war?

(Pat nods his head.)

We are not fighting this war to keep the world free of Nazis.

(Pat shakes his head.)

Or to maintain the British Empire.

(Pat shakes his head.)

We're fighting this war to keep the Liberal party in power.

(Pat nods his head.)

And that means you and me in power together, forever.

(Pat nods his head.)

Oh my dog can sing. Pat, sing us a song.

(The lights fade.)

Scene Twenty

(In another playing area the lights fade in. McNAUGHTON and SOLDIERS enter. BERNARD MONTGOMERY enters.)

McNAUGHTON: Forward.

MONTGOMERY: I am Bernard Montgomery, inspector general of all troops in the British army. Welcome to England.

McNAUGHTON: Thank you. We are ready to invade Europe. The Canadian army is a dagger pointed at the heart of Berlin.

MONTGOMERY: You and your troops will be transported to Aldershot where they will train with British troops.

McNAUGHTON: The Canadians will not train

with British troops. They will stay under Canadian command. The Canadians are not British troops.

MONTGOMERY: Then what are they?

McNAUGHTON: They are Canadian troops. I do not want Canadian divisions to be part of a British army. We want all the divisions to form a Canadian army. The Canadians fight better when they are together not in penny packets. Good day. Forward.

(McNAUGHTON and SOLDIERS exit.)

MONTGOMERY: I am going to destroy him.

(The lights fade.)

Scene Twenty-one

(In another playing area the lights fade in. KING is behind a forest of radio microphones.)

KING: Test ... is this working?

VOICE: *(Off.)* Yes, Mr. Prime Minister. Five seconds. Five, four, three.

KING: Brave Canadians, this is your prime minister speaking. In this election vote for the Liberal party. Vote for the Liberal party and there will be no conscription. Vote for me and there will be full employment. Vote for me and there will be no conscription. I repeat, no conscription. Did you hear that? Hello anyone out there.

(The lights fade.)

Scene Twenty-two

(In another playing area the lights fade in. JOE enters.)

JOE: Been here six months in jolly old England. The phony war they call it. That's exactly what it is. A phony war. No killing, no fighting, no shooting, no nothing. Just go on parade. Stand guard, then stand to, then stand down, then stand up. Makes you crazy.

(The lights fade.)

Scene Twenty-three

(In another playing area the lights fade in. KING and Pat enter.)

KING: It's a landslide, Pat, a landslide. We have formed a massive majority government. Oh my dog can sing. Pat, sing a song.

(The lights fade.)

Scene Twenty-four

(In another playing area the lights fade in. ROSE and VIOLET are making a tank. ROSE holds a big spanner. FRED enters.)

FRED: Get a leg on. Don't you know there's a war on? I can't go anywhere. Can't go dancing. Some lout steps on your foot and punches you in the face. Go to the restaurant? Same story. Take the wife to the movies? Can't do that. The only thing you know for sure is that either before, during, or after the movie someone is going to be kicking the crap out of you. My favourite is during. And the language they use. Oh my ears. And you're with the wife. But I've learned my lesson. It's not fair. Just because a woman can do my job doesn't mean the job is easy. I'm doing this job because I am vital to the war effort. I tried to join, I really did but they wouldn't take me. Flat feet. Now everybody spits on me, calls me chickenbelly, but I don't care. I do a good job, a good job. And you're going to do a good job 'cause I showed you.

(FRED exits.)

ANNOUNCER: *(Voice over.)* Attention workers! The phony war is over! The Germans have invaded Holland, Belgium, Luxembourg! It's blitzkrieg!

ROSE: This can't be happening.

VIOLET: This is unbelievable.

ANNOUNCER: *(Voice over.)* Attention workers! The Germans have invaded France! The French army has been annihilated! It's blitzkrieg!

ROSE: This can't be happening.

VIOLET: This is unbelievable.

ANNOUNCER: *(Voice over.)* The battle of France is over! The battle of Britain is about to begin!

ROSE: This can't be happening.

ANNOUNCER: *(Voice over.)* The battle of Britain is about to begin!

ROSE: This is a nightmare.

ANNOUNCER: *(Voice over.)* The battle of Britain is about to begin!

(The lights fade.)

Scene Twenty-five

(In another playing area the lights fade in. The sound of an air raid siren. JOE and JOHN enter. They look up. The sounds of aerial combat. McNAUGHTON and ROBERTS enter.)

JOE and JOHN: Ooooh ... Aaaah ... Ooooh ... Aaaah.

McNAUGHTON: Colonel Roberts, the German army has conquered Europe.

JOE and JOHN: Ooooh ...

McNAUGHTON: We will not be invading Europe.

JOE and JOHN: Aaaah ...

McNAUGHTON: We are now here for the defence of Great Britain.

JOE and JOHN: Ooooh ...

McNAUGHTON: German invasion is imminent.

JOE and JOHN: Aaaah ...

McNAUGHTON: Stand on guard, be alert.

JOE and JOHN: Ooooh ...

ROBERTS: The men are ready.

JOE and JOHN: Aaaah ...

(The lights fade.)

Scene Twenty-six

(In another playing area the lights fade in. RALSTON enters. CRERAR enters holding magazines featuring McNAUGHTON's face.)

CRERAR: Our beloved general is receiving accolades for his defence of Great Britain.

(CRERAR gives the magazines to RALSTON.)

RALSTON: "Star Weekly," "Macleans," "Life," "Time Magazine." Jesus. All with his ugly stupid face on it. They're making him into a hero. Well, we'll see, we'll see.

(The lights fade.)

Scene Twenty-seven

(In another playing area the lights fade in. KING, RALSTON, and LAPOINTE enter.)

LAPOINTE: Merde de cochon.

KING: What's the matter with you.

LAPOINTE: I am having a complete nervous breakdown. I am interning French-Canadiens who oppose the war effort. Have you any idea what that is like for a French-Canadien? Do you know what they call me? They call me merde de cochon, merde de cochon. I get chest pains when I least expect them. And now, the fall of France has been a terrible shock.

RALSTON: We want everyone between the ages of sixteen and sixty registered for home defence.

LAPOINTE: And now this. Oh mon dieu.

KING: I am declaring a state of national emergency. The defence of Canada is the primary issue. The invasion of Canada is a distinct possibility. Therefore the government of Canada will authorize the National Resources Mobilization Act which will mobilize all our human and material resources for the defence of Canada. The act relates only to the defence of Canada on our own soil.

LAPOINTE: I agree with this if it is for the defence of Canada only.

RALSTON: May I suggest conscription for the defence of Canada.

KING: I am horrified at that suggestion. Horrified. We are not here to invent ways of getting Canadians into action. We are here to protect lives. We are fighting the best kind of war. A war with no casualties. Active service means casualties, casualties mean reinforcements, and reinforcements mean conscription. And conscription means dissension, strife, disorder. Strife, disorder! That is not what we want. We want peace and order. I am horrified at that suggestion. Horrified.

RALSTON: I take back the suggestion.

KING: Excellent. We are agreed. You see with agreement there is peace. Oh peace. A lot of peace.

RALSTON: Yes.

(The lights fade.)

Scene Twenty-eight

(In another playing area the lights fade in. A loudspeaker voice is heard. FRED gives ROSE her first pay envelope.)

FRED: Sign here. Count it. Not bad, eh?

ANNOUNCER: *(Voice over.)* Buy war bonds. Buy war bonds. Buy war bonds. Buy war bonds.

(FRED gives VIOLET her first pay envelope.)

FRED: Sign here. Count it. Not bad, eh?

ANNOUNCER: *(Voice over.)* Buy war bonds. Buy war bonds. Buy war bonds. Buy war bonds.

(FRED exits.)

ROSE: I've never had so much money in my life.

VIOLET: Me neither.

ROSE: For the last ten years I've been eating beans and peas. I'm going to buy all the food I couldn't eat.

VIOLET: And clothes.

ROSE: Oh yes, and clothes.

VIOLET: And war bonds.

ROSE: That too.

VIOLET: And clean sheets, and ...

(The lights fade.)

Scene Twenty-nine

(In another playing area the lights fade in. McNAUGHTON and a SCIENTIST, wearing a lab coat, enter. MONTGOMERY enters.)

McNAUGHTON: I am building and supplying a Canadian army that will be capable of operating independently. The standard Bren gun magazine holds thirty rounds. But my new design holds one hundred rounds. I recommend that we go with the new design.

SCIENTIST: Very good.

McNAUGHTON: Now with the artillery. We need muzzle velocity of at least four thousand five hundred feet per second and specially devised armour-piercing shells.

MONTGOMERY: I have no idea what you are talking about.

McNAUGHTON: I am talking about guns with real killing power. Artillery will win the war. The country with the biggest factories that can make the biggest cannons will win. Oh that reminds me I will write a letter to C. D. Howe that we also need wireless receivers and transmitters, and tanks with six inch plate. Now, with regard to airburst ranging. The data has to be correct. I cannot stress enough the importance of correct data. Now lets get that letter off to C. D. Howe right now.

(McNAUGHTON and the SCIENTIST exit.)

MONTGOMERY: He is obsessed with technology. He is not really a general. He is too busy studying weapons and equipment.

(The lights fade.)

Scene Thirty

(In another playing area the lights fade in. HOWE enters.)

HOWE: That's right. I want factories to build guns, guns, guns! Bombs, bombs, bombs! Tanks, tanks, tanks! Planes, planes, planes! One aircraft today is worth ten in six months time. Who said that? Who cares? That's right we'll put ten thousand workers there to make Hurricanes. And we'll expropriate all that land. And put ten thousand there to make Spitfires. Tanks, tanks, tanks! We'll put five thousand there to make tanks. Jeeps, jeeps, jeeps! Trucks, trucks, trucks! What are you looking at? I'm busier than a whore working two beds. Get back to work. There's a war on you know. This country can make anything. Guns, guns, guns!

(The lights fade.)

Scene Thirty-one

(In another playing area the lights fade in. KING enters.)

KING: I am waiting for Franklin Roosevelt. Always waiting. I hope he doesn't ask me to go swimming with him. I can't do that. My hideous horrible body in a swim suit is too awful to contemplate. Splashing away. But I like to watch him swim. But the hands of the clock are on top of one another. A good sign. That means God is on my side.

(FRANKLIN DELANEY ROOSEVELT enters with cigarette holder and a martini.)

FDR: That is what I want done. Don't tell me

why it can't be done. Just do it. Mackenzie, how good to see you.

KING: Mr. President.

FDR: Mackenzie, we are concerned about the inadequacy of the defence of Canada on the Atlantic and Pacific coasts. If Germany invades Canada we will have to invoke the Monroe Doctrine and put Canada under our protection.

KING: Put us under your wing.

FDR: Yes we will put you under our wing.

KING: This is a military alliance between Canada and the United States.

FDR: How does it feel to be under the wing of an eagle?

KING: Oh it feels good, it feels good.

FDR: We will call this ... where are we?

VOICE: *(Off.)* Ogdensburg.

FDR: The Ogdensburg Agreement. Agreed to by Franklin and Mackenzie on a fine Sunday afternoon in August 1940.

KING: Yes ... The sun is so warm.

FDR: I can feel the rays. How about a swim? What do you say?

(The lights fade.)

Scene Thirty-two

(In another playing area the lights fade in. RALSTON and CRERAR enter.)

RALSTON: Mackenzie King is too cosy with the Americans. Too cosy.

CRERAR: It is important that the British Empire emerge from the war intact.

RALSTON: It can only emerge intact if we have an Imperial army with Canada as an active participant.

CRERAR: Yes. We have a request from the British government to garrison Hong Hong.

RALSTON: Send them.

CRERAR: I don't think we need to inform our beloved general of this.

RALSTON: Definitely not.

CRERAR: We can only create a great army by getting active.

RALSTON: And we can only get conscription by getting active.

CRERAR: Yes.

(The lights fade.)

Scene Thirty-three

(In another playing area the lights fade in: an English pub. JOE and JOHN are playing darts. A WOMAN sits at a table with an ENGLISHMAN.)

VOICE: *(Off.)* Time, gentlemen, time. Time, gentlemen, please.

ENGLISHMAN: Sitting in a snug with a mug. I just want some beer and some intelligent conversation.

WOMAN: I like to see myself as a class act.

ENGLISHMAN: Like another beer?

WOMAN: Well, just a little one.

ENGLISHMAN: Here have some of this.

WOMAN: Why thank you. You know there are bigger glasses. My husband doesn't like it when I drink.

ENGLISHMAN: Bartender.

(ENGLISHMAN exits.)

JOHN: Oh look at that.

JOE: Settle down. Show some discipline.

JOHN: Once I break the ice I'm a ball of fire, but I can never come up with the right line to break the ice. You can't go up to these English girls and say "I'd like to buy you a drink." They get very snooty.

JOE: Oh Miss, I don't mean to be rude, but my friend and I were wondering how old the church in this village is. My friend thinks it is eighteenth century, but I think it must be at least a thousand years old.

WOMAN: Oh at least. It's an Anglo-Saxon church.

JOE: Eighth, ninth century.

WOMAN: Now that I think of it, there's a plaque that says it was built in the seventh century.

JOE: Really?

WOMAN: Yes ... So you're from the Canadas.

JOE: Yes.

JOHN: I'm from Manitoba.

WOMAN: My Tommy's in the jungle.

(TOMMY enters.)

TOMMY: No he's not. He's right here. The neighbours said you were here.

WOMAN: I thought you were in Singapore.

TOMMY: Now you know.

JOE: The lady's with me.

TOMMY: That's no lady, that's my wife.

JOE: Sorry.

TOMMY: What do you mean by that?

(The sound of an air raid siren.)

JOE and TOMMY: Blast.

(The lights fade.)

Scene Thirty-four

(In another playing area the lights fade in. KING, RALSTON, and CRERAR enter.)

CRERAR: It is believed that the addition of two battalions to defend Hong Kong would render the garrison strong enough to withstand an extensive siege by Japanese forces.

KING: Who believes that?

CRERAR: Well.

RALSTON: The British government is requesting the despatch of two battalions.

CRERAR: Two.

RALSTON: For obvious reasons Britain cannot send two battalions.

CRERAR: Two.

RALSTON: I see no obvious military risk.

CRERAR: We are not at war with Japan.

RALSTON: Great Britain is not at war with Japan.

CRERAR: China is at war with Japan.

KING: But Hong Kong is in China, is it not?

CRERAR: Well.

RALSTON: Hong Kong is part of the British Empire.

KING: What happens if we are attacked?

CRERAR: They won't be attacked.

RALSTON: Japan would never dare to attack the British Empire.

CRERAR: This is a giant game of bluff.

RALSTON: Will they call my bluff?

CRERAR: Bluff me if you can.

RALSTON: Bluff me I dare you.

CRERAR: I recommend that the Canadian army take this on.

RALSTON: Me too.

KING: I agree to the despatch of two battalions as long as this agreement does not later afford an argument for conscription.

CRERAR and RALSTON: Oh no.

(The lights fade.)

Scene Thirty-five

(In another playing area the lights fade in: Mackenzie King conjures up Hong Kong. KING enters with a crystal ball.)

MALTBY: *(Voice over.)* Brave Canadians, welcome to Hong Kong.

(The lights fade.)

Scene Thirty-six

(In another playing area the lights fade in. MALTBY enters.)

MALTBY: Welcome, welcome. I am General Maltby. The British have held Hong Kong for one hundred years. Our job is to ensure that it remains part of the British Empire.

Hong Kong is a Chinese word. It means "fragrant harbour." Now, I am an expert on the Chinese. The Chinese are completely insane. All of them. They are beneath contempt. I would not insult a yellow dog by calling them one. Now where was I? Yes. There is a possibility that we will be attacked by the Japanese army. Do not worry about the Japanese. I am an expert on the Japanese. I am going to tell you a few things about them. The whole population of Japan is completely insane. They worship demons, eat insects, and can see in the dark. Now where was I? ... Yes.

(The lights fade.)

Scene Thirty-seven

(In another playing area the lights fade in. GENERAL LAWSON and SOLDIERS ONE and TWO enter. LAWSON smokes a Briar pipe.)

SOLDIER TWO: If they attack, they'll wipe us out.

SOLDIER ONE: It is a death trap.

LAWSON: Oh it's a pipe full.

SOLDIER ONE: I thought we were just going to be on garrison duty.

LAWSON: And we are.

SOLDIER TWO: So what do you think of Hong Kong?

LAWSON: Oh that'll take two pipes. Two pipes.

(The lights fade.)

Scene Thirty-eight

(In another playing area the lights fade in. SOLDIERS THREE and FOUR enter. A NURSE enters.)

SOLDIER THREE: Then I got Beriberi. Bloated up as big as a walrus. Couldn't sit, couldn't stand, just lay on my side, excrete sideways. What a mess.

NURSE: There, there. We'll clean you up. I like doing this actually.

SOLDIER FOUR: You're in good hands.

(SOLDIER FOUR and NURSE look at each other. The lights fade.)

Scene Thirty-nine

(In another playing area the lights fade in: a dance. Big band music plays on the radio. SOLDIER FOUR and the NURSE enter dancing. SOLDIERS ONE and TWO dance. LAWSON and MALTBY dance.)

SOLDIER ONE: He's got himself a nice piece of cherry pie. A nice piece.

SOLDIER FOUR: You are talking about the woman I love. Stop. Now.

SOLDIER ONE: A nice piece of cherry pie.

SOLDIER FOUR: When the war is over I have big plans for this woman. Big plans. Babies that turn into people. House, job, a real life.

SOLDIER ONE: A nice piece.

RADIO: *(Voice over.)* We interrupt this broadcast. Pearl Harbour has been attacked by Japanese forces. Bulletin, Pearl Harbour has been attacked by Japanese forces. President Franklin Roosevelt has declared December 7th, 1941 a day of infamy. This is the BBC. We now return to our previous programme.

SOLDIER FOUR: What can it mean?

LAWSON: Oh that's two pipes, two pipes.

MALTBY: This is not the war I wanted to see but it will do. The British Empire versus the world. That's a fair fight. To live and die like an Englishman. To battle stations.

(The lights fade.)

Scene Forty

(In another playing area the lights fade in. The Battle of Hong Kong. MALTBY enters.)

MALTBY: Now the Japs have taken the Gin-Drinkers line and Kowloon has fallen. The Japs have declared everybody a prostitute so that should keep them busy for a week.

(In another playing area the lights fade in. LAWSON enters holding a telephone. SOLDIERS ONE, TWO, and FOUR enter. The sound of artillery.)

LAWSON: General Maltby, we are under attack. The Japs have invaded Hong Kong.

(MALTBY picks up a telephone.)

MALTBY: That can't be.

LAWSON: We are under attack.

MALTBY: That can't be.

LAWSON: You bloody fool, you nincompoop. Listen.

(LAWSON holds the telephone up. The sound of artillery.)

MALTBY: That can't be happening.

(Lights fade on MALTBY.)

LAWSON: Hello ... hello. The Japs are attacking Wong Nei Chong Gap. Hello ... hello. The Japs are attacking.

SOLDIER TWO: See, that's how it's done.

SOLDIER ONE: I'm out of bullets.

SOLDIER TWO: There's some over there.

SOLDIER ONE: Where?

SOLDIER TWO: There.

SOLDIER ONE: No there's not.

SOLDIER TWO: Then look for them.

SOLDIER ONE: There's a mortar over there.

SOLDIER TWO: Get it.

SOLDIER TWO: I don't know how to fire it.

SOLDIER ONE: Learn.

(SOLDIER ONE exits.)

LAWSON: Hello ... is anyone there?

SOLDIER FOUR: Two of our boys have gone crazy in the head. The bombing has snapped their minds.

(JAPANESE SOLDIER ONE enters holding a grenade. He throws the grenade into the trench.)

SOLDIER TWO: Grenade.

SOLDIER FOUR: Grenade.

(SOLDIER FOUR shoots JAPANESE SOLDIER ONE. SOLDIER TWO dives on the grenade. There is a loud explosion. SOLDIER FOUR is wounded.)

LAWSON: Stretcher bearers, stretcher bearers.

(JAPANESE SOLDIER TWO enters and shoots LAWSON. SOLDIER FOUR shoots JAPANESE SOLDIER TWO. The lights fade.)

Scene Forty-one

(In another playing area the lights fade in. NURSE and SOLDIER THREE enter.)

SOLDIER THREE: If a bomb doesn't get us, the Japs will kill us in our beds. Butchered in my bed.

NURSE: Look on the bright side.

(SOLDIER FOUR enters.)

How are you feeling?

SOLDIER FOUR: After seeing you ... pretty good.

SOLDIER THREE: This is a hospital. It's Christmas.

SOLDIER FOUR: Merry Christmas.

SOLDIER THREE: Why don't they take a break? Here they come.

ALL: Here come the Japs.

VOICE: *(Off.)* Banzai!

(THREE JAPANESE SOLDIERS enter. JAPANESE SOLDIER ONE stabs SOLDIER FOUR. JAPANESE SOLDIER TWO bayonets SOLDIER THREE. JAPANESE SOLDIER THREE forces the NURSE to exit.)

SOLDIER FOUR: Stop, stop, stop!

(The sounds of the NURSE being raped. SOLDIER FOUR is stabbed by JAPANESE SOLDIER ONE. The sound of the NURSE screaming. The sound of the wounded men screaming.)

SOLDIER THREE: It's war. We'll get our turn. They'll get theirs, they'll get theirs.

(JAPANESE SOLDIER THREE enters holding the NURSE's uniform. The lights fade.)

Scene Forty-two

(In another playing area the lights fade in. KING looks up from the crystal ball.)

KING: Rape, murder, torture. The stories from Hong Kong are horrible, terrible, dreadful ... Truly awful. We are now at war with Japan. And now the Canadian people are clamouring for revenge against Japanese-Canadians. Beating them, spitting on them, kicking them. And that means strife and disorder. And I want peace and order. They will be interned. Interned. Put them in a concentration camp and then we'll have peace. A lot of peace.

(The lights fade.)

Scene Forty-three

(In another playing area the lights fade in. McNAUGHTON, JOHN, and a SOLDIER enter. MONTGOMERY enters.)

McNAUGHTON: We're going to have a picnic. We have devilled-egg sandwiches prepared with the loving hands of Mrs. McNaughton. There's goodness in every sandwich, gentlemen, goodness.

MONTGOMERY: My first contact with the Canadians was during the Great War when I was a captain. I never liked them. Always bragging. And this obsession with creating a Canadian army is ridiculous. The Canadians are Empire Troops and will be commanded accordingly or my name is not Bernard Law Montgomery. Just get on with it! If you have talent you will succeed. If you don't, you won't. Just get on with it. The Canadians should be fighting in a real army, the British army, not the Canadian army.

JOHN: You ever been fly fishing?

McNAUGHTON: Oh the stories I could tell.

MONTGOMERY: I am going to destroy him. His troops are going to be my troops.

(The lights fade.)

Scene Forty-four

(In another playing area the lights fade in. KING enters.)

KING: I am going to develop a closer relationship with Winston Churchill. And I will visit our armed forces and find out first hand their needs and requirements. I hope they like me.

(The lights fade.)

Scene Forty-five

(In another playing area the lights fade in. MUFFIN and ROSE enter. ROSE knits.)

MUFFIN: It's wartime, Mum. Wartime rationing is the law. What is the law? No more butter or bacon for me. That is the law.

ROSE: You are taking this too seriously. There is bacon in the fridge.

MUFFIN: I don't care. What is the law?

ROSE: What did you learn at school today?

MUFFIN: How many frying pans does it take to make a tank?

ROSE: I have no idea.

MUFFIN: I do. What is the law?

ROSE: Quiet.

MUFFIN: What's that your knitting?

ROSE: A sock.

MUFFIN: Oh that's a big sock.

ROSE: Yes.

(The lights fade.)

Scene Forty-six

(In another playing area the lights fade in. KING and CHURCHILL enter dancing.)

CHURCHILL: Oh darling, dance with me. Do you mind if I call you darling?

KING: No … He's tight most of the time.

CHURCHILL: Canada's war effort is magnificent, Mackenzie. Magnificent. C'est magnifique as you say in Canada. We all look to you as the link with America. You have saved the British Empire. Dance … left foot, left foot.

KING: He's drunk all the time.

CHURCHILL: Now Mackenzie, darling. The real purpose of the Americans in this war is, when the war is over, to be guardians of the British Empire minus Great Britain. We must discourage them of this idea.

KING: He's completely drunk. Now Winnie, do you need any more men?

CHURCHILL: I see no need for conscription, Mackenzie, no need. We do not need men. We need materials. Give us the tools and we'll finish the job.

KING: Yes.

CHURCHILL: Give us the tools and we'll finish the job.

KING: Yes. Yes.

CHURCHILL: World War Two is not a war of men. It is a war of machines.

KING: It makes me so happy to hear you say that.

CHURCHILL: The Canadian army belongs here in Britain. Don't save the world when you can save us. This is the only part of the world worth saving.

KING: He's drunk all the time. I am going to review the troops at Aldershot.

CHURCHILL: Oh good show, good show.

(The lights fade.)

Scene Forty-seven

(In another playing area the lights fade in. JOE, JOHN, and a SOLDIER enter.)

JOHN: I am an individual. I am completely different from everybody. I am not a number with a face. I am an individual.

JOE: It says here Virginia Woolf killed herself today.

JOHN: Who's she?

JOE: A famous lesbian.

JOHN: A lesbian. That's what I want to be. Have you ever met a man who's a lesbian?

JOE: Never.

JOHN: Well you have now.

(McNAUGHTON enters.)

McNAUGHTON: Attention. The prime minister of Canada is going to inspect the troops. Look sharp, look smart. Carry on.

(McNAUGHTON exits.)

SOLDIER: Mackenzie King is coming.

(The SOLDIERS put their hands under arm pits and make farting sounds. The lights fade.)

Scene Forty-eight

(In another playing area the lights fade in. KING enters. The sound of booing.)

KING: Brave Canadians. Brave men of the armed forces. I am here as your prime minister to tell you that the people of Canada are behind you.

(Lighting change. The booing ends.)

They booed me, hissed at me. They'll regret that. They'll regret that.

(The lights fade.)

Scene Forty-nine

(In another playing area the lights fade in. RALSTON, HOWE, and CRERAR enter.)

CRERAR: Now I will outline the salient details of the army programme.

RALSTON: Yes.

CRERAR: We will need at least two more divisions.

HOWE: Guns, guns, guns.

CRERAR: Then we will need an armoured division.

HOWE: Tanks, tanks, tanks.

CRERAR: Plus reinforcements.

RALSTON: Men, men, men.

CRERAR: And then …

RALSTON: Ah.

(The lights fade.)

Scene Fifty

(In another playing area the lights fade in. A PRIEST, LAPOINTE, and KING enter. The PRIEST recites the last rites.)

LAPOINTE: I am dying.

KING: Without you I would never have been prime minister.

LAPOINTE: Kiss me.

KING: Not in front of a priest.

LAPOINTE: What kind of man are you? Make me a promise.

KING: Anything.

LAPOINTE: No conscription.

KING: I promise.

LAPOINTE: Now kiss me.

KING: Who can replace you?

LAPOINTE: St. Laurent. Louis St. Laurent. Oh Louis, Louis, Louis.

KING: Louis St. Laurent.

LAPOINTE: Remember … no conscription.

KING: Louis St. Laurent.

(LAPOINTE dies. The PRIEST makes the sign of the cross. The lights fade.)

Scene Fifty-one

(In another playing area the lights fade in. HOWE and RALSTON enter.)

RALSTON: Well C. D. we now have two armies. One comprised of volunteers willing to serve anywhere. And one of conscripts limited to service in Canada.

HOWE: Who won't do anything?

RALSTON: They're alive but dead.

HOWE: Zombies.

RALSTON: Exactly. The zombie army. We need men for the army. Not zombies.

HOWE: We need men for industry. I have created twenty-eight Crown corporations. Because of me there is zero percent unemployment. Guns, guns, guns. War is good for business. In 1939 we had no women working in industry. Now we have eight-hundred thousand of them.

RALSTON: You can have them. I want the men. Men, men, men!

(KING and LOUIS ST LAURENT enter.)

KING: Gentlemen, this is the new Minister of Justice. Louis St. Laurent. Louis, take your place at the cabinet table. Well gentlemen, shall we discuss the disagreeable subject?

RALSTON: The army has a programme that cannot be filled by voluntary enlistment.

KING: The issue of conscription was decided in the general election of 1940. Conscription serves only to divide the country. It is playing into Hitler's hands.

RALSTON: Conscription indicates a total war effort and equality of sacrifice. Everybody suffers. Everybody.

KING: Yes.

RALSTON: Britain is conscripting men. The United States is now in the war and they are conscripting men. But in Canada, no conscription.

KING: We were elected on a no-conscription policy. Do you think we should have another election?

RALSTON: No, I want a referendum.

KING: A referendum. In a referendum we are asking for the people's verdict on conscription. It negates the concept of parliamentary democracy. Is that what you are suggesting?

RALSTON: Well, no.

KING: Then …

RALSTON: I want the French in the trench. All the slackers are going to contribute. All of them.

KING: Mr. St. Laurent.

ST LAURENT: With respect to French Canada, if the situation were reversed and the English were in a minority, with France the controlling interest, and we were being asked to send over men to France. You would have a very different attitude toward conscription. We must take all these facts into consideration.

RALSTON: Silvered tongues covered in honey are not going to persuade me I want a referendum on conscription.

KING: Gentlemen, we are a house divided. What about a plebiscite on conscription?

ST LAURENT: I agree to a plebiscite.

RALSTON: A plebiscite. Fine.

KING: Yes.

Scene Fifty-two

(In another playing area the lights fade in. HOWE enters holding a placard with the words "April 27th, 1942 Plebiscite on Conscription." KING enters.)

KING: The question: Are you in favour of releasing the government from any obligation arising out of any past commitments restricting the methods of raising men for military service? Yes or no. And now the result.

(RALSTON enters holding a placard with the words "Canada: 64% Yes, 36% No.")

Canada: sixty-four percent "yes," thirty-six percent "no."

(ST LAURENT enters holding a placard with words "Quebec: 24% Yes, 76% No.")

Quebec: twenty-four percent "yes," seventy-six percent "no."

RALSTON: The result of the plebiscite is decisive.

ST LAURENT: Not necessarily.

RALSTON: Canada has voted decisively for conscription. The people have spoken. The will of the people is binding.

KING: Only in a referendum. We have not had a referendum.

ST LAURENT: We have had a plebiscite. A plebiscite is a poll of opinion.

RALSTON: We've been had.

KING: The significance of the plebiscite. And I stress that word. Plebiscite! We consulted the views of the people. The plebiscite was not about conscription or no conscription. It was about having a free hand to alter the National Resources Mobilization Act.

RALSTON: We have a mandate to move forward.

KING: We have a mandate to alter the act if it is necessary to do so.

RALSTON: It is necessary to do so.

KING: There are some who want conscription even if it is not necessary. There are others who want no conscription even if it is necessary. Both are the wrong attitudes. The right attitude is to have no conscription unless it is necessary, and if it is necessary, then to have it.

RALSTON: What are you saying?

KING: I am saying … not necessarily conscription, but conscription if necessary.

RALSTON: I've had it. I resign.

(RALSTON holds up an envelope.)

KING: If you resign I resign.

RALSTON: What?

KING: If there is an attempt to bring conscription into force when it is not necessary, I will resign. The government will fall. You will be held responsible.

RALSTON: But if conscription is required for reinforcements overseas?

KING: We will seek the approval of Parliament for such a course of action.

RALSTON: Why tie our hands when we can do it now?

KING: Parliament will decide.

RALSTON: Conscription now or I resign.

(RALSTON holds up a letter.)

KING: A lack of confidence in Parliament is not good ground for resignation. We cannot fight a civil war while attempting to fight an international war.

RALSTON: I take back my resignation.

(Pat, the dog, enters, grabs the letter, and exits.)

KING: The only thing that would necessitate conscription would be terrible fighting where large numbers of lives were lost.

RALSTON: Yes.

(The lights fade.)

Scene Fifty-three

(In another playing area the lights fade in. RALSTON and CRERAR enter.)

RALSTON: Harry, you are leaving for England to replace General McNaughton.

CRERAR: Unfortunately, only temporarily. Our beloved general is fatigued and weary.

RALSTON: We need a victory. Get them into action at any cost.

CRERAR: I will.

RALSTON: I am determined that the men will see active service. Determined.

CRERAR: They will.

(The lights fade.)

Scene Fifty-four

(In another playing area the lights fade in. KING and Pat enter. Pat holds an envelope in his mouth.)

KING: What's that you got there? Always bringing me gifts. You're so good to me, Pat, so good to me. Oh it's Ralston's letter of resignation. Signed and undated at that. I'll keep it safe … for a rainy day. Oh Pat.

(Pat nods his head. The lights fade.)

Scene Fifty-five

(In another playing area the lights fade in. MONTGOMERY enters. HUGHES-HALLET and LORD MOUNTBATTEN enter.)

HUGHES-HALLET: Lord Mountbatten entering the room.

MOUNTBATTEN: General Montgomery. Operation Sledgehammer, the invasion of Europe, is cancelled.

MONTGOMERY: Thank God.

MOUNTBATTEN: But our American friends are insisting upon an invasion of France in 1942.

MONTGOMERY: It is a hopeless idea.

MOUNTBATTEN: Exactly. And yet if we do not invade, the Americans are threatening to abandon Europe and focus all of their attention upon the Pacific war with the Japanese.

MONTGOMERY: They can't do that.

MOUNTBATTEN: No. And to compound the conundrum, Winnie, while in his cups no doubt, has promised Stalin a second front. And now Stalin is demanding an invasion of Europe or he will make a separate peace with Hitler.

MONTGOMERY: He can't do that.

MOUNTBATTEN: No.

MONTGOMERY: This is what disasters are made of.

MOUNTBATTEN: So we have to demonstrate that an invasion of France is not on. And we have to demonstrate this with the minimum loss of life. Now what divisions do we have that are expendable.

MONTGOMERY: The Canadians are very keen.

MOUNTBATTEN: Really?

(The lights fade.)

Scene Fifty-six

(In another playing area the lights fade in. ROBERTS and CRERAR enter.)

ROBERTS: They're actually going to show us the plan.

CRERAR: Yes.

(MONTGOMERY enters.)

MONTGOMERY: Gentlemen. If we ever intend to invade France it is absolutely essential to mount a preliminary operation on a divisional scale. This is it.

(A map of Dieppe is projected on the scrim.)

Target: Dieppe. Object: destruction of target. I recommend a frontal assault. Here. Don't attack the flanks here and here. Attack here. Enemy resistance will not be strong. So attack here. Any questions? ... Good. Now you have the plan. If you have talent you will succeed. If you don't, you won't.

CRERAR: I recommend that the Second Canadian Division commanded by Major-General Hamilton Roberts, spearhead the assault.

MONTGOMERY: Excellent. Lord Mountbatten and the Combined Operations headquarters are currently preparing the plan of attack which you will have presently. From this moment forth I wash my hands of this operation. I am going to go to Africa and do great things. Good day.

(MONTGOMERY exits.)

CRERAR: Ooooh!

(MOUNTBATTEN and HUGHES-HALLET enter.)

HUGHES-HALLET: A little darkness, a lot of surprise and we can visit the poor man's Monte Carlo for at least a day. This is Lord Mountbatten. He is the commander of Combined Operations. He is the mastermind of the Dieppe operation.

CRERAR: Ooooh!

MOUNTBATTEN: Combined Operations is the only lunatic asylum in the world run by its own inmates. You excite and amuse me. Come to my room at midnight. No, seriously. Military intelligence, I realize that term makes no sense, but military intelligence tells us that Dieppe is lightly defended. We estimate one battalion of poor fighting quality. I hate people with blue eyes. You lucky Canadians have the great honour of serving as the spearhead of the British Empire. You can call me Dickie.

(The lights fade.)

Scene Fifty-seven

(In another playing area the lights fade in. JOE and JOHN enter. JOE holds a newspaper. JOHN plays at being a soldier.)

JOHN: Bang ... bang.

JOE: It says here that the British are going to open a second front in France later this summer.

JOHN: Maybe we'll finally see some action.

(The lights fade.)

Scene Fifty-eight

(In another playing area the lights fade in. ROBERTS and CECIL MERRITT enter. A map of Dieppe is projected on the scrim.)

MERRITT: You seem troubled.

ROBERTS: It's the plan, Colonel Merritt, the plan. The purpose of the raid is to see if it is possible to capture a major port in working order. Therefore a full frontal assault will be launched. It's the plan. It is too big for a raid and yet, too small for an invasion.

MERRITT: Yes, it's like an invasion and a raid all rolled into one.

ROBERTS: Yes that's exactly what it is like. What's the latest rumour?

MERRITT: I don't think you'll like this one.

ROBERTS: What is it?

MERRITT: That this is a sacrifice landing and the Second Division is completely expendable.

ROBERTS: What! How do rumours like that start? Who starts rumours like that?

MERRITT: Just a rumour.

ROBERTS: As commanding officer of the raid on Dieppe. It is within my power to cancel the raid. If we lose the element of surprise. I will do so.

MERRITT: Yes.

(The lights fade.)

Scene Fifty-nine

(In another playing area the lights fade in. MOUNTBATTEN and HUGHES-HALLET enter.)

MOUNTBATTEN: Now you will be with Commander Roberts on the HMS *Calpe*. It is a political imperative that the raid proceed forward. Under no circumstances is the raid to be cancelled. Under no circumstances.

HUGHES-HALLET: It will be done. The Canadians are in a skittish mood.

MOUNTBATTEN: Oh yes, yes, yes, yes. Oh the Canadians. When they are not bragging, they are complaining. I hate them. Just get them in the boats, get them in there and we'll see what happens. Who knows, maybe it will work.

(ROBERTS enters.)

MOUNTBATTEN: Oh, Commander Roberts.

ROBERTS: Sir, I have this terrible feeling.

MOUNTBATTEN: Get in the boats.

ROBERTS: This is going to be a complete disaster.

MOUNTBATTEN: Get in the boats.

ROBERTS: I think the raid should be cancelled.

MOUNTBATTEN: Whatever I say three times is true. Get in the boats.

ROBERTS: But—

HUGHES-HALLET: Get in the boats!

(HUGHES-HALLET takes ROBERTS' arm. They march forward.)

ROBERTS: Forward.

(MERRITT, JOE, and JOHN enter. The lights fade.)

Scene Sixty

(In another playing area the lights fade in: the HMS Calpe. *The sound of ship's foghorn and a boatswain whistle. HUGHES-HALLET and ROBERTS enter.)*

ROBERTS: There is a German convoy up ahead.

(There is a brief firefight with flares and searchlights. The sound of ships' guns firing.)

They'll tell the Germans at Dieppe that we're on the way.

HUGHES-HALLET: Sssshhh. Loose lips.

ROBERTS: But they'll tell the Germans.

HUGHES-HALLET: Nothing to be alarmed about. Proceed forward.

ROBERTS: But they'll warn the Germans.

HUGHES-HALLET: Proceed forward.

ROBERTS: Secrecy and surprise are supposed to be—

HUGHES-HALLET: We are proceeding forward.

(The lights fade.)

Scene Sixty-one

(In another playing area the lights fade in. JOE, JOHN, and SOLDIERS are in a landing craft. The landing craft door is upstage (as if the audience were in the back of the landing craft). A piper plays the bagpipes. The sound of artillery and machine guns. JOE and JOHN give the thumbs up gesture to the audience. The lights fade.)

Scene Sixty-two

(In another playing area the lights fade in. ROBERTS enters.)

ROBERTS: I can see the landing craft approaching the beach.

(The lights fade.)

Scene Sixty-three

(In another playing area the lights fade in. A landing craft, in profile, enters from stage right. The landing craft reaches centre stage and the landing craft door opens. JOE, JOHN, MERRITT, and SOLDIERS rush out.)

MERRITT: Forward.

(THREE SOLDIERS are shot. JOE, JOHN, and MERRITT exit stage left. The lights fade.)

Scene Sixty-four

(In another playing area the lights fade in. MERRITT, JOE, JOHN, and two SOLDIERS enter.)

MERRITT: Fight, keep fighting.

(SOLDIER TWO is shot. SOLDIER ONE holds up a radio.)

SOLDIER ONE: We have a radio.

MERRITT: Send a message. We have landed but

casualties are heavy. Get us out if you can. Forward.

(MERRITT, JOE, and JOHN exit. SOLDIER ONE cranks the radio set.)

SOLDIER ONE: We have landed—

(SOLDIER ONE is shot. The lights fade.)

Scene Sixty-five

(In another playing area the lights fade in. ROBERTS and HUGHES-HALLET enter.)

HUGHES-HALLET: We have landed.

ROBERTS: What else … what else?

HUGHES-HALLET: They have landed.

ROBERTS: All right. All right, send in the second wave. The next wave send them in. We will reinforce success.

(The lights fade.)

Scene Sixty-six

(In another playing area the lights fade in. FRENCH-CANADIAN SOLDIERS in a landing craft enter.)

FRENCH-CANADIAN: Mes amis. Let's show them what French-Canadiens can do.

(The landing craft door goes down. The FRENCH-CANADIAN SOLDIERS are killed by machine gun fire. The lights fade.)

Scene Sixty-seven

(In another playing area the lights fade in. ROBERTS and HUGHES-HALLET enter.)

ROBERTS: What's happening at Dieppe? Get that thing working.

HUGHES-HALLET: It's working but no message is being sent.

ROBERTS: What's happening?

HUGHES-HALLET: Hello, can you hear me?

ROBERTS: What's happening at Dieppe? What's happening at Dieppe? I have to know. How can I conduct the battle if I don't know what's happening?

HUGHES-HALLET: Hello, can you hear me?

ROBERTS: You are a … complete … fucking … asshole!!

HUGHES-HALLET: Hello, can you hear me?

ROBERTS: What's happening at Dieppe? What's happening at Dieppe?

(The lights fade.)

Scene Sixty-eight

(In another playing area the lights fade in. MERRITT, JOE, JOHN, and two SOLDIERS enter. SOLDIER ONE is shot.)

MERRITT: Don't move. If you move you've had it.

JOHN: It's an awful F.U., awful.

(SOLDIER TWO is shot.)

Stretcher bearer, stretcher bearer.

(JOHN is shot in the knee. JOE holds up a radio set.)

JOE: It works, it works.

MERRITT: Give it to me. Is there any chance of getting us off this beach? Hello, anyone out there?

(The lights fade.)

Scene Sixty-nine

(In another playing area the lights fade in. ROBERTS and HUGHES-HALLET enter. Radio static is heard, then MERRITT's voice.)

MERRITT: *(On the radio.)* Is there any chance of getting us off this beach? Hello, anyone out there? Is there any chance of getting us off this beach? Casualties are very heavy. It's a complete disaster. Hello, anyone out there?

ROBERTS: Evacuate them.

HUGHES-HALLET: We have been ordered to evacuate the troops from the beach.

(The lights fade.)

Scene Seventy

(In another playing area the lights fade in. MERRITT and a SOLDIER enter. JOE and JOHN enter. A SAILOR in a landing craft enters. The SOLDIER is shot.)

SAILOR: This is an evacuation. Do it in an orderly manner. We can take no more bodies.

(JOE and JOHN get into the landing craft.)

I will now cite the king's regulations on orderly evacuation.

JOE: Are you a man or a book?

SAILOR: No more, no more. There's too many, we're going to sink.

(The landing craft with the SAILOR, JOE, and JOHN exits.)

VOICE: *(Off.)* Achtung Schweinhund.

(MERRITT raises his hands. The lights fade.)

Scene Seventy-one

(In another playing area the lights fade in. HUGHES-HALLET and ROBERTS enter.)

HUGHES-HALLET: No further evacuations are possible. Those who cannot be evacuated will have to be abandoned. We have to withdraw. You must give the command.

ROBERTS: Very well. Withdraw.

HUGHES-HALLET: We have been ordered to withdraw.

(The lights fade.)

Scene Seventy-two

(In another playing area the lights fade in. JOE, JOHN, and a DOCTOR enter. MOUNTBATTEN enters. ROBERTS enters.)

JOHN: Oh my leg.

JOE: Give him the morphine.

(The DOCTOR holds up a syringe.)

ROBERTS: We were used as pawns to forward British imperial policy. Cannon fodder for the Empire. That will never happen again.

(ROBERTS exits.)

MOUNTBATTEN: Bloody Canadians, always complaining. Well, he's for home.

JOHN: Oh my leg, my leg.

DOCTOR: We're going to have to take it off.

JOHN: Not my leg.

DOCTOR: Hold him down.

(JOE restrains JOHN.)

JOHN: Not my leg.

(The DOCTOR holds up a saw.)

No.

(The DOCTOR starts to saw JOHN's leg off.)

Mother.

(Blackout.)

Scene Seventy-three

(In another playing area the lights fade in. The sound of a saw. John's MOTHER is chopping down the maple syrup tree. The tree falls. MOTHER mouths the word "no." Blackout.)

Scene Seventy-four

(In another playing area the lights fade in. MOUNTBATTEN enters. JOHN, JOE, and the DOCTOR enter.)

JOHN: No!

(DOCTOR holds up the stump of JOHN's leg. JOHN is restrained by JOE. HUGHES-HALLET enters.)

HUGHES-HALLET: Mission accomplished.

MOUNTBATTEN: Congratulations. Let Dieppe be a lesson to the people clamouring for an invasion of France. Badminton anyone?

HUGHES-HALLET: I'll play with you.

MOUNTBATTEN: How lovely.

(The lights fade.)

Scene Seventy-five

(In another playing area the lights fade in. KING enters. He looks in his crystal ball. KING gasps. The lights fade.)

Act Two

Scene One

(The lights fade in: 1943. KING is looking at his crystal ball. The lights fade.)

Scene Two

(In another playing area the lights fade in. RALSTON, MONTGOMERY, and McNAUGHTON enter.)

MONTGOMERY: General McNaughton, Operation Spartan, the dress rehearsal for the full scale invasion of Europe, was a fiasco. You commanded a fiasco.

McNAUGHTON: Mistakes were made, that is why we have exercises. That is how you learn.

MONTGOMERY: The hand that holds the dagger at the heart of Berlin is palsied.

RALSTON: It is a disgrace that the Canadians are not fighting. A disgrace.

McNAUGHTON: The Canadians were fighting at Hong Hong in 1941 and at Dieppe in 1942.

RALSTON: But this is 1943 and they are not fighting.

McNAUGHTON: I do not think we should put soldiers in the line just to keep them busy. Unnecessary casualties are to be avoided.

RALSTON: The men need battle experience.

McNAUGHTON: Without question.

RALSTON: I have recommended that the Canadians participate in the next operation. Operation Husky, the invasion of Sicily.

McNAUGHTON: I object strongly to a Mediterranean strategy.

RALSTON: We'll send the first Canadian division to Sicily, and the second and third divisions will remain in England.

McNAUGHTON: I object, if the Canadian government now believes in dispersion of the Canadian army, then they would be wise to put someone in control who believes in it.

RALSTON: Montgomery of El Alamein will command the Canadians.

McNAUGHTON: I think the Canadian army should be commanded by Canadians. I think it is important.

RALSTON: Noted.

MONTGOMERY: The Canadians will be under my command. I do not want you near the battlefield. If you come to Sicily I will have you arrested.

McNAUGHTON: They are my troops.

MONTGOMERY: I forbid you to visit them. Forbid you.

McNAUGHTON: This is outrageous.

MONTGOMERY: Forbid you.

McNAUGHTON: This ends the idea that Canada's contribution to the war can best be through her own army.

MONTGOMERY: Yes.

McNAUGHTON: The acid test of a country's sovereignty is who controls the armed forces.

MONTGOMERY: Yes.

(The lights fade.)

Scene Three

(In another playing area the lights fade in. There is a sign, "Pachino." GUY SIMONDS and a CAPTAIN enter. A Sicilian PEASANT enters jabbering in Sicilian.)

PEASANT: Infamata fungula stugatz.

SIMONDS: What's she saying?

CAPTAIN: She's saying "Welcome to Sicily, land of goats and monkeys."

SIMONDS: That's Cyprus. Get an education. It's not too late. You have everything to gain.

PEASANT: Infamata fungula stugatz.

SIMONDS: What's she saying?

CAPTAIN: She's saying how much she hates Mussolini.

SIMONDS: What else is she saying?

PEASANT: Infamata fungula stugatz.

SIMONDS: Get that old hag out of my sight.

CAPTAIN: This way.

(CAPTAIN pushes the PEASANT offstage. MONTGOMERY enters.)

MONTGOMERY: Soldiers, brave soldiers, gather 'round me. We have landed at Sicily. We will now conquer this island. You lucky Canadians will be lead by General Simonds. He is my protégé. Carry on.

(The CAPTAIN exits.)

I am going to teach you the art of war. Now, the first lesson. Someone always takes the fall. But never you. Make an example of him and then sack him. Sack him, sack him! Say things like, "Some of you officers I have no confidence in. And I am going to sack you, sack you, sack you! Others I will keep. Now here is how it works. I command and you obey all my commands. Anyone who does not obey my commands will be sacked, sacked, sacked! I will have his guts for garters." Now you.

SIMONDS: Some of you officers I have no confidence in. And I am going to sack you, sack you, sack you! Others I will keep. Now here is how it works. I command and you obey all my commands. Anyone who does not obey my commands will be sacked, sacked, sacked! I will have his guts for garters.

(MONTGOMERY nods his head in approval.)

MONTGOMERY: Oh you … very good. Now, on to Assoro.

(The lights fade.)

Scene Four

(In another playing area the lights fade in. ROSE and MUFFIN enter. Music from a radio plays.)

ROSE: So what did you do today, Muffin?

MUFFIN: Nothing. Well I collected more bottles for the Victory Bond. Oh the War Bond. What would we do without the War Bond?

ROSE: Quiet.

RADIO: *(Voice over.)* In the news today the Canadian army invaded Sicily. It is estimated that five hundred Germans were killed at Pachino. In further action the Canadian army—

ROSE: Turn that off.

MUFFIN: They're killing them. I'm so happy, I'm so happy. Dad's in Sicily killing everybody. I'm so happy, I'm so happy.

(The lights fade.)

Scene Five

(In another playing area the lights fade in. SIMONDS, JOE, DOUG, CAPTAIN, and a SOLDIER enter.)

SIMONDS: They've got us pinned down. Get down, get down. They've got us pinned down. We can't attack them head on. That is suicide. We have to climb this mountain and get behind them.

JOE: It's three hundred feet straight up.

SIMONDS: Up and at 'em!

(SIMONDS, JOE, DOUG, the CAPTAIN, and SOLDIER climb the mountain. The lights fade.)

Scene Six

(In another playing area the lights fade in. A GERMAN SOLDIER on sentry duty is singing lines from "Lili Marlene." Hands come out of a trench behind him. Then the CAPTAIN is revealed. He kills the GERMAN SOLDIER with a knife.)

CAPTAIN: All clear. Come on.

(Other hands are revealed coming out of the trench. SIMONDS, JOE, and DOUG enter.)

SIMONDS: Now, on to Assoro.

(They charge forward. The lights fade. The sound of a battle.)

Scene Seven

(In another playing area the lights fade in. PIMPOLINA enters.)

PIMPOLINA: Hey soldiers, welcome to Assoro. I am Pimpolina, welcome to Assoro.

(CAPTAIN, JOE, and DOUG enter.)

CAPTAIN: We have liberated the village of Assoro. For the next forty-eight hours everyone is a prostitute.

PIMPOLINA: Hey you want prostitute? I got prostitute. Look.

(PIMPOLINA opens a curtain. A gabble of voices are heard.)

JOE: Oh that's the clap for sure.

CAPTAIN: We want young girls—clean and wholesome.

PIMPOLINA: I am Pimpolina, the pimp. You want girls, I get you girls. You want boys, I get you boys. You want she-he, I get you that too. What you want, you know I got it. I am Pimpolina, the pimp.

SIMONDS: I want young girls. Clean and wholesome.

PIMPOLINA: What you want is what you want. It take.

(PIMPOLINA rubs his fingers together.)

SIMONDS: What do you think of Mussolini?

PIMPOLINA: I am not a Mussolini man. I hate Mussolini with deep passion. Deep passion. You want little girls, I get you little girls. That village Catania, everyone in that village Mussolini Fascista and they have nice little daughters. I get them for you.

CAPTAIN: That sounds like a good idea.

PIMPOLINA: Welcome to Sicily.

(The lights fade.)

Scene Eight

(In another playing area the lights fade in. CAPTAIN and JOE enter. PIMPOLINA enters with a young Sicilian GIRL.)

PIMPOLINA: You come with me. I teach you to say "Cigarettes for Papa. Chocolati for Mama."

(PEASANT enters.)

PEASANT: She had the Figue de Madonna. Figue de Madonna. Look what you did to my wonderful beautiful daughter! Infamata fungula stugatz.

PIMPOLINA: You get out of here.

(PIMPOLINA pushes the PEASANT offstage. The sound of a crash.)

You come with me.

GIRL: Cigarettes for Papa. Chocolati for Mama.

JOE: Look what they're doing.

CAPTAIN: I don't want to know what they're doing. They do what they do.

JOE: This is disgusting and disgraceful and I am ashamed.

CAPTAIN: It's war.

(JOE points his rifle at PIMPOLINA.)

JOE: Let that girl go or I will kill you.

(PIMPOLINA lets go of the GIRL.)

PIMPOLINA: I don't understand, you want bigger girls I get you bigger girls.

CAPTAIN: We have liberated Sicily.

JOE: And he's in charge.

CAPTAIN: He's on our side.

GIRL: Cigarettes for Papa. Chocolati for Mama.

PIMPOLINA: Welcome to Sicily.

JOE: Jesus.

(The lights fade.)

Scene Nine

(In another playing area the lights fade in. SIMONDS enters wearing a beret just like MONTGOMERY'S beret. [Note: During the course of the play SIMONDS becomes the spitting image of MONTGOMERY.])

SIMONDS: Oh you. Oh call me Pip. Snip, snip, snip. Clip, clip, clip. Zip, zip, zip. Goes the hair on my lip. Sicily was a difficult campaign. Very difficult, very difficult. Twenty-five hundred casualties. But the comb is in my hair so what do I care. I am like a boy with a smile. Oh General Montgomery. He is my hero. My hero.

(MONTGOMERY enters.)

MONTGOMERY: Soldiers, soldiers, gather around me. Gather 'round me.

(CAPTAIN and SOLDIER ONE gather around MONTGOMERY.)

Oh you magnificent specimens of manhood. Oh you magnificent Canadians. Oh! Oh you. I trust you have all enjoyed horizontal refreshment.

SOLDIERS: Yes!

MONTGOMERY: Oh it's so important. Brave Canadians, brave Canadians. You have invaded and conquered Sicily. Now you are going to invade and conquer Italy. The fleshpots of Rome await you.

(The SOLDIERS cheer.)

Oh you.

(The lights fade.)

Scene Ten

(In another playing area the lights fade in. ROSE and VIOLET are making a tank.)

FRED: *(Off.)* Keep working.

ROSE: My husband went to war four years ago I haven't heard from him since and then he sends me a postcard from Sicily. "Wish you were here" it says. What's that supposed to mean? I was married to him for fourteen years, I haven't seen him for the last four and they were the best years of my life and now I'm married to this. Squeezing the nuts of a tank. My life.

VIOLET: I like to do it like this.

ROSE: My life.

FRED: *(Off.)* Keep working.

VIOLET: Oh stay out of the moonlight. You're ripe.

ROSE: Oh I'm ripe all right. I'm ripe.

FRED: *(Off.)* Keep working.

VIOLET: He can get on your nerves.

ROSE: You'll get used to it.

VIOLET: God I hate that voice.

(FRED enters.)

FRED: Workers. Stop working. An important announcement from the Ministry of Defence. Workers. The Canadian army has landed in Italy. They are anniheeha …

ROSE: Annihilating.

FRED: They are annihilating the enemy. Victory follows victory. Now lets give the Canadian army a big cheer. Hip hip …

ROSE and VIOLET: Hooray.

FRED: Hip hip …

ROSE and VIOLET: Hooray.

FRED: Hip hip …

ROSE and VIOLET: Hooray.

FRED: And now I have an announcement of a personal nature. The army is taking anyone who wants to serve. So they have taken me.

ROSE and VIOLET: Hip hip hooray.

FRED: And now you Mrs. Rose Porter will be the new foreman.

VIOLET: Hip hip hooray.

(The lights fade.)

Scene Eleven

(In another playing area the lights fade in: Italy. JOE and DOUG enter.)

JOE: Here we are at the toe of the Italian boot.

DOUG: Look at the birds, look what they're doing. Just stick the old beak in.

(DOUG fires his rifle.)

JOE: What are you, completely nuts?

DOUG: They shouldn't be doing that.

JOE: Well they are.

DOUG: I can't stand it, I can't stand it. If I die will you bury me deep so the birdies won't poke out my eyes and eat them.

JOE: If you catch one I'll bury you.

(SIMONDS and DWAYNE enter.)

SIMONDS: Italy has just surrendered. The Italian army are throwing down their arms. It is beyond chaotic. The Italian partisans have begun reprisals against the Mussolini Fascists. But the Germans are still fighting. On to Potenza.

(SIMONDS exits.)

JOE: He's not human.

DOUG: That's it, I've had it. I can't do it, can't do it.

JOE: Fight for Canada.

DOUG: Ram it.

JOE: Remember your battalion.

DOUG: They're all dead.

DWAYNE: What a coward, beneath contempt.

JOE: You're the new recruit?

DWAYNE: Yes.

JOE: All right. I'm going to give you some wisdom. There are three stages to the war. Stage one: It can't happen to me. Stage two: It can happen to me. Stage three: It's going to happen to me. When you reach the third stage it's only a matter of time. When—

DWAYNE: Right. It can't happen to me.

(JOE nods his head and smiles.)

JOE: On to Potenza.

(The lights fade.)

Scene Twelve

(In another playing area the lights fade in: Potenza. Three CORPSES are on stage. JOE, DOUG, and DWAYNE enter.)

VOICE: *(Off.)* Are you alive or dead?

(The sound of a gunshot.)

This man is dead.

DWAYNE: What are they doing?

JOE: The Italian partisans are looking for Mussolini supporters.

(PARTISAN enters holding a gun.)

PARTISAN: Are you alive or dead?

(PARTISAN shoots CORPSE ONE in the head.)

This man is dead.

JOE: Some of Mussolini's men are pretending to be dead.

DWAYNE: Look at those corpses covered with maggots.

PARTISAN: Are you alive or dead?

(PARTISAN shoots CORPSE TWO in the head.)

This man is dead.

DOUG: We should stop them.

JOE: No, no, street justice. It's happening all over Italy.

PARTISAN: Are you alive or dead.

(CORPSE THREE sits up.)

CORPSE THREE: I'm alive. I'm a Mussolini man. I live for Mussolini, I die for Mussolini.

PARTISAN: Die Fascist die.

(PARTISAN shoots CORPSE THREE and then PARTISAN exits, SIMONDS enters.)

SIMONDS: Attention. I want three volunteers for burial duty. This is a health hazard. Three volunteers. One, two, three.

(SIMONDS exits.)

VOICE: *(Off.)* Are you alive or dead?

(The sound of a gunshot.)

This man is dead.

DWAYNE: Look at those bodies covered in maggots. Maggots. Makes me sick.

JOE: You'll get used to it. All right, we're going to bury them over there.

DWAYNE: You mean pick them up with my bare hands.

JOE: That's right. Give him a proper burial. Do it.

(JOE, DOUG, and DWAYNE lift up the three corpses. The lights fade.)

Scene Thirteen

(In another playing area the lights fade in. JOE, DOUG, and DWAYNE enter.)

DWAYNE: Ah maggots. I hate them. I gotta wash my hands. I got crushed maggots on my fingers. I gotta wash my hands.

JOE: Starting to get to you, eh?

DOUG: When I think I could have stayed in Canada and dicked all the broads. And here I am in a shit hole with you.

JOE: We all make choices. No one twisted your arm. I haven't seen my wife in four years.

DOUG: So what?

(A shot is heard. DWAYNE is hit in the shoulder.)

Bloody sniper. Did you see him?

JOE: Yeah. I saw him. He thinks he's real smart. Got his head all blacked out. But I see him, I see him. He is a dead man.

(JOE fires his rifle.)

DOUG: All right, another one bites it.

JOE: I can't even remember what my wife looks like.

(The lights fade.)

Scene Fourteen

(In another playing area the lights fade in. ROSE and MUFFIN enter. MUFFIN is painting stocking seams on ROSE's legs.)

MUFFIN: Why am I doing this? Painting your legs.

ROSE: There are no stockings.

MUFFIN: And then this line down the back of your legs?

ROSE: Keep it straight. It's supposed to be a seam.

(The lights fade.)

Scene Fifteen

VOICE: *(Off.)* Oooohhh!

(In another playing area the lights fade in. JOE and DWAYNE enter. The DOCTOR enters.)

JOE: We got shot by a sniper. He got bullet in arm. It's been unattended for three days.

DOCTOR: Now these wounds are on their way to becoming gangrenous, but there is a solution. I'm going to cover your wounds with maggots.

DWAYNE: No, not maggots.

(DOCTOR holds up a jar of maggots.)

DOCTOR: Don't make moral judgements about maggots. They do a good job. They eat necrotic flesh. They devour it. Can you open this for me.

(JOE opens the jar of maggots.)

DWAYNE: No.

DOCTOR: Or you're going to lose your arm. The choice is yours.

DWAYNE: Oh.

DOCTOR: Just don't look at them and you'll be all right.

DWAYNE: Get them off me, get them off me.

(FRED enters.)

FRED: What a baby, beneath contempt.

JOE: You're the new recruit?

FRED: Yes.

JOE: All right I'm going to give you some wisdom. There are three stages to the war. Stage one: It can't happen to me. Stage two: It can happen to me. Stage three: It's going to happen to me.

DWAYNE: Get them off me, get them off me.

DOCTOR: It's all right, they're working, they're working. Look at them work. They're just eating it, eating it.

DWAYNE: No.

JOE: When you reach the third stage it's only a matter of time. When—

FRED: Right. It can't happen to me.

(JOE nods his head and smiles. DWAYNE screams. The lights fade.)

Scene Sixteen

(In another playing area the lights fade in. ROSE and VIOLET are making a tank.)

VIOLET: Like they say in Elora, there's a lot of dickweed in this world and I'm going to get me some.

ROSE: You're actually going out with a zombie.

VIOLET: Actually, I am … I admit it.

ROSE: You'll be sorry.

VIOLET: It beats slapping mosquitoes.

ROSE: Nothing beats that. Zombies. I've seen them on parade, strutting about, leering and smiling, making filthy remarks and bum-pinching. Oh bum-pinching. They wouldn't fight in a fit.

VIOLET: I'm not going out with him so I can fight with him. Men are hard to find.

ROSE: We all make sacrifices. Go without.

VIOLET: No. You go without. I go with.

ROSE: All right this one's done. Move it forward.

(The tank moves forward.)

Next.

(The lights fade.)

Scene Seventeen

(In another playing area the lights fade in. The sound of a bell tolling. JOE, DOUG, DWAYNE, and FRED enter.)

DOUG: Ortona … Ortona. What a beautiful name.

FRED: Who is that bell tolling for? Who is that bell tolling for?

JOE: If anyone says "It's is tolling for thee" I will kill him with my bare hands.

FRED: I think it is tolling for all of us.

JOE and DOUG: Shut up.

DOUG: The only thing you know for sure is there is a Kraut up there having a great time ringing that bell.

FRED: Now what?

JOE: Now we sit here and wait for it.

FRED: Good, I'm tired of walking toward it. I'd rather sit and wait for it.

DWAYNE: Do you see any maggots on me?

JOE: No.

DWAYNE: I feel like they're inside me.

FRED: Well, they are actually. Like when we die we make our own maggots.

DWAYNE: Oh! I can feel them crawling around inside me.

JOE: Shut up … Here!

(JOE holds up a bottle of red wine and takes a drink and then passes it to DWAYNE. DWAYNE takes a drink and passes it to DOUG. DOUG takes a drink and passes it to FRED.)

FRED: I don't drink.

DOUG: You will.

(DOUG passes the bottle to DWAYNE. DWAYNE passes it to JOE. A shot is heard.)

JOE: Down, down.

(The lights fade.)

Scene Eighteen

(In another playing area the lights fade in. SIMONDS and DWAYNE enter. JOE enters at the side of a doorway. FRED and DOUG enter at the other side of the doorway.)

SIMONDS: All right the Germans are in those houses. We have to take them house by house. Room by room. Start with that one. Ready. Now.

(DOUG throws a grenade through the doorway a loud explosion and bright flash. Shrieks and screams.)

Now!

(DOUG goes through the doorway. GERMAN ONE enters the doorway and stabs DOUG. JOE shoots GERMAN ONE.)

JOE: Come on.

(JOE and FRED go through the doorway.)

JOE: *(Off.)* Down here … it's full of Kraut.

(The sound of gunshots, shrieks, and shouts. GERMAN TWO enters the doorway.)

Watch out he's right behind you.

(SIMONDS and DWAYNE shoot GERMAN TWO. JOE and FRED enter the doorway.)

JOE: Down here.

(The sound of gunshots, shrieks, and shouts. DWAYNE looks at the dead body of DOUG.)

SIMONDS: Private.

(SIMONDS goes through the doorway. The lights fade.)

Scene Nineteen

(In another playing area the lights fade in. JOE, FRED, and DWAYNE enter. JOE and FRED are shoveling dirt.)

DWAYNE: Look at those maggots.

FRED: What was his name?

JOE: Doug.

FRED: Doug what?

JOE: Just Doug.

FRED: Seems a shame to bury a man without a last name.

JOE: Just dig.

FRED: Here come the birdies.

JOE: Cover his head, cover his eyes.

FRED: Birdies got a right to eat.

JOE: Not him.

DWAYNE: You going to say a few words.

JOE: Ashes to ashes, dust to dust.

DWAYNE: Maggots to maggots.

JOE: Amen.

(The lights fade.)

Scene Twenty

(In another playing area the lights fade in. KING enters.)

KING: Nothing makes sense anymore. Everything is stonked. You want to fight fascism? Join the army. You want to attack Germany? Invade Italy. Oh Italy. The fighting in Italy is terrible. Horrible, dreadful, truly awful. The carnage at Ortona. The casualties, the casualties. Street by street, house by house, room by room. And now the long awaited invasion of Europe is being planned by Winston Churchill and Franklin Roosevelt at the Quebec Conference. And I am the host. Moi!

(The lights fade.)

Scene Twenty-one

(In another playing area the lights fade in. CHURCHILL and FDR enter.)

FDR: It will be called Operation Overlord. General Eisenhower will be the supreme commander.

CHURCHILL: And Montgomery will command the assault on Normandy.

FDR: D-Day will be sometime in early June.

(There is a knock on the door.)

CHURCHILL: Who's that?

FDR: It's Mackenzie. Entrez-vous, as you say in Canada.

(KING enters holding a tea pot.)

KING: Just me and the tea. Winston Churchill, Franklin Roosevelt and me. The big three.

CHURCHILL: Big two-and-a-half more like it.

KING: Tea?

FDR and CHURCHILL: Please.

(The lights fade.)

Scene Twenty-two

(In another playing area the lights fade in. FRED, a SOLDIER, and a CHAPLAIN enter.)

CHAPLAIN: All right what's your problem?

FRED: It's not a problem really. Don't get me wrong. It's not the horror and the bullshit. I don't mind the killing. I don't mind it at all. It's just … it's just … the chickenshit. I can't stand the chickenshit. Like we were on the line and the lieutenant got blown up, nothing left of him and the captain came in and started swearing a blue streak because the lieutenant had his receipts and he couldn't balance his mess bill unless he had his receipts. And he started calling down the lieutenant that he was stupid and irresponsible cause he didn't have his receipts, couldn't stop talking about his stupid receipts, didn't give a damn about the lieutenant. And then we're in a mine field and three of us got blown up and they're in the hospital and the colonel comes in and he wants them to stand up and salute him. They had no legs! It gets to you.

CHAPLAIN: You'll get over it.

FRED: Yeah. Thanks for listening.

CHAPLAIN: Next!

(FRED exits.)

What's your problem?

(The lights fade.)

Scene Twenty-three

(In another playing area the lights fade in. MONTGOMERY and SIMONDS enter.)

MONTGOMERY: I have just received word that I will be commanding the British forces during the invasion of Europe next summer. I want you to come with me.

SIMONDS: I would be honoured.

MONTGOMERY: I will see if I can arrange to have you command the Canadian forces under my command.

SIMONDS: Oh would, could you?

MONTGOMERY: What do you think of McNaughton?

SIMONDS: I hate him.

MONTGOMERY: You're learning.

SIMONDS: Yes.

MONTGOMERY: Oh you.

(The lights fade.)

Scene Twenty-four

(In another playing area the lights fade in. FRED and DWAYNE enter.)

FRED and DWAYNE: We are the D-Day Dodgers, out in Italy. Always on the vino, always on the spree. We are the D-Day Dodgers, in sunny Italy.

(SIMONDS enters holding a piece of paper.)

SIMONDS: We have just received word that we

have been posted to the big one. The invasion of France. D-Day!

(The lights fade.)

Scene Twenty-five

(In another playing area the lights fade in. MONTGOMERY and RALSTON enter.)

MONTGOMERY: We can't have McNaughton commanding the Canadians on D-Day.

RALSTON: Definitely not.

MONTGOMERY: I should command the Canadians on D-Day.

RALSTON: Definitely ... What about McNaughton?

MONTGOMERY: He's got to go. Awfully nice chap but stodgy. Definitely not a commander. He's not fit to command two men and a boy. He would be much happier pulling hair out of his nose than commanding an army.

RALSTON: Who will replace McNaughton?

MONTGOMERY: My doggie-boy would be nice.

RALSTON: Simonds? No too junior. We need a more senior commander.

(CRERAR enters.)

Crerar.

MONTGOMERY: He'll do.

(The lights fade.)

Scene Twenty-six

(In another playing area the lights fade in. ROSE enters.)

ROSE: Keep working. The minister of Supply and Munitions, C. D. Howe, is increasing the quota of tanks from two to three a day. Keep working. There's a war on don't you know? No slacking. That means you. Keep working.

(The lights fade.)

Scene Twenty-seven

(In another playing area the lights fade in: D-Day. CRERAR and SIMONDS enter.)

CRERAR: Now here's how it works. I command and you obey all my commands. Is that understood?

SIMONDS: Yes ... sir.

(A map of Normandy is projected on the scrim.)

CRERAR: This is the map of Normandy. D-Day. The Americans will be attacking here at Omaha beach and Utah beach. The British will be attacking here at Gold beach and Sword beach. We will attack here. At Juno beach. It is expected to be heavily defended. You can expect a crossfire of machine gun nests and minefields. After securing our bridgehead we march ten miles and take Caen. You will lead the assault.

SIMONDS: Have you worked out the wastage rates?

CRERAR: Seventy percent. Hopefully it won't be as high as that.

SIMONDS: Let's see. Third division. Fifteen thousand men that makes ...

CRERAR: Ten thousand five hundred casualties can be expected.

SIMONDS: Very good.

(The lights fade.)

Scene Twenty-eight

(In another playing area the lights fade in: D-Day, Juno beach.

SIMONDS, JOE, DOUG, FRED, DWAYNE, and a SOLDIER are in a landing craft. The landing craft door is upstage [as if the audience were in the back of the landing craft]. A piper plays the bagpipes. The sound of artillery and machine guns. JOE and DOUG give the thumbs up gesture to the audience. The lights fade.)

Scene Twenty-nine

(In another playing area the lights fade in. CRERAR enters.)

CRERAR: I can see the landing craft approaching the beach.

(The lights fade.)

Scene Thirty

(In another playing area the lights fade in. The landing craft, in profile, enters from stage right. The landing craft reaches centre stage and the landing craft door opens. JOE, DOUG, SIMONDS, and SOLDIERS rush out.)

SIMONDS: Forward.

(Two SOLDIERS are shot. JOE, DOUG, and SIMONDS exit stage left. The lights fade.)

Scene Thirty-one

(In another playing area the lights fade in. There is a signpost, "Caen." SS GENERAL KURT MEYER and GERMAN SOLDIERS enter. MEYER holds binoculars.)

MEYER: I see them. Gott in himmel. Donnerwetter nochmal. I see them. I am here to destroy and exterminate. If the Canadians are successful you can call me Schwartzjuden. I will have earned it. I see them, I see them. They are dead men. Forward.

(A German tank and TWO GERMAN SOLDIERS enter. MEYER, the SOLDIERS, and the tank cross the stage. The lights fade.)

Scene Thirty-two

(In another playing area the lights fade in. SIMONDS and MONTGOMERY enter.)

SIMONDS: We have met stiff resistance at Caen. Our advance has been halted.

MONTGOMERY: Don't worry. I will conduct the siege of Caen. It will be a brilliant victory, brilliant.

SIMONDS: Yes, yes.

MONTGOMERY: Why was El Alamein such a magnificent victory? Why was it such a success? Because everyone knew what they were doing. Someone who knew what they were doing was in charge. Who's in charge, that's the question.

SIMONDS: You are.

MONTGOMERY: Yes. Now the German army. We are going to wear them down, wear them out, and then destroy them utterly. We will begin with a three day artillery barrage and then a massed assault on the centre. Any questions? Good. Let the siege of Caen begin.

(The sound of a distant artillery barrage. The lights fade.)

Scene Thirty-three

(In another playing area the lights fade in. The sound of a thunderous artillery barrage. Four SOLDIERS enter. They cover their ears with their hands SIMONDS enters. He looks at his watch. He readies the men for an assault. SIMONDS looks at his watch.)

SIMONDS: Five ... four ... three ... two ... one.

(The artillery barrage ends.)

Now!

(SIMONDS and the SOLDIERS go over the top. Four SOLDIERS are killed by machine gun fire. SIMONDS exits. The lights fade.)

Scene Thirty-four

(In another playing area the lights fade in. MONTGOMERY and CRERAR enter.)

CRERAR: The casualties, the casualties. You are fighting a World War One battle with Canadian troops. A frontal assault is hopeless. We should send in the tanks.

MONTGOMERY: No, no, we are saving them. Strategy, strategy. We are putting our troops in the centre and our tanks on the flanks.

(SIMONDS enters.)

SIMONDS: The men are ready to go again.

MONTGOMERY: Go.

SIMONDS: Forward.

(The lights fade. Screams and shrieks. Artillery fire.)

Scene Thirty-five

(In another playing area the lights fade in. ROSE enters. A radio plays.)

RADIO: *(Voice over.)* In the news, Canadian and British forces began the thirtieth day of the siege at Caen.

(The lights fade.)

Scene Thirty-six

(In another playing area the lights fade in. JOE, FRED, and DWAYNE enter. FRED reads a letter. JOE holds a letter.)

DWAYNE: We've moved about eight hundred yards in one month.

FRED: The nerve.

JOE: My father told me about this kind of war.

FRED: The cheek.

JOE: You sit, you wait for it, eventually it comes, then your war is over.

FRED: The dishonesty. I write a letter to the wife informing her that I was going to be copulating with prostitutes and that I wanted her blessing.

JOE: And did she give it to you?

FRED: No, she wrote, quote "But don't you pay more than five dollars for it 'cause that's all I'm getting."

(JOE laughs.)

You think that's funny, that's not funny.

(SIMONDS enters.)

SIMONDS: Now be on your guard. The Germans are taking prisoners. Corporal.

(SIMONDS and JOE exit. The sound of a dog barking.)

DWAYNE: The Germans are taking prisoners.

FRED: So what? Only the dead hate war. I love it.

DWAYNE: Shut up. Listen … hear it?

FRED: A dog barking.

DWAYNE: Listen. It's barking in Morse code. It's telling the bloody Germans where we are.

FRED: Right. It's a German shepherd dog.

DWAYNE: Die bastard die.

(FRED and DWAYNE fire their machine guns Silence.)

Bloody German shepherd dog.

FRED: Bloody German shepherd dog.

(SIMONDS enters.)

SIMONDS: Be on your guard. The Germans are taking prisoners. Private.

(SIMONDS and DWAYNE exit. In another playing area the lights fade in. Two GERMAN SOLDIERS advance toward FRED. The lights fade.)

Scene Thirty-seven

(In another playing area the lights fade in. MONTGOMERY and CRERAR enter.)

CRERAR: The casualties, the casualties.

MONTGOMERY: Yes. A frontal assault is hopeless.We will attack the flanks. Here and here, not here, here and here.

CRERAR: The tanks.

MONTGOMERY: No, no, we are saving them.

CRERAR: But the casualties, the casualties.

MONTGOMERY: War is mass murder, General. If you do not have the stomach for it I know someone who does.

(SIMONDS enters.)

SIMONDS: General Montgomery.

MONTGOMERY: Speak.

SIMONDS: We have just received word that the German army tried to assassinate Hitler today.

MONTGOMERY: See, it's all falling apart. Only a matter of time, only a matter of time. Let's strike while the iron is hot.

CRERAR: The casualties, the casualties.

(CRERAR exits.)

MONTGOMERY: He doesn't have it.

SIMONDS: He never did.

MONTGOMERY: And he never will.

SIMONDS: I hate him profoundly. He's a snake, a backstabber.

MONTGOMERY: He's for home. He's got to go. He's not worth meeting and beating with a stick.

SIMONDS: Sack him, sack him, sack him!

MONTGOMERY: Oh you.

(The lights fade.)

Scene Thirty-eight

(In another playing area the lights fade in. MEYER and FRED enter. MEYER holds a bottle of schnapps.)

MEYER: July 20th … July 20th …

(A GERMAN SOLDIER enters.)

GERMAN SOLDIER: Obergruppenführer Meyer. We have taken fifty prisoners.

MEYER: Shoot them … No! Our wounded men need blood. Drain them of their blood. Every drop. Then shoot them.

(GERMAN SOLDIER exits.)

FRED: You'll be tried for war crimes for that.

MEYER: I will drink schnapps and weep. The great German poet Goethe once said that man only uses his intellect to outdo the beasts at being beastly. Goethe. You, of course are so stupid that you pronounce it "Go-eth," or some such stupid pronunciation that only you are capable of.

Fighting for Britain. How odd. Not fighting for your real masters, the Americans. But then you are too stupid to know that. I have come to realize that Canada is the stupidity capital of the world. You are too stupid to live. July 20th, 1944. That day will live in infamy. They tried to kill the führer today. Die Schweinhunden, Schweinhunden! But they failed. He is unkillable. The man of Destiny. I worship Hitler as a living god. A living god. I see you sneer. You will die for that. The tank, bring it forward.

(A German tank enters.)

Lay him down.

(A GERMAN SOLDIER enters and forces FRED to the ground.)

Forward.

(The tank runs over FRED.)

How you like that?

(FRED shrieks.)

Back up. Back up.

(The tank backs up. FRED shrieks.)

How you like that? Again.

(The lights fade.)

Scene Thirty-nine

(In another playing area the lights fade in. FRED's head is on a stick. The Caen sign hangs from a hook on the stick. JOE and DWAYNE enter.)

DWAYNE: The dirty bastards, look what they did. It's not right, it's not right.

JOE: No it's not.

(JOE puts a cigarette in the mouth of FRED's head.)

Now it's right ... That's how I remember him. So what do you think of war now? Do you like it?

(SIMONDS enters.)

SIMONDS: Brave soldiers, brave soldiers. Gather 'round me, gather 'round me. The village of Caen is ours. We have destroyed it utterly. The Germans have retreated to the Falaise area of Normandy. We are in the process of surrounding them. Afterwhich we will destroy them utterly. Assemble by that hedge row. Take that with you.

(SIMONDS exits.)

JOE: He's not human.

(JOE and DWAYNE exit with FRED's head on the stick. The lights fade.)

Scene Forty

(In another playing area the lights fade in. ROSE enters.)

ROSE: Dear Joe, Remember this, A kiss is just a kiss, A guy is just a guy, And when you went to war so did I. Hey Joe good-bye. Now I get paid to work. A jerk is still a jerk, On that you can rely. I don't know if I won or lost, But I'm the boss.

(The lights fade.)

Scene Forty-one

(In another playing area the lights fade in. MONTGOMERY, SIMONDS, and CRERAR enter.)

MONTGOMERY: General Simonds.

SIMONDS: The Falaise gap will be my killing ground. I will mass seven hundred tanks and fifty thousand troops here in four square miles of hell on wheels. American bombers will bomb the Caen-Falaise road into oblivion and then we will march forward, close the gap and destroy the enemy. Destroy them utterly.

CRERAR: This is completely unacceptable. I am the commanding general of the Canadian army. You can only communicate with General Simonds through me.

MONTGOMERY: General Crerar, you are not fit to command two men and a boy. And here you are commanding an army. You would be much happier pulling hair out of your nose than commanding an army. I have no confidence in you as a commander. You have no ideas. But young Guy Simonds. He has ideas. I want him to lead the assault on closing the Falaise gap. Him. Not you. Him.

CRERAR: Well.

(The lights fade. The sound of an artillery bombardment, shrieks and screams.)

VOICE: *(Off.)* There, there.

Scene Forty-two

(In another playing area the lights fade in. An OFFICER, DWAYNE, and a SOLDIER enter. The SOLDIER fires a machine gun up in the air.)

DWAYNE: There.

OFFICER: When the Germans bomb us, we take cover. When we bomb the Germans, they take cover. But when the American planes come over we all take cover.

(SIMONDS and CRERAR enter.)

CRERAR: It's chaos out there. It's chaos.

SIMONDS: It's not supposed to happen like this.

CRERAR: But it is.

SIMONDS: But it's not supposed to happen like this.

CRERAR: But it is.

SIMONDS: The yellow markers mark our positions?

OFFICER: No, the yellow markers mark the area to be bombed.

SIMONDS: No, the yellow markers mark our positions.

OFFICER: No, the yellow markers mark the area to be bombed.

SIMONDS: You're sacked. Those are our planes you are firing at.

DWAYNE: Well if they're going to drop bombs on us they're going to die.

SOLDIER: More planes.

DWAYNE: Die bastard, die.

SOLDIER: Die bastard, die.

SIMONDS: Those are our planes.

(SIMONDS puts his gun to DWAYNE's head.)

Stop. I order you.

DWAYNE: Well someone should tell them to drop their bombs on the Germans. Not us!

SIMONDS: You're sacked ... you're sacked ... you're sacked. Sacked. Sacked!

(The lights fade.)

Scene Forty-three

(In another playing area the lights fade in. MONTGOMERY and SIMONDS enter.)

MONTGOMERY: General Crerar is very critical of you.

SIMONDS: What are his criticisms? What can he question?

MONTGOMERY: He is questioning your sanity. This is serious. Deal with it.

SIMONDS: My sanity, my sanity. How dare he. I am completely sane!

MONTGOMERY: Do not underestimate Crerar. He is completely, utterly useless, but he is devious and vicious too.

SIMONDS: I hate him, loathe him, detest him.

MONTGOMERY: He has informed the Canadian government that I am interfering in the affairs of the Canadian army. The Canadian government has informed my government of same.

SIMONDS: What does it mean?

MONTGOMERY: It means I can never see you again. Never give you commands to obey. Never speak with you, never touch you.

SIMONDS: Oh no.

MONTGOMERY: Oh you.

(The lights fade.)

Scene Forty-four

(In another playing area the lights fade in. DWAYNE, an OFFICER, and a SOLDIER enter.)

DWAYNE I prayed to you before the battle that if you got me through I would be a good man. You were as good as your word and I will be as good with mine. Oh yes Lord, I hear you.

(CRERAR enters.)

CRERAR: Is this the result of the American bombing?

OFFICER: No RAF this time.

DWAYNE: You want me to do what? No more fornicating, Lord? Very well, no more fornicating.

CRERAR: The battle of the Falaise gap is a complete disaster. The German army has escaped from Normandy to Holland. And we had them, we had them.

DWAYNE: No more drinking! ... No more drinking.

OFFICER: Since D-Day we have taken twenty-five thousand casualties. We no longer have enough men to properly reinforce the army.

CRERAR: I will make a request for further reinforcements.

DWAYNE: No more lying! … No more lying.

CRERAR: This poor wretch.

DWAYNE: Don't sneer at me you stupid bastard.

CRERAR: Take that man to the hospital.

DWAYNE: I'm talking to God. What are you doing?

(The lights fade.)

Scene Forty-five

(In another playing area the lights fade in. DWAYNE and an OFFICER enter.)

DWAYNE: What are you looking at me for? Stop looking at me. Stop. Or I'll start looking at you. Here I'm looking at you. I'm looking right at you. You don't think I can see you. I can see you and it's not pretty.

(In another playing area the lights fade in. CRERAR enters.)

CRERAR: Colonel Ralston, based on current wastage rates, we need fifteen thousand trained reinforcements badly. We do not need volunteers who are not trained. We need trained men. That's right the zombies, we need them.

(DWAYNE covers his face with his hands.)

OFFICER: Now Private, we are going to rehabilitate you and put you back in the line.

DWAYNE: I'm so happy.

CRERAR: Sending untrained men into war is murder. They have a fifty percent chance of survival.

OFFICER: Take your hands away from your face.

DWAYNE: No. I'm so happy. I don't want anyone to see how happy I am.

CRERAR: We are able to take our wounded from the hospital and put them back in the line and rehabilitate our special cases.

OFFICER: Take your hands away from your face, that is an order.

(DWAYNE takes his hands away from his face. He grins like a demon.)

We're going to put you back in the line.

DWAYNE: I'm so happy.

(The lights fade.)

Scene Forty-six

(In another playing area the lights fade in. JOE and two SOLDIERS enter. They fight GERMANS stationed offstage. SOLDIER ONE is shot.)

JOE: War! There is no way out. You can die. Get wounded. Go mad. Keep fighting. Those are your choices.

(SOLDIER TWO is shot. JOE keeps fighting. The lights fade.)

Scene Forty-seven

(In another playing area the lights fade in. KING and RALSTON enter.)

RALSTON: Our duty is to kill Germans.

KING: No, our duty is to save lives. We are trustees of the people.

RALSTON: I have received reports that there is a reinforcement crisis in Europe. I am going to investigate this report personally.

KING: Just don't come back demanding conscription.

(RALSTON exits.)

He's going to come back demanding conscription. I can feel it, feel it.

(The lights fade.)

Scene Forty-eight

(In another playing area the lights fade in. JOE and TWO SOLDIERS enter. RALSTON and CRERAR enter. SOLDIER ONE is shot. RALSTON and CRERAR react. SOLDIER TWO is shot. RALSTON and CRERAR react. The lights fade.)

Scene Forty-nine

(In another playing area the lights fade in. KING and McNAUGHTON enter.)

McNAUGHTON: I was treated like a whipped cur, Mr. King, like a whipped cur.

KING: Yes. General McNaughton, would you be interested in serving in the cabinet?

McNAUGHTON: Yes. But I could never sit in cabinet with Ralston. If he stays in, I stay out.

KING: If Colonel Ralston were to resign as Minister of Defence would you be interested in serving in cabinet?

McNAUGHTON: Oh very much so.

KING: You are not motivated by revenge, I hope.

McNAUGHTON: I have no ego. When I am shaving I cannot even see myself.

KING: Yes.

(The lights fade.)

Scene Fifty

(In another playing area the lights fade in. RALSTON and HOWE enter.)

RALSTON: Oh C. D. the things I saw in Europe. Terrible, terrible. We're going to bell the cat. Are you with me or ag'in me?

HOWE: I am with you.

(KING and McNAUGHTON enter. KING holds Pat.)

KING: I trust you all know General McNaughton.

McNAUGHTON: Mr. Howe ... Colonel.

KING: Sit here. I have invited General McNaughton to attend this meeting because I value his expertise. Pat the letter.

(Pat exits.)

Well shall we discuss the disagreeable subject?

RALSTON: Mr. King, I want to speak about reinforcements. Fighting has been more intense than anticipated. The numbers in the reserve are less than anticipated. We cannot sustain the army without conscription.

KING: Perhaps we should reduce the size of the army.

RALSTON: The size of the army will not be reduced. The war will last until the spring of 1945. Everyone says so, Eisenhower, everyone. Even the High and Mighty Lord himself.

KING: God ... you spoke with God?

RALSTON: No. I meant Field-Marshall Montgomery.

KING: Who cares what he thinks, right, General?

RALSTON: The only thing that is certain is that Canadians will keep fighting. No let up, no rest. We must reinforce the Canadians. You have pledged to impose conscription if necessary. The facts indicate it is necessary.

RALSTON: We need fifteen thousand soldiers.

KING: General McNaughton.

McNAUGHTON: The original intention was that the Canadian army would fight in one theatre of war. Unfortunately we are fighting in two theatres of war, simultaneously. Therefore we do not have enough men. Some people find this surprising. We can solve our problems with volunteers.

KING: Yes.

RALSTON: It's time to get serious about the war effort.

KING: We have six hundred thousand men in uniform.

RALSTON: It's not enough. I demand conscription.

(Pat enters with an envelope and gives it to KING.)

KING: Thank you.

(KING takes the letter out of the envelope.)

Do you have a pen? What is the date today?

RALSTON: November 1st, 1944.

(KING writes on the letter.)

Many people think you are completely unacceptable as prime minister during wartime and should be replaced

KING: Any idea who the replacement should be?

RALSTON: Yes.

KING: Gentlemen. I have here Colonel Ralston's letter of resignation. Dated November 1st, 1944. General McNaughton you will assume the position of Minister of Defence for the government of Canada. On your way out close the door.

(RALSTON exits.)

McNAUGHTON: We can solve our problem with volunteers. I will make a personal appeal to all Canadians to join the army for my sake.

KING: Yes.

(The lights fade.)

Scene Fifty-one

(In another playing area the lights fade in. JOE and CHUCK enter. CRERAR enters.)

CRERAR: We are going to liberate Holland.

(CRERAR exits.)

JOE: Oh we'll get good cheese there.

CHUCK: There is no cheese in Holland.

JOE: What?

CHUCK: There's nothing in Holland. No food, no nothing. They're eating tulips.

JOE: No cheese in Holland. That's like no maple syrup in Canada.

VOICE: *(Off.)* We are going to liberate Holland.

(The lights fade.)

Scene Fifty-two

(In another playing area the lights fade in. McNAUGHTON enters.)

McNAUGHTON: Hi. General Andy here. Just doing my bit for Canada. You. Have you thought of joining the army? Too shy to speak? Put you in the army and you'll get over your shyness. And you, sir. You look like a big fine strapping man. Put you in a uniform and that'll make the woman you're with smile. How about you? Ever thought of fighting for Canada? Think about it. Patriotism is a great thing. It's the reason the sky is blue. Join your country's army for God's sake. What's the matter with you? Men are dying and need help. And only you can help them. If you won't do it for yourself, or you won't do it for Canada then do it for me. Ol' Andy ... What do you say?

(The lights fade.)

Scene Fifty-three

(In another playing area the lights fade in: the water rats. JOE, DWAYNE, CHUCK, and a SOLDIER are crossing the Scheldt. They hold their rifles above their heads. They are up to their waist or chest in water.)

CHUCK: Oh fighting on dykes and polders. Do you know what polders are? Polders are land that has been reclaimed from the sea. It is not really land.

JOE: I can't figure out if I am being macerated or marinated. If I make it back to Canada, I'll ask my wife, she'll know.

DWAYNE: You're being marinated. Meat is marinated. Fruit is macerated.

JOE: I'll ask the wife if you don't mind.

(The lights fade.)

Scene Fifty-four

(In another playing area the lights fade in. McNAUGHTON and KING enter.)

McNAUGHTON: Mr. Prime Minister, I regret to inform you that I have not been able to raise the fifteen thousand volunteers needed to reinforce the army. We will have to conscript all the cowards for general service.

KING: Send our zombies to Europe?

McNAUGHTON: Yes.

KING: Very well.

(The lights fade.)

Scene Fifty-five

(In another playing area the lights fade in. JOE, CHUCK, and two ZOMBIES enter.)

JOE: Attention. About face. Left turn. You. Right turn.

CHUCK: Zombies.

JOE: You're the new recruits. Don't tell me your names. Just nod. If you survive the next twenty-four hours tell me your names and where you come from. All of it.

(JOE holds up a Bren gun.)

JOE: How many of you know what this is? Well c'mon, speak up.

ZOMBIE ONE: What is it?

JOE: It's a Bren gun. How many know how to take it apart and put it back together again? Speak up.

ZOMBIE TWO: How do you fire it?

(ZOMBIE ONE picks up a grenade.)

ZOMBIE ONE: What's this?

JOE: That's a grenade.

ZOMBIE ONE: What happens when you do this.

(ZOMBIE ONE pulls the grenade pin.)

JOE: Asshole. Hold the hammer down.

ZOMBIE ONE: What hammer?

JOE: Run! Throw it!

(ZOMBIE ONE exits with the grenade. Offstage: a loud explosion and a shriek.)

Jesus.

ZOMBIE ONE: *(Off.)* Oh God, oh God.

JOE: Jesus, what a mess.

CHUCK: Look here's one of his fingers.

JOE: It's not a finger.

CHUCK: Right.

(The lights fade.)

Scene Fifty-six

(In another playing area the lights fade in. KING and Pat enter.)

KING: Franklin Roosevelt died today. Do you know what that means Pat? Just me, Hitler, and Stalin left, Pat. Just me, Hitler, and Stalin.

PAT: What about Churchill?

KING: Pat!

(The lights fade.)

Scene Fifty-seven

(In another playing area the lights fade in. JOE and CHUCK enter.)

CHUCK: The Brits and the Yanks get to liberate all the cities and what do we get to do?

JOE: We get to do what we're supposed to do. Kill Kraut. I spend every waking moment killing Kraut and when I'm sleeping, I'm dreaming about killing Kraut.

(CRERAR enters.)

CRERAR: Attention. We have a telegramme from the prime minister of Canada praising the liberation of Holland. He offers his congratulations for a magnificent job done.

JOE: Mackenzie King offers his congratulations.

(JOE and CHUCK put their hands in their armpits and make farting sounds.)

CRERAR: The Third Reich is collapsing. Now we are going to march forward into Germany.

JOE: On to Germany.

(The lights fade.)

Scene Fifty-eight

(In another playing area the lights fade in: Canadians at Buchenwald. The MAYOR enters.)

MAYOR: Valdaree, valdara, valdaree, valdara, ha, ha, ha.

(CRERAR, JOE, and SOLDIERS enter.)

Welcome to Buchenwald.

CRERAR: Well this is a very nice village. Very beautiful.

MAYOR: Ja. Buchenwald means "Wood of the beeches."

CRERAR: What's down there?

MAYOR: A beautiful lake.

CRERAR: And over there?

MAYOR: A wonderful forest.

CRERAR: And over there?

MAYOR: Uh ... I have no idea what's over there.

JOE: It's a camp of some sort.

CRERAR: All right. Go reconnoitre that area and give me a report.

(JOE exits.)

MAYOR: Would you like some beer and sausages? We have Knockwurst, Bratwurst, Weisswurst, Schwarzwurst, Jagwurst. Would you like some?

(JOE enters.)

JOE: Well I thought I had seen everything. You're not going to believe what you are going to see when you go over that hill.

(The lights fade.)

Scene Fifty-nine

(In another playing area the lights fade in. KING and Pat enter.)

KING: Hitler killed himself today. Do you know what that means, Pat? It means just me and Stalin, Pat. When the war is over, I'll be the only one left. Mark my words, Pat, mark my words. The new order. Me.

(The lights fade.)

Scene Sixty

(In another playing area the lights fade in. CRERAR, JOE, CHUCK, and three SOLDIERS enter.)

CRERAR: The war is over.

(The SOLDIERS celebrate. SOLDIER TWO throws his rifle to the ground.)

JOE: Now I can go to the Pacific and start killing Jap. Can't wait.

(The lights fade.)

Scene Sixty-one

(In another playing area the lights fade in. KING and Pat enter.)

KING: The new president of the United States, Harry Truman says he's going to drop a big bomb on Japan. So big it's going to end the war. I can't imagine how big a bomb like that must be. It must be gigantic.

(Pat nods his head. The lights fade.)

Scene Sixty-two

(In another playing area the lights fade in. An image of the atomic bomb exploding is projected onto the scrim. KING enters. The image looks like it is superimposed on KING's face and body. KING gasps. The lights fade. The end.)

Cast of Characters

New France:

Part One of
The History of the
Village of the Small Huts

AGONA: Huron wife of Atironta
AGOUHANNA: Huron demigod
ANADABIJOU: Montagnais chief
ATIRONTA: Huron chief
BEAUPORT: Jacques Beauport, Seigneur of New France
BOURGEOYS: Marguerite Bourgeoys, a nun, chaperone of Les filles du roi
BRÉBEUF: Jean de Brébeuf, a Jesuit priest
BRÛLÉ: Étienne Brûlé, Champlain's manservant
CARTIER: Jacques Cartier, French imperialist and explorer
CHAMPLAIN: Samuel de Champlain, founder of New France
CHAMPLAIN'S WIFE: a nun who married Champlain
DENONVILLE: Governor of New France
DONNACONA: Iroquois chief, gave Canada its name
FRONTENAC: Count Frontenac, governor of New France
GARAKONTIE: Iroquois chief
GARANGULA: Iroquois chief
GROSSEILLIERS: friend of Radisson
HÉLÈNE: une fille du roi
JOGUES: Isaac Jogues, a Jesuit priest
KIRKE: David Kirke, British imperialist
LALEMANT: Jesuit priest
LAVAL: Bishop of New France
LE BOEUF: Habitant
LE CARON: Recollet priest
LOUIS: fur-trader
MARIE: une fille du roi
MAURICE: fur-trader
MEMBERTOU: MicMac chief
ODODHARHO: Iroquois demigod
RADISSON: Pierre Radisson, a fur-trader
TAIGNOAGNY: Son of Donnacona
TALON: Jean Talon, Intendant of New France
TEGANNISSORENS: Iroquois chief
TESSOUAT: Huron warrior
TRACY: Alexandre Prouville, the Marquis de Tracy, Governor of New France

An ACTOR, an ENGLISH OFFICER, a HABITANT, an IROQUOIS WARRIOR, a MAN, a PRIEST, a SHAMAN, and various FACES, MUTINEERS, and offstage VOICES.

The British:

Part Two of
The History of the
Village of the Small Huts

The Plains of Abraham

AMHERST: Lord Amherst, Commander in Chief of the British army
BIGOT: François Bigot, Intendent of New France
BOUGAINVILLE: Colonel in the French army
BRIAND: Bishop of New France
FRASER: Sergeant in the British army
JENKINS: Private in the British army
LEVIS: Chevalier de Levis, Montcalm's second in command
MARIE: a habitante, wife of Pierre
MONTCALM: Loius-Joseph de Gozon, the Marquis de Montcalm, Commanding General of the French army
MURRAY: James Murray, a general in the British army
MADAME PEAN: Bigot and Vaudreuil's courtesan

MONSIEUR PEAN: a cuckold
PIERRE: a habitant, husband to Marie
PONTIAC: Chief of the Ottawa
RAMEZAY: Colonel in the French army
TOWNSHEND: Lord Townshend, a British general
VAUDREUIL: Pierre de Rigaud, the Marquis de Vaudreuil, Governor of New France
VERGOR: Bigot's lackey
WOLFE: James Wolfe, Commanding General of the British army

A NUN, various ENGLISH SOLDIERS and OFFICERS, FRENCH SOLDIERS and OFFICERS, and offstage VOICES.

The Conspiracy of Pontiac

BLACKHAWK: Ojibway chief
CAMPBELL: Captain in the British army
DALYELL: Captain in the British army
FRANÇOIS: fur-trader
GLADWYN: Henry Gladwyn, British Major commanding Detroit
JOHNSON: Sir William Johnson, Indian agent for the British army
MAHOGANNE: Algonquin maiden
MINAVAVANA: Ojibway chief
PONTIAC: Chief of the Ottawa, Algonquin leader
THAYENDANEGEA: Iroquois chief, later called Joseph Brant

An ASSASSIN, a SOLDIER, a WIFE, a WOMAN, and various ENGLISH OFFICERS and TOWNSPEOPLE.

The Loyalists

ARNOLD: Benedict Arnold, an American general
BONTEMPS: Charles Bontemps, Seigneur of Quebec
BRIAND: Bishop of Quebec
BURGOYNE: John Burgoyne, a British general
BUTLER: John Butler, founder of Butler's Rangers
CAMPBELL: John Campbell, a British colonel
CARLETON: Guy Carleton, later named Lord Dorchester, Governor-General of Canada
ELIZABETH: Elizabeth Simcoe, wife of John Graves Simcoe
GENET: French Jocabin
HALDIMAND: Frederick Haldimand, a British general, later Governor-General of Canada
JOHNSON: John Johnson, Upper Canada land owner
JOSEPH: Joseph Brant, Iroquois chief and ally of the British, formerly called Thayendanegea
LADY DORCHESTER: Wife of Guy Carleton
LAURA: Laura Secord, a United Empire Loyalist, married to James Secord
MME ST LAURENT: Mistress of Prince Edward Augustus
MOLLY: Molly Brant, Joseph's sister
MONTGOMERY: Richard Montgomery, an American general
PIERRE: Habitant
PRINCE: Prince Edward Augustus, son of King George III
SECORD: James Secord, a United Empire Loyalist, married to Laura Secord
SIMCOE: John Graves Simcoe, Lieutenant-Governor of Upper Canada
SQUAT: Diddley Squat, the American ambassador
WALKER: Thomas Walker, an English fur-trader
WALTER: Walter Butler, son of John Butler
WOOSTER: American captain

A LOYALIST, an ENGLISH SOLDIER, various AMERICAN SOLDIERS, and offstage VOICES.

The War of 1812

BOERSTLER: Richard Boerstler, an American officer
BROCK: Isaac Brock, a British general commanding Upper Canada
CHAPIN: American officer
DEARBORN: Henry Dearborn, an American general
DRUMMOND: Gordon Drummond, a British general
FITZGIBBON: James Fitzgibbon, a sergeant in the British army
HARRISON: William Henry Harrison, an American general
HULL: William Hull, an American general
LAURA: Laura Secord, an Upper Canada citizen, married to James Secord
OVERHOLSER: Jacob Overholser, an American immigrant
PIKE: Zebulon Pike, an American officer
PREVOST: John Prevost, a British general
PROCTOR: Henry Proctor, a British colonel
PROPHET: Brother of Tecumseh
ROBINSON: John Robinson, Family Compact Attorney General

SALABERRY: Charles de Salaberry, a Château Clique war hero
SCOTT: Winfield Scott, an American general
SECORD: James Secord, an Upper Canada citizen, married to Laura
STRACHAN: John Strachan, a parson
TECUMSEH: Shawnee chief
THOMAS: Private in the British army
WILLCOCKS: Joseph Willcocks, a citizen of Upper Canada

A RECRUIT, a WIFE, and various AMERICAN and BRITISH SOLDIERS, and offstage VOICES.

The Mackenzie-Papineau Rebellion:
Part Three of
The History of the
Village of the Small Huts

ALLEN: Duncan Allen, a Mackenzie supporter
ANDERSON: Anthony Anderson, a Mackenzie supporter
BALDWIN: Robert Baldwin, a lawyer
BONDHEAD: Sir Francis Bondhead, Lieutenant-Governor of Upper Canada
BONTEMPS: Charles Bontemps, a member of the Château Clique
BOURGET: Ignace Bourget, Bishop of Montreal
CHENIER: Jean-Olivier Chenier, a Patriote
COLBORNE: Sir John Colborne, Lieutenant-Governor of Upper Canada, and later Military Governor of Lower Canada
DURHAM: Lord Durham, author of the famous report
FITZGIBBON: James Fitzgibbon, a war hero from the War of 1812
FRENCH: Charles French, Mackenzie's apprentice
GORE: Charles Gore, a British general
GOSFORD: Earl of Gosford, Lieutenant-Governor of Lower Canada
HINDENLANG: Charles Hindenlang, an American mercenary
JOHNSTON: Bill Johnston, a pirate
JUNIOR: Son of a Family Compact member
LAFONTAINE: Louis Lafontaine, a lawyer
LITTLE PIERRE: Patriote
LOUNT: Sam Lount, a Mackenzie supporter
MACKENZIE: William Lyon Mackenzie, the Great Reformer
MACNAB: Family Compact member
MADAME PAPINEAU: Mother of the Great Patriote
MOFFAT: Member of the Château Clique
MRS MACKENZIE: Mother of William Lyon Mackenzie
O'TOOLE: Mackenzie supporter
PAPINEAU: Louis-Joseph Papineau, the Great Patriote
PIERRE: Patriote
POWNALL: Family Compact lackey
RENSELLAER: Leader of the Hunters Lodge
ROBINSON: John Robinson, a Family Compact member
ROLPH: John Rolph, Baldwin's law partner
SARAH: Sarah Lount, wife of Sam Lount
SQUAT: Diddley Squat, the American ambassador
STRACHAN: John Strachan, founder of the Family Compact
WEIR: Jock Weir, a British captain
WETHERALL: George Wetherall, a British colonel

A man from the ALAMO, a HABITANT, a REFORMER, a SERGEANT-MAJOR, a SHERIFF, and various ENGLISH SOLDIERS, PATRIOTES, and offstage VOICES.

Confederation and Riel:
Part Four of
The History of the
Village of the Small Huts

ALLAN: Hugh Allan, a capitalist, first holder of the CPR contract
ANDRÉ: Priest
BAD ARROW: Cree warrior
BARNABÉ: a doctor
BELLEAU: Narcise Belleau, a Pre-Confederation prime minister
BERNARD: John A. Macdonald's secretary
BIG BEAR: Leader of the Cree
BISHOP TACHÉ: Manitoba bishop, Riel's mentor
BLAKE: Edward Blake, Leader of the Liberal Party
BOULTON: Charles Boulton, a militia colonel
BOURGET: Ignace Bourget, Bishop of Montreal
BROWN: George Brown, Father of Confederation, Leader of the Clear Grits
CARTER: Newfoundland representative at the Quebec Conference
CARTIER: George-Étienne Cartier, Father of Confederation, a Quebec Conservative

COLE: George Cole, Prince Edward Island representative at Charlottetown
CROZIER: Northwest Mounted Police commissioner
MADAME CUVILLIER: George-Étienne Cartier's mistress
DELANEY: Indian agent in Saskatchewan
DONOGHUE: Manitoba Fenian
DUMONT: Gabriel Dumont, leader of the Métis people
EVELINA: Daughter of Barnabé
GALT: Alexander Galt, Father of Confederation
HOWE: Joseph Howe, Nova Scotia representative at Charlottetown
ISIDORE: Isoder Dumont, a Métis, brother of Gabriel Dumont
LADY MACDONALD: Wife of Sir John A. Macdonald
LAFLAMME: Rudolphe Laflamme, a lawyer, member of Le parti rouge
LAURIER: Sir Wilfrid Laurier, Leader of the Liberal Party
LÉPINE: Manitoba Métis
MACDONALD: Sir John A. Macdonald, Canada's first prime minister, Father of Confederation
MACKENZIE: Alexander Mackenzie, Canada's first Liberal prime minister
McDOUGALL: William McDougall, putative Lieutenant-Governor of Manitoba
McGEE: D'Arcy McGee, Father of Confederation
MIDDLETON: Frederick Middleton, commander of the Militia during the Northwest Rebellion
MONCK: Lord Monck, Governor-General during Confederation
MRS RIEL: Mother of Louis Riel
NORBERT: Métis
POPE: James Pope, Premier of Prince Edward Island
PRESTON: Sergeant Preston, a Northwest Mounted Police officer
QUINN: Indian agent in Saskatchewan
RIEL: Louis Riel, founder of Manitoba and Saskatchewan
SAMMY: American ambassador
SCHULTZ: Ontario Orangeman
SCOTT: Thomas Scott, an Ontario Orangeman
SMITH: Donald Smith, owner of the Hudson Bay Company and the Canadian Pacific Railway
TACHÉ: Étienne Taché, Pre-Confederation prime minister
TILLEY: Samuel Tilley, New Brunswick Father of Confederation
TUPPER: Charles Tupper, Nova Scotia Father of Confederation
WANDERING SPIRIT: Cree warrior
WOLSELEY: Garnet Wolseley, a British colonel, commanded the 1870 Red River Expedition

A CLERK, a DEFENSE ATTORNEY, a JUDGE, a PROSECUTOR, a MOTHER, DAUGHTER, FATHER and SON, a NUN, a MOUNTIE, the SPEAKER, a MÉTIS and MÉTISSE, and various MEN, WOMEN, SOLDIERS, and offstage VOICES.

Laurier:
Part Five of
The History of the
Village of the Small Huts

ABBOTT: J. J. Abott, a Conservative prime minister
LADY ABERDEEN: Wife of the Governor-General
LORD ABERDEEN: Governor-General of Canada
ANTOINE: Antoine-Aimé Dorion, member of Le parti rouge
ARMAND: Armand Lavergne, Wilfrid Laurier's son
BLAKE: Edward Blake, Liberal Leader of the Opposition
BORDEN: Robert Borden, Conservative Leader of the Opposition
BOURASSA: Henri Bourassa, Quebec Nationalist, grandson of Papineau
BOURGET: Ignace Bourget, Bishop of Montreal
BOWELL: Mackenzie Bowell, a Conservative prime minister
CARTIER: George-Étienne Cartier, Father of Confederation
DORION: Eric Dorion, a member of Le parti rouge
EMILIE: Emilie Lavergne, Wilfrid Laurier's mistress
MADAME GAUTHIER: Wilfrid Laurier's landlady
GREY: Earl Grey, Governor-General of Canada
GUIBORD: Joseph Guibord, a member of the Institut-Canadien
IVAN: Immigrant

JACQUES: Habitant
JEAN: Habitant
LA FLECHE: François La Flèche, a priest
LAFLAMME: Rudolphe Laflamme, a member of the Institut-Canadien
LAURIER: Sir Wilfrid Laurier, a Liberal prime minister
LAVERGNE: Joseph Lavergne, Wilfrid Laurier's law partner
MACDONALD: Sir John A. Macdonald, a Conservative prime minister
MACKENZIE: Alexander Mackenzie, a Clear Grit (Liberal) prime minister
McCARTHY: Dalton McCarthy, John A. Macdonald's brother-in-law
MERCIER: Honore Mercier, Premier of Quebec
MINTO: Lord Minto, Governor-General of Canada
MULOCK: William Mulock, a minister in Laurier's Cabinet
PAPINEAU: Louis-Joseph Papineau, the Great Patriote
RIEL: Louis Riel, Métis leader
SIFTON: Clifford Sifton, Laurier's Minister of Immigration
SMITH: Donald Smith, owner of the Canadian Pacific Railway and the Hudson Bay Company
TARTE: Joseph Israel Tarte, a member of the Castor party
THOMPSON: John Thompson, a Conservative prime minister
TUPPER: Sir Charles Tupper, a Conservative prime minister
ZOE: Zoe Lafontaine

A BUTLER, a DOCTOR, a SERVANT, the SPEAKER, and various offstage VOICES.

The Great War:
Part Six of
The History of the
Village of the Small Huts

ALDERSON: Edwin Alderson, a British general at Ypres
ARMAND: Armand Lavergne, Quebec Nationalist, follower of Bourassa
BORDEN: Sir Robert Borden, a Conservative prime minister
BOURASSA: Henri Bourassa, Quebec Nationalist, founder of *Le Devoir*
BOYLE: Russell Boyle, an officer in the Canadian Expeditionary Force (CEF)
BYNG: Julian Byng, a British general, commanded the CEF
CURRIE: Arthur Currie, a Canadian general in the CEF
DAVID: Private in the CEF
DUCHESS: The Duchess of Connaught, wife of the Governor-General
DUKE: The Duke of Connaught, Governor-General of Canada
DWAYNE: Soldier in the CEF
EDITH: Wife of Stephen
GEORGE: Lloyd George, a British prime minister
HAIG: Sir Douglas Haig, Commander-in-Chief of all British Forces
HUGHES: Sir Sam Hughes, Minister of Militia
JOHN: Soldier in the CEF
LAURA: Laura Borden, wife of the prime minister
LAURIER: Sir Wilfrid Laurier, Liberal Leader of the Opposition
MARTHA: John's mother
McNAUGHTON: Andrew McNaughton, a colonel in the CEF
MEIGHEN: Arthur Meighen, a minister in Borden's Cabinet
NELLIE: Nellie McClung, advocate of women's suffrage
OTTO: Otto Schlippenschloppen, a German officer
PIERRE: Habitant
ROBERT: Friend of Stephen, spurned lover of Edith
SCOTT: Frederick Scott, Chaplain of the First Canadian Division
STEPHEN: Friend of Robert, lover of Edith
YVETTE: Habitante

A BUTLER, a COURIER, a DOCTOR, a FATHER, a GERMAN PRISONER, a NURSE, a RECRUITER, a SERVANT, a SENTRY, a WHORE, a YANK, and various PATIENTS, SOLDIERS, and offstage VOICES.

The Life and Times of Mackenzie King:
Part Seven of
The History of the
Village of the Small Huts

ANDREWS: Alfred Andrews, a Winnipeg capitalist

BENNETT: R. B. Bennett, a Conservative prime minister
BISAILLON: Joseph Bisaillon, Customs Official
MRS BLEANEY: A fortune-teller
BORDEN: Sir Robert Borden, a Conservative prime minister
BRONFMAN: Sam Bronfman, a whisky maker
BUREAU: Jacques Bureau, Minister of Customs
COPPING: World War I veteran, later a member of the "Special Police"
DIXON: Fred Dixon, a union organizer
ETTA: Etta Wreidt, a spiritualist
GODFROY: Godfroy Patteson, husband of Joan Patteson
GOEBBELS: Nazi
HITLER: Adolf Hitler, a Nazi
JOAN: Joan Patteson, Mackenzie King's mistress
JOE: Working class hero
JUDY: Joe's wife
KING: Mackenzie King, a Liberal prime minister
LADY BYNG: Wife of the Governor-General
LAPOINTE: Ernest Lapointe, Mackenzie King's Quebec Lieutenant
LAURIER: Sir Wilfrid Laurier, a former prime minister
LORD BYNG: Governor-General of Canada
McNAUGHTON: Andrew McNaughton, a general in the Canadian army
MEIGHEN: Sir Arthur Meighen, a Conservative prime minister
MOLLY: Sid's girlfriend
RIBBENTROP: Joachim Ribbentrop, a Nazi
RUSSELL: Robert Russell, a union organizer
SID: Gangster
STEVENS: Harry Stevens, a Conservative Cabinet Minister
THOMPSON: World War I veteran and strike breaker
VINCE: World War I veteran, Joe's friend
WOODSWORTH: James Shaver Woodsworth, a socialist
ZANETH: Frank Zaneth, a Royal Canadian Mounted Police officer

A COMMUNIST, a CROOKED COP, a DAUGHTER, a DRIVER, a FOREMAN, a FRENCH-CANADIEN, a GARGOYLE, a HOBO, an INFORMER, an INSTRUCTOR, a LANDLORD, a MOTHER, a PEASANT, a REPORTER, a SERVANT, a SOLDIER, the SPEAKER, a VOLUNTEER, and various STOCKBROKERS, MOUNTIES, HOBOES, WOMEN, MEN, STRIKERS, GOONS, and offstage VOICES including a loudspeaker and radios.

World War II:
Part Eight of
The History of the
Village of the Small Huts

MRS BLEANEY: A fortune-teller
CHAMBERLAIN: Neville Chamerlain, a British prime minister
CHUCK: Soldier in the Canadian army
CHURCHILL: Winston Churchill, a British prime minister
CRERAR: Henry Crerar, a Canadian general
DOUG: Soldier in the Canadian army
DWAYNE: Soldier in the Canadian army
FDR: Franklin Delaney Roosevelt, an American president
FRED: Factory foreman, later a soldier
HITLER: Nazi
HOWE: C. D. Howe, Minister of Munitions and Supply
HUGHES-HALLET: Mountbatten's aide-de-camp
JOE: Canadian war hero, married to Rose
JOHN: Soldier in the Canadian army
KING: Mackenzie King, a Liberal prime minister
LAPOINTE: Ernest Lapointe, Mackenzie King's Quebec Lieutenant
LAWSON: Canadian colonel at Hong Kong
MALTBY: British general at Hong Kong
McNAUGHTON: Andrew McNaughton, a Canadian general
MERRITT: Cecil Merritt, a Canadian colonel at Dieppe
MEYER: Kurt Meyer, a general in the German S.S.
MONTGOMERY: Bernard Montgomery, Field Marshal of the British army
MOTHER: John's mother
MOUNTBATTEN: Lord Mountbatten, mastermind of the Dieppe assault
MUFFIN: Daughter of Joe and Rose
MUSSOLINI: Benito Mussolini, Italian Fascist
PIMPOLINA: Sicilian pimp
RALSTON: James Ralston, Minister of Defence
ROBERTS: Hamilton Roberts, a Canadian colonel at Dieppe
ROSE: Munitions worker, married to Joe

SIMONDS: Guy Simonds, a Canadian general
ST LAURENT: Louis St Laurent, Minister of Justice
TOMMY: British commando
VIOLET: Munitions worker, Rose's friend

A CAPTAIN, a CHAPLAIN, a CLERK, a DOCTOR, an ENGLISHMAN, a GIRL, the MAYOR of Buchenwald, a NURSE, an OFFICER, a PARTISAN, a PEASANT, a PRIEST, a SAILOR, a SCIENTIST, a WAITER, a WOMAN, and various CORPSES, SOLDIERS, ZOMBIES, and offstage VOICES, including a film announcer, a radio, and the voice of Pat the dog.

Production Credits

New France: Part One of The History of the Village of the Small Huts premièred at Theatre Passe Muraille on April 14, 1985, with the following cast:

Gary Farmer: ODODHARHO, IROQUOIS WARRIOR, MEMBERTOU, DONNACONA, ATIRONTA, SHAMAN, TEGANNISSORENS, LOUIS, GARANGULA
Arturo Fresolone: AGOUHANNA, TAIGNOAGNY, ANADABIJOU, ATIRONTA, TALON
Geza Kovacs: ATIRONTA, MAN, MUTINEER ONE, BRÉBEUF, GROSSEILLIERS, LE BOEUF, FRONTENAC
John Blackwood: TESSOUAT, CHAMPLAIN, LALEMANT, LAVAL, BEAUPORT, ENGLISH OFFICER
Robert Nasmith: CARTIER, HURON WARRIOR, IROQUOIS WARRIOR, GARAKONTIE, LE CARON, KIRKE, JOGUES, RADISSON, HABITANT
Michael Copeman: PRIEST, BRÛLÉ, ENGLISH OFFICER, MAURICE, TRACY, DENONVILLE
Jennifer Dean: MUTINEER TWO, CHAMPLAIN'S WIFE, HABITANT, AGONA, MARIE
Janet Burke: HÉLÈNE, ACTOR
Deanne Taylor: BOURGEOYS

Set and lighting design by Jim Plaxton
Props and costume design by Bobbe Besold and Shadowland
Music by Brent Snyder
Written and directed by Michael Hollingsworth
Produced by Shain Jaffe and Deanne Taylor

The British: Part Two of The History of the Village of the Small Huts premièred at Theatre Passe Muraille on January 21st, 1986, with the following cast:

The Plains of Abraham

Robert Nasmith: AMHERST, FRASER
Graham Greene: VAUDREUIL, FRENCH SOLDIER ONE
Gary Farmer: VERGOR, PONTIAC, PIERRE
Arturo Fresolone: BIGOT
Janet Burke: MME PEAN
Alan Bridle: MONSIEUR PEAN, MURRAY, HABITANT, FRENCH SOLDIER THREE
Paul Bettis: MONTCALM, JENKINS
Michael Copeman: LEVIS, BOUGAINVILLE, FRENCH OFFICER ONE, RAMEZAY
Patrick Brymer: TOWNSHEND, FRENCH SOLDIER TWO
John Blackwood: WOLFE, BRIAND, NUN
Jennifer Dean: FRENCH OFFICER TWO, MARIE

The Conspiracy of Pontiac

Gary Farmer: PONTIAC
Graham Greene: BLACKHAWK, MAHOGANNE, THAYENDANEGEA
Janet Burke: ENGLISH OFFICER ONE, WOMAN
Robert Nasmith: ENGLISH OFFICER TWO
Jennifer Dean: WIFE, SOLDIER
Paul Bettis: GLADWYN
Arturo Fresolone: MINAVAVANA, ASSASSIN
Patrick Brymer: CAMPBELL
Alan Bridle: DALYELL
Michael Copeman: FRANÇOIS
John Blackwood: JOHNSON

The Loyalists

Michael Copeman: CAMPBELL, WALTER, GENET
Paul Bettis: CARLETON, AMERICAN SOLDIER
Graham Greene: WALKER, JOSEPH
Arturo Fresolone: BONTEMPS, WOOSTER
Robert Nasmith: BRIAND, BUTLER, SECORD
Gary Farmer: PIERRE, SQUAT
Alan Bridle: JOHNSON, ARNOLD, MME ST LAURENT
John Blackwood: MONTGOMERY, AMERICAN SOLDIER, BURGOYNE, LOYALIST, PRINCE
Jennifer Dean: HALDIMAND, LADY DORCHESTER, LAURA
Janet Burke: MOLLY, ELIZABETH
Patrick Brymer: SIMCOE, ENGLISH SOLDIER

The War of 1812

Gary Farmer: TECUMSEH, SCOTT
Graham Greene: PROPHET, BOERSTLER, THOMAS
Michael Copeman: HARRISON, HULL, DRUMMOND
Paul Bettis: BROCK, AMERICAN SOLDIER TWO, WILLCOCKS
John Blackwood: STRACHAN, RECRUIT, OVERHOLSER
Patrick Brymer: ROBINSON, PREVOST
Arturo Fresolone: CHAPIN, SALABERRY
Janet Burke: WIFE, AMERICAN SOLDIER ONE
Robert Nasmith: PROCTOR, SECORD, PIKE
Alan Bridle: FITZGIBBON, DEARBORN
Jennifer Dean: LAURA

Battle scenes were performed by the entire company.

Set and lighting design by Jim Plaxton
Props and costume design by Shadowland
Music by Brent Snyder
Stage Manager: Keltie Creed
Written and directed by Michael Hollingsworth
Produced by Shain Jaffe and Deanne Taylor

The Mackenzie-Papineau Rebellion: Part Three of The History of the Village of Small Huts premièred at Theatre Passe Muraille on April 15th, 1987, with the following cast:

Paul Bettis: COLBORNE, ANDERSON, MRS MACKENZIE
Tom Butler: GOSFORD, FITZGIBBON, ALLEN, SERGEANT-MAJOR, RENSELLAER, DURHAM
Eric Keenleyside: MACKENZIE, GORE, SQUAT
Arturo Fresolone: PAPINEAU
Robert Nasmith: LOUNT, MME PAPINEAU, WEIR, LITTLE PIERRE, ALAMO
Daniel Chevrier: LAFONTAINE, CHENIER, HINDENLANG
Mario Romano: BOURGET, ROBINSON
Derek Keurvorst: PIERRE, MACNAB, ROLPH, HABITANT, BUTLER
Patrick Brymer: FRENCH, MOFFAT, BONDHEAD
Roger McKeen: STRACHAN, POWNALL, WETHERALL, O'TOOLE, JOHNSTON
Janet Burke: BONTEMPS, JUNIOR, SHERRIFF, BALDWIN, SARAH

Set and lighting design by Stephen Allen
Props and costume design by Shadowland
Music by Brent Snyder
Stage Manager: Arron Moses
Assistant Stage Manager: Jill Beatty
Written and directed by Michael Hollingsworth
Produced by Shain Jaffe and Deanne Taylor

Confederation and Riel: Part Four of The History of the Village of the Small Huts premièred at the Olympic Arts Festival, Calgary, Alberta in February, 1988, with the following cast:

Tom Butler: MACDONALD, SOLDIER TWO
Eric Keenleyside: BROWN, LAFLAMME, LÉPINE, ALLAN, QUINN, DEFENCE ATTORNEY
Derek Keurvorst: CARTIER, CROZIER, BARNABÉ, JUDGE, BOULTON, LAURIER
Janet Burke: MRS RIEL, POPE, LADY MACDONALD, MAN ONE, NUN, MÉTISSE, TRADER, MME CUVILLIER
Arturo Fresolone: RIEL

Robert Nasmith: MONCK, CLERK, SPEAKER, EVELINA, PRESTON, BAD ARROW, SOLDIER ONE, DONOGHUE, MOUNTIE
John Blackwood: BISHOP TACHÉ, TUPPER, TACHÉ, McDOUGALL, SMITH, MIDDLETON
Mario Romano: BOURGET, TILLEY, SCHULTZ, BERNARD, MAN TWO, WANDERING SPIRIT
Roger Mckeen: McGEE, COLE, BLAKE, ISIDORE, DELANEY, PROSECUTOR, SCOTT
Bruce Vavrina: GALT, MACKENZIE, MÉTIS, MISERABLE MAN, WOLSELEY, ANDRE, CARTER
Graham Greene: BELLEAU, SAMMY, HOWE, NORBERT, MAN THREE, BIG BEAR, DUMONT

Set and lighting design by Steve Allen
Props and costume design by Shadowland
Music by Brent Snyder
Stage Manager: Arron Moses
Assistant Stage Manager: Jill Beatty
Written and Directed by Michael Hollingsworth
Produced by Shain Jaffe and Deanne Taylor

Laurier: Part Five of The History of the Village of the Small Huts premièred at Theatre Passe Muraille on July 1st, 1991, with the following cast:

Stephen Ouimette: LAURIER
John Blackwood: GUIBORD, MACKENZIE, MACDONALD, LORD ABERDEEN, MINTO, GREY, MULOCK, JACQUES
Janet Burke: MME GAUTHIER, CARTIER, ANTOINE, LAVERGNE, McCARTHY, BORDEN, IVAN, LADY ABERDEEN
Jennifer Dean: ZOE, BOWELL
Arturo Fresolone: RIEL, PAPINEAU, LA FLECHE, TARTE, ARMAND
Robert Nasmith: BOURGET, BLAKE, THOMPSON, SIFTON, JEAN
Kim Renders: LAFLAMME, SMITH, TUPPER, BOURASSA
Deanne Taylor: DORION, EMILIE, ABBOTT

Set and lighting design by Jim Plaxton
Props and costume design by Teresa Przybylski and Shadowland
Music by Brent Snyder
Stage Manager: Leslie Lester
Written and directed by Michael Hollingsworth
Produced by Catherine McKeehan and Deanne Taylor

The Great War: Part Six of The History of the Village of the Small Huts premièred at the Theatre Centre on June 12th, 1992, with the following cast:

John Blackwood: BORDEN, MARTHA, BOYLE, BYNG, HAIG , WHORE, SOLDIER ONE, DWAYNE, PATIENT TWO
Janet Burke: LAURA, EDITH, DUCHESS, CABINET MINISTER, ALDERSON, NURSE, FRENCH-CANADIEN MOTHER, NELLIE, SOLDIER TWO
Alan Bridle: MEIGHEN, SERVANT, CURRIE, RECRUITER, SCOTT, SOLDIER THREE, PATIENT ONE
Mackenzie Gray: FATHER, JOHN, ARMAND, GEORGE, McNAUGHTON, SOLDIER FOUR, YANK
Cliff Saunders: DAVID, LAURIER, HUGHES, SOLDIER FIVE, PIERRE
Hugo Dann: ROBERT, DUKE, FRENCH-CANADIEN SON, SOLDIER SIX, GERMAN PRISONER
Alex Fallis: STEPHEN, BOURASSA, SENTRY, BRITISH SOLDIER, OTTO, SOLDIER SEVEN

Set and lighting design by Jim Plaxton
Costumes designed by Astrid Janson
Props designed by Astrid Janson and Peter Bowyer
Music by Brent Snyder
Stage Manager: Michael Carley
Written and directed by Michael Hollingsworth
Produced by Deanne Taylor and Leslie Lester

The Life and Times of Mackenzie King: Part Seven of The History of the Village of the Small Huts premièred at the Theatre Centre on February 25th, 1993, with the following cast:

John Blackwood: BORDEN, ANDREWS, SID, BISAILLON, ETTA, LAPOINTE, WELFARE MAN, RIBBENTROP, PEASANT
Alan Bridle: GARGOYLE, MEIGHEN, LAURIER, MRS BLEANEY, WOODSWORTH, DAUGHTER, INSTRUCTOR

Janet Burke: MOLLY, MOTHER, JOAN, JUDY, INFORMER
Layne Coleman: KING, FASCIST
Michael Copeman: VINCE, STEVENS, LANDLORD, FOREMAN, HITLER, HOBO, CONVICT, FASCIST
Mackenzie Gray: COPPING, RUSSELL, CROOKED COP, BUREAU, GODFROY, STOCKBROKER ONE, McNAUGHTON GOEBBELS, FASCIST, COMMUNIST
Geza Kovacs: JOE, DIXON, BYNG, STOCKBROKER TWO, REPORTER
Edward Roy: ZANETH, SAM, LADY BYNG, BENNETT, HOBO, THOMPSON, VOLUNTEER

Set and lighting design by Jim Plaxton
Costume design by Astrid Janson
Props design by Astrid Janson and Shadowland
Music and Sound design by Brent Snyder
Stage Manager: Michael Carley
Written and directed by Michael Hollingsworth
Produced by Deanne Taylor and Leslie Lester

World War II: Part Eight of The History of the Village of the Small Huts premièred at the Theatre Centre on March 31st, 1994, with the following cast:

Nancy Beatty: HITLER, MUFFIN, CRERAR, VIOLET, ZOMBIE ONE, NURSE, PEASANT
John Blackwood: MOTHER, LAPOINTE, McNAUGHTON, FDR, MERRITT, DOUG, MEYER, TOMMY
Alan Bridle: CHAMBERLAIN, WAITER, JOE, MONTGOMERY, PRIEST
Janet Burke: MRS BLEANEY, HOWE, ROSE, WOMAN, MALTBY, HUGHES-HALLET, GIRL, PARTISAN, CHAPLAIN, ZOMBIE TWO
Steve Cumyn: JOHN, CLERK, FRED, ST LAURENT, CAPTAIN, CHUCK
John Jarvis: KING, ROBERTS, LAWSON, SIMONDS, DOCTOR, GERMAN SOLDIER, ENGLISHMAN
Edward Roy: MUSSOLINI, RALSTON, CHURCHILL, MOUNTBATTEN, PIMPOLINA, DWAYNE, MAYOR

Set and lighting design by Jim Plaxton
Costumes designed by Astrid Janson
Props designed by Shadowland
Music composed by Andrew Paterson
Sound design and battle scapes by Greg Somerton
Lighting operated by Mark Ryder
Stage Manager: Paul Mark
Written and Directed by Michael Hollingsworth
Produced by Deanne Taylor and Leslie Lester

photo © Michael Cooper

Michael Hollingsworth with producer Deanne Taylor

Michael Hollingsworth has a personal history of upsetting the common notions most hold about what theatre can and cannot do. His previous theatre pieces include the acid-etched vision of *Strawberry Fields; Clear Light*, a play closed by the morality squad; and *Electric Eye*, a video-integrated drama with fifty televisions. His stage translations of Orwell's *1984* and Huxley's *Brave New World* have played in Toronto, Vancouver, Calgary and London, England. Mr. Hollingsworth is presently at work on a brand new project, *The Global Village.*